MAY 1 2 201

M000286634

Fields of War:
Battle of Normandy

Robert J Mueller

A Visitor's Guide to Historic Sites

 FRENCH BATTLEFIELDS
ARLINGTON HEIGHTS

French Battlefields
PO Box 4808
Buffalo Grove, Illinois 60089-4808
Fax: 1-224-735-3478
Email: contact@frenchbattlefields.com
Web address: http://www.frenchbattlefields.com

Copyright 2014 by Robert J Mueller
All rights reserved
Cover design by Vince Martinez
First Edition
Manufactured in the United States
Library of Congress Control Number: 2013953274
ISBN-13: 978-0-9823677-3-5   ISBN:-10: 0-9823677-3-2

Cover photographs:
Color: Mémorial des Parachutists and la Fiére Bridge
Time line: US 1st Infantry Division troops land at Omaha Beach on 6 June 1944. NARA
American howitzer shells German forces retreating near Carentan. NARA
German prisoners march under guard from Cherbourg. NARA
Spine: An American soldier's temporary grave marker at Pointe du Hoc. NARA

Abbreviations used for photographs:
AHEC: Army Heritage and Education Center, Carlisle, Pennsylvania
IWM: Imperial War Museum, London, England
LAC: Library and Archives Canada, Ottawa, Canada
NARA: National Archives and Records Administration, College Park, Maryland

Dedicated to:
Nora and Matt, Beth and Charles,
and Carrie and Peter

We are not doing this for ourselves...
> — Painted on the side of a barrack in Fort Irwin, California - 2010

Ours is a world of nuclear giants and ethical infants. We know more about war than about peace, more about killing than we know about living.
> — General Omar Bradley (Armistice Day speech 11 November 1948)

The soldiers' graves are the greatest preachers of peace.
> — Albert Schweitzer

Contents

Contents

Contents

Introduction

Ten years of touring European battlefields has brought a deep appreciation of how a commander's use of local terrain can significantly influence the outcome of military engagements. Defensive positions are strengthened by placement on high ground with clear lines of observation and fields of fire. Routes of advance are hidden by terrain or deception while attackers search for an enemy's weaknesses.

However, in the summer of 1944, terrain and even weapons superiority were not the determining factors in the battle of Normandy. Victory resided in the men who fought there. The difficult terrain where American, British, and Canadian forces pushed back and eventually destroyed the German Seventh Army reinforces one's respect for those ordinary men, from ordinary backgrounds, who did extraordinary things.

The combat infantrymen's burden was indeed heavy. For example, by 1944, only 20 percent of American troops were in combat divisions and of those in combat divisions only 65 percent of the men were fighting soldiers. By war's end some rifle companies had suffered over 200 percent casualties; in other words, statistically, every man in the unit had become a casualty – and each of their replacements. Frequently a battalion's original combat soldiers that survived the entire war unscathed could be counted on one's fingers.

It is with this in mind that *Fields of War: Battle of Normandy* identifies and describes the actions of individual soldiers, enlisted men and officers, whose unflinching dedication to their fellow soldiers motivated heroic actions, frequently at the cost of their lives. The Fields of War series is in tribute to the soldiers of all nations who, willingly or not, suffered the cold, hunger, fear, and hurt of battle.

How to Use this Book

This guide brings battlefield visitors to specific sites of important battlefield events, describes what happened there, and offers opportunities to view commemorations, visit museums, or inspect surviving relics of the battle. Part I, The Invasion, devotes chapters to each of the six infantry and three airborne divisions that established a fragile foothold in France on D-Day, 6 June 1944. Part II, Defeat of the German Army, presents chapters describing battles for key urban centers, large scale offensives that led to the ultimate German defeat in the Falaise Pocket, and, finally, the liberation of Paris by its citizens and the men of the 2nd French Armored Division. The book has been organized chronologically but makes compromises to travel efficiency.

Each chapter begins with a brief summary of the precipitating military events. A 'fact box' summarizes key information and a detailed battlefield map assists in following the action and locating selected sites. The 'Battle' section describes each commander's objectives and troop movements. An 'Aftermath' section notes results of the fighting and significant events which occurred after the engagement. The major section of each battle is devoted to the 'Battlefield Tour'. Each tour starts at an easy to locate town and has been designed to be taken in any order. Geographic coordinates (latitude, longitude), which can be entered into GPS locators, are given for each location allowing visitors to select only those sites of individual interest or to alter the order of visitation. Clear driving instructions, highlighted in boxes for easy reading, are designed to bring a visitor to various positions of importance on the battlefield. A brief explanation of the significance of the site includes descriptions of individual soldier's contributions to its ultimate outcome. Footnotes provide insights into mentioned soldiers' after battle lives.

The book has been written with the intent of touring battlefields by automobile.

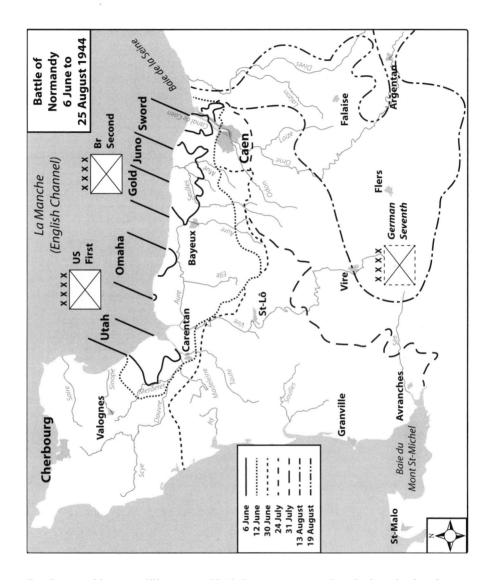

For those unable or unwilling to provide their own transportation, the invasion beaches are well serviced by tour companies which offer a reasonable alternative to driving and provide transportation, experienced guides, and sometimes arrange for meals and accommodations. Inland battlefields are not so well served. Public transportation to battlefields is seldom a viable option.

Besides the recommended tour routes in this guide, the blue NTL (*Normandie Terre-Liberté*) Totems which provide descriptions of local interest and define eight tour routes, each of which focuses upon a different period of the Battle of Normandy. These totems are noted in the text when encountered. A *Normandie Pass*, (See: http://www. normandiememorie.com/76.normandiepass) costing only one Euro, can be purchased at any of the sponsoring museums or attractions. It offers a small discount to entry fees at thirty-nine sites whose sponsorship is indicated at the end of each participating museum's entry in this book.

The indicated positions of military units on the battlefield maps presented in this book are approximated for ease of viewing and do not necessarily indicate headquarters locations. The maps show modern roadways; but they should never be considered a substitute for current highway road maps. Farm or forest roads are generally not drivable without four-wheel drive vehicles.

Comparative military ranks are presented in appendix A; appendices B through E offer additional information helpful to understanding unit sizes and their composition, German military terminology, and to compare statistics on armored vehicles.

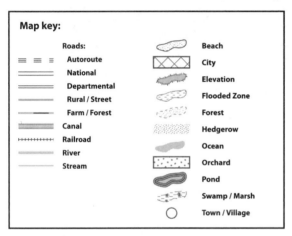

Map key:

Roads:			
	Autoroute		Beach
	National		City
	Departmental		Elevation
	Rural / Street		Flooded Zone
	Farm / Forest		Forest
	Canal		Hedgerow
	Railroad		Ocean
	River		Orchard
	Stream		Pond
			Swamp / Marsh
			Town / Village

Military Symbols
Unit Size (infantry example):

Squad		Brigade	
Platoon		Division	
Company		Corps	
Battalion		Army	
Regiment		Army Group	

Unit Type:

Airborne		Cavalry	
Airborne, Artillery		Engineering	E
Airforce		Infantry	
Armored (Panzer)		Infantry, Motorized	
Armored, Reconn.		Signals	
Artillery		Special Forces	
Artillery, Armored		Tank Destroyer	T D
German (infantry example)			

Custom Map Symbols:

Aircraft, Fighter		Crater	
Aircraft, Bomber		Farm	
Antitank Gun		Casemate	
Artillery		Fortification (Pre-20th Century)	
Battlefield		Machine Gun	
Bridge		Monument, Military	
Blockhouse		Museum, Military	
Castle or Chateau		Overlook	
Cathedral		Pillbox or Tobruk	
Cemetery, Military		Ruins	
Chapel, Church, or Abbey		Tank	
Citadel		Tobruk	
		Trenches	

General Tourist Information

Battlefield touring in Normandy brings tourists into beautiful countryside where one can view broad sand beaches, narrow stonewall-lined lanes through small villages, and the soaring towers of medieval churches. The dining opportunities are rampant with shellfish only hours from the sea; three famous Norman cheeses - Pont l'Évêque, Liverot, and Camembert; and powerful apple brandy known as Calvados.

Tourist offices can provide helpful information regarding accommodations, cultural and historic sites, walking or cycling routes, and hours of operation for museums. The offices are not included in the tours, but their addresses and contact information are provided at the beginning of each town's description. The Michelin Green Guide for Normandy is highly recommended for its presentation of general tourist information. It makes an excellent accompaniment to this book and offers general touring advice in addition to listing historic and cultural locations, market days, festivals, and public holidays.

Twenty-four hour military time is in use in Europe; therefore operational hours in this book are so presented. Outside of the major French metropolitan areas, tourist offices, many museums, most retail shops, and all banks honor the French custom of closing during midday. Weekday and Saturday morning hours are frequently restricted to 9:00 to 12:00 and 14:00 to 17:00. On Sundays and public holidays almost all establishments are closed with even many restaurants closing after the noon meal. Those sites open on weekends are frequently closed on Mondays or Tuesdays. Some variations exist, especially later closing hours during the summer tourist season. Few museums are handicap accessible; those that so advertise are indicated. Most British and American military cemeteries are handicap accessible. The information contained herein is believed to be accurate at the time of printing, but museum hours are notoriously subject to change. If access to a certain site is of paramount importance, it is best to contact it in advance.

American visitors must accommodate the use of the metric system as it is the measure used on local road signs and maps. Each year roadways are improved or re-routed and intersections reconstructed. France is now undergoing a renumbering of their National Roads, changing them from their historic 'N' designation to 'D' or departmental road identifier. Therefore, up-to-date road maps or GPS locators are a necessity. The 1:50,000 scale maps prepared by the *Institut Géographique National* (IGN) are available at many bookstores, autoroute service areas, or over the internet from www.ign.fr.

Local citizens are remarkably tolerant of battlefield visitors; however private property should be respected and never accessed without owner's permission. Crops are the farmer's livelihood and trampling planted fields should be avoided, although a field boundary often provides a useful walkpath. Forests may be the scene of the autumn shooting season and care should be exercised. Finally, an additional word of caution: abandoned bunkers or off-trail battlefield terrain frequently retain dangerous spikes, barbed wire, or even unexploded ordinance. Utmost caution must be exercised and independent exploration is discouraged.

Part One
The Invasion
6 June to 14 June 1944

Islands claim their own natural defenses, but by 1944, the British Isles had become a veritable fortress, brimming with military hardware, naval vessels, aircraft and their landing fields as well as personnel in training for the upcoming Allied invasion of Hitler's *Festung Europa*. The decision to invade France, made at the Quebec Conference in August 1943, was to be realized with a cross-channel, amphibious invasion of Western Europe, code-named NEPTUNE, part of the larger Operation OVERLORD, the plan to liberate Normandy. A guessing game regarding the actual site of the invasion continued through the spring of 1944, while Allied and German intelligence tried to ferret out the opposition's intentions amid false information and conflicting military opinions. Each studied the other's geographic limitations and monitored meteorological conditions.

The Allies selected the shores of Normandy's Seine Bay, from the Orne River to the east coast of the Cotentin Peninsula, as the invasion site. The area possessed excellent landing beaches and seemed less obvious than the strongly-defended Pas-de-Calais. The important issues of post-invasion supply and reinforcement had been resolved by constructing portable harbors – called Mulberries – which were floated across the English Channel to establish disembarking facilities until the ports at Cherbourg and le Havre could be liberated. Over 176,000 men, 3,000 guns, and 1,500 tanks, supported by 284 major naval combat ships and 4,300 landing craft, were poised to cross the rough waters of the Channel under an air umbrella of 7,770 aircraft. After training for as long as two years, all units encamped in closed and guarded compounds along Britain's southern coast to assure security.

The invasion force, commanded by British General Bernard Law Montgomery (later 1st Viscount Montgomery of Alamein), targeted five invasion beaches, code-named (from east to west) Sword, Juno, Gold, Omaha, and Utah. The beaches were further divided into sectors with code names such as Dog White and Queen Red. The British 3rd and 50th Divisions would land on Sword and Gold, and the 3rd Canadian Division would land on Juno – all supported by large contingents of commandos, demolition engineers, tank battalions, and special function forces. Omaha and Utah, on either side of the confluence of the Aure and Vire Rivers, were the landing sites assigned to the Americans. The US 1st and 29th Infantry Divisions would land on Omaha, and the US 4th Division would land on Utah. To capture and hold critical areas before the waterborne troop landings, the British 6th Airborne Division and the American 82nd and 101st Airborne Divisions would land by parachute and glider during the early morning darkness.

Hitler and the German High Command expected the invasion to occur in Pas-de-Calais, where the journey across the Channel was shorter and where Boulogne and Calais could provide port facilities. German generals disagreed on the utilization of Germany's panzer divisions against the invading forces. Generalfeldmarschall Erwin Rommel, as commander of Army Group B and the person holding responsibly for coastal defenses, thought that Germany's only chance of victory was to smash the invaders at the water's edge. Other military leaders, led by Generalleutnant Leo Freiherr Geyr von Schweppenburg, commander of Panzer Group West, argued for waiting until the Allied intentions became clearer before launching a counterstrike. The controversy, plus Hitler's personal control of the panzer troops, contributed to Germany's muddled reaction to the invasion. Rommel nevertheless led construction of the Atlantic Wall defenses, which included casemated

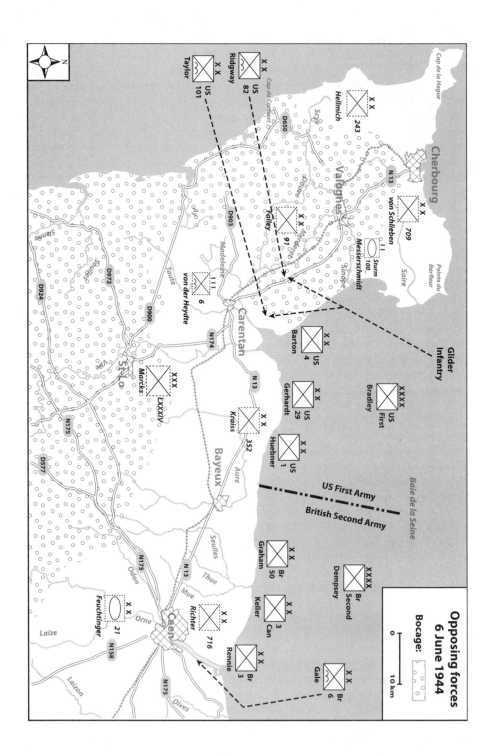

Opposing forces
6 June 1944

Bocage:

0   10 km

armaments, antitank walls, seaside pillboxes, *Widerstandsnesterter,*[1] millions of mines, and beach obstacles designed to sink landing craft as they approached France's shores.

The German Seventh Army was responsible for the coastal defenses in Normandy and Brittany. Although its II Parachute Corps and 21st Panzer Division were first-rate units, most of the other troops were decidedly second-rate, often containing Russians and ethnic Germans from conquered lands who had volunteered to fight for the Reich but had little combat experience or motivation.

In the early morning of 5 June, amid unsettled weather conditions that had already delayed the invasion for one day, the Supreme Allied Commander, General Dwight D Eisenhower, decided to proceed. He also wrote a note accepting full responsibility if the invasion failed and visited the airborne troops that would lead the invasion, fearful of the appalling casualty rates projected by his staff. He returned to his headquarters to await the outcome of the largest amphibious invasion in history, on a day that has since been called 'the longest day.'

---

1   *Widerstandsnest:* a resistance pocket specifically sited to protect a geographic feature such as beach, road, or bridge. Typically holding only light antitank or artillery weapons and with a complement of less than 100 men, German strategists expected resistance pockets to delay attackers for only several hours

Chapter One
British 6th (Red Devils) Airborne Division
6 to 13 June 1944

The eastern limit of the Normandy invasion zone was bounded by the Orne River and the Canal de Caen, which run a parallel course from the English Channel at Ouistreham to the city of Caen. In 1944, these waterways were crossed by only one set of bridges, near the rural village of Bénouville. A wooded ridge ran from Sallenelles southeast to Troarn and overlooked the Orne valley. The massive invasion's eastern flank was physically isolated by a German-created flood plain in the Dives Valley that restricted armored movements to the roads. The destruction of the bridges crossing the Dives and Divette Rivers would prohibit rapid movement westward by the forces of the German Fifteenth Army stationed in the Pas-de-Calais.

The British 6th Airborne Division was assigned the critical task of destroying gun positions and occupying key bridges and road junctions east of the Orne River. The 3rd Parachute Brigade, comprised of the British 8th and 9th Parachute Battalions and the 1st Canadian Parachute Battalion, sought to destroy the Merville Battery, which enfiladed Sword Beach, as well as the bridges across the Dives and Divette Rivers at Troarn, Bures,

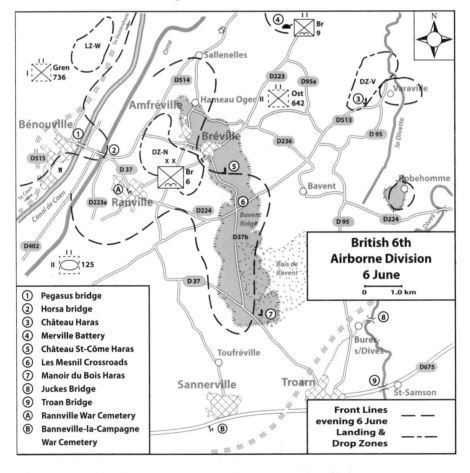

① Pegasus bridge
② Horsa bridge
③ Château Haras
④ Merville Battery
⑤ Château St-Côme Haras
⑥ Les Mesnil Crossroads
⑦ Manoir du Bois Haras
⑧ Juckes Bridge
⑨ Troan Bridge
Ⓐ Rannville War Cemetery
Ⓑ Banneville-la-Campagne War Cemetery

British 6th
Airborne Division
6 June

0   1.0 km

Front Lines
evening 6 June
Landing &
Drop Zones

Robehomme, and Varaville. Upon completion of those missions, they would withdraw to defend the Sallenelles-Thaon ridge against enemy counterattack from the south and east. The British 5th Parachute Brigade, comprised of the 7th, 12th, and 13th Parachute Battalions, drew the assignment to capture the bridges over the Orne River and Canal de Caen and hold them for use by British forces arriving from the landing beaches. Three battalions of the 6th Airlanding Brigade were to arrive by glider after dawn on 6 June to strengthen the division's positions. Also operating in the area was the independent 1st Special Service Brigade, which would land on Sword Beach, cross the captured bridges, and secure the coastal end of the 6th Airborne's area of operations.

D-Day Landings
6 June 1944

At 2256 on 5 June, six Halifax bombers towing Horsa gliders left Royal Air Force (RAF) Tarrant Rushton airfield in Dorset, England, on a dangerous – some thought foolhardy – assignment. The 180 men of the 2nd Battalion, Oxfordshire and Buckinghamshire Light Infantry Regiment (Ox & Bucks), were to land on a moonlit night in German-occupied France to capture two bridges critical to the success of the invasion. The Bénouville Bridge over the Caen Canal and the Ranville Bridge over the Orne River were strategically important because they were the only crossings of the two waterways north of Caen. The bridges were guarded by a unit of Grenadier Regiment 736 comprised of fifty, mainly eastern European, enlisted men led by German officers and non-commissioned officers (NCOs) and commanded by Major Hans Schmidt.

The Ox & Bucks Regiment had been formed in 1881 by combining the 43rd Regiment of Foot (Light Infantry) and the 52nd Regiment of Foot (Light Infantry). The unit had fought with considerable distinction in the First World War at Mons, Marne, Ypres, Loos, Somme, Passchendaele, and during the 1918 counteroffensive. Previously in the Second World War, it had been evacuated at Dunkirk. Its 2nd Battalion had been retrained as airborne glider troops in 1943, becoming part of the 6th Airlanding Brigade. Operation OVERLORD was the airborne unit's first action. Company D of the glider-borne Ox & Bucks Regiment became the first Allied unit to set foot upon French soil since the abortive Dieppe landings of 1942.

Objective	To capture and hold two bridges across the Orne River and Canal de Caen
Forces	
British	181 men of Company D, Oxs & Bucks Regiment (Major John Howard)
German	50-man detachment from Ostbatallion 642 (Major Hans Schmidt)
Result	Two bridges were quickly captured and held until relieved
Casualties	
British	2 dead; 14 wounded
German	Uncertain
Location	Bénouville is 9 km northeast of Caen.

Battle

The lead glider cast off its towline when it crossed the Norman coastline at 0007. Navigating only by stopwatch, compass, and airspeed gauge, the glider pilots performed a remarkable feat of flying, bringing the first three craft down at 0016 in a boggy field just meters away from the eastern end of the Bénouville Bridge and an enemy antitank pillbox. British troopers tossed grenades through the apertures of the machine-gun pillbox across the road, and a burst of fire killed one sentry on the bridge – but not before he had fired a warning Verey flare.[2] German troops in slit trenches on both sides of the canal jumped into action, but quick bursts from Sten guns and a few grenades ended their resistance. Meanwhile, the Ranville Bridge, 400 meters to the east, fell against only nominal opposition.

Pathfinders identified landing and drop zones for other elements of the division, which arrived in scattered drops starting at 0050. The 5th Parachute Brigade captured the high ground east of the bridges near Ranville and reinforced the Ox and Bucks to establish a firm perimeter west of the Orne. The 3rd Parachute Brigade also accomplished its missions as described below. Late in the day, gliders arrived with the remainder of the 6th Airlanding Brigade.

At approximately 2115, 2nd Battalion, The Royal Warwickshire Regiment, arrived. The bridges were now secure, and the Bénouville Bridge would afterward be known as 'Pegasus Bridge' after the airborne division's 'flying horse' emblem. Despite the early success, British forces did not advance more than 5 kilometers past the bridge toward Caen until the mid-August collapse of German resistance.

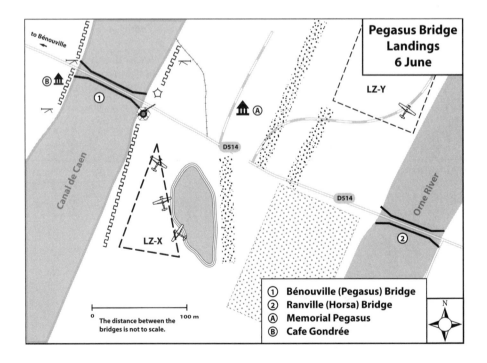

Pegasus Bridge Landings 6 June

LZ-Y

to Bénouville

Canal de Caen

D514

D514

Orne River

LZ-X

0   100 m
The distance between the bridges is not to scale.

① Bénouville (Pegasus) Bridge
② Ranville (Horsa) Bridge
Ⓐ Memorial Pegasus
Ⓑ Cafe Gondrée

N

---

2   Verey (or Very) flare: a distress signal fired skyward from a snub-nosed pistol.

Battlefield Tour

> Before touring the battlefields around Caen, a visit to Mémorial de Caen provides an excellent perspective on the Battle of Normandy as well as the entire Second World War. The museum is located on esplanade General Dwight Eisenhower; take exit #6 or #7 from the Caen ring road (Périphérique / E48 / N814) and follow the signs for '*Le Mémorial.*' See Chapter Thirteen for a description of the museum. (49.197908, -0.38376)
>
> The battlefield tour starts at the Mémorial Pegasus (museum), east of Bénouville. From Caen, leave the ring road (E46/N814) at exit #3a (Porte d'Angleterre) toward Ouistreham (D515). After 7.6 km, exit toward Bénouville; continue straight at the large roundabout (Av du Commandant Kieffer); cross over the bridge and turn left onto Av Major John Howard to access the museum. (49.242371, -0.272062)

Mémorial Pegasus

Avenue du Major Howard   14860 Ranville
Tel: +33 (0)2 31 78 19 44   Web: info@memorial-pegasus.org

Mémorial Pegasus contains artifacts from the capture of Pegasus Bridge (the renamed Bénouville Bridge) and other engagements of the British 6th Airborne Division in the area. The local Gondrée family collected many of the items over the years and augmented them with contributions from the participants, including Major John Howard, the assault team commander. The 1934 counterweighted drawbridge is now located on the grounds of the Pegasus Museum. The dent in its side stemmed from a German bomb dropped to destroy the bridge after its capture. The bomb was a dud and fell harmlessly into the canal. The grounds also hold an original Bailey bridge, other military equipment, and a full-size replica of a Horsa glider.

Open daily February and March, October and November from 10:00 to 17:00; April through September from 09:30 to 18:30; closed December and January. Admission fee; Normandie Pass accepted.

> A path leads from the parking area to the new **Pegasus Bridge**. (49.242448, -0.274315)

The original bridge was replaced in 1994 by a wider and longer version that retained the original design and mode of operation. The large block above the roadway is a wonderfully balanced counterweight that lifts the roadway with minimum effort.

> Do not cross the bridge, but proceed on Esplanade John Howard to the left along the canal.(49.242007, -0.273627)

Glider #91 containing Major Howard and Company D's 1st Platoon, commanded by Lieutenant Den Brotheridge, landed nearest the bridge. The glider was traveling at 160 km/h and at an altitude of 60 meters during its final approach. Two minutes before hitting the ground, the men linked arms and raised their knees in a protective sitting crouch. The aircraft bounced once, tearing off all three wheels, and skidded to a stop in a controlled crash. The two pilots were thrown through the plastic windshield, and every passenger was rendered unconscious – 50 meters from the east end of the bridge.

Glider #92, carrying 2nd Platoon, landed moments later, followed by #93 with 3rd Platoon. The pilots of the final aircraft made desperate efforts not to collide with #91. Their craft swerved toward the pond and its tail broke off upon hitting the ground. Three men, including the platoon commander, hurled through the cockpit and one man drowned in the pond. Remarkably, the noise of the three glider landings did not arouse suspicion, since the Allied air forces had provided another of their regular bombing raids on Caen when such nighttime sounds were not uncommon.

Although momentarily dazed, true to their training the soldiers immediately went on the attack. Corporal Jack Bailey[3] and two others pushed grenades into the pillbox's gun slits while Lt Brotheridge charged onto the bridge. One of the two sentries on the bridge, Soldat Helmut Romer,[4] was an 18-year-old draftee. He has the distinction of being the first member of the German military to encounter the Allied invasion. Romer crossed over the crown of the bridge and spotted the invaders. He shouted 'Fallschirmjäger!'[5] to the second sentry as he ran toward the slit trenches lining the western side of the canal. The second sentry had time to fire only a warning flare before Brotheridge killed him with a burst from his Sten gun.

Now alerted, German MG 34 machine guns opened fire and caught Brotheridge at the west end of the bridge as he threw a grenade to eliminate the machine gun to his right. Brotheridge went down and died a few minutes later.[6] Men from 1st Platoon followed and cleared the left machine gun and the underground bunkers along the canal bank.

Platoons from the other two gliders joined the assault, and by 0021 – five minutes after landing – the shooting stopped. Bénouville Bridge, afterward known as Pegasus Bridge, had been captured intact.

Near the canal bridge is one of the ten **Signal Monuments**, erected at strategic sites by Comité du Débarquement, the French agency created in 1946 to foster commemoration of the events in Normandy. Each monument is inscribed, 'Here, on 6 June 1944, the heroism of the Allied Forces liberated Europe.' This Signal Monument specifically adds:

'6 June 1944 – the banks
of the Orne first parts
of France are liberated
by the Allied forces.'

Esplanade John Howard connects three stone monuments that identify the actual glider landing sites amidst the swampy ground southeast of the bridge. Each monument bears a plaque naming the officers and men on each glider. A bust of **Major Howard**[7] stands next to the first stone and commemorates the occasion. (49.241632, -0.273639)

---

3   Corporal Jack Bailey survived the war.

4   Soldat Helmut Romer escaped from the fighting at Pegasus Bridge but surrendered to British soldiers on 7 June. He spent the war working on farms in England. He was still alive in 2004 and frequently attends D-Day reunions in Bénouville.

5   *Fallschirmjäger*: paratroopers

6   Lieutenant Herbert Denham Brotheridge is buried in Ranville Communal Cemetery.

7   Major Reginald John Howard served as an enlisted man and non-commissioned officer before the war. Recalled to duty in 1939, he quickly rose to command Company D, the Oxs and Bucks. For his leadership in capturing the bridge, he was awarded the Distinguished Service Cross and French Croix de Guerre. Major Howard never returned to combat after suffering serious injury in an automobile accident. After the war, he entered public service and frequently lectured on his wartime experiences. Howard died in 1999 at age 86.

On the banks of the canal, just beyond the first glider tablet, a stone **table of orientation** shows the location of the antitank cannon, Gondrée café, and the landing spots with respect to the canal and bridge. A small stone wall bears a plaque identifying this as stop 1 on the '**Pegasus Trail**' – ten locations on the battlefield of the 6th Airborne Division. Only three of the memorial plaques remain, but most of the ten sites have been included on this tour.

Return to the bridge where a German **50-mm antitank gun** stands in its tobruk[8] near the water's edge and below the bridge's modern control tower. A pillbox, which no longer exists, lay directly across the road, where Major Howard established his command post. (49.242105, -0.273793)

Cross to the western end of Bénouville (Pegasus) Bridge. (49.242407, -0.274921)

Musée de Pegasus Bridge
Av du Commandant Kieffer   Tel/Fax: +33 (0)1 43 25 29 67
Email: museedepegasusbridge@wanadoo.fr
Web: http://www.pegasusbridge.fr/

The small café across the bridge and on the left, renamed '**Pegasus Café**,' is still owned by descendants of Georges and Thérèsa Gondrée, who were the proprietors on 6 June. Madame Gondrée, a trained nurse, assisted British medics, who used the café as a first aide post. Monsieur Gondrée was helpful in his own way by digging up ninety-nine bottles of champagne he had buried in his garden when the Germans approached in 1940. The small museum displays artifacts and photographs of the bridge and surrounding area. Besides refreshments, a small shop offers souvenirs.

One plaque above the entrance to the café claims the building was the first house in France to be liberated in the last hour of 5 June (British Greenwich Mean time was two hours behind German Double Summer Time). The second plaque commemorates the use of the café for medical treatment of the wounded. The third plaque relates the relief of Major Howard's force by 7th Battalion, The Parachute Regiment, and the heavy casualties they suffered through D-Day.

The restored **Centaur tank** across the road carries a 95-mm howitzer gun. The tank landed at la Bréche d'Hermanville-s/Mer as part of the Royal Marine Commando Armoured Support Group on 6 June. Abandoned for thirty years, it was refurbished by the British Army and placed on exhibit near Pegasus Bridge. (49.242706, -0.274795)

Walk or drive east (Av du Commandant Kieffer) 250 m to the roundabout (place de la Libération). (49.243565, -0.278255)

The roundabout was a simple crossroads in 1944 with the village's *mairie*[9] on the southeast corner, where it still stands. Major Howard sent Lieutenant David Wood

---

8   Tobruk: a German defensive position widely used in Normandy. Constructed of an open, circular, concrete-lined pit with a reinforced concrete underground munitions chamber, they varied in size and design but accommodated a machine gun, mortar, or tank turret.

9   Mairie: a French town or village hall as distinct from a Hôtel de ville of a larger community.

with his 2nd Platoon to establish a defensive perimeter at this crossroads.[10] While the men approached, they could hear armored vehicles coming from the north and south. The 1st Company, *Panzerjäger* Battalion 716, headquartered only 6 kilometers away in Biéville led the German response followed by engineers from the 716th Infantry Division. While the first vehicle[11] slowly turned the corner, Sergeant 'Wagger' Thornton[12] fired a PIAT[13] shell that burst into flames on impact as fuel and ammunition ignited. Thinking that they faced a much larger force armed with antitank guns, the Germans withdrew to await more precise reconnaissance of the situation.

A stone cross memorial to the **7th Light Infantry Battalion**, The Parachute Regiment, (known as 7th Para) abuts the face of a destroyed fieldstone wall on the northeast quadrant of the roundabout. (49.243677, -0.277912) The inscription dedicates the memorial to those members of the unit who died defending the bridgehead. The 7th Para was dropped in the early hours of 6 June and took time to collect and organize. It arrived at the bridge at 0300 and expanded the perimeter to include the Château de Bénouville, visible to the south from the bridge, and le Port to the north. The 7th Para was under heavy pressure all day, and one company actually became surrounded near the chateau. It defeated numerous attempts by *Kampfgruppe*[14]*Rauch*[15] to recapture the bridge. At one point, a *PanzerKampfwagen* (PzKpfw)[16] IV reached the center of Bénouville before being destroyed by a Gammon bomb.[17] Their situation stabilized after the arrival of sea-landed infantry.

The village's war memorial stands in front of the *mairie*. The truncated obelisk appears as if the top has been shot off, obliterating the names of some First World War dead. (49.243338, -0.27803)

Return toward Pegasus Bridge, stopping in the parking area behind Café Gondrée. (49.24244, -0.275145)

As morning dawned, 7th Para and Howard's Ox & Bucks endured heavy pressure

---

10   Lieutenant David J Wood was severely wounded with three bullets in his leg. Although the wound kept him out of the rest of the war, he remained in the army, rising to the rank of Colonel. He died in 2009 at age 86.

11   The nature of this vehicle has raised much speculation. The Panzerjäger Battalion manned Marder IIs, a self-propelled antitank vehicle with a 75-mm PaK 40 gun mounted upon a PzKpfw II chassis, which made it appear to be a tank.

12   Sergeant Charles 'Wagger' Thornton was awarded the Military Medal. He survived the war.

13   PIAT: Projector Infantry Anti Tank weapon fired a high explosive charge but was also heavy, difficult to arm and aim, and had an effective range of only 50 meters.

14   *Kampfgruppe* – a temporary, combined-arms combat formation which included infantry, armor, and artillery elements usually assigned a specific purpose and frequently named after its commander.

15   *Kampfgruppe Rauch*: formed around 2nd Battalion, Panzergrenadier Regiment 192, and named after the unit's commander, Oberst Josef Rauch. Rauch fought throughout the war, rising to the rank of generalmajor and commanding the 18th Panzergrenadier Division in the Battle of Berlin. He surrendered to the Russians and was held as a POW until 1955.

16   PzKpfw: German tank models were designated by Roman numeral plus '*Ausführung*' (abbreviated *Ausf*) and a letter meaning a variant of that model. PzKpfw V was frequently identified by the name Panther and the PzKpfw VI was named Tiger.

17   Gammon bomb: officially #82 grenade designed by Captain RS Gammon for use by parachute and special forces. It was usually filled with high explosives and used against armored vehicles.

from German infantry with armored support. The perimeter was shrinking as German self-propelled (SP) guns forced the British to give ground. More misdropped paratroops arrived, and at noon the defenders heard the sound of bagpipes. The 1st Special Service Brigade with No 45 Commando crossed the bridge toward its objectives, followed by No 3 Commando. The fighting around the bridge continued for most of the day until the arrival of the 2nd Battalion, Royal Warwickshire Regiment.

In the parking area at rear of the café, a signboard commemorates the arrival of Brigadier Lord Lovat and his **1st Special Service Brigade**, heralded by legendary Piper Bill Millin.[18] Lovat's troops approached the bridge from the north, marching along the canal towpath behind a Centaur tank. Lovat crossed the bridge at 1202:30, 2 minutes and 30 seconds later than planned. Brigadier The bridge was not their objective, however, as they crossed the canal and the Orne River and turned north toward Sallenelles. (49.242446, -0.275138)

Return to Mémorial Pegasus to retrieve your vehicle and proceed east to Pont de Ranville (Ranville Bridge). (49.240319, -0.266874)

The Ranville Bridge over the Orne River was the second objective of the Ox and Bucks. As the attack upon Pegasus Bridge was starting, the first of three Horsa gliders landed in Landing Zone Y north of the bridge along the bank of the river. The 6th Platoon, commanded by Lieutenant Dennis Fox,[19] jumped from its aircraft as the alerted defenders raked the field with their MG 34 machine gun. An accurately placed 2-inch mortar round silenced the machine gun whereby Fox's men ran to the undefended western end of the bridge. Although the eastern end was protected by two machine-gun positions and a pillbox, the startled defenders broke and ran toward Ranville. The other two gliders landed 700 meters and 13 kilometers distant.

The German unit's commander, Major Hans Schmidt, informed of the action at the bridges, sped from Ranville to conduct a personal reconnaissance. As his half-track vehicle approached the bridge, Fox's men waited in ambush. The half-track was sprayed with machine-gun fire as it crossed the bridge and swerved out of control onto the embankment at the west end. Accompanying motorcycle riders were killed on the eastern approach. A wounded Major Schmidt was taken prisoner.

The Ranville Bridge has been renamed **Horsa Bridge** after the Horsa gliders that transported the men there. A modest highway bridge, built in 1971, replaced the original structure. A stele on the northern embankment at the west end commemorates the actions of the **Ox and Bucks** in quickly occupying the position and establishing a defensive perimeter. (49.240511, -0.267379)

Leave Horsa Bridge proceeding east (D514); at the first roundabout take the second exit toward Ranville (D37) and enter the town. After 1.2 km, turn left onto rue du 6 Juin (D223) and proceed. The tour will return to Ranville later. After 3.5 km, turn right toward Bavent (D236) and follow for 2.0 km. Turn left toward Deauville / Varaville (D513). Follow for 2.6 km to the junction with highway D95 on the southern outskirts of Varaville. (49.251735, -0.162252)

---

18   Piper William Millin, who landed at Sword Beach and inspired his comrades with his music, played his bagpipes unarmed. He died in 2012 at age 88.

19   Lieutenant Dennis Fox (later Major) was wounded in March 1945 but survived the war.

Varaville

The 1st Canadian Parachute Battalion, 3rd Parachute Brigade, dropped into drop zone (DZ) V between 0100 and 0130 on D-Day. The landings were widely dispersed, and much of the battalion's heavy weapons were lost. Eighty-four troopers were taken prisoner by the German garrison.

The **1st Canadian Parachute Battalion Monument** commemorates the capture of Varaville and the fierce fighting during the destruction of the Divette bridge. The brass plaque retells the story of the unit's landing and subsequent engagements. Erected by the veterans of the battalion, it also thanks the local citizens for the risks they took in helping their liberators.

> Reverse direction and proceed 450 m on highway D513; turn right onto a farm lane – no sign, but white wooden fences border both sides of the lane. (49.250566, -0.16833) Continue approximately 130 m, until the red-roofed buildings come into view on the right. (49.251756, -0.168947)

The horse farm on the right, le Château Haras, was a German strongpoint and marks the eastern edge of DZ V. While Royal Engineers supported by one platoon of Company C, 1st Canadian Parachute Battalion, destroyed the bridge over the Divette River on the eastern edge of Varaville along highway D27, the thirty remaining men of Company C attacked the well-defended chateau. The farm was surrounded by barbed wire and minefields; inside the perimeter were a 75-mm antitank gun, mortars, and machine-gun positions. A shell from the 75-mm gun detonated Canadian PIAT shells in the chateau gatehouse during a command conference killing the company commander, Major Murray MacLeod, among others.[20] The assault continued into the morning, with Captain John Hanson[21] assuming command. By 1030 the German pillbox was captured with forty-two prisoners taken; however, the unit was still subjected to incoming artillery fire into the late afternoon.

Despite this early success, the chateau and Varaville witnessed a change of fortune. After the Canadians withdrew to le Mesnil to form a defensive line against an attack from the south, the German Grenadier Regiment 857 reoccupied the village, which was not finally liberated until 17 August.

Merville Battery

The German battery south of Merville was a formidable gun emplacement. Four large casemates held 100-mm, Czech-made guns that had a range of 10 kilometers, capable of striking Sword landing beaches.[22] The casemates were constructed of 1.8-meter-thick reinforced concrete. The site included a command bunker and other fortifications for ammunitions storage. Inside the perimeter were numerous trenches, firing pits, 20-mm FlaK guns, and fifteen machine-gun positions. Although lacking natural defenses, the casemates were protected by an antitank ditch on the coastal side, a 5-meter-wide belt of barbed wire, and wide minefields. The garrison was manned by a detachment from I

---

20   Private William S Ducker was a medical orderly who entered the gatehouse under fire to give aide to those wounded by the shell that killed MacLeod. Private Ducker was awarded the Military Medal. He was killed on 19 June and is buried in Hermanville War Cemetery.

21   Captain John P Hanson was awarded a Military Cross for his leadership.

22   Allied military planners believed that the larger Casemate #1 held a longer range 155-mm gun.

Battery, Artillery Regiment 1716, commanded by Leutnant Raimund Steiner, who was in the forward fire-control bunker in Franceville at the time of the attack.

The mission to silence the guns was assigned to the 9th (Eastern and Home Counties or Essex) Parachute Battalion (9th Para), which had been retrained as paratroops from the 10th Battalion, Essex Regiment, in late 1942. The Essex Regiment formed in 1881 and fought in the Boer War as well as in the First World War at le Cateau, Ypres, Somme, Cambrai, and Gallipoli. Although Merville was its first operation, the unit had trained for the mission for two months, practicing assaults against a full-scale model of the Merville Battery.

Objective	To eliminate the battery's threat to troops landing on Sword Beach.
Forces	
British	9th Parachute Battalion (Lieutenent-Colonel Terence Otway)
German	I Battery, Artillery Regiment 1716 (Leutnant Raimund Steiner)
Result	The guns were silenced
Casualties	
British	85 killed or wounded
German	22 killed and 20 taken prisoner
Location	Merville is 20 km northeast of Caen.

Battle

The 9th Para, commanded by Lieutenant-Colonel Terence Otway,[23] experienced a disorganized drop in DZ V located between Gonneville-en-Auge and Varaville. The combination of a nighttime drop, severe winds, the nearby flooded marshes, and German antiaircraft fire and ground patrols proved fatal to some of the paratroopers and dispersed the rest of them. Although originally a force of 750, only 150 men reached the rendezvous point, 1 kilometer southeast of Gonneville. Most of their specialized equipment was missing: they had no explosives, mortars, antitank weapons, medical equipment or communications gear. They did have one medium-range machine gun and six Bangalore torpedoes[24]. Col Otway decided that the assault must be launched, regardless of the odds, because the invasion counted on it.

The detonation of the Bangalore torpedoes placed under the barbed wire was the attack signal. As dawn was breaking, Major Alan Parry,[25] Company A commander, led the 50-man main assault force while Otway remained with his meager number of reserves. Divided into four groups – one assigned to each casemate – the men charged through the openings in the perimeter wire and followed the faint scratches of the de-mining party through the minefield. The scene became chaotic as men fired in all directions. Grenade

---

23   Lieutenant-Colonel Terence Brandram Hastings Otway was awarded the Distinguished Service Order for his actions at Merville Battery and the days that followed. On 12 June, while preparing for the attack upon Bréville, Otway received a severe injury from a shell that landed nearby. He never returned to active service but remained in the War Office until 1948. He died in 2006 at age 92.

24   Bangalore torpedoes: connected sections of tubing which held an explosive charge. They were frequently slid under obstacles and detonated to clear an opening.

25   Major Allen James Maule Parry was awarded the Military Cross. He was wounded in the assault on Casemate #1 but returned to duty later to fight in Belgium, Holland, and Germany.

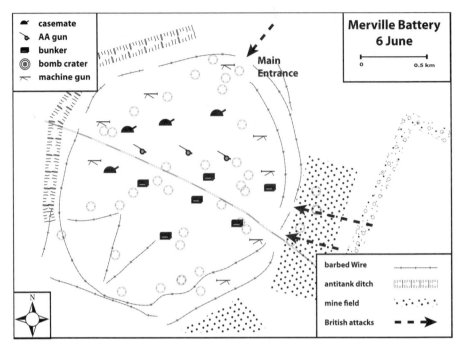

explosions added to the noise and dust as the paratroopers moved from position to position. Grenades tossed through open doorways and down ventilation pipes exploded in the casemates and bunkers. Each of the four guns was disabled, however, by destroying its breech.

Leutnant Steiner, hearing the explosions in his post 2 kilometers away, ordered counterfire from guns in Franceville onto his own battery, but the battle was already over. A yellow smoke flare alerted offshore naval vessels that the battery had been taken. The 9th Para had suffered 85 casualties in the assault with only 22 prisoners taken.

Aftermath

On 7 June, Allied commanders received a report that the guns at Merville were again active. No 3 Commando was sent to recapture the battery, but it found that the guns were indeed inoperative. Still, a strong German counterattack led by SP guns caused heavy casualties, including the unit commander, as No 3 Commando withdrew.

Battlefield Tour

From le Château Haras, continue on the farm lane approximately 1 km to where the lane makes a sharp left curve at the junction with an unpaved farm track on the right. (49.256196, -0.180244)

Drop Zone V was located between the Château Haras and this rural road junction. The exact rendezvous point was a hedgerow 200 meters north. Col Otway reached the rendezvous at 0130 and there learned of the disastrous landing. By 0250, he was leading his drastically reduced force northwest toward Gonneville.

Continue 1.0 km into Gonneville-en-Auge and turn right after the church in place de l'Église. Note: due to the many one-way streets, turn right again almost immediately to proceed along the north side of the church (becomes rue de la Mairie). After 440 m, turn right onto rue des Banques and continue 150 m to the intersection. (49.264218, -0.187494)

A three-man team led by Major George Smith[26] had dropped at 0017 and proceeded immediately to the battery for on-ground reconnaissance. He returned to meet Otway's main force at this intersection to report the extent of the minefields and the two routes he had selected as passageways. The final plans were revised and at 0400 the troops departed into the night.

A pink granite stele with gold lettering stands in what is now named **Carrefour du 9ème Bataillon**. From this crossroads, 9th Parachute Battalion started on its final march to the Merville Battery.

Turn right onto Chemin du Douet Philbert and proceed 600 m to the junction with highway D223. The embankments and ditches of this country lane provided cover for the advance of the attack group toward the battery. Turn right (unsigned), proceed 85 m, and turn onto the drivable farm track on the left. (49.267342, -0.193934)

In 1944, the ground to the north was wooded, as was a smaller area 50 meters to the south. The trees provided some cover as the attack force approached the battery perimeter and the lanes through the minefield as earlier marked by Major Smith's team. Both copses have since been removed. A diversion team, led by Sergeant Sidney Knight, moved 300 meters farther north to the entrance roadway to the battery. [27]

If the gate is open, continue forward; the dirt road passes through the Melville Battery grounds – now a protected nature preserve – but does not allow entrance to the battery structures. The final assault occurred parallel to this road through two breaches in the barbed wire 70 and 100 meters to the north. The road passes between Casemates #3 and #4 and provides an attackers perspective of the installation.

Proceed out of the battery grounds; turn right onto les Pâtis. After 200 m, turn right onto rue du Buisson, then after 150 m turn left onto rue des Mariniers After 190 m, turn right onto Av Alexandre de Laverge, and finally after 200 m turn right onto Av de la Batterie de Merville. (49.27009, -0.196375)

Batterie de Merville

place du 9ème Bataillon   14810 Merville-Franceville
Tel: +33 (0)2 31 91 47 53   Web: http://www.batterie-merville.com/

All four of the battery's casemates are accessible. Casemate #1, the first constructed and the largest, houses a museum containing photos and relics of the Atlantic Wall labeled in French and English. Its displays include a terrain map used by the British in preparation for the attack and a light table illuminating the 9th Para Battalion's assault. A light and sound

---

26   Major George Smith was awarded the Military Cross.

27   Sergeant Sidney George Knight was awarded the Military Medal for his aggressiveness in this and subsequent engagements on D-Day.

presentation replicates the attack. One can also enter the tobruk on the roof of Casemate #1. A bust of Lieutenant Colonel Otway stands outside across the pathway. Casemate #2 remains as a memorial to the 9th Battalion. It features a table of orientation on the roof, showing how the guns covered the landing beaches at Ouistreham and Sword Beach. Casemate #3 is dedicated to the Glider Pilot Regiment, No 3 Commando, No 45 Royal Marine Commando, and 1st Canadian Parachute Battalion. Casemate #4 commemorates the August 1944 action, which finally cleared the area of German troops. The museum also displays an authentic Douglas C-47 'Dakota' transport airplane.

Open daily 15 March through 15 October from 09:30 to 18:30; daily 16 October through 15 November from 09:30 to 17:30. Admission fee; Normandie Pass accepted.

Battle of Bavent Ridge
7 to 13 June 1944

After the spectacular *coup de main* operation against the two bridges at Bénouville and Merville Battery, the 6th Airborne Division adopted a defensive posture fighting as well-trained infantry. Constant pressure by first grade German infantry units continued until 13 June and inflicted much higher casualty rates than the more perilous airborne operations.

Objective	To prevent German counterattack from east of the Orne River.
Forces	
British	6th Airborne Division (Major-General RN Gale)
German	Grenadier Regiment 736 (Oberst Ludwig Krug); later strengthened by the 346th Infantry Division (Generalleutnant Erich Diester)
Result	The Bavent Ridge was captured and held despite heavy casualties
Casualties	
British	821 dead; 2,709 wounded; 927 missing (6 June to 16 August)
German	Uncertain
Location	Sallenelles is 15 km northeast of Caen.

Battle

By 8 June, the Germans were responding more aggressively with the arrival of Grenadier Regiments 856 and 857 of the 346th Infantry Division. Their objectives were to recapture the bridges at Bénouville and Ranville and to take back control of the west-facing edge of the Bavent Ridge that ran through Hameau Oger, Amfréville, Bréville, les Mesnil crossroads, and on to Troarn. Only probing patrols took place on 8 and 9 June, with the full-scale assaults on 10 June supported by tanks and SP guns. The British 6th Airborne Division responded by shifting its paratroop units to the areas of greatest enemy action. The key to the situation became the village of Bréville, which had been occupied by the Germans and formed a salient in the British line known as the Bréville Gap. It was finally assaulted and captured on 12 June.

Aftermath

After the attack capability of the German 346th Infantry Division was broken, a stalemate developed. The 51st (Highland) Division took up positions on the southern

front in preparation for attacks upon Caen. The 6th Airborne Division was reorganized and responsibilities redefined.

Battlefield Tour
      The individual actions are briefly described as the tour route travels from Sallenelles to Troarn along highways D37b and D37, which follow the crest of the Bavent Ridge from north to south.

> Leave the Merville Battery on Av de la Batterie Merville. Turn left onto Av Alexandre de Lavergne and carefully follow this street for almost 1 km to the roundabout with highway D514. Take the third exit toward Caen (D514). After 2.4 km, pass the *mairie* on the right.

      A monument to the **Belgian-Luxembourg Brigade Piron** lies behind the *mairie*. The unit liberated Sallenelles and Franceville-Plage during the Allied advance in August 1944. (49.264847, -0.226722)

> Continue 270 m to place Général Piron and turn left toward Amfréville (D37B). Continue 500 m to the memorial on the left. (49.259174, -0.231225)

      The D37B / D37 highway starts up the ridge at Sallenelles and continues roughly southeast along its crest for approximately 10 kilometers. Although difficult to see when driving south, two flag poles signal the location of a granite stele holding a brass plaque commemorating the men of the **4th Special Service Brigade**. The brigade, composed of four troops of Royal Marine Commandos and No 10 (Inter-Allied) Commando, came under the 6th Airborne Division on 11 June. The site marks the northern tip of the Bavent Ridge. Although notably barren of adequate parking, this location permits views to the west and north that prove the value of holding this high ground.

> Continue toward Amfréville (D37B) and enter the town. Before reaching the church, turn right onto rue Morice and after 140 m turn left and continue 35 m to the memorial on the left. (49.248832, -0.235742)

Amfréville
      After their noisy arrival at Bénouville, No 4 and No 6 Commando moved across the bridge and continued north into Amfréville, where they drove out a small German force and occupied the village. No 45 Royal Marine Commando continued into Sallenelles to attack the batteries at Franceville-Plage, but they were driven back to Hameau Oger on 8 June.
      A gray granite stele commemorates **No 3 Commando** and the liberation of the town on 6 June. The simple memorial to the unit's fallen dead is surrounded by shrubs on an unnamed street.

> Continue 170 m to the memorials on the left. (49.247384, -0.235224)

      The men of 12th Para were briefed before the attack upon Bréville in l'Église St-Martin, located in the center of the main square known as le Plein. A memorial place holds

a cross with a brass plaque commemorating the men of **1st Special Service Brigade**. A separate plinth holds a brass plaque commemorating the **British and French Commandos**, who fought their way inland as part of the brigade to secure the eastern flank against all enemy attacks.

> Continue and cross highway D37B at the south end of the square to enter a frontage road (rue des Champs St-Martin). Park near the entrance gate to the old farm. (49.245287, -0.233221)

The white, painted stele past the **NTL Totem**[28] commemorates **No 6 Commando** and its members killed in the fighting in Amfréville. The gateway to the right of the large house opposite was the entrance to an old farm used by Brigadier Lord Lovat and his 1st Special Service Brigade while occupying the town. A small plaque above a window on the left side of the entryway now identifies the structure as Ferme des Commandos. While the command staff watched the assault upon Bréville from this gate, an Allied shell fell short, killing Lieutenant-Colonel AP Johnson,[29] 12th Para commander. Brigadier Lord Lovat and the 6th Airlanding Brigade commander, Brigadier H Kindersley, were struck by shell fragments and seriously wounded.

Battle of Bréville
12 June 1944

Bréville sits on the western edge of the Bavent Ridge, overlooking British positions at Ranville and the Orne Valley. Until 10 June it was held by the German Grenadier Regiment 857 and was used as a base for attacks against Amfréville and the Bois des Monts.

Objective	To secure positions on the Bavent Ridge and end the threat of German counterattack from the east.
Forces	
British	12th Parachute Battalion (Lieutenant-Colonel AP Johnson)
German	Grenadier Regiment 857
Result	The village was liberated
Casualties	
British	162 dead
German	418 dead
Location	Bréville is 14 km northeast of Caen.

Battle

The 12th (Yorkshire) Parachute Battalion (12th Para) led a hastily-planned night

---

28   NTL: *Normandie Terre-Liberté* (Normandy, Land of Liberty): The local *départements* established eight color-coded tourist routes in Normandy covering sites of the battle. Each location is marked with a blue totem, which describes the local action and provides maps and directions to the next site. Special road signs also provide directions to the sites.

29   Lieutenant-Colonel Alexander Percival Johnson is buried in Ranville War Cemetery.

assault with support from Company D, 12th Battalion, Devonshire Regiment, tanks of the 13/18 Royal Hussars, and 100 guns from four field artillery regiments. With only a three-hour notice and ground troops 5 kilometers from the start line, a mad scramble ensued achieve jump-off positions before the 10-minute preliminary bombardment.

As the bombardment commenced, the German SP guns in Bréville started counterfire on the British lines. Against intense enemy machine-gun and artillery fire, the men of Company C, 12th Para, pressed forward. Only fifteen survived the 200 meters from Amfréville to the outskirts of Bréville. As Company B, 12th Para, and Company D, Devonshire Regiment, entered the field, Sherman tanks on either side broke cover and engaged the enemy guns. With the appearance of the British tanks, the German shelling quickly diminished. The fighting ended at 2245 as Company B took up defensive positions in German trenches in a field near the church, and Company C secured the crossroads to the south. The units involved suffered significant casualties: 12th Para lost 141 men, Devonshire regiment lost 36 men, and the Germans left 78 dead in the village plus an unknown number of wounded who escaped. To add to the death toll, British artillery inexplicably renewed its bombardment, with the shells falling upon their own men. The 12th Parachute Battalion was relieved the next morning.

Battlefield Tour

> Leave Amfréville by continuing on rue des Champs St-Martin for 450 m. Turn left toward Bréville (D37B) and continue 350 m to the churchyard entrance on the left. (49.240627, -0.226432)

The Bréville churchyard contains several broken pieces of concrete and grave markers and the ruins of the old church stand in silent testimony to the ferocity of the battle. Only a portion of the ornately-carved rear wall and a few foundation pillars remain. A new church now stands adjacent to the old church. Tilted and moss-covered gravestones frame the two Commonwealth graves.

> Proceed 110 m to the junction of highways D37B and D223 and the monument on the right. (49.240264, -0.226264)

A multicolored granite stele commemorates the people of Bréville and the men of the **12th Parachute Battalion** who died during the assault that drove out the German force on 12 June. The inscription notes that the 162 men who died are buried in Ranville War Cemetery. The road junction is now Carrefour 6th Airborne Division with an adjacent **NTL Totem**.

> Leave Bréville to the southwest toward Ranville (D223). Follow for 2.3 km and enter Ranville. Turn left onto rue du Stade (D37) and almost immediately a sharp right turn onto rue Airbornes 10. After 270 m, turn left onto rue du Comte Louis de Rohan Chabot and proceed 100 m to the cemetery entrance on the right. (49.23117, -0.257825)

Ranville

The 13th (Lancashire) Parachute Battalion effected a more successful drop than other units. By 0150, two-thirds of the battalion had reached the DZ N rendezvous point.

They marched into Ranville, where they drove off garrison troops from 7th Company, Panzergrenadier Regiment 125, commanded by Hans von Luck.[30] A counterattack by the 3rd Company, Panzergrenadier Regiment 125, supported by SP guns in the late afternoon of 6 June, was repelled. A stronger assault against the Bénouville and Ranville Bridges, however, took place on 10 June, as Grenadier Regiment 857 traveled across Landing Zone N, heading north and east of Ranville. The 13th (Lancashire) Parachute Battalion's concentrated fire and spirited bayonet charge finally drove back a persistent enemy. The Germans suffered over 400 dead with 100 taken prisoner.

The **Ranville War Cemetery** holds 2,235 British Commonwealth and 330 German burials with most of the casualties occurring during local fighting. To the left of the Cross of Sacrifice, a cross-shaped stele, erected shortly after the conflict, is dedicated to the **Royal Engineers** of the 6th Airborne Division and has a round plaque displaying its winged-horse emblem. The cemetery contains the grave of two brothers from the 1st Canadian Parachute Battalion, Lieutenants J Maurice and J Philippe Rousseau.[31]

Across the street and slightly north of the cemetery entrance, a fieldstone wall displays a map of the eastern bridgehead and displays the areas of operation for the airborne and commando brigades. (49.231298, -0.257507)

An old windmill tower stands directly to the south and displays a bronze plaque commemorating the members of the **Belgian Brigade Piron**, killed in the later August fighting. The Belgian 1st Infantry Brigade, named Brigade Piron after its commander, Major Jean-Baptiste Piron, fought in the Battle of Normandy with the 6th Airborne Division. The brigade was formed in 1942 from Belgian soldiers who had escaped to Britain in 1940. It eventually increased to 2,200 men and included a contingent from Luxembourg. The men arrived in Normandy on 30 July and liberated Franceville-Plage, Varaville, and numerous other towns along the French coast before fighting in Belgium and the Netherlands. (49.230986, -0.25761)

> Walk north along the roadway to place General Sir Richard Gale and enter the churchyard at the rear of the church. (49.231995, -0.257868)

The **Ranville Churchyard** next to the cemetery holds forty-seven British Commonwealth burials, including that of Lt Herbert Denham Brotheridge, the first British soldier killed on D-Day. The graves are positioned along the exterior wall immediately to the right of the entrance. Among the well-maintained row is the grave of a German soldier. The churchyard was used for the first burials on 6 June, before the Commonwealth War Graves Commission established Ranville War Cemetery.

> Leave the cemetery, cross rue Airbornes 10, and proceed east 50 m to the entrance of the *mairie* courtyard. (49.231909, -0.256885)

A bust of **General Sir Richard Nelson Gale** stands near the right rear corner

---

30   Major Hans von Luck fought on almost every front of the war. His unit was instrumental in stopping Operation Goodwood during the Battle of Caen. See Chapter Thirteen.

31   The Rousseau brothers were originally from Montreal, Quebec, Canada. Paratrooper J Philippe dropped near Gonneville-s/Mer on 6 June; his body was found the next day. J Maurice was killed in September 1944, after being captured by the enemy during a clandestine operation in the Vosges. His body was later moved next to his brother in Ranville.

of the courtyard, in front of the *mairie*. The bust, unveiled during the 50th Anniversary celebrations, commemorates the commander of the British 6th Airborne Division and his fearless leadership during the first days of the invasion. Gale landed by glider at 0330 on D-Day and established his headquarters in Ranville.

> Return to your vehicle and proceed north to rue Airbornes 10; turn right, go past the *mairie*, and continue 250 m to the next major intersection (place 6 Juin 1944, D37). (49.230923, -0.254008)

A memorial plaque commemorating the liberation of Ranville and claiming the honor of being the first town in France to be liberated decorates a stone wall in what is now place 6 Juin 1944. The plaque displays the insignia of the **13th (Lancashire) Battalion**, The Parachute Regiment, with its slogan 'Win or Die.'

> Turn past the 13th Para Monument toward Hérouvillette (D37). After 750 m, turn right onto Route d'Hérouvillette (D37C) and follow for 1.1 km into the village. Turn left onto Av de Caen and quickly turn right onto rue de la Paix. Stop at the entrance to the cemetery. (49.219524, -0.241478)

Hérouvillette was occupied by the Ox and Bucks on 7 June without incident. An effort to occupy Escoville, 1 km to the south, was initially successful, but the Ox and Bucks were driven out by an armor-led counterattack later in the day, at the cost of eighty casualties. In 1944 the road to Escoville ran through flat, open fields, and the unit's advance provided excellent targets for the Germans. The German counterattack, conversely, provided excellent targets for British antitank guns. The marble plaque with gold lettering on the cemetery wall behind the church commemorates those members of the **Ox and Bucks** who fought at Pegasus Bridge, Escoville, and Bréville-les-Monts.

> Reverse direction and return to Av de Caen and turn right, pass along the side of the church, and proceed 400 m (becomes Av de Cabourg). Carefully enter the slip road on the left and stop at the stone plinth. (49.222432, -0.23663)

The short stone wall marks stop 3 on the **Pegasus Trail** (stop 2 is along highway D514 and marks the eastern boundary of Drop Zone N) and overlooks the southern boundary of Drop Zone N. The main drops of 7th, 12th, and 13th Para arrived during the early morning darkness of 6 June in these fields. The first gliders of 6th Airlanding Brigade landed here shortly after noon. The water tower visible in the distance locates the Bois des Mont, a battle zone described below.

> Reverse direction and return to Av de Cabourg turning a sharp left. In 75 m turn left toward Deauville / Varaville (D513). After 1.6 km, turn left toward Bréville (D37b). Proceed 1.2 km and stop at the water towers on the left. (49.234723, -0.223109)

Battle of Bois des Monts and Château St-Côme
During the night of 7/8 June, the survivors of the 9th Parachute Battalion's attack upon Merville Battery occupied the Bois des Monts, across the road from the Château St-Côme, finally establishing their position at approximately 0130. Because they were

too small to defend both positions, the paratroopers utilized active patrolling to keep the Germans out of the chateau. Over the next few days, men who had missed their drop zones slowly accumulated at the position, increasing the complement to 270.

Battle

German patrols from Grenadier Regiment 857 started testing British positions by midday on 8 June. In fact, the first serious German assault on the Bois des Monts met mass rifle and machine-gun fire on 9 June. The Germans, nonetheless, placed two SP guns and substantial infantry on the chateau grounds. The attacks continued the next day, with three separate incursions repulsed with machine-gun and mortar fire. During the main attack, 105-mm SP guns moved along the chateau drive, flanked on both sides by infantry. The Allies held their position only with the help of naval gunfire. Eventually ,the Germans abandoned their assault that night.

On 11 June, 9th Para was reinforced by members of 5th Battalion, The Black Watch, detached from the 51st (Highland) Division, which had launched an attack on Bréville at 0430. Despite a preliminary artillery bombardment, the Highlanders were unable to penetrate the village, and its attack was repulsed, leaving behind three hundred casualties. The Germans countered with a strong, armor-supported attack against the chateau the next day. The Black Watch was driven from the grounds into the Bois des Monts, where the 9th Para was also under assault. The situation become perilous, and Company C, 1st Canadian Parachute Battalion, was dispatched from les Mesnil as reinforcements. The battle raged on, with British, Canadians, and Germans mixed together in the woods and chateau buildings. Finally, the Canadians reoccupied the chateau, and the Germans pulled back.

Battlefield Tour

The road opposite the water tower marks the entrance to the Château St-Côme Haras, which is now a private horse-breeding farm. Two memorials, however, adjoin the entrance. On the right, the **Bois des Monts battle stele** provides a good description of the engagements. On the left, a small slate plaque mounted on a stone plinth commemorates in Dutch and French the men of the **Princess Irene Brigade**, a Dutch unit which fought in the area in August 1944.

Across the highway and farther south, the life-sized casting of a Scottish piper commemorates the **51st (Highland) Division's** participation in the battle and its 110 killed. The forest behind the piper is the Bois des Monts, and although private, the density of the trees helps one imagine the close-in, heavy fighting that took place there in the early days of June 1944. (49.234562, -0.223171)

Reverse direction and proceed toward Troarn (D37b, becomes D37). After 1.3 km, turn toward the memorials on the right. (49.226248, -0.216492)

Battle of les Mesnil Crossroads
8 to 16 June 1944

After their fight in Varaville and the destruction of the bridge at Robehomme, the three companies of 1st Canadian Parachute Battalion rendezvoused at les Mesnil, as planned. This high-ground intersection was the key to protecting the division's positions along the Bavent Ridge.

Battle

At dawn on 8 June, German Grenadier Regiments 856 and 857, supported by tanks and SP guns, launched the first of several efforts to recapture the les Mesnil crossroads. Effective mortar fire and a PIAT round against the leading tank forced the attackers to retreat. The German losses were significant as attack and counterattack continued for much of the day. Sporadic fighting continued until 17 June, when the Canadians were relieved by the 5th Parachute Brigade. In ten days of fighting, the Canadians suffered 119 casualties.

Battlefield Tour

A stone block stele carries a plaque paying special tribute to the men of the **3rd Canadian Parachute Brigade**, which held this vital high-ground crossroads. A nearby stele dedicates the square to Brigadier James Hill[32] and the men of his **3rd Parachute Brigade**. The unit's headquarters, situated in the Poterie de Bavent, lies 200 meters west on highway D513.

Continue toward Troarn (D37) for 2.9 km. Park at the entrance to Manoir du Bois Haras. Walk 30 m farther to the two steles on the left. (49.201022, -0.211422)

Battle of Bois de Bavent

Battle

The 8th (Midlands) Parachute Battalion established a base behind the manoir in the Bois de Bavent and the adjacent Bois de Bures on 6 June. Separated from the rest of the division, the unit engaged the enemy in its own private war. From there it continued harassing the Germans with aggressive and wide-ranging patrols. Mine fields, tree bursts from artillery shelling, and snipers took their toll on both sides.

Battlefield Tour

A roadside stele commemorates the members of the **8th Parachute Battalion**, who fought in the Battle of Normandy. A memorial to the unit commander, Lieutenant-Colonel Alastair S Pearson,[33] stands beside the stele. The Manoir du Bois is now another of the region's private horse farms.

Side trip: Juckes Bridge

The pastoral setting and proximity to Bois de Bavent (5 kilometers east) make a side trip to one of the Dives River bridges destroyed by the 6th Airborne Division on 6 June a pleasant excursion.

---

32   Brigadier Stanley James Ledger Hill was a career soldier who oversaw the Dunkirk evacuation while a member of Lord Gort's staff. Hill was awarded a Distinguished Service Order and Légion d'honneur for service in Africa. He was awarded a second Distinguished Service Order for leading an assault in Normandy. Hill retired in 1949 and died in 2006 at age 95.

33   Lieutenant-Colonel Alastair S Pearson (later Brigadier) was a highly-decorated soldier who fought in North Africa, Sicily, and Normandy, earning the Military Cross and four Distinguished Service Orders. The final DSO was awarded for leading a party 6 kilometers behind enemy lines to rescue eight wounded paratroops. He died in 1995 at age 80.

Continue toward Troarn (D37). After 2.5 km, turn left toward Bures-s/Dives (rue des Bures). After 1.5 km turn left toward Bures-s/Dives (D95), then quickly turn right onto

rue du Capitaine Juckes. Follow the road for 250 m, then bear left (still rue Capitaine Juckes) and continue an additional 100 m. Turn right onto rue du Port and follow it to the end. (49.200579, -0.168384) Total distance: 8 km.

As part of the mission to deny the bridges over the Dives River to the Germans, 2nd Troop, 3rd Parachute Squadron, British Royal Engineers, under the command of Captain TR Juckes, arrived at this bridge at 0630 on 6 June. Whereas the Dives River is not a major waterway, its steep banks were sufficient to restrict the movement of armored vehicles to the roadways. The unit quickly prepared explosives and, after permitting the local farmer to bring his cattle across, destroyed both the road bridge and the railway bridge a short distance to the north. The company then returned to 8th Parachute Battalion positions in Bois de Bures. The rebuilt structure is now known as **Pont Capitaine Juckes.**[34] The **Juckes Bridge Memorial** stands on the left embankment. The current bridge is restricted to farm vehicles.

To return to the tour route, reverse direction and proceed to D37; turn toward Troarn. From the Bois de Bavent, proceed south toward Troarn (D37). In the center of town, enter a roundabout and take the third exit toward le Havre / Rouen (Route de Rouen, D675). Follow for 1.8 km to the small bridge on the Dives River. (49.184196, -0.16446)

Troarn Bridge

Col Pearson realized that he lacked sufficient forces to march through Troarn and destroy the bridge over the Dives River. He therefore sent a small team led by Major JCA Roseveare to Troarn in a medical jeep with a trailer full of explosives. In a daring maneuver, the team raced through Troarn – exchanging fire along the way with the alerted German garrison – to the bridge east of town. By 0500, the charges were set. They lit the fuse and blew a 6-meter gap in the metal truss structure. Knowing that the garrison had been alerted, Roseveare led his men back to Bois de Bavent through the countryside.

The strategic nature of Troarn is apparent. The town sits on the ridge crest, with road intersections coming from every direction. The highway to the east drops precipitously off the Bavent Ridge and overlooks the 1944 flood plain created by the Germans. This highway was the major corridor between Caen and Cherbourg to the west and between le Havre and Rouen to the east. A **stone stele** on the west bank of the Troarn highway bridge carries a plaque commemorating the actions of Major Roseveare[35] and his men.

To return to Caen, reverse direction and follow highway D675 for 9.1 km to the Caen ring road (*Periphérique*) or take highway D675 for 2.1 km to access Autoroute A13/E46 and continue 7.0 km to the ring road.

---

34   Captain Thomas Roland Juckes was awarded a Military Cross. He was killed by mortar fire on 28 June near Mesnil de Bavent and is buried in Ranville War Cemetery.

35   Major John Couch Adams Roseveare was awarded the Distinguished Service Order for his bravery.

Chapter Two
British 3rd (Iron) Infantry Division
6 to 9 June 1944

The capture of Caen was crucial to the success of Operation OVERLORD. The city was Lower Normandy's largest manufacturing and transportation center, and the open countryside, devoid of the hatred hedgerows faced by the Americans, provided ideal tank country. Armor and aerial superiority would facilitate a swift exit from the beachhead. The British 3rd Infantry Division's objectives were to land on Sword Beach, advance south, and capture Caen on D-Day.

The British Second Army's landing beaches – Sword, Juno, and Gold – were significantly different than those of the Americans farther west. Broad, flat stretches of sand stood before resort communities of oceanfront villas. Sword Beach, the easternmost of the three, extended from the mouth of the Orne River to near St-Aubin-s/Mer to the west. Although the entire beach was divided into four sectors – codenamed Oboe, Peter, Queen, and Roger – only Queen was selected for landing because of its gaps in the shallow offshore reefs. The bulk of British 3rd Infantry Division, therefore, would have to land within a 1.5-kilometer gap in front of the seafront community of la Brèche d'Hermanville-s/Mer.

The Atlantic Wall of Generalfeldmarschall Erwin Rommel was readying to repel any landing attempt. Strongpoints containing casemated cannon, machine guns, and mortars encircled by rows of barbed wire and minefields defended probable landing areas, especially those with southward roadways that offered quick exits from the beachfront. Six artillery batteries were positioned inland facing Sword Beach.

The ground troops, units of Grenadier Regiments 726 and 736 of the German 716th Infantry Division, were 'static' forces without motor transport and with contingents of unreliable *Ost* battalions and a high percentage of elderly soldiers. Supported by ninety-eight tanks of Panzer Regiment 100, the division covered a seafront of 45 kilometers. The 21st Panzer Division was stationed farther inland while it refitted after losses in Africa the previous year.

The British 3rd Infantry Division traces its origins to the Napoleonic Wars when it was formed by the 1st Duke of Wellington to fight during the Peninsula Campaign. It participated in the Battle of Waterloo, the Crimean War, and the Boer War. The 'Iron Division,' as it became nicknamed, had also spent four years on the Western Front during the First World War and had been part of the British Expeditionary Force during the 1940 Battle of France under then Major-General Bernard Montgomery. After the evacuation from Dunkirk, it spent four years waiting to return to the continent.

The division comprised three infantry brigades – each with its complement of Royal Artillery, Engineers and other services – and was augmented for the invasion by the 1st and 4th Special Service Brigades, the 27th Armoured Brigade's specialized armor, and engineering units of the 79th Armoured Division.

The invasion was led by Breaching Squadrons, LCTs[1] carrying AVRE[2]s, Sherman

---

1   LCT: Landing Craft, Tank, one of a variety of amphibious assault ships used during the invasion. An LCT could carry from three to nine tanks depending upon its size.

2   AVRE: Armoured Vehicle Royal Engineers, a Churchill tank modified to mount a 290-mm spigot mortar that fired a 40 pound shell against heavy fortifications. See appendix E.

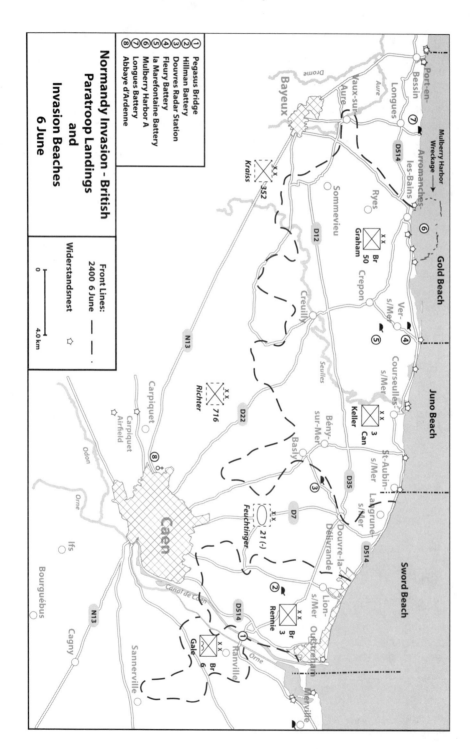

Normandy Invasion - British
Paratroop Landings
and
Invasion Beaches
6 June

① Pegasus Bridge
② Hillman Battery
③ Douvres Radar Station
④ Fleury Battery
⑤ la Marefontaine Battery
⑥ Mulberry Harbor A
⑦ Longues Battery
⑧ Abbaye d'Ardenne

Front Lines:
2400 6 June — — ·

Widerstandsnest ☆

0 ⊢———⊣ 4.0 km

Crabs,[3] dual drive (DD) Sherman tanks, and other specialized units, including squadrons from 79th Armoured Division (Hobart's Funnies[4]) designed to deal with any shore-gun emplacements that survived the naval and aerial bombardments. Assault infantry battalions landed a few minutes later, accompanied by engineer teams to clear gaps in the beach obstacles. Additional landings later on strengthened the infantry and added antitank and SP gun firepower.

D-Day Landings (Sword Beach)
6 June 1944

Objective	To establish a beachhead and to capture Caen.
Forces	
British	British 3rd Infantry Division (Major-General TG Rennie)
German	716th Infantry Division (Generalleutnant Wilhelm Richter)
Result	Although the landings were entirely successful, Caen was not captured.
Casualties	
British	683 casualties
German	uncertain
Location	Ouistreham is 15 km north of Caen.

Battle

The paratroop landings on the Cotentin Peninsula suggested to General Richter, commander of the German 716th Infantry Division, that the long expected invasion had begun, and at 0110 on 6 June he placed his forces on full alert. At 0530, Allied naval vessels started a preliminary bombardment. At 0725, exactly on schedule, the LCA[5]s of 2nd Battalion, East Yorkshire Regiment (E Yorks), hit the shore alongside Duplex Drive[6] Sherman tanks amid blazing small-arms crossfire. Companies A and B landed on Queen Red, directly in front of the guns of *Widerstandsnest* 20 (WN-20). Although casualties were high, the men reached the relative safety of the beach promenade while the tanks were torn apart by the guns. Queen White, where 1st Battalion, South Lancaster Regiment, led the assault, was fortunately not as well defended. AVREs followed the lane through the minefield created by the Flails. The defenders were easily overcome, opening the beach exit.

At 0820, No 4 Commando – including No 10 Inter-Allied French Commando, led by Commandant Philippe Kieffer – set foot on Queen Red. It fought through a campground to reach the east/west shore road and turned east toward their objectives. No 41 Commando landed in the teeth of WN-20. Once on the shore road, it turned west toward its objectives in Lion-s/Mer. By 0840, the other elements of Brigadier Lord Lovat's 1st Special Service Brigade were ashore and moving across open country and toward the Bénouville bridges.

---

3   Crab (or Flail): a Sherman tank equipped with a rotating cylinder of chains designed to safely detonate mines.

4   Hobart's Funnies: named after 79th Armoured Division commander Major-General Percy Hobart, proponent of the specialized tanks used by British forces during the invasion. See appendix E

5   LCA: Landing Craft, Assault, a shallow draft craft used to ferry assault troops from transport ships.

6   Duplex Drive (or DD): a British development for amphibious swimming tanks. The names refers to two drive mechanisms: standard land transmission and a secondary propeller for water crossings.

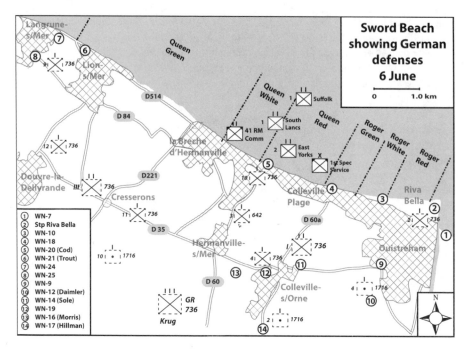

The landing was textbook – according to plan – with acceptable levels of casualties. However, the incoming tide, driven by an onshore wind, narrowed the available sand beach. Infantry and vehicles continued to land and units became intermixed; soon an enormous traffic jam paralyzed all movement off the beach. The tangled affairs on the beach delayed the movement of 185th Infantry Brigade, whose mission was to advance to Hermanville-s/Mer and continue down highway D60 to capture Caen. After waiting an hour for tank support, Brigadier KP Smith ordered the troops forward without accompanying armor. At 1300, the 1st Battalion, The Suffolk Regiment (Suffolks), easily overcame WN-16 but faced significant opposition at WN-17 (Hillman Battery) 1 kilometer to the south where they were held up for most of the day.

The 2nd Battalion, King's Shropshire Light Infantry (KSLI), proceeded down the Périers Ridge into strong resistance in Biéville. Lieutenant-Colonel FJ Maurice[7], the unit's commander, placed an antitank battery on the southern slopes of the ridge and a squadron of tanks behind its crest. Pushing against strengthening German resistance from the opposite side of a deep natural ditch, KSLI was stopped south of Biéville.

German Counterattack

Late in the morning of 6 June, Oberkommando der Wehrmacht (OKW) subordinated Generalmajor Edgar Feuchtinger's 21st Panzer Division to General Marcks[8],

---

7   Lieutenant-Colonel Frederick Jack Maurice was awarded the Distinguished Service Order for his leadership on D-Day. He was killed on 6 July 1944 at age 39 and is buried in la Delivrande War Cemetery.

8   General der Artillerie Erich Marcks was a Prussian career army officer killed by a fighter-bomber near St-Lô on 12 June at age 53. Marcks is buried in the Marigny German Cemetery in Normandy. He received the Knight's Cross of the Iron Cross with Oak Leaves posthumously.

LXXXIV Armeekorps commander, who ordered a move against the landing beaches from their positions east of Caen. Two *Gepanzerte Gruppe*[9] formed: one containing I Battalion, Panzergrenadier Regiment 125, and the 98 tanks of Panzer Regiment 22 commanded by Oberst Hermann von Oppeln-Bronikowski[10] moved against la Brèche; while the second with I Battalion, Panzergrenadier Regiment 192, led by Oberst Josef Rauch[11] targeted the British-Canadian gap between Lion-s/Mer and Luc-s/Mer. Essentially troops that had been moving against the British Airborne drops east of the Orne were ordered to reverse direction and attack the sea-borne landings west of the Orne, leaving only one company of tanks to face the paratroops. The units did not reach their assembly area near Lébisey until 1530.

Gepanzerte Gruppe Rauch began its counterattack by passing through the open country between Périers and Mathieu, heading toward la Delivrande. By 1900, the panzergrenadiers[12] reached the sea north of Lion-s/Mer, where they joined the garrison of WN-21. The arrival of armor support would have made the position practically impenetrable, but the tanks never arrived.

Major Martin Vierzig's II Battalion, Panzer Regiment 22, manning a mix of PzKpfw IV and French Souma tanks, prepared for its counterattack from the Bois de Lébisey north of Caen. It passed the right flank of KSLI and its accompanying tanks from C Squadron, Staffordshire Yeomanry. The guns on the older model PzKpfw IV had limited range: in open ground and at ranges of over two kilometers, the advantage belonged to the Sherman Fireflies and their 17-pounder guns. The guns of the British 20th Antitank Regiment joined the tank fire. Numerous losses drove the panzers farther to the west, toward A Squadron on the opposite flank. Vierzig[13] saw his regiment being destroyed and broke off his assault.

Major Wilhelm von Gottberg[14], commanding the panzer regiment's I Battalion, manning obsolete PzKpfw 38(t)s, was farther to the west and proceeding north, where he found the providentially-placed British 41st Antitank Battery and the Staffordshire's B Squadron on his flank around Point 61. Again Sherman Fireflies and M10 tank destroyers took a heavy toll on the panzers. In the two actions, 21st Panzer Division had 64 tanks destroyed or damaged.

Aftermath

Whereas German infantry threatened to drive a wedge between the British and Canadian beachheads, they were not strong enough to hold against mounting Allied strength. Their presence, however, paralyzed the British 9th Infantry Brigade, preventing

---

9   *Gepanzerte Gruppe*: similar to *Kampfgruppe* but one centered upon an armored contingent.

10   Hermann von Oppeln-Bronikowski came from a Prussian noble family and was highly decorated during the First World War, earning the Iron Cross First and Second Class. He went on to command the 20th Panzer Division and earn the Knights Cross with Oak Leaves and Swords. He survived the war to help establish Germany's Bundeswehr and died in 1966 at age 67.

11   Oberst Josef Rauch received the Knight's Cross of the Iron Cross for his leadership during the fighting at Caen. He was eventually captured by the Russians and held as a POW until 1955. He died in 1984 at age 82.

12   Panzergrenadier: the motorized infantry component of a panzer division.

13   Major Martin Vierzig survived the war and became a dental surgeon.

14   Wilhelm von Gottberg rose to command Panzer Regiment 22 in the final Battle of Berlin. He died in 1994 at age 80.

its attack on Caen. The D-Day objective was lost for the next six weeks.

At approximately 2100, troops of the 6th Airlanding Brigade started to arrive at Landing Zone W, southeast of Aubin-d'Arquenay. Oberst Rauch witnessed the delivery of the airborne force and believed his position around Lion-s/Mer to be untenable. Rauch withdrew to its original positions around St-Contest. One company joined the garrison at the Luftwaffe radar station near Douvres.

Battlefield Tour

The tour begins at Ouistreham and visits seafront sites before proceeding inland. The Mémorial de Caen is a good first stop. For its description, see Chapter Thirteen. (49.197908, -0.38376)

To start the tour from Caen, leave the ring road (E46/N814) at exit 3a (Porte d'Angleterre) toward Ouistreham (D515, becomes D514) and continue for 10.8 km to the large roundabout at the junction of D514 and D84. Take the 2nd exit (D84) and continue 750 m to the next roundabout. (49.270736, -0.255339)

To start the tour from Pegasus Bridge, proceed west to the interchange with highway D514 and turn toward Ouistreham (D514); proceed 2.5 km to the large roundabout at the junction of D514 and D84. Take the 2nd exit (D84) and continue 750 m to the next roundabout. (49.270736, -0.255339)

Ouistreham

Ouistreham has been a fishing port since the Middle Ages and is now the home of a ferry harbor which serves as the port for the city of Caen.

L'Office de Tourisme de Ouistreham (49.288846, -0.258498)

Jardins du Casino - Esplanade Lofi   14 150 Ouistreham-Riva Bella
Tel: +33 (0)2 31 97 18 63   Web: http://www.ville-ouistreham.fr/

In the center of the roundabout, the **Signal Monument** carries the inscription: 'Here on 6/6/1944, Europe was liberated by the heroism of the Allied forces.' A plaque on the Signal Monument is dedicated to the French and British soldiers of No 4 Commando who fell for the liberation of Ouistreham on 6 June 1944. Many similar commemorations of the liberation abound in Ouistreham.

Proceed straight at the roundabout (D84) and continue 1.0 km; turn right onto place du Général de Gaulle and follow through the canal area.

The locks for the Canal de Caen are on the right. A walk across the locks at their north end leads to a view of the Ouistreham Lighthouse. The last remnant of the German canal defenses, an **armored cupola**, is at the far end of Jetée Paul-Emile Victor, which extends north from the lighthouse. (49.283162, -0.246742)

Continue for 450 m, bear left onto rue des Dunes, and quickly bear right. The Brittany Ferries terminal is on the right after approximately 100 m. (49.283596, -0.249896)

Royal Navy and Royal Marine Monument stands in the parking area in front of the Brittany Ferry terminal entrance. The rough-cut stone bears a finely-detailed nautical anchor and commemorates those who manned the over 4,000 landing craft and gun- and rocket-firing ships.

Reverse direction and follow rue des Dunes south for 410 m; turn right onto Av Général Leclerc (D84). Follow for 2.2 km (becomes Route de Lion, D514); turn right onto rue Fontenelle. After 290 m, turn left onto Bd Aristide Briand and continue 270 m to the monument on right. (49.29305, -0.281085)

Colleville-Montgomery

Known before the war as Colleville-s/Orne, despite being more than 2.5 kilometers from the Orne River, the town's origins are somewhat vague. Located on the Roman road from Bayeux to Rouen, the town constructed redoubts in the last days of the French kings to protect the Orne estuary. The ruins of the Colleville redoubt can be seen on rue de la Redoute at the junction with rue Vauban. The Germans also fortified the site.

Office de Tourisme de Colleville Montgomery (49.292693, -0.282941)

Avenue de Bruxelles   14880 Colleville Montgomery
Tel: +33 (0)2 31 96 04 64   Email: ot.colleville.my@orange.fr
Web: http://www.colleville-montgomery.fr/

The beachfront **No 4 Commando Monument** commemorates the 1st Special Service Brigade's landing, which took place slightly to the west, in a graphic bas-relief depicting beret-wearing men struggling across the beach while shell explosions target the landing craft behind them. This monument marks the eastern end of Queen Red sector. All of the British landings occurred to the west of this point.

Across the road, the casemate on the southeast corner of the intersection formed part of **WN-18**. The strongpoint held a 75-mm gun, which could fire the entire length of the beach, and a 50-mm antitank gun. The now-sealed embrasure faces rue Vauban behind a massive protective wall. Much of the casemate has been incorporated into the adjacent house, and thick ivy covers the remains. The roofline was modified from the military sloped-and-soil-covered version into its present square shape after the war. The position was eliminated by several tanks firing high explosive rounds from close range. In front of the casemate is an **NTL Totem**.

Continue on Bd Maritime for 180 m. (49.293386, -0.283504)

The large parking area on the left now occupies the ruins of a holiday park that was the site of the 1st Special Service Brigade's landing. The commandos quickly penetrated through the park to access the lateral roadways (now rue du Commandant Kieffer and Route de Lion) and proceed toward their objectives to the east.

Continue an additional 140 m on Bd Maritime; turn left onto rue Georges Lelong. After 180 m, turn left onto Rue de Lion (D514). After 300 m, turn right onto rue de la Mer and continue around the small park to the parking area. (49.290695, -0.282396)

A statue of **Field Marshal Bernard Law Montgomery, 1st Viscount Montgomery of Alamein,** stands in a small park alongside the coastal highway. Montgomery is wearing his traditional beret and holding a sheaf of notes as if addressing his troops or explaining his invasion plan to Allied commanders.

> From the northeast corner of the park, walk across Route de Lion to view two more memorials on Av du 4ème Commando. (49.290995, -0.281501)

A stele backed by shrubs presents a memorial to **Commandant Philippe Kieffer**[15] and his men who landed and passed this corner on their route to attack the casino strongpoint. They proceeded east on Route de Lion.

The **Provisional Cemetery Monument** across the street marks the site of the first British burials on 6 June 1944. The monument also memorializes the British landings as well as Commandant Kieffer specifically as the first soldier to set foot upon France from the landings. The people of Colleville-s/Orne commend the soldiers for their courage, tenacity, and sacrifices in liberating Europe from the German oppressor. The inscription ends by renaming the town Colleville-Montgomery to remind future generations of the exploits of these heroes.

> Regain your vehicle and make successive right turns to arrive at the rue de Lion / rue de Riva-Bella (D514). Turn toward Ouistreham. Follow for 1.4 km; turn left onto rue Pasteur.

Two small plaques near house #64 commemorate the deaths of all of the **No 4 Commandos** and name two of the French commandos killed there. (49.288232, -0.259176)

> Continue and turn right onto place Alfred Thomas. After 200 m, take the 1st exit onto Av Victor Hugo and enter the large parking area. For convenience, park at the far west end.

Riva-Bella

Many of the seafront resorts have names separate from their commune. Riva-Bella is the resort community in Ouistreham as la Brèche is in Hermanville-s/Mer. The names are frequently interchanged.

The pre-war casino at Riva-Bella had been destroyed by the Germans and replaced with a fortified strongpoint – part of *Stützpunkt*[16] **Riva-Bella (Stp-08)** – which included bunkers, tobruks, pillboxes, and the usual ring of mines and barbed wire designed to defend the Orne River and Canal de Caen entrances. The beach approaches were defended by concrete 'dragon's teeth' that became prominent in later fighting along the German Westwall.

Commandant Kieffer's lightly-armed French Commando force drew the task of overcoming the casino strongpoint. It attacked from two directions: north along the

---

15   Commandant Philippe Kieffer was wounded twice during the invasion and was awarded the Légion d'Honneur, Croix de Guerre with four citations, and the British Military Cross. Kieffer died in 1962 and is buried with honor in Grandcamp-Maisy Communal Cemetery.

16   *Stützpunkt*: stronger base frequently comprised of several resistance pockets (*Widerstandsnest*) and equipped with field guns and antitank weapons. Manpower was approximately of company strength, 100-180 men.

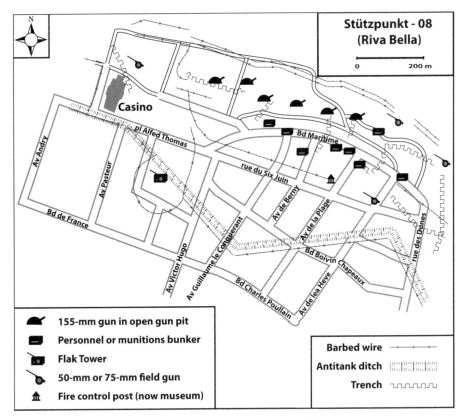

**Stützpunkt - 08
(Riva Bella)**

0   200 m

- Casino

Legend:
- ![155-mm gun] **155-mm gun in open gun pit**
- ![Personnel bunker] **Personnel or munitions bunker**
- ![Flak Tower] **Flak Tower**
- ![field gun] **50-mm or 75-mm field gun**
- ![museum] **Fire control post (now museum)**

Barbed wire	——+——+——
Antitank ditch	⊔⊔⊔⊔⊔
Trench	⊓⊔⊓⊔⊓

rue Pasteur and east along Bd du Maréchal Joffre (now Bd Kieffer). Machine guns in an armored cupola and 50-mm antitank guns inflicted numerous casualties. Two 20-mm FlaK guns fired from the roof of the demolished casino, and sniper fire was equally intense from the Flak tower to their rear. At 0925, the arrival of a Sherman DD tank (some reports state that it was a British Centaur) finally gave the Frenchmen the firepower they required. The first two shells hit the armored cupola and immediately silenced the enemy guns. The individual positions were then destroyed one by one.

A German **Flak tower** stands at the rear of the parking area. The painted white structure is accessed by stairs, and its top permits viewing over the beaches of Riva-Bella and the casino. (49.287596, -0.257483)

Access Place Alfred Thomas by foot and walk west to the museum. (49.288652, 0.25967)

Musée du 4ème Commando
place Albert Thomas   14150 Ouistreham
Tel: +33 (0)2 31 96 63 10   Email: info@musee-4commando.org
Web: http://www.musee-4commando.org/homepage_032.htm

This relatively small museum tells the story of the creation of Kieffer's 1st Battalion Fusiliers Marins Commando and the actions of its 177 members on 6 June 1944. The displays include uniformed mannequins, original memorabilia, and a multi-lingual film. A scale model of the casino strongpoint provides a good frame of reference. The **NTL Totem** stands in front of the museum.

Open daily 17 March through 7 November from 10:30 to 13:00 and from 13:30 to 18:30. Admission fee; Normandie pass accepted.

> The casino is directly across the street from the museum. (49.288985, -0.259525)

The modern casino, rebuilt on the original site, marks the center of the strongpoint, which stretched for some distance on either side down to the beach. A few small tobruks and dragon's teeth can still be found along the pathway leading from the casino to the beach.

> Return to your vehicle. From the parking area, return to place Alfred Thomas and proceed west past the museum (becomes Bd Kieffer). Take the first exit from the next roundabout (Bd Aristide Briand) and after 100 m, park on the right and walk ahead. (49.29058, -0.26232)

The '**Flame of Sacrifice**' monument stands upon an armored cupola of the casino strongpoint and is encircled by shrubs and French flags in recognition of the sacrifices of the Free French soldiers. The distance from the casino indicates the extent of the Stp Riva-Bella. The irregularly-shaped pink granite stones scattered about the site record the names of the **1st Battalion Fusiliers Marins Commandos** killed in the 6 June fighting; over thirty others from the 177-man force were wounded. An infosign identifies the location of each death.

> Continue west approximately 200 m and turn left on Bd Winston Churchill.

A small, almost hidden, stele commemorating the **death of four of Kieffer's men** at this location appears on Bd Winston Churchill, approximately 75 m south of Bd Kieffer on the right. (49.289131, -0.264283)

> Turn left onto Bd Kieffer and follow for 930 m (becomes place Alfred Thomas, then rue du six juin). Turn left onto Av de la Plage and park. (49.287497, -0.25231)

Le Grand Bunker – Musée du Mur de l'Atlantique

Avenue du 6 Juin   14150 Ouistreham
Tel: +33 (0)2 31 97 28 69   Email: bunkermusee@aol.com
Web: http://www.musee-grand-bunker.com/

The Grand Bunker, one of the better museum sites along the beach, is located inside an actual German fortification. The 17-meter-high, five-story, windowless bunker was the fire-control tower for batteries at Riva-Bella. The roof held a Flak gun, its only major armament. Although shelled and attacked on D-Day, the structure was practically impregnable. Commandos attempted to take the tower but were driven off by a hail of grenades thrown from the upper floors. On 9 June, Royal Engineer Lieutenant Bob Orrell and three men reconnoitered the building. After their first attempts to force open the armored door failed, they packed it with 7 pounds of explosives and blew it open. The garrison of 52 men then surrendered.[17]

The museum grounds display a German 88-mm gun and a V-1 'Flying Bomb', a British M7 'Priest' 105-mm self-propelled gun, and American M5A1 'Stuart' light tank and M3 Half-Track. The museum is fitted with German artifacts and demonstrates the operation of the tower, including its armory, sick bay, telephone switchboard, gas filters, and radio room. The top floor holds range-finding equipment and overlooks Sword Beach through an observation slit. Documents and photographs on the Todt Organization, the construction organization responsible for building the Atlantic wall, are also displayed.

Open daily February through March and October through December from 10:00 to 18:00; April through September from 09:00 to 19:00. Admission fee; Normandie Pass accepted.

Continue on Av de la Plage to Bd Maritime; turn left and park at a convenient place within the next 100 m. (49.288659, -0.251543)

No 4 Commando, less the French contingent, continued east to eliminate the six 155-mm gun battery manned by the German I Battery, Coastal Artillery Regiment 1260, on the Ouistreham beachfront. In a running, shooting attack, the commandos hit the battery defenses from every direction, clearing trenches and blowing-up barbed wire, only to find the gun pits empty. The guns had been moved to more sheltered positions inland.

The open gun pits of the **Riva-Bella Battery** are now covered with sand; however, glimpses of exposed concrete of some shoreline tobruks are still possible. More importantly, a walk across the dunes provides a perspective on how important the elimination of these guns was to the Allied planners and how exposed the guns would have been to Allied air power – the reason why Generalfeldmarschall Rommel ordered their re-location.

Proceed west on Bd Maritime for 2.3 km (becomes place Alfred Thomas, Bd Aristide Briand, Bd Maritime again). Turn left onto Av de Bruxelles, then take the next right onto rue du Commandant Kieffer. After 450 m, turn right onto rue de Pont l'Evêque and go to the seafront. (49.294736, -0.288563)

La Brèche d'Hermanville-s/Mer

Hermanville-s/Mer Syndicat d'Initiative (49.298063, -0.302349)

Place du Cuirassé Courbet   14880 Hermanville-sur-Mer
Tel: +33 (0)231361800   E-mail: accueil.hermanville@orange.fr

The large, grassy plain facing the waterfront was the location of Hauptmann Heinrich Kuhtz's **WN-20** (nicknamed Cod by the British); the enormous strongpoint was 350-meters wide and manned by 10th Company, Grenadier Regiment 736. One 88-mm PaK 43 and three 50-mm antitank guns covered the whole of the beach. The installation extended to the coastal highway, where beachfront houses now stand – although, in 1944, only a few large villas stood along this section of beach.

The 2nd Battalion, East Yorkshire Regiment, landed along this beachfront into the teeth of the German strongpoint. Despite the intense fire, the Yorks worked to the

---

17   Lieutenant Robert Orrell was awarded the Military Cross. He survived the war, was married for 59 years, and died in 2005 at age 86.

strongpoint's rear while tanks suppressed the bunkered guns with high explosive rounds. The infantry penetrated the barbed wire to gain access to the enemy trenches. Guns, grenades, and sometimes bayonets silenced one position after another. The Yorks lost 200 men on this stretch of beach.

> Unfortunately, driving along this section of beachfront is not permitted. Reverse direction and proceed 160 m before turning right onto rue Amiral Wietzel (D514); continue 400 m. Enter the open square on the right. (49.295821, -0.293283)

The square was the main beach exit for the first waves of infantry because the roadway continued south to Hermanville-s/Mer. One block to the east was the western end of WN-20. On the corner of the intersection with rue de Rouen, two houses that appear in many of the British landing photographs and films still stand. The street also marked the boundary between Queen Red and Queen White Beaches. Between WN-20 and WN-21 on the western side of Lion-s/Mer, the seafront villas had been converted into defensive positions. The windows were walled up, except for gun slits. The road to Hermanville is named the Bd de la 3ème Division d'Infanterie Britannique.

> Continue west on rue Amiral Wietzel for 500 m, then turn right onto rue du Docteur Turgis and park on the left. (49.296521, -0.300182)

A **Centaur tank** is almost hidden behind tall shrubs. This specialized vehicle carried a 95-mm howitzer to support Royal Commando landings. Obsolete by this stage in the war, they nonetheless provided mobile artillery until the Royal Artillery units landed. They were withdrawn from battle shortly afterward. The **NTL Totem** is adjacent to the tank.

The **Allied Navy Sailors Monument** stands along the beach at the far end of Av Felix Fauré. (49.297542, -0.29956) The Celtic Cross-topped, granite stone commemorates the men of the Royal, Merchant, and Allied Navies who fought and died along this seafront to land and supply the ground troops. Although this memorial is not well-known, the location provides good views of the broad sweep and gradual sandy slope of Sword Beach. Offshore at this spot stood **Gooseberry #5** – a smaller version of the massive artificial harbors or Mulberries built farther west. Large ships, including obsolete cruisers, were deliberately sunk to provide a breakwater for smaller craft landing matériel directly onto the beach. No remnant of the Gooseberry remains.

> Continue west by vehicle or on foot for 230 m to place du Cuirassé Courbet. (49.29785, -0.30251)

This square was another main exit off the beach and led to a highway to Hermanville-s/Mer (Av du 6 Juin, D60b). Unlike the troops landing at Colleville-Montgomery, the 1st Battalion, South Lancashire Regiment (Lancs), suffered few casualties on this lightly-defended sector.

The open space in front of the Syndicat d'Initiative holds numerous commemorations. The largest is the red triangle within a black triangle that forms the insignia of the **British 3rd Infantry Division**. A stele to its left commemorates **The South Lancashire Regiment** and the 288 officers and men of this battalion who sacrificed their lives on D-Day and in the subsequent campaign to free northwest Europe. Wall plaques pay tribute to the **East Yorkshire Regiment** and the **13/18 Hussars**. To the right, a white stone stele carries a gray plaque for the five regiments of the **Royal Artillery** that were part of the 3rd Division. Finally, a statue depicting a sailor hoisting a shell acknowledges the **Royal Norwegian Navy**, from which ten ships and one thousand men participated in the invasion. A bronze plaque in the center commemorates the construction of the Gooseberry harbor off this beach.

Exit place du Cuirassé Courbet to the west on Av Henri Gravier; turn left, then right to access the coastal highway toward Lion-s/Mer (D514, not signed). The coastal highway (D514) was the route taken by the Royal Marine Commandos in their attack against WN-21 (nicknamed Trout). Continue 1.7 km to the large roundabout and park. (49.305955, -0.324478)

No 41 Royal Marine Commando landed on the western end of Queen White Beach. It proceeded westward into Lion-s/Mer. Troops P and Y moved through the village against WN-21, but they were stopped short of their objective by heavy defensive fire. At 1100, three AVREs came up Bd Anatole France (D514) to their assistance, only to be knocked out by the strongpoint's 50-mm antitank gun. A second group of commandos moved against the Château de Lion-s/Mer to the south but were also unsuccessful.

Infantry from III Battalion, Grenadier Regiment 736, moved down the hillside shortly after noon under the cover of artillery fire from mobile 155-mm guns, attacked the commandos on their landward flank, and penetrated the commando line. Naval shellfire drove off the attackers, who retreated back up the hill.

The spear and sundial memorial hails **No 41 Royal Marine Commando**, who disembarked at the hour indicated by the stone on the sundial. A **Roll of Honour** lists the names of thirty British marines who died in the landings. Twenty-five were casualties on the beach, including the unit's second-in-command, Major DL Barclay.[18]

A plaque quotes the Four Freedoms from President Franklin Roosevelt's 1941 State of the Union Address: Freedom of Speech, of Worship, from Want, and from Fear. A **Churchill AVRE** tank stands nearby.

WN-21 (Trout), the strongest of the German defenses on Sword Beach, extended from the highway to the seafront. It held one 75-mm and two 50-mm antitank guns, but nothing now remains.

Reverse direction and proceed along the coastal highway (D514) toward la Brèche. After 1.8 km, turn right toward Hermanville-s/Mer / Caen (Av du 6 juin, D60b). After 1.0 km, continue straight on rue Hervé le Roy and after 280 m, turn left onto rue du Cimetière Anglais. (49.305955, -0.324478)

Hermanville War Cemetery contains 1,003 burials, many from the D-Day landings. The red triangle insignia of the British 3rd Infantry Division is embedded on the surface of the parking area. White crosses mark the graves of French commandos. The Suffolks assembled in this area prior to their attack upon strongpoints WN-16 and WN-17. All Commonwealth cemeteries are open at all times

---

18   Major David Lovat Barclay died at age 24; his name is inscribed on the Chatham Naval Memorial in Kent, England, since he had no known grave.

The strongpoint **WN-16 (Morris)** was located 500 meters to the west and consisted of three casemated 105-mm guns, with a fourth under construction. Only one of the casemates remains, standing at the western end of rue du Clos du Moulin. (49.273349, -0.307703) On 6 June, the 1st Battalion, The Suffolk Regiment, captured the position without resistance, along with 67 prisoners.

Reverse direction; after 300 m, turn left and continue on Grande Rue. After 800 m, turn left toward Colleville-Montgomery (D35). Proceed 1.1 km across the open terrain and then turn right onto Grande Rue (becomes rue des Marronniers, then rue Suffolk Régiment). Continue a total of 1.1 km to the bunker on the right. (49.264878, -0.309591)

Hillman Memorial and Museum

rue du Suffolk Regiment   14880 Colleville-Montgomery
Email: suffolk@amis-du-suffolk-rgt.com   Web: http://www.amis-du-suffolk-rgt.com

The Hillman strongpoint (WN-17) loomed as the strongest defensive position in British 3rd Infantry Division's sector, with twelve underground bunkers connected by a complex of tunnel and trenches. Only the bunkers' armored machine-gun cupolas extended above the surface. The large defensive perimeter held tobruks, trenches, and antitank guns – all surrounded by two wire entanglements – and housed the headquarters of Oberst Ludwig Krug's Grenadier Regiment 736 as well as 150 of his men.

At 1310, the attack by the 1st Battalion, The Suffolk Regiment, commenced with an artillery bombardment. The two wire entanglements were breached by Bangalore torpedoes under the cover of smoke, but the intensity of the machine-gun fire stopped

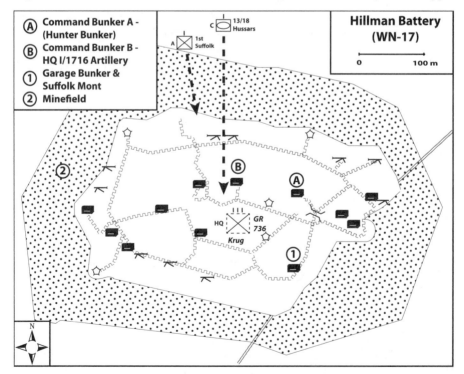

further progress. At 1600, tanks from C Squadron, 13/18 Hussars, approached by the road and added their power to the assault – all to no avail. A larger gap was blown in the wire, and Hussar tanks, ignoring the minefield, moved within the perimeter. Tank fire suppressed the armored cupolas while infantry occupied the abandoned trenches. They then methodically moved against the individual structures with grenades and automatic weapons fire. Resistance ended at approximately 2000, but Oberst Krug[19] did not open the door to his command bunker and surrender until 0645 the next morning. Seven-three enemy were taken prisoner.

The roadside bunker was the first to be cleared and now holds a memorial plaque to **The Suffolk Regiment** and its 35 D-Day casualties. The rooftop holds a heavy machine-gun tobruk, table of orientation, and a view of the installation. This building contained two storage bays for antitank guns or vehicles and a personnel shelter.

The command bunker, or **PC A**, is now known as '**Hunter bunker**' after its capturer, Private JR Hunter,[20] who single-handedly silenced its machine gun. The extensive underground structure boasted two levels and thirteen rooms for equipment such as ventilation, communications, and power generation. The armored cupola is actually on the bunker, despite being meters from the entrance door. The two entrances are protected by a firing slit in a narrow, concrete-lined 'alleyway.' The mortar tobruk retains images painted upon its interior wall, marking the ranges to important targets.

Slightly to the west is **PC B,** an administrative bunker with a design similar to the command bunker. To its left, a trench that connects to other positions extends into the field before gradually disappearing.

Hillman is well-signed, with each visitable site holding an explanatory plaque describing its construction and capture. Additional bunkers and several tobruks which were included in the original site, are now on private land and not visitable.

Open daily July through August, except Sundays, from 10:00 to 12:00 and from 14:30 to 18:30. Free guided tours are available every Tuesday, July through September at 15:00. Free admission to museum; the site is open at all times.

Continue south on rue Suffolk Régiment for 1.2 km. (49.25537, -0.31679)

The gray granite stele of the **Royal Norfolk Regiment** commemorates the 116 soldiers who died in this area from 6 June to 9 July 1944. The regiment advanced through the open fields parallel to the roadway and came under the guns of the Hillman strongpoint. The unit, forced to ground and to lie in the fields for two hours until Hillman was captured, suffered over 40 casualties. The fields to the west also mark the site of the British 41st Antitank Battery that inflicted heavy damage to Major Gottberg's Panzer Regiment 22.

Reverse direction and return into Colleville-Montgomery, passing the Hillman Museum. After 2.2 km, turn left onto rue de Caen (D60a). The intersection is unsigned and easy to miss, but occurs shortly after entering the 30kph zone. Follow for 1.5 km to the junction with highway D60 and park at a convenient spot. (49.265508, -0.319784)

Périers Ridge, the sloping hillside south of the landing beaches, adjoins the highest spot on the ridge, **Point 61**, near this intersection. By early afternoon on 6 June,

---

19   Oberst Ludwig Krug died in 1972 at age 78.

20   Private JR Hunter, wounded in the attack, was awarded the Distinguished Conduct Medal.

2nd Battalion, KSLI, along with two tank squadrons of the Staffordshire Yeomanry and M10 antitank guns from the 41st Antitank Battery, reached the lightly-defended location. As the first tanks crested the ridge, five were destroyed by a German 88-mm gun, and the I and II Batteries, Artillery Regiment 155, fired their 105-mm guns from near Périers-s/le-Dan onto the infantry. The German gun positions were attacked by a company from 2nd Battalion, KSLI. After a brief firefight, the artillerymen fled.

The site provides a panoramic view of the terrain that served the British armor so well on 6 June. The large structure seen in the distance to the south locates the city of Caen.

> Continue straight into Périers-s/le-Dan (D220); after 1.9 km, turn left toward Biéville (rue de Église, D222). Continue 350 m into Biéville to the memorial on the right. (49.257428, -0.339407)

A pink granite stele dedicated to the **British 3rd Infantry Division** stands in a small square east of the *mairie*. The monument celebrates the liberation of the village and commemorates the British soldiers who died during June and July 1944 to assure French liberty. Against the wall to the rear of the monument, a second similar stele remembers the Frenchmen of the village who died in the two world wars.

> Continue 650 m to the drive on the left. Park and walk past the cemetery on the right. (49.254837, -0.330341)

Église St-Ouen stands in the fields on the outskirts of the village. Historians speculate that this location may have been a place of worship since early Merovingian times. The current crumbling, roofless nave stems from the 11th century, making it one of the oldest in the region. The peculiar arrangement of stones used in its walls presents a fishbone pattern, an early Christian theme. The Gothic choir dates from the 13th century and contains wall paintings from as late as the 15th century.

> Continue (D222) and after 550 m, turn right toward Biéville-Beuville / Caen (D60). Continue through the villages for 2.7 km to the white stone memorial on the right. (49.227547, -0.33283)

The **Allied Soldiers Monument** is dedicated to the ideals of Peace and Liberty. The white-stone, free-form sculpture erected by the Commune of Biéville-Beuville commemorates the battles fought on these grounds. The steep gully ahead formed a natural antitank ditch for German forces to the south. The site is only 1.4 kilometers from German concentrations of the 21st Panzer Division that took place in Bois de Lébisey. After 6 June, the front lines in this sector barely moved for the next 34 days.

> Continue toward Caen (D60) into Lébisey. The highway climbs up the hillside that exposed the advancing Allied troops to German guns in the woods ahead. After 1.5 km, turn left toward Hérouville/Colombelles (D226) and stop at the small drive on the right. (49.215481, -0.338688)

Lt-Col Maurice sent KSLI's Company Y, led by Major PC Steel,[21] across the

---

21   Major Peter Crawford Steele, killed during the engagement, is buried in Ranville War Cemetery.

ditch located immediately beyond the Allied Soldiers Monument and into Bois de Lébisey. It encountered strong resistance and withdrew under threat of encirclement. Judging the British salient too exposed to continue, Maurice led his men back to Biéville. The British 3rd Infantry Division's advance had ended.

The terrain to the immediate south of the highway appears level; however, the horizon (which is the Périers Ridge) highlights the dramatic difference in height that the panzergrenadiers used to such good advantage.

Attack on Caen
7 June 1944

Battle

The British offensive on Caen resumed at first light on 7 June with an assault against Bois de Lébisey. The attack, led by 2nd Battalion, Royal Warwickshire Regiment (Warwicks), used the Dan Creek, south of Blainville, as its start line while armored units advanced out of Biéville. Unfortunately, the wood had been occupied by a battalion of Panzergrenadier Regiment 125 during the night, and when the two leading companies of the Warwicks approached the forest's edge, German small-arms fire thinned their ranks. The infantry then charged into the wood and engaged the enemy but made little progress against concentrated machine-gun and mortar fire. The 3rd and 4th Companies moved forward to join the melee. With the battle still raging into mid-afternoon, the 1st Battalion, The Royal Norfolk Regiment (Norfolks), advanced on the village west of the wood. The entrenched panzergrenadiers, however, continued delivering heavy fire, and by evening both regiments withdrew, at the cost of 204 casualties. Caen was not taken that day, either.

In early July, the 185th Infantry Brigade remained stalled before the Bois de Lébisey. At 0400 on 8 July, 2nd Battalion, Royal Ulster Rifles, after a one-day rest period behind the front lines, led the attack upon the forest. By 1000, the immediate objective was taken, and the brigade forces continued south to the heights overlooking Caen. Heavy and accurate German artillery fire prohibited additional progress.

Battlefield Tour

> The tour starts in the Bois de Lébisey. (49.215481, -0.338688)

The forest is considerably smaller than it was in 1944, with modern housing to the west and public buildings occupying portions of the remaining forest. The highway on the northern edge (Route de Colombelles, D226) now leads to a bridge over the Canal de Caen and the Orne River into Colombelles. In 1944, Colombelles was the site of a large factory district. During the July battles, the tall chimneys of the factories served as artillery observation posts directing German fire. Their small profile made them safe from British artillery and aircraft, but they were destroyed later by ground forces.

> Reverse direction and turn left toward Caen (Av du Général de Gaulle, D60). After 400 m, turn right toward Épron (Av de Garbsen, D226b). Follow carefully through two roundabouts for 2.7 km. In Épron, turn right toward Cambes-en-Plaine (unsigned, D7). Continue 800 m to the next roundabout and take the 4th exit toward Cambes (D79b).

Oberst Oppeln's Panzer Regiment 100 assembled on the ground to the right in preparation for its D-Day counterattack. (49.231275, -0.375509)

After 900 m, enter Cambes-en-Plaine, turn right onto rue du Chateau (D79b), and follow that street to the memorial on the right. (49.233072, -0.384956)

Battle of Cambes-en-Plaine
7 June to 8 July 1944

Battle

The I Battalion, SS Panzergrenadier Regiment 25, 12th SS Panzer Division (*Hitlerjugend*), had been marching throughout the previous day in response to conflicting orders. It eventually entered Cambes from the south, reaching the Bois de Cambes at the town's northern tip by 1700 on 6 June.

On 7 June, the reserve 9th Infantry Brigade advanced against Caen by way of Périers and Cambes-en-Plaine. Progress as far as le Mesnil 2.0 kilometers to the north was rapid, and from there the 2nd Battalion, The Royal Ulster Rifles (Ulsters), moved south against Cambes. The Ulsters attacked from the north without success behind an artillery barrage against the walled forest. They successfully attacked again two days later from the northwest and captured the wood but were unable to advance farther. The resulting stalemate lasted 30 days.

Battlefield Tour

Amid the trees in the center of the village, a white cement memorial bears plaques commemorating the village's liberators, the **59th (Staffordshire) Division**, **3rd Infantry Division**, and particularly the **Royal Ulster Regiment**. The area around the monument was the scene of particularly heavy fighting on 9 June, when the Ulsters sought to force the panzergrenadiers out of the ruins of the village chateau, which was within this now vacant, wooded area.

Walk or drive to the *mairie* ahead (rue de l'Espérance) on the left. (49.232655, -0.38524)

The courtyard of the Mairie holds a flame-shaped, blue-granite stone as a symbol of light and liberty in memory of the **soldiers and civilians** who died during the intense and prolonged fighting. Over 80 percent of the village was destroyed and its reconstruction took fifteen years. Cambes, therefore, offers a modern, suburban appearance, despite its founding in the 10th century. Across from the Mairie, the Romanesque **Église St-Martin** presents a dramatic, square bell tower. Similar bell towers were common constructed during the Hundred Years War for observation and warning local citizenry of approaching enemies.

From the 59th Division Memorial, proceed northeast on rue de l'Espérance as it curves to the left. After 400 m, turn right onto rue du Mesnil Ricard and proceed to the cemetery on the right. (49.236578, -0.38597)

Despite being captured by the Allies after heavy fighting by the Ulsters and the 1st Battalion, The King's Own Scottish Borderers (KOSB), the village remained under German bombardment until Operation CHARNWOOD on 8 July, when the British advanced into the northern outskirts of Caen.

The **Cambes-en-Plaine War Cemetery** occupies the heavily disputed wood, making it a true battlefield cemetery. Burials did not start until 8 July, after the front lines had moved south. More than half of the 224 burials are men of the 59th (Staffordshire) Division, which held this ground through much of the four-week stalemate.

Continue 100 m to the road junction (D220a). (49.237198, -0.385283)

The attack on 7 June by The Royal Ulster Rifles from le Mesnil occurred along the farm road straight ahead. Near this intersection, a white stone stele bears a polished granite plaque: 'In memory of all ranks of the **2nd Battalion, Royal Ulster Rifles** who captured the village of Cambes-en-Plaine on 9 June 1944 and gave their lives in Normandy in the cause of freedom – 6 June to 17 September 1944.'

Turn right at the intersection (rue du Lieutenant Lynn) and proceed 100 m to the monument on the right. (49.236578, -0.384709)

The remaining rubble from a stone wall that originally framed the forest holds a plaque to the **1st Battalion, Kings Own Scottish Borderers**, who held this section of the front for weeks while under attack from German forces only 500 meters down the road. The road is named after Lieutenant Lynn[22], who died during Operation CHARNWOOD on 8 July.

Continue 550 m, then turn left toward Caen (D79b); at the roundabout take the 3rd exit (unsigned) and continue 350 m to the monument on the right. (49.231737, -0.369651)

Château de la Londe was the site of close quarters fighting in late June. The British 3rd Infantry Division was attempting to expand its positions against the German-held trenches and gun pits at la Bijude, a small community immediately south of the previous roundabout. The area was captured on 28 June, but thirty German tanks denied additional advance. The area between the chateau and the copse to the north became known as the 'bloodiest square mile in Normandy' due to the combat that occurred here. The chateau and surrounding wood were destroyed but have been restored to their pre-war condition.

A monument dedicated to the **1st Battalion, The Royal Suffolk Regiment**, stands alongside a plinth holding a battlefield map at the entrance drive to the chateau.

Reverse direction and return to the previous roundabout and make a right turn toward Mathieu (D7). Follow for 5.4 km.

As the highway swings west to bypass Mathieu, it parallels terrain that was the path of the Panzergrenadier Regiment 192's counterattack against Lion-s/Mer on D-Day.

At the roundabout, take the 4th exit toward Courseulles-s/Mer / Musée du Radar (D404). After 2.5 km, turn right toward Douvres-la-Délivrande / Musée du Radar (D83) and proceed 400 m to the museum entrance. (49.285653, -0.403125)

---

22   Lieutenant Brian Freeman Lynn served in the Royal Canadian Infantry Corp attached to the North Staffordshire Regiment. Lynn died at age 21 and is buried in la Delivrande War Cemetery.

Musée du Radar Allemand et Base Secrète Allemande
Route de Basly   14440 Douvres-la-Délivrande
Tel: +33 (0)2 31 37 74 43 or +33 (0)2 31   E-mail: infos@mairie-douvres14.com
06 06 45

 The Luftwaffe radar station, code-named 'Distelfink' by the Germans, was part of the Atlantic Wall defenses. Its location was excellent, being only 2.5 kilometers from the Channel and 53 meters above sea level. The sea itself is visible to the northeast. A highway divided the installation into two sections. The northern section held the long-range 'Wasserman' radar, which had a tall, framed tower. The larger, southern section held the two intermediate-range 'Freya' radars and two short-range 'Würzburg' radars. The Freya looked like a waffled square and was capable of detecting approaching warplanes at a range up to 100 kilometers. The Würzburg was a parabolic dish used for gunnery targeting.

 The site commanded over eight concrete works holding flamethrowers, 38-mm FlaK guns, three 75-mm guns, and twenty machine guns – all surrounded by barbed wire, minefields, and an antitank ditch. The defensive capabilities of the station earned it the name Stp Douvres. The radar station was inoperative by D-day due to concentrated aerial

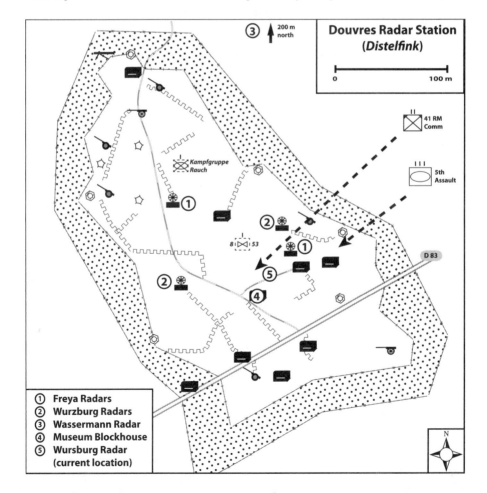

① Freya Radars
② Wurzburg Radars
③ Wassermann Radar
④ Museum Blockhouse
⑤ Wursburg Radar
(current location)

and naval bombardments. The Canadians briefly attacked the facilities but were repulsed and decided to bypass the area. The 258-man Luftwaffe contingent, strengthened by a company of panzergrenadiers from *Kampfgruppe Rauch*, resisted efforts by British forces to overcome the position. On 17 June, British 26th Assault Squadron, Royal Engineers[23] and No 41 Royal Marine Commando, supported by Flails from the 22nd Dragoon Guards, launched a massive assault during which tanks penetrated the minefields, resulting in the garrison's surrender.

Only a small portion of the original site is accessible; however, two of the six remaining bunkers are open. The **personnel bunker** accommodated 20 men in two large rooms and now houses displays on the history and development of radar. The **command bunker**, nicknamed 'Anton,' contained equipment to direct German fighter planes against Allied bombers. The structure, with twenty rooms on two levels, contains artifacts demonstrating life in an underground bunker and includes a scale model depicting the successful assault and models of the various radar receivers.

An excellent example of a **Würzburg Radar** remains on the site, one of only three still in existence. Though not used at Douvres, this unit was captured by the British and taken to England for use as a radio telescope before being relocated to Douvres for the 50th anniversary of the invasion. It is one of three such units in existence. The small structure on the rear of the dish is a postwar addition.

Open daily June through 19 September from 10:00 to 18:00. Admission fee; Normandie Pass accepted.

Continue into Douvres-la-Délivrande (D83); after 1.1 km, turn right onto rue Froide. Proceed straight through the roundabout (becomes rue de la Poterie). After 650 m, turn left onto rue d'Anguery and a sharp right onto rue Abbé Bellée. Turn left onto rue des Noyers, turn right onto rue Maître Colleville, and finally cross Route de Caen (D7) to park on rue de la Fossette. The cemetery's main entrance is on Route de Caen. (49.290342, -0.377634)

The 942 burials in **la Delivrande War Cemetery** resulted from the D-Day landings on Sword Beach and the early June attack upon Caen. The cemetery also holds 180 German graves, located in the right rear plot. Many of those graves bear markers that state 'Buried near this spot,' suggesting the actual grave locations are unknown.

To continue the landing beaches tour, return to Route de Caen (D7) and turn toward Luc-s/Mer (right). In the second roundabout, take the 1st exit toward Luc-s/Mer (D7c, becomes D83) and follow for 3.1 km. Turn left onto rue du Docteur Charcot (changes name, but remains D514) and follow into St-Aubin-s/Mer. (49.33259, -0.394692)

---

23   The assault was led by Royal Engineer Troop Commander, later Colonel and Doctor, David Pratt, whom the author had the pleasure of meeting at Douvres in 2006 when he was a spry 82 years old.

Chapter Three
3rd Canadian Infantry Division
6 to 11 June 1944

The Canadian assault force was assigned to 8 kilometers of flat sand beach code-named Juno, which ran from Courseulles-s/Mer (Mike Sector) on the west to St-Aubin-s/ Mer (Nan Sector) on the east. Beyond the low coastal dunes, open country with gently rolling fields provided excellent opportunity for rapid advancement.

Juno Beach was defended by the II Battalion, Grenadier Regiment 736, of Generalleutnant Wilhelm Richter's 716th Infantry Division. The unit was decidedly inferior with a collection of mismatched guns captured from various foreign armies; no motor transport to shift troops or resupply their static positions; and composed of troops that were too old, too young, too infirm, or not even German. Artillery support was by the division's I Battalion, Artillery Regiment 1716, which fielded sixty-seven guns of various calibers and manufacturers, most of which were still in open pits because their concrete casemates had not yet been completed.

The 3rd Canadian Infantry Division carried three infantry brigades each comprised of three battalions plus reconnaissance, artillery, engineer, and other support units. The 2nd Canadian Armoured Brigade, with its three regimental tank units, engineering units with their special purpose armored vehicles, and a beach control unit, provided additional support. No 48 Royal Commando was also under nominal command.

Canadian units in Second World War battle zones were all volunteers. Infantry regiments were frequently formed around regional peacetime cadres. The North Shore Regiment, for example, had mustered several local militia battalions from New Brunswick: the Régiment de la Chaudière was a French speaking unit from Quebec; the Queen's Own Rifles was from Ottawa; and the Winnipeg and Regina Rifles were from the open plains of Saskatewan and Manitoba.

The 15-inch guns of two battleships, HMS *Ramillies* and HMS *Warspite*, along with the various guns of twelve light cruisers, eleven destroyers, and forty modified landing craft carrying a variety of cannon and rocket launchers, provided pre-invasion firepower. Ninety-six 'Priest' self-propelled guns fired at resistance nests as their LCTs approached landfall. Centaur tanks fired their 95-mm guns once they reached the beaches. Seventy-six Sherman DD tanks added the firepower of their 75-mm guns.

D-Day Landings (Juno Beach)
6 June 1944

Objective	To eliminate beach defenses and move south to cut the Bayeux-Caen highway
Forces	
Canadian	14,000 men of 3rd Canadian Infantry Division (Major-General RFL Keller); 2nd Canadian Armoured Brigade (Brigadier RA Wyman)
German	1,500 men of II Battalion, Grenadier Regiment 736 (Hauptmann Deptolla)
Result	The landings were successful, but the highway was not captured
Casualties	
Canadian	366 dead, 548 wounded, and 47 missing

German	uncertain
Location	St-Aubin-s/Mer is 19 km north of Caen.

Battle

The Juno Beach assault was the last of the five seaborne landings on D-Day because off-shore reefs submerged only after mid-tide. The naval bombardment began at 0600 and continued for 90 minutes. The first troops were scheduled to land at 0745, but rough seas delayed them until 0758, an interval which gave the German defenders sufficient time to recover from the naval bombardment and man their weapons. As at the American and British beaches, the aerial and naval bombardments had little effect upon the German strongpoints. Most of the beach obstacles also remained intact. One-third of the infantry landing craft were struck by mortar fire or hit mines affixed to beach obstacles hidden by the incoming tide resulting in dreadful losses. Smoke and dust created by the bombardment hid most of the targets from the landing-craft-born artillery. Destroyed civilian buildings,

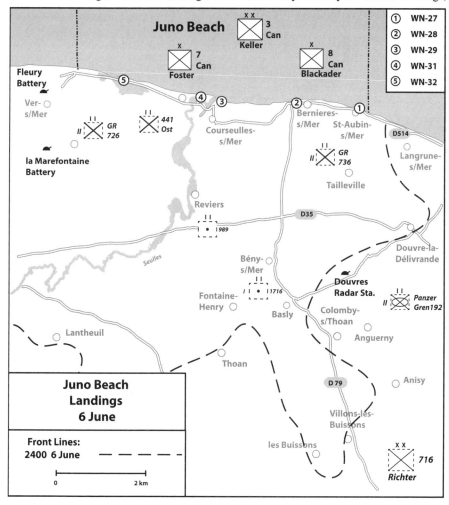

the result of bombing and rocket fire, created additional hiding places for German snipers and machine-gun teams.

The 3rd Canadian Division's 7th and 8th Infantry Brigades led the initial landings. Each company, supported by a troop of tanks, was assigned a particular beachfront objective. The landing locations had been selected to avoid the four resistance points (*Widerstandsnester*) at Vaux, Courseulles-s/Mer, Bernières and St-Aubin-s/Mer, but navigation errors, wind, and currents drove some landings off target.

The objective of the Royal Winnipeg Rifles was to eliminate WN-31 immediately west of the snake-like Seulles River, which ran along the western edge of Courseulles-s/Mer. The town and WN-29 became the objective of the Regina Rifles. Sherman tanks of the 6th Canadian Armoured Regiment (1st Hussars) provided armored firepower – A Squadron with the Winnipegs and B Squadron with the Reginas.

The Queen's Own Rifles landed on Nan White sector in Bernières against WN-28, and the North Shore Regiment came ashore to the left on Nan Red Sector in St-Aubin-s/Mer. The Nan Sector assault companies were supported by the tanks of B and C Squadrons, 10th Canadian Armoured Regiment (Fort Garry Horse).

The rough seas caused concern regarding the seaworthiness of the Sherman DD tanks. The Fort Garry Horse decided that the risk was too great and ordered the LCTs to launch the tanks directly onto the beach despite the potential for concentrated antitank fire. The 1st Hussars' Shermans were launched 3 kilometers from the beach requiring the marginally sea-worthy vehicles to struggle through the rough waters. Only ten of their nineteen vehicles reached the shore. The decisive support effort was from destroyers which ran close in to shore and found targets for their 4-inch guns.

No 48 Royal Marine Commando approached directly into the guns of WN-27 at St-Aubin-s/Mer. Three of their six LCIs struck beach obstacles, two were permanently hung up and their troops wiped out by enemy machine-gun fire or by drowning, and the unit suffered 40 percent casualties. With its force depleted and without heavy weapons' support, the commandoes could not penetrate the defenses of their objective at WN-26 in Langrune-s/Mer. Nor could they achieve the planned link to Sword Beach, where No 41 Royal Marine Commando had also stalled in front of its objective, WN-25, at Lion-s/Mer.

Despite these setbacks, the troops secured the beachfront and moved inland to establish a defensive perimeter and eliminate isolated pockets of enemy troops. *Ostbattalion* 441, comprised of mostly Russian POWs led by German NCOs, presented little resistance, and its men surrendered or disappeared farther inland. A promising start was confounded, however, by congestion on the beaches. As more troops and equipment landed on the tide-narrowed sand beaches, the beach exits and narrow village streets became a traffic nightmare, and the assault lost its initial momentum.

The 9th Infantry Brigade, led by the North Nova Scotia Highlanders and supported by tanks of the 27th Canadian Armoured Regiment (Sherbrooke Fusiliers), landed later in the day intending to pass through the lead units to cut the Bayeux-Caen highway – the main transportation route to the northwest – and capture Carpiquet Airfield. According to plan, the brigade started ashore near Bernières at 1140 and passed through the assault troops, who continued mopping up the beach defenses in Courseulles-s/Mer and St-Aubin-s/Mer. By noon, the leading units were several kilometers inland; however, small groups of ethnic German troops defended some isolated villages took their toll before being rooted out. The advance slowed as each enemy group stubbornly fought until it was about to be overcome – and then surrendered.

Late in the day, tanks of C Squadron, 1st Hussars, made the decision to strike out for their objective unsupported by infantry. The light Stuart tanks motored through towns and fields mostly devoid of enemy troops. They crossed the Bayeux-Caen Highway at Bretteville-l'Orgueilieuse and stopped 8 kilometers ahead of the nearest infantry support. Lacking protection from German infantry manning hand-held antitank weapons, they were ordered to return to Fontaine-Henry.

By the end of 6 June, although the North Shore Regiment was still battling the II Battalion, Grenadier Regiment 736, command post in Tailleville, the North Nova Scotia Highlanders sheltered at Villon-les-Buissons, only 5 kilometers from Caen. The Canadians had not achieved their wildly optimistic objectives but had progressed farther inland than any other Allied unit. They had effected linkage with the British 50th Division at Creully to the west, but a 6-to-10-kilometer gap remained between them and British troops to the east.

The 21st Panzer Division's attack against British 3rd Infantry Division (see Chapter Two) to the east convinced Lieutenant-General Miles C Dempsey, commander of British Second Army, that he dared not risk further advance with his flank thus exposed. He gave the order for all units on Sword, Juno, and Gold Beaches to dig in for the night. The panzer threat was eliminated by the 185th Infantry Brigade, but caution prevailed, momentum was lost, and so was the opportunity to capture Carpiquet Airfield – a lost opportunity for which the Canadians would later pay dearly.

Aftermath

The 3rd Canadian Infantry Division was successful in landing its three infantry brigades and associated units and securing a lodgment in Normandy. However, its flanking units had advanced farther than those in the center creating an enemy-held wedge along the Mue River valley. The division suffered more casualties than all other landing forces excepting the American troops that landed on Omaha Beach.

Battlefield Tour

The tour moves from east to west through the seaside villages before proceeding inland. The resort communities along the coast are well supplied with small restaurants and hotels. In the height of the tourist season, highway D514, which connects these villages, presents a driving challenge due to heavy vehicular traffic and numerous tour buses. Inland villages suffer from a lack of tourist amenities but are far less congested and present their own charm with their ancient stone buildings and massive Norman churches.

> The tour of the Canadian invasion battlefields starts in the coastal town of St-Aubin-s/Mer. Enter Aubin-s/Mer from the east on the coastal highway (D514, becomes rue Pasteur). The seafront becomes visible at the intersection with rue Bellevue. The round building on the right is the Office de Tourisme, but parking is not conveniently available. Continue to the parking area near the intersection with rue Canet immediately west of the pillbox and memorials on the right. (49.332436, -0.394505)

St-Aubin-s/Mer

St-Aubin was particularly hard hit by the invasion; 90 percent of its shoreline buildings were destroyed, and 40 percent of the town suffered damage.

Office de Tourisme (49.331798, -0.392917)
Dam Favreau   14750 St-Aubin-s/Mer
Tel: +33 (0) 231 973 041   Email: otsaintaubin@orange.fr
Web: http://www.tourisme-saintaubinsurmer.fr

The parking area and surrounding ground was the location of **WN-27**. The strongpoint included several machine-gun nests and three 81-mm mortars. Trenches protected riflemen firing upon avenues of approach. An underground barracks fitted with tunnels allowed the one hundred German troops manning the fortifications to move between positions.

Company B, North Shore Regiment, landed against WN-27 whose 50-mm AT gun was particularly successful in hitting tank-carrying landing craft during its approach. Despite the beach losses, the company used its Bangalore torpedoes to blow holes in the barbed wire and clear paths through minefields. After departing the beach, Company A circled St-Aubin and attacked from the south along rue Canet in a double envelopment with armored vehicles striking from the east along rue Pasteur (D514). For the next two hours, the Canadians searched the strongpoint and engaged in small fire fights with scattered German troops.

The 1944 resistance nest has been replaced by an automobile parking area and a heavy equipment yard. A ceremonial plaza with commemorative plaques and stones lies directly east. In front of the beach opening, a gray stele bears a plaque identifying the beach as landing site for the **North Shore Regiment** and **No 48 Royal Marine Commando**. Behind the stele, speckled-granite tablets on the left bear gold inscriptions of the names of the thirty-seven North Shore, fourteen Fort Garry Horse, six Royal Canadian Engineers, and three Royal Canadian Artillery troops killed in the landings. Similar tablets on the right bear the names of forty-four No 48 Royal Marine Commandos and twenty-one civilians lost. The civilian tablet identifies the beach as the landing place of French intelligence agent Maurice Duclos, known as St-Jacques, who had been smuggled into France on 4 August 1940.[1]

If the tide is out, accessing the beach at this point and looking back toward land presents the strength of the position and the height of the seawall, which was topped, in 1944, with barbed wire entanglements.

The eastern end of the resistance nest was anchored by a pillbox housing a **50-mm antitank gun** protected from naval fire by its thick concrete rear wall. Sherman DD tanks of the Fort Garry Horse arrived and brought the strongpoint under fire. The Germans knocked out two tanks before succumbing to the combined fire of a 95-mm Centaur tank gun and the prodigious firepower of an AVRE Petard. The pillbox retains the 50-mm antitank gun sited to provide enfilade fire east or west along the beaches. The seventy shell casings found around the emplacement testified to the gun crew's determination to resist the invasion.

The pleasant seafront promenade to the east offers refreshment at several cafés and restaurants. After 100 meters, a memorial stele to the **Fort Garry Horse** is barely visible among the shrubs in front of the round tourist office.

---

1   Maurice Duclos was an artillery soldier who fought in Norway. After escape to England, he established espionage circuits and engaged in sabotage missions in France. Duclos survived the war and became an officer of the *Legion d'honneur*, Officer of the Order of the British Empire, and received the French Croix de Guerre and British Military Cross. He died in Argentina in 1981 at age 74.

> Leave the west end of the parking area into the small roundabout and exit eastbound (toward the tourist office) onto rue de Verdun (D514). After 130 m, turn right onto rue Canet. At the 'T' junction, turn right onto rue du Maréchal Foch, then turn quickly left onto rue Abbé Bossard. Continue 200 m to the church.
> (49.329024, -0.395776)

Companies C and D, North Shore Regiment, formed their ranks in the fields around **Église St-Aubin**. The magnificent neogothic church appears to be a medieval, Norman structure, but do not be fooled. It was constructed in the 1840s while St-Aubin sought its religious independence from neighboring Langrune-s/Mer. Nonetheless, it is an impressive structure with a tall spire standing above the shell damaged bell tower.

> Leave St-Aubin by continuing south on rue Abbé Brossard. At the large roundabout, take the 1st exit toward Bernières-s/Mer (D7). After 800 m, continue straight onto highway D7b and continue to the junction with rue de Verdun (D514). Turn left and continue 1.2 km to junction with rue du Régiment de la Chaudière. Turn right to the small parking area. Walk to the seafront promenade and enter place du 6 Juin. (49.335421, -0.422888)

Bernières-s/Mer

The beach exit from Nan White sector was the main landing area for the Queen's Own Rifles of Canada. Wind and current pushed the five LCAs carrying Company B, the lead assault company, east and directly against the town's strongpoint, **WN-28**. The Germans held their fire while the LCAs approached the shore in a line and, with the naval bombardment over, a short-lived quiet settled over the boats. When released, the density of the defensive fire was horrific, but Lieutenant WG Herbert, Lance-Corporal René Tessier, and Rifleman William Chicoski survived the deadly crossing of the sand beach to find shelter from gunfire at the base of the 3-meter-high sea wall. The trio slowly edged along the wall until they brought fire from their Sten guns and grenades onto the strongpoint's gun embrasures.[2] Pillboxes and trenches defended by the 5th Company, Grenadier Regiment 736, were cleared in sequence as the tanks of the Fort Garry Horse began to arrive. In total, the Queen's Own lost sixty-five men taking WN-28; however, less than an hour later Royal Engineers had cleared two exits off the beach.

Place of prominence is now granted to the **Signal Monument** in the center of the beach exit. It bears the French and English inscription, 'Here on 6 June 1944 Europe was liberated by the heroism of the Allied forces.' The monument is accented by a low stone wall in the form of a giant 'V' reminiscent of the British 'Victory' symbol.

The large timbered house on the eastern corner of the place was a prime navigation aid and is featured in many of the landing photographs. It has become the **Maison de le Queen's Own Rifles of Canada.** The plaque posted before the house provides the details:

> This house was liberated at first light on D-Day 6 June 1944 by the men of the Queen's Own Rifles of Canada, who were the first Canadians to land on this beach. It may very well have been the first house on French soil liberated by sea-borne allied forces. Within sight of this house over 100 men of the Queen's Own Rifles were killed or wounded in the first few minutes of the landing.

---

2   Lieutenant WG Herbert was awarded a Military Cross; Lance Corporal René Tessier and Rifleman William Chicoski were both awarded Military Medals.

The North Nova Scotia Highlanders' landings took place adjacent to the boat launch ramp and life-saving station 100 meters west of the Signal Monument. A commemorate plaque on the wall of the life saving station identifies the site.

The beach to the east of the Signal Monument was the location of **WN-28**, although only the concrete structures built into the seawall remain. A mortar tobruk sited into the seawall 150 meters from the Signal Monument presents only its cemented opening to view from the promenade. Its seaward face carries a plaque to identify the landing site of Company B.

More prominently, a pillbox stands 60 meters farther along the promenade. The thick seaward face protected it from naval gunfire, and the 50-mm antitank gun enfiladed the beach as far as neighboring Courseulles-s/Mer. Only the mounting ring with its severed bolts remains in position, but it can be entered to gain the full extent of its defensive capability. Strongpoints like this pillbox were overcome only at a significant cost.

The pillbox holds several Canadian memorials: a campaign map depicting the movements of the **Queen's Own Rifles** during Normandy and northern European operations on its face; an attached granite stele topped with the unit's insignia that holds a plaque praising the unit's sacrifices; and a bronze plaque in memory of the 5th (Hackney) Battalion of **the Royal Berkshire Regiment,** which provided beach control.

Numerous memorial steles line the seawall in what has been renamed **place du Canada** including those to the **Fort Garry Horse** and a smooth granite block with two bronze plaques: one to all Canadian Servicemen who were killed on Juno Beach, and the other a table of orientation showing how the various Canadian units moved inland from the beach and the advanced positions they achieved by midnight of 6 June. A memorial to the dead of the **Régiment de la Chaudière** and its commander, Lieutenant-Colonel Paul Mathieu, stands atop a tobruk built into the seawall.

Continue east for another 150 meters, to where minefields, weapons trenches, and wire entanglements stretched 100 meters back from the seawall, which holds another tobruk. The close quarters fighting within those defenses cost Company B numerous casualties.

Return to the parking area and proceed south on rue du Régiment de la Chaudière for 350 m before turning right onto rue du général Leclerc. Park on the left before the church. (49.33131, -0.423607)

The 11th century **Église Notre-Dame de la Nativité** is noted for its 13th century bell tower, which stands 67 meters above the town. The tower was a beacon for landing craft crews searching through smoke and haze for their assigned landing beaches. The steeple, a naval target to deny its use by enemy observers, survived only slightly damaged. The church retains its ancient Gothic glory and dominates the place de l'Église.

The street – rue du général Leclerc (D7) – around the square displays numbered period photographs showing Canadian troops advancing through the town. The photographs provide an interesting view of Bernières in 1944. The stone walls, narrow streets, and stoutly constructed buildings of the town provided snipers with abundant cover and greatly slowed Canadian units exiting from the beach area.

Exit Bernières by following the street (rue du général Leclerc, D7) around the church entrance to the roundabout. Take the second exit onto rue Léopold Hettier (D7) to the junction with the coastal highway (D514). Turn toward Courseulles-s/Mer and follow for 2.3 km into Courseulles. Continue straight onto place du Six Juin – across the intersection with Quai des Allies – and park in the large square. (49.335732, -0.45774)

Courseulles-s/Mer

Office de Tourisme (49.33475, -0.45795)

5 rue du 11 Novembre   14 470 Courseulles-s/Mer

Tel. +33 (0)2 31 37 46 80   Fax 02 31 37 29 25

Email: tourisme@courseulles-sur-mer.com

Web: http://www.courseulles-sur-mer.com/tourisme_courseulles/ office_de_tourisme. html

Courseulles-s/Mer was the most heavily defended Juno Beach sector; in fact, it was the most heavily defended sector along the entire British Second Army landing area except perhaps for Ouistreham. Within its three resistance nests lay six large caliber guns and twelve machine-gun positions. The two assault battalions of the 7th Canadian Infantry Brigade landed on either side of the harbor entrance.

Of the nineteen Sherman DD tanks launched by the 1st Hussars against Courseulles harbor defenses, ten made the beach eleven minutes before Company A, Regina Rifles Regiment. They engaged the 6th Company, Grenadier Regiment 736, and its one 88-mm and two 75-mm guns housed in the concrete casemates of WN-29. The advance of the Canadian infantry was delayed by having to repeatedly clear the area of enemy as a warren of tunnels and trenches permitted German infantry to reoccupy abandoned positions.

The large parking area north of the Quai des Alliés and east of the harbor entrance formed the west end of **WN-29** and now holds several artifacts from the invasion. The **Duplex Drive Sherman tank** on display was originally lost by the 1st Hussars Regiment in the rough seas. It was salvaged and restored after resting for twenty-six years beneath the waves of Juno Beach. The tank carries plaques and remembrances from numerous units engaged in the liberation of Normandy. An **NTL Totem** stands nearby. (49.335638, -0.457982)

The short street behind the tank is named after Sergeant Léo Gariépy (see below). The area is a popular tourist stop for its restaurants, shops, flower displays, and children's carousel.

A short distance west, a **50-mm antitank gun** has been preserved near its original position beside the river estuary. In 1944, this weapon sat slightly nearer to the harbor entrance in a concrete lined pit with only the gun and shield exposed above ground level. The shield still displays the effect of the shell that killed the German crew and put the gun out of action. (49.335778, -0.458379)

Walk along the estuary to the flower-bedecked platform standing before the entrance to the Maison de la Mer. The estuary marked the boundary between Mike Red and Nan Green sectors and also between the Royal Winnipeg Rifles to the west and the Regina Rifles to the east. The platform holds a monument commemorating the **Allies'** landing to liberate France and the return to France of **général Charles de Gaulle** on 14 June 1944. (49.336148, -0.457716)

Proceed east to the opening in the sea wall flanked by memorials to units that fought in Normandy, although not all of these units landed on D-Day. The key plaque identifies

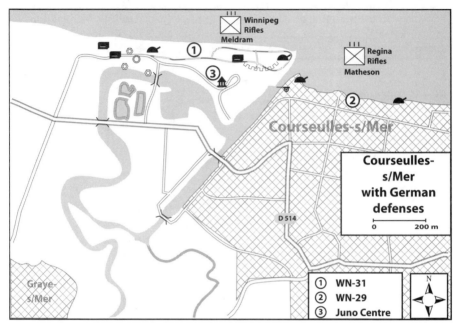

this beach as the landing point of **Company A**, **Regina Rifles**, and it commemorates the regiment's 458 men killed during the ensuing northern European campaign. Access the beach and move to the west. (49.336143, -0.456914)

WN-29 was anchored on its western end by a massive casemate where the Bar de la Mer now stands. It held an 88-mm PaK 43/41 antitank gun and perhaps a 75-mm field cannon. The 88-mm gun stood behind 1.3 meters of reinforced concrete flanked by machine-gun pillboxes. The embrasure aims along Nan Green sector to the east. Company A landed directly into the guns of this strongpoint and paid a dear price crossing the beach. (49.336444, -0.457193)

Company A survivors were strung along the seawall when Lieutenant Bill Grayson found himself among the narrow lanes behind the seafront villas. After throwing a grenade through a pillbox opening, he kicked open the door in time to see surviving enemy troops frantically leaving through a second door. The final German rolled a grenade across the floor toward Grayson, who picked it up and hurled it after the retreating enemy. Armed with only his pistol, Grayson followed the trench system that led to the rear of the 88-mm pillbox. The enemy within surrendered and thirty-five men were taken prisoner and an 88-mm gun silenced – with a pistol![3] The gun was destroyed by high explosives shells fired through the embrasure opening by a Sherman DD tank.

A tall steel cross stands on the opposite side of the estuary. Beyond the cross, the wreckage of a German casemate that was part of WN-31 stands tilted on the sand dunes. This emplacement, the closest to the harbor entrance, had twin embrasures allowing two 50-mm guns, similar to the one already visited near the estuary, to fire east at the harbor entrance or west along the length of Mike Beach.

Return to the beach promenade and continue east. An impressive wooden dagger stands at the seawall 170 meters east of the beach exit. This unusual memorial lionizes the

---

3   Lieutenant William Grayson was awarded the Military Cross.

Royal Winnipeg Rifles and identifies what was the center of the expansive WN-29. The Winnipegs actually landed on the opposite side of the harbor, but this location was selected for their memorial. (49.335853, -0.455139)

A large public swimming pool is visible 250 meters farther east where the seaside promenade curves to the north before continuing east. (49.335523, -0.451711) The pool now occupies the site of a pillbox that held a 75-mm field cannon. The gun held out until Sgt Léo Gariépy of the 1st Hussars landed his tank and brought it right up to the blockhouse. Gariépy fired five rounds at point blank range and destroyed the emplacement. He then drove his tank parallel to the dunes, eliminating entrenched enemy riflemen as he progressed.[4] The power of WN-29 is now fully evident, a heavily-defended beach front with powerful guns covering each flank. Fortunately, the initial assault by Company B, Regina Rifles, occurred a short distance farther east allowing them to escape the well-fortified beach front and enter the town.

From the beach exit at the wooden dagger, pass through the parking area flanking rue Pierre Villey to Av de la Combattante. Defensive positions, trenches, gun pits, and minefields filled the space to the avenue where an antitank ditch blocked access to the town proper.

Proceed west on Av de la Combattante to return to the car park, noting the two white memorials almost hidden beneath a shrub on its eastern edge. The stones commemorate the participation of the **French destroyer *Combattante*** (after which the avenue is named) in the D-Day bombardment. The ship sank later in the war after hitting a mine. (49.335799, -0.457027)

Proceed south on Place du Six Juin; after 170 m, turn right (rue du maréchal Foch, D514). Follow for 700 m across the swing bridge over the harbor entrance, and turn right onto rue de Marine Dunkerque. Continue to the bridge over the River Seulles. (49.336246, -0.465074)

Company B, Royal Winnipeg Rifles, fought through the sand-dune defenses of WN-31 and left the beach area on this bridge, which crosses a sweeping curve in the Seulles River. A replacement bridge was built by the **Royal Engineers 85th Field Company** and nicknamed 'Nottingham Bridge.' A stele carrying a memorial plaque to the engineers stands near the southwest corner of the bridge.

Cross 'Nottingham Bridge' and turn right onto Voie des Français Libres. Continue to the Juno Centre parking area. (49.336561, -0.461168)

Juno Beach Centre

Voie des Français Libres
14470 Courseulles-s/Mer
Tel: +33(0)2 31 37 32 17

BP 104
Email: contact@junobeach.org
Web: http://www.junobeach.org

Juno Beach Centre is noted for its architecture, the six sections of which represent Juno, Gold, Omaha, Utah, Sword and Canada connected in a star fashion around a center that houses the reception area. A unique sculpture of soldiers, their bodies rising out of a single mass with blank faces and wearing the traditional British-style helmet, stands in

---

4   Sergeant Léo Gariépy returned to Courseulles after the war and is now buried in the local community cemetery.

front of the Centre entrance. The museum's rooms cover the invasion of Normandy and Canadian participation in the entire war – on the home front and in Europe. In a hallway, the names of the Canadian soldiers killed in the Second World War are projected across the curved ceiling, a feature that takes 13 ½ hours for all of the 45,000 names to appear.

Open 1 April to 30 September from 09:30 to 19:00; March and October from 10:00 to 18:00; and February, November, and December from 10:00 to 17:00. Guided tours led by Canadian students are available six times per day during the summer season, twice per day during the spring and fall. Admission fee; Normandie Pass accepted; handicap accessible.

> Leave the Juno Centre and proceed on foot toward the water to the walkpath that parallels the seafront.

The landing zone for Company B, Royal Winnipeg Rifles was particularly deadly because it faced one 75-mm and two 50-mm guns and numerous machine guns and mortars in **WN-31,** which stretched from the harbor to a pillbox 550 meters to the west. The armaments on WN-31 were formidable. The casemated guns brought their fire upon the approaching tanks of A Squadron, 1st Hussars, which hit the beach six minutes after the infantry. Captain John W Powell's attention focused upon advancing among the Teller mines on the beach obstacles when his tank's gun was sliced through by a 50-mm antitank shell. Despite additional hits upon his tank, Powell continued forward with only his machine gun operational. Although wounded, Powell positioned his tank such that his crew could fire through the enemy's embrasure and kill the German gun crew.[5]

The German positions started to fall to the determined attacks, coordinated by their fearless company commander, Captain PE Gower, who strode up and down the beach directing his men.[6] Rifleman Emil Saruk crossed the beach and slipped behind one pillbox; its gunfire soon ceased. Later, Saruk's body was found near the entrance door, and the pillbox held a cluster of dead Germans.[7] The assault was successful, but only twenty-six men survived the ordeal unscathed.

Numerous fortification artifacts remain for visitors to understand the nature of a German resistance nest. Memorials and informational signs stretch along the sand dunes. A German **observation bunker** stands immediately in front of the Juno Centre. As part of the Atlantic Wall defense system, the fire of other bunkers and casemates around Courseulles were coordinated by observers in an armored cupola on the roof, which has been since removed, but a steel ring indicates its location and size. The cupola also held a machine gun. The Juno Centre offers guided tours to view the bunker's interior; however, the exterior can be readily examined without a tour. Although it appears today that observation of offshore ships was blocked by dunes, in 1944 the dunes had a considerably different configuration. (49.337029, -0.460718)

A memorial to the **Canadian Navy** stands near the path slightly to the east and commemorates all of the Canadian naval officers and men who served during Operation OVERLORD and the entire war.

A covered trench connected the observation bunker with the double casemate near

---

5   Captain John W Powell was awarded the Military Cross.

6   Captain Philip E Gower was awarded the Military Cross.

7   Rifleman Emil Saruk is buried in Bény-s/Mer Canadian War Cemetery. He died at age 27.

the harbor that was entrance viewed from the opposite side of the estuary. The trenches' concrete roof or, farther east, large stones placed in the sand, identify the trench's path through the dunes. One may follow the path to the double casemate, but interest resides only in its location. The casemate has been considerably tilted due to eroding sand, and entrances and embrasures have been barred over safety concerns. (49.336694, -0.459934)

> Return to your vehicle and proceed west on Voie des Français Libres past the access bridge to park at a convenient spot. Find the beach exit framed with metal portrayals of attacking soldiers. Walk across the beach to a casemate. (49.337386, -0.465406)

The R612-style casemate west of the Juno Centre held a 75-mm field cannon that guarded the beach exit codenamed M1. The Royal Winnipeg Rifles, who landed along this stretch, came under its fire. The powerful gun knocked out the first 1st Hussar tank to approach it. German machine guns, raking the five-man crew as it bailed from the vehicle, killed the men. Two other tanks that landed nearby dealt with both the gun and then the German infantry – without mercy. An infosign identifies this position as '**Cosy's Bunker.**' Lieutenant WF (Cosy) Aitken led his 15-man platoon of Company B, Royal Winnipeg Rifles, in an assault on the fortification. They captured the position, but during the assault Aitken was shot in the lungs.[8]

The wing wall pointing toward the sea separated two embrasures that allowed the single gun to fire to the west and machine guns to fire to the east. The enormous shell damage above the embrasure suggests that it may also have been hit by naval gunfire. The tilt of the casemate has resulted from sand shifting during demolition efforts. (49.337106, -0.458336)

To the west, a stainless steel **Cross of Lorraine** stands amid a small amphitheater that looks out to the English Channel. It commemorates the return of général Charles de Gaulle to France, who had landed a short distance from this location. This site also marks the boundary between Courseulles-s/Mer and Graye-s/Mer. (49.337491, -0.467595)

Farther west, a **R630-style blockhouse** contained three machine guns: two internal MG34s or MG42s within one large embrasure pointed to the northwest and a third machine gun mounted in a tobruk on the roof. The filled rooftop tobruk is plainly visible; however, shifting sand has filled the blockhouse's doorways and embrasures. (49.337658, -0.468153)

Continuing west, a **Signal Monument** stands at beach exit M2 from Mike Red sector. The path through a minefield and across a blocking tank ditch, forged by the Royal Engineers of 79th Armoured Division, was imperative because ground to the west was flooded as part of the German defensive plans. (49.337784, -0.469204)

A 75-mm field cannon sited 1.8 kilometers west of the Signal Monument constituted the only permanent fortification of WN-32 designed to cover Mike Beach from the west. The powerful weapon was the first objective of Company C, Canadian Scottish Regiment, which was attached to the Winnipegs for the landing. However, it had been destroyed by naval gunfire from HMS *Diadem*. The Scots found only a few German corpses, and the gun was not a factor in the battle. The Scottish proceeded to clear minefields and attack toward Château Vaux. The crumbled concrete casemate remains fully exposed along the seafront with its embrasure aimed east toward Courseulles. It offers little interest, and

---

8   Lieutenant William Forsythe Aitken survived his wounds and the war. He was Mentioned in Dispatches for heroism.

the level of destruction makes the site extremely dangerous. (49.341944, -0.493076)

From the Signal Monument, turn south away from the water and pass through the beach exit to the tank on the left. A **Royal Engineer AVRE Petard tank** advanced to the south before sliding into a broken culvert near the far end of the parking area ahead on the left. Unable to pull the tank out of the ditch and still under enemy fire which killed three members of the tank crew, engineers placed a bridging AVRE across the gap, using the sunken tank as a pier, and the advance continued. As the day progressed, the original tank sank deeper into the sand until it was completely bulldozed over. After thirty-two years, the original AVRE was recovered, refurbished, and now forms the **79th Armoured Division Memorial**. The tank is wonderfully preserved and presents one of the best examples of these unique vehicles on the invasion beaches. (49.33719, -0.46914)

Turn left and proceed east along Voie des Français Libres. The memorial on the right in the parking area's northeast corner commemorates the landings of the **Royal Winnipeg Rifles** and **Canadian Scottish** and the casualties they suffered in securing this beach exit. (49.336896, -0.468614)

A large personnel shelter stands slightly above the roadway on the left. Its actual function is uncertain, but the structure's extra thick walls suggest a command or communications post. An **NTL Totem** is to its right. (49.337218, -0.468206)

A machine gun tobruk, almost completely hidden by blowing sand, sits slightly above road level on the left. It held an MG42, which rotated upon the mounting ring embedded in the tobruk's round opening. This position and the double tobruk described below were sited to defend the resistance nest against land attack from across the river. (49.337204, -0.467691)

The large diameter concrete ring across the road from M1 beach exit identifies an open-pit gun position. The gun was initially installed here while the casemate was under construction. (49.336966, -0.465932)

An unusual double tobruk, slightly to the east and below road grade, is readily visible by walking farther east and down the boat launch ramp to the river. The tobruks are of differing sizes because one was designed to hold a 50-mm mortar and the other a machine gun. (49.336812, -0.465825)

Other scattered pieces of concrete among the dunes mark openings to underground troop shelters, ammunition stores, more tobruks, or just part of the tank defenses, minefields, gun pits, and machine-gun positions dotting the resistance nest.

Leave Courseulles by continuing west along Voie des Français Libres. Continue straight across the coastal highway (D514) on Av du général de Gaulle (D112c) into Graye-s/ Mer. Turn left onto rue Grande (D112c); after 400 m turn right on rue de Banville, then a quick left toward Courseulles (D12). After 750 m enter a large roundabout and take the 1st exit toward Caen (D79). After another 750 m, enter another roundabout and again take the 1st exit toward Reviers / Thaon (D170, Route de Reviers). Follow for 2.6 km into Reviers; turn toward Tailleville (D35).

Before exiting Reviers, pass the small stele passed on the right, which commemorates the **Regina Rifles** who died liberating the town. (49.301427, -0.4616)

Continue for 850 m to the cemetery on the left. (49.302411, -0.45059)

The **Bény-s/Mer Canadian War Cemetery** holds 2,048 graves of men who died during the Normandy fighting. All are Canadians except for four British and one Frenchman. The site originally held two temporary cemeteries that were later combined. A tree-lined entry path leads to sixteen grave plots that, taken together, form the square cemetery. The plots hold the bodies of nine pairs of brothers and, in one of the saddest events of the invasion, one group of three brothers. Thomas, Albert, and George Westlake were all riflemen. Albert and Thomas served in the Queen's Own Rifles of Canada, and both died on 11 June. They are buried in adjacent graves. George joined the North Nova Scotia Highlanders and died on 7 June.[9]

Two shelters flank the entrance path, and both allow visitors to ascend a stairway to a viewing platform from which impressive views of the cemetery are possible. It is possible to see Juno Beach 4.5 kilometers to the north from this high ground atop a north-south running ridge. The left shelter holds a plaque dedicated to the **Cameron Highlanders of Ottawa**.

Continue toward Tailleville (D35) for 3.1 km. In Tailleville, turn left toward At-Aubin-s/Mer (D219) and, after 400 m, stop near the far end of the buildings on the left. (49.307147, -0.407202)

Tailleville

The chateau in Tailleville held the headquarters of Hauptmann Deptolla of II Battalion, Grenadier Regiment 736, and was defended by the battalion's 8th Company. Two of the unit's four companies held the beachfront defenses attacked by the Canadians while its weapons company was stationed between Tailleville and Reviers, where 2nd Company, *Ostbattalion* 441, was likewise garrisoned. The grenadier's 7th Company and the *Ostbattalion's* 1st Company lay west of Vaux.

Tailleville had been transformed into a fortress – identified as WN-23 – with tunnels, trenches, minefields, and pillboxes on the chateau grounds and to its north. The town was surrounded by a 4-meter-high, 1-meter-thick stone wall. The upper levels of the chateau provided excellent observation of the landing beaches at St-Aubin, 3 kilometers to the north

Believing the town to be empty, infantry Companies A and C, North Shore Regiment, moved in a line in the fields on either side of the road followed by a troop of Fort Garry Horse tanks on the roadway. German machine guns and mortars started to pound the advancing line, and Canadian tanks took identifiable targets under fire. Company C approached the village on the west side of the road as several machine guns raked the line of men until a mortar-carrying Bren carrier scored accurate hits upon all but one of the machine guns. Private Herbert Butland leapt forward and charged across the field against the remaining MG42. Despite a long burst, the German gun missed Butland, who killed its crew with a burst from his own Bren gun.[10]

The Canadians achieved the stone wall but were now trapped and unable to surmount the wall. Three more tanks arrived, and the now six vehicles drove around the village firing over the wall where possible. The tanks were stymied until they found a

---

9   Five Westlake brothers grew up parentless supporting each other in Toronto, Canada. The two remaining brothers did not join the army. At least three other examples of families that lost three brothers fighting in the all-volunteer Canadian Army are recorded.

10   Private Herbert Butland received the Military Medal.

large wooden gate. One tank battered the gate down and entered the chateau courtyard followed by streaming infantry. They discovered that the town was an underground fortress with tunnels connecting buildings, pillboxes, and firing trenches. After a difficult six-hour fight, much of it in darkened underground rooms and corridors as the Germans moved between the buildings using tunnels to appear behind the Canadians, German troops started to surrender after their line of withdrawal to the south was blocked. Sixty enemy troops were taken prisoner and an equal number killed. The delay cost the opportunity to capture the radar station at Douvres-la-Délivrande (see Chapter Two).

The wall on the northern side of the chateau grounds marked the first line of defense. Although now partially obscured by piles of rubbish, the wall provided protection for German machine guns. Near the western end of the wall, two pillboxes and a mortar tobruk remain. These positions held underground passages allowing movement underneath the wall to and from the chateau grounds.

The open gateway immediately behind the wall was that blown open by the tanks of the Fort Garry Horse in their assault upon the chateau. The roadway is public and leads to a courtyard frequently used as a storage area and flea market. One of the German firing slits is visible in the wall to the left of the short section of wall. A view of the red brick and stone façade of the **Chateau Tailleville** is possible from the courtyard. The building's northern face still displays the bullet and shell marks of the intense fire required to overcome the German resistance. Above-ground German installations no longer exist, and the underground positions are not accessible.

Reverse direction and proceed approximately 170 m to the large 'S' curve. (49.306063, -0.408919)

A buried German machine gun tobruk, now frequently used as a flower planter, sits near the roadway. Lieutenant-Colonel DB Buell, commander of the North Shore Regiment, came under fire from a German gunner as he sheltered in the nearby gateway. He was rescued by the appearance of a Canadian tank, which eliminated the enemy. Behind the tobruk is a memorial to Felix Cassignuel, who owned the farm accessed through that gateway. In the confused fighting that occurred during the clearing of the numerous German positions, Cassignuel was accidentally killed by a Canadian grenade.

The west side of the roadway, south of the farm, is place Alphonse Noël, named after a Canadian soldier of the North Shore Regiment who was wounded here on 6 June during the liberation of the village.[11]

Continue to the junction with highway D35. Turn toward Revières (D35), and follow for 2.1 km. Turn toward Bény-s/Mer (D79), and continue to the parking area on the left before the church. (49.291742, -0.432962)

The Régiment de la Chaudière progressed due south from Bernières-s/Mer along highway D79a (becomes D79) to enter Bény-s/Mer from the north. The unit was hit by accurate 88-mm fire as it moved upon Bény-s/Mer; the town, however, was captured around noon on D-Day by Company C. Continuing, the unit was hit by shells from a 100-

---

11   Alphonse Noël survived the war and returned to Canada. On the 40th anniversary of the battle, he returned to Tailleville and discovered the family of Felix Cassignuel. Cassignuel's son was now the mayor, who led a campaign to dedicate the small square to Noël and the North Shore Regiment.

mm gun battery positioned west near the village of Moulineaux. The guns were eliminated by accurate salvos from the 4.2-inch guns of HMCS *Algonquin*, which was anchored offshore. Entrenched infantry defending the guns' positions were a more difficult problem. A badly depleted Company B assaulted the field positions but was unable to make progress until a gap was discovered in the wire entanglements. Two platoons charged through, and fifty-four enemy troops quickly surrendered.

A simple concrete stele, overlooked by the flags of Canada and France, commemorates the liberation of the village by the **Régiment de la Chaudière** at 1530 on 6 June.

> Continue toward Basly (D79) and follow past the rear of the church to the small monument on the right. (49.278985, -0.423886)

After overcoming the German resistance about Bény-s/Mer, the Régiment de la Chaudière's Company C moved through undefended Basly. The red granite stone, beautifully sculpted into the shape of a maple leaf, stands in the small park behind the church beside the First World War memorial. The stone commemorates the liberation of the village on 6 June by the French-speaking Canadians.

> Continue following highway D79 into Colomby-s/Thaon. Turn toward Fontenay-Henry (D141). Stop after 170 m at the *mairie* on the left. (49.265226, -0.411201)

After the village's capture by the Régiment de la Chaudière, the North Nova Scotia Highlanders, mounted upon tanks of the Sherbrooke Fusiliers, took over the advance toward Carpiquet airfield. The French-Canadian force needed the rest, having fought all day up the sloping terrain from the beach to the ridgeline that runs through Colomby and Anguerny. From its crest, they saw the airfield ten kilometers distant across the open fields.

The liberation of this beautiful Norman village on 7 June by the **Régiment de la Chaudière** is commemorated by a simple stone stele and plaque placed in front of the *mairie*. Appropriately for the French-speaking unit, the plaque reads in French only.

> Reverse direction, and continue 300 m into Anguery to the stele on the left. (49.265655, -0.404906)

Near the school parking area, a stele commemorates **Capitaine Michel Gauvin**, commander of the Chaudière Regiment's Bren carrier platoon. Gauvin negotiated the surrender of a twenty-man German antiaircraft gun detachment located in la Mare d'Anguerny.[12]

> Continue 500 m to the roundabout near the church. (49.267041, -0.401366)

The 11th century Romanesque **Église St-Martin de Anguerny** is on rue du Régiment Queen's Own Rifles of Canada. The structure, surrounded by its ancient graveyard, stands above the **Rond-Pont du Régiment Fort Garry Horse**. The church wall continues along the road toward Douvres-la-Délivrande (VC1) and holds a beautiful dark black granite stone plaque dedicated to the **Queen's Own Rifles of Canada** '...who

---

12   Capitaine Michel Gauvin was awarded a Military Cross for this action. He died in 2003 at age 84.

gave their lives to take and hold Anguerny.'

Leave the roundabout toward Mathieu (D141) and follow for 2.6 km as the roadway becomes a frontage road for the high-speed highway D7. Continue to the junction with highway D220. At the roundabout, take the 1st exit toward Anisy, and stop after 350 m at the monument on the right. (49.25089, -0.387843)

The white stone stele carrying a cut-out of the Canadian Maple Leaf stands immediately before entering the village and is dedicated to the **Queen's Own Rifles of Canada**. The stele marks the limit of the unit's D-Day advance from Nan White beach at Bernières-s/Mer and, indeed, the farthest point of the entire 8th Canadian Infantry Brigade.

Continue into and through Anisy for 1.1 km. Turn left toward Caen (D79). After 950 m, stop at the memorial on the right. (49.239758, -0.39848)

A beautiful memorial to **Norwegian airmen and sailors** who participated in the European campaign stands on open ground slightly above the intersection of highway D79 and rue de Cambes. The rough stone obelisk carries a plaque depicting air, sea, and ground forces during the invasion. The beautifully landscaped site was chosen with regard to the Norwegian Spitfire pilots stationed at a temporary airfield near Villons-les-Buissons.

Turn toward Villons-les-Buissons (unsigned, but passes in front of the Norwegian memorial). Turn left toward Buron (rue des Sherbrooke Fusiliers, D220), and continue 1.1 km to the memorial wall on the right. (49.233294, -0.414015)

Bren carriers mounted by a platoon of Company C, North Nova Scotia Highlanders passed the curve at Villons-les-Anisy as three German machine guns in the village opened fire. After a brief firefight, most of the German platoon was killed. However, darkness was rapidly approaching, and the mobile force was still seven kilometers from Carpiquet. Major-General Keller sent out orders for each unit of the 9th Brigade to stop and establish defensive positions to repel an expected German counterattack. His decision would have dramatic consequences for the Canadians. Accordingly, the North Nova Scotia Highlanders and Sherbrooke Fusiliers formed a fortress position around the road junction of highways D79 and D220.

The **Hell's Corner Memorial** identifies the farthest advance of 9th Canadian Infantry Brigade troops on D-Day. On 7 June the North Nova Scotia Highlanders moved south across the Bayeux-Caen Highway only to the beaten back to this point (see below). For the next 32 days this position represented the Canadian advance position, and it became the target of frequent German artillery and mortar attacks, hence earning its nickname from the Canadian troops.

German Counterattack
7 June 1944

The fighting of 6 June had essentially wiped out the 716th Infantry Division. Its commander, Generalleutnant Wilhelm Richter, still sheltered in his headquarters north of Caen, had little to command and no radio contact with any of his regimental commanders. The 21st Panzer Division had split its counterattack into two efforts, one on each side of the Orne, and neither was successful.

At 1500 on 6 June, Adolf Hitler finally released additional armored troops in reaction to the invasion. He placed the 12th SS Panzer (Hitlerjugend) and Panzer Lehr divisions under Seventh Army control. Minutes later, Hitler placed the front from Bayeux to Caen under I SS Panzer Corp's SS-Oberstgruppenführer Josef (Sepp) Dietrich. Seventh Army Commander Generaloberst Friedrich Dollman ordered the panzer divisions to proceed to the Caen area in preparation for a counterstrike to the invasion beaches.

The German convoys embarked upon a fearful trip under frequent aerial attack by Spitfires and Typhoons which caused delays and significant loss of troops and equipment. While the 12th SS Panzer Division was strung out along the highways of Normandy, SS-Standartenführer Kurt Meyer was ordered to form a *kampfgruppe* from any divisional units that were available and launch a counterattack to the north by the afternoon of 7 June. Late in the evening of 6 June, his headquarters was established in the medieval Abbaye d'Ardenne, 2 kilometers from Richter's headquarters and northwest of Caen.

Objective	To defend Carpiquet airfield and sever Allied links between Sword and Juno Beaches.
Forces	
Canadian	9th Infantry Brigade (Brigadier DG Cunningham)
German	SS Panzergrenadier Regiment 25 (SS-Standartenführer Kurt Meyer)
Result	The Germans stopped the Canadian advance toward Carpiquet airfield.
Casualties	
Canadian	110 killed, 64 wounded, and 128 taken prisoner
German	86 killed, 50 wounded, and 27 missing
Location	Buron is 8 km northwest of Caen

Battle

At 0745, the North Nova Scotia Highlanders and the Stuart tanks of the Sherbrooke Fusiliers' Reconnaissance Troop, supported by the machine-gun platoon of the Cameron Highlanders of Canada, left Villons-les-Buissons and moved south. After a short fight against two 88-mm gun positions west of Villons-les-Buissons, the troops overcame weak resistance in Buron from remnants of the 716th Infantry Division and then continued on into Authie, where the leading Company C was under mortar and artillery fire from the east as the Sherbrooke Fusilier Stuart tanks continued on to Franqueville only 2 kilometers from the Carpiquet Airfield.

Observing the Canadian troop movements from a turret of the abbey's church building, Kurt Meyer did not believe his eyes. Despite orders to attack northwards, this was an opportunity that he could not pass up. The Canadian advance was oblivious to the presence of *Kampfgruppe Meyer* only 1.5 kilometers distant on its uncovered flank. Meyer sent III Battalion of his panzergrenadiers and a company of PzKpfw IVs crashing into the Sherbrooke Fusiliers in Franqueville. Taking advantage of their higher ground, German tanks and antitank guns poured fire into the Sherbrooke armor. Three companies of grenadier infantry then swung around to the west of Authie and overran Company A, North Nova Scotia Highlanders, which had dug in between Authie and Gruchy. In addition, II Battalion hit Buron from the southeast. For two hours a tank battle raged in the fields

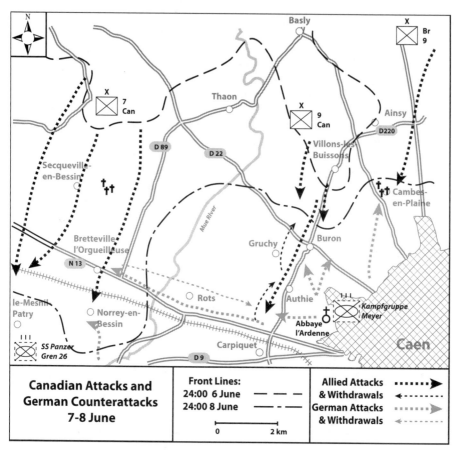

Canadian Attacks and German Counterattacks 7-8 June

Front Lines:	
24:00 6 June	— — —
24:00 8 June	— · —

0   2 km

Allied Attacks & Withdrawals	● ● ● ● ● ● ▶
	◀ - - - - - - -
German Attacks & Withdrawals	● ● ● ● ● ▶
	◀ - - - - - - -

between Authie and Buron. The Canadians lost twenty-one tanks in the engagement; the Germans reported only six tanks lost. The Canadians were pushed back to Villons-les-Buisson, but as Meyer's force was also engaged against the British 3rd Division in Cambes-en-Plaine, he halted the pursuit.

Battlefield Tour

The tour continues from Hell's Corners. Follow highway D220 1.8 km into Buron and stop at the square on the left. (49.217329, -0.421311)

The village was liberated early on 7 June as the North Nova Scotia Highlanders and Sherbrooke Fusiliers advanced toward the Bayeux-Caen Highway. The German counterattack drove the Canadians back to Villons-les-Buissons and, although recaptured the same day, Buron was abandoned as undefendable with the troops available. The village remained in German hands until early July.

Memorial steles to the **Sherbrooke Fusiliers** and the **Highland Light Infantry of Canada** are located in a park in the center of town. The large Sherbrooke plaque is affixed to a stone stele under the gentle shade of low trees. The engraving commemorates the seven years of war and the men from Sherbrooke, Quebec, Canada, who fought during the period. The Highland Light Infantry was a reserve regiment of the 9th Infantry Brigade that was not significantly engaged in the early June battles; however, it was among the first Allied troops to enter Caen the following month.

> Continue toward Authie (D220) and, after 1.5 km, stop at the memorial on the right. (49.206526, -0.431526)

The modern appearance of Authie reflects the intense fighting that took place in and around the village especially in this intersection and around the village church to the west. The village was mostly destroyed in June 1944 as II Battalion, SS Panzergrenadier Regiment 25, attacked the advancing North Nova Scotia Highlanders.

A memorial to **North Nova Scotia Highlanders** stands on the corner marked by the French and Canadian flags. The gray stone-block stele carries a brass plaque commemorating the soldiers and civilians who lost their lives on 7 June in the heated battle in and around the village. An **NTL Totem** stands nearby. The square has been renamed 'place des 37 Canadiens' in memory of those Canadian POWs executed along this street by the SS.

> Leave the center of Authie to the east on rue de l'Abbaye (D220c). After 1.5 km, leave the roundabout at the 1st exit onto rue du Régiment du 1er Hussard. Continue 410 m past the abbey entrance gate to a small parking area on the left. Walk back to the Porte de Bayeux for a view into the medieval courtyard. (49.19689, -0.415084)

The chapel of the medieval Premonstratensian **Abbaye d'Ardenne** was constructed in 1121 with other buildings added, as required, over the centuries. The abbey was looted by the English during the Hundred Years War and King Charles VI used it during his siege of English-held Caen. Heavily damaged during Second World War fighting for Caen, almost all of the buildings required complete reconstruction. The site became the property of the regional government in 1994 and is now dedicated to literary research. The church functions as its library. Access to the grounds is limited.

The abbey became the headquarters of the SS Panzergrenadier Regiment 25 on the night of 6/7 June as the leading element of the 12th SS Panzer Division[13] arrived. The octagonal turrets atop the church's façade made for excellent observation posts with a view from the landing beaches to the north and over the plains to the south. During the morning of 7 June, *Kampfgruppe* commander Kurt Meyer observed the Canadians' southward advance from one of these turrets.

Visitors must now walk south along the roadside from the Porte de Bayeux on the rue d'Ardenne to enter **le Jardin des Canadiens** through an opening in the wall between the main entrance and the stables. (49.19659, -0.415439) A memorial to twenty Canadian soldiers executed during the next several days by SS troops is located on the left against the exterior of the abbey wall. A vinyl mural attached to the wall reveals photographs of sixteen of the victims, apparently executed at the wall and buried in a trench at its base. All but two of the soldiers' bodies were accidentally discovered months later as reconstruction

---

13　The 12th SS Panzer Division held a large complement of untested teenage boys who had been raised believing in the Nazi tenets of Aryan superiority. They were described as well-trained and well-armed fanatics led by NCOs who had been brutalized in Eastern Front fighting. Perhaps this was the basis for their savagery to captured enemy.

started. The bodies were relocated to Bény-s/Mer Cemetery.[14]

> Return to Authie and turn left toward Franqueville (D220). Stop at a convenient spot. (49.200554, -0.43396)

Kampfgruppe Meyer's attack upon the exposed flank of the Sherbrooke Fusiliers took place along this road. Once past the distant trees on the right, the white structure of the abbey church is visible to the east.

During 7 June, SS-Standartenführer Wilhelm Mohnke brought his SS Panzer-grenadier Regiment 26 onto Meyer's left flank to face the 7th Canadian Infantry Brigade, which had advanced across the Bayeux-Caen Highway to occupy Norrey-en-Bessin and Putot-en-Bessin. Mohnke's objective was to eliminate the Canadian positions that protruded into the German front as a preparation for a full-scale counterattack by 12th SS, 21st Panzer, and Panzer Lehr divisions between Bayeux and Caen toward the channel.

The Canadian positions offered few defensive advantages. The gently rolling agricultural land held mature, but as yet unharvested, grain standing over one meter in height. The farming villages generally sat in low ground, easily overlooked from surrounding low hills.

German Counterattacks
8 to 11 June 1944

Objective	To cut off Canadian spearhead and to regain control of the Bayeux-Caen Road and rail lines
Forces	
Canadian	7th Canadian Infantry Brigade (Brigadier HW Foster)
German	SS Panzergrenadier Regiment 25 (SS-Standartenführer Kurt Meyer) and SS Panzergrenadier Regiment 26 (SS-Standartenführer Wilhelm Mohnke)
Result	The Canadians held their positions forcing a stalemate.
Casualties	
Canadian	500 killed, 468 wounded, 35 missing, and 186 taken prisoner
German	222 killed, 459 wounded, and 62 missing
Location	Bretteville-l'Orgueilleuse is 14 km northwest of Caen

Battle

After *Kampfgruppe Meyer* drove back the 9th Canadian Infantry Brigade from Authie and Buron, the Regina Rifles commander, Lieutenant-Colonel FM Matheson, became concerned about his exposed flanks and ordered the Regina Rifles to consolidate in defensive positions around Bretteville-l'Orgueilleuse and Norrey-en-Bessin. Early on

---

14   Kurt 'Panzer' Meyer was convicted of war crimes at his trial in December 1945, as having ultimate responsibility for the conduct of his men. Although he received a death sentence, it was never carried out, and his life sentence was also commuted. He was released in 1954 and died in 1961.

The murders at Abbaye d'Ardenne were not the only killings committed by SS troops during this battle. Thirty-seven Canadian POWs were executed around the villages of Buron and Authie on 7 June 1944, twenty-six at Château d'Audrieu, and forty northeast of Fontenay-le-Pesnel. All told, the 12th SS Division killed 156 prisoners.

8 June, Mohnke, supported by tanks of the SS Panzer Regiment 12, struck against the 7th Canadian Infantry Brigade front. The Regina Rifles in Norrey-en-Bessin held, but the Royal Winnipeg Rifles in Putot-en-Bessin did not.

Over the next several days, German tank attacks attempted to force the Canadians from their defenses which blocked the path of the planned German armored offensive. Positions hardened as both sides suffered severe losses, and the first stage of the Anglo-Canadian drive on Caen came to a close. Although the beachhead was firmly established, the principle goal of Carpiquet was beyond the Canadians' reach.

Battlefield Tour

Tourist information and services are more difficult to obtain in these small farming villages. French Battlefields recommends obtaining general information from the tourist offices in Caen or Bayeux. Because the fighting devolved into a series of individual engagements, each will be described and toured in turn.

> From Franqueville, continue south through the large roundabout toward Caen/Carpiquet (D14) and pass under the autoroute. Follow for 1.3 km into Carpiquet; turn right toward Tilley-s/Seulles (D9). Follow for 5.4 km, passing along the edge of the airport to the junction with highway D83. The junction lies between Cheux 2.0 km to the south and St-Manvieu-Norrey 1.0 km to the north.

Battle of Norrey-en-Bessin
8 to 10 June

Wilhelm Mohnke established his headquarters in Cheux. At 0330 on 8 June, his I Battalion moved through St-Manvieu without artillery or tank support in preparation for an attack upon Norrey-en-Bessin. Once past St-Manvieu's buildings and on the downward slope into the lowland between the villages, his company drew rifle fire from Regina Rifles outposts. On the up slope, mortar and artillery fire intensified, and the attack broke down with the 3rd Company taking up positions hidden in the tall grain. The battalion's 2nd Company, advancing farther west, swung west of the village and moved into a farm south of Cardonville.

On 9 June, after the failed tank attack against Bretteville (see below), Kurt Meyer launched the Panther (PzKpfw V) tanks of 3rd Panzer Company against Norrey from the east. Shortly after noon, twelve Panthers passed under the railway line at Villeneuve, turned east, and formed a single line. The broad front of tanks sped across the open fields, but they exposed their flank to the Sherman Fireflies of the 1st Hussars. The Panther advance stuttered and stopped as tanks exploded in flames. Having lost seven tanks, the Germans withdrew.

On a third attempt, Norrey fell to Pionier[15] Battalion 12 on 10 June. Starting at front line positions established on 8 June south of the village, they advanced during the pre-dawn darkness despite heavy mortar fire to the edge of town. Machine guns shredded the leading company's command team, and the attack collapsed.

---

15   In the German Army, Pionier units were specially trained in construction and demolition activities. They were frequently used as emergency infantry.

Turn right toward Bretteville-l'Orgueilleuse (D83). The highway follows the German attack of 8 June. After 1.9 km, turn left toward Norrey-en-Bessin (D172). The 10 June attack started in the fields on the left. Follow for 750 m to the intersection in front of the church. (49.197296, -0.513935)

A pink granite stele boldly inscribes a golden Canadian Maple Leaf and bears the insignias of the **Regina Rifles** and **1st Hussars**. The **Église Notre-Dame de Norrey-en-Bessin** is a prime example of 13th century Norman Gothic architecture with its wooden ceiling nave and vaulted transepts. The church was almost totally destroyed during the intense fighting. The rebuilt church did not include its steeple, thus creating the unusual flat top to the bell tower.

From the intersection in front of the church, proceed east (rue du Village) for 450 m. Turn left toward Bretteville-l'Orgueilleuse at the 'T' junction (not signed) and continue 800 m to the bridge over the railway line. (49.202892, -0.509952)

The tank attack of 9 June approached from the east with the Panthers in a north/south line. They reached a point approximately at this postwar bridge before being engaged by the 1st Hussars positioned to the north. The elevation of the railway bridge offers a view

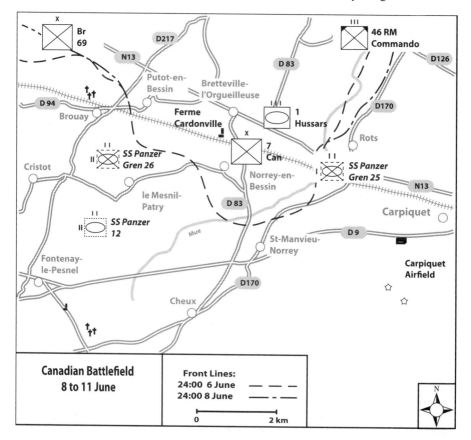

Canadian Battlefield
8 to 11 June

Front Lines:
24:00 6 June — — —
24:00 8 June — - — -

0   2 km

N

of the terrain of the tank battle.

> Continue toward Bretteville (D83) for 450 m to the large roundabout. Take the 1st exit – the slip road; do not enter the autoroute – and immediately park on the left. (49.207014, -0.511218)

A white stone pathway bordered in roses leads to a white-stone winged memorial dedicated to the varied units of the **3rd Canadian Infantry Division, Royal Canadian Artillery, and British 43rd, 15th, and 50th Infantry Divisions** and the liberation of the surrounding communities. Glass plaques attached to the curved surfaces list the dates of liberation for each of the communes and each participating unit.

> Reverse direction and return to the roundabout; take the 4th exit onto rue de la Gare. After 170 m turn right onto rue de la Liberté, then in 500 m left onto rue du Commando D. A plaque is mounted on the wall on the right. (49.205626, -0.519447)

After being repulsed on 8 June, Mohnke's 2nd Company again attacked la Ferme de Cardonville at 0500 on 9 June. Company D, Regina Rifles, commanded by Major (temporary) Gordon Brown, resisted their repeated attacks. During the five-hour engagement, Major Brown's riflemen held off the attackers until radio communication was re-established. Subsequent intense artillery fire from the 13th Field Artillery Regiment forced the SS troops to abandon their attack and withdraw toward le Mesnil-Patry. The rifle company fielded only thirty-seven effectives at the end of the battle with fifty-one dead or wounded.[16]

Once a linen factory surrounded by stone walls that made for an excellent fortress, the site has developed into a light manufacturing district and bears little resemblance to the rural farm of 1944. The memorial plaque to **Company D**'s stout defense bears the regiment insignia above a brass plaque that describes the events of the battle for the farm. A short distance past the memorial, the rail line passes the south wall of the farm enclosure.

> Reverse direction and return to the large roundabout. Take the 4th exit toward Bretteville (D83) and proceed 450 m to the center of the town. Turn right onto rue de Caen (D613) – a difficult turn as the roadway curves around the church into a busy intersection. Park near the NTL Totem ahead on the left. (49.209756, -0.509735)

Battle for Bretteville-l'Orgueilleuse
8 June

During the evening of 8 June, the Reconnaissance Company of SS Panzergrenadier Regiment 25 and two companies of Panther tanks left Franqueville, bypassed Rots to the south, and attacked Bretteville-l'Orgueilleuse along the Bayeux-Caen Road. They met the 3rd Antitank Regiment's antitank guns and Cameron Highlanders machine guns at the edge of town. A swirling six-hour night battle ensued around the eastern outskirts of the village. Overrunning the advance outposts, German troops blasted their way into the village. One platoon of panzergrenadiers entered the town by circling around to the north. Six men survived to enter the church. They fired a signal flare for the Panthers to advance. Although

---

16   Major Douglas Gordon Brown was awarded a Distinguished Service Order for his leadership during the war. He died in 2008 at age 89

five Panthers were destroyed, two managed to enter the town and charge the battalion headquarters before the lead tank was destroyed and the second withdrew. Two of the men in the church were killed in an attempt to return to their lines. The remaining four spent the next six days hiding in a hollow in the cemetery until they were able to dig a hole through the wall. Three made their escape; the fourth man, too weak to run, surrendered.

The entrance gate to a farm courtyard behind the 13th century Église St-Germain bears a plaque identifying it as the **Regina Rifles** headquarters during the German assault. One of the Panther tanks attacking the town reached a position 25 meters to the east before being set alight by a PIAT antitank weapon fired from close range by Rifleman JE Lapointe,[17] who hid behind a stone wall. The following tank sprayed the roadway with cannon and machine-gun fire as it reversed and made its escape. The **NTL Totem** stands across the road.

> Reverse direction and proceed 400 m and then turn right into place des Canadiens. Continue 95 m to the rear of the place and turn left; the memorial is ahead on the left. (49.212141, -0.514649)

The open square has been dedicated as **place des Canadiens** for their stout defense of the village against superior armor. A flower and flag encircled memorial at the far end of the square holds a commemoration to the **Regina Rifles'** sacrifice. Flanking a pink granite Maple Leaf, English and French language plaques on the face of the gray stone stele remind residents that the '…brave soldiers from the Regina Rifles died…' for their freedom. In front of the stele, a black stone carries the unit's insignia listing the intense battles the regiment participated in during the two world wars including Vimy, Passchendaele, Cambrai, Orne, and Falaise.

> Complete the loop around the place and return to rue de Bayeux (D613). Turn right; after 500 m, turn left toward Putot-en-Bessin (D94), and follow for 1.7 km. Bear left onto rue de l'Église and continue 240 m to the memorials on the right. (49.210962, -0.538834)

Battle of Putot-en-Bessin
8 June

Putot-en-Bessin was the D-Day objective of the Royal Winnipeg Rifles, a target they achieved early on 7 June. The regimental commander, Lieutenant-Colonel John Meldram, placed Company A on the rail bridge known as the Pont de Brouay and Companies C and D between the rail line and the village. Company B, practically wiped out on Juno Beach, was held in reserve. Putot's unique position between the Bayeux-Caen Road and the deep rail cut which acted as an effective tank ditch against armor coming from the south, the made it imperative that the village be held. British troops were supposed to be in neighboring Brouay, but Col Meldram found his right flank completely open. A troop of towed 17-pounder antitank guns was ordered to la Bergerie farm to cover the open ground.

The II Battalion, SS Panzergrenadier Regiment 26, assault began at 0630 on 8 June, as its 6th and 7th Companies moved in night-battle formation from le Mesnil-Patry to strike in a two company front. Major Fred Hodge, commanding Company A at the Brouay rail crossing, permitted the Germans to approach the bridge before opening fire with his platoon of riflemen and the Vickers machine guns of the supporting Cameron Highlanders.

---

17   Rifleman Joseph E Lapointe was awarded the Military Medal.

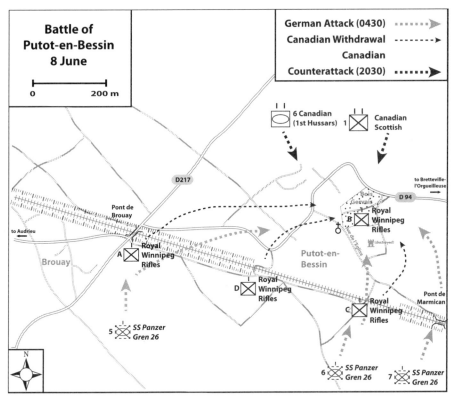

A six-pounder antitank gun knocked out two armored vehicles, and the bloodied Germans withdrew.

At 1000, a renewed assault preceded by artillery and mortar fire ensued and, despite fierce resistance, the Winnipegs could not stop infantry from penetrating over the rail line and into the village. By afternoon, German snipers had penetrated in the village's buildings and overrun platoon after platoon. The three forward companies' survivors withdrew under smoke to the east to join the remnants of Company B. Forty-five Canadian prisoners taken in this engagement were murdered by SS troops at Abbaye d'Ardenne (see above) or Château d'Audrieu (see below).

As darkness approached, the Canadian Scottish, supported by 1st Hussar Sherman tanks, advanced under a creeping artillery barrage from their reserve positions near Secqueville-en-Bessin to renew the fight. Despite heavy German machine-gun and mortar fire, they retook the Pont de Brouay, but efforts to establish positions across the railway line were fiercely repelled. The panzergrenadiers established new positions 300 meters south of the railway line. In their turn, the Canadian Scottish established a concentrated fortress position east of the railway bridge.

Battlefield Tour

Monuments to the **1st Battalion, Canadian Scottish,** and the **Royal Winnipeg Rifles** hold a position of honor in place des Canadiens near the rear of the village church. The pink granite and gray stone steles carry plaques the two units. An infosign describes the locations of the various units and the path of the German attack.

> Reverse direction, and turn left onto rue du 7 Juin (D94). Carefully follow the highway for 1.0 km through the village to the railway bridge. Park on the slip road to the left on the far side of the bridge. (49.211271,-0.553663)

The rail bridge – known as the **Pont de Brouay** – figured heavily in the fighting for Putot as it controlled the railway cutting that bordered the village. The deep rail cutting, which formed a natural tank ditch, extends east of this bridge along the southern edge of the village. The German attack came over fields south of the cutting, where German units later took up defensive positions after the battle.

Side trip: Canadian Memorial in Audrieu

> From the slip road, reverse direction and cross over the highway (D217) toward Brouay (D94). Follow through Brouay and toward Audrieu for 3.2 km. In Audrieu, turn left on rue du Moutier (D82), pass the church, and stop at the memorial on the left. (49.20659, -0.5953) Total distance: 7 km.

Canadian POWs were taken by the members of the III Battalion, SS Panzergrenadier Regiment 26, to the grounds of Château Audrieu 350 meters farther south. The battalion commander, Major Gerhard Bremer, was an ardent Nazi who had fought in Poland, France, and Russia. Bremer interrogated the Canadian prisoners three at a time. When they refused to answer his questions, Bremer had the trio taken to nearby woods and shot. Bremer eventually gave up his interrogations, but the killing continued.[18] Altogether, the execution of twenty-six Canadian and British prisoners was witnessed by two French farmers.[19]

The chateau is now a hotel, but commemoration of the event occurs on a plaque on a wall opposite the village *mairie*. The plaque lists the names of sixty-six victims from killings at Audrieu and northeast of Fontenay-le-Pesnel.

> Return to the tour route by reversing direction back through Brouay to the junction with highway D217 before the railway crossing. Leave the Pont de Brouay south toward Cristot (D217). After 2.1 km, turn left toward le Mesnil-Patry (D172) and follow for 1.8 km to the memorial on the right. (49.194243, -0.546154)

Battle of le Mesnil-Patry
11 June

At 1430 on 11 June, the Queen's Own Rifles and 1st Hussar tanks moved from Bray in a masking advance as British units farther west attempted to flank and capture Caen. The men of Company D rode upon the tanks of the Hussars B Squadron across the grain fields southwest of Norrey toward le Mesnil-Patry. The German 1st Company,

---

18   Gerhard Bremer escaped the Falaise Gap to later fight in Holland, Ardennes, and Hungary. Captured at the end of the war in Austria, he was imprisoned by the French for six years but never brought to trial for war crimes. He died in Spain in 1989 at age 71.

19   SS-Standartenführer Wilhelm Mohnke was suspected of instigating the atrocities. Captured by the Russians in Berlin in 1945, Mohnke spent 10 years in Soviet prisons. Released in 1955, he returned to civilian life and died in 2001 at age 90.

Pioneer Battalion 12, engaged the tanks with machine guns and mortars. The Canadians jumped from the tanks, and a confused, close-quarter engagement ensued. Hussar tanks searched out enemy trenches, and the German troops responded with *Panzerfausts*[20] and magnetic mines. The Sherman tanks of B and C Squadron continued their advance until reaching the northern outskirts of the village. They believed armor approaching from the east of le Mesnil came from a neighboring British unit. In fact, the vehicles were Panther tanks from II Battalion, Panzer Regiment 12. As thirty-four Hussar tanks burst into flames across the battlefield, the Canadians were forced to withdraw after suffering almost 200 casualties. Le Mesnil was liberated on the night of 16/17 June after the Germans withdrew because of flanking actions by British troops to the west.[21]

Memorials to the **Queen's Own Rifles of Canada** and to the **1st Hussars** stand opposite the churchyard near the intersection. The twin polished granite slabs list the names of those killed in the engagement. The left-hand tablet, dedicated to the Queen's Own Rifles, includes the names of Albert and Thomas Westlake.

> Continue on the rue de l'Église (D172) for 3.0 km, through the south edge of Norrey-en-Bessin to the junction of highway D83. (49.195987, -0.508375)

The road proceeds in the opposite direction to that of the Queen's Own Rifles of Canada's attack on 11 June across the broad open fields, so typical on this part of Normandy, that exposed advancing forces to enemy cannon fire. The first German tanks appeared on the right; moments later more tanks had circled around le Mesnil and attacked from the west.

> Turn left toward Bretteville-l'Orgueilleuse (D83). Follow the highway for 1.7 km along the same route as already used into Bretteville and again turn right toward Caen (D613).

Highway D613 is the original Route National 13 or Bayeux-Caen Highway, site of fierce fighting in June 1944. Replaced by the nearby E46/N13 Autoroute, the original road section between Bretteville-l'Orgueilleuse and Villeneuve is little changed from 1944.

> Follow the Bayeux-Caen Road for 1.6 km; turn left on Chemin du Hamel and continue 650 m to the memorial on the left. (49.208333, -0.485061)

Battle of Rots
11 June

Rots had been occupied by a company of I Battalion, Panzergrenadier Regiment 26, since 9 June. Antitank guns and Panther tanks were stationed at strategic locations within the town. However, by 11 June, the initiative had shifted back to the Canadians. No

---

20   *Panzerfaust*: a cheap, single-shot recoilless antitank weapon that could be fired by one person. The weapon was effective at ranges up to 60 meters.

21   Three Canadian prisoners were executed at le Mesnil-Patry. Post-war reports claim that this event served as retaliation for the execution of nine officers and men of Panzer Artillery Regiment 130, who had been captured near Cristot by members of the Inns of Court Regiment. Nonetheless, SS-Sturmbannführer Bernard Siebken and SS-Untersturmführer Dietrich Schnabel, both of II Battalion, SS Panzergrenadier Regiment 26, were tried and found guilty of murder. They were hanged on 20 January 1949.

46 Royal Marine Commando and a squadron of Fort Garry Horse tanks advanced against German positions in the Mue Valley to close the gap between the two Canadian salients. After easily moving south against initial weak opposition, they met fierce opposition in Le Hamel and Rots, where a fight continued into the night while Shermans and Panthers dueled in the square in front of the church. Although suffering horrendous losses including six tanks, the Canadians pushed the panzergrenadiers to the south.

A stele in place du 46ème Royal Marine Commando commemorates the men of **No 46 Royal Commando** who fought in the battle for Rots. A black plaque at the right end of the stone wall records the names and ages of twenty-two Royal Marine Commandos who perished during that fighting.

Continue 650 m, then turn right onto Chemin de la Cavée and continue 270 m to the memorial on the right. (49.211358, -0.476824)

An unusual **memorial to the dead of Rots** presents a few destroyed stone walls framing a beautifully landscaped garden of shrubs and flowers. Although slightly off the main path, it deserves a brief stop and moment of reflection.

This concludes the tour of the 3rd Canadian Infantry Division invasion battlefields. The 3rd Canadian Infantry Division's participation in the defeat of the German Army in Normandy is continued in Chapter Thirteen (Battle of Caen). The tour of the British Second Army landing beaches continues with the British 50th Infantry Division in Ver-s/Mer.

To continue the landing beaches tour, continue on Chemin de la Cavée for 120 m; turn left onto rue Froide (D170) and follow for 3.6 km. In Cairon, turn left toward Arromanches/Creully (D22) and follow for 8.8 km. In Creully, turn left onto pl Edmond Paillaud (D93), then after 200 m sharply right toward Courseulles/Arromanches (D22). Follow for 4.1 km (becomes D65). In the roundabout in Crépon, take the 2nd exit toward Ver-s/Mer (D112) and follow through the town to park in front of the museum in place de l'Amiral Byrd. (49.336742, -0.52537)

Chapter Four
British 50th (Northumbrian) Infantry Division
6 to 7 June 1944

The strengthened 50th Infantry Division Group, assigned to land at Gold Beach, was to eliminate enemy coastal batteries; push inland seizing the high ground; cut the Bayeux-Caen highway; capture the historic city of Bayeux; capture Arromanches-les-Bains as the future site of the Mulberry Artificial Harbor, which was expected to be the main supply port at least until Cherbourg was liberated; and provide linkage between the Canadians to the east and the Americans to the west.

Although Gold Beach extended some 18 kilometers from Ver-s/Mer to Port-en-Bessin, steep cliffs faced the western sectors, broken only with strongly defended draws at Port-en-Bessin and Arromanches. The eastern sectors, code-named Jig and King, provided the broad, gradually-sloped sand beaches suited for large scale amphibious operations. However, this area also had its drawback with marshy ground directly behind the beach that could severely limit inland movement. Thus, capture of roadways through Ver-s/Mer (actually almost 3 kilometers from the shoreline despite its name) and Asnelles carried prime importance.

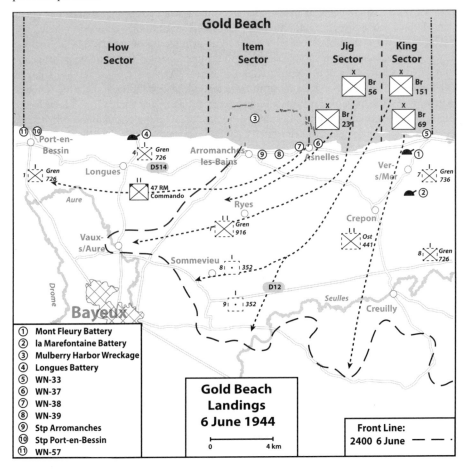

Gold Beach

| How Sector | Item Sector | Jig Sector | King Sector |

Gold Beach Landings 6 June 1944

0   4 km

Front Line: 2400 6 June

1. Mont Fleury Battery
2. la Marefontaine Battery
3. Mulberry Harbor Wreckage
4. Longues Battery
5. WN-33
6. WN-37
7. WN-38
8. WN-39
9. Stp Arromanches
10. Stp Port-en-Bessin
11. WN-57

Sectors of Gold Beach were defended by units of the German 352nd and 716th Infantry Divisions supported by batteries of their respective artillery regiments in field emplacements or casemates. The only nearby German reserves were *Kampfgruppe Meyer*[1], composed of Grenadier Regiment 915 and Füsilier Battalion 352 in three groups south and east of Bayeux and three companies of 88-mm antitank guns from 21st Panzer Division deployed near the Bayeux – Caen highway.

Fifteen strongpoints or resistance nests, protected possible landing sites along the coast line. Although the construction of many of these defensive positions had not yet been completed, many of the pillboxes, casemates, mortar and machine-gun tobruks, minefields, and barbed wire entanglements had been installed. The beaches between high and low tide were studded with a variety of hedgehogs, Belgian gates, mined vertical poles, and other defensive devices.

A naval flotilla of five cruisers, one gunboat, and thirteen destroyers started its bombardment of selected German targets at 0530 on 6 June. The German batteries at Longues and Marefontaine were special targets for the cruisers. By 0630, squadrons of American heavy bombers added their tonnage against German shore defenses. Finally, as the assault craft neared the shore, rocket-firing and artillery-mounted landing craft added their firepower. The intensity of the bombardment shocked defending garrisons into silence.

The experienced British 50th (Northumbrian) Division, which had been considerably strengthened by additional attached infantry, armor, and artillery units, had encountered the Germans earlier in the war by launching a flank attack against General Erwin Rommel's leading spearhead in the 1940 Battle of France. The ferocity of that attack may have contributed to the German High Command's hesitancy to assault the Dunkirk beachhead. The unit was evacuated from Dunkirk and, after refitting, transferred to North Africa in 1941 as part of the British Eighth Army. It later participated in the invasion of Sicily. The 50th Infantry Division presented a solid core of experienced junior officers and NCOs led by the highly decorated Major-General Douglas Graham.

D-Day Landings (Gold Beach)
6 June 1944

Objective	To land and overcome seafront defenses, establish contact with the Americans to the west and Canadians to the east, and move inland to cut the Bayeux – Caen Highway.
Forces	
British	50th (Northumbrian) Infantry Division (Major-General Douglas Graham)
German	Elements of Grenadier Regiment 726; Grenadier Regiment 916; and Artillery Regiment 352 (Oberst Walter Korfes)
Result	While they failed to satisfy all initial objectives, the British secured a substantial lodgment.
Casualties	
British	350 killed and 750 wounded or missing
German	1,000 taken prisoner

---

1   Oberstleutnant Karl Meyer, not to be confused with SS-Standartenführer Kurt Meyer, commander of SS Panzergrenadier Regiment 25

Location	Bayeux is 30 km northwest of Caen; la Rivière is 18 km northeast of Bayeux

King Sector

King Sector, near la Rivière, the beach front community within the commune of Ver-s/Mer, was the landing beach for the British 69th Infantry Brigade composed of the 5th Battalion, East Yorkshire Regiment, and 6th and 7th Battalions, The Green Howards.

La Rivière, within the German Coastal Defense Sector 'Caen,' was defended by elements of the 7 Company, Infantry Regiment 736. In addition to the coastal resistance nests WN-33 and WN-34 at la Rivière, inland gun batteries were concentrated about Ver-s/Mer at Mont Fleury and Marefontaine (WN-32).

Battle

The landings at King Sector occurred as planned. At 0725, LCTs carrying armored units of X and Z Breaching Squadrons disembarked the Royal Engineers who had responsibility for clearing beach obstacles. A few minutes later, 5th Battalion, East Yorkshire Regiment, landed west of la Rivière and 6th Battalion, Green Howards, landed at le Paisty Vert, an undeveloped beachfront west of la Rivière. The air and naval bombardments had been precise and effective, and the dazed Germans were slow to respond. The suppression of antitank defenses allowed the successful landing of armored units. Infantry moved quickly against German strongpoints, which were overcome with a minimum of British casualties.

Only WN-33, a casemated 88-mm gun position supported by machine guns in seafront houses, offered sustained resistance. Its fire destroyed two AVREs and inflicted casualties to the 5th East Yorkshire companies landing on that section of the beach. Resistance in la Rivière and Mont Fleury Battery was momentary, and by late morning all three of the brigade's battalions were progressing inland against four companies of Ostbattalion 441; however, the foreign troops showed little inclination to fight and generally surrendered at the first opportunity. The Germans quartered in Ver-s/Mer did not surrender their positions easily either, stubbornly fighting from house to house. However, the German commander, Hauptmann Gustav-Adolf Lutz, commanding 7th Company, Grenadier Regiment 736, had no answer for British armor. The AVRE's powerful 290-mm spigot mortars blew defensive positions apart. By 1100, the remaining garrison of forty enemy troops had surrendered.

Battlefield Tour

The tour starts near the eastern limit of Gold Beach in Ver-s/Mer. From Bayeux leave the Bayeux ring road (D613/Bd Winston Churchill) northeast of the city toward Courseulles-s/Mer (D12/Route de Courseulles). After 3.2 km, enter Sommervieu and continue straight toward Ver-s/Mer (D205, becomes D112). Continue 11 km into Ver-s/Mer; be aware that in Crépon the road turns left to join the Route d'Arromanches (D65) for 450 m before exiting a roundabout toward Ver-s/Mer. Park in front of the museum in place de l'Amiral Byrd. (49.336742, -0.52537)

Ver-s/Mer

Musée American Gold Beach
2, place Amiral Byrd   F14114 Ver-s/Mer
Tel: +33 (0)2 31 22 58 58   Web: http://www.goldbeachmusee.fr/

As implied in its name, this museum celebrates two entirely separate events. The first was the first mail flight of the Ford Trimotor 'America' from the United States to France. Although the intended destination was Paris, thick fog caused the plane to ditch in the channel off Ver-s/Mer. Displays present the history of transatlantic mail service.

The second section of the museum commemorates the landing of the 69th Brigade on the beaches north of Ver-s/Mer. Displays present plans for Operation NEPTUNE, how the invasion on Gold Beach unfolded, models of aircraft, and miniature dioramas of resistance nests.

Open every day in July and August; open every day, except Tuesday, April through June and September though October from 10:30 to 17:30. Admission fee; Normandie Pass accepted.

Leave the museum by returning to highway D112; then turn left onto rue de la 8ème Armée (D112, becomes Av du 6 Juin). After 650 m pass rue du Pavillon where the Mont Fleury Lighthouse (49.340147, -0.5189) stands 100 m to the east. The lighthouse grounds were fortified as WN-34, although nothing of note remains. Continue an additional 350 m and then turn left into the parking area behind the armored vehicle. (49.34334, -0.516615)

The **Espace Robert Kiln**[2] is named after an officer in the 86th (Hertfordshire Yeomanry) Field Regiment, Royal Artillery, which supported the landing of 5th East Yorkshires on King Red Beach. The Hertfordshires gave covering fire from their landing craft as infantry approached la Rivière. In the center of the park is the regiment's **Sexton self-propelled 87.5-mm (25-pounder) gun**, donated by Dr Matthew Kiln in memory of his son. The gun fired a high explosive shell a maximum of 12 kilometers against targets identified by forward observers. Infosigns around the site explain the actions of the unit and describe the Gold Beach landings.

A 3-meter-tall stele stands across the highway from Espace Robert Kiln in memory of the **Royal Artillery Regiments** of the British 50th (Northumbrian) Division. (49.343607, -0.516564) The white-stone column holds a bronze plaque, which lists the participating units. A second white-stone column, beautifully inscribed with the stag emblem of the **2nd Battalion, The Hertfordshire Regiment**, stands on the corner of the intersection of the coastal highway (D514) and Av Colonel Harper. (49.343649, -0.5161) Lieutenant-Colonel JR Harper was the unit's commander during the time it was headquartered in Ver-s/Mer. The house to the east with the gated entrance and red trim was one of the few buildings to survive the battle and became headquarters for Admiral Bertram Ramsay, the Naval Commander in Chief of the Allied Expeditionary Force, as the gray plaque on the gatepost attests. (49.343272, -0.515896)

---

2   Major Robert John Kiln was a famed Lloyd's underwriter and amateur archeologist. He landed in Ver-s/Mer on D-Day and later in the war lost a leg in fighting outside Antwerp. He died in 1997 at age 77.

> Cross the coastal highway (D514), turn north on Av Colonel Harper (becomes rue de la Mer), and stop at the waterfront amid abundant parking. (49.344967, -0.514979)

The lifeguard tower stands upon an octagonal foundation in the seawall that once held a 50-mm antitank gun. This was the eastern end of *Widerstandsnest* (WN-33); the casemate visible to the west formed the western end of the resistance nest.

> Proceed west 210 m along Bd de la Plage to the second casemate. (49.345204, -0.517918)

The western end of WN-33 held a casemated 88-mm PaK43 gun. The two embrasures faced east and west along the beach with a thick concrete wall protecting against naval fire. The position presented the stiffest resistance to the King Beach landings and its gun destroyed two AVREs. Machine guns in seafront villas and the 88-mm gun forced British infantry to huddle along the seawall until a Sherman Crab commanded by Captain Roger Bell[3] fired two rounds through one of the casemate's gun embrasures. With the gun knocked out, German machine-gun fire weakened and 5th East Yorkshires, led by their commander, Lieutenant-Colonel GW White,[4] charged over the seawall and cleared the houses of defenders.

> Continue west following the road as it curves south (rue du Corps de Garde); after 150 m turn right onto Voie du Débarquement and continue 650 m to the road junction to the south. (49.345302, -0.527998)

The small ramshackle structure on the right was a train stop serving a light railway line that ran along the old coastal road. Capture of roadways that permitted travel inland was a critical issue with Allied planners. Thus, despite the rural location, substantial infantry and armor secured the capture of this now-isolated intersection. Believing the hut to have been a German pillbox, the area was subjected to naval bombardment by two artillery-carrying landing craft and two destroyers. The hut survived all of that firepower unscathed. Shortly after 0730, Company D, 6th Green Howards, landed immediately to the west and marched along the beach to this location. German resistance, up until that time, had been non-existent.

This lonely structure now holds an infosign describing the actions of the Green Howards and CSM Stanley Hollis (see below), who won distinction in receiving the only Victoria Cross awarded on D-Day. Across the intersection, an info sign is the first of nine that identify the **69th Brigade britannique les sentier de la liberté** (Path to Freedom), a hiking route that retraces the steps of the British 69th Infantry Brigade. Slightly farther west, a sign identifies the landing spot of Commander (later Rear Admiral) Richard Byrd on 1 July 1927 as described in Musée America Gold Beach.

The houses seen upon the ridgeline to the south were not present in 1944, but they provide perspective to the Mont Fleury Battery, which was approximately 200 meters farther south on the opposite side of the ridge and thus well hidden from direct naval fire.

---

3   Captain Roger Francis Bell was awarded a Military Cross. He survived the war.

4   Lieutenant Colonel GW White was wounded later on 6 June. He survived the war.

Optional visit: Widerstandsnest 35

WN-35 lays 1.1 kilometers to the west, where the broken concrete of its casemate and pillboxes remains in an abandoned condition. Despite the heavy preliminary bombardment, German defenders repelled an attack by Company A, 6th Green Howards, led by Captain Frederick Honeyman[5] until three AVREs arrived. After the AVREs's petards neutralized the emplacement's 50-mm gun, Honeyman led his infantry against the strongpoint, quickly silencing the opposition. (49.34579, -0.542243)

> Proceed south on Voie de la 50e Division d'Infanterie (becomes Av Franklin Roosevelt). The roadway passes through cultivated fields where on 6 June an antitank ditch ran roughly east-west on both sides of the road. After 750 m, turn right onto rue Hector Berlioz and proceed to its end. (49.338392, -0.52994)

Mont Fleury Battery held four 122-mm Russian field guns manned by 3rd Company, Army Coastal Artillery Regiment 1260. Only one of the casemates was complete, however; the other three casemates were only cement block shells with their guns in open emplacements in a field approximately 250 meters to the southwest. The entire position was heavily shelled by HMS *Belfast* during the preliminary bombardment securing numerous hits. The three exposed guns never fired a round.

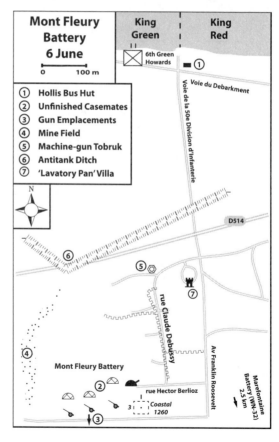

The completed casemate stands at the end of rue Hector Berlioz. Even though the casemate had been allegedly hit with a 500 lb bomb, it still managed to fire a few shells on D-Day. Two of the three incomplete casemates are visible in the field at the end of the track.

Company D, 6th Green Howards, left the beach area and proceeded south along what is now Av Franklin Roosevelt. The ground between the casemates and the new coastal road (D514) was defended by bunkers connected by a communications trench that ran where rue Claude Debussy now passes through a new subdivision. On 6 June, two bunkers were attacked in succession by CSM

---

5   Captain Frederick Honeyman was awarded the Military Cross. He was killed on 11 June during an attack upon Cristot. Honeyman was 23 years old and is buried in Bayeux War Cemetery.

Stanley Hollis. Hollis rushed the first bunker, firing his Sten gun as he ran through a hail of machine-gun bullets. He climbed onto the roof and tossed grenades through the firing embrasure. After taking the concussed enemy prisoner, Hollis moved south along the communications trench until he encountered the second bunker. Its twenty-six inhabitants, in no mood for a fight, surrendered. The action reduced the defensive strength of Mont Fleury Battery, and the position offered only light resistance before completely surrendering.[6]

Return to Av Franklin Roosevelt and turn right. After 350 m, merge right toward Crépon (D112, rue de la Libération). After 1.4 km, turn left onto rue Marefontaine and continue 700 m to the casemates in the field. (49.322863, -0.52876)

Crépon

Marefontaine Battery (WN-32) consisted of four large casemates, each holding 100-mm Czech guns manned by 6th Company, Artillery Regiment 1716. The installation was not complete and lacked many of its planned ground defenses. The site had no view of the beach and relied upon a remote firing command post located on the Meuvaines heights (WN-35b) near Maromme 2.5 kilometers to the west.

Like Mont Fleury Battery, Marefontaine was also shelled during the morning by HMS *Belfast*. The garrison of fifty men quickly surrendered when faced with two Churchill Crocodiles[7] of the 141st Royal Armoured Corps and Company C, 7th Battalion, Green Howards.

A rutted, but drivable, farm road approaches dark shapes atop the high terrain where four casemates of identical construction are located. Three of the casemates, inside a barbed-wire fence, are not accessible; the fourth is outside the fence but barred closed. A sign identifies the site as a stop on the 69th Brigade britannique les sentiers de la liberté and explains its function and capture.

Reverse direction and return to D112; turn left and follow D112 for 1.4 km to the large roundabout. Take the 2nd exit toward Crépon-centre (D65) and continue 400 m to the monument on the left. (49.315639, -0.55003)

A beautifully executed bronze statue perched upon a stone plinth commemorates the **6th** and **7th Battalions, Green Howards**. The tired, bare-headed soldier holds his bayoneted rifle to his side while his other hand grabs the strap of his camouflaged helmet as he sits upon a low wall. The plaque on the plinth outlines the units' advance from the landing beaches and the courage of CSM Hollis. A stone wall behind the statue holds eight plaques presenting the Roll of Honor of those from the two battalions who died during the Battle of Normandy.

Perhaps the most evocative memorial in Normandy, the Roll of Honor celebrates

---

6   Company Sergeant Major Stanley Hollis was award his nation's highest honor, the Victoria Cross, for this action and other actions performed near Crépon later in the day. It was the only such award received for action on D-Day. Hollis was wounded in September and returned to England. He died in 1972 at age 59 and is buried in Acklam Cemetery, Middlesbrough, England.

7   Churchill Crocodile: another of Hobart's Funnies in which a Churchill tank was modified with a flamethrower in place of the hull machine gun. An armored trailer was towed behind the tank carrying 1,800 liters of fuel.

one of Britain's oldest regiments. The Green Howards originated in 1688 in support
of William, Prince of Orange. The name 'The Green Howards' first appeared in 1744,
although its official title became 'The Green Howards (Alexandra, Princess of Wales's
Own Yorkshire Regiment)' only in 1920. The regiment fought in numerous wars including
the American Revolution, Crimean War, Indian Mutiny, South African War, and both
World Wars.

Two large infosigns across the road relate the exploits of **Command Sergeant
Major Hollis**, including his participation in the taking of the Mont Fleury Battery;
comments on the Victoria Cross; the Green Howards' landing and advance to Crépon; and
action at Ferme du Pavillon, the location of WN-36a. This location is also part of the 69th
Brigade britannique les sentiers de la liberté itinerary.

Proceed south for 85 m and then turn right toward Bayeux (Route de Bayeux/D112);
continue for 550 m to Crépon's western outskirts. Stop at the old farm buildings on
the left immediately before the house with bright blue shutters (unfortunately it is not
signed). (49.3143, -0.556993)

Crépon was the site of CSM Stanley Hollis' second heroic action on D-Day.
Company D, 6th Green Howards, was conducting a search of the town when Hollis led

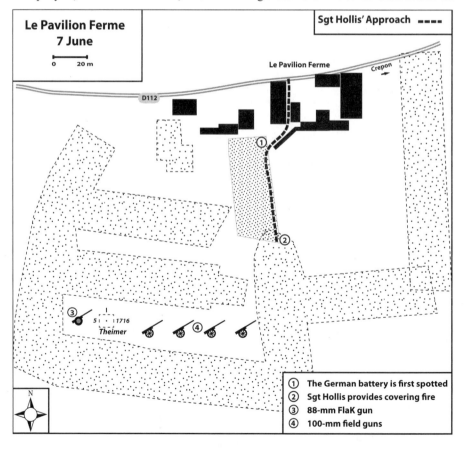

his men through the gateway entrance to **Ferme du Pavillon**. They encountered a strong German force with field artillery in the orchard behind these farm buildings. Massively outgunned, Hollis ordered his men to withdraw, but, upon reaching safety, he found some of his men pinned down by German small-arms fire. Hollis grabbed a Bren gun and returned to the orchard where he stood in full view and provided covering fire as his men withdrew, thus saving three men's lives. The position, WN-36a, was not taken until the following morning. The farm is private property and should not be entered.

> Reverse direction and turn right to proceed south toward Creully (D65). After 2.5 km, continue straight although the road becomes highway D22; after 800 m, stop at the memorial on the left. The road from Crépon to Creully, code-named 'Hudson Highway,' identifies the route taken by 7th Green Howards. (49.286953, -0.540293)

The Green Howards, with seventeen tanks of 4th/7th Royal Dragoon Guards, overcame German opposition 500 meters south of Crépon and by mid afternoon of D-Day had crossed highway D12 heading toward Creully. The leading troops found the Seulles River bridges intact and entered the town to find it occupied by Canadians from the Royal Winnipeg Rifles.

A memorial wall carrying the unit insignia and a bronze plaque profiling a tank commemorates the men of **4th/7th Royal Dragoon Guards** (8th Armoured Brigade), some of whom returned to France on that day after having been withdrawn at Dunkirk in 1940. The Guards landed the first amphibious Sherman tanks on Gold Beach at H-5 minutes. In addition, stainless steel plaques mounted on the base of the monument recall the advance of the Royal Dragoons toward Creully and provide an extensive list of their casualties. An impressive view of the chateau from the river valley near the memorial is available.

The regiment dates from 1685 and 1688 with the 4th (Royal Irish) Dragoon Guards and 7th Dragoon Guards (Princess Royal's) respectively. The 4th Dragoons were the first British unit to engage the enemy north of Mons in August 1914. The 7th Dragoons exercised the last cavalry charge of the war minutes before 1100 on 11 November 1918. After serving separately in First World War, the units merged in 1922. The regiment became a tank unit in 1938.

> Continue south (D22) into Creully; turn left into place **Edmond Paillaud** and park. A small archway a little west of the hotel with a sign 'To Chateau' provides access to the chateau grounds. A bridge crosses over what was once a defensive moat. (49.286332, -0.539604)

Creully

Château de Creully
37 place Edmond Paillaud   14480 Creully
Tel: +33 (0)2 31 80 18 65   E-mail: chateau@creully.fr

The chateau dates from the 11th and 12th centuries and was fortified during the Hundred Years War due to its position overlooking the Seulles River valley. It was demolished and rebuilt in the 15th century and expanded in the 16th and 17th centuries. The 12th-century lower hall retains its ancient architectural details. One of the towers, used by radio journalists such as Edward R Morrow to report on the Battle of Normandy, retains a collection of old radio equipment.

Open weekdays in July and August from 10:00 to 12:30 and from 14:30 to 17:30. Admission fee with guided tour.

Note: this is not the Château de Creully where General Montgomery established his headquarters on 8 June. Montgomery was actually at Château de Creullet, 500 meters to the north, but also in the commune of Creully. Although listed as a French historic monument, the Château de Creullet is private.

Walk east on rue de Tierceville to the chateau parking area on the left. (49.286021, -0.538027)

A plaque on the wall to the left adjacent to the parking area honors the **Royal Winnipeg Rifles Regiment** and commemorates its liberation of the town. That two units claim that honor is not unusual as the enemy withdrawal permitted Allied forces to enter the community from opposite directions.

Leave Creully toward Tierceville (D93). After 1.6 km, turn right toward Courseulles-s/ Mer (D12) and continue 280 m to the roundabout. (49.294953, -0.527344)

A statue-topped column stands in the grassy center of the roundabout as a monument to the **Royal Engineers**. The figure is a cement copy of Eros, similar to the one topping the column in Piccadilly Circus in London. The monument was erected by the **179**th **Special Field Company** in August 1944, one of the earliest memorials on the battlefield as the war was still being fought only 50 kilometers away.

The surrounding area was an encampment for the Royal Engineers, who arrived shortly after D-Day to clear roads and bridges and to build airfields. **B3 Aerodrome**, the first British-fighter landing ground operational in Normandy, was constructed in fields 2.5 kilometers to the north and saw the first Spitfires arrive on 10 June.

Reverse direction and leave the roundabout toward Bayeux (D12). After 3.1 km, turn right in the western edge of Villers-le-Sec toward Bazenville / Ryes (D87). Continue 2.6 km to the cemetery on the right. (49.299774, -0.601137)

The **Ryes War Cemetery**, in the Commune of Bazenville, holds 652 Commonwealth burials – mostly British – and 326 German graves. Burials started only two days after D-Day and many were casualties on the landing beaches, thus accounting for the number of Royal Navy and Merchant Navy personnel. Located in the Norman countryside along a minor road, the site provides quiet and solitude not often found in other cemeteries.

Jig Sector

The large flooded zone between le Paisty Vert and Asnelles precluded any landing between those two points. Asnelles, however, was critical because it controlled one of the few improved roadways that led south from the coast. Its capture fell to the 231st Infantry Brigade, commanded by Brigadier ABG Stanier. Asnelles was overlooked from the east by a southwest running ridge line east of Meuvaines and from the south by a north-south ridgeline west of le Carrefour and St-Côme-de-Fresné.

Battle

WN-37 was not neutralized by the naval bombardment, and its 75-mm gun played havoc with the breaching teams in Jig Green sector consequently beach obstacles and minefields were not cleared Thus, much of the armor either did not arrive or was promptly destroyed. Casualties among senior officers and the loss of communications equipment threw the landings into disarray.

Fortunately, the initial infantry assault units, 1st Battalion, Hampshire Regiment, and 1st Battalion, Dorsetshire Regiment, landed well east of their intended beaches. The 1st Hampshires landed in front of WN-36, which it stormed and captured, but its attempt to move west along the beachfront was stopped by deadly fire from WN-37.

Strengthened by the arrival of 1st Devonshire Regiment and the capture of farms south of WN-36, the troops moved inland at 0915. The Hampshires fought small groups of defenders as it entered Asnelles from the southeast. Elements of 2nd Battalion, Devonshire Regiment, moved cross-country southwest toward Ryes, a small town with a road network necessary to the Germans for a possible counterattack. Naval fire suppressed German mortars and guns near Ryes and Meuvaines, thereby relieving the pressure upon troops moving inland. By late afternoon, British troops overcame resistance at WN-37 and the beach at Jig Green was open.

Battlefield Tour

From Ryes War Cemetery, proceed northwest toward Ryes (D87). After 350 m, turn right toward Crépon (D112) and follow 4.3 km into that town. Turn left toward Crépon-centre (D65) and pass through the village to the large roundabout. Continue toward Arromanches (D65). After 2.1 km, turn right toward Asnelles (D65A); then, after 220 m, bear right on rue du Débarquement (unsigned, C2). Follow for 1.0 km across the coastal highway (D514) and continue on the country lane for 700 m with the marshy area on the right to the waterfront parking area. (49.341916, -0.583338)

Asnelles

Office de Tourisme d'Asnelle
Cafe de l'Essex Yeomanry   14960 Asnelles
Tel: +33 (0)2 31 21 94 02   Email: contact@tourisme-asnelles.com
Web: http://www.tourisme-asnelles.com/

WN-36 marked the boundary between Jig Green East and Jig Green West. The 1st Hampshire battalion were to land along 750-meter stretch of beach to the west. Although now the beachfront community of Roseau Plage occupies the land, in 1944 it was uninhabited marsh. Company A, 1st Hampshires, attacked WN-36 from across the beach. Although the fighting was hand-to-hand, it was of short duration, and German defenders were killed or captured.

The ruins of WN-36 are slowly being reclaimed by the sea and are, therefore, uninteresting. Its location, however, demonstrates German coverage of the beachfront between WN-36 and WN-37, visible to the west. The concrete shelter lying atilt in the sand probably held a 50-mm gun from a PzKpfw III. The position also held a 37-mm antitank gun and three machine-gun emplacements.

> Reverse direction and within 100 m, turn right on rue Royal Hampshire Regiment. Continue 1.0 km (becomes rue The Dorset Regiment) to the junction with the coastal highway (D514). (49.339853, -0.585762)

A stone and concrete wall dedicated to **231st Infantry Brigade** and Brigadier Alexander Stanier[8], the commanding officer of the 231st Brigade and leader of the Jig sector invasion force, fronts the left of the road junction marked by a row of Allied flags. The inscription carries a dedication to the town's liberators and is topped by the 'double T' insignia of the 50th Infantry Division representing the rivers Tyne and Tees, which defined the division's original recruitment area.

Place Alexander Stanier is immediately west along the coastal highway (D514). A stele's inscription in Welsh, English, and French commemorates the **2nd South Wales Borderers**' landing at Asnelles on D-Day. The nearby metal **Cross of Lorraine** commemorates the 18 June 1940 proclamation by General Charles de Gaulle to the French people: 'France has lost a Battle! But France has not lost a war!'

> Proceed west on the coastal highway only 75 m before turning right (north) on rue de Southampton. After 140 m, turn right onto rue Xavier d'Anselme, then left onto Bd de la Mer and into place Maurice Mosnier. Le Hamel is the beachfront community west of Asnelles, but it is nonetheless in the Commune of Asnelles. Company B, 1st Hampshires, attacked WN-37 following this route. (49.342034, -0.584507)

WN-37 held a powerful 75-mm field cannon, which some sources identify as an 88-mm PaK 40, and a 50-mm antitank gun supported by five machine-gun emplacements. The Germans had also fortified a multi-story seafront children's sanatorium, which no longer exists. The resistance nest was manned by a platoon of infantry from Grenadier Regiment 916. Both cannons were positioned to enfilade the beach to the east and were responsible for disabling six British tanks. Company A, 1st Hampshires, attacked the position head on but could not overcome the intense defensive fire. The company commander was killed and most of its officers and senior NCOs became casualties. With leadership and communications absent, the assault was abandoned.

In the early afternoon of 6 June, Major David Warren's[9] Company B, 1st Hampshires, attacked the resistance nest from the south. Between 1500 and 1700, an AVRE, commanded by Lance-Sergeant HM Scaife,[10] threw two spigot mortars into the sanatorium causing the surrender of its German defenders. A round from the 25-pounder SP gun by the 147th Field Artillery Regiment's Sergeant RE Palmer disabled the gun in

---

8   Brigadier Sir Alexander Beville Gibbons Stanier was a well-connected career officer and 2nd Baronet of Peplow Hall. He received the Military Cross in the First World War and was awarded a Distinguished Service Order for his leadership of Welsh and Irish Guards during the evacuation of British forces from Boulogne in 1940. Stanier received a bar to his DSO for action defending against German counterattacks in the Rhine Valley. Active in postwar relations, he was awarded the Légion d'honneur by France and several other awards from Belgian and the United States. He retired from military service in 1948 and became active in local politics. He died in 1995 at age 95.

9   Major David Warren was awarded a Distinguished Service Order for his part in the D-Day landings; he had earlier been awarded a Military Cross for leading an attack upon a German armored column in Sicily. He retired as a brigadier. Warren died in 2012 at age 82.

10   Lance-Sergeant Herbert Matthew Scaife was awarded a Distinguished Conduct Medal.

the casemate while Scaife's AVRE attacked the rear of the position with another petard round.[11] The thirty surviving Germans surrendered to Company B, which itself had been reduced to fifty men during the engagement.

The still imposing casemate central to WN-37 remains as the major D-Day site in Asnelles. The pock-marked southern face of the casemate, reminders of the furious small-arms fire of the attacking 1st Hampshires pays testimony to the ferocity of the combat. A bronze plaque on the sealed gun embrasure remembers the **147th (Essex Yeomanry) Field Regiment, Royal Artillery**, and its members who died in the liberation of Europe. A separate plaque recalls Sgt Palmer's actions to disable the position's gun. A machine-gun tobruk is located in the seawall to the east. The coast guard tower to the west was built atop another of the German installations.

The place Maurice Mosnier holds several informational signs describing the attack upon WN-37 by 231st Brigade. The children's sanatorium, which the Germans incorporated into the resistance nest, has been torn down. Snipers located in its upper floors were a special threat to attacking infantry. A map shows the landing sites of the brigade and a photograph of the shoreline as viewed from the beach. A **NTL Totem** is nearby.

The eastern arm of the **Mulberry Harbor** was centered upon Arromanches-les-Bains and its wreckage is still present on the beach at low tide and offshore. An upside down anchor embedded in concrete on the beach moored unloading ships that had docked inside the artificial harbor.

> Proceed west along the seafront on Bd de la Mer (after 350 m it curves to the left and becomes rue de la Marine). At the junction with the coastal highway, turn right toward Arromanches. After 500 m, turn right and proceed to the seafront pillbox. (49.340469, -0.595536)

The intact and open pillbox on the western end of the seafront promenade was part of **WN-38**. The structure shows its strong reinforced concrete back to naval fire, but a 180-degree opening permitted its 50-mm antitank gun to enfilade east or west along the beach. It was attacked by Lance-Sergeant Scaife's AVRE, supported by infantry of the 1st Hampshires. The AVRE's heavy gun destroyed positions in nearby fortified houses, and twenty Germans duly surrendered.

This structure is one of the most complete on the landing beaches and is a fine example of seafront defenses. Views of the entire western end of Gold Beach as far as the heights west of Arromanches are possible from the partially-enclosed gun platform.

> Return to the coastal highway and turn right toward Arromanches. After 850 m, turn left onto Allée de la Fontaine; stop at a convenient location. (49.33863, -0.607413)

The two casemates that formed part of **WN-39** held 75-mm and 50-mm field guns able to hit landing craft. Naval shelling by the gunboat *Flores* had little impact. About 1500, Company D, 1st Hampshires, led by Major J Littlejohns[12] and assisted by several tanks, attacked from the southeast. Although the position sported several machine-gun emplacements, it offered little resistance whereby thirty Germans quickly surrendered.

---

11   Sergeant-Major Robert Edwin Palmer was awarded a Military Medal.

12   Captain (temporary Major) Johns Leslie George Littlejohns was awarded a Military Cross.

The view from the hilltop overlooking Asnelles presents the town's complete exposure to these guns. They fired over one hundred rounds on D-Day and the numerous armored vehicles destroyed or damaged crossing the beach attest to their accuracy.

Return to the coastal highway and again turn toward Arromanches. Turn into the large cliff top parking area on the right. (49.339399, -0.615149)

Capture of Arromanches-les-Bains

Battle

The Allied plan purposely avoided a direct assault upon Arromanches harbor because the beach needed to be kept free of all wreckage in order to rapidly construct the artificial harbor. Although considered to be a strongpoint to the German Army, Stp Arromanches, situated atop the seaside cliffs east of the town, was manned by naval personnel who had no training in infantry warfare. It was attacked in late afternoon of 6 June by Company D, 1st Hampshires. The defenders quickly surrendered.

Major Littlejohns, now occupying the eastern heights above Arromanches, launched an attack upon the town at 2000 after a short naval bombardment. The town's defenders offered little resistance, deciding instead to flee. WN-43 and WN-44 were easily occupied.

Battlefield Tour

Arromanches-les-Bains

Arromanches, a major destination for visitors to the western British landing beaches, is frequently teaming with tourists. Its museum, numerous monuments and commemorations, the remains of the famous Mulberry B Harbor, and tourist conveniences make it a popular stop.

Office de Tourisme d'Arromanches (49.34007, -0.622356)
2 Rue Mar Joffre   14117 Arromanches les Bains
Tel: +33 (0)2 31 22 36 45   Web: http://www.ot-arromanches.fr/

The parking area is not in Arromanches but in St-Côme-de-Fresné where *Stützpunkt* **Arromanches** was located on the headlands above the town. The site holds numerous memorials and artifacts of the invasion. An elevated, observation platform holds a **table of orientation** that also explains how the Mulberry was constructed. The grand sweep of Mulberry Harbor wreckage extends from west to east centered roughly upon Arromanches.

Traces of a Kriegsmarine radar station remain near the panoramic table, including a trapezoidal concrete structure used as the base for a German **Würzburg Radar**. The station was destroyed by Allied air forces weeks before the invasion. A coastal **fire-control bunker** has been closed as dangerous. Bits and pieces of concrete locate various German positions used for antiaircraft guns, underground personnel bunkers, and other unknown purposes. The coastal cliff can be extremely dangerous and should be avoided.

Follow the walkpath (Esplanade de Général de l'Armée Aérienne Michael Fourquet) west to the cinema entrance passing memorials along the way.

The **Royal Engineers Monument** presents the insignias of the twenty-nine units assigned to the D-Day landings and an engraved stainless steel map of the British invasion areas. A simple stone stele pays homage to French Air Force général Michel Fourquet,[13] leader of the famed '**Lorraine Squadron**' who led his unit on bombing runs on D-Day. The pathway from the observation platform to the Cinema 360 is lined with touching photographs – mostly close-ups of soldiers – taken during the fighting. Each is labeled '**The Price of Freedom**.' A beautiful view awaits onlookers peering down into Arromanches.

Le Cinéma Circulaire Arromanches 360 (49.338859, -0.617525)

Chemin du Calvaire   14117 Arromanches les
Tel: +33 (0)2 31 06 06 44   Email: contact@arromanches360.com
Web: http://www.arromanches360.com

This surround cinema features a twenty-minute film titled 'The Price of Liberty,' which mixes modern footage with archival photographs and film to present the D-Day landings. The film is shown twice every hour.

Open daily February through November from 10:10 to 17:10; later in summer season. Admission fee.

Following the walkpath down into the town of Arromanches is possible, but the walk back up is strenuous. A stone plaque mounted upon an obelisk commemorating the centennial of **naval combat at Arromanches** during 7-8 September 1811 is near the upper end of the path. (49.3397, -0.617061)

> Leave the parking area and turn right onto the coastal highway toward Arromanches-les-Bains (D514). After 900 m, turn right onto rue du Petit Fontaine and follow to the large parking area in front of the museum. (49.340213, -0.620926)

Musée du Débarquement Arromanches

Place du 6 Juin   14117 Arromanches
Tel: +33 (0)2 31 22 34 31
E-Mail: info@arromanches-museum.com
Web: http://www.musee-arromanches.fr/

The museum is dedicated to the Normandy Beach landings and the technology of the Mulberry Harbors. A trilingual guided tour presents working, scale models of the design, construction, transportation across the channel, and operation of the harbor elements. The tour is supplemented by a 15-minute film presented in nine languages. A short light-and-sound show explains the beginnings of the D-Day invasion in six languages and various displays identify key commanders.

Open generally from 09:00 to 19:00. Admission fee; Normandie Pass accepted.

The museum entrance is flanked by two fine examples of **British 25 pounder guns**. Around the right side is a **German 88-mm gun** in desert camouflage paint. In the parking area stands an **American M3 armored half-track**, a widely used transportation and assault vehicle. Manufactured in numerous variations, the M3 typically mounted a

---

13   Général Michel Martin Leon Fourquet joined Free French Air Force in 1940, earning a Distinguished Flying Cross and French *Légion d'honneur*. He became one of Charles de Gaulle's chief military advisors during de Gaulle's presidency. He died in 1992 at age 78.

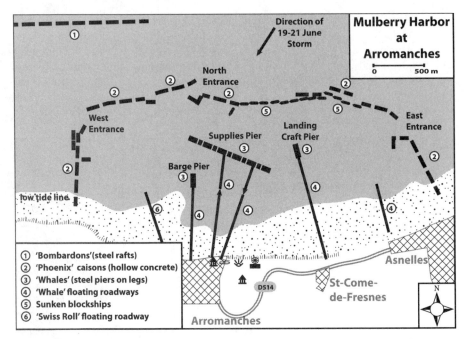

.50-calibre machine gun and frequently .30-calibre machine guns were added by the troops. A **Bofors 40-mm antiaircraft gun** is stationed on the waterfront side of the museum. The stone wall embankment descending to the beach holds several plaques recognizing the contributions of **Logistics, Royal Navy, Royal Marines,** and **Merchant Seamen** to the success of the invasion. A beachfront **observation platform** provides viewpoints of the Mulberry remains.

The **Mulberry B Monument** stands to the left toward the waterfront. Its three stones hold bronze plaques commemorating those responsible for their formidable technological feat and describe the operation of the floating harbor. Remains of Mulberry piers and floating caissons remain in a broad sweep offshore; some sections, in fact, lie only a few hundred meters from the seawall and can be approached at low tide. A memorial stele to **Brigadier Alexander Stanier** stands along the waterfront.

Walk up the rue de la Batterie to the pillbox. (49.340023, -0.618617)

A **M4A2 Sherman tank**, once part of général Leclerc's French 2nd Armored Division, stands atop the bunker of **WN-43**. The position mounted a 105-mm mountain gun behind the now-barred embrasure.

From Arromanches, regain the coastal highway (D514) and proceed approximately 6 km into Longues-s/Mer. Turn right onto D104 and continue 900 m to the battery entrance on the left. (49.343156, -0.691355)

Longues Battery
6 to 7 June 1944

Battle

In the early morning hours of 6 June, the battery (WN-48) was bombed by Allied planes. Although targeting was erratic, the bombs cut underground telephone cables to the command bunker, which significantly reduced the battery's accuracy. Before dawn, it was shelled by the French cruiser *Georges Leygues* and battleship USS *Arkansas*. As the sun rose and targets became visible, the battery opened fire on the invasion armada, eventually engaging in a 20-minute duel with British cruisers HMS *Ajax* and HMS *Argonaut* at a range of 11 kilometers. In a remarkable feat of naval gunnery, Ajax's 6-inch guns put shells through the embrasures of two casemates. The battery resumed sporadic firing in the afternoon, but hits from the *Georges Leygues* silenced it completely.

The battery was attacked by elements of 2nd Devonshire Regiment shortly after 0800 on 7 June after a further short naval and air bombardment. The German garrison was disorganized by the heavy shelling and its resistance was feeble. The entire position was overcome by 1100 with 184 prisoners taken.

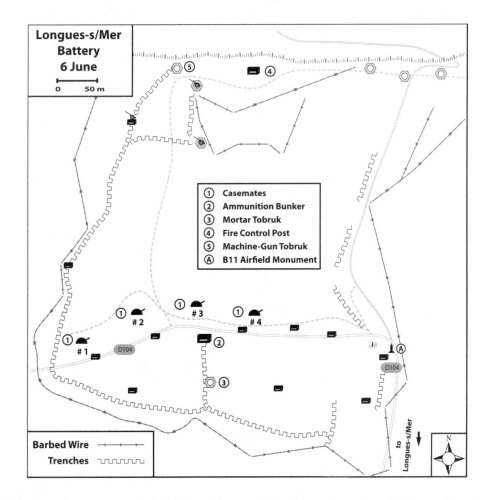

Longues-s/Mer Battery 6 June

0   50 m

① Casemates
② Ammunition Bunker
③ Mortar Tobruk
④ Fire Control Post
⑤ Machine-Gun Tobruk
Ⓐ B11 Airfield Monument

Barbed Wire
Trenches

N

Battlefield Tour
Office de Tourisme de Longues-s/Mer
Site de la Batterie   14400 Longues-sur-Mer
Tel: +33 (0)2 31 21 46 87   Email: longues@bayeux-tourism.com
Web: http://bayeux-bessin-tourisme.com/en/visiteguidee/batterie-de-longues-sur-mer/

The **Longues Battery** located immediately north of Longues-s/Mer, consisted of a seafront fire-control post and inland four casemates, each holding a 150-mm naval gun capable of striking targets as far as 20 kilometers away. The battery was manned by Army Coastal Artillery Battalion 1260, the same unit manning batteries at Mont Fleury, Pointe du Hoc, and Ouistreham.

The four casemates, stretching in a line to the west from the battery entrance, may be viewed, entered, and explored at will. **Casemates #1, #2, and #3** hold intact guns, a rarity among Atlantic Wall defenses. The left side of casemate #3 shows the results of its duel with HMS *Ajax*. **Casemate #4** suffered a gun malfunction on D-Day when a shell exploded in its breach. The resulting detonation fired stored ammunition, and the tremendous explosion blew out the rear of the casemate. The shattered remains of its gun lie under the embrasure opening. The site was protected by ten tobruks and held numerous underground personnel and ammunition bunkers, but most have been filled and are no longer visible. The grass-covered rectangular mound behind the tourist office locates an underground **ammunition storage**. A trench that provided entry into the store is visible near the road.

Walk across the field to the north to view the **command bunker/fire-control post** on the cliff edge 60 meters above the channel. The lower level provides entry through the back of the bunker; but viewing much of the ocean from this level is difficult because the bunker is partially underground. A perilous climb up steel bars inserted into the concrete wall achieves the upper range-finder room. Beautiful views of the surrounding oceanfront and the harbor at Arromanches are possible. In an unusual construction, the roof of the upper observation level is a one-meter thick reinforced concrete slab supported by four metal posts. (49.345889, -0.693415)

One-hour guided tours presented in French and English are available daily in July and August or weekends April through June and September through October starting at 10:15 and 14:15. Despite a fee for the tours, because the positions are in open fields, they may be visited at any time without admission charge. The Longues coastal battery is among the best preserved in Normandy and is a must-see for anyone visiting the landing beaches.

A stele displaying a Spitfire aircraft stands at the entrance to the battery and commemorates **British airfield B11** built 300 meters east of this location. The stele also commemorates Free French pilot Sergeant Pierre Clostermann,[14] an ace with 33 downed aircraft to his credit.

Return to the coastal road (D514) and proceed west toward Port-en-Bessin.

---

14   Sergeant Pierre Henri Clostermann joined the Free French Air Force in 1942, flying the Supermarine Spitfire in an RAF squadron. He was awarded the Grand-Croix of the French *Légion d'honneur*, French Croix de Guerre, British Distinguished Flying Cross and bar, and American Distinguished Service Cross, Silver Star, and the Air Medal among many others. After the war he wrote several successful books on his experiences. Clostermann died in 2006 at age 85.

Battle for Port-en-Bessin
6 to 8 June 1944

Port-en-Bessin was a small fishing harbor whose significance lay in its location between the British and American landing beaches and designation as a site for one of the terminals of the underwater gasoline pipeline.

The port was defended by units of Grenadier Regiment 726, which manned concreted positions on the eastern and western highlands overlooking the village. While the guns were not among the heaviest on the Atlantic Wall, they possessed enough firepower to repel small landing craft attempting to enter the harbor. The task of capturing the port was assigned to Lieutenant-Colonel CF Phillips[15] and the men of No 47 Royal Marine Commando. Aware of the extensive seafront defenses, Phillips decided upon an assault from the landward side. Because the nearest landing beach was Jig Green, 11 kilometers to the east, the commando unit landed there, assembled, and marched cross-country to Port-en-Bessin on 6 June.

No 47 Royal Marine Commando was divided into five troops (A, B, Q, X, and Y) and operated as an independent force under the command of 4th Special Service Brigade. The total complement was 420 men. The unit was formed from other Royal Marines in August 1943 and received extensive commando training in Scotland. Operation NEPTUNE was its first action.

Objective	To capture the small harbor town of Port-en-Bessin and establish link to American forces coming from Omaha Beach
Forces	
British	No 47 (Royal Marine) Commando (Lt-Col CF Phillips)
German	1st Company, Grenadier Regiment 726 (Hauptmann Hiesekorn)
Result	The harbor defenses were overcome.
Casualties	
British	46 killed, 68 wounded, 6 captured, and 28 missing
German	Over 100 taken prisoner
Location	Bayeux is 30 km northwest of Caen; Port-en-Bessin is 9 km northwest of Bayeux

Battle

At 0950, No 47 Royal Marine Commando landed on Jig sector of Gold Beach near the seafront community of le Hamel. During the approach, and as with many Allied landing craft on that day, wind and current swept the commando's LCAs well east of their intended landing beach. The landing craft, approaching the shoreline in column, turned to achieve the correct landing beach, thus exposing the craft to German shore batteries. The easy targets, plus mines, congestion, and uncleared beach obstacles led to five LCAs sunk and five damaged. The unit suffered seventy-six casualties during the landing.

Although scheduled to rendezvous at the church in le Hamel, it was still in German hands. Therefore they circled around to the south and east. By 1100, they were marching to their primary objective at Port-en-Bessin. The unit stopped for the night atop Hill 72 near Escures, less than 2 kilometers south of Port-en-Bessin.

---

15   Lieutenant Colonel Cecil Farndale Phillips was awarded a Distinguished Service Order.

Communications were finally established with 231st Brigade during mid-morning on 7 June, and plans to support the commando assault with naval gunfire and air support commenced. As the ground assault started, the troops came under fire from Château Maisons, also known as Fosse Soucy, 900 meters to the south, which was headquarters for the I Battalion, Grenadier Regiment 726.

A Troop, under cover of smoke shells, passed through Port-en-Bessin west of the inner basin and moved up the western headlands against WN-57. However, under enemy fire from artillery barges anchored in the harbor, frontal fire from the resistance nest defenders, and rear fire from Stp Port-en-Bessin on the eastern headlands, the attack quickly broke down and the troops retreated into the town.

At 2230, armed motor boats from two destroyers breached the outer harbor net defense and engaged the floating flak barges. No return fire was forthcoming. Upon boarding all three were found abandoned. About the same time A and Q Troops attacked the eastern head emplacements in a running gun battle which resulted in a German surrender. Early the next morning, the western headlands and WN-57 were likewise abandoned.

Battlefield Tour

Port-en-Bessin

Office de Tourisme
Quai Baron Gérard
Tel: 33 (0)2 31 22 45 80

14520 Port-en-Bessin
Email: port@bayeux-tourism.com

Port-en-Bessin has been occupied as a port since Roman times because of its location in a wide draw, which provided shelter from storms and access inland. Bessin refers to an ancient region which derived its name from a Gallic tribe. It was included into the Duchy of Normandy in 924. William the Conqueror maintained a shipyard there, which constructed portions of his invasion fleet. It continues to be known as a fishing port as the large inner basin and shipyards attest.

At the entrance to Port-en-Bessin, a plain, gray, stone stele on the right side of highway D514 near the college holds a brass plaque dedicated to **No 47 Royal Marine Commando** and bears the '6 Juin 1944' date. (49.342082, -0.745026) Continue to the junction with highway D6. (49.343418, -0.752628)

An anchor and plaque dedicate the small roundabout to Captain Terence Cousins, who died leading the attack upon the eastern headlands on 7 June. The communal cemetery, a rallying point for British attacks on the western headlands, is a short distance to the west.

Proceed north on Av du Général de Gaulle (becomes Quai Général de Gaulle) and continue along the western side of the inner basin. After 350 m, pass the partial dike that separates the two basins. In 1944, this was the basin's full extent. Continue to the port; turn left onto Quai Letourneur and after only 50 m, left again (rue du Nord). After 40 m, turn right onto rue de la Mer (becomes rue Torteon) and follow 180 m to the parking area. (49.34951, -0.759274)

Western headlands:
A parking area at the end of rue Torteron provides easy access to a picnic area

with views over the harbor. The German bunker on the hillside above the picnic area comprised part of **WN-57** and was a fire-control post.

Reverse direction back to rue du Nord. Turn right, and then rapidly right again onto rue du Phare (becomes le Sémaphore). Follow 350 m up the hill to the walk path on the right; parking nearby may be difficult. Follow the walkpath to the right without entering onto the golf course to the gateway and garden on the edge of the cliff top. (49.349382, -0.760873)

The **No 47 Royal Marine Commando Memorial Garden** stands on top of one of the two German casemates of WN-57 that housed 57-mm Skoda cannons. The enclosure holds two lectern-style memorials to the commandos. The first lectern displays brass tablets mounted on a gray stone block plinth. The center plaque maps the town and the direction of the British attacks upon the western and eastern headlands. The side plaque describes the events of 7 June 1944. A second lectern, of gray granite stone, holds plaques listing the Roll of Honour of the twenty-eight troopers who died in the initial landing near Asnelles and a second Roll of Honour listing the eighteen names of those who died during the attack upon

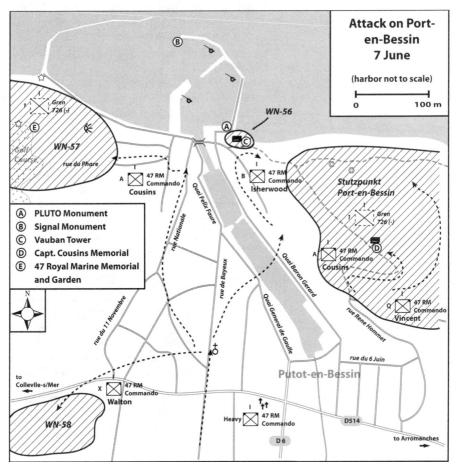

the port. A special plaque honors Professor John Forfar, who served as the unit's medical officer during the invasion and later wrote the unit history. Below, the structure of the outer and inner harbors and the extended inner basin, as well as the entire eastern headlands battlefield, are visible across the town. In good weather and with binoculars, visitors can see the Mulberry Harbor at Arromanches in the distance. Moreover, descending the stairs at the rear of the garden into the casemate to view the harbor through the gun embrasure presents the position's field of fire.

Reverse direction down the hill back to Quai Letourneur. Turn right and cross the bridge over the inner basin to a large parking area.

Harbor Area:

An inscribed stone tablet commemorating the 50th Anniversary of the invasion stands near the base of the eastern harbor mole. The port was one of the **PLUTO** (Pipe Line Under The Ocean or Pipe Line Underwater Transport of Oil) terminals for the undersea pipeline from England that supplied the Allied armies with gasoline. The tablet depicts the pipeline and resultant distribution of jerry cans of gasoline throughout Normandy. Large storage tanks were constructed on the hillside where the golf course currently sits. Despite numerous engineering problems and unforeseen issues, PLUTO eventually was supplying one-million gallons of gasoline per day. (49.349216, -0.755385)

A **Signal Monument** commemorating the liberation of Europe stands at the end of the eastern harbor mole. (49.352222, -0.756437)

The Germans installed a blockhouse at base of the hill that protected the harbor with its 57-mm cannon. Although now sealed, its wall holds a plaque to the **No 47 Royal Marine Commando** and the men of French cruisers *George Leygues* and *Montcalm*. (49.34929, -0.754312)

A tower overlooking the harbor was built in 1694 to protected it from pirates and English invasions. The round structure, named after the famous French military engineer Sébastien le Prestre de Vauban, is known as **Vauban Tower** and still stands above the German blockhouse, its twentieth-century equivalent. A second tower once stood on the top of the cliff, but it was destroyed during the battle. (49.349042, -0.7542)

Steps built into the hillside, which at times can be treacherous, lead up to the tower and provide access to its viewing platform. The path continues up the hill to the level plateau, the site of Stützpunkt Port-en-Bessin, but the steep, slippery slope makes the climb difficult. An easier approach from the opposite side of the hill as described at the next stop is available. (49.348437, -0.75104)

Leave the harbor area along the east side of the inner basin on Quai Baron Gérard. At the southeast corner of the inner basin, continue straight on rue des Chantiers. After 40 m, turn left on rue du 6 Juin and follow into the roundabout. Take second exit to rue René Hommet. After 240 m and immediately before the sweeping curve to the right, turn left and park. A walkpath initially starts north but zigzags 350 m up the hill. (49.346781, -0.749602)

Eastern Headlands

After an earlier reconnaissance, Captain Terence Cousins, A Troop commander, led A and Q Troops on this zigzag track up the southern slope of the eastern headlands, which was manned by 1st Company, Grenadier Regiment 726. Despite mines and a wire fence, the men approached the summit unobserved. Captain Cousins advanced with four men against the German bunker that stands on the landward side of the gently sloped plateau. Unfortunately a German grenade thrown from the bunker managed to kill Cousins.[16]

With a mighty cheer and the firing of a red Verey light, the remaining twenty-one troopers stormed over the crest, firing Bren guns and throwing grenades. A Troop moved to the left in the direction of the Vauban Tower while Q Troop swept to the right across the flat plateau. Pillboxes were attacked and wire barriers cut. Within minutes, A Troop approached the northern cliff line where it took cover in the empty trench lines. Q Troop ran forward roughly 100 meters before stopping for fear of entering a mine field. Q Troop then moved along the cliff edge with a captured German *oberleutnant*, who called for his men to surrender. Unsure of the size of the attacking force due to the growing darkness, they obliged. The POWs, in turn, were led down the path to the quay below.

A brass plaque mounted upon a blue stone stands below the entrance doorway to the bunker. The plaque is dedicated to **No 47 Royal Marine Commando** and describes the attack and the death of Captain Cousins.

The mortar tobruks and cliff side trenches of *Stützpunkt* **Port-en-Bessin** remain. Paths across the pasture's grass lead to the various gun emplacements. The zigzags of the cliff-side trenches are unmistakable despite the tall grass that partially hides them. The plateau can be carefully explored, although the tangled brambles sometimes make leaving the defined paths difficult. The GR de Pays Tour du Bessin follows these cliffs to the east for several kilometers.

Return down the zigzag path and reverse direction back to the Quai Baron Gerard; turn left and follow as it curves around the south edge of the basin. Turn left on Av du Général de Gaulle and continue south 700 m to the large roundabout on highway D6, where the large sculpture presenting a globe with surmounted 'V' commemorates the meeting on 10 June between British Generals Montgomery and Dempsey and American forces commander General Omar Bradley. (49.338721, -0.756276) Exit the roundabout south toward Bayeux (D6). After 600 m, find the entrance to the museum on the left. (49.333974, -0.757027)

Musée des Épaves sous-marines du Débarquement (Underwater Wrecks Museum)
Route de Bayeux   14520 Commes (Port-en-Bessin)
Tel: +33 (0)2 31 21 17 06
Web: http://www.cheminsdememoire.gouv.fr

The museum pays tribute to the underwater exploration of the waters off the Normandy coast and the numerous ships, tanks, aircraft, and other debris left from the invasion fleet. A film presents the risks and successes of the underwater exploration. Several of the recovered pieces are visible in the courtyard even when the museum is closed. A **NTL Totem** is located there as well.

Open weekends and holidays in May and daily June through September from 10:00 to 12:00 and from 14:00 to 18:00; closed October to April. Admission Fee.

---

16   Captain Terence Frederick Cousins was awarded the Military Cross for leading his men against the bunker east of the harbor. He was 22 years old and is buried in Bayeux War Cemetery.

50th Infantry Division Moves Inland
7 June 1944

The Germans counted few tactical reserves available for counterattack. Early on D-Day, *Kampfgruppe Meyer* was ordered to respond to American paratroop landings on the Cotentin Peninsula, and it spent the day racing west where I Battalion, Grenadier Regiment 915, was committed against the US 1st Infantry Division landings at Omaha Beach. The II Battalion and Füsilier Battalion were later recalled to attack Crépon.

Battle

Additional units of the British 50th Division continued to land on Gold Beach strengthening its infantry, armor and artillery contingents. The division's troops moved south without strong opposition. They crossed the Seulles River and the British 69th Brigade destroyed the 700-man Füsilier Battalion 352 at St-Gabriel, where Oberstleutnant Meyer[17] was killed. The 151st Brigade landed and progressed south of Sommervieu toward Bayeux, the key city in the area, which was not secured as planned and posed a severe threat to British plans if occupied by a substantial German force. On 7 June, units of the 56th Brigade entered Bayeux and found it undefended. They continued southwest to the Drôme River, where the 2nd South Wales Borderers were repulsed on attempts to cross the Drôme at Sully.

German resistance stiffened on 8 June with the arrival of elements of SS Panzergrenadier Regiment 26 and mechanized infantry from Panzer Lehr. In addition, armored units' easy advance over open ground was ending. South of Route Nationale N13, the British were entering terrain more favorable to the Germans – the infamous bocage.

Aftermath

Although the 50th Division had fallen short of accomplishing its D-Day objectives, 25,000 men landed on Gold Beach at the cost of a fewer than expected 1,100 casualties. They punched through the thin, but well armed, veneer of beachfront defenses and advanced inland over 7 kilometers. The sites of future supply harbors at Arromanches and Port-en-Bessin were secured, and the important Norman city of Bayeux captured. A junction with Canadian troops advancing inland to the east was achieved.

Battlefield Tour
Bayeux

Bayeux traces its origins as a capital of an ancient Gallic tribe. It became a sizable town under Roman rule and was part of coastal defenses against pirates. By the late 9th century it had been captured and plundered by Bretons, Saxons, and Vikings. One of the ancestors of the dukes of Normandy was from Bayeux, but William the Conqueror moved the capital to Caen. The town was repeatedly pillaged during the Hundred Years War until the French victory in the decisive Battle of Formigny only 16 kilometers to the northwest.

Bayeux was fortunate not to have suffered damage during the war. Therefore, its old houses and narrow cobblestone streets, especially in the cathedral district, provide the medieval feel of old Normandy.

---

17   Oberstleutnant Karl Meyer was 46 years old. He is buried in St-Desir-de-Lisieux German Military Cemetery.

Office de Tourisme (49.27681, -0.700947)
Pont St-Jean　　　　　　　　　　　　14400 Bayeux
Tel: +33 (0)2 31 51 28 28　　　　　　　Web: http://www.bessin-normandie.com

> From Port-en-Bessin, proceed toward Bayeux (D6) until the junction with the ring road (D613). Turn right toward Vaucelles / Cherbourg (D613) and proceed 450 m to the large roundabout (Rond-point Vaucelles). (49.282616, -0.71939)

A **memorial wall** surrounded by the flags of the Allied nations is located in the center of the roundabout. Its inscription includes figures representing the people of Bayeux, as identified by their cathedral in the background, greeting the entrance of général Charles de Gaulle, backed by the gods of war, and British, French, and American troops debarking from landing craft. The monument commemorates the relationship between de Gaulle and the city of Bayeux and stands at the western entrance to the city.

> Continue to follow the ring road (D613) as it proceeds south and east around the city changing names several times. Pass the British cemetery as it will be visited later. After 1.4 km enter the museum parking area on the left. (49.273104, -0.711247)

Musée de la Bataille de Normandie
Boulevard Fabian Ware　　　　　　　14400 Bayeux
Tel: +33 (0)2 31 51 46 90
E-mail: bataillenormandie@mairie-bayeux.fr
Web: http://www.mairie-bayeux.fr/index.php?id=230

The museum is one of the premier military museums in Normandy. Its two large galleries present exhibits and maps explaining the Battle of Normandy from the beach landings to the Battle of Falaise in two-or-three-day increments. Equipment and weapons of all nations are divided by themes such as artillery, air force, propaganda, or small arms. Dioramas display scenes of equipment in use. Personal mementos of the fighting men of all nations are on display. The variety of exhibits is substantial. A film covering the Normandy fighting is captivating. Please leave at least two hours to tour this informative museum.

Even when closed, the museum is worth a visit to view the heavy equipment displayed on the surrounding lawns. Included are a British Churchill MK VII (flamethrower) tank, American M4A1 Sherman tank, American M10 tank destroyer, German *Jägdpanzer* (tank destroyer) 'Hetzer,' and a German quad 20-mm FlaK gun. The grounds also hold several memorials including a gray granite memorial stele to the **Nottinghamshire (Sherwood Rangers) Yeomanry** and a polished black stele commemorating the **2nd Battalion, Essex Regiment,** who were the first to enter Bayeux on 7 June 1944. A round stone carries a plaque to the **Corps of Military Police** who died in the Battle of Normandy.

Open daily May through September from 09:30 to 18:30; October through April from 10:00 to 12:30 and from 14:00 to 18:00. Admission fee; Normandie Pass accepted.

> The British cemetery is 300 m back northwest on Bd Fabian Ware. Walk from the museum as parking near the cemetery is limited. (49.274098, -0.714058)

Bayeux War Cemetery is the largest Commonwealth Second World War Cemetery in France with 4,182 bodies from ten Allied nations and 466 Germans buried within its walls, most from the Battle of Normandy. The vast majority of the Allied burials come from United Kingdom troops. Bayeux was not a battle ground, but the cemetery was started for those who had died of wounds in local hospitals. Later it expanded as an accumulation cemetery with bodies collected from temporary graves across Normandy. The Cross of Sacrifice is located at the far rear of the cemetery; the German graves reside at the left boundary and are distinguished by their slightly different tombstones. The cemetery is wheelchair accessible.

The **Bayeux Memorial to the Missing** is across the road from the cemetery. It commemorates the 1,808 Commonwealth servicemen who died in the period from the landings to the advance to the Seine River and who have no known grave. The frieze on the memorial presents a unique Latin inscription that refers to William the Conqueror: 'We, once conquered by William, have now set free the Conqueror's native land.' (49.274357, -0.713704)

From the museum parking area, continue 200 m southeast on Bd Fabian Ware (D613). Turn left on rue St-Loup (D96A). After 400 m, turn left onto rue de la Poterie (D96); then after 190 m, take the 1st exit from the roundabout onto rue des Terres (becomes rue Royale). After 400 m, turn left on rue St-Patrice and park at a convenient location north of rue St-Patrice or rue St-Malo or rue St-Martin.

Cathedral District:

Because of the narrow cobblestone one-way streets and the delightful opportunity to explore Norman Bayeux, parking and walking in this district is recommended.

Proceed to the large park in place Charles de Gaulle. It can be located by walking south on rue Royale or rue du Général de Dais. A stone pillar marking the site of **Général de Gaulle's speech** to the French people on 14 June 1944 recalls the general's spirited directive, which rallied the French people to support its allies in the fight for France's liberation. (49.276317, -0.707567)

Leave the place Charles de Gaulle to the southeast on rue Bourbesneur. (49.275204, -0.706022)

Musée-Mémorial Général de Gaulle
10 rue de Bourbesneur   14400 Bayeux
Tel: +33 (0)231924555

The 15th-century Gouveneur Hotel became the first headquarters of the French Army. The building now houses a museum recording the life and career of général de Gaulle in Bayeux through documents and photographs.

Open daily from 10:00 to 12:00 and from 14:00 to 18:00. Admission fee, but entry included in the price of Musée de la Bataille de Normandie.

Continue southeast; turn left on rue des Chanoines and proceed to the cathedral. (49.275722, -0.704144)

Cathédrale Notre-Dame de Bayeux
Rue des Cuisiniers   14400 Bayeux
Tel: +33 (0)2 31 92 01 85
Web: http://cathedraledebayeux.voila.net/

The original Norman-Romanesque cathedral was completed in 1077, but only the towers and crypt remain from the original structure. The Gothic spires were added to the towers in the 13th century. The three entrance doors serve the west end, but the rear of the cathedral presents the most impressive sight with its flying buttresses and two shorted bell towers.

Inside the cathedral, the traditional plaque commemorating **British First World War casualties** is in the left aisle; below it is a **56th Infantry Brigade** plaque remembering those who died in the campaign for the liberation of Northwestern Europe. An American flag in the right aisle locates a stone plaque dedicating one of the chapels to Lieutenant Colonel A. Peter Dewey.[18]

The central aisle presents highly decorative arches, triforium, and clerestory. The three-story chancel, surrounding ambulatory, and radiating chapels are magnificent. The crypt is barren, but the short columns are topped by floral capitals above which are restored frescoes.

Open daily 08:30 to 17:00 and later in the summer. No admission charge.

Proceed along the south (right) side of the cathedral on rue LL le Forestier. A plaque dedicated to the **50th Northumbrian Division** graces the wall adjacent to an arched gate that is the entrance to a small park opposite the cathedral. The plaque recognizes the sacrifices of the troops that landed on Gold Beach and fought through the fields of Normandy to liberate the city of Bayeux on 7 June 1944. (49.275162, -0.703876)

Continue on rue LL le Forestier (becomes rue de Nesmond) to the museum entrance. (49.274245, -0.700786)

Musée de la Tapisserie de Bayeux – Centre Guillaume le Conquérant
13 bis rue Nesmond   BP 21215 14402 Bayeux
Tel: +33 (0)2 31 51 25 59   Web: http://www.tapisserie-bayeux.fr/

The medieval artistry of the world famous Bayeux Tapestry depicts events surrounding the Battle of Hasting in 1066 when William the Conqueror's army defeated that of King Harold. The linen cloth with wool embroidery is on display in a dim display hall to protect the cloth from the deteriorating effects of light. Audio guides in fourteen languages provide a self-paced explanation of the historical significance and often purposeful irony of each of the fifty-eight scenes on the 70-meter long embroidery. A second floor presents life in Normandy and England at the time of the Battle of Hastings.

Open daily 15 March to 15 November from 09:00 to 17:45; 16 November to 14

---

18   Lieutenant Colonel A Peter Dewey was a relative of New York Governor and presidential candidate Thomas E Dewey. In 1940, while in France reporting for a Chicago newspaper, he enlisted in the Polish Military Ambulance Corps. After the French defeat, he escaped through Portugal. In August 1944, Dewey parachuted into France with the OSS to report German troop movements. For his service, he was awarded the *Légion d'honneur*, *Chevalier de l'ordre de la légion d'honneur*, and Croix de Guerre. He became the first American killed in Indochina on 26 September 1945 while part of an OSS delegation. His body was never recovered, thus, his name is listed on the Wall of the Missing in the Manila American Cemetery.

March from 09:30 to 11:45 and from 14:00 to 17:15; closed first three weeks in January and Christmas and New Year holidays. Admission fee.

From the Musée de la Tapisserie, walk north on Allée des Augustines, then Allée de l'Orangerie to rue St-Jean. The Aure River, home to the tanners and dyers who used the water for their processing of leather and cloth, passes through Bayeux one block west of the cathedral. The short, frequently dead-end streets in this district offer many beautiful views of the river, old buildings, and the cathedral which towers above them.

Return to the vehicle by turning left on rue St-Jean (becomes rue St-Martin, then rue St-Malo, then rue St-Patrice). A particularly impressive **half-timbered house** with overhanging upper stories stands on the corner of rue St-Martin and rue des Cuisiniers. (49.277304, -0.702857)

Proceed southeast on rue St-Patrice (changes names several times) for 1.5 km. Unfortunately, the streets are in a busy commercial district, but it is the most straightforward route to the final site on this tour. Turn right on the ring road (Bd Maréchal Montgomery, D613). Proceed 130 m to the large roundabout; where parking may be a problem. (49.272075, -0.690368)

The **Rond-point Eisenhower**, at the eastern end of Bayeux, lies diametrically on the opposite side of the city as the général de Gaulle Monument. A statue of General Dwight Eisenhower stands off to the side of the center of the park. The statue portrays Eisenhower looking right down highway N13 toward Caen with his hands on his hips as if he is frustrated waiting for something – perhaps Montgomery to take Caen. A raised stone patio in front of the statue assumes the shape of a five-pointed star.

This concludes the British 50th Division invasion beaches' tour. The tour of British Second Army battlefield sites continues in Chapter Thirteen.

Chapter Five
US 1st (Big Red One) Infantry Division
6 June 1944

Omaha Beach was a broad crescent bound at either end by rocky cliffs and faced with steep 60-meter-high bluffs. A strip of brush-covered low dunes separated the beach and the bluffs, the latter penetrated by small valleys or draws, which allowed exit from the beach up to flat farmland farther inland. The 6.5-kilometer-long landing beach held five such draws, each leading to villages along a coastal road now designated highway D514. The tide was ferocious in this part of Normandy, rising and falling as much as seven meters in a few hours. Low tide exposed a broad tidal area as wide as two-hundred meters. The high tide line was marked by a 2.4-meter-high wall of water-smoothened stones called 'shingle.' The eastern sector of Omaha Beach that extended 2.5 kilometer from below Cabourg to St-Laurent-s/Mer was empty, and the sandy shoreline was not disturbed by development. The western sector beach to Vierville-s/Mer held a few seafront villas.

Rommel recognized the strong possibility that the Allied invasion centered about Normandy. He therefore created the strongest possible defenses for the potential landing areas, especially at Omaha Beach. These defenses concentrated at the beach exits since he

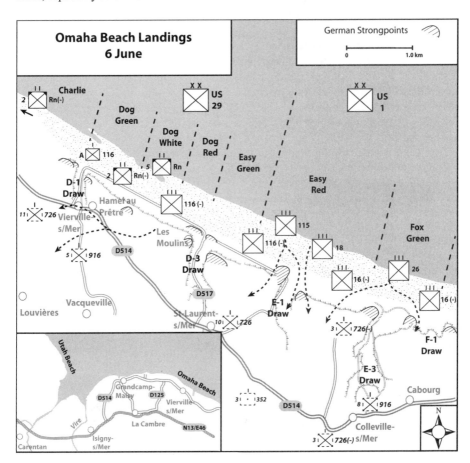

knew that they would be necessary to move troops and armor inland. In all, the Germans planned six semi-independent strongpoints or *Widerstandsnester* (WN) numbered 60 to 65, but by 6 June not all of the individual concrete shelters had been completed. Nonetheless, they held casemates, pillboxes, antitank guns, mortar tobruks, artillery emplacements, rocket launchers, and machine-gun emplacements. Additionally, they were all protected by antitank ditches, minefields, and barbed wire.

Omaha Beach was defended by Grenadier Regiment 726, 716th Infantry Division, whose twelve companies stretched to cover 41 kilometers of seafront from Courseulles-s/ Mer in the east to Grandcamp in the west. This division, however, was definitely third rate and included many non-German 'volunteers' from conquered countries. As such, it was confined only to 'static' defense. Unknown to Allied planners, weeks earlier the Omaha defenses from Colleville to Vierville were augmented by four companies of II Battalion, Grenadier Regiment 916, 352nd Infantry Division, supported by the I and IV Battalions, Artillery Regiment 352.

Although many references describe the 352nd Infantry Division as a first rate unit, it was not. The division was better equipped and more mobile than the so-called 'static' units in Normandy, and it did not have the less dependable non-ethnic Germans among its ranks; however, most of its soldiers were 17-year-old conscripts, and ammunition shortages had limited their live-fire exercises. Nonetheless, even average troops could be very effective when provided with well-designed defense works.

The US 1st Infantry Division is the oldest in the United States Army, and its 16th Infantry Regiment traced its lineage back to the American Revolution. In 1917, the division was the first American unit to arrive on the First World War battlefield, fired the first artillery shot of the American Expeditionary Corps, and suffered the first three soldiers killed. In April 1918, the division's 28th Infantry Regiment launched American troops' first offensive operation against the village of Cantigny. In September, the entire division was committed in the Battle of the Mihiel Salient and only two weeks later in the decisive Meuse-Argonne Offensive, during which it fought as far east as Sedan. The original unit insignia provided its nickname, the 'Big Red One.' The division entered the Second World War when it landed near Oran, Algeria, on 8 November 1942. It fought in North Africa until the surrender of German forces in Tunisia. In July 1943, it landed in Sicily and fought in the brutal mountain campaign. The 1st Infantry Division was America's most experienced infantry unit, but despite being a veteran unit, many new recruits were to see their first action.

D-Day Landings (Omaha Beach)
6 June 1944

Objective	To land on the Normandy coast, secure the beachhead, and move inland.
Forces	
American	34,250 men of 1st Infantry Division and temporarily attached units (Major General Clarence Huebner)
German	Grenadier Regiment 726 (Oberst Walter Korfes) and Grenadier Regiment 916 (Oberst Ernst Goth)
Result	Although stiffly resisted, the landings were successful

Casualties	
American	1,240 killed, wounded or missing
German	uncertain; 1,200 killed or wounded in Grenadier Regiment 916
Location	Bayeux is 30 km northwest of Caen; Colleville-s/Mer is 16 km northwest of Bayeux.

Battle

June 6th was a dismal, dark morning on the wave-tossed English Channel. The first infantry companies transferred into their landing craft while still thirteen kilometers from shore. By the time they reached the beach, the men had been in their landing craft for almost five hours. Most of them were sick from the heavy seas generated by the strong northwest wind or from the terror of the approaching battle.

German positions were bombed by 450 heavy bombers of the Eight Air Force, shelled by eighteen Navy warships in the channel, and bombarded by thousands of rockets launched from modified landing craft. The smoke and dust they raised obscured any seafront landmarks to be used by approaching landing craft.

Sixteen demolition teams composed of specially trained army engineers and naval underwater experts were to arrive at H-Hour plus 3 minutes. Their mission was to blow channels through the beach defenses for use by following amphibious Sherman tanks. Their arrival was delayed and before they could explode the beach obstacles, the landing craft arrived. The teams reverted to fighting as infantry.

Thirty-two tanks of the 741st Tank Battalion were to land minutes before the infantry assault to surprise the enemy and commence shelling of any remaining defense works. The Duplex Drive tanks were outfitted with collapsible skirts to provide buoyancy; however, the rough seas and crashing waves were too much for the 33-ton machines. Of the first thirty-two tanks, twenty-seven sank before reaching the beach. The remaining sixteen tanks supporting the 1st Battalion landed directly on the beach from their LCT.

All of the men and material expended to prepare Omaha Beach for the landing troops had failed; the naval bombardment had failed to destroy enemy pillboxes; the aerial bombing had failed to provide the bomb craters to shelter the landing troops on the beach; the demolitions teams had failed to provide safe passage through the beach obstacles; the tanks had failed to provide the supporting fire of the their 75-mm guns.

Four companies totaling 750 men of the 16th Regimental Combat Team[1] comprised the first wave and were to be landed by twelve American LCVPs[2] and twelve British LCAs at regimental objectives code-named Easy Red and Fox Green. By the time the first landing craft had approached the shoreline, they were hundreds of meters off target. German defenders were under orders to hold their fire until the first invaders touched the shore. As the ramps dropped, the infantrymen of the first wave drew the interlocking fire of well-placed German machine guns. Mortar and artillery fire sought out the trailing landing craft forcing some to stop too far from the beach. As troops debarked into the water that was frequently too deep, they entered what was, quite literally, a bath of blood. Some drowned; others sought shelter behind German beach obstacles, only to find them topped

---

1   Regimental Combat Team: essentially an infantry regiment and supporting tanks, artillery, engineers, supply, and other attached units.

2   LCVP: Landing Craft Vehicle, Personnel or Higgins Boat was a flat-bottomed, shallow draft boat capable of carrying thirty-six men or one vehicle.

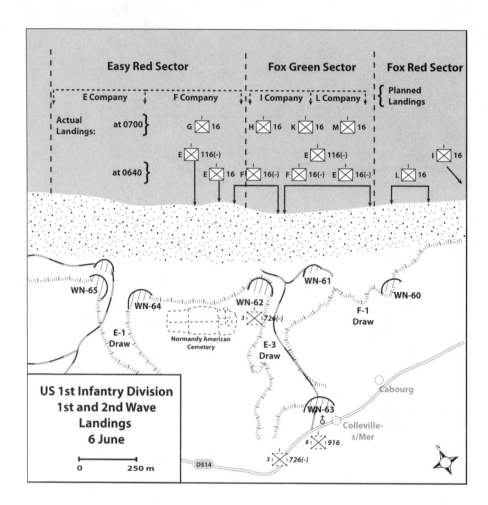

with explosives or mines. After struggling through 90 meters of water, the overloaded infantrymen were faced with crossing 130 meters of open beach while still facing withering machine-gun fire, shells, and accurate snipers. Those few who survived huddled up against the shingle field, stripping their rifles to remove the sand and salt water. Clusters of men drew well-aimed German mortar fire. The 16th Infantry Regiment was being slaughtered.

Waterlogged radios eliminated contact with the naval ships and unit commanders. Success or failure was out of the hands of the planners and beyond the orders of the generals. As the incoming tide narrowed the strip of beach, junior officers, sergeants, and privates would crack open Hitler's *Festung Europa* – or not.

Lieutenant John Spalding, commanding a section of Company E, and Captain Joseph Dawson, commanding a much-reduced second wave Company G, landed between the well-defended Colleville and St-Laurent draws. They were the first to realize the futility of attempting to force the draws, but fortune had landed them where they could execute an alternative plan. By 0800 both groups were on the bluff above the beach and attacking entrenched German defenders from their vulnerable rear.

By 0830 the Navy beach master signaled to hold all landings. The beach was blocked by floundering or sunken landing craft from the first two waves. The battleship *Arkansas* moved closer to shore to take the German pillboxes under direct fire. Eight destroyers moved to within 700 meters of the beach and, directed by forward observers on shore, acted as the infantry's field artillery.

The regimental commander, Colonel George A Taylor, landed about 0815. He roamed up and down the beachfront attempting to create order out of chaos. To the tired, hungry, wet, frightened men cowering behind the shingle sea wall he roared, 'There are two kinds of people who are staying on this beach – those who are dead and those who are going to die. Now let's get the hell out of here!' And they did by attacking and clearing enemy positions while bypassing those too strong to be directly overcome.

The 115th Infantry Regiment was originally targeted for the les Moulins draw, but the beaching lanes had not yet been cleared. Its LCI pulled back and landed 1.5 km to the east. The regiment moved up the same trails as Spalding and Dawson. The 18th Infantry Regiment did the same. By day's end, 5,000 infantrymen had cracked open the German defenses by way of a steep but weakly defended gap.

By 1700, German units were starting to feel the pinch of dwindling ammunition stocks. An hour later, General Kraiss's 352nd Infantry Division headquarters informed German Seventh Army that troops fortified with tanks had penetrated the coastal defenses. Rommel's 'destroy the enemy on the beach' strategy had already failed.

As night fell on 6 June – late because of the long summer days in northern Europe – American troops and equipment flooded the beach even though it was not fully secure from German snipers and harassing artillery fire. They had established a beachhead, but everyone knew that the fighting had just started.

Aftermath

On D-Day, the 1st Infantry Division suffered 186 killed, 620 wounded, 358 missing, and 76 other casualties for a total of 1,240. The German 352nd Infantry Division suffered an almost equal number. Although initial objectives were not taken, Omaha Beach saw the landing of 34,250 men on D-Day.

German shore defenses were completely disorganized, and German troop movements to reinforce the 352nd Division had been mauled by Allied fighter bombers. The US 1st Division moved rapidly through the farms, orchards, and villages of Normandy, each advanced marked by small, intense fire fights until the enemy had been killed or surrendered. By 7 June, the 26th Regimental Combat Team met the British 50th Infantry Division southwest of Port-en-Bessin, unifying the two Allied beachheads east of the Vire River. The 16th Regiment, which had suffered the worst of the D-Day losses, entered reserve while the 18th and 26th Regiments pushed for Caumont l'Éventé, a strategic market town 230 meters above sea level which controlled seven intersecting roads. Caumont was liberated by the leading 1st Battalion, 26th Regiment, on 13 June. The division halted as the British to the east and the US 2nd and 29th Infantry Divisions to the west had not kept pace. As a dangerous salient formed, Caumont remained the Allied Army's deepest penetration from the beach until late July. On 13 July, the 1st Infantry Division was relieved and sent to rear areas for rest.

Battlefield Tour

From the Bayeux ring road (D613), exit to the northwest toward Port-en-Bessin (D6). Follow for 7.2 km to a roundabout. Take the 1st exit onto Av du général de Gaulle (Toutes Directions) and continue for 650 m. At the roundabout take the 3rd exit toward Grandcamp-Maisy (D514) and follow for 6.8 km to Colleville-s/Mer. Stop at the small parking area and overlook on the right. (49.348654, -0.845625)

Colleville-s/Mer

A parking area near the center of the village provides an opportunity to stop and view the full distance of Colleville draw. Noticeable on the skyline is the spike of the 1st Infantry Division obelisk, which identifies the location of WN-62. WN-63, meanwhile, consisted of a line of emplacements from the head of the draw to the center of the village where the small stone *mairie* flies the French and American flags above the doorway. The building itself was used as German headquarters on D-Day.

Large panels erected at various sites in Colleville present photographs of village locations taken during or shortly after the battle. Photographic panel #5 is located in the corner of the *mairie's* courtyard and depicts the village a few years after the battle. Panel #6, depicted on a stone building across the road and 50 meters west, shows military police and an amphibious DUKW transporter exiting from the draw roadway.

A minor road, opposite the *mairie*, is signed to Plage de Colleville-s/Mer. Turn north towards the *Plage* and continue for 1.6 km. The gated doorway seen on the left as you leave Colleville was the entrance to WN-63, the 8th Company, Grenadier Regiment 916, command post. Continue and follow the curve to the left under the high-vehicle barrier and into a gravel car park. (49.36087, -0.846462)

The road follows the **Colleville draw**, the American troops' most important objective in the eastern sector of Omaha Beach. This exit from the beaches and entrance to the coastal highway was particularly wide and less steep than the other draws, thereby allowing easy passage for armored vehicles. Just as critical for the German defense, it was defended by WN-61 to the east and WN-62 to the west.

Walk down to the sand beach.

At low tide one can walk out onto **Omaha Beach** and look up at the bluff for an over-awing experience. Depending upon the time of day, low tide may expose the expanse of surf and beach that they had to cross while under enemy fire. The slopes above the parking area hold WN-62, to which we will return later. The American cemetery is atop the bluff to the west and located by its flagpole on the bluff's horizon. A small marker identifies the boundary between Easy Red and Fox Green landing beaches. The men of Companies E and F, 16th Infantry Regiment, and Company E, 116th Regiment, US 29th Infantry Division, landed and died on this beach.

Proceed by foot along the beach to the east. (49.35943, -0.83892)

WN-61 was not up the bluff face as most other resistance nests but lower along the beach. Its enormous casemate housed a deadly German 88-mm PaK43 antitank gun and approximately twelve soldiers from Grenadier Regiment 726. The German gun put three American tanks out of action in rapid succession. The defenders pinned down elements of Companies E and F 16th Regiment, and the drastically off target Company E, 116th Regiment. Technical Sergeant Raymond F Strojny, Company F, seeing that the officers of his company had been killed or wounded, took command. He shifted the men down the beach where better cover was available and then proceeded to fire six bazooka[3] rounds at the casemate's gun embrasure. The last round entered the structure and detonated stored ammunition, ending its resistance. Strojny,[4] despite being wounded by sniper fire, led his men through the wire and minefield and up the hill.

Much of **WN-61** sits upon private property and cannot be visited; however, its proximity to the beach makes it readily visible and provides a sharp image of Sergeant Strojny's courage in attacking such a formidable fortification. The structure is nearly intact and displays the wing wall that was common to these casemates to protect the gun embrasure from possible naval fire. The gun embrasure is aimed directly at the beach in front of Colleville Draw. The concrete platform for a 50-mm antitank gun sits behind the casemate. On the east side of the casemate and slightly behind it is a tobruk which held the 37-mm gun turret of a French Renault tank. The structure now appears to have been incorporated into a house. A well-preserved example of a machine-gun tobruk stands near the beachside rental building. Other elements of the resistance nest remain, but they are not visible from public land.

Side Trip: WN-60

To achieve WN-60, follow the shoreline track to the east past WN-61. After approximately 400 meters, the track curves south and starts to climb the Cabourg Draw. Continue an additional 400 meters to a second track on the left that reverses direction back north. It leads to the emplacements of WN-60. (49.356286, -0.832365) Total distance: 1.8 km

While elements of 2nd Battalion, 16th Infantry Regiment, were trying to overcome opposition at WN-62, Company L of the unit's 3rd Battalion landed along a narrow beach overlooked by low cliffs on Fox Red sector. They were assigned to Fox Green sector, but, like other units, they drifted to the east of their original target. The unit's commanding officer had been seriously wounded during the approach.

Recognizing their perilous position, 1st Lieutenant Jimmie Monteith led his platoon through machine-gun fire to the heavy barbed wire below **WN-60** where he directed the placement of a Bangalore torpedo and blasted an opening. Two mine fields were under fire from machine-gun emplacements and a pillbox. Monteith led a small patrol forward along **Cabourg Draw (F-1)** while two Sherman tanks from the 741st Tank Battalion and the 5-inch guns of destroyer USS *Doyle* intermittently suppressed enemy fire from the strongpoint. Company L quickly overcame the strongpoint from the rear using grenades and satchel charges, occupying the position by 0900 and taking thirty-one prisoners. Although not the unit's assigned objective, it was the first German position to be

---

3   Bazooka: a two-man, portable recoilless, rocket-firing antitank weapon usually operated by a loader and a firer. The weapon's effective range was limited and it was frequently considered the weapon of last resort against approaching enemy armored vehicles.

4   Sergeant Raymond F Strojny was awarded the Distinguished Service Cross for his actions; he had already been awarded a Silver Star in Sicily, and he later was awarded a Bronze Star for actions in Germany. Strojny died in Washington at age 90.

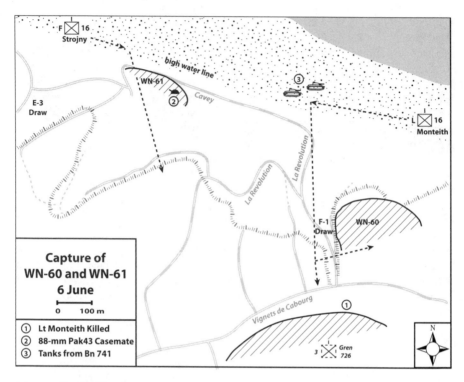

**Capture of
WN-60 and WN-61
6 June**

0   100 m

① Lt Monteith Killed
② 88-mm Pak43 Casemate
③ Tanks from Bn 741

taken on Omaha Beach.

After establishing a defensive position on a hill near the trail behind WN-60, Monteith and his men repulsed repeated enemy counterattacks. Monteith dangerous exposed himself to enemy fire as he directed the defense of the nearly surrounded unit. He personally eliminated two enemy machine-gun positions, one with a rifle grenade and the second with a hand grenade. He was killed while moving across 200 meters of open ground to attack a third machine-gun emplacement. His determination to hold the advantageous position directly contributed to the opening of Colleville draw.[5]

WN-60 is frequently overlooked by D-Day visitors since it is considerably more difficult to approach along a 1.0 kilometer uphill farm track. Concreted tobruks and cement-lined entrances to underground trenches are still present among its tangled vegetation. An extremely dangerous pillbox remains in evidence. The real attraction, however, is the commanding view of Omaha Beach. From this elevated position, the entire sweep of the curved beachfront stretches to its western end at Vierville-s/Mer. From WN-60, forward observers for I Battalion, Artillery Regiment 352, had an unobstructed view of the length of Omaha Beach. Its elimination greatly reduced the effectiveness of their artillery fire.

Return to the parking area. Exit the parking area by walking south and following the track up the slope towards WN-62. This is the north entrance to WN-62. A water-filled, **antitank ditch** started immediately below the parking area and extended to the east for approximately 220 m before turning sharply south. (49.360401, -0.847256)

---

5   Lieutenant Jimmie Monteith Jr was awarded the Medal of Honor and is buried in Normandy American Cemetery. He has been called one of the greatest heroes in American military history.

Companies E and F, 16th Infantry Regiment, had trained to attack the St-Laurent draw on Easy Red sector. They studied sand tables and photographs to memorize the landmarks; however, the men on eleven of twelve of their LCVPs jumped into 1.3 meters of water at 0640 at the mouth of Colleville draw instead. Enemy machine guns, rifles, and mortars fired as they struggled to wade through the surf and across the open beach. Survivors sought shelter behind the rock shingle gasping for breath while they were sought out by the plunging fire from German mortars. To their front, coils of barbed wire barred forward movement. Attempts to cut through the wire with cutters or Bangalore torpedoes met with intense enemy fire. The 16th Regiment's first wave remained trapped on the beach as machine guns ripped through their ranks. Company F suffered 80% casualties.

As the day progressed, fire from the seemingly impregnable WN-62 continued to inflict casualties and suppressed American efforts to open the draw. However, while other units secured Grand Hameau to the east and St-Laurent to the west and pressured German troops in Colleville and Cabourg, the WN-62 defenders became more isolated. The gathering strength of American fire, especially from destroyers and beach-landed tanks, also took a toll. Nevertheless, enemy small arms and artillery fire continued into Colleville draw throughout the day even as combat engineers cleared the landing wreckage, removed mines, and bulldozed roadways.

WN-62 was not captured by a mass assault or individual heroics but was slowly ground down as the American attackers became stronger and the German defenders became weaker. By mid-morning, most of WN-62's heavy weapons had been silenced by tanks or mortars. Supporting artillery fire ended at approximately noon when ammunition at batteries farther inland was fully expended. Automatic weapons fire also slackened due to dwindling ammunition stocks. By 1430, resistance ended when the last defenders surrendered.

WN-62 had been manned by only twenty-eight German soldiers of the 3rd Company, Grenadier Regiment 726, and thirteen forward observers of 1st Battery, Artillery Regiment 352, fighting as infantry. Only three of the Germans escaped alive or uninjured, and even they were captured the next day. On the beach below, hundreds of GIs had been killed or wounded, ten tanks destroyed, and over a dozen landing craft were burning. It is incredible that forty-one soldiers, albeit in well-established positions, caused such carnage on the beach.

Because of its extraordinarily strong defenses, **WN-62** was the deadliest for American troops. The first curve in the path up the hill from the parking area passes a tobruk on the right which housed an MG 34. No sign remains of the two rows of barbed wire that extended down the beach to the east. The path continues directly to two casemates that each held a 76.5-mm Czech-made cannon. The guns were positioned to fire to the west along Omaha Beach. Both casemates are accessible but are generally muddy and damp. It is more informative to mount the roof of either casemate and grasp the dramatic views down Omaha Beach to the west and the Colleville draw to the east – the same views that the positions provided to the German defenders. Their gun embrasures retain the damage wrought by American naval and tank fire. The upper casemate had been hit by twenty-seven rounds before being silenced by tank fire.

American engineers used the well-known beach shingle to fill antitank ditches and as base for the construction of exit roadways. Their heroic actions, performed while under enemy fire, are commemorated by the **5th Engineer Special Brigade Memorial** erected atop the upper casemate. The sides of the monument hold plaques dedicated to

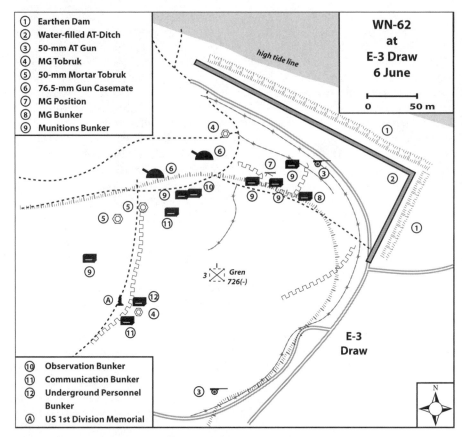

①	Earthen Dam
②	Water-filled AT-Ditch
③	50-mm AT Gun
④	MG Tobruk
⑤	50-mm Mortar Tobruk
⑥	76.5-mm Gun Casemate
⑦	MG Position
⑧	MG Bunker
⑨	Munitions Bunker

WN-62
at
E-3 Draw
6 June

0   50 m

high tide line

3 ⊠ Gren
726(-)

E-3
Draw

⑩	Observation Bunker
⑪	Communication Bunker
⑫	Underground Personnel Bunker
Ⓐ	US 1st Division Memorial

N

the brigade and to the 20th, 146th, 299th Engineer Combat Battalions. The 5th Engineer Special Brigade plaque lists the names of the ninety-six who died in the 6 June assault. Special plaques are dedicated to the 20th and 146th Engineer Combat Battalions, both of which were awarded Presidential Unit Citations for actions in support of the 16th Infantry Regiment on D-Day. (49.360286, -0.847964)

A barely discernible complex of antiaircraft machine gun positions, two MG 34 machine guns and artillery observation, telecommunications, and ammunition storage bunkers are east of the casemates.

From the upper bunker continue uphill along a walkpath, which parallels a German trench line and whose characteristic zigzag pattern is discernible in the tall grass. Near the lower end of the trench is a tobruk for a 50-mm mortar; a second such position is to the right slightly farther uphill. The **1st Infantry Division Memorial** stands upon a bunker used to house communications gear for the resistance nest. The 10-meter polished granite obelisk is the same design as used in all five 1st Division memorials on Second World War battlefields. Engraved on the memorial are the names of 627 officers and men killed during the period 6 June to 24 July 1944. The five soldiers[6] of the division awarded the Medal of

---

6   The five are: Private Carlton W Barrett, Staff Sergeant Walter D Ehlers, Staff Sergeant Arthur F Defranzo, 1st Lieutenant Jimmie W Monteith Jr, and Technician 5th Class John Pinder Jr. Defranzo, Monteith and Pinder received their awards posthumously.

Honor[7] have their names inscribed with gold lettering. The memorial is centered upon a circular brick courtyard which holds benches for those wishing to sit and contemplate the events of that day. (49.359179, -0.84819)

> Return to the parking area and return up the hill. Keep to the right and enter the parking area for Normandy American Cemetery Visitor Center. (49.358696, -0.851902)

Normandy American Cemetery Visitor Center
14710 Colleville-s/Mer   E-mail: info@abmc.gov
Tel: (US) 703-696-6900

The center opened in 2007. Its low profile and position on a wooded site in a vast underground construction, in no way detracts from the solemnity of the cemetery. The orientation pavilion offers several fine quotations from world leaders regarding the invasion; however, the only quotation which came from an enlisted man states:

> You can manufacture weapons and you can purchase ammunition, but you can't buy valor and you can't pull heroes off an assembly line. – Sergeant John B. Ellery, US 1st Infantry Division

The center is not an artifacts museum, but rather an interpretive area that explains the invasion and the subsequent battle for Normandy. The exhibit space is strong on audio/ visual displays relating the story of courage and sacrifice of Allied forces. Many displays tell, in brief form, the personal histories of individual soldiers who participated in the landing and the subsequent fighting.

The visitor center is open daily from 09:00 to 18:00 from April 15 to September 15, and from 09:00 to 17:00 the rest of the year. No admission fee.

> Exit the visitor center up the hill via a landscaped pathway to the cemetery.

The **Normandy American Cemetery and Memorial,** destination for over one million visitors each year, is the premier site for visitors to Omaha Beach. Among its finely manicured lawns and shrubs lie 9,387 men and women, including 307 who remain unidentified. All but 8 are Americans. The precisely aligned graves feature white marble headstones in the shape of the Star of David for those of the Jewish faith or the Latin Cross for all others. Among the graves are those of three Medal of Honor recipients, identified by the gold lettering on their headstones.

> Continue to the Omaha Beach Overlook on the right. (49.360185, -0.853093)

Between the St-Laurent and Colleville draws, the bluff was less strongly defended. At 0640, one 32-man section of Company E, commanded by 2nd Lieutenant John Spalding, landed 1000 meters east of its objective. The section lost much of its equipment in the struggle out of the deep water. The soldiers faced barbed wire once they achieved the seawall. Sergeant Curtis Colwell stuffed a Bangalore torpedo under the wire and detonated its twenty pounds of explosives.[8] The men rushed through the resulting gap and, with only

---

7   Only 464 such awards were made in all theaters of the Second World War.

8   Staff Sergeant Curtis Colwell received a Distinguished Service Cross for his actions.

two casualties, reached the sand dune near a demolished stone house. Between them and the hillside bluff was a minefield.

Sheltering behind the stone ruins, Spalding sent Technical Sergeant Philip Streczyk to find a path through the mine field to the German front. Streczyk reported that it was impenetrable but that he had spotted a path running along a protected defile a few meters to the east. Terrain protected it from fire from a pillbox 400 meters farther east. Spalding and Streczyk led their men up the slope to the very edge of the bluff where they were stopped by machine-gun fire coming from a foxhole. After suffering several casualties, Streczyk led a charge which overwhelmed the lone Polish gunner.[9] The first American troops had scaled the top of the bluff. It was now roughly 0800 hours.

At 0700, Captain Joseph Dawson, commander of Company G, landed in the second wave. Dawson was the first man off his landing craft followed by two of his staff. When they entered the water, a shell hit the boat and killed the other thirty men. Dawson reached the shingle and collected Company G men from other landing craft. He and Pfc Frank Baldridge explored a path up the hillside in the same defile used by Spalding, slightly farther to the east, until they came under the fire of a machine-gun emplacement. Dawson moved among the brush until he achieved the crest of the ridge and then destroyed the machine gun with a fragmentation grenade.[10] The machine guns eliminated by Streczyk and Dawson flanked the draw to the left and right. Shortly after 0800, Captain Dawson

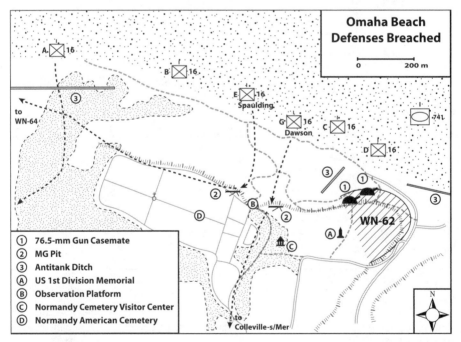

Omaha Beach Defenses Breached

0   200 m

① 76.5-mm Gun Casemate
② MG Pit
③ Antitank Ditch
Ⓐ US 1st Division Memorial
Ⓑ Observation Platform
Ⓒ Normandy Cemetery Visitor Center
Ⓓ Normandy American Cemetery

---

9   For his actions on 6 June, Sergeant Philip Streczyk was awarded the Distinguished Service Cross and Britain's Military Medal. In all, Streczyk fought in Tunisia, Sicily, Normandy, and Hürtgen battlefields receiving four Silver Stars. He survived the war.

10   Captain Joseph Dawson received the Distinguished Service Cross for his actions on D-Day. He later won more acclaim for his actions at Aachen, Germany, where the battle ground is now referred to as Dawson's Ridge. He died at age 84 in Corpus Christi, Texas.

joined Spalding's group to plan their next moves. Dawson led his group for Colleville while Spalding headed west towards St-Laurent.

The **Omaha Beach Overlook** stands at the top of the defile used by Spalding, Dawson, and others to surmount the bluff. Spalding climbed up from the left and Dawson from the right. Here the German defenses at Colleville draw cracked and were gradually pried open. The overlook provides a table of orientation and views of the expanse of Omaha Beach. The overlook also provides the perspective of the German defenders while they awaited the landing of the first American invasion forces and the exposed nature of American troops as they struggled, overloaded and wet, to cross the beach.

Do not be intimidated by the low, bolted gate. It is designed to keep animals out of the cemetery, not the visitors in. One is allowed to step over the gate and take the smooth asphalt and stone steps down the hill, but the trek can be arduous with little of note to see. The demolished house and the stone walls that hid troops before they ascended the bluff are long gone. A wooden walkway crosses the marshy area at the bottom of the hill to exit directly onto Omaha Beach.

> Walk west along the asphalt path that follows the top of the bluff and the edge of the grave plots.

The cemetery path roughly follows the route of Spalding and his men as they attacked the German trenches along the top of the cliff edge. Theirs was a feat of small unit maneuver, rapid fire, and raw courage as trenches were cleared, machine-gun emplacements overcome, and enemy captured or killed. By 0900, Spalding had crossed the orchards and hedgerows now occupied by the cemetery plots. Spalding and Streczyk encountered the first defenses of the incomplete **WN-64** at the far end of the cemetery path. They attacked an underground dugout capturing six to eight Germans and an unmanned 81-mm mortar. For the next hour, they attacked other elements of the strongpoint with hand grenades and small arms fire eliminating an antiaircraft gun, three more concrete shelters, two pillboxes, five machine guns and captured twenty German prisoners.[11] The ruins of that strongpoint are lost in the undergrowth northwest of the cemetery boundary.

The waves of the English Channel crash against the sands of Omaha Beach, the most difficult and deadliest of the landing sites. Strong winds invariably blow inland, providing an appropriate hushed whisper among the pine trees lining the pathway above the beach code-named Easy Red.

> At the end of the seaside walk, turn left and proceed to the central mall, then continue towards the eastern end of the cemetery. (49.361016, -0.860463)

Two Italian granite figures representing the United States and France mark the western end of the cemetery. As one proceeds east, two Medal of Honor awardees are on the right: Lieutenant Jimmie W. Montieth (plot I, row 20, grave 12) and T/Sgt Frank Peregory (plot G, row 21, grave 7). The circular rotunda in the center of the graves area is a **Memorial Chapel**, and inscriptions commemorating the sacrifice of those who died in

---

11   For his leadership and courageous actions on 6 June, 2nd Lieutenant John Spalding received the Distinguished Service Cross. He was wounded in fighting in the Hürtgen on 27 September but recovered to later fight in Belgium. Unfortunately, the stress of leading men in combat haunted him for the remainder of his life.

the Normandy landing are on the outside wall. The interior holds a black and gold marble altar. (49.360387, -0.857985)

Second Lieutenant Robert Niland and Sergeant Preston Niland, two of the three Niland brothers killed in the same week and who inspired the motion picture *Saving Private Ryan*, are buried a short distance ahead and to the left in plot F, row 15. Tragically, thirty-eight pairs of brothers are buried in the cemetery. Father and son Colonel Ollie Reed and Lieutenant Ollie Reed Jr are buried in plot E, row 20. Farther ahead, Medal of Honor holder Brigadier General Theodore Roosevelt Jr is buried on the end of plot D, row 28, next to his brother, Lieutenant Quentin Roosevelt, a pilot who died in the First World War and who is the only serviceman from that war buried in an American Second World War cemetery.

Normandy American Memorial (49.359262, -0.853372)

A semicircular memorial with a loggia behind the reflecting pool at the eastern end of the cemetery houses battle maps of the Western European campaign with inscriptions describing its events. In the center of the open arc is a 7-meter bronze statue representing 'The Spirit of American Youth Rising from the Waves.'

Behind the memorial lies the **Garden of the Missing**, upon whose curved walls are 1,557 names of those who gave their lives for their country and whose graves were never located. Included are the Morelands, twin brothers who were both killed on 6 June while serving with the 149th Engineer Combat Battalion. The spaces between the memorial and the wall are landscaped with American Peace rose bushes.

Return to the car park; follow the exit signs from the cemetery and proceed to the junction with highway D514. Exit the roundabout toward Colleville-s/Mer and stop at the church at the west end of the village. (49.348554, -0.848085)

Local German commanders recognized the threat to their beach defenses and dispatched 700 men of the II Battalion, Grenadier Regiment 915, from Bayeux. They arrived in Colleville-s/Mer at noon. Dawson and his men moved directly across the fields and hedgerows towards Colleville-s/Mer, engaging small groups of German soldiers along the way. At 1530, upon reaching the village, the men took up defensive positions in the farm courtyard across the road from l'Église Notre-Dame de l'Assomption de Colleville. German troops controlled the remainder of the village. Because they used the church steeple as a forward observation post, Dawson and two men entered the walled-in cemetery grounds surrounding the church. As they passed into the church, they were greeted by enemy fire from a sniper in the belfry who killed one of Dawson's men. Dawson and his other man eliminated the sniper and the artillery observers.

Later, a dramatic firefight developed when German troops counterattacked the unit in the farm courtyard. Although beaten back and surrounded, Dawson and his men fought off the attack. Later an enormous naval bombardment targeted the church steeple. Dawson was irate at the casualties his *ad hoc* unit suffered as a result of their own naval fire. As darkness fell, the Americans occupied a small portion of the western end of the village, and the Germans held most of the rest.

Panel #2 on the western wall of the churchyard depicts American troops as they walked past the ruined church. Panel #3 presents the church after its reconstruction in 1950. Panel #4 on the farmyard wall shows American Sherman tanks moving through the village. The obelisk to the west is the village's First World War memorial.

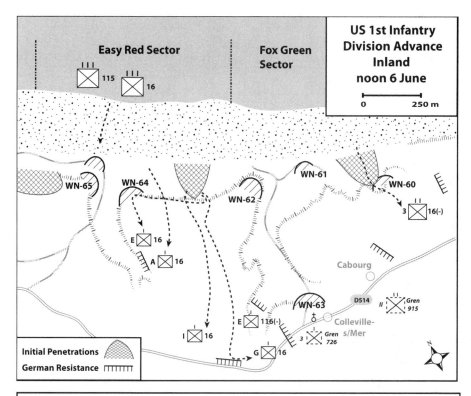

Reverse direction and proceed 300 m west; stop at the museum on the left. (49.347158, -0.851011)

Big Red One Assault Museum

Hameau le Bray D-514   14710 Colleville-s/Mer
Tel: +33 (0)2 31 21 53 81
Web: http://www.bigredonemuseum.com

All of the artifacts in this private museum derive from the owner's private collection when, at only nine-years old he started scavenging the battlefield for memorabilia. He researched their original owners and the exhibits relate the stories of the men of the 1st Infantry Division in Normandy. The collection is rotated each the year bringing in different material for the next season. An excellent example of the metal beach barrier known as a Belgian Gate is on the lawn outside of the museum.

Open daily from 10:00 to 19:00 in June through August; open daily except Tuesday from 10:00 to 12:00 and from 14:00 to 18:00 in September through November and in March through May. Admission fee.

Continue 2.5 km west on D514 into St-Laurent-s/Mer and turn right on Rue Quincangrogne; after 750 m stop at the stone memorial on the left. (49.361317, -0.867105)

The large marble-streaked, granite stone holds a plaque commemorating the location and construction of **Airfield A21c**. The grass field, located slightly northwest of the monument, was first operational on 8 June 1944 to provide emergency services for Allied aircraft. By the next evening, specialized Dakota aircraft were removing the critically wounded to England. Thereafter, 11,030 injured men were evacuated in June and July.

> Follow the road 550 m to the parking area below the small pillbox.
> (49.364559, -0.863714)

St-Laurent draw (E-1) was headed by woods and dense brush. Its exit was a dirt track which wound up its western face to St-Laurent. WN-64, eliminated early in the day by Lt Spalding and his men, cannot be visited or even seen from the roadway below. However, **WN-65**, positioned directly above the parking area, held a much stronger position. The concrete casemate housed an effective 50-mm antitank gun. An antitank ditch extended parallel to the beach roughly along the line of the roadway. The beachfront held a machine-gun tobruk and two open-air machine-gun emplacements. On the bluff behind the casemate and extending to the west sat three more machine-gun emplacements. Finally, the draw exit was protected by a second 50-mm antitank gun in the wooded uplands.

WN-65 was taken by a frontal assault led by Lieutenant Colonel George Gibbs,[12] commander 7th Field Artillery Battalion, who reorganized the confused men and found a

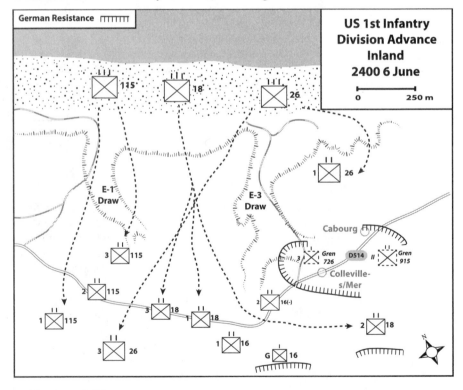

---

12   Lieutenant Colonel George W Gibbs was awarded the Distinguished Service Cross. Gibbs retired from the US Army as a colonel and died in 1976.

breach in the wire entanglements. While tanks of the 741st Tank Battalion, an M15 half-track with 37-mm gun, and the destroyer USS *Frankford* fired upon the strongpoint, Gibbs' *ad hoc* unit crossed the minefield. They overcame the pillbox and entered the underground tunnels shooting anyone who resisted while capturing twenty-one enemy.

First Lieutenant Robert P Ross of the 37th Engineer Combat Battalion assumed command of a leaderless infantry company and led them and his engineering platoon up the slopes behind the pillbox. At the crest they engaged two enemy machine-gun emplacements and eliminated both, killing forty of the enemy.[13]

By noon, St-Laurent draw was in American hands, the only draw to be opened on that day by assault from the beach. The dreaded casemate became the 37th Engineer Combat Battalion's command post while the unit cleared the minefield and pushed a lane through the shingle for tanks and other vehicles. They moved inland toward St-Laurent, and by 1500, E-1 draw was open to traffic.

WN-65 remains one of the more well-known resistance nests because of its easy access. The **50-mm antitank gun**, with its shattered defense plate, still sits in the casemate with its barrel protruding from the gun embrasure facing to the east. The shell-pocked roof shows the effects of the American naval bombardment. Above the embrasure opening is a plaque to the **467th Antiaircraft Artillery Automatic Weapons Battalion**, which landed on this beach on the morning of 6 June. The battalion suffered heavy casualties in the neutralization of the enemy positions guarding this beach.

A plaque mounted on the side of the bunker facing the beach is to the **Provision Engineer Special Brigade Group** and lists all of its various units. In front is a stele to the **2nd Infantry Division** displaying its Indian Head insignia mounted upon a star, which in turn is mounted upon a shield. The division landed here on 7 June.

An information plaque provides this area's proper name as 'le Ruquet' valley and briefly describes the events of the day. Cement steps lead down to the **NTL Totem** below the casemate.

Visitors gain a good perspective of the position's importance by walking behind the pillbox and following the steps and a sometimes slippery path a short distance up the hill.

From WN-65, continue on the road, which becomes the rue de la 2ème Division US as it curves to the west and follows the bluff. After 550 m, the road curves to the beach front seawall. Stop in the parking area at the junction between Easy Red and Easy Green sector and the 1st and 29th Infantry Division boundary as identified by a small sign. (49.368094, -0.870967)

---

13   1st Lieutenant Robert P Ross was awarded a Distinguish Service Cross for his leadership in this action. Two bulldozers operators, Private Vinton Dove and Private William J Shoemaker, both of the 37th Engineer Combat Battalion, received the same award for clearing the beach exit and filling the antitank ditch while under direct enemy fire.

Chapter Six
US 29th (Blue and Grey) Infantry Division
6 to 9 June 1944

The western sector of Omaha Beach is the mirror image of the eastern sector. The beachfront is backed with low dunes before a cliff face rising between 55 and 70 meters. Its western end terminates in sheer cliffs that reach down to the water closing off the beach. Differences include a seafront roadway that parallels the water and the beachfront communities of les Moulins and Vierville-s/Mer. The German defenses incorporated fortified buildings in les Moulins along D-3 draw whereas Rommel ordered the houses along the waterfront to be destroyed to improve lines of fire, but a few yet remained on 6 June.

As in the east, the 29th Infantry Division's sector was also defended by partially completed strongpoints, which held a variety of heavy weapons and small arms positions. WN-66 through WN-74 targeted the seafront cliffs and the exits from the beaches. The Moulins draw presented a narrow exit from the beach and one that could be easily defended. The draw forked into east and west branches before reaching the village of St-Laurent-s/Mer. The Vierville draw was the most significant to Allied planners because it offered a paved highway to the nearby coastal road, a fact not lost on German planners who made it one of the most strongly defended.

The US 29th Infantry Division was known as Blue and Grey because of its composition from National Guard units from the Civil War border states of Maryland, Pennsylvania, and Virginia. The unit was originally formed to fight in the First World War and suffered almost 6,000 casualties during 21 days in the Meuse-Argonne Offensive. After the first war, it was demobilized and reverted to National Guard status until reactivated in February 1941. Operation OVERLORD was its first combat action.

D-Day Landings (Omaha Beach)
6 June 1944

Objective	To land on the Normandy coast, secure the beachhead, and move inland.
Forces	
American	29th Infantry Division (Major General Charles H Gerhardt)
German	726th Grenadier Regiment, 716th Infantry Division (Oberst Walter Korfes) and 916th Grenadier Regiment, 352nd Infantry Division (Oberst Ernst Goth)
Result	Although stiffly resisted, the landings were successful
Casualties	
American	1,272 casualties
German	unknown
Location	Bayeux is 30 km northwest of Caen; les Moulins is 21 km northwest of Bayeux.

Battle

The first wave was comprised of 740 infantrymen of Companies A, E, F, and G, 116th Infantry Regiment, preceded by armor from the 743rd Tank Battalion. The first tanks were to land at 0624 with the infantry three minutes later. Also in the first wave was Company C, 2nd Ranger Battalion. Their special objective was to land west of Vierville draw and to proceed west to destroy the guns and radar station at Pointe de la Percée. The air, naval, and rocket bombardments were just as ineffective on this sector of Omaha Beach as they were to the east despite the presence of significant beachfront markers, such as a three story house at les Moulins and the Chateau Hardelay in Hamel au Prêtre.

As happened to the 1st Division in the eastern sector, the first-wave landing craft were driven east by wind and current. Company E ended up 1.5 kilometers east in front of Colleville draw where it suffered high casualty rates. Companies F and G landed in front of les Moulins draw. The ill-fated Company A arrived on target.

As in the eastern sector, the landings were a bloody mess. Units found themselves on the wrong beach and intermixed with unfamiliar partners. Because the overpowering German defenses retained control of the beaches, combat engineers, antiaircraft battalions, and antitank gunners lost their equipment and their cohesion. Their units suffered appalling levels of casualties during the landings, and the survivors spent the day as infantrymen.

The first senior commander to report to General Omar Bradley was Brigadier General Willard Wyman, the 1st Division assistant commander, who communicated at 0900: 'Situation difficult; information limited; progress low.' Bradley considered transferring the subsequent landings to Utah Beach or the British beaches; however, additional units continued to land and some found themselves in weakly defended areas.

Despite coils of barbed wire and fields of mines defending the seafront roadway,

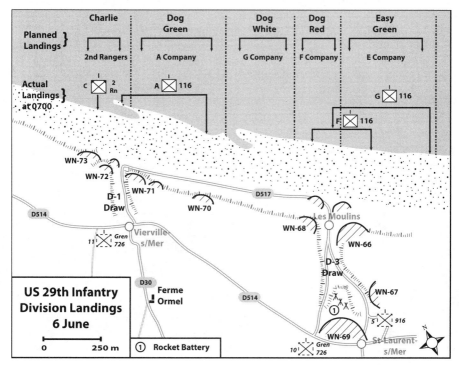

troops made their way up the cliff face. By noon, the entire 3rd Battalion, 116th Regiment, had landed between les Moulins and St-Laurent draws and had moved inland. The 115th Regiment was mislanded east of the St-Laurent draw but moved inland and to the west. It crossed the draw to join the 3rd Battalion and remnants of the severely reduced 2nd Battalion in capturing St-Laurent-s/Mer.

Two companies of 2nd Ranger Battalion scaled the cliffs to Pointe du Hoc and, after an intense fire fight, located and destroyed the German field guns that threatened the entire invasion fleet.

Meanwhile, the 5th Ranger Battalion and two companies of the 1st Battalion, 116th Regiment, entered Vierville-s/Mer from the east. Although the Vierville draw defenses were pounded by naval fire including the big guns of the battleship USS *Texas,* the draw was captured by a small group coming from landward. Strong German resistance west and south of the town, however, stopped farther progress from Vierville.

Almost every aspect of the invasion had gone wrong, but the troops were ashore and the draws were open.

Aftermath

Little of the invasion was executed according to the original plan; indeed, many of its elements produced disastrous results. On the other hand, the German defenses were incomplete due to shortages of men and materiel. The element of surprise, moreover, confused the German High Command and it held most of their re-enforcements in place. Nonetheless, American success on Omaha Beach was due to overwhelming numbers and the extraordinary quality of its assault troops – especially its junior officers and NCOs.

Battlefield Tour

From WN-65, as described at the end of the previous chapter, in the St-Laurent draw, continue on the road, which becomes the rue de la 2ème Division US as it curves to the west and follows the bluff. After 550 m, the road curves to the beach front seawall. Stop in the parking area at the junction between Easy Red and Easy Green sectors and the 1st and 29th Infantry Division sectors as identified with a small sign. (49.368094, -0.870967)

At 0740, 3rd Battalion, 116th Regiment, landed on an empty beach at **Easy Green**, the most lightly defended sector of Omaha Beach. The battalion crossed the sand almost intact, and the men sought shelter behind the 2-meter-high shingle wall. They were only temporarily safe from rifle and machine-gun fire, as plunging fire from German mortars was sure to search them out. Beyond the shingle were two coils of barbed wire. They lost no time blowing a hole in the wire and heading up the cliff.

The **'Bloody Omaha' information panel** at the far end of the parking area identifies the 1st / 29th divisional boundary and speaks to the death and destruction wrought here.

Continue northwest 450 m to the next seaside parking area. (49.369768, -0.876396)

On D-Day, sections of Companies F and G, 2nd Battalion had the misfortune of landing directly opposite the Moulins draw. The Germans held their fire until the twelve LCVPs had discharged all of their troops. The men started to cross 400 meters of open beach, partially obscured by the smoke from burning brush; then enemy machine-gun fire caught the men in deadly crossfire. Casualties were high.

The **round concrete platform** near the eastern end of the parking area held an open-air 50-mm PaK 38 antitank gun, which was part of WN-66. The gun's line of fire along the beachfront targeted tanks and landing craft.

A white, two-story building with large seaward-facing windows occupies the site of a three-story house known locally as the 'Villa les Sables d'Or,' one of the few structures not cleared by the Germans. Its Luftwaffe observation post served as a beacon to landing craft in this area. Amid the carnage wrought by the enemy, Major Sidney Bingham, 2nd Battalion commander, gathered up as many Company F men as could shake off the shock of battle. Bingham eventually abandoned attempts to occupy the villa and force Moulins draw. Instead, he moved to the east where his much reduced 2nd Battalion climbed the cliff paths used earlier by the 3rd Battalion.

Continue northwest 280 m to the roundabout and park. (49.370709, -0.879751)

Les Moulins, or **D-3 Draw** offered a direct path off the beach and into St-Laurent-s/Mer, but the firepower of the strongpoints sited on the draw's shoulders decimated any troops attempting a direct assault. Units landing in front of the draw attempted to escape by moving east or west.

At the center of the beach exit is a **Signal Monument** with inscriptions to the 1st Infantry Division and the 116th Regimental Combat Team which landed on D-Day. Its side is engraved with images of men dying among the waves, lying on the beach, and fighting inland.

A stainless steel artwork titled '**Les Braves**' stands on the beach directly behind the monument and marks the center of Omaha Beach. Nine meter Wings of Hope and Wings of Fraternity are on the right and left as they represent the hope for a better world and commitment to humanity. In the center, Standing Liberty commemorates the courage of men who fought against totalitarianism. In total, the work remembers the bravery of soldiers who landed on these beaches. In the words of the sculptor, Anilore Banon:

> I created this sculpture to honour the courage of these men: sons, husbands, and fathers, who endangered and often sacrificed their lives in the hope of freeing the French people.

Proceed south on Av de la Liberation (D517).

The roundabout marks the approximate position of a water-filled antitank ditch zigzagging across the draw and parallel to the waterfront. Farther south, access to the beach along this roadway was blocked by Belgian gates, which were closed at night. The houses on the east side of the draw were linked by tunnels and trenches offering German riflemen with a variety of shooting positions. Scattered fire from these positions continued until 8 June.

Continue to the museum parking area on the right. (49.367092, -0.881991)

Musée Mémorial d'Omaha Beach

Avenue de la Libération   14710 St-Laurent-s/Mer
Tel: +33 (0)2 31 21 97 44
Email: musee-memorial-omaha@wanadoo.fr
Web: http://www.musee-memorial-omaha.com/

The museum's extensive collection of artifacts from the invasion beaches includes weapons, uniforms, life-size dioramas, photographs, maps, and other materials. Displays also describe life under the German occupation. A moving film presents recollections of American veterans. The entrance is marked by a fine example of an M4A4 Sherman tank and the only American 155-mm 'Long Tom' cannon in Normandy.

Open daily mid-February to mid-March from 10:00 to 12:30 and from 14:30 to 18:00; mid-March to mid-May from 9:30 to 18:30; mid-May to mid-September from 9:30 to 19:00 (later in July and August); and mid-September to mid-November from 9:30 to 18:30. Admission fee; Normandie Pass accepted.

Continue south, and after 700 m, bear left onto rue de Val; after 190 m, turn right onto rue de l'Église and proceed to the church. (49.359626, -0.877908)

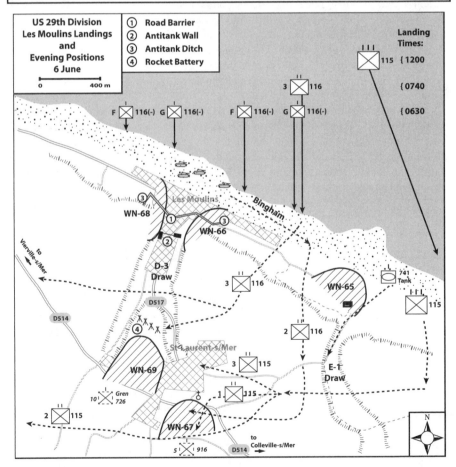

St-Laurent-s/Mer

Église St-Laurent, founded in 1065, was named after St-Laurent Auvray, a companion of Robert the Magnificent, the father of William the Conqueror. The present structure's nave dates from the 13th century, and the tower from the 14th century. The 1944 shells seriously damaged the tower, which was rebuilt to its original design. The churchyard holds four Commonwealth War Graves (see Operation AQUITINT, below).

St-Laurent-s/Mer was a strong defensive position centered about the village church, with a machine gun and observation post in its steeple. A machine gun was also installed on the roof of a house on the north side of the coastal highway near the western exit of the draw. The village held the command post of 10th Company, Grenadier Regiment 726, which had recently been augmented by 5th Company, Grenadier Regiment 916. WN-69 was 400 meters west of the village center on slightly higher ground.

The church steeple was destroyed by naval fire, but the village's underground tunnels and communication trenches aided the German defense. Still, the 2nd Battalion, 116th Regiment, and the entire 115th Regiment launched a heavy attack from the east at 1515. Effective direct fire from 105-mm SP howitzers cleared village buildings of enemy troops, but 3rd Battalion, 115th Regiment, attempting to move southwest and bypass St-Laurent, ran right into WN-69. By 2015 the church had been cleared, but the junction of the coastal road and the highway to Formigny (D517), which was the beach defenders last remaining exit route, held out. The fighting continued into the night.

The open ground passed on the right on the approach from the beach into St-Laurent held the Nebelwerfer Battalion 100. Wooden structures supporting forty 320-mm rocket launchers echeloned across the field from northwest to southeast. Although not very accurate, the rocket emitted a terrifying screaming sound in flight, and its explosion amidst the beach shingle sent shards of metal and pebble across a large kill radius. The Nebelwerfers were put out of action by fire from USS *Thompson* at 1213.

Reverse direction and return to the beach front roundabout. Continue west stopping to view the small plaque on the seawall at the western exit of the roundabout. (49.371084, -0.880671)

The memorial plaque commemorates Major Gustavus March-Phillipps and the eleven men of **Operation AQUITINT**, a landing on the night of 12/13 September 1942 of British No 62 Commando to perform reconnaissance near Port-en-Bessin. After landing at the wrong site, the group encountered a German patrol whence a fire fight broke out. The commandoes were hopelessly outgunned. Three men including March-Phillipps, were killed and four were immediately captured, two of whom were never heard from again. One of the escapees, Captain Graham Hayes, evaded immediate capture only to be taken prisoner as he attempted to cross the border into Spain. He was executed by the Gestapo in a Paris prison. Four of the bodies, including that of Major March-Phillipps, are buried in the St-Laurent churchyard.

Company G landed in the first wave at this section of Dog Red sector directly under the guns of les Moulins draw. Though many of their officers became casualties, the survivors moved west in an attempt to reach their targeted assault area. Blocked by breakwaters which extend like comb's teeth along this beachfront, they remained isolated for much of the battle.

Only the barest remnants of the breakwaters remain visible because most of the structures have been erased by years of pounding surf and shifting sand.

> Continue west for 400 m to the small monument slightly below road level on the left. (49.372758, -0.885724)

The numerous bodies scattered about the beach posed a health hazard and psychological threat to landing troops. St-Laurent Cemetery #1, atop the cliff near Colleville, was still under occasional enemy fire. Burial details selected his site as temporary **St-Laurent Cemetery #2**, and bulldozed trenches to inter 456 invasion casualties. Within weeks they had been removed to St-Laurent Cemetery #1, later renamed Normandy American Cemetery. The small monument marks the site.

> Slowly proceed west and observe the broad expanse of Dog Red and Dog White landing beaches and the sharp inland bluffs, which held partially manned German trenches. After 700 m, stop in front of the large building at #90 Bd de Cauvigny (D517). (49.375716, -0.894302)

Dog White Sector became the most successful of Omaha's landing zones on D-Day. At 0730, a LCVP carrying Assistant Division Commander Brigadier General Norman Cota and the command group for the 116th Regiment landed among elements of the 116th Regiment's Companies B and C. Cota's arrival was quickly followed by that of Lieutenant Colonel Max Schneider[1] and his 5th Ranger Battalion, temporarily designated as Ranger Force C – comprised of 700 of America's best fighting men – as a contingency force. If Ranger Force A captured Pointe du Hoc, it would be re-enforced by Force C landing below the cliffs. If Pointe du Hoc was not captured, Force C was to land to the east, march overland, and attack the point from the inland side. After witnessing the destruction of Company C, 2nd Ranger Battalion, at Vierville (see below) and receiving no message from Force A's destroyed radios, Schneider suggested that the Royal Navy officers land his troops 800 meters farther east. They did so at 0740, and the Rangers joined with elements of Companies B and C to create a cohesive fighting force at a weakly defended stretch of beach.

Although the various units had incurred few casualties in landing, General Cota had to get the men moving; they had to get off the beach before the Germans brought their mortars and howitzers to bear. Cota was the right man in the right place to make that happen. Fearlessly striding up and down the beach, Cota conferred, ordered, and encouraged his men – all the while waving his Colt .45 pistol in the air.

Beyond the shingle was a single coil of barbed wire, a seaside roadway, two more coils of wire, 150 meters of open ground (probably mined), and finally steep bluffs that afforded little shelter. At 0750 Company C began to move. Private Ingram Lambert[2] jumped the first strand of wire, crossed the road, and placed a Bangalore torpedo under the double wire coil before he was shot and killed. Lieutenant Stanley Schwartz[3] followed and detonated the charge. The first two soldiers attempting to run through the gap were killed, but others were successful and they entered a German communications trench that led

---

1   Omaha Beach was Lieutenant Colonel Max Schneider's fifth amphibious assault. Schneider was awarded a Distinguished Service Cross for his leadership under fire. Hewas killed in the Korean War.

2   Private Ingram Lambert was an only child; he is buried in a family plot in Ramsey, New Jersey. Twenty-four men of the 116th Regiment were awarded Distinguished Service Crosses for their actions on 6 June; Lambert was not one of them.

3   Lieutenant Stanley Schwartz was killed later that day in fighting west of Vierville.

them through the dunes to the foot of the bluff. After conferring with Col Schneider, Cota barked, 'Rangers, lead the way!'[4] Within minutes, the Rangers blew four more breaches in the barbed wire and were filtering into the grassland south of the roadway. Schneider and his 5th Ranger Battalion reached the top of the bluff and continued due south, cutting the coastal road.

Company C, 743rd Tank Battalion also came ashore in this area; however, once landed the tanks became magnets for German antitank fire. Those that survived sheltered in the shallow surf or deeper runnels and came forward to fire at identified targets before reversing back to their meager shelter.

The large brick and stone building at #90 was the wartime location of **Chateau Hardelay**, owned by a wealthy local businessman. Behind the structure a zigzag path leads up the slope to WN-70, which held machine gun emplacements and a 75-mm gun. Company A, 2nd Ranger Battalion, landed at 0740 into a hail storm of small arms fire. Nearly 50% of its men became casualties on the beach. With all of its officers dead or wounded and now led by sergeants, the men of Company A climbed the steep bluffs and eliminated enemy positions along a cliff edge trench system. Company B, 2nd Ranger Battalion, also came ashore in front of this position. The Germans fired directly into the landing craft when the ramps dropped, but the survivors leapt over the side and struggled across the beach. After attempting to move west, the company returned east to attack and overcome the strongpoint. Those two companies of 2nd Ranger Battalion suffered 102 casualties out of a total complement of 136 men. Later in the day, the survivors were combined into one unit and put in reserve.

Captain Ned Elder,[5] commanding Company C, 743rd Tank Battalion, ordered the battalion's tanks to be landed directly onto the beach because of the threat of heavy seas swamping the DD Shermans. Thus, unlike the scene on the eastern sector, the infantry on the western sector had the support of the tank's 75-mm guns.

General Cota, after climbing the bluff, accompanied Company C due south across the fields to rue du Hamel au Prêtre, which they then followed west arriving in Vierville-s/Mer at 1000. Proceeding cautiously, they entered the village without opposition. Vierville was the first of the coastal villages to be liberated.

Proceed to Vierville draw and park near the large casemate. (49.379158, -0.902885)

Vierville draw (D-1) was protected by two enormous casemates near the water's edge. The eastern casemate held a deadly 88-mm PaK 43 antitank gun. Combined with the gun in the casemate at WN-61 at the opposite end of Omaha Beach, these two powerful weapons covered the complete range of the beach. A massive concrete antitank wall, measuring three meters high, two meters thick, and thirty-eight meters long, stretched from the eastern casemate to cross the seafront roadway and provided an impassible barrier to units leaving the beach. The shoulders of the draw each held additional strongpoints. The eastern shoulder now holds a blue and white house with rows of seafront windows. The house was built upon the foundation of a pillbox holding two machine guns capable of firing on the beach to east and west. Farther back from the cliff, but not visible from the roadway, three tobruks were built (two for mortars and one for antiaircraft machine guns)

---

4   'Rangers lead the way' became the motto of American Ranger units.

5   Captain Ned S Elder was awarded a Distinguished Service Cross for his action on D-Day. He was killed on 11 July 1944 and is buried in Normandy American Cemetery.

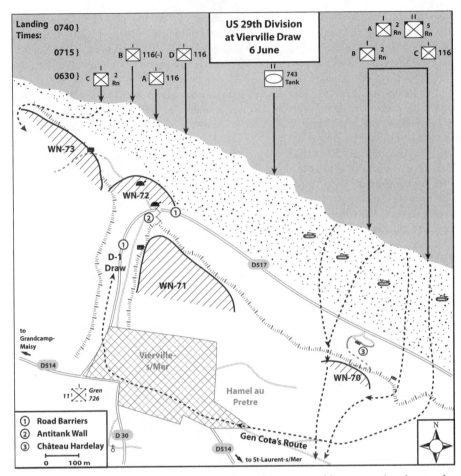

supported a final bunker built into the hillside with two machine guns aimed onto the roadway. On the western shoulder, a light weapons bunker provided shelter for riflemen. This position, located behind the Hotel du Casino, is also no longer visible from below.

The assignment of breaching the formidable defenses of Vierville Draw was given to Company A, 116th Infantry Regiment. Company A was a Virginia National Guard unit and many of the company's 210 men came from the foothills of the Blue Ridge Mountains near Bedford, Virginia. One of its six British manned LCAs swamped one kilometer from shore and another was destroyed by German artillery. The remaining five boats were right on time and on target – unfortunately.

The Germans held their fire while the men of Company A filed off their craft into the chilly waters. The infantrymen waded through the surf and onto the beach. They fell prone on the sand to catch their breath and access the beach obstacles ahead. All was quiet. Their LCAs, now empty, turned and made their way back out to sea. On its way back to its transport ship, one craft rescued the men left bobbing in the water from the swamped LCA.

Suddenly machine-gun fire erupted everywhere. The bullets ripped into men standing, lying, squatting or trying to hide. Within minutes Company A – Virginia's finest – was no more. Of the 155 men to leave their five landing craft, 100 were dead and almost all of the others were wounded. The few survivors floated in with the tide; a couple drifted to the west and sheltered at the foot of the cliff. Only two privates from Company A later engaged the enemy. The destruction was so complete that commanders decided to close Dog Green Sector to further landings.

Supporting fire for the infantry landing at Vierville was to be supplied by sixteen tanks of Company B, 743rd Tank Battalion. One LCT carrying four tanks landed directly in front of a casemate containing an antitank gun. The German guns sank the LCT, killing the company commander and two lieutenants. A second LCT was sunk on its approach, thus reducing the number of tanks to eight, which landed successfully farther east.

The eastern casemate holds the **National Guard Memorial** commemorating the sacrifices of the men of America's National Guard units, which served with distinction amid such considerable loss in the invasion. The three-sided monument, built on top of the casemate, has its interior walls covered with inscriptions. One, in English and French, describes how the National Guard answered the call to arms in 1917 and in 1940 and throughout the continuation of both of those wars. The front of the memorial posts a quote from President Franklin D Roosevelt from 19 June 1941:

> We too, born to freedom and believing in freedom, are willing
> to fight to maintain freedom. We, and all other who believe
> as deeply as we do, would rather die on our feet than live on
> our knees.

A plaque near the embrasure identifies the numerous National Guard units that participated in the amphibious assault on D-Day and their originating states.

Despite the American occupation of Vierville, the draw was still in German hands. At noon, another thirty-minute naval barrage including shells from the 14-inch guns of the battleship USS *Texas* induced thirty casemate defenders to surrender to engineers on the beach.

Shortly after noon, Cota led a small five-man contingent of staff and officers of 121st Engineer Combat Battalion through Vierville and down the exit road. They responded to rifle fire from the double embrasure bunker on the eastern cliffs with fire of their own and took five prisoners. Fifty-four additional prisoners were later taken from caves dug into the hillside. Remarkably, the fearsome Vierville draw had been captured by a general – coming from the wrong direction.[6]

However, the exit road was still blocked by the antitank wall. Cota moved down the beach to the east looking for a way to blow open the barrier. He found a bulldozer with cases of TNT tied to its top and found a volunteer to drive it to the wall. The 121st Engineer Combat Battalion was the recipient of Cota's gift. At 1500, it detonated one thousand pounds of TNT destroying the barrier. Vierville draw was open for business and American tanks finally moved inland. The embankment opposite the casemate holds a plaque to the **9th Squad, 3rd platoon, Company C, 121st Engineer Combat Battalion,** which destroyed the wall.

A second, slightly lower casemate rests on the opposite end of the beachfront

---

6   Brigadier General Norman 'Dutch' Cota was awarded the Distinguished Service Cross for his unfailing leadership and repeatedly exposing himself to enemy fire. Many thought that he desired a Medal of Honor, but the Supreme Allied Command was reluctant to award the highest honor to general officers. They did, however, make an exception for Brigadier General Theodore Roosevelt Jr, who was awarded a Medal of Honor for his leadership under much less trying circumstances on Utah Beach. Cota later commanded the 28th Infantry Division in the Battle of the Hürtgen Forest.

promenade. This position held a 50-mm PaK 38 antitank gun with two embrasures, which allowed it to fire either east or west. The mountings of a Renault tank turret, is visible in the parking area. An **NTL Totem** is immediately adjacent and describes events near Vierville. Slightly farther east, a small stone stele holds a plaque to the **58th Field Artillery Battalion**, which landed on 6 June and fought as infantry after having lost all of its weapons to enemy fire.

Along the beach an 850 ton ancillary platform from **Mulberry Harbor A**[7] provides access to a postwar pier that extends over the tidal beach. From its far end, one gets a perspective of the seafront defenses as they appeared to the men of Company A.

> From the end of the roadway, walk or drive the short distance to the west. Walk up the hillside on the left along the pedestrian pl du Débarquement to the pillbox above. (49.380609, -0.905921

The final strongpoint, located on the Pointe de la Percée 1.5 kilometers to the west, held two Czech-made Skoda 75-mm mountain guns. Although the guns were not in hardened casemates, the weapons provided the Germans partial enfilade fire on sea approaches to the mouth of the Vierville draw. Nearby was a radar station with two Würzburg and one Freya radar systems capable of scanning the channel for approaching craft. The radar site was bombed by RAF Mosquito aircraft twice in late May, and the radars played no part on the landings.

Sixty-five Rangers from Company C, 2nd Ranger Battalion, under the command of Captain Ralph Goranson, were assigned to Charlie sector. Their objective was the German strongpoint atop Pointe de la Percée. The Rangers had to take the advantageous position to prevent its firing into the flank of the Vierville landings. The two LCAs holding Company C were the western-most of the Omaha Beach landing craft. They came in just below WN-73, situated on the headlands immediately west the Vierville draw.

Before all of its troops exited the landing craft, one ship was destroyed by four hits from German artillery. The second LCA was hit twice and came under heavy small arms fire. By the time the survivors reached shelter of the base of the cliff, nineteen were dead and eighteen injured. The company had not fired a single shot.[8]

The survivors moved west about 300 meters where the first man to the top was Private First Class Otto Stephens[9] who had anchored a rope for the Rangers below, then, without waiting, attacked enemy positions. Others climbed the cliff face by thrusting their bayonets into the soft chalk. Once the full force reached the top of the cliff, they moved east to reach the fortified house that marked the western limit of WN-73. Captain Goranson felt he had no choice but to attack eastward to relieve the fire falling upon the units in front of the Vierville draw. Advancing Rangers exchanged rifle fire and grenades with the enemy while they pushed east along the cliff edge trenches. As a machine gun in a pillbox was

---

7   The St-Laurent Mulberry Harbor A was similar in construction to Mulberry Harbor B at Arromanches. After the 'Great Storm' of 19 June destroyed the Mulberry Harbor A, supplies continued landing directly onto the beach. In fact, Omaha Beach would remain the major logistical port for American troops for the next five months.

8   The terrifying opening scenes from the 1998 motion picture *Saving Private Ryan* realistically depicted Company C's assault.

9   Private First Class Otto Stephens was awarded a Distinguished Service Cross; he was killed on 6 December 1944 in Germeter during the Battle of the Hürtgen Forest.

spraying the troops on the beach, Sergeant Julius Belcher kicked in the door and threw in a white phosphorous grenade. The enemy soldiers attempting to flee were shot. The Rangers, joined by a stray assault section from Company B, 116th Regiment, destroyed the remaining WN-73 positions, accounting for sixty-nine enemy dead at the cost of two additional casualties.[10] That night the Rangers and infantrymen bivouacked in the first hedgerows beyond the cliff. Unknown to them, the original objective at Pointe de la Percée had been eliminated during the day by naval gun fire.

The pillbox built into the hillside was the eastern-most element of **WN-73**. Company C, 2nd Rangers came ashore slightly to the west of this position. This bunker held a 75-mm PaK 40 antitank gun which was primarily responsible for the destruction of Company A, 116th Infantry Regiment. The fortification offers a view from the German perspective of craft and tanks landing near the Vierville draw. Moreover, treacherous, steep stone steps above the bunker punctuate the side of the hill to approach a grassy area that provides a wonderful view of Omaha Beach and a slight view of another bunker higher up the hillside. A dangerous trench line running west along the cliff face held other fighting and storage structures taken by the Rangers. To move to the fortified house on the western end of the strongpoint, is not possible.

The point of land visible to the west is frequently mistaken for Pointe du Hoc. It is actually Pointe de la Percée, the target of Goranson's company. The site cannot be accessed due to the collapse of sections of the seafront cliffs.

> Proceed by car or on foot up the Vierville draw to view a number of monuments commemorating the battle.

Highway D517, which has been given the honorary title of **Avenue de Bedford Virginie USA** in memory of the men of Company A, follows the west side of the draw whereas the east side holds the residential rue de la Mer. A memorial stele in memory of Jean Roger stands at the junction of the two roads. 'Sainteny,' an adopted name used by Roger along with his code name 'Dragon,' was a leader of the French Resistance who escaped after capture by the Gestapo in 1943. He was arrested again on 7 June 1944 in Paris, tortured, hospitalized, and again escaped.[11] (49.378859, -0.903583)

A stele dedicated to the **29th Infantry Division** lies between the two roadways 120 meters south of the National Guard Memorial. The various divisional units are listed down the sides the monument, and on the back its Second World War campaigns. In the course of the war the division suffered 19,814 killed, wounded, or missing. (49.378336, -0.904084)

The **double machine gun bunker**, part of WN-71, is visible on the eastern cliff side a few meters south of the stele. One of its embrasures points directly across the draw, and the other centers up the draw to the south. Cota and his party were fired upon from those positions.

A small parking space 30 meters ahead allows a stop in front of a plaque to the **5th Ranger Battalion** mounted upon the roadway embankment. The inscription, in

---

10   Captain Ralph E Goranson was awarded a Distinguished Service Cross for his successful assault of enemy positions. He was awarded a Bronze Star for actions later in the war. He returned to his native Illinois and was alive at age 91.

11   Jean Roger was awarded the *Légion d'honneur*. He died in 1978 at age 71.

English and French, notes General Cota's now famous order: 'Lead the way, Rangers' and commends the unit for achieving the breakthrough that captured Vierville and eventually opened the draw.

A stele in a similar position 80 meters farther south is dedicated to all of the varied units of the **6th Engineer Special Brigade**. This monument, surmounted by the US Army Engineer's castle, features a quotation from commanding officer Col Paul W Thompson: 'The fight for the first thousand yards.' Dedicated November 1944, this looms as one of the earliest Omaha Beach memorials. Not visible from the roadway but demonstrating the depth of the German defenses, a mortar tobruk remains in the field atop the cliff immediately to the east. (49.377386, -0.904401)

Along the west side of highway D517, the Musée D Day Omaha has preserved one of the **Mulberry floating roadway** sections that were part of the artificial harbor at St-Laurent-s/Mer. Also displayed are examples of German beach defenses including three tetrahedra. (49.376544, -0.905189)

Continue to the intersection with the coastal road, Route de Grandcamp (D514). Turn left toward St-Laurent-s/Mer; after 120 m, turn south toward Formigny (D30). After 210 m, turn right toward the church. (49.372733, -0.904763)

Vierville-s/Mer

The 12th-century parish church of St-André was mistakenly believed to house a German observation post. It was shelled by the destroyer USS *Harding*, inflicting serious damage to the church, cemetery, and presbytery. The church, since then, has been faithfully reconstructed.

A plaque on the exterior of the churchyard wall to the east commemorates the men of the **81st Chemical Mortal Battalion** who landed in the second wave at 0740. The unit fought across France, in the Ardennes, and into Central Europe. Nearby is a plaque to the **Battery B, 110th Field Artillery Battalion**, which came under heavy enemy shelling on 7 June while positioned next to this church.

The command post of the German 11th Company, Grenadier Regiment 726, was stationed in the farm 300 meters southwest of the church. Efforts by Company C, 116th Regiment, and Ranger Company B to move west of Vierville were stopped by German resistance nests positioned across the coastal road. Attempts by elements of 5th Ranger Battalion to move south overland were blocked by German groups of 5th Company, Grenadier Regiment 916. The Rangers adopted defensive positions for the night south of the coastal road. (49.372132, -0.907423)

Continue 400 m toward Formigny (D30) to Ferme Ormel. (49.369282, -0.905535)

Lieutenant Walter Taylor[12] commanded a boat section from Company B, 116th Regiment. His group was among the first to cross the grassy dunes and to follow German communication trenches to a faint path up the cliff. Swiftly moving cross country, Taylor found Ferme Ormel occupied by a small German detachment. After a quick fire fight, the Germans surrendered, and Taylor sent them back to the beach under guard. Two captured

---

12   Second Lieutenant Walter Taylor was awarded a Distinguished Service Cross for his personal bravery and dedication to duty. Taylor survived the war, retired from the Baltimore police department, and died in 2003.

German medical men tended the wounded and remained in the farm. Taylor continued south to the next crossroads where he encountered three truckloads of German infantry. Severely outnumbered, Taylor's unit fought a hasty retreat to the farm buildings. The enemy attacked, but the ancient stone walls held fire slots and provided superb protection against small arms fire.

Company A, 5th Ranger Battalion, with Lieutenant Charles Parker[13] commanding, was well ahead of the other Ranger units in advancing toward their objective of Pointe du Hoc. Lt Parker and his men fought through fields and orchards festering with enemy. After several hours, the twenty-three survivors achieved the rallying point at Ferme Ormel. Parker found Taylor and his twenty-five men already in the farm buildings. Faced with the Ranger's added firepower, the attacking Germans withdrew.

Parker left the farm continuing west, then north, but became increasingly isolated with every step in the maze of hedgerows. The Rangers survived a brief fire fight and entered into Ranger lines at Pointe du Hoc at 2100 (see below). The small group was the only re-enforcements received that day.

The **Ferme Ormel** manor building dates to 1632 and was once a stop on the pilgrimage route to Santiago de Compostela. The structures still retain small architectural details especially above the doorways and windows. Because they are privately owned, visitors cannot enter without invitation. A German artillery position was under construction in the orchard to the north, whose site can still be identified through an opening in the farm wall.

Return to the coastal road (D514) and turn toward Grandcamp. After 300 m, turn into the museum parking area. (49.375178, -0.908303)

Musée D-Day Omaha
Route de Grandcamp   14710 Vierville-s/Mer
Tel/Fax: +33 (0)2 31 21 71 80   Web: http://www.dday-omaha.org/

The museum's location is identified by the heavy weapons displayed in the parking area. Most noticeable are an German 88-mm PaK 43 gun, American landing craft, and an armored observation bell from a German coastal battery. Inside is the most wonderful, if somewhat haphazard, array of military artifacts in the landing beach area. The displays of equipment seem to present one of everything along with numerous items not frequently seen in other museums. Much of the equipment is of German origin, which, as such, typically did not survive the war. Among them are a quad 50-mm machine-gun, range finding equipment, automatic flamethrower, Goliath miniature remote-control tank, paratrooper motorbike, sabotage weapons, and much more. The Quonset (Nissan) hut housing the museum is itself historic. It was once right on the beach at the end of the Mulberry and served as an Army hospital. The structure was later acquired by the museum owner and moved inland.

Open daily March through May and September from 10:30 to 12:30 and from 14:00 to 18:00; June through August from 9:30 to 19:00; October through 11 November from 10:00 to 18:00. Admission fee.

---

13   First Lieutenant Charles H Parker was awarded a Distinguished Service Cross for extraordinary heroism against the enemy on 6, 7, and 8 June.

Continue west toward Grandcamp (D514) for 6.5 km to the entrance road to Pointe du Hoc. (49.389357, -0.991302)

Battle of Pointe du Hoc
6 to 8 June 1944

Pointe du Hoc was a sharp arrow's point aimed directly at the heart of the American invasion. The geographic structure and positioning of this small piece of chalk cliff presented the Germans a strategic position for the installation of heavy field guns that could strike at potential Allied landings either to the east or to the west. The cliff point offered unequalled observation over English Channel shipping or an approaching invasion fleet.

The Germans saw the advantages and installed a battery of six French-made 155-mm guns, which had a range of over 20,000 yards (18 kilometers or 11 miles). The guns were placed in open positions to permit a 360-degree firing arc; however, Allied air superiority forced the Germans to begin construction of re-enforced concrete casemates to protect guns as exposed as those at Pointe du Hoc.

The Allies had to eliminate the risk that the guns presented to the entire American invasion force. Pointe du Hoc was bombed by the Ninth Air Force on 15 April, 22 May, and again of 4 June. Giving it any more attention risked compromising the invasion. Although it dropped a total of 3,264 bombs, the level of destruction wrought by the bombings was uncertain. The only way to assure that the long range guns could not jeopardize the invasion required that troops occupy the position, whereby a *coup de main* became necessary. Still, Pointe du Hoc was not an easy target. Near vertical cliffs lined the seafront. Two machine gun emplacements topped the eastern cliffs with at least two others on the inland boundary of the fortified zone. Three 37-mm FlaK emplacements occupied concrete shelters. Old 240-mm artillery shells, suspended along the steep seaside gradients, rolled down the incline when triggered and exploded with devastating effect. The point was enclosed on the landward side by mine fields and barbed wire. The fortified area held eighty-five men of the II Battery, Artillery Battalion 1260, and one hundred twenty-five infantry from I Battalion, Grenadier Regiment 726, organized as WN-75.

The 2nd Ranger Battalion was an elite, all-volunteer US Army organization formed in spring 1943 for just such operations. The battalion, under command of Lieutenant Colonel James E Rudder, was to land by sea below the 30-meter-high cliffs, scale to the top, engage the enemy, and destroy the guns. After the guns had been neutralized, the Rangers were to move inland and cut the coastal road connecting Grandcamp and Vierville-s/Mer. The Rangers were to then wait for re-enforcements from 5th Ranger Battalion. For this specialized assignment, the Rangers had trained using free ropes, toggle ropes[14] and tubular ladders. Four DUKWs had been specially adapted to mount London Fire Brigade ladders capable of reaching the 30-meter heights.

As an important part of the plan, the larger Ranger Force C, composed of 5th Ranger Battalion and two additional companies of 2nd Ranger Battalion, would remain at sea to await word of the attack's success. If the code word had not been received by H+30 minutes, the larger group would land behind the 116th Infantry Regiment at Vierville-s/ Mer and proceed overland to Pointe du Hoc.

---

14   Toggle ropes: ropes with evenly spaced, spring-loaded bars that release after the rope is extended and that can be used as foot steps to assist with the climb.

Objective	To silence the heavy artillery located on the Pointe du Hoc
Forces	
American	Companies D, E, and F, 2nd Ranger Battalion (Lieutenant Colonel James E Rudder)
German	Elements of I Battalion, Grenadier Regiment 726 and II Battery, Coastal Artillery Battalion 1260 (Oberleutnant Brotkorb)
Result	Although the guns had been relocated by the Germans, they were found and destroyed.
Casualties	
American	81 killed and 54 wounded of a total force of 225 men
German	unknown
Location	Bayeux is 30 km northwest of Caen; Pointe du Hoc is 30 km northwest of Bayeux

Battle

The men of Colonel James Rudder's D, E, and F Companies, 2nd Ranger Battalion, were transported by ten LCAs designated to land at 0630; however, like much of the invasion plan, events proved different. One LCA sunk in the heavy seas, its men were picked up and eventually returned to England. As luck would have it, navigation gear failed, and in the dim morning haze the British gunboat leading the mission confused Pointe de la Percée with the intended target and was leading the entire force to the wrong location. Col Rudder recognized the error and forced his boat to veer west. The others followed, but the lost time presented severe repercussions.

In their three-mile run from Pointe de la Percée to Pointe du Hoc, the slow moving craft sailed abreast of the German guns. One of the four DUKWs was badly damaged and remained offshore, dead in the water. The force reached the point thirty-eight minutes late – all on the eastern side, not spread on both sides of the point as originally planned. The late arrival cancelled the element of surprise. The three remaining long-ladder DUKWs stalled among the bomb craters on the beach and proved to be useless. The ropes shot from mortars were too wet to reach the top, but hand-held rope grenades sufficed, and men climbed the near vertical surface hand-over-hand. As the Rangers started their ascent, they faced hand grenades dropped from above, whereupon the USS *Satterlee* raked the cliff edge with its 5-inch guns. An explosion of an artillery shell suspended from the cliff face (or perhaps naval fire) caused a collapse of the chalk cliff face and created a 12-meter debris pile at the foot of the cliff. Using the pile and connecting sections of 3-meter-long ladders, the first man climbed over the lip of the cliff. Others quickly followed.

The first troops found few defenders and in thirty minutes all of the Rangers had scaled the slope. By 0730 the coded message indicating that the Rangers were up on the cliff was sent to no response. The maneuver appeared almost too easy – and it was.

The assault was too easy because the heavy field guns were gone. The concrete casemates were not yet finished. German gunners had moved the cannon farther inland. The gun emplacements held only decoy guns fashioned from wooden poles.

Small Ranger groups fanned across the point searching out their objectives and returning scattered German fire. The shell and bomb craters offered excellent cover for the fast-paced advance despite sniper fire from enemy troops hidden among the trenches and tunnels. Movement across the fortified area was swift because German infantry had been oriented for landward attack, determining that the steep cliff precluded a sea-borne attack. Groups of Rangers crossed the fortified area and achieved the coastal highway by 0815. Although, the Germans also retained possession of a Flak position 300 meters to the west.

Patrols were sent out to search for the big guns, which were discovered in an apple orchard south of the coastal highway and quickly destroyed. The Rangers had accomplished their mission, but the real threat to them was just materializing. The repercussions of the thirty-eight minute delay in reaching the point were now felt.

The local German command had been active. By midafternoon, the Germans had reorganized and their artillery and mortar rounds pounded the fortified area. A German machine-gun squad launched a counterattack from the direction of St-Pierre-du-Mont. They were ambushed by a Ranger BAR team and finished off by Ranger mortars. Changes in assignments released a company of I Battalion, Grenadier Regiment 914, to add their firepower to the Pointe du Hoc garrison's counterattack.

As evening approached, only Lt Parker's twenty-man platoon from 5th Rangers had arrived. By night, Rudder had only eighty men south of the coastal highway in an 'L'-shaped formation. Two-man outposts fronted the main line of resistance. Mortar and grenade ammunition was almost exhausted, and rounds for automatic weapons were in short supply. The Rangers, then, started to use German weapons.

From midnight on, the Germans launched three attacks against the forward line, each coming from the southwest. Each attack included heavy use of mortars, grenades, and machine guns. The third attack at 0300 was the strongest and started to roll up Company E's line. Nineteen Rangers were killed or captured. Confusion reigned as friend and foe became intermixed in the darkness, made worst by both sides using weapons that sounded

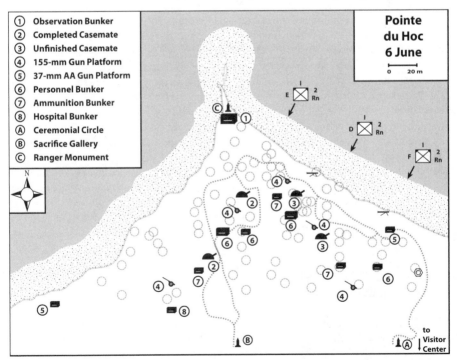

alike. Rudder ordered the men to fall back.

By dawn on 7 June, Rudder commanded only ninety men occupying a strip of Pointe du Hoc running between #3 and #5 gun positions. Rudder's men were heartened by the arrival of sixty men from 5th Ranger Battalion who had been transported by ship from Omaha Beach. More importantly they brought supplies of water and ammunition and evacuated the seriously wounded. For most of the day, naval fire kept the Germans at bay as Rudder's men awaited further re-enforcements.

A mixed unit of 250 infantry and Rangers from St-Laurent was assigned to re-enforce Rudder. Eight tanks from 743rd Tank Battalion added their firepower to the relief force. By noon, continuing toward Pointe du Hoc from St-Pierre-du-Mont, two tanks succumbed to minefields. When the men got within 800 meters of the fortified zone, the force came under heavy German artillery fire. As the tanks retreated to Vierville-s/Mer, the men dug in around St-Pierre.

A significantly stronger force assembled on 8 June with the entire 5th Ranger Battalion, all of the reduced 116th Infantry Regiment, and two companies of tanks. The Germans quickly gave way to the vastly superior force, and by noon the linkup was accomplished. Three days later, 2nd Ranger Battalion was in V Corps reserve.

Battlefield Tour

From the large roundabout on the Grandcamp-Vierville coastal road (D514), proceed north on the Pointe du Hoc approach road (rue Talbot) to the visitor center's large parking area befitting the enormous number of visitors to be found here at any time of the year. (49.393288, -0.986538)

Pointe du Hoc Visitor Center
Normandy American Cemetery   14710 Colleville-s/Mer
Tel: +33 (0)2 31 51 62 00

In 1979 the land was ceded by the people of France to the Unites States government in gratitude and in perpetuity. Since then, Pointe du Hoc has been maintained by the American Battle Monuments Commission. It is without question the best preserved Second World War battlefield in Europe. Unfortunately, although manned during the day, the visitor center offers little in the way of interpretative materials, but it does display the memorial plaque to Col Rudder[15] that once hung in the observation bunker. Another memorial plaque lists the names of all those killed during the assault. Considering the remote location of Pointe du Hoc, the restrooms are a welcome relief.

Open daily April through September from 09:30 to 13:00 and from 14:00 to 18:00; open Friday, Saturday and Sunday, October through March from 10:00 to 13:00 and from 14:00 to 17:00.

The Pointe du Hoc battlefield holds no signs or informational panels other that the one directly outside of the Visitor Center. The site and restrooms are accessible even when the center is closed. Although entering the bunkers and climbing around the craters

---

15   Lieutenant Colonel James E Rudder, wounded twice during the Pointe du Hoc fighting, was one of the most decorated soldiers of the Second World War, receiving the Distinguished Service Cross, Legion of Merit, Silver Star, *Légion d'honneur*, Croix de Guerre and Palm, and Order of Leopold (Belgium), among other awards. He retired from the US Army Reserves as a Major General. After the war he became President of Texas A&M University. Rudder died in 1970 at age 60.

can be tricky, a great deal of this site is wheelchair accessible by staying on the stone path. Touring the entire 30-acre site takes at least one hour.

Alongside the crushed stone path toward the battlefield, a **Ceremonial Circle** holds a 120-degree-arc of bronze plaques in French and English honoring the D-Day landings and displaying a top secret diagram of the German gun locations.

Passing the last shrubbery and gaining the first view of the battlefield is always a shock. The terrain still displays the results of the pre-invasion bombings and D-Day shelling. Craters cover the landscape in an interlocking pattern that leaves little of the flat, level earth of the original field. The German installations have been retained in their ruined state. The battle site remains strewn with blocks of concrete and sections of reinforcing wire with only grass and rain softening the edges of the bomb and shell craters. Although difficult to determine from the several and varied piles of broken concrete, visitors will find only two completed casemates for the six guns, uncertain if those two had ever been installed. The ruins of underground troop and ammunition shelters and trench lines that connected the various positions are still visible between the casemates and gun positions.

On the left, a **tobruk** where a FlaK gun was sited is filled with sand and soil, but at the time it was a position commanding the eastern approach to the installation. To the left and right of the path were once double rows of barbed wire. The ruins of **gun position #1** are 100 meters directly west. Its central platform held the 155-mm cannon and the niches in the surrounding wall held the gun's powder and projectiles.

Continue toward the cliff face to the substantial emplacement that held 37-mm FlaK guns. The **eastern Flak position** had been attacked three times on 6 June by Rangers without success. Finally it was silenced by the 5-inch guns of the destroyer *Satterlee* at 0837. Rudder established his command post in a shell hole under a partially collapsed German bunker. Though erosion has barred visiting Rudder's shell crater headquarters, the gun emplacement has been adapted for use as an observation platform for tourists and provides a beautiful view of the point, the Ranger Memorial, and the cliffs scaled by the three companies of 2nd Ranger Battalion. The troop quarters under the observation platform are accessible, but only with caution.

Continue along the seaside path that winds past large and small bomb craters and overlooks the cliff scaled by the assault teams. Two machine-gun emplacements were located among the coiled barbed wire that still lines the cliff edge. **Gun positions #2 and #3** are to the left and may be visited for closer inspection.

The concrete **observation bunker** (49.39722, -0.989306) stands at the point of the fortified zone. A boat section, led by Lieutenant Theodore Lapres,[16] made its assault on the tip of the point. Reaching the top, his troops faced the undamaged concrete observation post. German machine-gun fire from the OP slit met with three Ranger hand grenades. The machine gun went silent, but rifle fire continued until it met with a bazooka round through the slit.

The small force dashed around to the entrance on the landward side to find men from a different boat section attacking. Lieutenant Joseph Leagans'[17] small group had come up from the southeast. After driving a lone German into the bunker, it occupied a nearby shell hole, effectively sealing the OP. The standoff lasted until the next day when two

---

16   Lieutenant Theodore E Lapres was awarded a Silver Star; he stepped on a mine at Hill 400 in the Hürtgen Forest and lost a foot. He died in 1997.

17   Lieutenant Joseph Leagans was killed at Pointe du Hoc during the nighttime German attack upon the main defensive line south of the coastal highway.

satchel charges exploded against the entrance. Eight unwounded Germans surrendered; only one had been killed.

In 1944 the observation post was covered with rock, soil, and grass to make it almost indistinguishable from the surrounding terrain. Unfortunately, cliff erosion closed the bunker site for nine years; however, after successful stabilization efforts, the bunker site was reopened on 6 June 2011.

The inspirational granite dagger of the **Pointe du Hoc Ranger Monument** was erected by the French people and commemorates the assault of 2nd Ranger Battalion and the subsequent defense against repeated enemy attacks. Tablets at the monument's base note, in English and French, the heroism of the three Ranger companies and their commander who assaulted and took this point. Views toward Omaha and Utah Beaches are possible depending upon weather conditions.

The bunker is open to visitors. The stairway down to the entrance is guarded by two machine gun embrasures that made the metal door unapproachable by attackers. Inside the bunker are several rooms used for troops and communications equipment. The hardware attached to the walls held supports for bunks. The wooden beams supporting the roof are charred, thereby indicating some level of fire within the structure. The observation room holds an observation slit spanning 180 degrees, which provides a wide-angle view of the English Channel.

Behind the observation bunker, the enclosed casemate for **gun position #4** shows the effects of naval fire from destroyer USS *Satterlee* and battleship USS *Texas*. This casemate also provides an observation platform The intervening ground is spotted with large bomb craters.

Between the casemates for gun positions #4 and #5 – and only partially visible from the ocean – is a large troop, or ammunition bunker, that has a tobruk on the roof. Visitors may enter the structure from the protected back side down the cement stairs to view the machine gun ports covering the two entrances and two large interior rooms illuminated by single dim bulbs.

Continuing southerly, tourists will discover a huge crater containing enormous blocks of concrete immediately behind the **casemate for gun #5**. A munitions storage bunker located here had been detonated after the battle. An open-air **gun position #6** is behind the bunker and, behind it, a hospital bunker. One of the 155-mm coastal artillery guns has been relocated to a small field a short distance to the east.

At the far western edge of the fortified zone is a second **37-mm FlaK gun position**. The surrounding area is not nearly as crater-pocked, indicating that it did not receive the same level of attention from Allied bombers. A constant threat to the Rangers near the western gun pits, it remained the main German resistance point for two days. Apparently, the German battery commander had established his command post in that bunker. The rear of the structure shows some damage, demonstrating that it had been hit from the landward side, perhaps by tank fire. Like the first antiaircraft position, it has crew quarters underneath, but this position is more difficult to enter.

The straight path back to the parking area is known as **Sacrifice Gallery**, where personal stories are presented.

Return to the parking area and return along the approach road to the roundabout on the Grandcamp-Vierville Road (D514).

A small Ranger contingent took up positions 100 meters to the east to stop

German movement and communications between Grandcamp and Vierville-s/Mer. On the night of 6 June, the Rangers established a defensive line 200 meters down the farm track to the south. (We will visit the opposite end of the lane later in the tour.)

A second Ranger group took up similar positions 400 meters to the west. A line of shrubbery starts into a field to the south approximately 250 meters to the west of the roundabout. A two-man patrol of First Sergeant Leonard Lomell[18] and Sergeant Jack Kuhn[19] proceeded down this lane because it offered better cover than crossing open fields. Spotting fresh tracks in the soft earth, the men proceeded cautiously. After creeping forward 200 meters, they found the five guns aimed at Utah Beach in a camouflaged swale between hedgerows. They were unguarded although the gun crew was 100 meters away across an open field. Why the guns were left undefended was never determined, but the speed with which the Rangers advanced, despite their small number, may have been a factor. Kuhn stood guard as Lommel put thermite grenades in two of the guns' moveable gears. Lommel then smashed the sights on all five guns before returning to the western roadblock to gather more thermite grenades. Fortunately, thermite grenades are silent and, upon his return, the guns were still unguarded. Lommel and Kuhn destroyed the remaining weapons by placing grenades wherever they saw moving parts. The sixth gun was discovered and destroyed by a second patrol. A third patrol found the battery's powder supply along the hedgerow-lined lane and detonated it. By 0900 the heavy gun threat to the invasion was neutralized. They had not fired one shell.On 9 June the same orchard became the site of General Omar Bradley's first command post in France.

Note: The next instructions trace the area of the Ranger defense and complete the Ranger tour. With no visible remnants of the battle and the narrow and difficult roadway, it can be skipped if desired. The continuation of the 29th Infantry Division tour begins at the small bridge before Grandcamp-Maisy 2.3 kilometers to the west on highway D514. (49.389538, -1.019851)

Proceed 700 m west of the roundabout and turn south toward Cricqueville-en-Bessin (La Montagne) and follow the narrow country lane, (La Montagne) as it follows the shoulder of high ground overlooking the marshy Véret River valley to the south. After 800 m, the road approaches a farm complex that spreads across both sides of the lane. (49.384259, -0.996076)

On the left is a tree-shaded farm lane, which once continued to the coastal highway but no longer goes through. Coming from its opposite end, Lommel and Kuhn found the German guns along this lane. One can walk up the lane but it offers little to be seen. The

---

18   For his actions on D-Day, First Sergeant Leonard G 'Bud' Lomell was awarded a Distinguished Service Cross, the British Military Medal, and the French *Légion d'honneur*. He would later receive a battlefield commission and was awarded a Silver Star for his leadership in attacking Hill 400 in the Hürtgen Forest and a third Purple Heart. After the war he utilized the GI Bill to receive a law degree, opened a law firm in his native New Jersey, and became a community leader. He was honored by the residents of Grandcamp-Maisy with a monument in his home town of Point Pleasant, New Jersey. Lommel died in 2011 at age 91.

19   Staff Sergeant Jack E Kuhn was awarded a Silver Star as well as British and French awards. He ended the war as a First Sergeant. He served in the Marine Corps in the Korean War, after which he returned to his hometown of Altoona, Pennsylvania, where he eventually retired as chief of police. He died in 2002 at age 83.

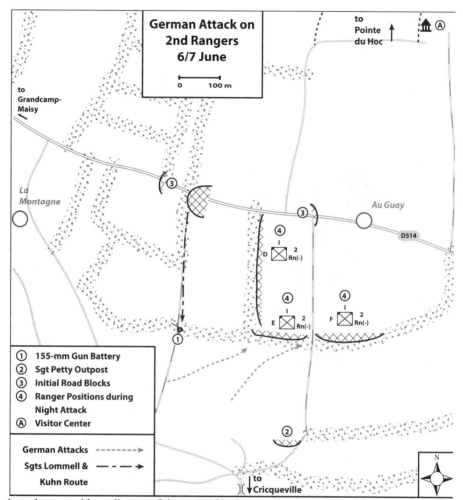

The map legend reads:

German Attack on
2nd Rangers
6/7 June

0   100 m

1 155-mm Gun Battery
2 Sgt Petty Outpost
3 Initial Road Blocks
4 Ranger Positions during
   Night Attack
A Visitor Center

German Attacks ----------->
Sgts Lommell & — — — →
Kuhn Route

lane does provide a glimpse of the type of hedgerow-lined fields so typical of Normandy, an impediment that became such a problem for advancing American troops in the weeks to come. The German attacks during the night of 6/7 June came from the southwest and fell against the Ranger main line of resistance formed approximately 200 meters to the north.

Continue 260 m to a small side road on the left (Le Callouet). Immediately ahead is a bridge over the narrow Veret River, and from there the road enters the lowlands. It may be appropriate to park here and walk 180 m up the hill to the sharp curve to the left where the pavement ends. (49.383847, -0.990368)

The side road sinks almost three meters below the fields as it climbs back up the hill. A Ranger outpost on the west side of the track near the lone farmhouse offered a natural defensive position and overlooked the road, bridge, and marshlands.

The outpost was manned by Sergeant William 'L-Rod' Petty. Petty had a clear field of fire over the valley to the south and the inland road that went to a 716th Infantry

Division battalion headquarters at Jucoville. The outpost became a death trap for German soldiers moving away from or around the Rangers' positions. Petty reportedly killed or wounded thirty Germans that day, with forty taken prisoner.[20]

The main defensive line occupied by Companies E and F, situated on an east/west line approximately 200 meters north of the outpost, marks the opposite end of the farm lane of the Ranger roadblock. One can walk up the lane, but little remains visible.

Side Trip: Colonel Rudder Memorial

For those with a special interest in Colonel Rudder, continue on la Montange for 700 m across the bridge and lowlands to the junction with highway D194. Turn toward la Cambe (D194) and continue 350 m to the church in Cricqueville-en-Bessin (49.377075, -1.000518) Total distance: 3.2 km
Otherwise return to the Grandcamp-Vierville road (D514) and proceed west to the small road bridge. (49.389538, -1.019851)

A **Memorial to Colonel Rudder,** erected in the 13th-century Église Notre-Dame de Cricqueville-en-Bessin, consists of a white marble plaque on an interior wall with the simple request: 'not to forget the American soldiers who risked and sacrificed their lives for you on the 6 June 1944.' A sea-green marble plaque with Colonel Rudder's profile in *bas-relief* stands above the plaque. Though, the church is frequently locked, a memorial service commemorates his leadership and sacrifice on the Sunday nearest the date of his death on March 23.

Follow D194 along the side of the church toward Grandcamp-Maisy for 1.9 km to the junction with the coastal highway (D514). Stop at the small bridge immediately to the right. (49.389538, -1.019851)

Securing the Beachhead
7 to 9 June 1944

The post-invasion zone of operation for the 29th Division was bound by the English Channel, the Vire River to the west, and the Aure River to the south. Both the Vire and Aure Rivers, moreover, had been blocked to create large flooded zones that restricted Allied movement to the few improved roads.

On 7 June, V Corps commander Major General Leonard T Gerow gave the 29th Infantry Division the mission to capture Isigny-s/Mer, the key to a link between the two American invasion beaches. The fishing village at the mouth of the Vire River became the prime objective of the division's recently landed 175th Infantry Regiment. The advance was supported by the two companies from the 747th Tank Battalion. The force was to proceed via Englesqueville, la Cambe, and Osmanville.

Generalleutnant Dietrich Kraiss, commander of the German 352nd Infantry Division, had committed all of his reserves. His mission was to delay the American advance until re-enforcements arrived from the French interior. With few exceptions, he ordered the bulk of his forces to withdraw south of the Aure River. One of the exceptions was the fishing harbor at Grandcamp-Maisy – known as Grandcamp-les-Bains in 1944.

---

20   Sergeant L-Rod Petty was to receive a Silver Star for his actions during the defense of the Ranger positions.

Objective	To establish linkage between the Omaha and Utah beachheads
Forces	
American	29th Infantry Division (Major General Charles H Gerhardt)
German	352nd Infantry Division (Generalleutnant Dietrich Kraiss)
Result	The mission was accomplished with the capture of Isigny-s/Mer
Casualties	
American	Uncertain
German	Unknown
Location	Bayeux is 30 km northwest of Caen; Grandcamp-Maisy is 33 km northwest of Bayeux

Battle

On the night of 7 June, the entire 175th Infantry Regiment left its assembly area at Gruchy in columns by battalion led by tanks of the 747th Tank Battalion. The troops followed a narrow gravel track southward until they encountered National Route 13 east of la Cambe, then followed the highway west toward Isigny-s/Mer. The 2nd Battalion peeled off to eliminate German guns at Cardonville while the leading 3rd Battalion marched through the night before halting in front of a mine field short of Isigny. With frank encouragement from General Gerhardt, the tanks and infantry moved forward and entered the town at 0300 on 9 June without opposition. By 10 June the leading units were crossing the flatlands of the Carentan estuary. The junction with airborne troops occurred at Auville-s/le-Vey.

After the relief of Colonel Rudder's force at Pointe du Hoc on 8 June, 2nd and 3rd

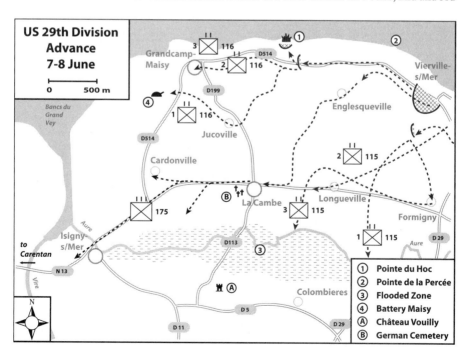

Battalions, 116th Infantry Regiment, continued west toward Grandcamp-les-Bains. The eastern approach was limited to the narrow coastal road because the area to the south was intentionally flooded by the Germans to act as an invasion barrier. Company I led the way into the town with the remainder of the two battalions following. The town was cleared by mid-afternoon.

The 1st Battalion, 116th Regiment, led by the tanks of Company A, 743rd Tank Battalion, moved against nearby Maisy by way of Jucoville through country empty of enemy troops. The approach into Maisy met with a strong enemy position west of the village from which the leading tanks received 88-mm antitank and mortar fire. The attack stalled for the night. The next morning the strongpoint was bombarded by the 58th Armored Field Artillery Battalion, but it required two full days to clear out the enemy resistance. The 116th Infantry Regiment, badly reduced in manpower by losses on Omaha Beach, entered divisional reserve.

Battlefield Tour

The coastal highway crossed the Véret River over a small bridge east of Grandcamp. The bridge was left intact by the Germans, but between the town and the bridge, the Germans had established WN-78 based upon two concrete pillboxes near the coastal cliffs which had extensive fields of fire from their higher ground. The leading 5th Rangers were stopped at the bridge lacking the heavy weapons necessary to deal with the enemy positions. British cruiser HMS *Glasgow* added some weight to the attack by firing on the town, but it avoided the resistance nest due to the proximity of friendly troops.

In late afternoon Companies K and L, 3rd Battalion, 116th Regiment, resumed the attack strengthened by tanks from the 747th Tank Battalion. One tank was lost to a mine, but the 3rd Battalion rushed across the bridge ignoring the mines. They were met by bursts from machine guns. Rifle and tank fire mixed with machine guns and mortars fueled a wild skirmish. The German strongpoint could not be overcome until Sergeant Frank Peregory crept into an abandoned German trench. He moved along the trench until he encountered the squad manning an MG 42. He rushed it while throwing grenades followed by rifle fire. He captured the three survivors and turned them over to members of his squad. Not satisfied, he repeated the process, eliminating a second machine-gun nest and capturing thirty-two more prisoners.[21]

The small bridge over the **Véret River** can easily be missed because the structure and the water it crosses are relatively inconsequential. The positions attacked by Sgt Peregory lie in the field to the north approximately even with the town sign where two accumulations of bushes and brambles are visible. The top of one pillbox is readily recognizable; a second pillbox is closer to the cliff and has been mostly destroyed and hidden by vegetation. One of three tobruks remains in the field while a second tobruk clings to the seaside cliff edge. Depending upon the season, the field can be crossed, but offers little in return to encourage the effort.

Proceed 800 m to the large Peace Park in Grandcamp-Maisy. (49.387932, -1.031116)

---

21   Sergeant Frank Peregory received a Medal of Honor for his lone attack. He was killed six days later and never knew of the award. He is buried, with great honor, in Normandy American Cemetery.

Grandcamp-Maisy

Grandcamp-Maisy became one of Normandy's best known beaches during the Belle Époque (1880 – 1930) when modern transportation permitted the residents of Rouen, Paris, and other cities to seek the invigorating sea air. The construction of villas and beach hotels followed. The First World War, the abandonment of the railway connections, and changing tastes led to the town's decline. A few of the elegant structures remain, and the town is still famous for its seafood restaurants.

Office de Tourisme de Grandcamp-Maisy

118, rue Aristide Briand   14450 GRANDCAMP-MAISY
Tel: +33 (0)2 31 22 62 44   Email: grandcamp.tourisme@ccigi.fr

The prominent feature in the Peace Park is a 10-meter polished metal sculpture of a woman entitled **'Statue de la Paix – Statue of World Peace'** surrounded by a well-landscaped garden dedicated in 2004. The statue was created by Chinese Artist Tao Yuan and donated by the Peoples Republic of China to commemorate the Pointe du Hoc battle. Its design is similar to others erected in Beijing, Korea, and Russia.

The **National Guard Monument** at the tip of the park commemorates the actions of Sgt Peregory in overcoming German resistance and his receipt of the Medal of Honor. The irregularly shaped stone was erected by the US National Guard Association.

The communal cemetery, hidden behind shrubs and a stone wall across the road from the Peace Memorial, lies around the ruins of the church, destroyed during the fighting in the area and never rebuilt. The cemetery contains the **grave of Commandant Philippe Kieffer**[22], the commander of the French contingent of No 4 Commando that landed at Sword Beach. The main cemetery entrance and large parking area is to the north on rue Gambetta. To find Kieffer's grave, pass through the large gate and proceed south into the cemetery. Commandant Kieffer is on the left with a magnificent granite tombstone flanked by flagpoles generally flying the British and French flags. (49.388624, -1.031508)

> Continue west on the coastal highway (D514) for 800 m; turn north on rue Docteur Boutrois (D199) and continue 85 m to the town hall. (49.387765, -1.041191)

A **Ranger Monument** in front of the *mairie* commemorates the capture and defense of Pointe du Hoc. The inscription, in French and English, reads: 'For no one is to forget the heroism of those men who defied the impossible for our freedom.' Prominent in the center of the curved cement bar is a grappling hook stuck into a piece of reinforced concrete representing the efforts made to climb the cliff.

Likewise, a stele commemorating a speech given by Général Charles de Gaulle upon his return to France on 14 June graces the garden in the place de la République to the right of the *mairie*.

---

22   Philippe Kieffer was born to an Alsatian family in Port-au-Prince, Haiti. After a formal education he entered banking in New York City. The day after the start of the war and despite his age, he volunteered for the French Navy and participated in events at Dunkirk. In 1941 he founded the French Commando unit that he was to lead. He participated in the Dieppe Raid of August 1942 among numerous raids into France and the Netherlands. After Normandy, the unit participated in attacks on various Dutch locations. Kieffer received numerous French military awards and the British Military Cross. He died in 1962 at age 63.

> Continue to the sea front promenade; the museum is 150 m west. (49.389133, -1.043798)

Musée des Rangers

Quai Crampon

Tel: (*mairie*): +33 (0)2 31 92 33 51

14450 Grandcamp-Maisy

E-mail: grandcamp-maisy@wanadoo.fr

This is one of the few museums that we have not toured. The displays are dedicated to the Ranger Battalions focusing upon the action at Pointe du Hoc. Some visitors comment that the displays and 18-minute Ranger film may be dated.

Open hours 15 February through 30 April from 13:00 to 18:00, closed Tuesdays; May through October from 10:00 to 13:00 and from 14:30 to 18:30, closed Tuesdays and Monday mornings. Admission fee; Normandie Pass accepted.

An **NTL Totem** stands outside of the museum.

> Continue 250 m farther west to the junction with Quai Henri Chéron.
> (49.389476, -1.047027)

The very prominent **French Heavy Bombers Monument** stands on the eastern side of the harbor right where the seafront road turns landward to go around the harbor. The three-meter gray and black stone commemorates the two French squadrons identified as Guyenne and Tunisie as part of the Royal Air Force's Bomber Command. They flew heavy bombers in the day and night destruction of Nazi Germany and the D-Day bombing of the nearby Battery Maisy. The cost was high as one of every two aircrew perished.

The three-story white building behind the monument served as the local Kriegsmarine headquarters. Today, it remains a private villa. Turning south along Quai Henri Chéron offers an opportunity to view a working French fishing port with its boats and fish market. The massive sluice gates maintain the water level in the harbor during low tide.

> Follow the road around the south end of the harbor, rejoining the coastal highway. Bear right onto rue du Joncal and continue for 450 m. Turn north on rue du Fort Samson and continue to the end. (49.390802, -1.056833)

The beachfront casemate of **WN-81** held a 50-mm cannon which could fire in either direction. Tobruks held two 25-mm FlaK guns, one machine gun, and a tank turret. The ruins stand on a small point which once was the site of Fort Samson,[23] designed by Vauban to guard the coast against English invasion. The casemate is gradually sinking into the beach sand as channel tides and currents slowly bury the concrete structure. While not the most visitable such site, its location demonstrates the thoroughness of German defenses for the port of Grandcamp.

> Reverse direction and continue south to the junction with the coastal highway. Turn southwest (right); after 650 m, turn right onto a narrow country lane (Les Perruques) where a temporary sign indicating Battery Maisy may or may not be present. (49.377487, -1.058759)

---

23   Fort Samson was the subject of an 1885 painting by Post-Impressionist artist Georges-Pierre Seurat.

1. The replacement Pegasus Bridge at Bénouville retains the design of the original, now in the museum nearby. A German antitank gun is positioned in the tobruk in the right foreground.

A Centaur tank stands opposite the Gondrée Café on the west end of Pegasus Bridge. The tank did not participate in the defense of the bridge but was part of the Royal Marine Commando Armoured Support Group that landed on 6 June. Its 95-mm howitzer was used effectively against German beachfront defenses.

2. The largest of the Merville Battery casemates now houses a museum containing artifacts of the engagement. A Douglas C-47 aircraft is partially visible behind the casemate.

A life-size Scottish piper commemorates the British 51st Division's participation in fighting in and around Bois des Monts.

3. The 'Flame' monument and memorial to the French Commandos under the command of Commandant Philippe Kieffer stands on Sword Beach in Ouistreham.

Statue of Field Marshal Bernard Law Montgomery in Colleville-Montgomery, below left.
The exhausted image of a Green Howard soldier presents the regiment's difficult combat on D-Day.
The statue stands at a road junction in Crépon, below right.

4 The Sundial Memorial commemorates the landing of No 41 Royal Marine Commando in Lion-s/Mer. A Churchill AVRE tank stands to the left rear. (left)

Memorial to the Royal Merchant and Allied Navies stands on Sword Beach in Hermanville-s/Mer (la Brèche). (below)

The command bunker or PC A at Hillman Battery is now known as Hunter Bunker. The bunker's armored cupola, to the right, was the only element above ground level. A machine-gun tobruk is centered above the two entryways.

5. Troops of Le Régiment de la Chaudière at a German machine-gun position in Bernières-s/Mer on 6 June. LAC

Troops of the Highland Light Infantry land on Nan White sector of Juno Beach at Bernières-s/Mer at approximately 1140 on 6 June. The tide-narrowed beach forced congestion of men and vehicles with only a single ramp constructed to surmount the seawall. LAC

6. German 50-mm antitank gun, which was part of WN-27
in St-Aubin-s/Mer as it appears today, above.
The same position was inspected by soldiers after its capture,
insert. IWM

Post-invasion wreckage of a P-47 fighter aircraft rests on
Juno Beach in St-Aubin-s/Mer. A disabled Sherman DD tank
was behind and to the right of the plane. US Air Force

7. Landing obstacles at Asnelles including steel-concrete hedgehogs, left center, and tetrahedra, left foreground. Arromanches-les-Bains is in the distance ,center). Photo by 1st Lt Albert Lanker, 10th Photo Reconnaissance Group on 6 May 1944. AHEC

Command and observation bunker of Longues Battery. Metal rods provide the only support for the reinforced concrete roof. The site is completely accessible athough changes to the terrain have limited sight lines from the observation level.

8. Wreckage of a floating concrete caisson rests in shallow water along the beach at Arromanches-les-Bains.

The village and harbor at Port-en-Bessin as viewed from the eastern headlands. The Vauban tower is visible, center. The western headlands are to the left in the distance.

9. Omaha Beach before E-3 draw as in appears today at high tide. The trees on the horizon locate Normandy American Cemetery. The 5th Engineer Special Brigade Memorial, center, stands upon a German pillbox. The obelisk on the horizon, left, is the US 1st Division Memorial.
An LCVP with troops from 1st Battalion, 16th Infantry Regiment, 1st Infantry Division during its approach to Omaha Beach. Note the plastic sheathed rifles and the boat team leader looking over the bow ramp, insert. NARA

Normandy American Cemetery holds 9,387 graves of service personnel who died in Normandy. The path on the right runs along the bluff edge overlooking Easy Red sector of Omaha Beach and was the location of the German trenchline.

10.   A memorial obelisk to the US 1st Infantry Division stands above WN-62 in the Colleville-s/Mer, or E-3, draw. The resistance nest's two tobruks and remnants of a concrete underground trench line are visible nearby.

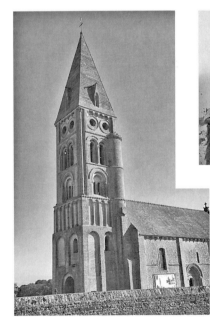

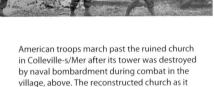

American troops march past the ruined church in Colleville-s/Mer after its tower was destroyed by naval bombardment during combat in the village, above. The reconstructed church as it appears today, left.

11.   A German soldier's view of the Omaha Beach invasion is shown in this captured personal photo. The water plumes are from explosions of Nebelwerfer rockets. The broad sand beach indicates that the photo was taken early on D-Day. Belgian gates are clearly visible as is the tangle of barbed wire in the foreground. The exact location is uncertain but it is believed to have been Dog White sector. Solonieff Collection, AHEC

D-1 draw at Vierville-s/Mer retains the resistance nest's two waterfront casemates. The left casemate now supports the US National Guard Memorial. Taken at high tide, the photo shows the complete absence of beach before the seawall. The headlands held additional strongpoints and the modern building seen on the high ground to the left was partially constructed upon a German bunker.

12.   The cliffs at Pointe du Hoc that were scaled the three companies of US 2nd Ranger Battalion. The dagger-like stone pillar of the Ranger Memorial stands upon the roof of the German observation and fire control bunker.

German 270-mm artillery shells were suspended along the cliff side as defensive munitions, as shown in the photograph on the right. NARA

The shell-pocked terrain of Pointe du Hoc displays the intensity of the Allied air and naval bombardments, below. The myriad of depressions, trenches, and underground bunkers offered the enemy a multitude of defensive positions during the two day engagement.

13. The Manoir de la Fière and the unassuming Merderet River bridge as viewed from the causeway into the western setting sun. The manoir retains much of its 1944 appearance when compared to the insert photograph taken shortly after the battle. The heavily damaged structure to the upper right on the 1944 photo was demolished and not replaced.

The central memorial in the US 507th Parachute Infantry Regiment's park in Amfreville, right.

Three stones that commemorate the engagement at Timmes Orchard and the paratroopers who fought there stand before a replanted Timmes orchard, below.

14.   One of two German Sturmgeschütz 40 destroyed as the self propelled guns approached Ste-Mère-Église by a 57-mm antitank gun of Battery A, 80th AA Battalion. The second StuG 40 is visible in the distance along the road to Neuville-au-Plain. NARA

Paratroopers take aim at a sniper in the tower of the church in Ste-Mere-Église. The riflemen appear rather casual in what may have been a photograph staged after the event, below left. NARA
A comparable scene as it appears today showing how little has changed since 1944, except for the removal of the foreground structure, below right.

15. Numerous memorials to men of the US 101st Airborne Division are to be found on its Normandy battlefields. Shown are those at Champ de Hancock, upper left, to the defense of the 'Cabbage Patch' by Company C, 502nd PIR; at Beuzeville, upper right, to paratroopers and airmen who died in a plane shot down early on 6 June; at Brécourt Manor, lower left, to the men of Company E, 506th PIR who destroyed four German guns firing upon Utah Beach; and at Les Moulins, lower right, where 3rd Battalion, 506th PIR and Company C, 326th Engineer Battalion denied Douve River crossings to the enemy.

The church in Angoville-au-Plain where medics Robert Wright and Kenneth Moore, 501st PIR, treated wounded Americans, Germans and civilians alike during a ferocious three-day battle for the village. The church's window commemorating the 60th anniversary of the event is shown in the insert.

16.   Bridge #1 over the la Jourdan River shows the character of the original four bridges along Purple Heart Lane into Carentan. It has been preserved as it was in 1944. The other three bridges have been replaced by modern highway structures.

American soldiers, probably 101st Airborne Division paratroopers, relax after the battle around Carentan's war memorial in the place de la République, below left. Archivesnormandie 39-45
The Signal Monument in Carentan pays special tribute to the 101st Airborne Division for its liberation of the town, below right.

Battery Maisy

Route des Perruques   Grandcamp-Maisy
Tel: +33 (0)67 80 45 6 25   Email: gary@maisybattery.com
Web: http://www.maisybattery.com/home.html

Until just a few years ago Battery Maisy, or WN-83, was an unknown but it is now a highlight of this part of the tour. Historical investigation of German military maps by Englishman Gary Sterner determined that a major militarized zone had once been on this land. He reasoned that it had been buried shortly after the battle to prevent reoccupation by German forces. There it lay for sixty years until unearthed. Sterner bought the land and has been slowly uncovering its past. Its history is open to much speculation, but it offers visitors the rare opportunity to witness a German strongpoint that has not been destroyed by war or weather.

Originally the 44-hectare site held six French Schneider 155-mm Model 1917 howitzers – four in gun pits and two open-air, all manned by the 9th Battery, Artillery Regiment 1716, 716th Division. The site included three underground personnel bunkers, command bunker, and an underground field hospital. It was protected by minefields, barbed wire, and twelve 88-mm FlaK guns. This strongpoint and a second, WN-84, only 650 meters farther on this road, were capable of shelling Utah Beach, Pointe du Hoc, and even Omaha Beach at the extreme limit of the guns' range. These guns were probably responsible for much of the artillery fire on Rudder's force on Pointe du Hoc.

The installation was attacked on 9 June from the east by Companies A, C, and F of 5th Ranger Battalion supported by heavy mortars and armored half-tracks of the Rangers' 2nd Battalion and elements of the 29th Infantry Division. It was captured only after a five-hour battle that raged through its trenches.

Only one-third of the installation has thus far been uncovered, with a number of positions still buried under the landscape. The tour is self-guided and follows a 1.5 kilometer trench line giving visitors a unique opportunity to walk around the site and enter bunkers and tunnels. The gun positions hold later version 150-mm German howitzers, not their original French guns. This relatively new site is a must-see.

Open daily from Easter to 1 November; hours vary. Admission fee; Normandie Pass accepted.

The coastal ground west and south of Grandcamp overlooked entrances to the Grand Vey waterways and marshlands. In the communes of Grandcamp-Maisy and Géfosse-Fontenay, the Germans built WN-84 through WN-92. Although ruins of most strongpoints remain, those nearest the water are slowly being reclaimed by the sea. Most are on private land, and many offer little interest except to the most ardent 'bunker hunter.' Battery Maisy is far superior in every criterion.

Return to the coastal highway and turn northeast. After 250 m, turn toward la Cambe (D113a, becomes D113). After 4 km the highway turns south and becomes very straight.

The flat land in either side of the highway provided excellent locations for Allied airfields, and memorial stones beside the narrow country lanes mark several such sites. The **354th Fighter Group** based in la Grande Lande to the northeast; a stele to **Airfield A2** identified les Vignets to the east, and a stele to **Airfield A3** marks the junction of D199 and D199a to the west.

> After a total 5.7 km from Maisy, turn east toward la Cambe (D613). After 800 m, turn south toward Monfréville/Vouilly (D113 again). Follow the signs to Cimetière Militaire Allemand along the E46/N13 frontage road going west. (49.34309, -1.026728)

La Cambe German Military Cemetery is the largest of its kind in Normandy and holds the graves of 21,222 German soldiers, the vast majority of the bodies from the Normandy fighting between 6 June and 20 August 1944. La Cambe was originally established on 11 June 1944 as the 29th Infantry Division cemetery. By its dedication on 23 July, five days after the liberation of St-Lô, the cemetery held 2,000 dead from the division. German war dead were buried in adjacent fields by the American Graves Registration Service. In 1945, the Americans were relocated to Normandy American Cemetery. After an agreement with the French government in 1954, la Cambe became an accumulation cemetery for over 12,000 soldiers buried in fields and churchyards. It is one of the six permitted German war memorials in Normandy.

The six-meter-high mound in the center, topped by granite cross and solitary figures, is a mass grave for 296 bodies. Scattered throughout the cemetery grounds are clusters of five stone crosses, which are not grave markers but common German military cemetery memorials. The graves are identified by stones set at ground level. Among the well-known German soldiers buried here is Tiger tank ace Hauptsturmführer Michael Wittmann.

The **Information Center and Peace Garden** is located across the parking area. Established in 1996, the objective of the information center's trilingual exhibits is to show what war does to the people of all countries and especially to the civilian population. Computer kiosks permit searching for the name and location of every American, British, and German soldier buried in Normandy and the names of all French civilian war victims. An adjacent grove of 1,200 Maples trees was planted as a Peace Garden and is intended to send a signal for peace.

The cemetery is open daily from 08:00 to 19:00; the Information Center open daily from 08:00 to 12:00 and from 13:00 to 19:00.

> Return to the autoroute intersection, cross over the Autoroute (E46/N13), and continue into la Cambe to the junction with old National Route, now renumbered D613. Turn west and proceed 2.7 km to the junction with highway D199. (49.342796, -1.043766)

Just before dark on 8 June, the 175th Infantry Regiment commander, Colonel Paul Goode, being pushed by Generals Gerhardt and Cota to move more quickly into Isigny-s/Mer, started his unit along this road. Ahead on the right and hidden behind a wall of shrubs lies Arthenay, a small village comprised of a few houses and horse barns. The Germans had established a delaying team ambush in the stout stone walls of these buildings. Using several machine guns and a hidden 88-mm antitank gun, they ambushed the leading units of the column. After the loss of six tanks, the Americans spotted the 88-mm gun and knocked it out. The remaining German forces retreated as tracer bullets ignited the barns.

Continue west (D613) and follow it into Isigny-s/Mer. For a faster route, enter the limited access National Route 13 (E46) exiting on D197a to regain D613. Cross over the triple-arched Aure River Bridge and proceed to the central square. (49.318482, -1.101277)

Isigny-s/Mer

Isigny-s/Mer controls the bridges over two rivers: the Aure, which runs immediately east of the town, and the Vire, a major river in Lower Normandy which runs 3.5 kilometers west of the town. Both rivers follow canalized banks to flow into the Banc de Grand Vey and thus into the English Channel. Before the construction of sluice gates and dikes, the town could become virtually surrounded by water. Its location promoted it as a fishing harbor, commercial center, and defensive point. Today Isigny is known for its dairy and cheese production, and it is now a market town with most tourist conveniences.

Isigny was occupied on 7 June by the German *Ostbattalion* 621 manned by Mongolian POWs under German officers and NCOs. As they approached the town, the 29th Division called in Allied bombing and naval gun fire to force the enemy from the town. The bombardments set the town center on fire, and the city was 60 percent destroyed.

Office de Tourisme Intercommunal d'Isigny – Grandcamp
(49.319129, -1.100553)
16 rue Emile Demagny   14230 Isigny-s/Mer
Tel: +33 (0)2 31 21 46 00   Email: isigny.tourisme@ccigi.fr

The only way into Isigny from the east was the Aure River bridge. Inexplicably, it was not destroyed by the retreating Germans. When American troops entered the city at 0430 on 9 June, they found that the main body of enemy troops had withdrawn, but it took several hours to rid the town of numerous machine-gun nests and snipers. Over 200 prisoners were taken.

The central square presents another **Signal Monument** and **NTL Totem** at its eastern end. The large stone commemorates the speech made by général Charles de Gaulle to the people of the town on 14 June 1944. An inscription added on the 25th Anniversary of the invasion bears homage to the valiant Allied liberators.

A plaque honoring the **29th Infantry Division, 175th Infantry Regiment,** and **747th Tank Battalion** hangs on the rear wall of the 13th-century Église St-Georges, which is 170 meters west of the Signal Monument. The plaque memorializes the link between the American and French people in their mutual move of liberty. Only one of the church's stained glass windows survived the bombings. The windows have been slowly restored, as has much of the destroyed church, with one window bearing the 29th Division's 'ying-yang' insignia. (49.317293, -1.102313)

Leave Isigny toward Carentan (D613) and stop at the Vire River Bridge. (49.308665, -1.14011)

Company K had been ordered to cross the Vire River to seek a link with American troops from Utah Beach. The **Vire River bridge** had been blown by the Germans, and its opposite shore was lined with barbed wire. Although machine guns offered some resistance, it was half-hearted, and the infantry crossed using rubber boats. On 10 June, elements of the 175th Regiment including the 29th Division Reconnaissance Troop made contact with members of the 327th Glider Infantry Regiment north of Catz 6.5 kilometers west of Isigny and 2.7 kilometers south of Brévands. The Utah and Omaha beachheads were now linked, and a major phase of the invasion in this sector of Normandy was completed.

So ended the Omaha Beach segment of the 29th Infantry Division's story. More hard fighting was yet ahead for the division whose battlefields are further presented in Chapter Eleven (Battle of St-Lô). The tour of D-Day invasion sites continues in Chapter Seven in Ste-Mère-Église, 20 kilometers to the northwest.

Continue for 5.0 km on highway D974, then enter the Autoroute (N13/E46). After 14 km exit and follow the signed into the town. (49.408488, -1.316804)

Chapter Seven
US 82nd (All-American) Airborne Division
6 to 10 June 1944

In northwest Normandy the Cotentin Peninsula, a 40-kilometer-wide finger of land, extends into the English Channel and points directly at England's southern coast. The terrain is mainly orchards and dairy pastures, and the major shipping port of Cherbourg lies on its north coast, only 130 tantalizing kilometers from Portsmouth, England. The peninsula is isolated from the rest of Normandy by the marshy terrain of the Marais du Cotentin.

The objective of American assault forces was to cut off and capture the Cotentin Peninsula by landing on the sandy beach of la Madeleine (code-name Utah), north of mud flats formed by the estuaries of the Douve and Vire Rivers and driving across the base of the peninsula. Allied planners considered the German Army's well-regarded aptitude in launching rapid counterattacks as the most serious threat to success. The denial by American forces of the strategic transportation routes for a German counterstrike was critical to the success of the amphibious landing. Thus, two American airborne divisions assumed the task of blocking or at least delaying the expected counterattacks, an effort which required the largest parachute drop in history – into enemy-held territory and at night. Theirs was a high risk gamble, but then so was the entire invasion plan.

The Merderet River, a 36-kilometer-long tributary of the Douve River, flows predominantly north and south approximately 8 kilometers inland from Utah Beach. As they had in many lowland areas of Normandy, the Germans had closed drainage gates to inundate the marshy banks of the river, creating a water barrier ranging from 1 meter to 5 meters deep and spreading up to 1.5 kilometers wide. Few roadways traversed the marshy area before the war; the bridges across the Merderet River at la Fière and Chef-du-Pont and their respective causeways crossing the flooded areas were tactical objectives for the Allies. Whoever controlled this ground controlled access to Utah Beach. The German Army could not be allowed to bring its armored units against the vulnerable landing forces. The market town of Ste-Mère-Église was the key since it sat astride the Route Nationale 13 – the Cherbourg-to-Bayeux highway – and the main north-south transportation artery of the Cotentin Peninsula.

Besides flooding the lowlands, the Germans had installed wooden poles in high ground pastures to destroy landing aircraft. The main defensive weapon, however, was the land itself – the bocage, Normandy's centuries-old maze of small pastures and orchards divided by impenetrable 1- to 2-meter-high walls of vegetation that offered stubborn defenders a myriad of ambush opportunities. Anticipating the possibility of an Allied airborne assault in the area and to augment the rather weak local infantry units, the German 91st Airlanding Division, a unit specially trained to repel airborne assaults, was stationed in the highlands west of the Merderet.

An experienced unit, the 82nd Airborne Division had distinguished itself as a fighting force in Sicily and Italy. After suffering heavy casualties, however, in the fierce engagements at Salerno and Anzio – where it earned a Presidential Unit Citation – the division was withdrawn from Italy in anticipation of the attack upon northern Europe. The 504th Parachute Infantry Regiment (PIR) was held in reserve while the highly-trained, but as yet untested, 507th and 508th PIRs and the 325th Glider Infantry Regiment (GIR) joined the experienced 505th PIR for the airborne assault. American parachute regiments each fielded three battalions plus special units totaling approximately 1,300 men. The glider regiment was similarly configured but slightly larger with a compliment of 1,700 men. American airborne battalions held three companies rather than the four companies of infantry battalions.

D-Day Landings
6 June 1944

Before midnight on 5 June, 378 C-47 transport planes left airfields near Nottingham, England, carrying the three parachute infantry units to their assigned targets. Their mission was vital to the success of the seaborne invasion at Utah Beach. The 505th PIR would land east of the Merderet River and capture the crossroad village of Ste-Mère-Église and the Merderet bridge at la Fière; the 507th PIR would land northeast of Amfreville to protect the northwest flank of VII Corps; the 508th would land near Picauville to seize and destroy the bridges across the Douve River at Étienville (a small village west of Pont l'Abbé) and Beuzeville-la-Bastille.

Objective	To secure the western flank of the Allied invasion and prevent a German counterattack against forces landing on Utah Beach.
Forces	
American	82nd Airborne Division (Major General Matthew Ridgway)
German	91st Airlanding Division (Generalleutnant Wilhelm Falley)
Result	All objectives achieved; enemy 91st Airlanding and 265th Infantry Divisions destroyed
Casualties	
American	1,142 killed; 2,373 wounded; 840 missing; and 1,081 non-battle casualties (totals to 8 July 1944)
German	1,500 killed; 2,189 captured (potentially understated as no credible statistics exist)
Location	Carentan is 75 km east of Caen; Ste-Mère-Église is 14 km northwest of Carentan

Battle

On 6 June, the first pathfinders landed at 0121 and set up beacons to identify three drop zones (DZ) for the main force, scheduled to arrive thirty minutes later. Despite these beacons, low cloud cover, intense German antiaircraft fire, and inexperienced pilots resulted in planeloads or sticks of eighteen men to be scattered across the southern Cotentin Peninsula. Many died from German fire or drowned after landing in flooded fields. Nevertheless, defying predictions of losses exceeding 75 percent, the paratroopers landed, found weapons and ammunition, coalesced into mixed units, and established leadership. Groups roamed the countryside trying to find their units, assembly points, and unit objectives, or, being completely lost, just caused havoc. Engagements with the enemy were mere skirmishes compared to the pitched battles that occurred later. These small unit actions, however, would determine the success or failure of the Allied invasion. As such, they grew in importance out of all relationship to the number of men involved.

At 0130, a battalion commander in the German 709th Infantry Division reported a large number of aircraft over his headquarters in St. Floxel, east of Montebourg. At

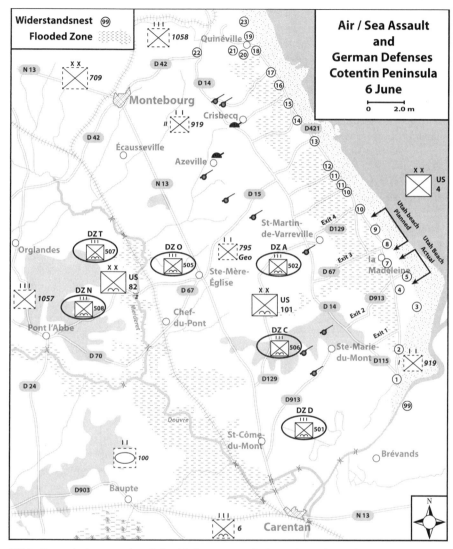

0215, Seventh Army ordered the highest state of alarm throughout the LXXXIV Corps sector, which included all of the invasion beaches. By 0300, Generalmajor Max Pemsel, Seventh Army chief-of-staff, had already concluded that the long-heralded invasion had begun and that he had correctly located the points of main effort near Carentan and Caen. The paratroopers' dispersed landing, however, yielded an unexpected benefit. Although it had warned German commanders of the impending attack, it also caused them to overestimate the size of the American force and created uncertainty regarding the objective. In fact, Generalfeldmarschall Gerd von Rundstedt (OB West commander), Generalfeldmarschall Hugo Sperrle (Third Air Force commander), and Generalmajor Dr Hans Speidel (Generalfeldmarschall Erwin Rommel's chief-of-staff) all disagreed with local commanders considering the paratroopers to be a diversion from the real landing farther northeast at Pas-de-Calais.

The 505th PIR benefited from its experience of combat jumps in Sicily and Italy. Most of its units landed near their intended DZ O. The other two regiments' drops were widely scattered, with some sticks being as far as 20 km from their intended DZ's. They started the battle where they landed, however, accumulating into larger and larger groups to take the fight to the enemy. One such small group of fourteen men, led by Lieutenant Malcolm Brannen,[1] encountered a German staff car speeding along the highway north of Picauville. The unit stopped the car with a burst of automatic weapons fire, killing all of its occupants, including the commander of the 91st Airlanding Division, Generalleutnant Wilhelm Falley.[2]

Ste-Mère-Église fell to the Allies, and furious enemy counterattacks from north and south were driven back. East of the village the bridge at la Fière was captured and held against heavy counterattack and artillery bombardments. The western end of the causeway was secured only after a furious charge into the teeth of German machine-gun and artillery fire. The lightly-defended bridge at Chef-du-Pont was taken and held against enemy armored attacks. Isolated groups at Hill 30 and Ferme Jules Jean were surrounded but, despite heavy casualties and shortages of ammunition, withstood enemy firepower.

Aftermath

By 10 June, despite stubborn resistance and heavy losses, the 507th and 508th had established a firm beachhead west of the Merderet River, and were eventually relieved by the 90th Infantry Division. Fighting north of Ste-Mère-Église continued for two more days until the 505th was also relieved.

The 507th PIR rejoined the battle on 14 June north of Picauville, where it and the 90th Infantry Division attacked to the west astride highway D15 and captured St-Sauveur-le-Vicomte in the Americans' first attempt to cut the Cotentin Peninsula. Due to the 90th Division's failure to advance, three battalions of the paratroopers were attacked on their exposed left flank near la Bonneville. The next day, the 505th PIR came out of reserve and passed through the 507th to continue the offensive toward St-Sauveur, which they captured on 16 June with the help of a massive time-on-target[3] artillery barrage.

The Allies needed a port to increase delivery of men and matériel to the growing beachhead. The limited supplies available were diverted to the units fighting north to capture Cherbourg; thus, the 82nd Airborne Division consolidated its positions and entered a period of light patrol activity. On 3 July, it began an offensive toward La-Haye-du-Puits, which sat astride the main north-south highway on the western side of the Cotentin, with an attack against Hill 131. Both Hill 131 and Hill 95 on the western end of the la Poterie Ridge were taken the next day.

Finally, virtually drained after thirty-three days of almost constant combat, with the men still wearing their jump uniforms and after suffering 46 percent casualties without replacements, the depleted 82nd Airborne Division entered Corps reserve on 8 July. It had effectively destroyed the German 91st Airlanding Division and the 265th Infantry Division as fighting forces, and satisfied all of their assigned objectives despite shortages

---

1   Lieutenant Malcolm Brannen (later Lt Col) survived the war and fought in Korea. He died in 1999 at age 88 and is buried in Arlington National Cemetery.

2   Generalleutnant Wilhelm Falley was the first German general officer to be killed during the Normandy landings.

3   Time-on-Target: artillery guns of different caliber and at different distances from the target adjust their firing times so that all of the shells reach the target simultaneously for a devastating effect.

of ammunition, food, and medical supplies. By 11 July, the survivors were returning to England.

Battle of Ste-Mère-Église
6 to 7 June 1944

Objective	To capture the important road junction
Forces	
American	2nd Battalion, 505th PIR (Lieutenant Colonel Benjamin Vandervoort)
	3rd Battalion, 505th PIR (Lieutenant Colonel Edward Krause)
German	Infantry Regiment 1058 (Oberst Kurt Beigang)
Result	Successfully captured the town and held it against repeated enemy attacks
Casualties	
American	186 killed; 656 wounded; and 111 missing (505th PIR casualties for the entire Normandy Campaign)
German	At least 414 killed; 408 captured
Location	Carentan is 75 km east of Caen; Ste-Mère-Église is 14 km northwest of Carentan

Battle

During the late evening of 5 June, a fire broke out in a house along the village square of Ste-Mère-Église, across from the church. The church bell announced the threat, and villagers organized a bucket brigade to bring water from the nearby town pump. The flames and bright moonlight illuminated the first of the American transport planes as they flew from west to east toward their drop zones. The noise aroused the German occupation troops, whose Luftwaffe Flak battery and machine guns poured shells at the apparitions in the sky. At 0151, 82nd Airborne Division paratroops were released over the village. The mortar squad of 2nd Platoon, Company F, 505th PIR, drifted helplessly beneath its canopies as the

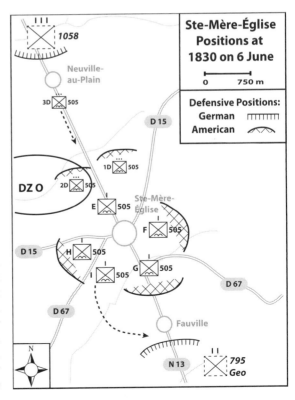

Ste-Mère-Église
Positions at
1830 on 6 June

0   750 m

Defensive Positions:
German
American

alerted enemy soldiers fired at the troopers. Most were killed before reaching the ground; many of the bodies remained suspended from their harnesses, the parachutes snagged on trees, telephone poles, and even the church steeple. One paratrooper actually drifted into flames of the burning building. A few misdropped members of the 101st Airborne's 506th PIR suffered the same cruel fate.

Elements of the 3rd Battalion, 505th PIR, landed southwest of Ste-Mère-Église. At approximately 0400, Lieutenant Colonel Edward Krause led 180 paratroopers along the Chef-du-Pont road (D67) and then into the village along the parallel rue des Écoles. Shortly before dawn, the German garrison returned to its beds, and the Flak battery inexplicably left. Colonel Krause ordered his men to attack with stealth, using mainly knives, bayonets, and grenades. The only rifle flashes were those of the enemy. A short engagement, in which ten German soldiers were killed and thirty captured, secured the town. The Allies located and cut the main German communications cable and mined the approach roads.

During the remainder of the early morning hours, groups of the regiment's 2nd and 3rd Battalions accumulated in the village, including the 2nd Battalion commander, Lieutenant Colonel Benjamin Vandervoort. Shortly after dawn, heavy German shelling hit Ste-Mère-Église from the III Battalion, Infantry Regiment 1058, stationed to the south near Fauville. At 1000, the attack stopped near the southern outskirts of the village courtesy of a single 57-mm antitank gun, which eliminated the German self-propelled (SP) guns. Whereas the German unit did not threaten the village again, it still occupied Hill 20 between Fauville and les Forges, overlooking Landing Zone (LZ) W. The next day German infantry destroyed many of the gliders transporting the reinforcing 325th GIR, causing numerous casualties.

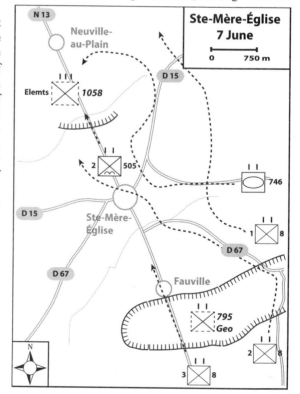

Over the next twenty-four hours, despite repeated artillery shelling, the hastily-assembled groups of paratroopers repulsed attacks by reinforced battalions of German infantry who had penetrated the outskirts of Ste-Mère-Église from the north astride the N13 highway. By midday on 7 June, infantry of the US 4th Infantry Division and the spearhead of the armored support force entered Ste-Mère-Église from the southwest along the Chef-du-Pont road after bypassing the Germans at Fauville. Generalleutnant Karl-Wilhelm von Schlieben, commanding the German 709th Infantry Division, withdrew most of his forces northward to defend Cherbourg, thus freeing units of the 82nd Division to join in the attack upon the causeway across the Merderet River.

Battlefield Tour

  The tour of 82nd Airborne Division battlefields starts in Ste-Mère-Église, the first objective of the American paratroopers and where tourist services for this sector of the Cotentin and an excellent museum are available. The wartime location of the Route Nationale 13 (N13) has been modified by construction of a limited access highway that bypasses Carentan yet still has the N13/E46 identification, causing some confusion. In 1944, the N13 followed the course of the now N2013, which still bears some old N13 road signs, from Carentan north though both St-Côme-du-Mont and Blosville and on to Ste-Mère-Église. The modern N13/E46 occasionally follows the same route, especially sections north of St-Côme-du-Mont.

> Exit N13/E46/E3 at highway D67 toward Ste-Mère-Église; however, at the first crossroads, continue straight onto rue de Richedoux and continue along rue général de Gaulle to the central square (place du 6 Juin) in front of the church. Park here and tour the village on foot. (49.4085, -1.3169) Enter the church. (49.408704, -1.316675)

Ste-Mère-Église

  Ste-Mère-Église is a typical Norman market town founded in the 11th century and which witnessed both the passage of William the Conqueror leaving for England in 1066 and Edward III's invading troops arriving in 1346 during the Hundred Years War. The town was occupied by the Germans on 18 June 1940 without a fight by a panzer division commanded by General Erwin Rommel. Today, with numerous memorials, shops, and restaurants catering to the needs of battlefield visitors, it records the events of 6 June 1944.

Office de Tourisme Communautaire de Ste-Mère-Église
6, rue Eisenhower   50480 Ste-Mère-Église
Tel: +33 (0)2 33 21 00 33
Web: http://www.sainte-mere-eglise.info/en/index.html

  The 12th-century chapel of Courtomer Abbey took four hundred years to become the gray stone parish church of Ste-Mère-Église. During the morning of 6 June, a German sniper fired at the gathering Americans from its massive square tower until troops rushed the church's entrance and killed the sniper.

  The church, renamed **Notre-Dame de la Paix**, displays two stained glass windows commemorating the battle. The larger window, above the door at the rear of the church, depicts the Virgin Mary and Christ Child above the burning village, with paratroopers landing on either side of her; the second window, in the north transept, was donated by Veterans of the 505th PIR and depicts Saint Michael, patron saint of paratroopers, surrounded with military emblems and commemoration dates of the battle.

  Leave the church and observe the southwest corner of the church tower. Private John Steele, in an incident made famous by the book and movie *The Longest Day*, saw the suspension lines of his parachute snag on the steeple of the church. He slid down the slate tiles and, feigning death, hung on the edge of the roof as the battle raged below. Temporarily deafened by the ringing church bell, he was discovered to be alive and was captured when

Germans in the tower went to search his body for papers. Steele escaped several days later.[4] The event is memorialized by the village each year by hanging a **uniformed mannequin suspended from the steeple** by a parachute. (49.408732, -1.31638)

Proceed across the square to the southeast to a hand pump along rue Traversiere, which runs behind the church. The large stone in the church square is apparently of Roman origin and marked the intersection of two Roman roads. (49.408729, -1.315795)

The hand-operated **water pump** used by the townspeople to fight the early morning fire is near the rear of the church. It stands under the trees that line the large square near what was once the local meat market – the same square whose trees held six lifeless bodies of troopers of Company F. Nearby is the first of **fifteen signboards** erected in the village that present a comparison of wartime images with today's appearance. The comparisons demonstrate how little the village has changed since 1944, and the period photographs bring to life the danger and destruction of the battle. Across the street from the pump, on what was the location of the burning building, stands a museum dedicated to airborne forces.

Musée Airborne (49.408434, -1.315366)

14 rue Eisenhower	Ste-Mère-Église
Tel: +33 (0)2 33 41 41 35	Email: infos@airborne-museum.org
Web: http://www.airborne-museum.org/	

The Musée Airborne (formerly Musée des Troupes Aéroportées), whose entrance is guarded by a US Sherman M4 tank, is one of the best in Normandy. Dedicated to the two American airborne divisions, it displays a significant collection of memorabilia in two specially-shaped buildings. One building shows the appearance of an open parachute and includes an original American Waco glider, which, along with the British-built, wooden Horsa glider, was one of two types used during the landings. The second building resembles a delta-style parachute and contains a C-47 (Dakota) transport, the military version of the civilian Douglas DC-3 airliner. The collections include countless personal effects, remembrances, and a 20-minute film describing the battle.

Open February through March, October through November, and during the Christmas holidays from 09:30 to 12:00 and from 14:00 to 18:00; April through September from 09:00 to 18:45. Admission fee; Normandie Pass accepted.

Leave the museum and turn left on rue Eisenhower back in the direction toward rue du général de Gaulle. The white-stone gate post at 4 rue Eisenhower bears a plaque to Private First Class Clifford Maughan and mortar squad of Company F, the first men to land in Ste-Mère-Église and who were either killed or captured in the effort. Pfc Maugham was luckier than his comrades, having been captured by a German officer who later surrendered to Maughan.[5] The house and courtyard are typical of the village during the battle. (49.408052, -1.316857)

Turn right at the intersection of rue Eisenhower and rue du Général De Gaulle. As shown in **signboard #7**, rue du Général De Gaulle was and still is the main street of Ste-

---

4   Private John Steele made four combat jumps: Sicily, Italy, Normandy, and Holland. He survived the war, achieved local notoriety for his D-Day exploits, and became an honorary citizen of Ste-Mère-Église. He died in 1969 at age 53.

5   Private Clifford Maughan survived the war. He died in 1990 at age 70 and is buried in the National Cemetery in California.

Mère-Église. Modern conveniences have changed the street slightly – mainly to allow for tourist traffic – but next-generation trees still surround the square and shade the sidewalk. With its current appearance, it is difficult to imagine how this thriving market town looked in 1944, with intermittent shelling and machine-gun bursts or with dead bodies on the ground and hanging from these trees. (49.408094, -1.317128)

Continue walking northwest along rue du général de Gaulle. The gray stone **Signal Monument** directly in front of the church reads, 'Here, on June 6th 1944, the heroism of the Allied Forces liberated Europe.' **Signboard #8** shows the threat of a German sniper hidden in the church tower and the soldiers detailed to eliminate him. (49.408495, -1.317388)

Continue on the opposite side of the street to the intersection of rue du général de Gaulle (D67, also rue Cap de Lainé) and rue de Verdun (D15, also rue Division Leclerc). This intersection formed the central crossroads of Ste-Mère-Église; thus, whoever possessed it controlled troop movement to or from the beaches to the east and between Cherbourg and Carentan. Looking down rue Division Leclerc (to the east) and comparing the building roof lines with the photograph on nearby **signboard #11**, one sees how little these buildings have changed. Although subjected to brief German shelling, the village did not experience the total destruction that other communities in Normandy suffered later. (49.408865, -1.318059)

Continue west to the Hôtel de ville. (49.409708, -1.318485) At 0630, Colonel Krause entered the **Hôtel de ville** and from an open window hung the same American flag that he had flown over the Main Post Office in Naples, Italy, signifying that the village was the first one in France to be liberated by American forces. The flag still adorns the inside of the building.

The small flag-ringed square in front of the building displays various memorials of the liberation. A memorial stele to **Generals Matthew Ridgway and James M Gavin**, commander and assistant commander, respectively, of the 82nd Airborne Division, is to the right. **Borne '0'** marks the beginning of the 1,446 kilometers Voie de la Liberté, the highway route between Normandy and Bastogne, Belgium, which follows the route of Lieutenant General George S Patton Jr's Third Army and, perhaps more important to the French, général Jacques-Philippe Leclerc's 2nd French Armored Division as it liberated France and Belgium.[6] Similar bornes dot every kilometer along the route and frequently are seen beside the highways. Behind the borne is a stele listing the names of the forty-five French civilians who died during the village's liberation.

> Return to your car and proceed northwest on rue du Cap de Lainé (D974, becomes Route de l'Église) for 2.6 km to Neuville-au-Plain. Do not enter the autoroute, but remain on the frontage road. Park near the church. (49.429649, -1.330107)

The 91st Airlanding Division headquarters received reports of widespread paratroop landings shortly after midnight. The I Battalion, Infantry Regiment 1058, was ordered to leave positions near Montebourg at 0230 and proceed against landings sighted near Ste-Mère-Église. The unit's commander, however, was slow to organize his troops and did not approach Neuville-au-Plain until noon.

On the morning of 6 June, a 41-man platoon of Company D, 2nd Battalion, 505th

---

6   The route extends from Ste-Mère-Église to Cherbourg, Avranches, St-Malo, le Mans, Chartres, Reims, Metz, Verdun, and Bastogne. A small separate route runs from Utah Beach to Ste-Mère-Église.

PIR, commanded by Lieutenant Turner Turnbull, hastened north to Neuville-au-Plain to block the Cherbourg road. Soldiers positioned themselves near the chateau on the north side of the hamlet and were strengthened with a 57-mm antitank gun which arrived later in the morning. A column of soldiers approached the crossroads on the N13 from the north, giving the appearance of being German prisoners guarded by a small number of American paratroopers. In fact, it was quite the opposite. The feint was detected, and a intense firefight broke out. Two German self-propelled guns were set afire by the antitank gun. The roadblock platoon, however, was grossly outnumbered and, as the German infantry worked its way around the unit's flanks, the paratroopers executed a fighting withdrawal. Radio contact was established with Colonel Krause, whose naval observer was able to call in a devastating bombardment from the battleship USS *Nevada*. The German attackers then withdrew, and the crossroad was abandoned by both sides, but Lt Turnbull's platoon had delayed the reinforced German regiment for an entire afternoon.[7]

Neuville-au-Plain is a quiet, old village with a stone chapel and the 18th-century Château Grandval at the intersection of highway D15e1 and the rue de l'Église. A **plaque** on the wall of the chateau garden across the road from the church commemorates the stopping of the German attack upon Ste-Mère-Église. Lt Turnbull had stationed his men facing north behind a hedgerow along the rural road past the chateau entrance to the west. His bazooka team and the 57-mm gun found some concealment from a nearby house. Other members of the forty-three-man unit were in an orchard on the west side of the N13, currently not accessible from this side of the highway. As 1st Platoon, Company E, provided covering fire, Turnbull, with his unit now reduced to sixteen men, withdrew down the highway. One of those killed was squad leader Sergeant Robert Niland, one of the three Niland brothers whose deaths became the basis for the movie *Saving Private Ryan*.[8]

> Return 2.3 km to Ste-Mère-Église and stop south of the Maison de Retraite at highway D974 & rue de la Cassinerie to view signboard #15 on the east side of the highway. (49.41134, -1.319781)

At dawn on 7 June, a second, stronger German force comprised of I and II Battalions, Infantry Regiment 1058, 91st Airlanding Division; a special *Sturm*, or Assault, Battalion; and a battalion of seven self-propelled guns approached Ste-Mère-Église from the north. The German infantry moved through the fields east and west of the highway while the self-propelled guns advanced along the roadway. As the force fought its way to the northern outskirts of the village, two of the SP guns were stopped by the courageous actions of paratroopers manning a 57-mm antitank gun at the very edge of town. The Germans halted to reconsider their attack plan.

Lieutenant Waverly Wray led one platoon of Company D around the left flank of the German positions. After positioning his men, he moved alone from hedgerow to hedgerow to reconnoiter and discovered a group of Germans sheltering in a sunken lane around a communication post. Wray stood his full height to shoot over the hedgerow

---

7   Lieutenant Turner B Turnbull, known among his men as 'The Chief' because of his Choctaw Indian heritage, was killed the next day in Ste-Mère-Église. He was awarded a Silver Star and is buried in Normandy American Cemetery.

8   Sergeant Robert J Niland and his brother, 2nd Lieutenant Preston Niland, 22nd Infantry Regiment, 4th Infantry Division, who was killed on 7 June near Utah Beach, are buried in Normandy American Cemetery.

and down into the sunken lane, killing all six men before spinning around to kill two guards who had appeared in the field behind him. Wray had single-handedly eliminated the commanding officer and entire staff of a German battalion. His platoon now brought devastating mortar and machine-gun fire down upon the German infantry clustered farther down the sunken lane. The leaderless battalion fled north, exposing the left flank of the *Sturm* Battalion, which then also withdrew.

In 1944 rue de la Cassinerie formed the northern edge of Ste-Mère-Église, and Lt Wray's exploits took place in fields to the north approximately near the current Musée de la Ferme on rue de Beauvais. **Signboard #15** presents photos of two armored vehicles destroyed at the northern entrance of the town. The period photos are compared to a matching contemporary photo. The area has been developed since the engagement, and most of the hedgerows have been removed; however, the tour pauses here to recognize Lt Wray's platoon's actions: one understrength platoon, through courage and daring, stopped the attack of two armor-reinforced battalions.[9]

By 1715 that afternoon, the German attack force, less the routed I Battalion and *Sturm* Battalion, were still facing three platoons of airborne troops on the outskirts of the town. The German II Battalion, Infantry Regiment 1058, was in the fields and sunken roads around le Haras. An *ad hoc* platoon of misdropped airborne troopers, designated as 2nd Platoon, Company E, and commanded by Lieutenant James J Coyle, swung around to the west and crept through the fields and over the hedgerows to outflank the German unit. The Americans, with two tanks that had just arrived from the beachhead, caught the Germans full enfilade and unleashed a terrifying barrage of tank, mortar, and machine-gun fire. In 15 minutes the fight was over, and the German survivors were surrendering by the score. For the second time that day, a German battalion had been routed by an understrength platoon. German casualties from the two engagements amounted to 414 dead, 408 captured, and an untold number of wounded carried away during the hasty retreat.

The engagement occurred among the hedgerows of le Haras, located west of the N13 highway. The site is accessible only by a difficult route back into the village along a frontage road to the west, but nothing remains to mark the engagement. How close the German thrust came to entering the center of Ste-Mère-Église and capturing the vital N13/D15 crossroads is remarkable.[10]

Continue 300 m into Ste-Mère-Église, then leave the village heading west toward Picauville/Pont l'Abbé (rue de Verdun; D15), also signed as toward *Mémorial des Parachutistes*. After 2.6 km, cross the railroad line that the scattered groups of paratroopers used as a guide to the highway. From here they moved west to approach la Fière, 1 km ahead. A foxhole dug for commanding General Gavin and from which observers directed American artillery fire during the battle is on the left at a large curve in the road (49.400634, -1.361862). Upon reaching the memorial site immediately before the Merderet River, turn onto the side road to the right and park. (49.401493, -1.362812)

---

9   Lieutenant Waverly Wray was posthumously awarded a Distinguished Service Cross, America's second highest award for valour in the face of the enemy. He was killed in action on 19 September 1944 during Operation Market Garden. He was 24 years old.

10   Both Lieutenant Colonel Edward C Krause and Lieutenant Colonel Benjamin H Vandervoort earned Distinguished Services Crosses for their actions in capturing and holding Ste-Mère-Église.

Battle of la Fière Bridge
6 to 10 June 1944

Objective	To capture and hold the road bridge
Forces	
American	Various elements of 505th, 507th, 508th PIR, and 325th and 401st GIR
German	Infantry Regiment 1057 (Oberst Sylvester von Saldern)
Result	Successfully taken against a considerably stronger force
Location	Carentan is 75 km east of Caen; Ste-Mère-Église is 14 km northwest of Carentan; la Fière Bridge is 3.6 km west of Ste-Mère-Église

Battle

The 1st Battalion, 505th PIR, dropped relatively close together in the fields northeast of their intended objective, the bridge at la Fière. On 6 June, they and several misdropped elements of the 507th and 508th PIRs marched west toward the roadway. Company A, 505th PIR, commanded by Lieutenant John 'Red Dog' Dolan,[11] engaged German forces in the area around the memorial. After failing to flank the German positions located in this open field, paratroopers engaged in an hour-long firefight which cost the company numerous casualties, including several officers. Eventually the enemy withdrew, and the company established its positions in this field, which they held against enemy assault and artillery fire for the next four days.

As Company A held the field, the main force of Company G, 507th PIR, approached la Fière through the bocage fields south of the main road from Ste-Mère-Église and headed for their objective at Amfréville. Lieutenant John Marr[12] led his scouts around the south side of *le Manoir de la Fière* to seek a crossing

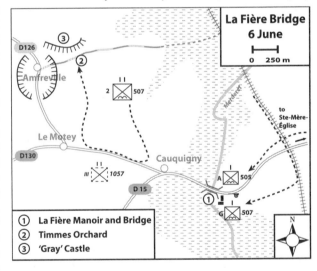

① La Fière Manoir and Bridge
② Timmes Orchard
③ 'Gray' Castle

of the river. Approaching the stone buildings along the river's edge, they were fired upon by a German machine gun located in the farm's cattle-feed lot. They destroyed it with grenades and proceeded onto the causeway, where they eliminated two more machine guns, easing pressure on Company A in the field to the north.

---

11   First Lieutenant John J Dolan was awarded a Distinguished Service Cross for extraordinary heroism. Dolan was severely wounded near Mook, the Netherlands, during Operation Market Garden when his jeep ran over a landmine. He survived his injuries to become an attorney in Boston, Mass.

12   Lieutenant John Marr retired from the US Army as a Colonel.

Suddenly German fire broke out from the second floor windows of the *manoir* aimed at Company B, 508th PIR, coming down the slope of the roadway from the east and another firefight developed. Twenty-eight men, a platoon of German Infantry Regiment 1057, which had moved into the building on the previous night, held up 300 Americans for hours until Lieutenant Homer Jones, moving along a sunken lane leading to the manoir, entered the solidly-built stone structure and engaged the enemy in a mad scramble through the multi-storied building while both sides fired through wood doors and floors. Several more Americans arrived in the house to add firepower, and the Germans waved a white flag.[13] By 1430, the manoir and east end of the causeway were secure, but German troops had occupied the west end.

At 1600, three light German tanks, armed with 37-mm guns, crossed the causeway with infantry support. A 57-mm antitank gun placed beside the Ste-Mère-Église road at the bend east of the manoir knocked a track off the lead tank, blocking the causeway's east end, but the tanks' guns continued to fire. Two bazooka teams had been placed in the ditches at the east end of the causeway. They exposed themselves to intense small-arms and machine-gun fire as they put round after round into the three tanks, eventually destroying each of them. A battalion of infantry with tank support had been stopped by one rifle company.

By the morning of 7 June, more German troops had arrived west of the causeway with reinforcing armor. They established artillery positions in the fields south of Cauquigny, a small hamlet near the western end of the causeway. Under supporting artillery – including the dreaded 88-mm gun – and mortar fire, they launched four unsuccessful attacks to cross the causeway. Sporadic shelling continued for the remainder of the day.

On 9 June, with the American position now reinforced by the arrival of 2nd Battalion, 401st GIR[14], General Gavin ordered the fresh but inexperienced unit to attack across the causeway. The battalion commander[15] considered the attack a suicide mission and claimed illness; he was immediately relieved. The battalion's companies accumulated behind the stone wall that ran parallel to the river at the manoir, south of the bridge. A 30-minute artillery barrage started at 1030, and 15 minutes later the first troops moved from behind the stone wall to assault the causeway. The men were particularly inspired by the presence of Generals Ridgway and Gavin on the causeway in the midst of the battle.

Three companies of glider infantry poured onto the narrow, 500-meter-long roadway and the ditches on either side. The first group of thirty men, led by Captain John Sauls, Company G commander, crossed the causeway while American artillery kept the

---

13   Lieutenant Homer Jones was awarded a Silver Star for his actions. He was seriously wounded on 4 July 1944 near le Haye-du-Puits but survived the war to live into his 80s.

14   The 401st Glider Infantry Regiment was reassigned in March 1944. Its 1st Battalion fought as 3rd Battalion, 327th Glider Infantry Regiment, 101st Airborne Division. Its 2nd Battalion fought as 3rd Battalion, 325th Glider Infantry Regiment. They are, however, frequently referred to by their original unit designations.

15   Lieutenant Colonel Charles Carrell, a West Point graduate, was transferred to the 90th Infantry Division. Carrell believed Gavin's reaction to have been precipitous and unfair. He retired from the army in 1947 and died in 1990.

enemy sheltering in their foxholes. First Platoon commander Lieutenant Don Wason[16] eliminated a German machine gun positioned to fire straight down the roadway. The Germans, however, had the platoon in their crossfire from machine guns positioned to the north and south on the river banks. Lieutenant James Johnson[17] of 1st Platoon, Company E, reached the western end as the artillery barrage subsided, and more German gunners added their fire

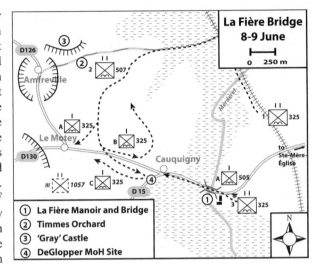

against the attack. Grenades blew up the machine gun on the northern bank. The men of Companies G and E fanned to the north and south, attacking gun positions along the river banks. Company F and paratroopers from the 507th PIR joined the assault. The enemy positions in the church and cemetery were eliminated, the bridgehead was expanded to the west toward le Motey, and the battle was over by noon.

Battlefield Tour

Walk up the hill toward the ***Mémorial des Parachutistes***, passing the four plaques dedicated to the casualties suffered by the units (508th PIR, 80th Airborne Antiaircraft Battalion, 325th GIR, and 505th PIR) engaged here. The fourth plaque specifically commends the 114 men of Company A, 505th PIR, 'whose exact D-Day mission was to seize la Fière Bridge and to prevent the enemy crossing easterly; despite heavy losses, Company A stood fast – no armed enemy ever crossed this bridge.' Another plaque honors the individual heroism of Private First Class Charles DeGlopper, which is described below.

The impressive bronze statue, known as '**Iron Mike**' and which is a replica of the one at the US Army Infantry School at Fort Benning, Georgia, commemorates all of the airborne forces of D-Day and stands in the field occupied by Company A on 6 June. The statue, rifle at the ready, peers pensively upon its objective, la Fière Bridge. From this point, viewers observe the entire battlefield. The Merderet is once again a narrow stream held within low banks, not the intimidating sight of a wide body of water of unknown depth as presented to the troopers in 1944. An enormous bronze **table of orientation** provides positions for the units engaged in the battle and features a German tank attempting to cross the causeway. A large, bronze **memorial stele** sitting upon a concrete base presents an open book, the pages of which state, in French and English, 'To pass on the memory, to remind that today we live in peace, freedom, and dignity because others gave their life for us.'

---

16   Lieutenant Donald B Wason died in the assault and was posthumously awarded a Distinguished Service Cross. He is buried at Long Island National Cemetery.

17   Lieutenant James Johnson was wounded in the la Fière action. He was later taken prisoner in Holland and spent most of the remainder of the war in German POW camps.

Walk to the bridge. The unassuming, single-arch, gray-stone **bridge** is almost disappointing in size and construction. Its appearance and location over a lazy stream in quiet pastures belies the fighting and death that surrounded it, but as frequently happens with military objectives, its importance in wartime was out of proportion with its peacetime use. (49.400981, -1.364121)

Across the roadway is the ***Manoir de la Fière***, now a dairy farm and *chambres d'hôtes* (B&B). The repaired stone buildings appear much as they did in 1944, except the largest and easternmost, which was heavily damaged and not rebuilt. A repaired stone wall still parallels the river bank, marking where American paratroopers passed during their attack upon the causeway on 9 June.

A sign on the bridge names it **Voie Marcus Heim**. Private Heim was one of the bazooka men who held their ground in the face of the approaching German tanks on 6 June. The lead tank, immobilized by a shell from the 57-mm gun stationed near the curve in the road behind this position, was still firing its cannon and machine gun at paratrooper positions until loader Heim and gunner Private First Class Lenold Peterson launched several rockets at the tank, setting it on fire. Heim and Peterson continued firing until all three tanks were ablaze.[18]

Drive across the bridge and causeway; park near the infosigns at the western end of the causeway in **square Capitaine Rae**. (49.402798, -1.370397)

At 1130 on 6 June, men of Company D, 507th PIR,[19] attacked from the west and occupied the chapel at Cauquigny, but they remained under fire from German troops hiding in the flooded ground to the south. German Renault and Hotchkiss tanks of Panzer Battalion 100 appeared on highway D15 with intent to cross and capture the causeway. The Company D men, under Lieutenant Lewis Levy, eliminated one tank with bazooka fire as it entered the crossroads (intersection of highways D15 and D126). The other two tanks were destroyed with grenades, thus effectively blocking the western end of the causeway. Levy and his men came under intense German machine-gun and rifle fire from the south and abandoned their position to join Lieutenant Colonel Charles J Timmes (see below).

The infosigns display photographs and text which describe the horrific nature of the battle. Cauquigny still consists of little more than the chapel and six dwellings from 1944. The chapel was heavily damaged in the fighting that raged around the hamlet and in the cemetery. Though rebuilt after the war, the structure and graveyard stones still show signs of bullet damage. The chapel wall bears a small bronze plaque to the **507th PIR**. (49.403196, -1.370673)

---

18   Private Marcus Heim and Private First Class Lenold Peterson, along with the second bazooka team of Private First Class John D Bolderson and Private Gordon Pryne, were each awarded Distinguished Service Crosses. All survived the war. Private Heim died in 2003 at age 78 and is buried in Middleburgh, New York. Private Peterson died in 1989 and is buried in Ft Snelling National Cemetery. Private Bolderson was promoted to staff sergeant, awarded the Silver Star, and received awards from the French, Dutch, and Belgian governments. Although wounded five times, he survived the war and died in 1974 at age 52. Sadly, his brother Marvin was with the US Rangers and died in July 1944. Private Pryne died in 2006 at age 81.

19   Captain Robert D Rae was awarded the Distinguished Service Cross for leading the 507th PIR assault across the causeway. He survived the war.

On the left fork toward Picauville (D15), proceed 300 m to the DeGlopper Infosign on the right. (49.403196, -1.370673)

On 8 June, American forces west of the river were strengthened by the arrival of 1st Battalion, 325th GIR, which moved south to the main highway between Cauquigny and Amfréville (D126) in the early-morning darkness of 9 June. The unit attacked toward the causeway with one company on either side of the highway. Company B, on the north side of the road, was stopped by intense machine-gun fire in the orchard east of the Hameau aux Brix road. One platoon of Company C, which was proceeding east in the fields south of the main highway, crossed highway D15 to accept a phony German surrender. German troops in the field opened fire and machine guns to the north and south fired down the roadway, decimating the trapped platoon.

German flanking action threatened the survivors who were sheltering in a roadside ditch. Private First Class Charles DeGlopper left the shelter of the ditch and entered the roadway, firing upon German positions with his BAR[20] while the remainder of his platoon escaped through a hedgerow opening to the rear. Although grievously wounded, he continued to fire clip after clip. Wounded again, he continued firing. Hit a third time, he fell to one knee but maintained burst after burst until killed. Meanwhile, the survivors of his unit made their escape from the German trap. Intense German fire continued upon the remaining units of Company C, eventually forcing the company commander and small groups to surrender.

DeGlopper's bravery is commemorated on a bronze plaque at the *Mémorial des Parachutistes* and by mention in the signboard at Cauquigny. At the actual location of the event, a roadside signboard presents his photograph and mentions his award citation.[21]

Return to Cauquigny and turn left toward Amfreville (D126). After 1.1 km, stop at the memorial park at the intersection with highway D130. (49.405671, -1.386589)

Early in the morning of 10 June, the US 90th Infantry Division's 358th Infantry Regiment crossed the causeway and the airborne units entered into reserve. The **507th PIR Memorial** celebrates the unit's actions on the battlefields of Europe with steles holding maps indicating their positions in Normandy, the Ardennes, and the Crossing of the Rhine into Germany. A white-stone monument displays a parachutist descending to the ground. This newly-constructed and attractive park marks the limit of the regiment's advance at le Motey before its relief by the 90th Infantry Division.

Continue toward Amfreville (D126) for 700 m and, immediately before entering the town, turn right at the tourist sign indicating '*Vergers Timmes.*' After 110 m, turn right on Route du Tiers and continue for 750 m to the memorial steles. (49.411259, -1.380458)

---

20   BAR: Browning Automatic Rifle, a bipod-mounted, air-cooled light machine gun that utilized a 20-round magazine and was carried by infantry squads.

21   Private First Class Charles N DeGlopper was awarded America's highest honor for bravery, the Medal of Honor. DeGlopper is buried in Maple Grove Cemetery, Grand Island, New York. He was 22 years old.

Battle of Timmes Orchard
6 to 10 June 1944

Lieutenant Colonel Charles J Timmes, commander of 2nd Battalion, 507th PIR, was assigned the task of landing on the west side of the la Fière bridge to provide support to the troops coming from the east. He encountered heavier-than-expected opposition and was driven away from the bridge by German forces. By the end of 6 June, Col Timmes had collected a force of one hundred men and had established defensive positions in an orchard near Ferme Jules Jean. He continued to present a danger to the German flank, thus diverting enemy manpower away from the main battle against the paratroopers at la Fière.

7 June passed uneventfully, but Timmes had been identified as an extreme threat to a German headquarters at le Château, known to the Americans as the Gray Castle, less than 1 kilometer to the northwest. At 0800 on 8 June, German troops launched the first of four attacks that day upon Timmes's men; all of which were beaten back. Col Timmes sent Lt Marr to establish communication with the 82nd Airborne Division headquarters. Marr found a walkable ford across the Merderet River and returned with a battalion of 325th Glider Infantry as reinforcements. One company feigned an attack on the Gray Castle to distract the enemy while two companies of the fresh infantry moved south to attack the la Fière causeway from the west.

Early in the morning of 9 June, those two companies of the 325th GIR unsuccessfully attacked German positions in Cauquigny as described above. Survivors of that failed attempt, many of them wounded, returned to rejoin Timmes's group. Despite being surrounded and low on ammunition, medical supplies, and food, Timmes's force resisted repeated attacks by a stronger German force. Finally, success at capturing the causeway relieved German pressure on Timmes.[22]

The narrow, sunken road is now paved but still shows the vegetation on both sides that would have caused difficulty for troops in 1944. At the end of the road, three large rocks hold black granite plaques commemorating the men of the 507th PIR, 508th PIR, and 325th GIR who fought here under the command of Col Timmes. The battlefield now known as '**Timmes Orchard**' remains behind the monuments.

Return to D126 and turn right toward Amfreville. Continue 1.9 km through Amfreville to the intersection highways D126 and D69 in Gourbesville. (49.420726, -1.409689)

The small park at the intersection of the two highways has been dedicated to the three hundred men of the **82nd Airborne Division** and the **90th Infantry Division** who died liberating Gourbesville. Behind the monument, the square tower of the village church rises. An adjacent signboard relates two of the many individual accounts of the D-Day air drops. Two privates engaged the enemy: one was wounded, treated by a German doctor and survived; the other died and was buried initially in the church graveyard. These stories are typical of that first week of the invasion – most are forgotten, some are passed from generation to generation, and a few are memorialized like the stories of privates James Hattrick[23] and RB Lewellen.

---

22   Lieutenant Colonel Charles Timmes was awarded the Distinguished Service Cross. He rose to the rank of major general, earning two Distinguished Service Medals, the Silver Star, and two Bronze Stars. He also served in Korea and Vietnam. He died in 1990 at age 83.

23   In 1948 the body of Private James R Hattrick was removed from the temporary American Cemetery near Ste-Mère-Église and returned to Charlotte, North Carolina.

Side Trip: Orglandes German Cemetery and Hémevez Massacre Memorial
    If desired, this location is convenient for touring these two sites. They are not key 82nd Airborne Division battlefields.

Continue west on highway D126 for 3.1 km and turn right toward Orglandes (D24). Continue 450 m through Orglandes to the cemetery on the left. (49.42589,-1.4477) Total distance: 16 km.

Orglandes German Cemetery
    Enter through a stone gatehouse adjacent to a steeple-topped chapel of similar construction. Originally a burial place for American and German soldiers who died during the Cotentin fighting, the American bodies were removed to Normandy American Cemetery in 1945. The cemetery now contains 10,152 German burials; many of the dead were collected after the war from individual graves scattered across the area. Generalleutnant Wilhelm Falley is buried in this cemetery. The graves are marked by gray stone German crosses, with two-to-six names per cross. The expansive grounds have been landscaped with randomly placed trees, per the German tradition, which make a spectacular display in the fall.

Leave the cemetery and proceed north toward Hémevez (D24). After 3.6 km, enter Hémevez and bear right on le Bourg. After 350 m, turn right (D271) and follow for 400 m. Another right turn on le Château leads to the churchyard in 150 m. (49.459237, -1.435851)

Hémevez Massacre Memorial
    On 6 June, fourteen paratroopers of the 1st Battalion, 507th PIR, landed along the Cherbourg-Paris rail line, north of the rural village of Hémevez, far from their target drop zone. While Private Ashton Landry and two others who were sent to reconnoiter hid from a German patrol in a stable on le Castel farm, a firefight erupted between the main group and German troops stationed at a local headquarters. The troopers were overcome and captured. Landry's patrol was also eventually captured and added to the weakly-guarded paratroopers held in a small copse 200 meters south of le Castel. That night he and his two-man patrol escaped to find American lines, but seven others were not so lucky. For reasons unknown, they were executed by a shot in the back of the head. A French farmer discovered the bodies hidden near a hedgerow, and he and local citizens buried them in the church graveyard. After the fighting had passed, the townspeople informed American personnel, who relocated the bodies to Normandy American Cemetery.
    The incident was forgotten for fifty years until a local citizen began a conversation with a returning member of the 507th PIR and revealed that he had witnessed the killings. After several years of research, the Frenchman located and communicated with Private Landry.[24] Through this effort the story became known.
    An infosign located outside the churchyard gate describes the events of the execution and displays a map showing Landry's movements as he attempted to avoid German patrols and eventually make his escape. In 2004, a memorial stone on the place of their initial burial in the churchyard paid homage to the seven dead men. Their names are

---

24   Private Ashton J Landry died in 2003 at age 81. He is buried in Fountain Memorial Gardens, Lafayette, LA.

listed on the reverse side. Symbolically, this memorial stands only a few meters from the commune's memorial to its First World War dead.

To continue the tour, return to Gourbesville and turn right toward Picauville (D69) From Gourbesville, proceed south toward Picauville (D69). After 3.3 km, a stele on the left commemorates **Airfield A8**, which had been located in the adjacent field to accommodate Ninth Air Force fighter planes. (49.392821, -1.418846) After 1.3 km, cross the intersection with highway D15. Less than 1 km to the north is **Château de Bernaville**, headquarters for the German 91st Airlanding Division and more recently a hospital. German General Falley was ambushed and killed along this road on 6 June. Continue 1.1 km into Picauville. (49.385446, -1.406572)

In the center of Picauville, at the rear of the 13th-century St-Candide church, the **Ninth USAAF Memorial** describes the severe danger of a nighttime air drop. Five planes crashed in local fields between 0114 on June 6 and 0617 on June 7. Surviving pilots reported that antiaircraft fire was particularly heavy in the Étienville area, 1.5 kilometers to the west, and that this fire was responsible for downing the planes. Four of the planes held members of the 101st Airborne Division. One plane was empty except for its aircrew. A stone wall holds plaques presenting emblems, plane numbers, and the names of each of the crew members and paratroopers killed, missing, or taken prisoner. A map shows the location of each crash. The memorial includes an engine from a C-47 transport in a protective case and a model of the same plane mounted upon a stone shaft.

Follow highway D69 for 1.9 km through Picauville, turn left toward Chef-du-Pont (D70) and continue 2.5 km across the causeway and Merderet River to the memorial park on the right. (49.377169, -1.353051)

Battle of Chef-du-Pont Bridge
6 to 10 June 1944

Objective	To capture the road bridge
Forces	
American	Company E, 507th PIR (Captain Roy Creek) Elements of 508th PIR
German	Infantry Regiment 1058 (Oberst Kurt Beigang)
Result	Successfully captured and held against repeated enemy attacks
Location	Carentan is 75 km east of Caen; Ste-Mère-Église is 14 km northwest of Carentan; Chef-du-Pont is 4 km southwest of Ste-Mère-Église

Battle

Soon after landing on 6 June, General Gavin sent 150 men of the 507th PIR to attack the village of Chef-du-Pont and the bridge to its west. At first, German resistance in the town was light, but it increased as the paratroopers approached occupied foxholes near the bridge. The force launched two attacks that cleared the east side of the bridge, but they could advance no farther. The bulk of the American force was called back to la Fière, reducing the contingent to approximately thirty-four men under the command of Captain Roy Creek, Company E, 507th PIR.

From the west side of the causeway, German troops used mortars and a 75-mm gun to shell Creek's force, further reducing it to twenty men. A glider-delivered 57-mm antitank gun arrived, and C-47s began dropping ammunition, including a 60-mm mortar. With enemy artillery fire suppressed by the antitank gun, eleven men stormed and captured the bridge.

During the night, German commanders assembled their forces and attacked the western approach to the causeway at dawn. They were beaten off by a mixed group of paratroopers dispatched by Lieutenant Colonel Thomas Shanley of the 508th PIR from his positions on Hill 30, less than 2 kilometers to the northwest. The next day a stronger attack, supported with Renault tanks and Sturmgeschütz III self-propelled guns, was also beaten back in fighting that was at times hand-to-hand. Finally, on 10 June, the US 90th Infantry Division crossed the causeway to continue the attack.

Battlefield Tour

A gray granite stone identifies the **508th PIR Memorial Garden** as dedicated to the men of the regiment who participated in the battle to hold the Chef-du-Pont bridges against repeated German attacks. The large **creamery complex**, immediately east of the park, converted during the defense to an observation post and casualty treatment center. On the south bank of the river, a signboard identifies the reconstructed bridge as **Pont du Capitaine Roy Creek**[25] and dedicates it to him and the men of the 507th PIR. The photograph on the signboard shows the three-span, humpbacked nature of the 1944 bridge. Between the river and the garden on the opposite side of the roadway, a stele commemorates the 508th PIR.

> Continue into Chef-du-Pont and turn right toward Ste-Marie-du-Mont (Route des Laitiers, D70). After 3.7 km, stop at the stele on the right. (49.381011, -1.301123)

The key D70 and N13 crossroad, known as les Forges, was occupied by 3rd Battalion, 8th Infantry Regiment, 4th Infantry Division, by noon on 6 June after having arrived from Utah Beach. Most of the battalion moved a few hundred meters north to face German positions on Hill 20. The 746th Tank Battalion arrived later in the day. The crossroad was the center of LZ W for the 325th GIR. However, between les Forges and Ste-Mère-Église was a reinforced German infantry battalion, whose slightly elevated position on Hill 20, immediately south of Fauville, enabled observation of and firing upon the entire landing zone. Efforts by Sherman tanks to dislodge the Germans met accurate fire from 88-mm guns, knocking out three of the American tanks. Right on schedule at 2100, the American gliders arrived and landed amidst the German mortar, artillery, and heavy machine-gun fire. Over 160 glider troops were killed. The next morning, the 8th Infantry Regiment attacked and overran the German positions.

American dead were buried in the field to the southeast of the crossroad, and for years a monument marked it as one of the three temporary American military cemeteries constructed immediately after the battle. After the war, the dead were either returned to the United States or reburied in Normandy American Cemetery, according to the wishes of the next-of-kin. The monument was relocated recently to the east side of the field to avoid the traffic of the autoroute interchange. The fieldstone stele bears a plaque that identifies the pasture behind it as **Blosville US Temporary Cemetery #3**, the original burial ground for

---

25   Captain Roy Creek rose to the rank of colonel and survived the war. He is still alive and in his 90s.

6,000 American soldiers.

Return to Ste-Mère-Église by turning left toward les Boutemonts before the autoroute underpass and continuing along the frontage road for 2.6 km, passing through Fauville, the site of the German strongpoint. Do not reenter the autoroute; instead, remain on local roads, turning right then left toward Ste-Mère-Église (D974).

See Chapter Eight to tour the final 82nd Airborne Division site in Graignes.

Chapter Eight
US 101st (Screaming Eagles) Airborne Division
6 June to 12 June

A vast marsh separated the dry sand dunes of the 4th Infantry Division's landings at Utah Beach from higher ground 1.5 kilometers inland. Only four elevated causeways crossed the flooded ground. The 101st Airborne Division's objectives were to seize the western ends of the four causeways between St-Martin-de-Varreville and Pouppeville and to secure the invasion's southern flank along the Douve River estuary. The key to the southern Cotentin Peninsula was its largest city, Carentan, which sat at the base of the estuary and controlled any movement onto the peninsula and any junction between US VII Corps on Utah Beach and US V Corps on Omaha Beach.

The eastern Cotentin peninsula between the Merderet River and the sea was defended by I Battalion, Grenadier Regiment 919, of the German 709th Infantry Division, a so-called static unit which lacked motorized transportation. The unit was questionably strengthened by *Ostbattalion (Georgian)* 795 near Foucarville directly behind Utah Beach. The three divisional artillery battalions were stationed far to the north around Cherbourg. The elements of the 91st Airlanding Division's Infantry Regiment 1058 was garrisoned around St-Côme-du-Mont, with *Fallschirmjäger*[1] Regiment 6 lying south of Carentan.

The 101st Airborne Division was activated in August 1942. The D-Day invasion signaled its first combat assignment after almost two years of training in the United States and England. The unit fielded three parachute infantry regiments, the 501st, 502nd, and 506th, plus the 327th Gilder Infantry Regiment.

The 501st Parachute Infantry Regiment (PIR) was to land near Angoville-au-Plain to destroy two bridges on the main Cherbourg-Bayeux highway and the railroad bridge to its west and to seize the la Barquette lock, which controlled the water levels on the flooded terrain along the Merderet and Douve Rivers. The 502nd PIR targeted causeway exits #3 and #4 after landing east of Ste-Mère-Église. Two battalions of the 506th PIR were to land west of Ste-Marie-du-Mont to secure exits #1 and #2. The 3rd Battalion, 506th PIR, was to land near Vierville to establish a bridgehead over the Douve River by capturing two bridges at le Port. Finally, the 327th Glider Infantry Regiment (GIR) constituted a seaborne reinforcement delivered through Utah Beach.

D-Day Landings
6 June 1944

Objective	To secure the exit roads from Utah Beach and to protect the 4th Infantry Division's northern and southern flanks.
Forces **American**	6,600 men of 101st Airborne Division (Major General Maxwell D Taylor)
German	Units of 709th Infantry Division (Generalleutnant Karl-Wilhelm von Schlieben) and Fallschirmjäger Regiment 6 (Major Friedrick Freiherr von der Heydte)
Result	All objectives were accomplished despite a high casualty rate

---

1   *Fallschirmjäger*: parachute troops; in this case, fighting as ground infantry

Casualties	
American	868 killed; 2,303 wounded; 665 missing or captured
German	Over 3,000 killed or wounded
Location	Carentan is 75 km east of Caen; Ste-Mère-Église is 14 km northwest of Carentan

Battle

During the night of 5/6 June, 490 C-47 transport planes carried the men of the 101st Airborne Division to France. Pathfinders, assigned to mark the drop zones with lanterns and by radio, jumped at 0015, approximately five minutes before a British glider-borne assault took place on the invasion's eastern flank at Bénouville. Minutes later, paratroopers exited their planes into what appeared to them as a solid wall of tracer bullets. Most of them were eager to escape the sickeningly-rolling, easy targets of the low and slow transport aircraft. At 0300, gliders began to arrive to deliver heavy weapons, vehicles, medical teams, and division staff.

The drops of the 101st Airborne Division were badly scattered. It took most of the night before large forces located each other, organized, determined their location, and moved toward assigned objectives. By dawn, when the seaborne landings were to start, not one objective had been accomplished, and the Germans had been fully alerted.

Major Friedrick von der Heydte[2] commanded the elite and over-strength German *Fallschirmjäger* Regiment 6 (Green Devils) – young, tough, and well-trained. Aroused by reports of enemy landings, he put his men on alert at 0300, but for hours he was denied specific instructions due to the destruction of German communication lines. At 0600 von der Heydte received orders to assemble his troops southwest of Carentan, but his unit's actions were severely hindered by a lack of motorized transport. Proceeding ahead of his lead units, von der Heydte entered Carentan and found it empty of German troops. He reached St-Côme-du-Mont after 1000 and found a battalion of Grenadier Regiment 1058 dug in. After establishing his command post south of the town, he gave his troops orders. 1st Battalion was to establish a line from St-Côme-du-Mont to Ste-Marie-du-Mont; 2nd Battalion was to advance on Ste-Mère-Église; 3rd Battalion was to establish itself in Carentan.

The first day of the invasion saw numerous small, but intense, engagements. Utilizing their training and individual initiative, the paratroopers destroyed pockets of enemy, especially artillery batteries, and quickly secured the causeway exits. The Germans, attempting to defend everywhere, dispersed small detachments, with the exception of the *Fallschirmjäger* Regiment 6, and their resistance was fragmented.

By D-Day night, Major General Maxwell Taylor, the 101st Airborne Division's commander, knew that two of the major missions had been accomplished. The northern flank was secured by the 502nd PIR at Foucarville, the causeways had been secured, and 4th Infantry Division was moving inland. His concern was the southern flank where German *Fallschirmjäger* units had gathered in strength around St-Côme-du-Mont and la Barquette.

---

2   Major Dr Friedrick-August, Freiherr von der Heydte was born to a noble Bavarian military family and became a highly decorated Luftwaffe officer who held the Knight's Cross with Oak Leaves, German Cross, and Iron Cross 1st and 2nd Class. After the war, von der Heydte became a lawyer and a Bavarian politician and attained the rank of Brigadegeneral in the post-war German Bundeswehr Reserve Army. He died in 1994 at age 87.

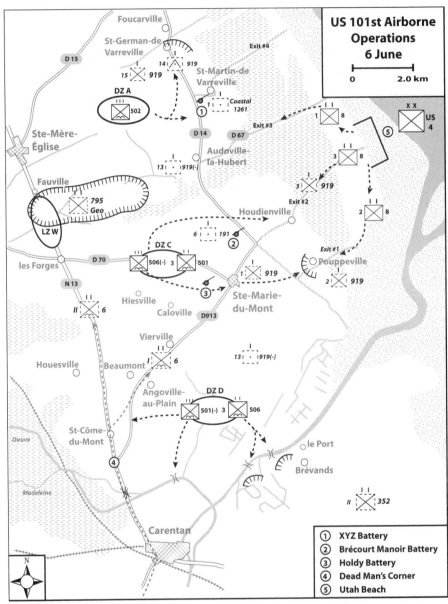

On the morning of 7 June, the landing of additional glider troops strengthened American positions in the Angoville / Ste-Marie-du-Mont / Hiesville area and the I *Fallschirmjäger* Battalion was slowly being surrounded. American naval shelling inflicted heavy casualties to any large concentration of German troops. Lacking heavy weapons and expending antitank ammunition, the *Fallschirmjäger* battalion began a fighting withdrawal to the southwest, attempting to bypass American concentrations near the Barquette locks.

Battlefield Tour

The 101st A/B Division battlefield is especially rich in notable sites in keeping with the intensity and importance of the fighting. Recent films about Company E, 506th PIR, have dramatically increased the interest in this unit, sometimes to the detriment of other units. This tour presents the achievements of the entire division. The 101st Airborne Division tour begins in Ste-Mère-Église; for a full description of Ste-Mère-Église, see Chapter Seven.

> Leave the center of Ste-Mère-Église along the southeast side of the church toward Beuzeville-au-Plain (becomes rue général Gavin, D17). After 1.6 km, at a country lane crossroads (49.418731, -1.303071), a red sandstone stele on the left commemorates the location of the **552nd AAA AW Battalion** and the **'La Londe' airfield**, which operated in this field from 12 June to 26 July. The name comes from the large farm to the northeast. The site has long since returned to its original condition and is now a pasture. Continue 1.9 km to the church in Beuzeville-au-Plain. (49.431258, -1.285669)

A white-stone memorial in the shape of an airplane tail wing stands at the rear of the Beuzeville-au-Plain church. It presents a too-often repeated story of that early June night. The memorial is dedicated to the five-man, C-47 crew[3] from the **439th Troop Carrier Group (TCG)** and Lieutenant Thomas Meehan III[4] and 16 parachutists of **Company E, 506th Regiment**, who died when their plane was set aflame by German antiaircraft fire and crashed in a field near the church. The attached bronze plaque lists the names of the dead soldiers and airmen.

A search of the village will reveal that the small community does not have a First World War Memorial. It is one of three in France to have been so fortunate because each of its fourteen soldiers returned after the November 1918 Armistice.

> Continue toward Foucarville (D17). After 2.8 km, turn right away from Ravenoville (D14).

This segment of highway is named Pugach Road after 1st Lieutenant Joseph J Pugach.[5] Forty-three of the roadways in the vicinity of Utah Beach have been dedicated to men in or attached to **1st Engineer Special Brigade**. White plaques with blue lettering positioned along the roadsides identify the dedications.

> After 1.9 km, stop at the intersection with highway D423. (49.426761, -1.24697)

Coastal Artillery Regiment 1261 manned **WN-108**, composed of Russian-made 122-mm guns that had been captured on the eastern front. The battery was located opposite a roadside cross in fields to the east toward St-Martin-de-Varreville. The site, ideally

---

3   First Lieutenant Harold A Capelluto, the aircraft's pilot, is buried in Normandy American Cemetery.

4   First Lieutenant Thomas Meehan III was Company E's commander. Lt Meehan had enlisted before the United States entered the war. His remains were recovered after the war and are now buried in Jefferson Barracks National Cemetery, near St. Louis. He was 22 years old.

5   First Lieutenant Joseph J Pugach, a member of the 286th Signal Company, was awarded a Silver Star. He was killed on 11 June and is buried in Normandy American Cemetery.

positioned to shell the approach along causeway exit #4 and much of Utah Beach, was the objective of Lieutenant Colonel Steve Chappuis[6] and his 2nd Battalion, 502nd PIR. Although injured on the jump and at DZ C instead of the planned DZ A, Chappuis gathered a dozen men and made for the battery. When he arrived hours later, he found it abandoned, the guns removed, and installations heavily damaged by air bombardments that occurred on the nights of 28/29 May and 5/6 June.

Remnants of eleven concrete structures remain in the fields, but they are on private property and of little interest except to enthusiasts.

> Turn right toward Turqueville (D423) and continue into les Mézières.
> (49.425023, -1.252946)

The barracks housing the battery personnel lined the highway. **Point WXYZ**, as it was identified by allied planners, was the assigned mission of Lieutenant Colonel Patrick J Cassidy's 1st Battalion, 502nd PIR. Objective W, the house at the crossroads west of St-Martin-de-Varreville, was unoccupied, and Col Cassidy therefore established his headquarters and aide station in it. A mixed group of fifteen men led by Staff Sergeant Harrison Summers moved east on the road toward position XYZ, in the small hamlet of les Mézières. Accounts vary, but what followed was an attack by Summers upon a much larger and sheltered enemy force. Although his men initially failed to follow him, Summers kicked open the door of the second house in the hamlet and sprayed its occupants with his Thompson submachine gun, killing four while the rest escaped to the fourth house along the road. Private William Burt joined Summers and set up a machine gun to fire on the fourth house while Summers repeated his attack, killing six more occupants. Private John Camien joined Summers as they repeated the procedure through the next five houses, killing thirty or more and taking no prisoners. They then approached a larger building used by the artillery garrison as a mess hall. When Summers burst in, the occupants were in the midst of a breakfast they would never finish. Summers killed all fifteen. Finally, Summers, Camien, and a few others who had now joined them attacked the final, two-story stone barn used as a barracks building. The artillery-men were not so easy to conquer this time. Pvt. Burt fired tracer bullets into an adjoining haystack, setting it and stored ammunition on fire. When the explosions started, enemy troops raced out the door and windows to escape only to find Summers and his men waiting for them. Thirty more German troops were killed. A bazooka round set the roof on fire and approximately one hundred troops made for the nearby woods. By this time elements of the 4th Infantry Division were arriving to add additional fire power. The entire German detachment was killed or captured. [7]

Les Mézières, a community of old french farmhouses in 1944, has grown and been modernized since, but many of the original structures remain. The white building with a red roof hugging the road was the first building attacked in Summers's account. The German mess hall was in the long, two-story chateau building behind the cement gate posts

---

6   Lieutenant Colonel Steve A Chappuis was awarded a Distinguished Service Cross for heroism against the enemy during the siege of Bastogne in December 1944. Colonel Chappuis died in 2008 at age 95.

7   Staff Sergeant Harrison Summers was awarded the Distinguished Service Cross and a battlefield commission for his exploits which were, to some, reminiscent of the exploits of the first war's Sgt. Alvin York. Summers was wounded in Holland and again at Bastogne but survived the war. He died in 1983 at age 65.
Private John Camien also survived the war; however, Private William Burt was killed five days later.

on the right farther to the west. The stone barn was destroyed in the battle, but it has been rebuilt in its original configuration and location. All of the buildings in les Mézières are private residences, whose owners are not generally welcoming to trespassers.

> Return to the intersection with highway D14, turn right, and continue 2.1 km to Audouville-la-Hubert. Stop at the intersection with highway D67. (49.408921, -1.242077)

Lieutenant Colonel Robert Cole landed near Ste-Mère-Église, wandered eastward collecting men from various regiments, and engaged and defeated a small German convoy. He easily secured the lightly-defended exit #4 and moved against exit #3. At 0930, Colonel Cole engaged Germans retreating from the beaches near Audouville-la-Hubert. In a sharp engagement they killed fifty-to-seventy-five enemy troops without loss. By 1300, they made contact with 1st Battalion, 8th Infantry Regiment, 4th Infantry Division. The two northern causeways were secure.

La Herguerie Ferme sits 70 meters west of the intersection along highway D67. (49.408579, -1.243558) Rumors persist that men of the 101st, believing that they had no facilities for holding prisoners, executed thirty German POWs from the *Ostbattalion* 795 on the farm's grounds on 6 June. Atrocities such as this did result from the brutal, close-range fighting during the Battle of Normandy but are generally not well documented. The shootings are not officially recognized, but perhaps they should be.

> Continue 2.6 km on highway D14 toward Ste-Marie-du-Mont. Pass through the small community of Le Grand Chemin and stop at the memorial on the right. (49.391647, -1.222497)

The German 6th Battery, Artillery Regiment 191, had installed four 105-mm howitzers in the field near Brécourt Manoir. The guns had been undetected by Allied intelligence and were sited to fire directly down causeway exit #2. They were protected by a detachment of fifty paratroopers from von der Heydte's I Battalion. Their effect upon the landings could have been deadly.

At 0830, eleven men under Lieutenant Richard Winters[8], acting commander of Company E, 506th PIR, attacked the fifty-man contingent at the battery. The enemy had established fields of fire for machine guns and mortars concealed among the hedgerows and connected by trenches. Using bravado and training, Winters' group and a flanking group led by Lieutenant Lynn Compton[9] eliminated the guns during a three-hour running gun and grenade battle that killed fifteen enemy. Winters and his men were still significantly outnumbered and thus withdrew, taking with them twelve captured enemy soldiers and documents detailing German defensive positions in the Cotentin. The remaining Germans,

---

8   Lieutenant Richard Winters received the Distinguished Service Cross for his leadership. Winters survived the war to live and retire in Hershey, Pa. He died in 2011 at age 91. Other members of the assault team received Silver Stars or Bronze Stars.

9   Lieutenant Lynn D Compton was awarded a Silver Star for his actions in disabling the guns. He was wounded in Holland and fought in the Ardennes. After the war, Compton returned to California where he had been a star athlete at UCLA before the war. He served in the Los Angeles Police Department while earning a law degree. He was the lead prosecutor in the Sirhan Sirhan trial for the murder of Robert F Kennedy and later joined the California Court of Appeals. He died in 2012 at age 90.

who were laying down murderous fire from around the manoir house, were later eliminated by two 4th Infantry Division tanks that arrived from the beachhead.

The polished black granite stele commemorates the action of the men of **Company E, 506th PIR**, during the D-Day battle and lists the names of all Company E men killed during the invasion. The accompanying **table of orientation** presents a brief description of the action and a hand-drawn sketch of the arrival of 4th Division tanks.

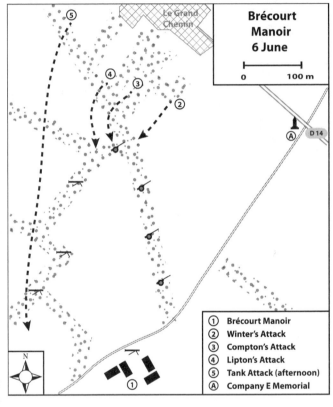

Brécourt Manor, a farm complex used by the artillerymen as a barracks and headquarters, is 500 meters down the country lane to the left of the monument. Nothing remains to identify the site of the German guns except ditches along the hedgerows that once were German trenches. The four German guns stood on the opposite side of the hedgerow at the rear of field #1 behind the monument. Three machine guns held positions along the hedgerow in field #2 west of the guns.

Brécourt Manor
6 June

0   100 m

① Brécourt Manor
② Winter's Attack
③ Compton's Attack
④ Lipton's Attack
⑤ Tank Attack (afternoon)
Ⓐ Company E Memorial

Continue toward Ste-Marie-du-Mont (D14); after 500 m, turn left toward Utah Beach (D913) and continue approximately 400 m to the statue of the left. (49.391452, -1.213582)

A new memorial, known as the **Richard Winters Leadership Monument**, was dedicated on 6 June 2012. The statue presents Major Winters as a leader of men, but it includes all those who led the way on D-Day. The plinth carries a quotation from Major Winters: 'Wars do not make men great; but they do bring out the greatness in good men.'

Continue on highway D913 to the statue on the right. (49.403392, -1.195858)

The statue of an old Danish seaman standing upon a stone plinth framed by the French and Danish flags memorializes the **800 Danish sailors** who participated in the landings as members of Allied boat crews.

This highway is **Causeway exit #2** and proceeds directly from la Madeleine, the US 4th Infantry Division landing beach, to Ste-Marie-du-Mont. The proximity of the guns at Brécourt Manor demonstrates the powerful effect those guns could have had on invasion operations and the inland movement of 4th Infantry Division.

Reverse direction and return to the intersection with highway D14. Turn left away from Audouville-la-Hubert (now D115). Continue 1.6 km, then turn left and continue into Pouppeville.

At 0600, General Taylor, Brigadier General Anthony McAuliffe, Colonel Julian Ewell, and 58 officers and men mostly from 3rd Battalion, 501st PIR, moved along this road toward Pouppeville along **Causeway exit #1**. When they approached the village, they found it held by 60 men of the German Grenadier Regiment 1058, 91st Airlanding Division. They engaged the enemy in a three-hour gun battle through the streets and houses of the small village before driving the remaining forces into the village schoolhouse. After a few bazooka rounds impacted the building, thirty-eight enemy soldiers surrendered while a few made their escape along the causeway heading toward the beach.

From the center of Pouppeville, proceed east (D329) for 750 m and stop.
(49.388121, -1.183965)

At 1110, a patrol commanded by Lieutenant Eugene Brierre found the Poupeville escapees hiding under a small bridge over la Grand Crique Rau, more a drainage ditch than river, 750 meters northeast of Pouppeville. Lt Brierre took them prisoner.[10]

A tank appeared coming from the direction of the sea. Stopped by rifle fire pinging upon its armor, the tank displayed an orange recognition panel. Lt Brierre answered with an orange smoke grenade. The paratroopers had made contact with Captain George Mabry,[11] 2nd Battalion, 8th Infantry Regiment, 4th Infantry Division. Causeway exit #1 was secure.

Mabry dispatched the two remaining tanks of the regiment's 70th Tank Battalion – three had been destroyed by German mines along exit #1 roadway, which explains why they approached so cautiously – to accompany Lieutenant Lewis Nixon to eliminate the remaining resistance at Brécourt Manoir.

The actual meeting place was at this small, barely noticeable culvert east of Pouppeville. A commemorative plaque has been erected approximately 650 meters farther east on the right side of the road. (49.390258, -1.176106)

Reverse direction and, after 2.1 km, turn right toward Ste-Marie-du-Mont (D115); after 1.6 km, turn left (D913) and proceed into the center of Ste-Marie-du-Mont. (49.378835, -1.22629)

---

10   Lieutenant Eugene Donnaud Brierre survived the war and became an attorney in his native New Orleans, Louisiana. He died in 2002 at age 78 and is buried in Metairie Cemetery, New Orleans.

11   Captain George Lafayette Mabry, Jr was awarded a Distinguished Service Cross for his actions in eliminating German resistance on Utah Beach. Later in the war, Mabry, then a lieutenant colonel, was awarded the Medal of Honor for leading an attack through a minefield and capturing three German bunkers in the Battle of the Hürtgen Forest. He survived the war as the second most decorated American soldier of the Second World War. He died in 1990 at age 72 and is buried in his home state of South Carolina.

Ste-Marie-du-Mont

Ste-Marie-du-Mont, only 5 kilometers from the landing beaches, controlled the road intersection on causeway exit #2, the critical roadway by which the 4th Infantry Division was to relieve the airborne troops. The II Battalion, Artillery Regiment 191, 91st Airlanding Division, was headquartered in Ste-Marie and commanded two batteries of four 105-mm guns, one at Holdy and the other at Brécourt Manoir.

Before dawn, a mixed group of six or seven paratroopers landed near the town, quietly made its way to the village square, and entered the church. Part of the force occupied the church's steeple from which they engaged German snipers. As the morning progressed, the American force grew and participated in small engagements with the town's German garrison, a company from 709th Infantry Division. After the capture of the Holdy battery (see below), Captain Lloyd E Patch of the 1st Battalion Headquarters Company and Captain Knut H Raudstein of Company C led their troops against the village but were stymied by a German machine-gun team securely positioned behind a stone wall south of the church. By early afternoon an American tank arrived from the beachhead, scattered the German defenders, and secured the town.

Église Notre-Dame de l'Assomption is a building of many eras with a Romanesque nave, Gothic chancel and transept, Flamboyant choir, and a multi-story bell tower of Gothic and Renaissance origins topped with Moorish-design dome. The earliest sections date from the 11th century, but the church was not completed until centuries later. The bell tower, the highest point in the Cotentin, invites tours in the summer. The 196-step effort promises magnificent views of the countryside and the 101st Division's battlefield.

Twelve panels around the place de l'Église describe, in French and English, the individual duels between American paratroopers and German defenders as the Americans landed among the gardens and courtyards of the village. Each hunted the other in the early morning gloom and shadows, moving stealthily along a garden wall or hiding behind the town war memorial. These simple stories, told on panels that dot the front or side of the church, bear attention. A plaque celebrating the liberators of the village, moreover, is on the right corner of the *mairie*.

Musée de l'Occupation (49.378486, -1.224852)
36, place de l'Église   50480 Ste-Marie-du-Mont
Tel: +33 (0)2 33 71 57 14

This building's faded murals, painted by German occupants in the old restroom attest to its use by the German garrison. The rooms are presented as they were in 1944 with artifacts and uniformed manikins portraying life during the four-year German occupation.

Open every day from 15 April to 15 September from 10:00 to 12:30 and from 13:30 to 18:30. Admission fee.

Musée de la Liberté (49.379024, -1.226376)
4, place de l'Église   50480 Ste-Marie-du-Mont
Tel +33 (0)2 33 71 56 54   Email: museedelaliberation@orange.fr

This small museum displays a collection of equipment, weapons, and personal items used by U.S. soldiers.

Open from 1 April to 11 November from 10:00 to 12:00 and from 14:00 to 18:00. Admission fee.

The narrow country lanes to the next three sites may be by-passed by proceeding directly to Angoville-au-Plain. To do so, leave Ste-Marie-du-Mont toward Vierville (rue 101ème Airborne, D913). After 3.8 km, turn left toward Angoville (rue de l'Église). (49.352386, -1.257634)
For the more daring, leave the place de l'Église toward Chef-du-Pont (D70). After 800 m, turn left onto a country lane toward Hiesville (D329e1). After 350 m, stop at the fork in the road. (49.377469, -1.237807)

Batterie du Holdy
Tel +33 (0)2 33 44 81 20
Web http://www.batterie-du-holdy.com/#accueil.A

Unknown to Allied planners, an enemy 105-mm howitzer battery manned by Artillery Regiment 191 poised along a nearby road. On the morning of 6 June, men of the 506th PIR, with some lost troopers of the 82nd Airborne Division, engaged the German troops but made no headway against the enemy positions. Colonel Robert F Sink, 506th PIR commander, gradually assembled an additional seventy-five-man unit from the 1st Battalion at his command post in Caloville[12] and sent them forward under Captains Lloyd Patch and Knut Raudstein.[13] When the reinforcements approached, the Germans withdrew to the earth revetments of the gun emplacements. They were trapped by a double envelopment with a bazooka team on one flank and a machine gun on the other. Rockets fired into the position ignited some of the stored cannon ammunition; then Patch and Raudstein moved the infantry in from two sides overrunning the position. The result was a bloody sight with fifty-to-sixty dead artillerymen and the remains of numerous paratroopers who were unlucky enough to land among the alerted Germans earlier in the morning. After Patch and Raustein left to attack Ste-Marie-du-Mont, an American lieutenant, doubtful of his ability to hold the gun position with his reduced force, destroyed three of the four guns before being instructed to stop.

The Battery du Holdy headquarters is now a B&B which offers tours of invasion sites by Jeep (by appointment only). The guns were located in the ramshackle pasture northeast of the fork in the road. Captain Patch's attack commenced from the direction of the stone house and crossed the road. A field on the opposite side of the hedgerow is the site of the famous picture of a crashed 82nd Airborne Division glider with a line of dead paratroopers. Eighteen were killed and fourteen injured in the disastrous incident.

Proceed and after 350 m jog right; continue for 850 m (rue du Limarais), then turn left toward Hiesville (D329, Route de Francqueville). Follow for 1.2 km into the small village, stopping at the first farm entrance on the right. (49.371636, -1.263041)

Hiesville was occupied without a fight on 6 June. At 0900, Ferme Franqueville became **General Maxwell Taylor's first headquarters** in France. A plaque on the farm gatepost marks the site; easier to notice, a bronze 'Screaming Eagle' details the other

12   Military histories refer to this town as Culoville or Coulaville; it shows on modern French maps as Caloville.

13   Captain Lloyd E Patch and Captain Knut H Raudstein were awarded Distinguished Service Crosses. Patch rose to the rank of lieutenant colonel and later commanded the 3rd Battalion, 506th PIR.

gatepost.

The **first Allied Field Hospital** in Normandy was established by 326th Airborne Medical Company in the Château de Colombières 550 meters north of the village on Route des Goueys. The French occupants stoically moved into one bedroom as the milk house converted into an operating room, with the wounded attended to in the other rooms. On 9 June, near midnight, German planes dropped three bombs on the area, killing eleven and wounding fifteen. The hospital was relocated. A grey stone column across the road from the chateau entrance identifies the site. (49.375814, -1.262119)

Leave Hiesville to the south on rue de Rabey. After 1.2 km, stop at the stele on the right. (49.365712, -1.273652)

At the intersection with highway D129, a roadside monument to Brigadier General Don Pratt marks Landing Zone E, which was across highway D129 and to the north. The glider carrying General Pratt, the 101st Airborne Division's Assistant Division Commander, was riddled by machine-gun fire while it circled to find a landing spot at 0345 on 6 June. The Waco glider landed but failed to stop in the small field, sliding on the wet grass until it crashed against the hedgerow at the end of the field. General Pratt[14] was killed and became the first American general officer to die in the invasion.

Turn left toward la Croix Pam (D129); after 140 m, turn left on rural road (unsigned, but rue des Vaucelles). After 1.5 km, turn left, then after 850 m, left again toward Angoville-au-Plain (D913). After 600 m, turn right (rue de l'Église) and proceed to the square in front of the church. (49.348954, -1.25345)

Battle for Angoville-au-Plain
6 to 8 June

The village was situated 400 meters east of DZ D where 1st and 2nd Battalions, 501st PIR, and 3rd Battalion, 506th PIR, were to land. The 506th PIR's drop was one of the most accurate that night but also one of the most disastrous since the *Fallschirmjäger* Regiment had anticipated the potential of the field as a landing site and was waiting for the unfortunate parachutists. German troops had ringed three sides of the field with machine guns and ignited a barn on the fourth side to illuminate the falling men making them easy targets. The battalion commander and his executive officer were among the dead, which included over half of the battalion.[15] The few survivors were those whose descent missed the drop zone.

Nonetheless, Angoville was occupied by 326th Airborne Engineer Battalion in the early morning of 6 June. Two medics, Privates Robert Wright and Kenneth Moore, established an aid station in the church. The village come under attack by a larger force of German paratroopers and was recaptured that morning. Although the engineers abandoned the village, the two medics chose to remain, treating American and German wounded and one injured French child. When the fallschirmjäger stormed the church, they discovered

---

14   Brigadier General Don F Pratt is buried in Arlington National Cemetery.

15   Killed were 3rd Battalion 506th PIR commander, Lieutenant Colonel Robert L Wolverton, and his executive officer Major George S Grant. Wolverton is buried at the US Military Academy, West Point. He was 30 years old. Major Grant is buried in Normandy American Cemetery. He was 26 years old.

the aid station. They offered assistance and throughout the remainder of the battle respected the sanctuary of the church. The battle over Angoville raged for the next two days, and the village changed hands several times while the medics continued to minister to their patients whose number grew to eighty. Finally, a determined attack by Col Sink's 506th PIR secured the village.

Prominent in the square is the gray stone stele dedicated to **Robert E. Wright** and **Kenneth J. Moore**[16] of 2nd Battalion, 501st PIR, who, throughout the three-day engagement, continued to care for a civilian child and wounded combatants. Descriptive panels explain the fight for the village and the heroics of the two medics.

The village church is across the square. A simple stele to the right of the church gate identifies the square as **place Toccoa**, named after the 101st Airborne Division's training camp in Georgia. The 12th-century stone church retains its ancient appearance with a steep-roofed tower in the center of the structure, simple wooden pews, wooden vaulted ceiling, and plain stone walls. The only modern additions are two stained-glass windows, one dedicated to medics Wright and Moore and the second honoring American parachutists. Less noticeable are the remains of war damage. The center of the church floor has a stone cracked from the impact of a mortar round that entered through a window but failed to explode. Several of the church pews retain dark stains from wounded soldiers' blood where they were treated by the medics.

> Leave Angoville-au-Plain to the south on rue de l'Église. After 300 m, continue straight on the very minor road, rue des Presles. After 650 m, stop at Delaunay Ferme B&B on the left. (49.341734, -1.259673)

On 6 June Lieutenant George Schmidt, Company E, 501st PIR, led thirty men through the fields to the east of the road from Angoville against a strong German position in farm buildings at **les Droueries**. While the group advanced, it came under heavy enemy mortar fire. Lieutenant Walter Wood, Company C, led 20 men around from the west against the building south of the crossroad. Lt Schmidt's attack was successful in capturing the farm buildings, but Schmidt[17] was killed by a sniper.

A black plaque mounted upon a white stele describes, in French and English, the D-Day attack led by Lt Schmidt. The 101st 'Screaming Eagle' and 501st emblems top the plaque. The building's wall remains bullet-riddled, and the sniper's hole remains in the side of the building.

> Proceed southeast on Vlg de la Haute Addeville for 650 m passing through Haute Addeville. Turn left and follow rue du Bel-Esnault for 1.0 km through Basse Addeville to a junction immediately before the N13/E46/E3 underpass. Turn left. The roadway parallels the E3/E46 for 850 m and then curves left. Continue 1.1 km to the junction with the minor road on the left. (49.329206, -1.24109)

---

16   Combat Medics Robert E Wright and Kenneth J Moore were awarded Silver Stars and survived the war.

17   Second Lieutenant George E Schmidt was awarded a Distinguished Service Cross for his outstanding courage. He is buried in Normandy American Cemetery.

Battle of the Douve Bridges
6 to 8 June 1944

Objective	To capture bridges across the Douve River.
Forces	
American	1st Battalion, 501st PIR (Colonel Howard Johnson)
German	I Battalion, *Fallschirmjäger* Regiment 6 (Hauptmann Emil Priekschat)
Result	The bridges were not captured.
Casualties	
American	uncertain
German	775 killed or captured
Location	Carentan is 75 km east of Caen; Barquette locks are 2 km northeast of Carentan

Battle

In the darkness of early 6 June, the 1st Battalion, 501st PIR, was badly scattered, most of its command structure killed, wounded, or lost in the marshes. By dawn, regimental commander Colonel Howard Johnson had collected a mixed force of roughly 150 men which moved against la Barquette, quickly capturing the undefended locks.

By midday on 7 June, Col Johnson's force had grown to 250 men, but they were receiving sporadic artillery fire from the direction of Carentan. About 1500, a large body from I Battalion, *Fallschirmjäger* Regiment 6, was seen approaching through the swamp from the north. Johnson swiftly and quietly shifted his men from facing south to facing north to address the new threat. One hour later, the enemy force of unknown size was within range, whereby, Col Johnson unleashed his ambush. An intense firefight erupted broken by periods of quiet. Parley attempts eventually convinced the Germans to surrender to the 'superior American force.' Johnson's men took 350 prisoners and accounted for 150 killed at a cost of 40 casualties. On 9 June, the men, at what was now known as 'Hell's Corners,' were relieved by the 506th PIR.

Action at La Barquette Locks 6 to 9 June

0 ⊢————————⊣ 300 m

E 46

1 ⊠ 501 Johnson

Ⓐ

Douve

Ⓐ Tour Stop

Battlefield Tour

La Barquette locks regulate the level of the wetlands about Carentan and the water level in the Douve River. They can be opened to drain the interior at low tide and closed to prohibit sea water from flowing inland at high tide. The locks are simply hefty doors that, in 1944, were manipulated by hand cranks on the walkways across the top of the structure. Unfortunately, admission to the locks is prohibited. Col Johnson's front line, facing the German troops on 7 June held an arc approximately 150 meters north of the last 1 kilometer of the just traveled roadway. The enemy advance initiated across the flat wetlands from the northeast.

The second location for the Battle of the Douve Bridges is near le Port and, because of lack of a nearby roadway crossing the river and canal, will be visited later in the tour.

Reverse direction and return to rue du Bel-Esnault. Turn left, pass under the autoroute, and continue for 700 m to Dead Man's Corner. (49.328325, -1.268256)

By the end of D-Day, the division's organized strength had grown to 2,500. Meanwhile, over 4,000 paratroopers, still scattered across the countryside, were fighting as members of other units, captive, or dead. Despite the reduced strength, however, the division attained its objectives. The four causeways from Utah Beach had been secured and handed over to 4th Division; roadblocks had been established on the northern flank of the invasion along highway D17 west of Foucarville; and, unknown to the unit's commander, the Douve bridges were in paratrooper hands.

Battle of St-Côme-du-Mont
7 to 8 June

Objective	To eliminate German forces in St-Côme-du-Mont.
Forces	
American	1st and 2nd Battalions of 506th PIR, 3rd Battalion, 501st PIR, and newly arrived 3rd Battalion, 327th GIR (Colonel Robert F Sink)
German	III Battalion, *Fallschirmjäger* Regiment 6 (Hauptmann Horst Trebes)
Result	The town was taken, but many of the enemy troops escaped to Carentan.
Casualties	
American	uncertain
German	unknown
Location	Carentan is 75 km east of Caen; St-Côme-du-Mont is 4 km north of Carentan

Battle

By the morning of 7 June, Col Sink had assembled a sizable but mixed unit force near Caloville. Led by the 1st Battalion, 506th PIR, it marched through Vierville and Beauville, stopping frequently to clear farms and villages of harassing enemy riflemen. By 1830, it achieved the crossroads east of St-Côme, where they were stopped by heavy machine-gun fire from Hauptmann Horst Trebes' *Fallschirmjäger* battalion.[18]

---

18 Hauptmann Horst Trebes was awarded the Knight's Cross of the Iron Cross for his actions during the 1941 airborne capture of Crete. Trebes was also rumored to be responsible for the execution of one hundred civilians. He was stripped of all awards and sentenced to death for the accidental death

Company D passed to the south where its leading support tank was destroyed by a rocket at the road junction south of St-Côme. (See Dead Man's Corner, below). Still, the 2nd Battalion cleared Vierville of infiltrating enemy troops and eliminated enemy resistance in Angoville-au-Plain. Col Sink called his extended and exposed forces back to Beaumont for the night to repeat the advance the next day with a more-concentrated strength.

A full-scale assault upon in St-Côme-du-Mont started at 0445 on 8 June with American forces attacking along a line from Beaumont to east of les Droueries, supported by a rolling artillery barrage and a handful of light tanks. The 501st PIR's 3rd Battalion moved south, then east, and claimed the Carentan road near the intersection with the Beaumont road (D913/N2013). The battalion was then suddenly attacked by German forces coming from the north. During the course of the day, it repulsed five such attacks, often fighting in close quarters among the hedgerows. The fifth German effort was so strong that only the timely arrival of three tanks and a spirited flank attack from troops positioned earlier on the west side of the highway retained the position. By mid-afternoon, after regrouping, the battalion withstood a second all-out attack on St-Côme-du-Mont, only to find the town abandoned as German forces had moved south along the rail line to the west of the town. During the day's fighting, the Germans had blown the second of the four highway bridges leading into Carentan.

Battlefield Tour

On 7 June, several light Stuart tanks accompanied by Company D, 506th PIR, approached the road junction from the direction of Beaumont. The lead unit was hit by German antitank fire at the intersection, killing the crew and leaving the body of the tank commander hanging halfway out of the turret. For several days, the tank, with its gruesome display, remained under enemy fire, giving the location its name, **Dead Man's Corner**. The American advance stalled, and its troops withdrew toward Beaumont to regroup. The road junction was captured during the coordinated assault on the following day. **Circuit Historique 1944 panel #2** stands beside the entrance gate to the museum.

The Centre Historique des Parachutistes US du Jour-J in conjunction with the Office de Tourisme des Marais de Carentan has erected thirteen **Circuit Historique 1944** information signs. Each green sign identifies and describes invasion events in or around Carentan. This tour does not follow its suggested route, nor does it include all of the sites, but they are worthy of notice.

Centre Historique des Parachutistes US du Jour-J
(Dead Man's Corner Museum)

2, village de l'Amont   50500 St-Côme-du-Mont
Tel +33 (0)2 33 42 00 42   Email: carentan.101@orange.fr
Web: http://www.paratrooper-museum.org

The museum lodges in a house at the crossroads where the Americans suffered losses to liberate St-Côme-du-Mont. It served as a German paratroop command post and then as an aid station. The museum houses a collection dedicated to American and German paratroopers. Full-scale dioramas present men and equipment from the battle. The collection of original artifacts is impressive. Looking to the south from an upper window offers an impressive view of the causeway into Carentan, later referred to as 'Purple

---

of a fellow officer during an all-night drunken party. He career was redeemed by the intercession of Hermann Goering. Trebes was killed on 29 July 1944 in fighting near St-Lô. He was 27 years old.

Heart Lane.' This private museum also features an attached shop selling original and reproduction military equipment and uniforms. A rusted German 88-mm FlaK gun in front of the building stills guards the intersection.

Open daily from 10:00 to 18:00; closed Sundays 1 October to 30 April and Christmas/New Year holidays. Admission fee; Normandie Pass accepted.

> Leave Dead Man's Corner by going up the hill into St-Côme-du-Mont (D974). Stop at the church. (49.335638, -1.272579)

Early in the morning of 6 June, the headquarters of German *Fallschirmjäger* Regiment 6 at Périers received orders to respond to reports of enemy parachutist landings. At midday of 6 June, Major von der Heydte arrived in St-Côme-du-Mont and climbed the church steeple[19] being used as an artillery observation post. The view of the English Channel 11 kilometers away was breathtaking. Warships of every description were pounding targets selected by their forward observers. The beach approaches were littered with landing craft disgorging men, equipment, and vehicles. He knew that this was the long-anticipated invasion.

The 12th-century **Église St-Côme-St-Damien** was heavily shelled by Allied naval vessels because its elevation provided extraordinary observation of the Utah Beach invasion. The structure has been rebuilt and is a registered historic landmark. The south portal should be viewed as well as the interior, if, that is, the church is open.

Circuit Historique 1944 Panel #1, in the village square at the entrance into the cemetery, tells the story of paratrooper demolitions expert Staff Sergeant Joseph Beyrle, who was forced to jump short of DZ D and landed on the church roof. Before daybreak, Beyrle destroyed a mobile generator and attacked a group of Germans who had gathered nearby. He then crawled over a hedgerow and stumbled into a well-defended German machine-gun position and was captured.[20] A brass plaque attached to the side of the church also tells Beyrle's story.

> Leave St-Côme-du-Mont toward Carentan (D974). After 1.8 km, turn into the parking area on the right and walk back north, crossing the original la Jourdan bridge and proceeding to the German pillbox. (49.321206, -1.265531)

---

19   Many histories of the battle state that this incident took place in Ste-Marie-du-Mont. In interviews conducted after the war, von der Heydte described climbing the church tower in St-Côme-du-Mont and that he was 11 kilometers from Utah Beach. The distance corresponds to St-Côme-du-Mont. By that time on 6 June, American paratroops held the Ste-Marie-du-Mont church tower.

20   Staff Sergeant Joseph 'Jumpin' Joe' Beyrle spent seven months in German POW camps. He escaped only to be re-captured and tortured by the Gestapo, who thought that he was a spy. After being transported to an Eastern Front POW camp, he successfully escaped again. Beyrle met and joined a Soviet tank unit with which he utilized his demolitions expertise. Wounded, Beyrle was moved to Moscow where he reported to the US Embassy to find that he had been reported dead by the War Department. Beyrle returned to his hometown of Muskegon, Michigan, and was married in the same church that earlier had held his funeral mass. He is thought to be the only American soldier to have also fought in the Soviet Army during the Second World War. He died in 2004 at age 81 and is buried in Arlington National Cemetery. His son, John Beyrle, became US Ambassador to Russia in 2008.

Battle of Carentan
10 to 11 June 1944

Carentan remained the key to further invasion progress. Its position on the Cherbourg-Bayeux highway and its rail and highway bridges across the Douve controlled movement between the Utah and Omaha invasion beaches and linkup of V Corps and VII Corps. Generals Eisenhower and Bradley met on 7 June and gave first priority to the city's capture.

Objective	To cross the causeway bridges and assault Carentan.
Forces	
American	3rd Battalion, 502nd PIR (Lieutenant Colonel Robert G Cole)
German	III Battalion, *Fallschirmjäger* Regiment 6 (Hauptmann Horst Trebes)
Result	The four bridges and the German headquarters were taken after a series of violent engagements.
Location	Carentan is 75 km east of Caen

Battle

By 9 June, the 506th PIR sat astride the Carentan highway south of St-Côme with the 502nd PIR on its right. The only approach to Carentan lay across the extended 800-meter causeway and the four bridges that crossed the flooded marshes. Shortly after midnight on 10 June, Lieutenant Colonel Robert Cole's 3rd Battalion, 502nd PIR, moved south against Carentan in what became the bloodiest engagement in the Cotentin Peninsula. For two days his battalion fought a close-quarters assault against a determined, well-positioned enemy. After suffering heavy casualties on the extended causeway, Cole led a ferocious charge to finally capture the *Fallschirmjäger* Regimental headquarters.

Battlefield Tour

The four causeway bridges formed simple single spans crossing a small Douve tributary called la Jourdan, the Douve (the bridge blown by the Germans on 8 June), a small backwater of the Douve known as le Groult, and another small tributary of the Douve named la Madeleine. The approach and all four bridges crossed two-to-three meters above the treeless, flooded marshes and were thus completely without cover. The west embankment fell sharply into the water; the east embankment was less steep and offered the possibility of passage but greater exposure to enemy fire.

The current causeway and bridges are of post-war construction, but the stone bridge and its approach roadway are original. The bridge crosses the Jourdan River, easily captured on the night of 9 June. The **German pillbox** controlled the strategic crossings, but it was probably abandoned by German troops before the second bridge was blown. An **NTL Totem** is nearby.

> Leave the parking area and proceed toward Carentan, crossing the Douve bridges. After 600 m turn left onto a very minor side road (les Breneuries) and stop to view the bridges. (49.321206, -1.265531)

On 9 June, a reconnaissance patrol crossed the Douve by boat, and the third bridge to find the fourth bridge barred by a metal gate. During the day artillery support in the form of twelve 75-mm pack howitzers and eighteen 105-mm SP guns took positions in St-Côme-du-Mont. Von der Heydte moved his regimental headquarters to Ingouf Farm and established machine-gun and mortar positions in the farmyard and nearby orchards. German artillery and mortars were positioned on Hill 30 southwest of Carentan.

By 1400 on 10 June, a wobbly footbridge had been constructed across the piers of the destroyed bridge #2 and, with little interference by the enemy, Col Cole's battalion crossed in single file during the next three hours. Suddenly the enemy came alive with small arms and machine-gun fire from the right front where a large stone farmhouse and surrounding hedgerows offered ideal cover. German snipers had also deployed to the left front with deadly effect.

The men inched forward, hugging the shallow ditches astride the highway while enemy bullets

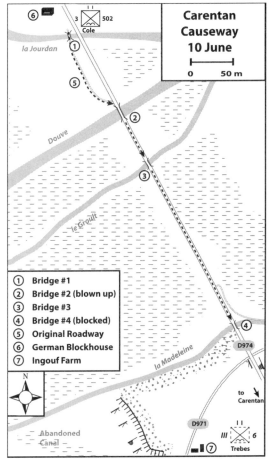

ricocheted off the asphalt surface and metal gate barring the final bridge. The number of dead and wounded mounted as the Americans brought machine guns and mortars into action against the enemy.

From the side road, **la Madeleine Bridge** (bridge #4) stands immediately ahead before the large traffic circle. The terrain to the west of la Madeleine bridge appears today much as the entire area did in 1944. The small islands of dry land protruding above the flood waters hid machine guns and snipers. German guns focused on the iron gate blocking bridge #4, where each paratrooper had to squeeze through a narrow opening under a hail of bullets. The standoff continued for four hours; as daylight waned, most of the battalion was trapped between the footbridge over bridge #2 and the gate at bridge #4. At 2330 two German dive bombers appeared flying along the line of the highway at low altitude. The planes dropped six-to-eight antipersonnel bombs and strafed the paratroopers huddled along the road, inflicting thirty more casualties in seconds. The night became quiet.

Walk to the roundabout to view the terrain to the southwest. (49.31445, -1.259587)

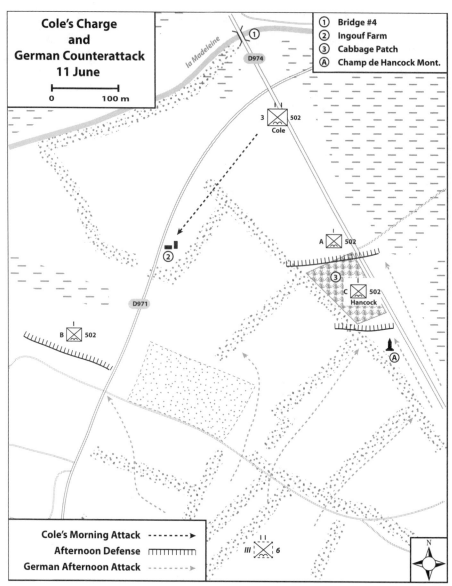

Cole's Charge and German Counterattack 11 June

0   100 m

① Bridge #4
② Ingouf Farm
③ Cabbage Patch
Ⓐ Champ de Hancock Mont.

la Madeleine

D974

3 ⨯ 502
Cole

A ⨯ 502

③

C ⨯ 502
Hancock

D971

B ⨯ 502

Ⓐ

Cole's Morning Attack ┄┄┄►
Afternoon Defense ⊓⊓⊓⊓⊓⊓⊓⊓
German Afternoon Attack ┄┄┄┄►

III ⨯ 6

N

By first light on 11 June, three of Col Cole's four companies had crossed la Madeleine. At 0530 he ordered the artillery to put down smoke in an arc centered upon the farmhouse from the Madeleine River to 400 meters down the main highway. The paratroopers reloaded their rifles and attached bayonets. At 0615 Colonel Cole gave the command, and seventy men, led by Cole himself, and his executive officer, Major John Stopka,[21] left the ditches and charged across the swamp and vegetable fields toward the

_____

21   Major John P Stopka was awarded a Distinguished Service Cross for continuously exposing himself to heavy enemy fire. He died in fighting at Bastogne and is buried in Luxembourg American Cemetery.

Ingouf farmhouse. At first only a few of Cole's men heard the order. While Cole ran forward firing his Colt-45, more of his men raced to catch up to the leaders while others fell to enemy fire. When the farmhouse was captured, German machine guns on the higher ground behind it pulled back. The barrier into Carentan had been broken by the first bayonet charge in Normandy.

The scene from the roundabout looking to the southwest is now of commercial establishments. The old farmhouse visible among the new buildings on the left roadside was the Ingouf Ferme and German headquarters. The famous charge started from the road junction now occupied by the roundabout and continued southwest on both sides of rue Américaine (D971).

Drive toward Carentan (D974) for 600 m and then turn right into the commercial parking area. A monument, easy to miss when traveling south sits along the roadside. (49.311009, -1.256733)

As Cole and his men desperately fought off determined German counterassaults against Ingouf Ferme, Lieutenant Colonel Patrick Cassidy's[22] 1st Battalion took up positions along a line from Ingouf farm back to the main highway ending in what was then a field of vegetables. For much of the afternoon, Captain Fred Hancock's Company C fought a relentless duel in the fields between the hedgerows southeast of the roundabout; at times the combatants lined opposite sides of the same hedgerow. For more than six hours Hancock's[23] men held firm as their numbers dwindled and German bodies piled up in front of American machine guns, in a scene reminiscent of the First World War.

A small park and memorial stone that commemorates Hancock's stubborn defense is almost lost among the buildings and parking areas of the commercial zone north of Carentan. Now known as **Champ de Hancock**, it identifies where Company C staged its defense in the hedgerow fields. Most of the hedgerows have been destroyed during construction of the commercial buildings, and only a portion of the **Cabbage Patch** remains behind a car dealership.

Reverse direction toward St-Côme-du-Mont; take the third exit from the large roundabout going southwest (Route Américaine, D971). After 190 m, turn left near the farm driveway. (49.312572, -1.260845)

At noon, an hour-long truce interrupted the fierce fighting as wounded of both sides were recovered. When the truce ended, German troops pressed forward along the four lines of hedgerows between the Ingouf Ferme and the cabbage patch. By late afternoon, the weakening American fire convinced Cole, who was still defending the farmhouse, that the battle was lost. While he was considering plans for a withdrawal, American artillery near St-Côme-du-Mont was re-supplied and brought its guns to bear upon the enemy. Five minutes of heavy bombardment dissipated the German attack. Von der Heydte eventually withdrew his men to the southwest and established a new line near Donville. He left one

---

22   Lieutenant Colonel Patrick J Cassidy was awarded a Distinguished Service Cross for leadership and personal bravery. Cassidy eventually attained the rank of Lieutenant General. He died in 1990 at age 75 and is buried in Fort Sam Houston National Cemetery.

23   Captain Fred A Hancock was awarded a Silver Star. He was wounded in Holland on Hell's Highway. He died in 2004 at age 94.

company in Carentan as rear guard. Cole's 700-man battalion had been reduced to 132. [24]

The **Ingouf Ferme**, center of the German resistance, still shows remnants of bullet holes received during the engagement. A plaque, identifying the farm as headquarters of Lt Col Cole, Medal of Honor recipient, is attached to the gate of the farm and is visible from highway D971. The plaque is slightly incorrect as the charge was launched toward the farmhouse, not from the farmhouse as the plaque states. **Circuit Historique 1944 panel #7**, near the entrance driveway of the private farm, presents Cole's medal citation. The period aerial photograph on the sign illustrates the open nature of the terrain in 1944. A row of shrubs perpendicular to and on the opposite side of the highway marks the hedgerow behind which German troops manned mortars, machine guns, and a 37-mm antitank gun – all aimed toward bridge #4.

For convenience, the route proceeds to Bloody Gulch, where the Germans almost succeeded in retaking Carentan. The final capture of Carentan will be described later in the tour.

Continue on rue Américaine (D971) for 1.2 km to the large roundabout near the livestock market. Take the second exit, which curves around the south side of a parking area, and follow toward le Couppeville. After 1.1 km, stop at the farm lane on the right. (49.299218, -1.277853)

Battle of Bloody Gulch
13 June 1944

The Germans realized that the loss of Carentan was a critical blow to the defense of the Cotentin Peninsula. Since 6 June, the 17th SS Panzergrenadier Division had been making slow progress from its positions south of the Loire toward the battlefield. By late afternoon of 12 June, the 506th and 501st PIRs were positioned in a broad arc from the railway line south of the Douve to across the Périers Road southwest of Hill 30. The 2nd Battalion, 506th PIR, advanced as far as Douville, where it met German forces preparing for a counterattack against Carentan. After an initial skirmish, both sides dug in for the night.

Objective	To continue the advance to the west.
Forces	
American	506th PIR (Colonel Robert Sink)
German	Elements of 17th SS Panzergrenadier (*Götz von Berlichingen*) Division (Generalleutnant Werner Ostendorf) and III Battalion, *Fallschirmjäger* Regiment 6 (Hauptmann Horst Trebes)
Result	The paratroops delayed a vastly larger armored force.
Location	Carentan is 75 km east of Caen; Bloody Gulch is 2.6 km west of Carentan.

---

24   Lieutenant Colonel Robert G Cole was awarded the Medal of Honor for his utter disregard for his own safety. He never knew of the award as he died by a sniper's bullet near Best, Holland, in September 1944. He was 29 years old. Cole is buried in Netherlands American Cemetery, Margraten, the Netherlands.

Battle

At 0530 on 13 June, two battalions of SS Panzer Grenadier Regiment 37, 17th SS Panzergrenadier Division, and remnants of the re-supplied *Fallschirmjäger* Regiment 6 counterattacked Carentan from the direction of Baupte, supported by thirty-seven self-propelled guns from the SS *Panzerjäger* Battalion 17. The 501st and 506th had planned their opposing attack for 0500 supported by only nine light tanks. A confused battle raged in an extended line as artillery, machine-gun, mortar, and rifle fire erupted from both sides. The American line started to crumble from left to right under the concentrated attack of German armored SS troops. The attack finally was repulsed at 1630 by the arrival of lead elements of Combat Command A (CCA) of 2nd Armored Division reinforced by P-47 Thunderbolt fighter-bombers. The increased American firepower drove the Germans back from what was their last effort against Carentan.

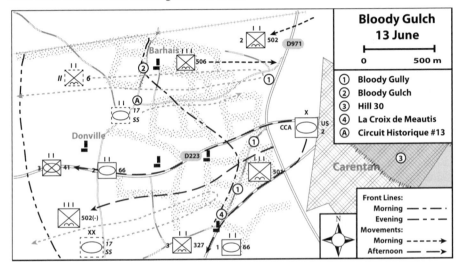

Battlefield Tour

Few drivable roads and the closed nature of the private pastures limit opportunities to view the exact sites of the battle's events.

Circuit Historique 1944 panel #13, along the farm lane, identifies this track as **Bloody Gulch**. Its likewise describes the attack of the re-enforced *Fallschirmjäger* Regiment 6. Not having the weapons to counter the *panzerjäger* battalion's 'Marder' 75-mm self-propelled guns, the American paratroopers were forced back toward Carentan through the fields passed in approaching this site. The farm track slopes downhill with high verges on both sides limiting views into the fields on either side. The 506th PIR was positioned in the fields to the right and the attacking Germans came from the left. The rail line, which formed the right flank of Company E, 506th PIR, is 500 meters ahead. A small tunnel under the rail line remains.

Continue 550 m, then turn left and proceed toward Carentan (D223, becomes rue d'Auvers, D903). Proceed into Carentan along route d'Auvers until it forms a slanted T-junction with the route de Périers (joining from the right) and rue Holgate (continues to the left). (49.300923, -1.249542)

This was the direction of attack of 2nd Battalion, 506th PIR, into Carentan on 12 June. The house (**Bar du Stade**) facing the route d'Auvers sheltered the German machine gun that pinned down Lt Richard Winters' troops during the attack as depicted in *Band of Brothers*. (49.300911, -1.249523)

Continue on rue Holgate for 250 m to the junction with rue de la Guinguette. The last building on the left had served as an airborne troop aide station. (49.30288, -1.248166) Turn right and follow for 350 m along the rail line and station. Turn left to cross the rail line. After 150 m, turn left on Bd de Verdun. Stop at the park near the Signal Monument on the right. (49.302894, -1.245301)

Battle of Carentan (continued)
12 June 1944

Battle

The final assault upon Carentan began during the night of 11/12 June when VII Corps artillery, naval guns, 4.2 inch mortars, and assault guns bombarded the town. In the darkness, two battalions of the 506th crossed the Carentan causeway and marched cross-country to the dominant high ground near the village of la Billonnerie known as Hill 30. The 1st Battalion, 506th PIR, took up defensive positions facing south. At 0600, Carentan was attacked from the north by 1st Battalion, 401st GIR, and from the south by 2nd Battalion, 506th PIR. Fighting against the enemy's rear guard, they quickly eliminated the last resistance and met near the town center.

Battlefield Tour

Carentan

Carentan is barely above sea level and virtually surrounded by marshes, waterways, and canals. Gallic settlers appreciated its position on the Douve estuary and established a small community. The town retains little of is old charm due the extensive damage suffered during the Battle of Carentan. The high-speed E46/N13 now bypasses Carentan to the north, dramatically going under the Carentan Bessin, a harbor for pleasure boats.

Office du Tourisme des Marais de Carentan (49.302898, -1.246079)
Boulevard de Verdun   B.P. 204
50500 Carentan   Tel +33 (0)2 33 71 23 50
Web: http://www.ot-carentan.fr/en/index.html

A stop at the **Hôtel de Ville** is warranted by the beautiful grounds fronting what was originally an old convent that was converted for public use. A **Signal Monument** dedicated to the liberation of Europe by the Allied Forces and the liberation of Carentan by the 101st Airborne Division stands in front of the Hôtel de ville. A plaque honoring the **101st Airborne Division** for its sacrifices to liberate Carentan stands at its base.

Continue north to the next intersection and turn right onto rue Holgate. Follow as the street curves to the right and enters **place de la République.** (49.304482, -1.24366)

The airborne forces met in this square following the liberation of the city. Along one side of the place are the remaining **14th-century arcades**, once a covered market. A statue representing the town's war memorial is in the center of the place, although it is frequently obscured by parked automobiles.

> At the far end of the place de la République, turn left onto the rue de l'Église and continue to the church. (49.305528, -1.243601)

Sections of the **Église Notre-Dame** date from the 12th century. The many changes and additions over the centuries are apparent since the church was not completed until three hundred years later. The south side of the church, built in the Flamboyant Gothic style, is of particular note. A stained glass window remembers the parachutists of the 101st Airborne Division, one of whose depicted religious figures holds the 'Screaming Eagle' emblem.

> Leave Pl de la République by car to the east on rue du Château. After 200 m, turn left on rue du Quai à Vin (becomes rue Sivard de Beaulieu). Turn right (rue de Caligny, D89e) and follow north out of the city and pass under the autoroute. After 450 m, the roadway crosses a tributary flowing into the canal over an original **Bailey Bridge** built at this location in June 1944 to replace a bridge destroyed by the Germans.
> (49.317318, -1.225426)
> Continue 2.1 km before turning right on a small side road. A memorial stands at the road junction. (49.331779, -1.206887)

Battle of the Douve Bridges (continued)
6 to 8 June 1944

Battle

The 3rd Battalion, 506th PIR, landed in the hottest drop zone in Normandy. The Germans ringed target field and American casualties were high before they fired a shot. The battalion operations officer, Captain Charles Shettle, took command and collected troops while the group moved toward its objective – the wooden bridges over the Douve River near le Port. By 0430, now numbering fifty-four men, the force moved against the bridges. Private First Class Donald Zahn[25] crossed one bridge under enemy machine-gun fire. Followed by Private First Class George Montilio,[26] they established a fire base while small teams crossed the river. Together the small force killed thirteen and destroyed three machine guns. As the day progressed, enemy fire steadily increased and forced Shettle's men back across to the western bank.

On 7 June the isolated group received occasional artillery and mortar fire. Unaware that the bridge was held by paratroopers, Col Sink ordered that the bridge be destroyed by air. A flight of P-47s bombed and strafed enemy and paratroopers alike and destroyed the two bridges. During the afternoon, a German force approached from the rear, causing rolling skirmishes to brake out. Under the impression that they faced a vastly superior paratroop

---

25   Private First Class Donald E Zahn was awarded a Distinguished Service Cross for his 'intrepid actions and personal bravery' and later received a battlefield commission. Lt Zahn fought in the defense of Bastogne. He now lives in Idaho and has nine children and twenty-three grandchildren.

26   Private First Class George Montilio was awarded a Distinguished Service Cross for daring and aggressiveness under intense enemy fire. He was killed in Germany on 19 April 1945, less than three weeks before the end of the war.

force, small groups of the enemy started to surrender. By nightfall, 60 to 70 enemy troops had been killed and 255 had surrendered.

At 1900 on 8 June, the 327th Glider Infantry Regiment took over and occupied Brévands the next morning. The two separate battles for Douve River locks and bridges had sealed the last withdrawal route of the I Battalion *Fallschirmjäger* Regiment 6. All but 25 of the 800-man battalion were killed or captured.

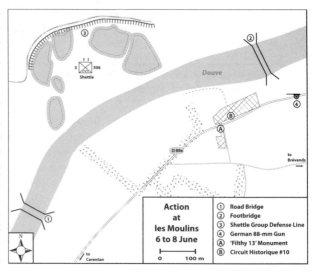

Action at les Moulins 6 to 8 June	
①	Road Bridge
②	Footbridge
③	Shettle Group Defense Line
④	German 88-mm Gun
Ⓐ	'Filthy 13' Monument
Ⓑ	Circuit Historique #10

0   100 m

Battlefield Tour

The community of le Moulin is little more than a few farm buildings where a chain ferry once transported people and animals across the Canal de Carentan. The western of the two bridges, 600 meters back toward Carentan, was a prefabricated design constructed in 1943 by the German Army to carry vehicles across the river; the eastern bridge 200 meters ahead toward le Port was merely a footbridge built in 1942. Neither of the bridges remains.

The memorial commemorates the actions of **3rd Battalion, 506th PIR,** and **Company C, 326 Airborne Engineer Battalion**, both of 101st Airborne Division, who denied these crossings to the enemy. Although Shettle's team crossed to this side of the canal, its defensive positions were on the opposite side of the canal. A polished black stone plaque describes the 'Filthy 13,' which was the nickname for Demolitions Platoon, Regimental HQ Company, attached to the 3rd Bn, 506th PIR, during its assignment to capture or destroy the bridges. An information panel describes the entire engagement.

Walk 30 meters to the east on highway D89e, turn to the left and pass around the side of a barn to find **Circuit Historique 1944 Panel #10** and its retelling of Captain Shettle's efforts to control the canal crossing. Pass through the arched gateway to mount the estuary's earthen, grass-covered dike. The footbridge was located approximately 150 meters to the east. Proceed along the canal embankment to the west. Captain Shettle maintained positions on the opposite side of the canal along an arc from the footbridge to the road bridge approximately 600 meters ahead. The concrete foundations of the road bridge remain, but the track to the site is overgrown and muddy. A pontoon bridge built by the 238th Combat Engineer Battalion 125 meters to the east of the damaged footbridge on 12 June was removed later in the war.

Continue northeast on rue du Moulin (D89e) 1.2 km to 'T' junction. Turn right and then, after 300 m, left to Brévands church. (49.331394, -1.190879)

The 12th-century Romanesque **Église St-Martin de Brévands** stands upon high ground, a rare commodity among the surrounding wetlands and a fact that had not passed unnoticed by the Germans. A small detachment from 352nd Infantry Division was stationed around Brévands as WN-98, but the strongpoint was much less well developed than others along the Normandy coast. German troops engaged the paratroopers after their crossing of the wooden bridge but later were driven off by the much larger glider regiment force.

> Proceed 90 m south from the front of the church in Brévands, turn left on rue des Avenues. After 600 m, turn right at the 'T' junction on D89. After 2.0 km, pass through Catz. (location is approximate)

On 10 June, the 327th Glider Infantry Regiment advanced south of Brévands nearing Catz and met units of the 116th Infantry Regiment advancing from Isigny-s/Mer to secure a linkage between Omaha and Utah Beaches.

This completes the tour of the 101st Airborne Division in Normandy. After the Battle of Bloody Gulch, the division spent the next sixteen days strengthening defensive lines to the south and southwest. On 29 June, it was relieved by the 83rd Infantry Division.

> To return to Carentan, continue into Banville; turn right toward Carentan (D974) and follow for 5.3 km into the town.

Side trip: 82nd Airborne Division in Graignes

> To view the final 82nd Airborne Division site, continue south through Banville; pass under the autoroute and proceed into the small village of St-Pellerin. Turn right 'vers N174' (D544). After 850 m, turn left away from Carentan (unsigned, but E3). After 3.5 km, enter a roundabout and take first exit (unsigned). At the next intersection turn right toward Graignes (D89) and follow for 5.2 km across marshes and the old Vire canal into le Vieux Bourg. Turn right onto place de la Libération 12 Juillet 1944 and stop near the **NTL totem**. Proceed on foot into the ancient cemetery. (49.244024,-1.206066) Total distance: 20.3 km

Battle of Graignes
10 to 12 June 1944

Objective	The troops at Graignes missed their DZ by a wide margin and engaged a vastly superior force in a battle for survival.
Forces	
American	181 men of 507th PIR, 82nd Airborne Division (Major Charles Johnston)
German	17th SS Panzergrenadier Division (Generalleutnant Werner Ostendorff)
Result	The town was overrun and destroyed.
Casualties	
American	33 soldiers killed or executed; 28 civilians killed and 4 executed
German	estimated at 500 killed or wounded

| Location | Carentan is 75 km east of Caen; Graignes is 12 km south of Carentan |

Battle

In the early hours of 6 June, sticks from the 82nd Airborne Division's 507th PIR landed more than 32 kilometers from their intended drop zone and fell near the village of Graignes. Many drowned in the marshes while survivors struggled to higher ground around the church. They were truly lost, as the village was not even on their maps. Originally only 60 men, they continued to collect stragglers growing to a force of 181. Major Charles D Johnston, the unit's executive officer, took command and, with the help of the villagers, collected weapons and ammunition and set up defensive positions around the village. The French civilians risked execution by feeding the soldiers and collecting intelligence regarding German movements in the area.

After several skirmishes during the previous night, on 11 June, elements of the German 17th SS Panzergrenadier Division launched two attacks which were beaten off with help from the town's citizens who redistributed ammunition and cared for the wounded. At dusk, the German force launched a more determined attack, accompanied by heavy mortar and 88-mm antitank-gun fire. It eventually overran the paratroopers, but not before the troopers inflicted an estimated 500 casualties. Major Johnston died in the burst of an 88-mm shell.

American survivors sought refuge in the flooded lowlands and tree-covered hillocks that surrounded the village. Eight-seven survivors spent the next two days in the marshes and barns before escaping to 101st Airborne Division positions near Carentan. The Germans took their reprisals by executing twenty-four wounded soldiers and thirty-two civilians for their role in helping the Allies. An additional forty-four townspeople were imprisoned,[27] the town was burned, and the church was blown up.

The delay imposed upon the 17th SS Panzergrenadier Division played a factor in the capture of Carentan. Without the fighting at Granges, the SS units could possibly have arrived at Carentan earlier, strengthening *Fallschirmjäger* Regiment 6 and making the capture of the city significantly more costly.

Battlefield Tour

The Commune of Graignes lies on a spit of ground that extends into the marshes of the Marais du Cotentin 8 kilometers south-southeast of Carentan. As such, it was bordered on three sides by flooded lowlands, and the only dry exit was the highway to the east toward St-Jean-de-Daye.

Only the tower of the destroyed 12th-century church was rebuilt, the ruined walls left as a dramatic reminder of the sacrifices of the soldiers and civilians. The parish priest, Curé Albert Leblastier, murdered in the reprisal, is buried under the surviving segment of the church roof. A **memorial plaque** erected in 1949 commemorates the events. A larger stone plaque lists the names of paratroopers and civilians killed in the action. The far end of the cemetery offers dramatic views over the Park Naturel Régional Marais du Cotentin du Bessin.

| Reverse the driving directions to regain highway D974 to Carentan. |

---

27   In 1986, eleven villagers were presented with the Distinguished Civilian Service Medal by the Unites States government. Six of those awards were posthumous.

Chapter Nine
US 4th (Ivy) Infantry Division
6 June to 14 June

The western-most seaborne assault zone, code-named Utah Beach, lay at the base of the Cotentin Peninsula immediately west of the Bancs du Grand Vey, where the Douve and Vire Rivers flow into the English Channel. The gradually sloped beach exposed over 700 meters of sand at low tide and faced a concrete seawall two-to-three meters high. A narrow strip of dunes fronted flooded marshlands, which extended inland for some 2 kilometers, before solid ground appeared along an uneven ridgeline approximately 30 meters above sea level. Slightly elevated causeways crossed the inundated areas, and four such routes were selected by Allied planners as exits from the beachfront.

The shore from Grand Vey in the south to Quinéville in the north was protected by a line of nineteen *Widerstandsnest* and *Stützpunkt*, which usually included re-enforced concrete gun positions, mortar or machine-gun tobruks, personnel shelters, mine fields, and wire entanglements. The beaches were littered with thousands of defensive structures of various designs, all intended to puncture, capsize, or explode beneath potential landing craft. The seawall was topped with barbed wire, and minefields were planted in the dunes. German troops in the invasion area included two battalions of the 709th Infantry Division. The I Battalion, Grenadier Regiment 919, headquartered near Foucarville. The *Ostbattalion* (Georgian) 795, a static infantry unit composed of Russian prisoners of war who 'volunteered' to fight in the German Army under the command of German officers and NCOs, was stationed near Turqueville. Heavy weapon support came from three batteries of the I Battalion, Artillery Regiment 191, headquartered in Ste-Marie-du-Mont, and the casemated batteries of the I Battalion, Coast Artillery Regiment 1261, headquartered near Foucarville. Additional units were posted inland and farther to the north.

The US 4th Infantry Division troops and their attached support units navigated the Channel in three US Navy attack transport ships. The accompanying naval armada of Task Force U numbered 865 ships, including the battleship USS *Nevada* and five cruisers. The division's objectives were to secure the beachhead, move inland, and proceed north to capture the port of Cherbourg, the only established seaport in Normandy large enough to handle the high volume of traffic required to supply the Allied army with the men, material, equipment, and fuel necessary to conduct further operations. The Allies divided Utah Beach into sectors bearing the coded names Tare Green and Uncle Red.

The 4th Infantry Division, a regular army unit, served with distinction in the First World War during the Battles of St-Mihiel and Meuse-Argonne. It adopted the 'Ivy' nickname from its four-leafed insignia. Deactivated in 1920, it reactivated in 1940 with three regiments of three battalions each.

D-Day Landing (Utah Beach)
6 June

Objective	To land on the coast of Normandy, establish contact with airborne forces, and secure a beachhead
Forces	
American	23,250 men of 4th Infantry Division and attached units (Major General Raymond O Barton)

German	12,230 men of 709th Infantry Division (Generalleutnant Karl Wilhelm von Schlieben)
Result	The landings and junction with airborne troops were successful
Casualties	
American	197 killed or wounded
German	Unknown
Location	Carentan is 75 km east of Caen; Utah Beach is 16 km northeast of Carentan

Battle

Although by 6 June much of the German radar network in Normandy had been destroyed by Allied bombers, German batteries detected the Allied armada at 0505 and commenced firing fifty-five minutes later. At 0550, the naval guns started their bombardment of the German beach defenses. Minutes later, 276 B-26 Marauder bombers of the Ninth Air Force dropped 4,404 two hundred fifty-pound bombs on seven objectives on the beach. The bombers were relatively ineffective, however, as concern over the safety of the landing forces led to dropping much of the ordinance several miles inland.

At 0435 the first waves of mainly LCVPs set off toward the beach. The days waiting in the harbors of England, the sleepless crossing of the channel, and the rough seas intensified their emotions. The time taken to launch and organize the landing craft seemed interminable to the soldiers. Launched 5 kilometers from the shoreline, it was not until two hours later that the 8th Regimental Combat Team (RCT), a temporary arrangement of the 8th Infantry Regiment supported by attached heavy weapons units, hit the beach at la Grande Dune near the hamlet of la Madeleine. Its support came from LCTs carrying M4 Sherman tanks or M7 Priest 105-mm self-propelled guns. Other LCTs had been converted to carry a variety of special weapons including antiaircraft guns, 4.7-inch naval guns, and 5-inch rocket launchers.

The landings on Utah Beach proved a resounding success and incurred a remarkably low 197 casualties, including 60 men lost at sea – a result partially attributable to the stronger than expected ocean currents and off-shore winds that drove the landing craft almost 2 kilometers farther southeast than planned to a less-well fortified section of beachfront. The naval and landing craft bombardments had destroyed most of the beachfront heavy weapons, and the surviving defenders were stunned into inaction by the violence of the assault. The daring and costly inland parachute landings of the 82nd and 101st Airborne Divisions were successful in limiting the response of inland German units and in securing the beach exit causeways.

By the end of the day, 4th Division units had established contact with the 101st Airborne Division, but not with the 82nd Airborne Division farther to the west, and it had crossed the Cherbourg-Bayeux highway, cutting the main German transport link in the eastern side of the Cotentin Peninsula.

Battlefield Tour

Leave Carentan toward St-Côme-du-Mont (D974); 3.2 km from the center of Carentan, turn toward Ste-Marie-du-Mont (D913) and continue on that road 12.5 km through Vierville and Ste-Marie-du-Mont directly to Utah Beach.

The flag-bordered main approach to Utah Beach is along Daniel Road (D913), designated as causeway exit #2 for the American invasion. (49.415748, -1.175162)

Utah Beach

At almost exactly H-Hour, twenty LCVPs lowered their ramps 100 meters from shore, and six hundred men of the 2nd Battalion, 8th Infantry Regiment, 4th Infantry Division, walked through the surf to shore. The regiment's 1st Battalion followed a few minutes later. Although their target was the causeway identified by Allied planners as exit #3, they had landed opposite exit #2. Brigadier General Theodore Roosevelt Jr, 4th Infantry Division's assistant commander and son of America's 26th president, Theodore 'Teddy' Roosevelt, landed with the first wave. Realizing that the landing had missed its assigned sector, Roosevelt performed his own reconnaissance to locate the causeway exits and proclaimed to his battalion commanders that 'We'll start the war right here.' The arthritis-plagued Roosevelt walked up and down the beach with the aid of his cane while he personally directed following units to their altered objectives. His steadfastness and grasp of the landing situation contributed mightily to the success of the landings.[1]

The landing faced WN-5,[2] which was manned by 3rd Company, I Battalion, Grenadier Regiment 919, and commanded by Leutnant Arthur Jahnke, a veteran of Eastern Front fighting where he had been awarded the Knight's Cross of the Iron Cross. Less than one month earlier, Jahnke had shown the fortifications to Erwin Rommel. The destructive force of the naval bombardments had shattered much of Jahnke's defensive capability. His 75-mm and 88-mm guns were damaged and ammunition bunkers exploded; wire entanglements were destroyed and machine-gun positions buried in the sand; rocket-firing planes had knocked out two 50-mm guns. Many of his men were emotionally dazed or concussed. Only a few machine guns and one 80-mm mortar remained functional. His company offered no contest against the American infantry regiment.[3] The strongpoint at WN-4, located 1.3 kilometers to the southeast, had survived the naval bombardment but was quickly cleared after its defenders offered only token resistance.

Within an hour, army and naval engineers and demolition teams had cleared the beach approaches as two more battalions of infantry landed ashore. Units of the 1st Engineer Special Brigade landed, blew gaps in the seawall for the passage of armored vehicles, and began the arduous task of clearing the causeway roads of German mines. By 0800, exits #1, #2, and #3 each had a battalion of infantry moving inland. However, not until 1200 was the last of the enemy at WN-5 captured and their guns silenced.

Although the struggle to secure the beachhead at Omaha Beach was more costly and the success of its landings in doubt for much of the day, Utah Beach became the traditional location for American commemoration ceremonies and victory memorials. In contrast, Omaha is a more somber location containing Normandy American Cemetery and more thoughtful memorials. The atmospheres of the two sites are distinctly – and

---

1   Brigadier General Theodore Roosevelt Jr, was awarded the Medal of Honor for his leadership and presence in the very front of the attack. Unfortunately, he did not live to receive the award as he was stricken with a fatal heart attack on 12 July. He is buried in Normandy American Cemetery next to his brother, Lieutenant Quentin Roosevelt, an allied pilot who had been shot down in the First World War.

2   Historically, two numbering systems were used to identify Widerstandsnest on the Cotentin coast; thus the defenses at Utah Beach were known as WN-5 and alternatively as WN-104.

3   Leutnant Arthur Jahnke was captured unhurt only to be injured by German fire while a POW; he survived the war.

appropriately – different.

Between the parking area and the museum is an unusually large **tobruk** designed to accommodate an 80-mm mortar. The alcoves in the exterior walls and the separate room to the left housed ammunition storage. Unfortunately, they have been sealed during recent reconstruction activity at the site. (49.414847, -1.17514) Near the entrance museum, a granite obelisk stands sporting the four Ivy Leaf insignia, dedicated to the men of the **4th Infantry Division** and commemorating their assault on these beaches on 6 June 1944. The monument was inaugurated in 1964 by General Omar Bradley. (49.41521, -1.175097)

Musée du Débarquement d'Utah Beach (49.415278, -1.174888)
Utah Beach   50480 la Madeleine
Tel: +33 (0)2 33 71 53 35   Email: musee@utah-beach.com
Web: http://www.utah-beach.com

The museum was constructed over remains of WN-5. Its artifacts, personal contributions of equipment, documents, film, and military hardware present an account of the events of 6 June. A scale model of the beach invasion helps establish perspective. A major feature of its interior is a tobruk bearing a 37-mm Renault tank turret, which was one of the few operating heavy weapons that survived the naval bombardment. The turret's machine gun kept firing until overcome by infantry. Full length glass windows offer a view onto Utah Beach.

The museum has been recently expanded to include a large hanger-style building containing a two-engine B-26G Marauder bomber aircraft, nicknamed 'Dinah Might,' and a truck from the Red Ball Express. Because of the new museum, tanks and landing craft that once were near the museum entrance have been temporarily relocated.

Open daily February, March, and November from 10:00 to 17:30; April, May, and October from 10:00 to 18:00; and June through September from 09:30 to 19:00. Admission fee; Normandie Pass accepted.

Leave the museum to the right. The **NTL Totem**, standing in front of a **M4 Sherman tank**, describes the beach landing. To their left, **Borne 00** identifies the opening in the antitank wall that provided exit from the beach and which passed immediately onto causeway #2. Like the borne previously noted in Ste-Mère-Église, it marks one of the four Voie de la Liberté routes from the invasion sites to Bastogne, Belgium. They can be separately identified by the varying colored rectangles near the marker's top. This one carries the simple inscription 'Here the American Armies Landed 6 June 1944.'

Pass through the dune opening to walk along Utah Beach. The ruin of a casemate that held a 50-mm cannon possibly taken from a PzKpfw III rests along the beach southeast of the museum. The gun replied to American naval shelling until it was hit and its crew killed. The concrete structure is slowing being buried by shifting sand. (49.414861, -1.173775)

Return through the beach opening and ascend the wooden stairs on the right to the roof of one of six German personnel blockhouses, three on each side of the access road, built along the backside of the dunes. The **US Navy Monument** is dedicated to the men and ships of that service who participated in the landings; the statue of three sailors presents their very different roles on D-Day – a seaman, a gun loader, and a demolitions expert fighting ashore with gun and explosives. A stele on the platform commemorates

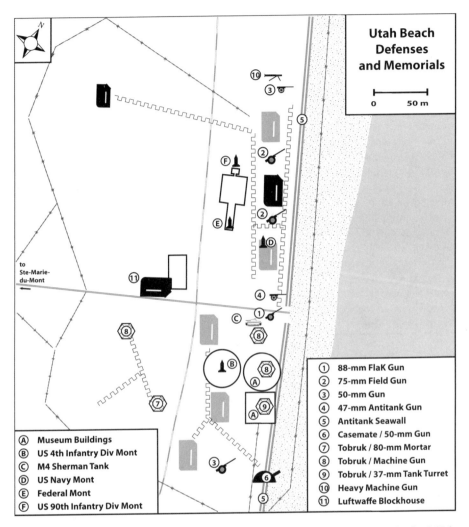

Utah Beach Defenses and Memorials

①	88-mm FlaK Gun
②	75-mm Field Gun
③	50-mm Gun
④	47-mm Antitank Gun
⑤	Antitank Seawall
⑥	Casemate / 50-mm Gun
⑦	Tobruk / 80-mm Mortar
⑧	Tobruk / Machine Gun
⑨	Tobruk / 37-mm Tank Turret
⑩	Heavy Machine Gun
⑪	Luftwaffe Blockhouse

Ⓐ	Museum Buildings
Ⓑ	US 4th Infantry Div Mont
Ⓒ	M4 Sherman Tank
Ⓓ	US Navy Mont
Ⓔ	Federal Mont
Ⓕ	US 90th Infantry Div Mont

the death on 6 June of Pilot Jacques Joubert des Ouches,[4] who flew a Spitfire in the 345th Lorraine Group Squadron.

Continue to the top of the main ceremonial platform, built over the center blockhouse. The 50-mm cannon mounted in a tobruk was used a shore battery. A stone obelisk commemorating the **1st Engineer Special Brigade**, holds plaques on three sides listing specific sub-units which provided services such as engineering, ordinance, transportation, demolitions, quartermaster, military police, etc. A low wall around the memorial and gun displays arrow-shaped plaques indicating the positions of various ships which participated in the invasion.

Descend the stairway to enter the blockhouse that holds several additional memorial plaques, including one to Major General Eugene Caffey, commander of the 1st

4   Lieutenant Jacques Joubert des Ouches flew 160 offensive missions during the war. His plane developed engine trouble while over St-Vaast-la-Hougue and crashed. His body was never found. He was a *Chevalier de la Légion d'honneur* and awarded the Croix de Guerre.

Engineer Special Brigade on D-Day.[5] Additional plaques list the names of those members of the special brigade who were killed. On the outside wall a plaque commemorates the **US Coast Guard** members who participated in the landings. (49.416346, -1.175856)

Ahead on the left, an 8-meter polished red granite obelisk known as the **Federal Monument** was erected on the 40th Anniversary of the invasion. The monument commemorates the landing and the liberation of the Cotentin Peninsula by US VII Corps and bears the inscription 'Humble tribute to its sons who lost their lives in the liberation of these beaches.'

A stone memorial to the **90th Infantry Division** stands across the plaza. The 90th Division landed at Utah after the 4th Division. Nicknamed 'The Tough 'ombres,' the unit fought in five campaigns across Europe. The insignia represents a stylized 'TO.'

Across the roadway, the privately-owned le Roosevelt Café adjoins a Luftwaffe blockhouse captured on D-Day and used thereafter as the **US Navy Communication Center**. The plaque on its side wall lists names of the forty-one men who directed the landing of 836,000 men and 220,000 vehicles on Utah Beach between 8 June and 31 October. The bunker is similar in construction to the bunker upon which the ceremonial platform stands. (49.415486, -1.17602)

Leave Utah Beach toward Ste-Marie-du-Mont (D913). After only 750 m, turn right onto a narrow road toward la Madeleine Chapel (not signed), which is 550 m ahead on the right. (49.417206, -1.186523)

Chapelle de la Madeleine was built over the ruins of an 11th-century chapel, which had been originally constructed by a Viking king who survived a nearby shipwreck. Field fortifications around the chapel comprised WN-7 and drew American naval fire. Its defenders were easily overcome by Company B, 8th Infantry Regiment. Although heavily damaged during the engagement, the chapel has been restored. The interior is extremely plain with a low-vaulted ceiling. The baptismal fount in the front of the church dates from Viking times.

Continue for 1.3 km to D67 (causeway exit #3), turn right away from Audouville-la-Hubert and toward the English Channel. Continue into the parking area in front of the dune opening. (49.428955, -1.190917)

By 0930, 3rd Battalion, 22nd Infantry Regiment, was ashore along the beachfront facing an old windmill north of la Madeleine. The unit's commander, Lieutenant Colonel Arthur Teague,[6] conferred with General Roosevelt before continuing with his objective of overcoming the string of beach defenses to the north. Teague's men cleared the dunes, utilizing prisoners to identify German minefields. A platoon of medium tanks from 746th Tank Battalion joined the infantry. Taking automatic weapons fire from WN-8, one Sherman tank closed to within 25 meters of the steel turret mounted atop a pillbox and blew it off with one round. The remainder of the garrison surrendered.

---

5   Major General Eugene Caffey was career military officer who graduated from West Point and University of Virginia Law School. He retired from military service in 1956 and died in 1961 at age 65.

6   Lieutenant Colonel Arthur ST Teague was awarded the Distinguished Service Cross for his personal bravery in actions on 14 June. He was wounded in action on 17 November in the Hürtgen Forest.

WN-8, which is identified on modern maps as 'Ancient Blockhouses,' stands on both sides of the parking area and represents the most accessible of the Utah Beach German defenses. Its main armaments consisted of a 47-mm Skoda-made antitank gun and a 75-mm field gun, both sited near the dune opening. Two bunkers to the south were personnel shelters for the approximately sixty troops manning the position. Each shelter had a machine-gun tobruk built into its roof. The bunkers were not of re-enforced construction as its walls and roof were only 0.6 meters thick; however, the positions are hidden by dunes and not visible from the sea. A large ground-level tobruk across the coast highway from the southernmost bunker probably housed a mortar. Two open-air 50-mm cannon positions are atop the dunes behind the southern personnel bunker. Minor vestiges of trench which linked these positions are visible, although they have become rather overgrown.

Leave the parking area and continue 1.1 km north toward Ravenoville-Plage (D421) to blockhouses immediately north of the Dune d'Audouville. (49.435699, -1.201715)

Only partially visible from the roadway, the extremely strong STP-9, was located along these dunes, is not deserving of a visit, and the intervening ground is fenced and private, but their presence demonstrates the thoroughness of German defenses along these beaches. Mostly collapsed by wave action, two casemates housing 88-mm guns, one mortar tobruk, a 47-mm field gun, a Renault tank gun, a beachfront bunker housing a 150-mm searchlight, and assorted machine guns, minefields, and barbed wire once completed the site. One casemate and the searchlight bunker remain in fair condition but cannot be entered. The strongpoint was eliminated by advancing infantry of the 22nd Regiment.

Continue northwest (D421) approximately 1.1 km to the parking area on the right. (49.443694, -1.20973)

The Leclerc Monument commemorates the landing on 1 August of the 2nd French Armored Division commanded by Major General Philippe Leclerc.[7] The M4A3 Sherman tank, M3 half-track personnel carrier, and M8 armored car seen near the monument were used by Leclerc's division while it moved across France as part of General Patton's Third Army. The NTL Totem to the right of the parking area describes the site. Leclerc's vehicles frame the dune opening and the Signal Monument, which also commemorates Leclerc's landing. Rows of new granite stones commemorate General Leclerc, the 2nd French Armoured Division, and their battles. Also present is Borne 1, inscribed St-Martin-de-Varreville to Strasbourg. A section of floating platform from a smaller Mulberry harbor is visible on the beach, depending upon the tide level. While the actual landings took place farther south, these dunes served as a major disembarkation point for men and equipment.

Les Dunes-de-Varreville was codenamed Tare Green sector in the original plan for the D-Day landings and directly accesses causeway exit #4 only 250 meters ahead. Pillboxes and bunkers along the beach were part of WN-10, which defended this section of beach. This resistance nest was a complex of cannon, tobruks for machine guns and mortars, flamethrowers, and beachfront casemates housing 47-mm and 88-mm guns. Much of the installation can be explored along the beachfront and among the inland dunes.

The 3rd Battalion, 22nd Regiment, and a platoon of medium tanks approached

7   A pseudonym used by Philippe François Marie, comte de Hautecloque to protect his family, which remained in German-occupied France.

the strongpoint from the south, but intense small arms fire stopped the infantry advance. Tank rounds had little effect upon the concrete emplacements. Finally, naval gun-fire hailed down upon the position followed by a storm of infantry. The surviving enemy surrendered. The battle to overcome this strong position was intense as demonstrated by the visible shell strikes on the fronts of several casemates.

Breaking the German Resistance
7 June to 14 June

Objective	To penetrate the German main line of resistance
Forces	
American	Three regiments of 4th Infantry Division and one regiment of 9th Infantry Division (Major General Raymond O Barton)
German	*Kampfgruppe von Schlieben* (Generalleutnant Karl Wilhelm von Schlieben)
Result	The line was broken and German troops withdrew toward Cherbourg
Location	Carentan is 75 km east of Caen; Utah Beach is 16 km northeast of Carentan; les Cruttes is 2.5 km north of Utah Beach

Battle

The 7 June objective of the 4th Infantry Division's 8th Infantry Regiment was the main body of troops of the *Ostbattalion* 795, trapped in a pocket south and east of Ste-Mère-Église. With the 1st Battalion holding its attention with an attack from the east, 2nd and 3rd Battalions moved northward from les Forges. Caught in a vise, the surviving 174 enemy troops quickly surrendered.

As the 4th Infantry Division moved inland and to the north, it escaped the flooded lowlands, but the gently rising hills with their hedgerows did present the Germans with opportunities for effective defense from commanding heights. Late in the day on 7 June, Generalleutnant von Schlieben determined that he did not have the strength to eliminate the American beachhead without strong panzer forces. He was also separated by American forces from LXXXIV Corps headquarters 60 kilometers away in St-Lô. Thus, he decided to form a defense line across the middle of the Cotentin Peninsula along east–west ridgeline along what is now highway D42 from Quinéville to Montebourg and le Ham. Elements of the 709th and 243rd Infantry Divisions and the coastal battery garrisons were given orders to retreat to this line and were formed into *Kampfgruppe von Schlieben*.

The US 12th Infantry Regiment moved in between the 8th Regiment to the west and the 22nd Regiment to the east. The 8th Infantry Regiment advanced northwest between the Cherbourg–Bayeux highway and the rail line to its west, overcoming German strongpoints near Mangeville, Écausseville, and Eroudeville before encountering strong German artillery fire. On their left flank, the 505th PIR took Montebourg Station and the 325th GIR took le Ham. On the opposite flank, the 22nd Regiment ran up against German strongpoints at Azeville, Crisbecq, and Ozeville. Each had to be taken or neutralized. In the middle, the 12th Infantry Regiment moved rapidly forward, creating a salient north of St-Foxel. They paid the price of exposed flanks after running into elements of German Infantry Regiment 1058 and were forced to retreat.

Each unit faced a hard, slogging battle from hedgerow to hedgerow. Tanks led the advance until stopped by antitank gun fire. New attacks took place daily. Casualties

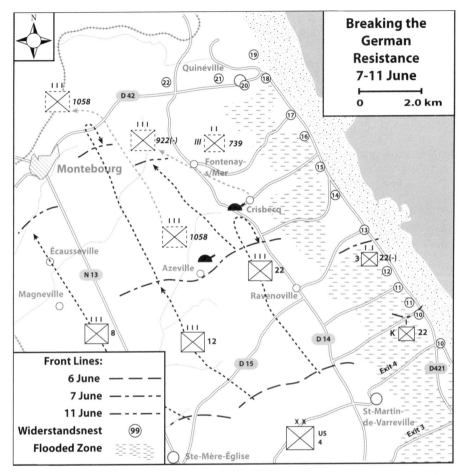

mounted with one regiment losing two thirds of its compliment. By 12 June, the three regiments, augmented by the 39th Infantry Regiment of the 9th Infantry Division moving along the coastal headlands, achieved the forward German outposts, roughly following a line from Hameau de Fontenay through Fontenay-s/Mer and St-Floxel to la Gare de Montebourg (Montebourg Station). On 14 June, the 12th, 22nd, and 39th Regiments moved north and shifted east to break through the main line of resistance and capture Quinéville. The German defenses on the Cotentin had been broken.

Battlefield Tour

Leave the Leclerc Monument to the northwest toward Ravenoville-Plage (D421).

The 3rd Battalion, 22nd Infantry Regiment, moved up the coast against I Battalion, Grenadier Regiment 919, encountering numerous concrete blockhouses containing artillery and machine guns. The Germans used underground telephone cables to call down fire from artillery batteries farther inland. The reduction of each position was a slow process; infantry waded through the waist-deep water of the flooded lowlands to approach positions from the rear against enemy small arms and battery fire while tanks and 57-mm AT guns fired from close range.

By the evening of 7 June the battalion neared the fortifications of WN-11 at les Cruttes, which were surmounted by machine guns and protected by mine fields, wire, ditches, and infantry pillboxes. Company K remained along the seafront to isolate the position while the remainder of the battalion was ordered to move inland (see below).

Not until 11 June, did Company K determine from prisoners that when one strongpoint was under attack, the defenders used underground tunnels to escape to a second strongpoint. They finally captured the two German strongpoints at les Cruttes (WN-11) and at St-Hubert (Stp-12) after firing antitank rounds first against one position and then shifting rapidly to fire against the second position. Ninety-three prisoners were taken.

The coastal highway moves closer to the beach as one progresses north. After traveling 2.0 kilometers northwest of the Leclerc Monument, the first elements of **WN-11** at les Cruttes become visible with a seawall tobruk that accommodated a Renault tank turret. (49.457752, -1.225314) A ringstand for a 50-mm cannon is nearby. Continuing northwest, the sea wall holds several additional tobruks and personnel blockhouses in fields on the inland side of the highway – generally on private land and not accessible. After a farther 600 m, a casemate noted for the multiple shell hits on the landward side wall, stands astride the seawall as part of **Stp-12** at Ravenoville-St-Hubert. (49.462215, -1.230099) The casemate housed a 50-mm cannon and a lower level machine gun both facing south and a second machine gun firing north.

Follow highway D421 northwest for 4.7 km through Grand Hameau des Dunes, and Hameau du Sud to the intersection with highway D69 and passing the locations of the following action. (49.493267, -1.264265)

Leaving les Cruttes under the fire of an augmented company on 7 June, Lt Col Teague led the remainder of the 3rd Battalion inland. Learning from a German prisoner that the garrison along the seafront at Grand Hameau des Dunes Ravenoville was stunned by intense naval bombardment and might surrender, he redirected his men back across the flooded fields to approach the strongpoint from the rear. The prisoner was sent forward, eventually returning with the entire eighty-two-man garrison. Much of **WN-13** has been destroyed, leaving only uninteresting beachfront foundations.

The 1st Battalion, 39th Infantry Regiment, joined Colonel Teague's battalion for the attack upon the defensive strongpoint known as **Fort St-Marcouf (WN-14)**. Following a heavy air attack, it found the blast door of the first bunker blown open and all of its inhabitants dead from concussion. While preparing an attack upon a second bunker, the command group came under fire from German artillery. The troop called American fire upon the narrow strip of beach, raking it with fire from sixteen 155-mm artillery pieces, 3-inch and 4-inch naval guns, mortars, and machine guns – all to no avail as the shells bounced off the 2-meter-thick concrete walls. An attempt by Company G to flank the position through the inundated area found the water to be chest deep and exposed to enemy fire. They were repelled. Finally, Company E, proceeded north on the road behind a tank destroyer to reach the bunker. The men pried open a vent cover and threw in a 5-pound TNT charge killing everyone inside. Now, only a few tobruks remain in an area of new housing.

North of Hameau du Sud, turn left toward Crisbecq (D69) and continue 2.8 km to the battery parking area on the right. (49.479617, -1.295738)

Batterie de Crisbecq

Route des Manoirs   50310 St-Marcouf de l'Isle
Tel: +33 (0)6.68.41.09.04   E-mail: contact@batterie-marcouf.com
Web: http://www.batterie-marcouf.com/

St-Marcouf Naval Coastal Battery (*schwere Marine-Küsten-Batterie-Abteilung 260 'Marcouf'* or *MBK 'Marcouf'*), also known as **Crisbecq Battery**, was an extensive installation of re-enforced concrete casemates, open-air gun positions, and numerous bunkers, pillboxes, and tobruks. Built in 1942 by the Todt Organization, the battery's guns were capable of hitting targets as far away as the Grande Vey. Its 300-man garrison was composed of naval reservists under the command of Oberleutnant-zur-See Walter Ohmsen. The main weapons were three 210-mm Skoda guns and one 150-mm gun supported by six French 75-mm antiaircraft guns and three 20-mm antiaircraft guns, all of which were in the open. In addition, its land defenses included seventeen machine guns and a 300-meter-wide minefield with triple rows of barbed wire. By 6 June, only two of the casemates for the 210-mm guns had been completed; the third gun still lay in an open position.

Before dawn on D-Day, the battery garrison captured twenty miss-dropped 82nd Airborne paratroopers. Oberleutnant Ohmsem was the first German officer to sight the invasion fleet from the battery's fire-control bunker at 0500 on 6 June. His report to superiors at Kriegsmarine headquarters in Cherbourg provided the first alarm to installations on the Cotentin Coast. The battery, considered the greatest threat to the Utah Beach invasion fleet, was the target of 600 tons of bombs in early morning RAF bomber raids. The casemated guns were not affected; however, many of the unprotected antiaircraft weapons were destroyed. At 0555 the battery fired its first rounds at Allied warships.

By 0700, naval shelling from the battleship USS *Nevada* and cruiser USS *Quincy* put casemate #1 out of commission but not before St-Marcouf's fire had sunk the destroyer USS *Corry*. Battleships USS *Arkansas* and USS *Texas* added their 14-inch guns to the attack on the battery. One hour later the *Nevada* scored a direct hit on casemate #2 killing the entire crew and destroying a second 210-mm gun.

Despite the damage to its heavy guns, the casemated batteries at Crisbecq and Azeville (see below) provided the Germans with well-fortified positions. By 7 June, Marcouf was surrounded but able to beat-off several American infantry attacks, frequently by calling down fire from nearby Azeville battery. In addition, the casemate #1 gun had been repaired and again began firing upon unloading activities at Utah Beach. The III Battalion, Grenadier Regiment 919, advanced south into the village of St-Marcouf, where it was repelled by 1st Battalion, 22nd Infantry Regiment. The Americans, in turn, attempted to take the battery by attacking through St-Marcouf. They encountered strong resistance from wire obstacles, and a German spoiling attack from the northwest drove them back to Dodainville, taking 98 prisoners. A nighttime German counterattack was routed by Allied naval gunnery.

A repeated attack on 8 June effected the same result, Azeville again providing heavy covering fire. After the fall of Azeville on 9 June, the Americans by-passed Crisbecq, leaving a small force to maintain pressure on the battery. On 12 June, the newly arrived 9th Infantry Division entered the battery to find only twenty-one wounded; the remaining 78

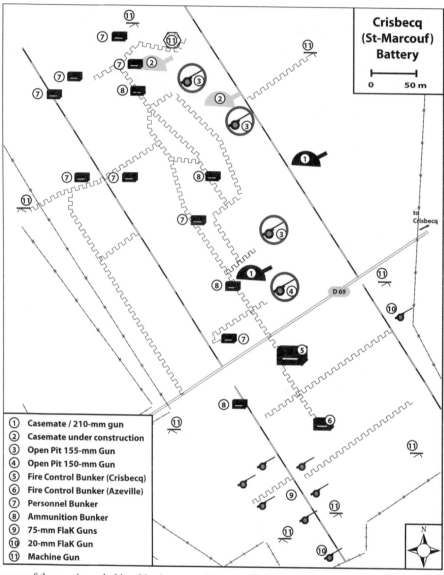

Crisbecq (St-Marcouf) Battery

0   50 m

① Casemate / 210-mm gun
② Casemate under construction
③ Open Pit 155-mm Gun
④ Open Pit 150-mm Gun
⑤ Fire Control Bunker (Crisbecq)
⑥ Fire Control Bunker (Azeville)
⑦ Personnel Bunker
⑧ Ammunition Bunker
⑨ 75-mm FlaK Guns
⑩ 20-mm FlaK Gun
⑪ Machine Gun

men of the garrison, led by Oberleutnant Ohmsen, had escaped during the previous night.[8]

The self-guided tour of the battery installation provides an opportunity to visit a fairly complete installation. Trenches that connected the buildings have been converted into wide, crushed-stone, paths some one meter below ground level. Some structures, still in good condition, are accessible, without hard climbing, but not with wheelchairs. The entire plan is easy to follow, and visitors can walk through passageways linking the

8   Oberleutnant-zur-See Walter Ohmsen was awarded the Knights Cross of the Iron Cross for his defense of the battery. He was later captured during the fall of Cherbourg and survived the war as a POW. After a brief postwar political career, Ohmsen rejoined the German Navy, rising to the rank of Fregattenkapitän. He died in 1988 at age 76.

underground shelters, which present the feel of wartime action.

A large casemate still retaining its **210-mm Skoda cannon** with camouflage netting lies immediately inside the gate. The damage was not the result of Allied bombardment but of post-battle experiments by engineers to test methods of attacking such structures in the future. An **open-air gun platform** capable of holding a 210-mm cannon adjoins the casemate. Various azimuths have been pre-identified and code-named with red paint around the inner circle of the position. A personnel bunker for twenty men contains two dioramas depicting everyday life of gunners and their difficult living conditions. And so the tour continues: ammunition stores, infirmary, five additional open-air gun platforms, and two uncompleted casemates.

The battery's command and **fire control bunker** is on the opposite side of the road. A stairway accesses the rooftop observation platform. From that vantage point, seeing the English Channel and even Utah Beach to the southeast – weather depending – stirs the imagination.

Open daily April, October, and November from 11:00 to 18:00; May, June, and September from 10:00 to 18:00; and July and August from 10:00 to 21:00. Admission fee; Normandie Pass accepted.

Continue on highway D69 for 1.3 km; turn left toward Azeville (D269). After 1.1 km turn right still toward Azeville (D269). After 400 m, enter the battery parking area on the left. (49.460935, -1.307137)

La Batterie d'Azeville
D269   50310 Azeville
Tel: +33 (0)2 33 40 63 05   Email: musee.azeville@cg50.fr
Web: http://www.sitesetmusees.cg50.fr

The four concrete casemates at *schwere Heeres-Küsten-Batterie* **Azeville** each housed a 105-mm Schneider gun manned by 2nd Battery, I Battalion, Coastal Artillery Regiment 1261, under Oberleutnant Hans Kattnig. Defenses included underground trenches, antiaircraft guns, machine-gun tobruks, minefields, and barb wire. The entire installation was manned by 170 men. The sea is not visible from this location; thus, the Crisbecq fire control bunker provided firing instructions to the Azeville Battery.

On 6 June, Azeville came under fire from the heavy ships of the Allied invasion fleet. Later that day, a ground attack by American paratroopers was defeated. On 7 June, the Sturm Battalion 7 fell back to Azeville after its defeat by the 82nd Airborne north of Ste-Mère-Église. While the 1st Battalion, 22nd Infantry Regiment, attacked Crisbecq Battery, the 2nd Battalion unsuccessfully attacked Azeville Battery. A repeat attack on 8 June was supported by artillery and naval bombardment, but again failed to take the position. During the naval bombardment, a shell from the USS *Nevada* entered casemate #3 through the gun embrasure, passed through the rear wall, and imbedded itself in the ground behind the casemate without exploding. The resulting concussion killed everyone in the casemate. Fifty years later, demolitions experts were called to remove the rediscovered and still dangerous shell.

On 9 June, American tanks moved west on the road through Cibrantot, south of the battery. Their attack came from the southwest, or rear of the casemates, focusing tank rounds and bazooka rocket fire upon the two-meter-thick concrete walls without effect. German small arms fire was light, reflecting their failure to clear fields of fire in that direction. Americans soldiers picked their way across the mine fields. A satchel charge of 40 pounds of TNT was placed against the rear blast door of the nearest casemate – to little result. Finally, Private Ralph G Riley scampered 75 meters against enemy small-arms fire with an explosive container of jellied gasoline on his back. Sheltering in a shell crater, he manually ignited the flamethrower and aimed its entire charge under the door of the nearest casemate. Shortly thereafter, the sound of exploding small arms ammunition rocked the bunkers, and Oberleutnant Kattnig displayed a white flag.[9] One hundred-sixty-nine prisoners were taken when all four casemates surrendered.[10]

The four large casemates flank the roadway just east of Azeville. A multi-language, audio-guided tour includes the small museum in casemate #4, which was the command bunker, explains the construction, use, and history of the casemates, and leads visitors through 350 meters of underground passages which connected the casemates. A 25-minute film provides a view into local life in the French village during the German occupation and the use of local labor to build the Atlantic Wall defenses. It is possible to view the exterior of the casemates outside of tour hours. Not handicap accessible.

Open daily April and October from 14:00 to 18:00; May and September from 11:00 to 18:00; and June through August from 10:00 to 19:00. Admission fee; Normandie Pass accepted.

Side trip: Hangar à Dirigeable

Leave Batterie d'Azeville through Azeville (D269) for 1.8 km to the junction with highway D115. Turn right toward Émondeville and continue 1.7 km. In Émondeville, turn left toward E46/N13 (D214). Enter the roadway and continue 1.4 km to the Joganville/Ecausseville exit (D69). Follow toward Ecausseville for 350 m then turn right toward Ecausseville (D510). The hanger is 1.4 km southwest of Ecausseville toward le Ham (D510). (49.451471, -1.383505) Total distance: 8.1 km.

Hangar à Dirigeable

La Lande   50310 Ecausseville
Tel: +33 (0)2 33 08 56 02   Email: contact@aerobase.com
Web: http://www.aerobase.fr/

The Hangar à Dirigeable housed dirigible airships engaged in fighting the German submarine threat in French coastal waters during the First World War. The first hanger, completely wooden, began construction between January and August 1917. The second concrete and cast iron hanger was started in 1917 but was not completed until August 1919. France abandoned hydrogen airships in 1936, but the location then housed Heavy Coastal Artillery and accompanying antiaircraft batteries.

The Germans occupied the site from 1940 to 1944, but they were driven out by the 8th Infantry Regiment on the night 10/11 June. Americans used the surviving concrete hanger for warehousing and vehicle repair. In 2003, the hanger was classified as a monument, and an association of local volunteers now maintains the site.

The enormous 150-meter-long by 30-meter-high hanger can be seen from some distance. While generally a large empty enclosed space, its construction was unique for the

---

9   Oberleutnant Hans Kattnig was captured and held in a POW camps in Great Britain and the United States until after the war. He died in 1988 at age 77.

10   Private Ralph G Riley received a Silver Star.

early 20th century because its walls consisted of 520 concrete slabs, weighing almost 3,000 pounds each. An intricate network of concrete posts forms the interior support and divides the interior into bays. Bay #7 has fading chalk drawings of wartime graffiti. A supply hut posts descriptions of local life under Nazi occupation and events related to modern balloon experiments.

Open April, May, and October on Wednesday, Saturday and Sunday from 14:00 to 18:00; June and September open daily except Friday from 14:00 to 18:00; open daily July and August from 10:00 to 18:00. Admission Fee.

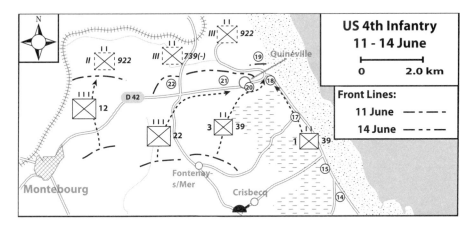

To regain the tour route: reverse direction and continue through Écausseville. Turn right away from Éroudeval (D69) and follow across the E46/N13 motorway. Immediately east of the motorway, turn left toward Montebourg (D974). After 2.7 km on the near side of Montebourg, turn right toward Quinéville (D42) and follow 7.2 km to the blockhouse described below.

From Batterie d'Azeville: reverse direction away from Azeville; turn left toward St-Marcouf de l'Isle (D269). After 1.1 km, turn right toward St-Marcouf de l'Isle (D69); 950 m ahead, turn left toward Fontenay-s/Mer (D14). After 650 m, observe the side road to the left. (49.480784, -1.305528)

On 9 June, the 2nd Battalion, 22nd Regiment, attacked another German strongpoint at **Château de Fontenay**. The chateau was headquarters for 3rd Battery, Coastal Artillery Regiment 1261, and was the location of six 155-mm guns. The defenders held out for two days, inflicting a serious level of casualties on the 22nd Regiment before evacuating during the night of 11 June.

The ruins of the chateau are 950 meters down the straight farm road and are in a dangerous condition because they remain as they were after the battle. The land is private and signed to prohibit visitors.

Continue 3.7 km, then turn right toward Quinéville (D42). After 2.0 km, stop at the casemate on the right near a rural road that goes to the Hôtel Restaurant du Château de Quinéville. (49.512034, -1.295727)

Battle of Quinéville
14 June 1944

The drive east toward Quinéville, provides a panoramic view over countryside to the south where the German main defensive line was established along the high ground of this ridge line. The church and *mairie* mark the eastern nose of the heavily defended ridge. From there, the terrain drops 30 meters to the harbor to the east.

A dirt- and grass-covered bunker east of the church in the old village of Quinéville was part of **WN-20** manned by the 8th Company, Grenadier Regiment 919. It still stands guard over the harbor below. Remnants of rusted hooks near the edge of the top probably held down camouflage netting. The bunker's large gun embrasure is aimed directly toward Quinéville harbor. A second bunker, seen on the field to the left of the highway 190 meters ahead, faces south. Both bunkers held 88-mm antitank guns. The view to the south presents the hedgerow country of checkered small pastures and orchards defined by narrow sunken lanes that were then so prevalent in 1944 Normandy. (49.512278, -1.293377)

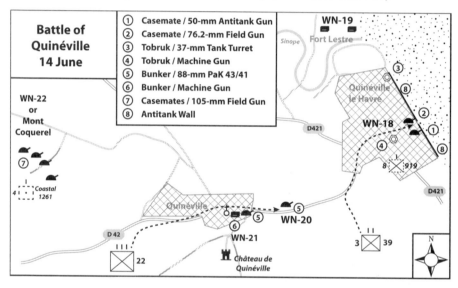

Two more fortified positions line the rural road from the bunker. Although the area is fenced and private, one pillbox is directly behind the *mairie* and is visible from the rural road with its aperture facing west. (49.511724, -1.296247) A second pillbox is slightly to the south and acted as a fire control post for the two bunkers. The church is west of the *mairie*, and from the rear of the churchyard one can see a German trench line zigzagging parallel to the church wall. The trench line connects the rear entrances of the two pillboxes and continues west. The pillboxes are hidden from this perspective because they have been built into the hillside.

Continue toward Quinéville; after 650 m (from the hotel entrance road) turn right on Av. de la Plage and continue 240 m to the museum on the right. (49.515161, -1.286312)

Quinéville

Quinéville's small harbor, shown on most maps as 'le Havre,' was at the eastern end of the German resistance line along the ridge of highway D42. Quinéville had been an important support point for German coastal defenses and was classified as a regional command post.

On 14 June, General Barton, 4th Infantry Division commander, ordered an attack by all three battalions of the 22nd Regiment plus the attached 3rd Battalion, 39th Infantry Regiment, 9th Infantry Division. The 22nd Regiment's battalions, preceded by a bombardment of multi-caliber weapons, moved forward and to the east to capture strongpoints on the inland ridges overlooking the town and its harbor. The men of the 39th Regiment achieved highway D42 southwest of le Havre and moved along that route into the harbor district. When leading Company K approached the seafront, it encountered a tank ditch covered by mortar and antitank fire from the strong beach defenses which claimed numerous casualties. Their supporting tanks were also driven back. The other three companies in the battalion were held up by minefields and wire entanglements. Finally, the impasse broke when a heavy smoke barrage was called down upon the German positions allowing Company K to rush the pillboxes and, after a five-and-one-half-hour battle, the surviving enemy troops surrendered.

A **NTL Totem**, **Voie de la Liberté borne**, and rough-cut, rose-granite stele commemorating the liberation of the town by the **39th Infantry Regiment** are near the museum entrance.

Mémorial de la Liberté Retrouvée
18, Avenue de la Plage   50310 Quinéville
Tel - Fax: +33 (0)2 33 95 95 95
E-mail: memorial.quineville@wanadoo.fr
Web: http://www.memorial-quineville.com

The museum is constructed partially in an Atlantic Wall blockhouse and is not the expected collection of military artifacts. Instead, it presents a peek into the lifestyle of civilian France during the Nazi occupation. Full-size dioramas are aligned along a village street allowing the visitor to walk among the darkened houses of a wartime French village. The museum walls hold very interesting propaganda posters of the French occupation. The view through the glass covered embrasure that once contained a 50-mm antitank gun provides a perspective of the gun's firing range along the beach.

Open daily 22 March to 11 November from 10:00 to 19:00. Admission fee; Normandie Pass accepted.

Walk down to the beachfront and pass through the opening cut into the impressive antitank wall to view the open beach. The structure on the left of the opening was a camouflaged bunker which held a north-facing 76.2-mm gun. The seawall held a 37-mm Renault tank turret. Around to the right, the south-facing museum blockhouse gun embrasure, which housed the antitank gun, is visible. From the beach, the tower at La-Hougue and the large fortified island in the harbor of St-Vaast can be seen to the north.

To return to Ste-Mère-Église, leave Quinéville toward Montebourg (D42). In Montebourg, follow signs toward Ste-Mère-Église / Carentan (D974) and follow for 9.6 km into the town or after 3.8 km enter the E46/N13 motorway. Remain on the motorway for 7.1 km, exiting toward Ste-Mère-Église (D67) and follow into town.

To continue the 4th Infantry Division tour in its battle to capture Cherbourg and defeat the German Army on the Cotentin Peninsula, follow the battlefield tour instructions in Chapter Ten (The Battle of Cherbourg).

Part Two
Defeat of the German Army
18 June to 21 August 1944

By 18 June, the American and British beachheads had merged to create a single front. All of the initial D-Day objectives, with the notable exception of the capture of Caen, had been accomplished. The buildup of men and material necessary for the retaking of France was taking place within the Normandy pocket. Assault divisions were receiving replacements for their casualties, and new formations were arriving. The US XIX Corps became operational on 13 June, and the British Second Army started landing its VIII Corps on 15 June. These formations added three armored and three infantry divisions to the Allied manpower base. By 17 June, the Allies had 557,000 men in Normandy.

Additional German troops were also arriving. The 17th SS Panzergrenadier Division had already made an appearance at Carentan as had Panzer Lehr at Tilly-s/Seulles. Additional infantry and armored units were on their way from across France. Notably, two armored and several infantry division remained stationed in Pas-de-Calais to repel a still expected Allied second invasion.

While the German Army was on the defensive, its superiority in weapons – machine guns, tanks, mortars, and rocket launchers – and the willingness of its soldiers to fight meant that an Allied victory was not certain. Neither American Sherman tanks nor British Cromwell or Churchill tanks were near to a match for the German Panther. The modified Sherman Firefly with its upgraded 17-pounder gun came close in fire power, but it was available in only limited numbers. And as for the German Tiger tank, it was practically invincible in combat. Fortunately, its numbers were limited, and they suffered from mechanical reliability issues.

The difficulty of fighting against a well-trained enemy in terrain that favored defense became more apparent. German defenses consisted of small groups of infantry supported by a tank or antitank gun in a well-camouflaged position. Whether British or American, Allied tanks could not overcome the position because of the antitank weapon, and infantry could not eliminate the antitank weapons because of the German infantry's machine guns. New tactics would have to be developed and, in the meantime, men died.

British efforts to capture Caen by direct assault (Chapters Two and Three) had failed. While General Dempsey conduced Montgomery's 'set piece' battles to take Caen, Bradley set his sights upon Cherbourg and St-Lô.

Allied air superiority and, seemingly to the Germans, unlimited materiel and supplies would eventually be the Allies' winning factors, not before, however, a long war of attrition and a gradual grinding down of the enemy's ability to resist. Certainly, more difficult fighting would ensue before the German Army was defeated.

Chapter Ten

Battle of Cherbourg
22 June to 29 June

After the breaking of the German defensive lines along the Quinéville ridge, American attention shifted south to focus along the Douve River and efforts to cut the Cotentin peninsula. Action in the north became relatively quiet. After a four-day lull, the drive on Cherbourg was restarted with three infantry divisions abreast – the US 4th Division on the right, the US 79th Division in the center, and the US 9th Division on the left. The 24th Cavalry Squadron was assigned to the eastern coastline.

By the evening of 19 June, General von Schlieben recognized that his men could no longer stop the American advance. He ordered units to withdraw north into Fortress Cherbourg – a ring of hills that ran 6-to-8 kilometers from the city, among which the Germans had established strongpoints of machine guns, antitank weapons, 88-mm guns, and tank barriers. During the four-year occupation, the French forts guarding the harbor were strengthened. The strongest position was Fort du Roule, sited upon a massive rock outcropping at the southern edge of the city.

At midnight on 19 June, a violent storm struck the Normandy coast. Winds and high seas drove small and large ships against each other, against the artificial Mulberry harbors, and onto the beaches. Landing craft were totally helpless against the ever-increasing swales. Off-loading of men and supplies was impossible. For three days Task Force U was fighting to stay afloat. Despite the misery added by the wind and rain and short supply of ammunition, the infantry advance continued. Moving through the more open fields on the western side of the Cotentin, the 9th Infantry Division made rapid progress against only

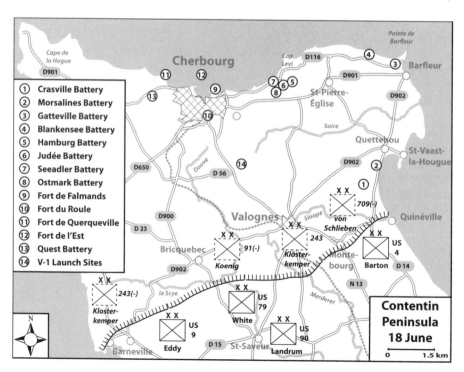

1. Crasville Battery
2. Morsalines Battery
3. Gatteville Battery
4. Blankensee Battery
5. Hamburg Battery
6. Judée Battery
7. Seeadler Battery
8. Ostmark Battery
9. Fort de Falmands
10. Fort du Roule
11. Fort de Querqueville
12. Fort de l'Est
13. Quest Battery
14. V-1 Launch Sites

Contentin Peninsula 18 June

light resistance. It arrived at the German defensive ring by 21 June. Moving up the middle of the peninsula, the 79th Infantry Division fought off several German counterattacks but also achieved the defensive ring on the same date. The 4th Infantry Division, however, had a tougher time. Montebourg and Valognes were captured but only after the former was completely obliterated by days of American artillery fire.

With the Germans trapped in a narrowing perimeter, cut off by land and sea, General Collins broadcast a surrender ultimatum to General von Schlieben. Schlieben did not reply but sent his engineers to start destruction of the city's harbor facilities. Hitler had declared Cherbourg a fortress city; in Nazi parlance, that meant that it was to be defended to the last man.

Objective	To capture the port of Cherbourg
Forces	
American	4th, 9th, and 79th Infantry Divisions of US VII Corps (Major General Joseph 'Lightning Joe' Lawton Collins)
German	21,000 men of *Kampfgruppe von Schlieben*: 243rd and 709th Infantry Divisions, the Cherbourg garrison, and Kriegsmarine, Luftwaffe, and Todt Organization units (Generalleutnant Karl Wilhelm von Schlieben)
Result	Cherbourg garrison surrendered on 29 June
Casualties	
American	2,811 killed, 13,564 wounded, 5,665 missing, 79 captured (VII Corps from 6 June)
German	over 29,182 prisoners taken
Location	Cherbourg is 125 km northwest of Caen at the northern tip of the Cotentin Peninsula

Battle

On 22 June, General Collins launched a general assault upon Cherbourg starting with bombing and strafing by ten squadrons of RAF Typhoons and Mustang aircraft and bombing by groups of fifty US Ninth Air Force aircraft attacking in five-minute intervals. A concentrated aerial barrage by 387 light and medium bombers followed against eleven identified German strongpoints. Whereas the air armada was impressive, the effect upon the well-fortified enemy was minimal.

Moving from positions northwest of Bois de Coudray and Bois de Roudoux against *Kampfgruppe Rohrbach*, the 4th Division made headway to Tourlaville, on the eastern outskirts of Cherbourg. Initial resistance was stiff, and the enemy was expert at infiltrating behind advancing American units; but determined American ground attacks cleared pillboxes and strongpoints. While 8th and 12th Infantry Regiments continued pressing toward the city, the 22nd Infantry Regiment contained the enemy in the Gonneville-Maupertus Airport area seven kilometers to the east. The two regiments advanced swiftly with the only significant resistance coming from WN-209 east of Fort des Flamands. Automatic weapons fire from pillboxes stopped the 12th Infantry which, frustrated, watched the explosions of the port facilities in the distance. The next morning, the appearance of American tanks induced the 350 defenders to surrender. The 'Ivy

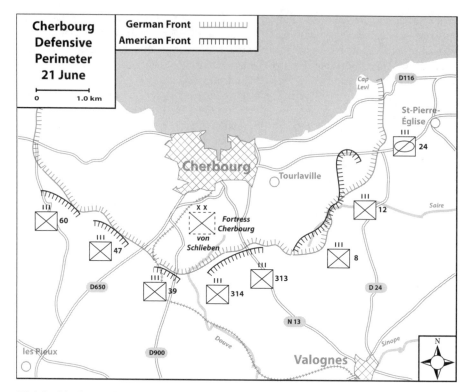

Division' had completed its assignment.

Early on 26 June, the 79th Division moved along the Valognes-Cherbourg highway and against the remaining city strongpoints, each being eliminated by antitank fire. Fort du Roule was overcome only after stiff fighting and individual heroics. On the same day, General von Schlieben and Konteradmiral Walter Hennecke were captured by the 39th Regiment in a vast underground command bunker in rue St-Sauveur. The next morning the last remaining German stronghold at the old arsenal surrendered although small groups in the jetty forts held out for two more days. The 9th Infantry Division was forced to fight for several more days to eliminate resistance in the Cap de la Hague at the northwest tip of the Cotentin. German demolition teams, however, had done their worst: the harbor facilities were a scene of devastation, and the port was not operational again until mid-August. By November 1944 the port was only capable of handling one-half of Allied shipping requirements.

Battlefield Tour

The tour starts by visiting the chateau where the fighting officially ended before continuing north to review locations in and around Cherbourg.

From Quinéville, exit the town toward Montebourg (D42). In Montebourg, follow signs toward Valognes (D974), and after 2.5 km enter the E46/N13 motorway. Remain on the motorway for 6.8 km, exiting toward Bricquebec (D902). After 850 m turn left toward Château de Servigny, 300 m ahead on the left. (49.497852, -1.497906)

Generalleutnant von Schlieben,[1] commander of Fortress Cherbourg, and Konteradmiral Walter Hennecke,[2] representing Kriegsmarine forces, signed the **Cherbourg surrender agreement** at the Château de Servigny before American Major General J Lawton Collins[3] on 26 June 1944. The event is commemorated by a plaque on the chateau's gatehouse located near the American flag. The chateau is in private ownership, but it is a B&B. Residential guests are invited to view the surrender room and the desk used for the signing.

Reverse direction and return to the E46/N13. Unfortunately, this interchange does not allow northwest-bound entrance to the motorway. Enter the motorway southeast toward Montebourg; leave the motorway at the first exit, cross over the motorway and re-enter toward Cherbourg. Proceed 11.3 km before exiting toward Flamandville (D56). (49.564165, -1.56817)

Highway D974/N13 from Valognes toward Cherbourg marked the axis of advance of the 79th Infantry Division's attack upon Cherbourg. The Germans established Cherbourg's defensive perimeter roughly along highway D56 to the south and southeast of Cherbourg. It was among these fields that the rapid American advance from a line Quinéville, Montebourg, Barneville-Carteret halted on the evening of 21 June.

Additional Site: V-1 Bases

After leaving the motorway, turn toward le Theil (D56). Continue for 2.5 km to the rural road on the left and proceed to the structures described below. (49.579833, -1.544094)

Three rather intact **V-1[4] launch sites** remain in this area. One sits to the rear (east) of the Château de Pannelier, which is 750 meters north on Route de la Brûlette (D121), immediately to the left upon exiting the motorway. The property is currently private and the access roads are gated.

The second site, known as la Boissais after a nearby farm, sits at the highest elevation south of Cherbourg. The site is visitable since a public highway bisects the farm.

---

1   General Karl Wilhelm von Schlieben was an old-school Prussian military officer who fought in both world wars. On the Eastern Front he was adjutant of the 4th Panzer Division, which was destroyed at Stalingrad, and commander of the 18th Panzer Division, which was destroyed during the Battle of Kursk. After his surrender, he was held for the remainder of the war as a POW before being released in 1947. He died in 1964 at age 69.

2   Konteradmiral Walter Hennecke was also held as a POW for the remainder of the war. After the fall of Cherbourg, he was awarded the Knight's Cross of the Iron Cross *in absentia* for his destruction of the Cherbourg port facilities. He died in 1984 at age 86.

3   Major General J Lawton Collins graduated from West Point in 1917 but did not see action in the First World War. Collins led the US 25th Infantry Division against the Japanese on Guadalcanal before assuming command of VII Corps in Europe. He held numerous postwar military assignments and became chief of staff of the United States Army during the Korean War. He died in 1987 at age 91 and is buried in Arlington National Cemetery.

4   V-1 (from the German *Vergeltungswaffe* 1 or retaliatory weapon #1, and also known as Fieseler Fi103): was the world's first guided missile; it was propelled by a pulse-jet engine and carried 1,900 pounds of explosive. The distinctive pulsing engine gave rise to the nicknames 'Buzz Bomb' and 'Doodlebug.' The first launch occurred on 13 June 1944 and, by March 1945, 9,521 V-1s had been sent against England and an additional 2,448 against targets in Allied controlled areas of Belgium.

Its structures are typical of such storage and launch area in the northern Cotentin.

The la Boissais site – sometimes referred to as la Sorellerie – was constructed during 1943/4 to accommodate V-1 flying bombs to be sent against southern England's seaports. Because it had no means of course adjustment, the V-1 therefore ignited on a launch ramp aimed at a fixed target, in this case Bristol, England. The site received its share of welcome from RAF bombers and, because of the Normandy landings, it never became operational. The la Boissais V-1 site was captured by US 8th Infantry Regiment on 21 June.

The access road and connecting roadways are original. The fixed launch ramp is in the field to the right. The building nearest the launch ramp contained no metal since it was used as the site of final adjustments to the V-1's sensitive magnetic compass. The blockhouse near the farm probably stored propellant. Bomb and tank shell damage is still visible on some of the structures.

> To reach the third site, continue east on highway D56; turn left at the next intersection (D87). After 500 meters, turn left onto the approach road to L'Orion Ferme. The V-1 structures are on both sides of this road. (49.590016, -1.517835)

A concrete building stands in the field only 30 meters before the access road and on the opposite side of highway D87. It alledgedly housed a searchlight and was part of L'Orion defenses. L'Orion V-1 site is less interesting than la Boissais. The launch ramps along with other ruined structures remain to the right (north) of the access road; however, hedgerows and vegetation make them difficult to identify.

> Return to motorway E46/N13 and continue towards Cherbourg. After 4.7 km enter a large roundabout; the motorway exits to the right and by-passes the city to its east by going directly to the port facilities. Instead, exit the roundabout toward Cherbourg / la Glacerie-Centre (N2013) and continue 3.8 km toward the center of the city stopping at the junction with highway D900, which occurs shortly after a broad 'S' curve. (49.625863, -1.616943)

Capture of Cherbourg
22 to 29 June 1944

Cherbourg was a fortress in Roman times. An enemy occupation of the harbor was first recorded in the days of the Vikings. The British held the fortress in 1758 during the Seven Years War. The construction and fortification of an enlarged harbor began in 1784 with the sinking of ships and rubble to develop the breakwaters and causeways that formed the harbor and eventually formed the largest artificial harbor in the world. Masonry fortifications were constructed to protect the harbor entrances.

Maison du tourisme de Cherbourg et du Haut-Cotentin (49.638771, -1.621621)
2, Quai Alexandre III   50100 Cherbourg-Octeville
Tel. +33 (0)2 33 93 52 02   Fax. +33 (0)2 33 53 66 97
E-mail: tourisme@ot-cherbourg-cotentin.fr
Web: http://www.ot.cherbourg-cotentin.fr

Notice the famous concrete letters on the right announcing the city limits of **CHERBOURG**. The location gained notoriety in 1944 when a broadly circulated

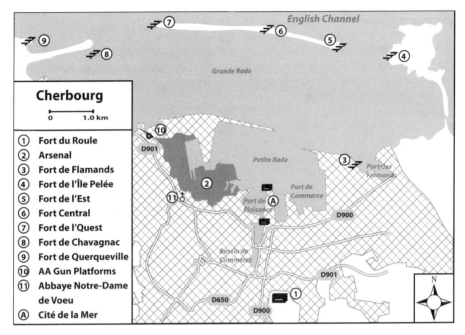

Cherbourg

0 ————— 1.0 km

① Fort du Roule
② Arsenal
③ Fort de Flamands
④ Fort de l'Île Pelée
⑤ Fort de l'Est
⑥ Fort Central
⑦ Fort de l'Quest
⑧ Fort de Chavagnac
⑨ Fort de Querqueville
⑩ AA Gun Platforms
⑪ Abbaye Notre-Dame
    de Voeu
Ⓐ Cité de la Mer

photograph showed dejected German POWs being marched past this sign and into captivity guarded by battle-weary American infantrymen.

> At this intersection the highway becomes D900; follow for 700 m before turning right (Av. Étienne Lecarpentier) and following the signs up the hillside to Musée de la Libération-Fort du Roule. A metal doorway, which bars the tunnel entrance to theunderground fortifications, is visible at the extreme of the fourth hairpin turn. Continue through the fort's gateway where a few parking spaces are located at the very top of the hill. (49.630387, -1.614089)

Fort du Roule (Stützpunkt-272), built upon a steep 125-meter promontory south of the city center, dominates the city and harbor of Cherbourg and the main highway from the south. Its 105-mm U-boat guns were in casemates build into the rock face and aimed toward the sea. The upper levels held mortar and machine-gun pillboxes, which were protected from infantry attack by fire from other German batteries in the city's western outskirts at Octeville.

Because of the steep rock cliff, the sole approach was a ridge from the south. The land attack was undertaken on 26 June by the 2nd and 3rd Battalions of the 314th Infantry Regiment, 79th Division. The 2nd Battalion first overcame a line of defensive positions and an antitank ditch, which were along an east-west trail that is now highway D410.

The American advance was stopped by fire emanating from a pillbox until Corporal John Kelly of Company E, 2nd Battalion, crawled forward under heavy automatic weapons fire to place a ten-foot-long pole charge containing fifteen pounds of TNT at the base of the pillbox. As the blast was ineffective, Kelly repeated the action. This time the blast damaged the ends of the guns. Kelly repeated the operation a third time to blast open the door, and then he threw handgrenades into the position forcing its survivors to surrender.[5]

The 3rd Battalion passed through the 2nd battalion and pushed on against the western side of the fortifications. Company K was facing a combined position of machine guns strengthened by an 88-mm FlaK gun. Company commander Lieutenant Carlos Ogden, armed with his rifle, hand grenades, and a grenade launcher, moved alone up the hill. Although wounded twice during the action, he destroyed the 88-mm gun with a rifle grenade and two machine guns with hand grenades. The attack was so devastating that the enemy on the top level of the fort surrendered.[6]

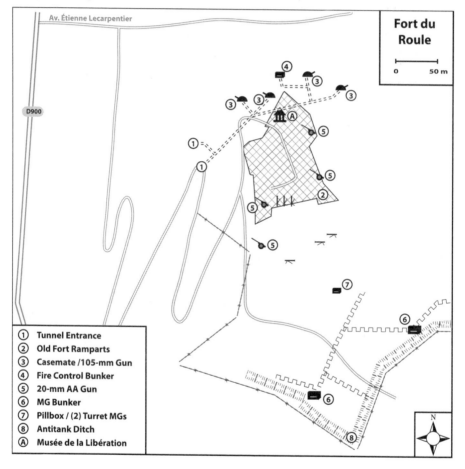

Fort du Roule

0   50 m

D900

① Tunnel Entrance
② Old Fort Ramparts
③ Casemate /105-mm Gun
④ Fire Control Bunker
⑤ 20-mm AA Gun
⑥ MG Bunker
⑦ Pillbox / (2) Turret MGs
⑧ Antitank Ditch
Ⓐ Musée de la Libération

Av. Étienne Lecarpentier

N

5   Corporal John D Kelly was awarded the Medal of Honor for his actions. The award was given posthumously as Kelly was killed in action on 23 November 1944 at age 21. He is buried in Épinal American Cemetery, Épinal, France.
In recognition of its actions, the 2nd Battalion, 314th Infantry Regiment, 79th Infantry Division was awarded a Presidential Unit Citation.

6   Lieutenant Carlos C Ogden was also awarded the Medal of Honor. He survived the war rising to the rank of major. He died in 2001 at age 83 and is buried in Arlington National Cemetery, Arlington, Virginia.

Musée de la Libération – Fort du Roule
Montée des Résistants   50100 Cherbourg-Octeville
Tel: +33 (0)2 33 20 14 12   Email: musee.liberation@wanadoo.fr
Web: http://www.ville-cherbourg.fr

The Liberation Museum, the oldest military museum in Normandy, occupies the upper levels of the Fort du Roule on the Montange du Roule. The fort was built in 1852 by order of Napoleon III to defend the port and the southern approaches to the city. Occupied by the Germans in 1940, the fort's defenses were modernized with the construction of four casemates, an observation bunker, and connecting underground passages in the side of the cliff below the fort.

Within the museum's arc-roofed casemates, displays depict the history of the Second World War from the Fall of France to the Liberation and its effect upon the daily lives of the citizens of Cherbourg. An illustrated map shows the final assault upon the city's defenses. A theater presents a rotating series of films. The view of the city of Cherbourg and its harbor from the fort's exterior terrace is spectacular. A small plaque on the wall of the ticket office commemorates the memory of General Joseph L Collins, who is an honorary citizen of Cherbourg.

Open October through April on Wednesday through Sunday from 14:00 to 18:00; daily May through September from 10:00 to 12:00 and from 14:00 to 18:00, except closed Sunday and Monday mornings. Admission fee; Normandie Pass accepted

> Return down the hill and turn right on Av de Paris (D900, becomes Av Carnot, then eventually Av Aristide Briand) and continue north toward the port. After approximately 500 m, park and view Fort du Roule from below. (49.63612, -1.6169)

The four German installed casemates and the fire-control bunker are clearly visible on the hillside below the fort. The lower levels of Fort du Roule remained troublesome despite the surrender of the top level since the men of 4th Battery, Kriegsmarine Artillery Battalion 260, continued to shell American positions with their four 105-mm guns. Connected by internal tunnels, which were blocked against access from above, the guns were difficult to eliminate. Attempts to place satchel charges against the casemate openings and antitank-gun fire from below failed to dislodge the enemy. Finally, bazooka fire neutralized guns protecting the western entrance; the security doors, which were passed on the approach up the hill, were blown open, and the fort capitulated later that evening.

> Continue north (D900) until the roadway ends in a large roundabout containing a statue of the ancient Roman god Minerva in the center. Exit the roundabout to the west on Quai Général Lawton Collins. After only 120 m, bear right toward Cité de la Mer. Stop after 170 m in the large parking area. (49.643422, -1.617785)

Sporadic sniper fire from buildings lining the streets approaching the dock area delayed the American advance through the city for hours. Four heavy pillboxes sited along the docks withstood direct fire by the 75-mm guns of Sherman tanks. The pillboxes were eventually battered into surrendering by fire from 57-mm antitank guns from the 1st Battalion, 313th Regiment.

One such pillbox is sited on the grassy area between the two parking lots of the Cité de la Mer. Surrounded and partially obscured by shrubbery, the bunker provides vivid evidence of German efforts to protect harbor facilities from landward attack. Its entrance door and protective machine gun openings are clearly visible as well as a rooftop tobruk. Its partially obscured embrasure once held a 47-mm Skoda antitank gun.

La Cité de la Mer (49.644767, -1.617592)

Gare Maritime Transatlantique   50100 Cherbourg
Tel : +33 (0)2 33 20 26 26   Email: informations@citedelamer.com
Web: http://www.citedelamer.com/

From the 1930s to the early 1950s, the Gare Maritime had been a train terminus feeding passengers to transatlantic liners steaming between Southampton and New York. The terminus was severely damaged by Allied bombings and German efforts to block the port. Although rebuilt after the war, it never regained the elegance of the pre-war period. It now houses the Cité de la Mer, a large aquarium and seafaring museum with special exhibits on the liner RMS *Titanic* and the history of deep-sea submersibles. *Le Redoutable*, the first French nuclear-powered submarine, stands in a dry dock outside the museum building and audio-guided tours are available in French and English.

Open daily 09:30 to 18:00 (later in summer; closed Mondays during off-season). Admission fee.

> Continue north along Allée du Président Menuit to its northern end. (49.648494, -1.617115)

Two casemates at the end of the pier at the Gare Maritime housed 105-mm Schneider cannon. Their 15-kilometer range protected approaches to the harbor entrance. The only remaining casemate is used as a viewing platform for *le Redoubtable*.

> Return to Quai Général Lawton Collins and continue south 350 m; turn right and cross Pont Tourant, which separates the inner and outer basins. After crossing the bridge, turn right onto Quai Caligny and follow the divided highway (changes names several times) for 1.5 km. Turn right (Av de l'Enseigne de Vaisseau Mangold) and enter the parking area in front of the arsenal entrance. (49.64601, -1.635278)

The **Cherbourg Arsenal** began in 1740 as a private shipyard building sailing schooners. Expanded during the Napoleonic era, by 1899 the arsenal specialized in building submarines, which it continues to do to this day. During the war the arsenal was the German base for two flotillas of 'S' or 'Schnell' boats, which were torpedo-carrying patrol craft similar to American PT Boats. These boats cruised the English coast, usually at night, seeking targets of opportunity or infiltrating spies.[7]

The **Portail de l'Arsenal,** the decorative frieze and gateway that once was the entrance to the naval yard, has been relocated to an attractive corner of the parking area. Access to the military port is absolutely prohibited.

---

7   At 0200 on 28 April 1944, eight LSTs were transporting a follow-up force of engineers and quartermaster troops toward a practice landing at Slapton Sands on the coast of Devon, England. Nine S-boats on patrol from Cherbourg were directed to the site by the interception of heavy Allied radio traffic. They torpedoed three LTSs; one burst into flames, one sank almost immediately, and the third limped to port. A total of 749 Allied sailors and soldiers died. The tragedy was hidden from public knowledge until after the war

> Return to the divided highway (becomes D901) and continue for 850 m; turn right leaving the divided highway at rue des 3 Hangards, then another right turn onto an access road. (49.647427, -1.640798)

The **Abbaye Notre-Dame de Voeu** was founded in 1145 on land donated by Empress Matilda, William the Conqueror's granddaughter. It rose to prosperity in the 12th century only to suffer repeated lootings during the Hundred Years War. It was rebuilt and then entered a slow deterioration during the French Religious Wars. Used as a military hospital during and after the French Revolution, it fell into disuse and was damaged during shelling in 1944. It is currently the subject of a long-term renovation plan.

> Return to the divided highway (D901) and continue for 750 m; turn right leaving the divided highway at the traffic light opposite the rue Vauban and stop. Walk north into the park to view the concrete structures. (49.655363, -1.650009)

Four **open-air gun platforms** were constructed by the Germans west of the Arsenal to house antiaircraft guns to protect the arsenal and four 240-mm railway guns positioned where the highway now passes. The platforms stand in a large park from which the western harbor opening can be seen.

> Return to the divided highway (D901, becomes D45) and continue west along the harbor for 3.1 km Turn right on rue du Port and continue 500 m to a parking area. (49.669077, -1.682174)

The harbor's historic fortifications can be viewed near **Fort de Querqueville**, which marks the western end of the great harbor. Although the plan of the fort stems from the reign of Louis XVI, it was not finished until 1852. The semi-circle of thirty-six casemates opens to the rear into a central courtyard. The bastion is separated from land by a moat. The 19th-century fort was incorporated into German defenses for Cherbourg by the addition of platforms mounting tank turrets capable of all-around defense. Although many of the buildings have become dilapidated, the grounds are still utilized by branches of the French National Marine École de Fourriers (Quartermasters), and access is usually only possible during Heritage Days.

Walk along the jetty that runs east of the fort. The rusted structure standing above the water in the harbor 30 meters from the jetty was part of the temporary harbor facilities built by American engineers after the capture of Cherbourg. German destruction of the harbor was so complete that the original unloading facilities could not be used for months and temporary facilities were constructed as clearing operations continued.

Fort de Chavagnac can be seen near the end of the 1-kilometer-long jetty, which is now used by fishermen and the occasional pleasure craft. The triangular fortification with rounded points was constructed behind the breakwater to defend the western entrance to the harbor.

Fort de l'Ouest is 1.1 kilometers to the east on the opposite side of the western harbor opening. This 19th-century fort was the last holdout in the battle for Cherbourg for thirty-eight German seamen, who sailed to this fort from the arsenal. Their intention was to detonate demolition charges and destroy the western end of the harbor. Shell fire from American 155-mm artillery pieces was successful in penetrating the fort's stone walls and breaking the detonation wires; the small group was the last to surrender on 29 June.

Numerous German batteries and fortifications were sited in the hills that rise up behind the fort. Cherbourg has expanded considerably since 1944, and much of that growth has been among these hills, making the task of finding and visiting these fortifications a difficult task with very little reward.

Reverse direction on rue du Port and continue across D45. Almost immediately bear right (rue Roger Glinel). Follow for 750 m; turn left (rue du Général Leclerc, D118), then very shortly turn right (rue de l'Église) and continue past the church to park. (49.664644, -1.698324)

Walk past the front of the church to the small **Chapelle St-Germain,** a brown stone building with a square steeple. The 10th-century chapel, built upon an even older structure destroyed during a Viking invasion, is the oldest in the Cotentin. The bell tower dates from the 17th century, replacing an older tower that was in danger of collapsing. Good views of Fort de Querqueville, Cherbourg harbor, and the forts in the harbor are possible from behind the ancient chapel.

This completes the Battle of Cherbourg tour.

Side trip: German Coastal Defenses

The northern shore of the Cotentin peninsula is studded with fortifications, some dating to the Napoleonic era. Many of the sites were updated before the war to offer protection from more powerful and longer range naval guns. For the most part, they were designed to protect Cherbourg from attack from the sea, although some open-air guns were capable of 360-degree defense at the cost of protection from aerial bombardment. After the French defeat of 1940, these positions were enhanced and expanded by the German Todt Organization as part of the Atlantic Wall defenses, often incorporating already existing French structures into their plans. Because of their size and re-enforced concrete construction, many of these structures remain. Some are on private land and therefore inaccessible, but others are on public land and offer opportunities for visits to those interested in Atlantic Wall structures. Their current state of disrepair varies; most have some damage from wartime bombardments or post-war demolitions experimentation. All have had their guns removed as well as most other salvageable materials. A few remain almost pristine, their only damage being the spray paint graffiti of local youths.

We recommend three sites, selected for their ease of access, nature of the emplacements, and natural beauty of the location. They can be visited after the Cherbourg tour by proceeding along the eastern seashore to return to the base of the peninsula or before the Cherbourg tour by leaving Quinéville and progressing north along the eastern coast of the peninsula to approach Cherbourg from the east.

Coastal Battery North of the Maupertus-s/Mer Airport

From the Chapelle St-Germain, reverse direction to regain the coastal highway (D45). After 550 m, enter a large roundabout and exit toward Cherbourg-centre (D901). Continue through the city of Cherbourg and out its eastern environs (D901, joins E46/N13).

After 11.3 km, remain on highway D901 as it exits the motorway to the east toward St-Pierre-Église. After 1.1 km, turn left toward Becquet (D122). After 1.5 km, turn right toward Bretteville-en-Saire (D116). After 6.4 km turn right onto a very narrow lane (Chemin du Pied Sablon) and drive to a 'T' junction. Turn right onto Chemin du Bruley and proceed to the entrance gate of the Cap du Brick nature area. (49.673863, -1.474893) Total distance: 23.0 km.

The **Batterie Seeadler**, originally of French construction and named *Batterie du Brûlé*, held four 194-mm French-made naval guns in open emplacements sited in a rough line 600 meters from the shoreline atop a level promontory. Nearer to the shore is a multi-level fire-control bunker also originally of French construction. The Germans felt that the open gun emplacements were too easily targeted by enemy aircraft and they built another fire-control bunker and gun casemates (*Batterie Osteck*) on the hills to the south, which are not readily accessible. Although the position was unoccupied on D-Day, the German 5th Battery, Artillery Regiment 1709, moved guns into its positions during their withdrawal up the Cotentin Peninsula.

Seeadler Battery is now part of the Pointe du Brick coastal conservatory and is therefore publicly accessible. The level hill top is covered by head-high vegetation mainly of fern, gorse, and heather. Paths have been cut through the dense and prickly foliage to allow access to the fire-control bunker and the four gun positions. It is not handicap accessible.

From the entrance gate, proceed west 140 meters to the first pathway on the right. Take it toward the fire-control bunker visible to the north. Within 75 meters, a side path goes to open **gun emplacement #1**. An earthen berm permits climbing atop the circular protective wall. The position retains its gun mounts within the circular enclosure. Separate alcoves built into the sides of the wall provided storage for shells and propellant. (49.674391, -1.476953)

Continue on the path toward the sea. The **fire-control bunker** is visible from the coastal road since it dominates the bluff above the highway. Although battle damage is apparent on its southern side and it is graffiti marred, this structure is an absolutely magnificent example of a tri-level observation post. With some physical dexterity, its levels can be entered to view its range of observation along the ocean front. The lighthouse and Napoleonic fort at Cap Levi is to the northeast and to the west are Cherbourg and its harbor fortifications. (49.676231, -1.480579)

Leave the fire-control bunker to the southwest, and at the T-junction proceed south to the access road. Open **emplacement #2** is 20 meters to the east. It shows damage, perhaps from engaging Allied ships approaching Cherbourg or from French naval experiments after the war. (49.673724, -1.478498)

Proceed west 70 meters on the access road to a path on the right. Open **emplacement #3** is in relatively good condition, and the walls and interior are easily accessible. (49.673412, -1.48029)

Continue on the path past to a T-junction and turn left to open **emplacement #4**, which retains the shell hoist used to lift shells from delivery trucks and place them into the storage shelters. A German soldier's painting remains on the ceiling of one of the alcoves. (49.673648, -1.481985)

Coastal Battery at Pointe de Néville

> Return to the coast highway (D116; this may be easiest by proceeding east on Chemin du Burley for 1.4 km into le Mont Tereire. Follow highway D116 for 11.3 km to the eastern side of Neville-s/Mer. Turn left toward Point de Neville (D514) and follow for 1.5 km to a small shore road on the right; turn and proceed to the battery. (49.701447, -1.332371) Total distance: 14.0 km from *Batterie Seeadler*.

Batterie Blankensee de Néville-s/Mer (WN-126), well-armed with four casemated 94-mm British Vickers Flak guns and four French-made 155-mm guns in open positions, was manned by 2nd Battery, Kriegsmarine Artillery Battalion 260. The German garrison may have destroyed the positions on 18 June and escaped to Cherbourg before the 24th Reconnaissance Squadron occupied the area on 20 June. US Army engineers also contributed to the damage during the testing of methods to attack fortified positions.

The site provides no restrictions to exploring the area because it is now a nature preserve; however, the structure can be very dangerous and should not be entered. The major installations are sited between the sea and the roadway which passes along the inland side of the casemates. Damage is evident on all of the casemates; huge blocks of concrete have been blown off; massive holes are in the walls; and an entire casemate is cracked and broken. Collapse looks imminent, but so they have sat for 70 years. Gun mounts have been salvaged, but circular rings on the floor mark the gun locations. The site is handicap accessible to a limited extent from the roadway.

The defence zone is accessible past a roadside sentry bunker at the main gate of the facility. Walk to the beach and continue north along the sea.

To the east is a small open-air gun position, which held either a 50-mm cannon or 20-mm antiaircraft gun. The metal rods are a postwar addition by local fishermen. West of this position is an undamaged machine-gun tobruk. The first of four casemates, which sheltered the Vickers antiaircraft guns, is ahead. The casemates were originally built as open-air positions; a concrete covering was added later to form an enclosed shelter.

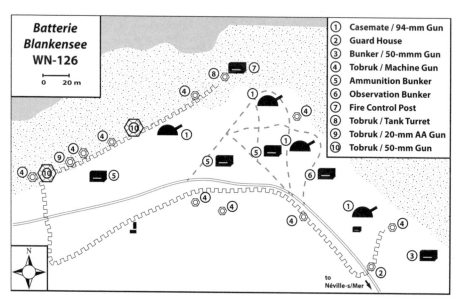

Batterie Blankensee WN-126

0   20 m

①	Casemate / 94-mm Gun
②	Guard House
③	Bunker / 50-mmm Gun
④	Tobruk / Machine Gun
⑤	Ammunition Bunker
⑥	Observation Bunker
⑦	Fire Control Post
⑧	Tobruk / Tank Turret
⑨	Tobruk / 20-mm AA Gun
⑩	Tobruk / 50-mm Gun

to
Néville-s/Mer

Continuing westward to the next structure, the narrow slit below the low profile roof identifies an fire-control post. Concrete covered tunnels, seldom seen elsewhere, are especially prevalent in this area. They were constructed by digging trenches, cementing the sides and floor, covering the trench with concrete panels, and camouflaging them with a covering of gravel and sand. Wind and waves have exposed these to view. **Casemate #2** is less damaged in front, but the jumble of broken concrete to its rear held the ammunition supply. It was detonated by retreating Germans or occupying Americans. **Casemate #3** looks almost intact compared to the others. The complete wreckage near the point of land was once the **fire control post**. The explosion within it was violent enough to blow the roof completely off and turn it over!

The final **casemate (#4)** is southwest of the fire control post. Behind it are the remains of its exploded ammunition storage building. The ground to its front is littered with sections of tunnels, tobruks, and defensive gun emplacements. The destruction is so complete that only experts can identify the remains. The octagonal concrete ring held a 50-mm cannon for close-in defence.

Coastal Battery at Pointe de Barfleur

Reverse direction and return to Neville-s/Mer. Proceed east toward Barfleur (D116) for 4.1 km. In Gatteville, turn left toward le Phare (D10) and follow for 400 m to the center of the village. Park and walk north on the Chemin de Roubary. The first installations are only 170 m ahead. (49.688594, -1.28215) Total distance: 6.4 km from Pointe de Néville.

The town of Gatteville-le-Phare sits two kilometers inland from the Pointe de Barfleur, the northeastern tip of the Cotentin Peninsula where a lighthouse sits upon rocks beyond the point. Between the town and the lighthouse were the casemates of ***Batterie Gatteville*** (**Stützpunkt-152**), whose four French-made 155-mm guns had a range of 20 kilometers and were manned by 7th Battery, Coastal Artillery Regiment 1261. In addition to the four casemates, the battery manned six open-air gun emplacements, a fire control post, and ammunition and accommodation bunkers. This was a massively defended area since it controlled the sea lanes around the northeast coast of France. Smaller positions were to the east (WN-123) and to the north (WN-125). Since the guns were pointed north toward the sea, they could not provide interdiction fire onto Utah Beach or against advancing allied ground troops. The battery surrendered to the 24th Reconnaissance Squadron on 21 June.

The positions sit on private land, and several have been converted for use as summer beach cottages; however, a public walk path goes through the center of the installation, and most of the positions are visible from the path. Two casemates are on each side of the path, numbered from west to east. One open-air gun emplacement is to the west; the other five are in a rough line to the east. Please respect private property.

The path first passes between two closely spaced accommodation bunkers. The right bunker is visible as a low, grass-covered mound showing only the inland wall and its entrance doorways. The number of doorways indicates that this was a twin accommodation bunker. Only 40 meters ahead on the right, the second of six open-air gun emplacements appears as part of a farm complex. The massive concrete circle is broken by an access opening on the landward side. This is not a small position as can been seen by the thickness of the surrounding walls. **Open-air emplacement #1** is 65 meters to the west and **casemate #1** is immediately west of it. The attached satellite TV dish on the casemate indicates that it is inhabited. The four casemates are identical in design, and each retains two concrete 'wings' on either side of the back of the structure. **Casemate #2** is to the left front and 45 meters across a pasture; its rear wall shows the impact of numerous tank or artillery shells fired from inland. **Open-air emplacement #3,** with its machine-gun tobruk clearly visible, is approximately due east of casemate #2 on the right side of the path. Beyond it and mostly hidden by vegetation is the **fire control bunker.**

Continuing north, **casemate #3** is immediately adjacent to the path. It presents a good perspective of the gun opening, which in this case has been enclosed to make the casemate livable. **Casemate #4** is ahead on the right and father into the field; its rear is shrouded in trees and shrubbery. Windows have been fitted into the gun embrasure and drapes can be seen incongruously hanging inside the sealed gun opening. The roof shows some damage probably inflicted by naval gun fire. Open-air **emplacements #4, #5,** and **#6** are to the east, hidden by terrain and vegetation.

The lighthouse (**Le Phare de Gatteville**) is clearly visible to the northeast. Still active and the third tallest lighthouse in the world, its 365 steps can be ascended for views of the coast line and channel. It can best be reached by car by continuing north on highway D10 and walking the final 200 m. (49.695118, -1.267601)

Chapter Eleven

Battle of St-Lô
9 June to 20 July

After the junction of Utah and Omaha beachheads, the US 29th Division's objective became the departmental capital city of St-Lô. The city's importance was not only political but also geographical since it was located at the junction of several important highways connecting it to Cherbourg, Bayeux, Coutances, Vire, and Périers.

American troops entered terrain requiring a different style of fighting. Walls of stone and vegetation known as hedgerows divided the gently rolling hills into small fields and pastures. Farm tracks that separated the fields had typically sunk beneath the level of the surrounding ground by centuries of erosion. The hedgerows offered excellent opportunities for concealed strongpoints and formed perfect fortresses. The hedgerows also limited maneuver and the use of tanks, which could not penetrate the tangled brush, tree roots, and stone barriers and were, at the same time, susceptible to short-range antitank weapons such as the German *Panzerfaust*. American infantrymen felt greeted by the searing noise of a German MG 42 at every field or road junction. A few enemy troops with a well-placed machine gun could hold up an entire company – and then disappear. The European war, for the Americans, was about to enter its most dangerous phase.

Expanding the Beachhead
9 to 11 June

On 9 June, with the fighting strength of the German 352nd Infantry Division reduced to 2,500 men and with much of its artillery lost, General Kraiss ordered a withdrawal behind the Elle River, a placid country stream that flows in a generally northwest direction from its source east of St-Lô into the Vire River near St-Fromond.

Battle

On the morning of 8 June, the 115th Infantry Regiment moved off the beachhead against no opposition but with orders to cross the Aure River. Only a few feet above sea level, the Aure valley was marshy ground in the best of times. That spring the Germans had dammed the river to create an impassible shallow marsh. As only one north-south causeway crossed the flooded area, it could be easily defended. By noon the lead battalion entered Longueville and, later in the day, Canchy. Although observation of the valley disclosed no enemy troops, it also did not reveal a viable route across the marsh.

Battlefield Tour

The Battle of St-Lô tour starts from Isigny-s/Mer where the 29th Infantry Division tour ended in Chapter Six. Isigny-s/Mer is 12 kilometers east of Carentan.

From Isigny-s/Mer proceed east toward la Cambe (E46/N13). Exit toward Vouilly (D113) and continue south. (49.336938, -1.009305)

The narrow D113 highway was the only road to cross the Aure flooded zone. After slightly more than 1 kilometer the road crosses le Aure Inférieure and enters the Marais Suhard. The entire lowland area is now the **Parc Naturel des Marais du Cotentin**, which extends from Isigny-s/Mer on the west to almost Trévières on the east. During

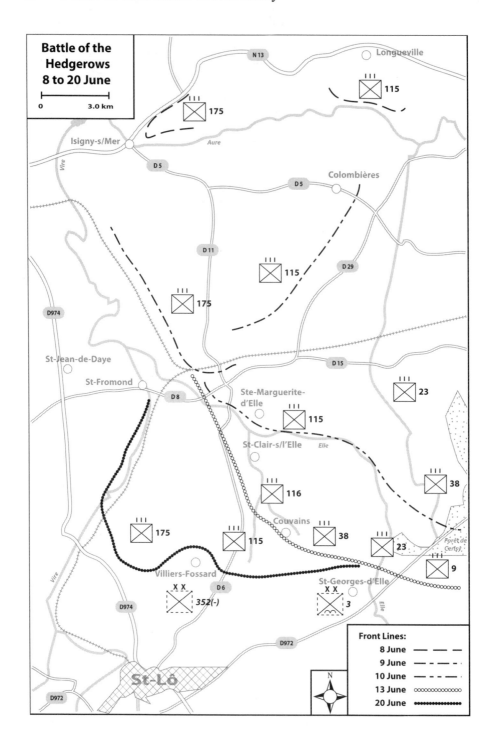

normal weather conditions, this lowland is not flooded although it was completely under water during storms as recently as 1995.

> After 3.6 km, bear left onto highway D113B; continue for 1.6 km to the Château Vouilly. (49.295072, -1.023552)

Le Chateau de Vouilly
James et Marie Jo Hamel   14230 Normandie
Tel: 33(0) 02 31 22 08 59   Email: chateau.vouilly@wanadoo.fr
Web: http://www.chateau-vouilly.com/

The moated 18th-century Château de Vouilly stands upon the foundations of a 12th-century fortress. Originally headquarters for the *Panzerjäger* Battalion of the 352nd Infantry Division, after D-Day the chateau housed the US First Army's Press Camp. Broadcasters and journalists including Ernie Pyle, Walter Cronkite, Robert Capa, Andy Rooney, and John Thompson filed their reports from here. A plaque of the main building's façade commemorates the event. The chateau is now operated as a dairy farm and bed and breakfast. Its dining room presents a small display of correspondent memorabilia.

> Continue 450 m to junction with highway D5. Turn left toward Colombières and continue 3.1 km into the village. Stop at the church. (49.296758, -0.981603)

A plaque on the south wall of the 13th-century Église St-Pierre de Colombières behind the village war memorial commemorates the **115th Infantry Regiment**, which liberated Colombières on 8 and 9 June 1944.

> From the church, proceed toward Trévières (D29a); after 400 m, turn north toward the Chateau de Colombières and continue to the entrance drive.(49.301873, -0.975552)

Chateau de Colombières
Comte Etienne de Maupeou d'Ableiges   14710 Colombières
Tel: +33 (0)2 31 22 51 65
E-mail: colombieresaccueil@aliceadsl.fr
Web: http://www.chateaudecolombieres.com/

The fiefdom of Colombières dates to the 11th century when it was created as a reward for comrades of William the Conqueror after his invasion of England in 1066. The oldest parts of the present structure date from the late 14th century. The massive twin towers were added after the Battle of Formigny at the end of the Hundred Years War.

On the morning of 6 June, the 2nd Company, *Panzerjäger* Battalion 352, consisting of 15 Marder antitank guns, suddenly left its camouflaged position under the elm trees of the chateau's drive and headed toward Colleville-s/Mer to face the Allied invasion. Headquarters personnel and a small detachment remained.

The chateau is now operated as a bed and breakfast with guided tours of the moat, courtyard, and main rooms available.

Open weekdays in July and August and weekends in September from 14:30 to 18:30. Fee.

> From the chateau, return south approximately 150 m and then turn east on la Basse Rivière. After 600 m, turn north onto la Poterie and continue 350 m to the small stele on the left. (49.304594, -0.965627)

Late on the afternoon of 8 June, platoon leader Lieutenant Kermit Miller of the US 115th Infantry Regiment set out from Longueville on patrol to search out a crossing of the flooded valley. Five hours after entering the swampy, stagnant water, the twenty-eight men reached Colombières, 4 kilometers on the opposite side. In the darkness they captured three German sentries. A local French woman told them that the chateau was a German headquarters. Miller's men, now supported by French Resistance fighters, surrounded the chateau and, after a brief firefight, captured the headquarters and accounted for forty-six dead enemy troops. Mindful of the route across the swamp that they had discovered, the platoon returned to regimental headquarters with eleven prisoners.[1]

On 9 June, the 115th Regiment followed Miller's route, the troops aided by footbridges constructed by the 121st Engineer Combat Battalion over the deeper streams. After crossing the swamp, the battalion spread toward its individual objectives.

The dark granite stele records the arrival of Lt Miller's platoon and the assistance given to it by the local French Resistance leader Albert Moulin and his son. The trackless Aure Valley to the north is now mostly pasture because the mucky soil is too difficult to plow.

Battle of the Elle
12 to 13 June 1944

After the 115th Infantry Regiment's three battalions crossed the Aure flooded zone, they fanned out with St-Lô as their objective. Because German resistance had melted away, apparently the city, only 27 kilometers distant, could be easily captured. Despite the absence of organized resistance, the regiment's 2nd Battalion suffered a disastrous encounter with retreating Germans and was almost destroyed. Nevertheless, the 115th Regiment continued to move south, and by early on 11 June, the regiment entered Ste-Marguerite-d'Elle only 12 kilometers from St-Lô.

On 12 June, two companies of the 29th Division's 175th Infantry Regiment were separately ambushed near Montmartin-en-Graignes while attempting to strengthen control of the Vire River Valley. The next day another of its companies mistakenly attacked a larger German force. The Germans reacted aggressively, dispersed the company, and forced the regimental and company commanders to surrender. In two days on separate battlefields, major elements of the 115th and 175th Regiments had suffered serious casualties. Manpower levels were quickly re-established, but the new recruits lacked the operational experience of the older, veteran members of the other battalions.

Objective	To press south toward the heights overlooking St-Lô
Forces	
American	29th Infantry Division (Major General Charles Gerhardt)
German	352nd Infantry Division (Generalleutnant Dietrich Kraiss); 30th Mobile Brigade (Oberleutnant Hugo Freiherr von und zu Aufseß)

---

1   Lieutenant Kermit Miller was posthumously awarded a Distinguished Service Cross for his exploits. Miller was killed the next day. He is buried in Normandy American Cemetery.

| **Result** | The advance was slow and costly as American troops fought entrenched defenders in each field and over every hedgerow. |
| **Location** | Bayeux is 30 km northwest of Caen; Colombières is 25 km west of Bayeux. |

Battle

German resistance stiffened while the 29th Division approached the Elle River. At 0500 on 12 June, 1st Battalion, 115th Regiment, launched its attack against the now-stabilized German front. Preceded by a barrage from four artillery battalions that inflicted little harm to Germans sheltering in their slit trenches and foxholes, the GIs came down the north slope of the creek embankment near rue du Pont de la Pierre into withering machine-gun fire. After six hours, twenty-five were dead, seventy-five wounded, and not one soldier had reached the narrow stream. Two platoons of tanks were sent forward but stopped when three of the tanks were destroyed in quick succession by well-camouflaged antitank guns. That evening the attack was resumed by the 116th Regiment, and the stream crossed by 2200.

The 3rd Battalion, 115th Regiment, was one kilometer to the east advancing where the front lines had been registered by German artillery and mortars. Two rifle companies – I and L – managed to cross the Pont Jourdan and proceed 2.4 kilometer to les Fresnes, unaware that flanking units had made no progress. Isolated and under continuous German artillery fire, they moved back to the start line – less 130 dead and the wounded troops they abandoned.

Despite the setbacks, on 13 June St-Clair-s/l'Elle and Couvains were captured from the Germans. The cost was high at 547 casualties. On 14 June, the 29th Division joined the recently arrived 30th and 35th Infantry Divisions in the newly created XIX Corps commanded by Major General Charles Corlett.

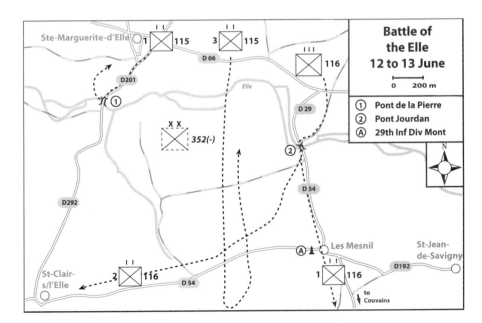

Battlefield Tour

The tour begins south of the Aure flooded zone after the 115th Regiment crossed it near Colombières. The paved roads in this part of the tour are narrow country lanes, only slightly changed from the dirt paths of 1944. They demonstrate that the wartime road network was not capable of supporting large mobile or armoured forces, forcing a type of warfare not suited to Allied strengths.

> From Colombières, proceed southeast toward Le-Molay-Littry (D5). After 800 m, turn south toward Lison (D202) for 6.3 km to the intersection with highway D113b at le Carrefour des Vignes aux Gendres. (49.248619, -1.018295)

The weary 2nd Battalion, 115th Regiment, had been marching for almost twenty hours when it advanced south along highway D113b to this intersection and halted for rest at 0200 on 10 June. Its officers chose two pastures south of the crossroads community of **le Carrefour des Vignes aux Gendres** as bivouac for the 600 men. The exhausted, hungry soldiers literally collapsed into sleep. However, they neglected to install basic defensive precautions. The sentries assumed that vehicle noise they heard was from the nearby 3rd Battalion. It was not.

German infantry, an accumulation of various elements of the 352nd Division attempting to withdraw to the Elle, infiltrated to within a few meters of the American encampment. Suddenly, flares erupted to provide an eerie light over the sleeping men. Machine-gun, rifle, and mortar fire filled the pastures. Three Sturmgeschütz III self-propelled guns roared down the road firing their 75-mm guns at point-blank range. Infantrymen attempting to escape over the hedgerows were gunned down. The battalion commander, Lieutenant Colonel William Warfield, and his staff had been meeting in one of the stone houses when the attack began. They ran outside to organize a defense and were killed on the roadway. Twenty minutes later the engagement was over: fifty were killed, one hundred were wounded or captured, and the remainder of the battalion scattered.

Only a few houses remain at the road junction known as le Carrefour (literally, 'The Crossroads'). To the south the terrain drops toward the valley of a minor stream. On the side of the intersection a grey, granite stele stands on a small cobblestone court. The stele commemorates the event, the casualties, and the death of the regimental commander, Lt Col Warfield.[2]

Accounts differ as to the exact location of the bivouac varying from 200 meters to 900 meters south of the intersection. The discrepancy matters little as the fields have a wearying similarity. Some accounts suggest Lt Kermit Miller was killed in this engagement; other accounts disagree. Regardless, the day after his efforts to safely advance the regiment, he was dead.

> Leave the intersection toward Lison (D202). After 1.3 km, turn south toward Ste-Marguerite-d'Elle (D201) and continue 4.6 km into the town. At the stop sign with the church on the left, the road jogs slightly to the left around an ancient stone building that displays its centuries of wear and repairs. Continue south on rue du Pont de la Pierre (D201) for 500 m to the bridge. (49.20386, -1.024389)

---

2   Lieutenant Colonel William E Warfield is buried in Normandy American Cemetery. He was the recipient of a Silver Star and Purple Heart.

The rue du Pont de la Pierre passes between incredibly high hedgerows and then along a gradual curve down the side of the hill before crossing the Elle River. **Pont de la Pierre** looks little changed from its 1944 appearance; the stone abutments have been rebuilt, but it remains a country-creek crossing. The roadway looks original. Although the approach is not particularly steep, it is fully exposed to the tree and brush-covered opposite hillside. The vegetation provided superb cover for prepared German antitank gun and automatic weapon positions. Advancing American troops were fully exposed and absorbed numerous casualties during the five-hour battle to cross the river.

Continue 1.5 km toward St-Clair-s/Elle (D201, becomes D292) to the junction with highway D54. Bear right after the church to continue west on highway D54 to the junction with highway D6. (49.190595, -1.041126)

A **29th Infantry Division Memorial** stands west of St-Clair beside the Isigny-St-Lô highway (D6) at the junction with highway D54. The rough granite stone, split by a white marble wedge embossed with the division's ying-yang insignia, professes eternal gratitude from the citizens of the local communities to the men of the division.

Reverse direction and proceed 2.7 km through St-Clair to the memorial wall on the right immediately before the intersection with highway D192. (49.195223, -1.005936)

After the capture of St-Lô, the 29th Division bivouacked in the vicinity of St-Clair. The men, warmly greeted by the local citizens, formed immediate friendships. A roadside site, lying east of the village and 600 meters south of the **Pont Jourdan** where the 3rd Battalion crossed the Elle River, was chosen to commemorate the sacrifices of the division in liberating France. The **29th Infantry Division Monument** is a long, low fieldstone wall forming a central arc with straight extensions on each side. It holds numerous brass and bronze plaques dedicated to various groups and individuals. It forms a central memorial to the division where units are remembered for service during all phases of the Normandy Campaign. Many of the individual commemorations include epitaphs from family members and make for poignant reading. One such plaque carries the simple statement, 'A soldier who did his job.'

Continue 200 m before turning south (right) toward Couvains (D59). Continue 3.7 km to the south side of the church in Couvains. (49.164673, -1.007845)

Couvains was first attacked by American forces on 12 June. The town was liberated the next day, but the 13th-century Église Notre-Dame was destroyed in the process. The 29th Division turned the area over to the 2nd Infantry Division, which then began its month-long struggle through hedgerows to the southeast toward St-Georges-d'Elle and eventually Hill 192. The 29th Division moved southwest toward St-Lô. Both divisions met fierce opposition in attempting to advance through the fields south of Couvains. Any forward movement met with counterattack, and from this point the pace of the advance slowed.

In the village of Couvains, the enormous, rebuilt stone church stands directly in the path of the north/south road (D59), which curves around the church and churchyard to the right. A small memorial sign to Sergeant Frank Peregory, who was awarded a Medal of Honor for his actions east of Grandcamp-Maisy, stands in a square directly to the south of the church. He was killed on 14 June in the action to liberate Couvains. The square was renamed **place du Lt Charles D Curley**,[3] Company E, 38th Regiment, 2nd Infantry Division, who led his platoon on the attack upon Hill 192 (see below).

Return back to the junction in the center of town. Leave Couvains southwest toward Villiers-Fossard (D92) and follow for 4.7 km into Villiers-Fossard. (Note: highway D92 takes a large jog left onto and then off highway D6).Turn south in the direction of 'vers D6' and, after 40 m, stop at the memorial past the *mairie*. (49.155869, -1.060309)

Battle of Hill 108
16 to 18 June 1944

German re-enforcements arrived as *Kampfgruppe Heinz* from the German 275th Infantry Division while *Kampfgruppe von Böhm* from the German 353rd Infantry Division advanced from Brittany. German troops marched much of the distance at night severely hampered by Allied fighter-bomber aircraft which struck trains, bridges, and truck convoys. Therefore, their units entered the battlefield in a piecemeal fashion. In addition, the elite, all-volunteer 3rd *Fallschirmjäger* Division was assigned to bolster Kraiss's exposed right (eastern) flank and was approaching from western Brittany. As a newly formed unit, most the German paratroopers had never seen combat, but their level of training, fearlessness, and vast superiority in automatic weapons and mortars were well-suited to establish fire superiority during the close-in bocage combat.

Objective	To capture the ridgeline north of St-Lô
Forces	
American	1st Battalion, 175th Regiment, 29th Infantry Division (Lieutenant Colonel Roger Whiteford)
German	352nd Infantry Division (Generalleutnant Dietrich Kraiss); *Kampfgruppe von Böhm* (Major von Böhm)
Result	The ridge was captured and held against German counterattacks
Casualties	
American	60 killed and 190 wounded
German	uncertain
Location	St-Lô is 60 km west of Caen; Villiers-Fossard is 6 km north of St-Lô

Battle

The 175th Infantry Regiment commenced an attack toward St-Lô on 16 June after penetrating the weak German line near Moon-s/Elle. Led by its 1st Battalion, commanded by Lieutenant Colonel Roger Whiteford, the regiment continued to press forward against enemy resistance until it secured Hill 108 after two days of fighting. An advance patrol entered le Mesnil-Rouxelin on 17 June forcing General Kraiss to withdraw his headquarters to St-Lô, which loomed within the Americans' grasp.

On 18 June, one of the worst days for the division in Normandy, the recently arrived

---

3   Major Charles D Curley Jr received *Chevalier de la légion d'honneur*. He died in his native Richmond, Virginia in 2009 at age 88.

Kampfgruppe von Böhm launched its two battalions upon positions of the 175th Regiment on Hill 108. The engagement started with the heaviest German artillery and mortar bombardment since Omaha Beach and continued through the day with hand-to-hand fighting for each hedgerow while hand grenades flew in both directions. No flank support came forth because the regiment had far outpaced neighboring units. Combat continued for almost twelve hours broken only by German calls for the unit to surrender. At the last minute, contact with a supporting artillery battalion was re-

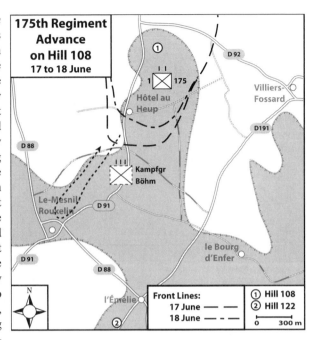

established and heavy fire dissolved the German pressure. The 1st Battalion was relieved the next morning by the regiment's 3rd Battalion.[4] The height became known as '**Purple Heart Hill**.' Unfortunately, it was only one of many such battlefields to earn that nickname during the course of the war.

Battlefield Tour

A 3-meter by 1-meter white marble tribute to the **175th Infantry Regiment** stands behind the *mairie* in the village of Villiers-Fossard. On it, a bronze plaque describes the history of the regiment from its founding in 1774 during the American Revolution, through the War of 1812, American Civil War, and First World War. The presentation continues with a detailed description in English and French of the regiment's exhausting fight west of Villiers-Fossard. The descriptions ends with the 29th Division's motto, 'Twenty-nine, let's go.' This relatively new monument was dedicated in 2009 and is beautifully appointed.

Reverse direction and proceed toward la Meauffe (D92). After 1.5 km turn left toward le Mesnil-Rouxelin (D91).

After leaving Villiers-Fossard, highway D92 climbs to northern edge of the ridge and passes along the north side of the finger-shaped ridge that held **Hill 108**. A few small orchards remain among the new home construction of Hameau Tubois. While this piece of land may have looked important on military maps, in actuality it offered little practical value as an observation post.

4   The 1st Battalion, 175th Infantry Regiment, received the French Croix de Guerre with Silver-Gilt Star and a Presidential Unit Citation for 'steadfastly refusing to yield.' Lt Col Whiteford was wounded in the fighting and evacuated.

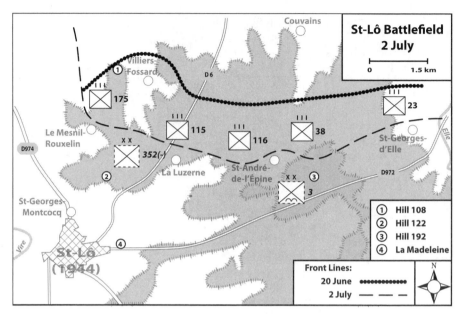

After turning toward le Mesnil-Rouxelin, the roadway sinks 2 to 3 meters below the level of the neighboring fields. The east side of the road is lined with classic Norman hedgerows that block most views of the ridge. After 750 meters, the highway passes Hôtel au Heup on the left; the few buildings marked the front line until the final push into St-Lô on 11 July. The roadside ditches and pits dug at the base of the hedgerows provided the only shelter for troops during that period. After 260 meters, the highway crosses an example of the deeply shaded and overgrown rural lanes that provided a clever enemy with camouflage and impossible-to-detect ambush positions. This junction marks the limit of the 175th Regiment's advance on 17 June. The road continues south slowly losing elevation as it enters le Mesnil-Rouxelin.

Battle of St-Lô
11 to 20 July 1944

The 29th Division's western flank along the Vire River was now held by the US 35th Infantry Division while the US 2nd Infantry Division manned its eastern flank.

The Great Storm of 19 June acerbated the Allied supply problems and caused a delay in offensive operations since American attention and supplies had focused upon the capture of Cherbourg. General Bradley ordered the advance toward St-Lô halted. The rest period was well appreciated by the front line troops, who were cycled back to rear areas for hot food, their first shower since boarding boats in England, and mail from home. The delay also gave replacements an opportunity to become acclimated to the battlefield.

During the quiet period, General Cota trained his men in methods to attack the deadly hedgerows with tanks modified to ram the hedgerows with prongs welded to its front.[5] Either the force of the tank collapsed the hedgerow, or engineers placed explosives

---

5   While units attempted different equipment to blast through the hedgerows, Sergeant Curtis Culin, 2nd Armored Division, received credit for building the prototype 'Rhino' or 'Hedgecutter' tank by welding steel teeth to the front of a tank. Sergeant Culin was awarded the American Legion of Merit for his initiative. Four months later he lost a leg in the Hürtgen Forest. He died in 1963 at age 48.

17.   Men of the 8th Infantry Regiment, US 4th Infantry Division land on Utah Beach. Some move over the crest of the hill while others take shelter behind a concrete seawall, below left. NARA
German pillbox on Utah Beach after the battle, below right. AHEC.

The ceremonial platform at Utah Beach, which was built atop German blockhouses, holds numerous memorials to the landing and support troops. The column on the right is the Federal Monument, erected on the 40th anniversary of the invasion.

18. Troops leave la Madeleine Chapel after services, below left. Archivesnormandie 39-45 The chapel's modern appearance, below right.

Casemate #2 at Crisbecq Battery still retains its 210-mm gun. The camouflage netting on the roof cleverly hides post-battle damage incurred during combat engineer training exercises as demonstrated by comparison to the 1944 photograph, insert. AHEC

19.   A German fortification, part of Stützpunkt-12 at Ravenoville-St-Hubert, remains along the seacoast north of Utah Beach. A sealed tobruk is visible in the left foreground. The installation is examined by two soldiers in 1944, insert. NARA

The V-1 launch ramp, built to deliver Hitler's vengeance weapon against the people of Bristol, England, sits in what is now a pasture grazing cattle at la Boissais .

20.   The famous sign at the outskirts of Cherbourg stands up well when compared to the 1944 photograph in the lower right of this book's cover.

Fort du Roule towers above the city of Cherbourg. On the hillside below it, four casemates and an observation bunker that were added to the fort's defenses by the Germans remain.

21. US infantrymen firing over a hedgerow during the advance upon St-Lô. The soldier on the left has just used his rifle to launch a grenade. NARA

German soldiers examine a captured Sherman 'Rhino' tank with its modifications to cut through hedgerows. Solonieff Collection, AHEC

22.   American troops, led by a French civilian, hunt enemy snipers and artillery observers in the ruins of St Lô as they warily pass the destroyed Église Notre-Dame. NARA

The elaborate memorial to the honorary 'mayor of St-Lô', Major Thomas Howie.

23.   The destruction wrought upon retreating German troops in Roncey is displayed as an elderly French woman walks past the village church and two destroyed German Jagdpanther 'Hetzer' tank destroyers. AHEC

The memorial to the US 116th Infantry Regiment stands upon Hill 203 above the city of Vire. The 29th Infantry Division's ying/yang insignia adorns the main stone flanked by tableau which name each of the 112 casualties suffered by the regiment's 2nd Battalion in capturing the hill.

24. Lieutenant General George S Patton Jr is honored in this memorial in place Patton, Avranches. The central column recognizes Patton's Third Army as the liberators of the city. The Sherman tank 'Thunderbolt' honors the 37th Tank Battalion. A Voie de la Liberté bollard stands on the right.

The monument to the US 30th Infantry Division stands in an opening among the trees atop Hill 314 at Mortain, below left. The inscription honors the unit's valor, sacrifice, and courage in holding the strategic height for five days against vastly superior enemy forces.
The Petit Chapelle stands upon a rock outcropping above the town of Mortain, below right.

25. The Jérusalem War Cemetery holds only forty-eight graves and is sited near a high-speed highway, but shrubs and other plantings protect the picturesque graveyard from the noise of passing vehicles, left.

The Musée de la Bataille de Tilly-s/Seulles occupies a 12th-century chapel sited in a swale near the center of the modern town, right. A monument to twenty-six civilians killed in the fighting fronts the chapel.

A Churchill tank of the Royal Tank Regiment, below, occupies a place of honor on Hill 112 near the stone block monument to the 43rd (Wessex) Division, left. The division fought for two days to capture the commanding height southwest of Caen in one of the more horrific engagements of the Battle of Normandy.

26.   Machine gunners from the Cameron Highlanders of Ottawa fire through hedge in combat near Carpiquet, below left. LAC
Canadian troops carefully work their way through the rubble strewn rue St-Pierre in Caen in July 1944, below right. LAC

A monument located near Cagny commemorates all members of the British Guards Division who perished attacking across these open fields during Operation Goodwood. The monument detail depicts a Sherman Firefly tank and celebrates the destruction of the first German King Tiger tank on 18 July by Lieutenant John Gorman of the Irish Guards.

27.   The stout walls of Ferme Troteval provided the German defenders with protection from small-arms fire. The polished black monument commemorates the capture of the farm buildings by the Canadian Fusiliers Mont-Royal.

The chapel in Verrières marked the limit of the Royal Hamilton Light Infantry advance during the battle for the village. The memorial plaque commemorates the unit's seven day defense against tanks of the German 1st SS Panzer Division.

28.   Allied troops observe the bombing of the Caen-Falaise road in August 1944 in this damaged but fearsomely graphic plate. LAC

All that remains of the intensely contested terrain south of Caen; a few memorials and the quiet Canadian War Cemetery at Bretteville-s/Laize where 2,792 grave markers carry the Canadian Maple Leaf insignia.

29.   Major David Vivian Currie, far left with pistol in his hand, accepts the surrender of German soldiers in an event which earned him the Victoria Cross, insert. LAC
The Pont de l'Église in St-Lambert-s/Dive near the 11th-century church after which it was named was the final escape route for German armor.

The muddy ford across the Dive River known as Gué de Moissy remained a final hope for escaping German men and vehicles, below right. A road east of Chambois is completely blocked with wrecked enemy transport destroyed by RAF Typhoon aircraft, insert. AHEC.

30.   Wreckage of German armor stands upon the streets of Chambois. NARA
A monument to the closing of the Falaise Pocket carries the insignia of the 1st Polish Armoured
Division and the US 90th Infantry Division, insert.

The flags of the United States, Poland, France, Great Britain, and Canada fly over the façade of the
Montormel Memorial to the Battle of the Falaise Pocket. The viewing platform overlooks the valley
through which the German Seventh Army attempted escape from the encircling Allied armies.

31.   Dramatic photograph of members of the Forces Françaises de l'Intérieur firing their machine gun from the window of a Paris apartment, left. AHEC
Parisians intent upon halting the movement of German troops block streets and are prepared to shoot. Note the drawings of the hated Hitler and Nazi collaborators on the front of the paving stone barricade, below. AHEC

Civilians celebrating the entry of allied troops into Paris scatter as a sniper opens fire in the place de la Concorde, below. The Ministère de la Marine is the structure on the right. AHEC
A glum General der Infanterie Dietrich von Choltitz signs the surrender document, insert. AHEC

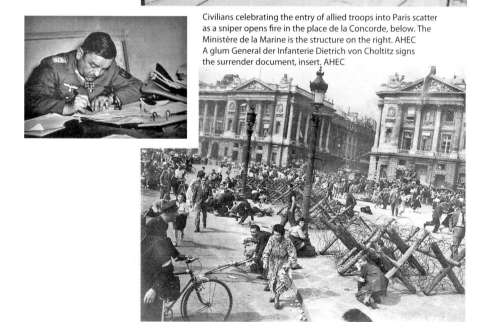

32. The unusual memorial to a man of mystery is almost hidden in a park near the Avenue des Champs-Élysée, Paris.
Jean Moulin, insert. Courtesy of Musée Jean Moulin

The memorial to those killed on 25 August 1944 is almost lost around the corner from the place de la Concorde in Paris. The niches, usually holding flowers or wreathes, were barren when this winter-time photograph was taken.

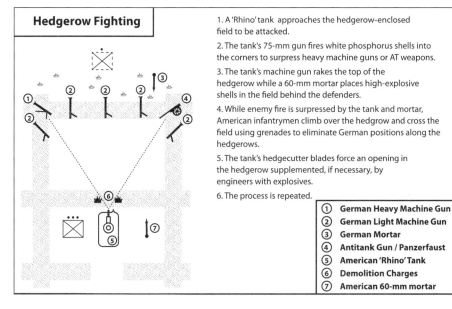

Hedgerow Fighting

1. A 'Rhino' tank approaches the hedgerow-enclosed field to be attacked.

2. The tank's 75-mm gun fires white phosphorus shells into the corners to surpress heavy machine guns or AT weapons.

3. The tank's machine gun rakes the top of the hedgerow while a 60-mm mortar places high-explosive shells in the field behind the defenders.

4. While enemy fire is surpressed by the tank and mortar, American infantrymen climb over the hedgrow and cross the field using grenades to eliminate German positions along the hedgerows.

5. The tank's hedgecutter blades force an opening in the hedgerow supplemented, if necessary, by engineers with explosives.

6. The process is repeated.

①	**German Heavy Machine Gun**
②	**German Light Machine Gun**
③	**German Mortar**
④	**Antitank Gun / Panzerfaust**
⑤	**American 'Rhino' Tank**
⑥	**Demolition Charges**
⑦	**American 60-mm mortar**

in the resulting holes and blew an opening. The tank then entered the enclosed field with cannon and machine guns blazing and infantry close behind.

The lull in fighting also allowed the Germans to regroup. The 352nd Infantry Division had been almost eliminated as a viable fighting force, its manpower reduced from 7,500 to less than 2,000 men. It remained a weak battle group leaving the main defense of St-Lô to the full strength 3rd *Fallschirmjäger* Division.

Although reduced to rubble by repeated Allied bombing missions, St-Lô still controlled eight major highways and an important bridge across the Vire River. Hills to the north, east, and west dominated the city. Without possession of St-Lô, American Army movements in the sector would stall and, without possession of the hills, holding St-Lô would be impossible.

To the Germans, loss of St-Lô meant loss of the road network that facilitated the movement of their troops and supplies. It also provided the Americans with offensive options to the southeast toward Vire or to the southwest toward Coutances, thereby increasing the German problem in utilizing their limited forces to guard against a breakthrough into more tank-friendly terrain.

Objective	To capture the city of St-Lô
Forces	
American	XIX Corps (Major General Charles H Corlett)
German	352nd Infantry Division (Generalleutnant Dietrich Kraiss); 3rd *Fallschirmjäger* Division (Generalleutnant Richard Schimpf)
Result	The city was liberated after four weeks of brutal fighting.
Casualties	
American	3,706 casualties

German	3rd *Fallschirmjäger* Division: 4,064 casualties; other combat groups: 986 casualties
Location	St-Lô is 60 km west of Caen

Whereas each battle was an integral part of the drive to capture St-Lô, the engagements are reviewed separately and toured in a convenient rather than chronological order.

Battle of Hill 122
15 to 17 July

Hill 122 is the last height looking down upon St-Lô from the north. From it the Germans laid down effective artillery fire across an eight-kilometer arc to the north. Hill 122 was a hedgerow-covered, gently sloping terrain when approached from the north. However, the ground dropped sharply toward St-Lô and provided extensive overviews of the city. Its loss would make the German hold on St-Lô untenable.

Objective	To capture Hill 122
Forces	
American	134th Infantry Regiment, 35th Infantry Division (Colonel Butler Miltonberger)
German	Elements of 352nd and 226th Infantry Divisions and 30th Mobile Brigade (Generalleutnant Dietrich Kraiss)
Result	The hill was captured and held.
Casualties	
American	283 killed and 1.050 wounded (15 to 30 July)
German	Uncertain
Location	St-Lô is 60 km west of Caen; le Mesnil-Rouxelin is 4 km north of St-Lô

Battle

The taking of Hill 122 fell to the 35th Infantry Division's 134th Infantry Regiment, a former Nebraska National Guard unit. The hill was defended in depth by experienced hedgerow fighters. At 0515 on 15 July, a creeping barrage in front of the American advance did little to the German troops sheltering in their foxholes along the hedgerows. In response, they applied withering crossfire on American troops advancing along highway D191. Despite the resistance, the American infantry crossed minefields and silenced enemy machine-guns with handgrenades, but its casualties were high. At 1250, the 1st Battalion, now facing the highest section of the hill, renewed the attack to capture the village of l'Émélie. It had advanced 2.1 kilometers when exhaustion and casualties brought the unit to a halt. The 3rd Battalion attempted to provide support, but a tank-led German counterattack pushed the 3rd Battalion back toward Villiers-Fossard to a farm known as Hôtel Durant. Although now isolated from the rest of the battalion, Companies A and B launched a final assault in the creeping twilight. The summit was taken and then lost again amid intense combat and enemy infiltration.

For the entire next day, the 3rd Battalion struggled against fierce enemy resistance to move forward on the right flank of the 1st Battalion while 2nd Battalion maintained pressure on the regiment's left flank. Finally, on 17 July, tanks from the 737th Tank Battalion, a platoon from 654th Tank Destroyer Battalion, and a company of 60th Engineer Battalion provided the firepower to blast the enemy's hedgerows emplacements. The hill was taken.[6]

Battlefield Tour

> Continue into le Mesnil-Rouxelin and stop at the junction with highway D88.
> (49.147529, -1.085616)

The tour begins in le Mesnil-Rouxelin, where a recently-erected memorial stele commemorates Lieutenant Colonel Alfred Thomsen, commander of 3rd Battalion, 134th Infantry Regiment.[7] The small village marked the right-hand boundary of the 134th Regiment's advance upon Hill 122.

> Leave le Mesnil-Rouxelin 'ver D6' (D88) and continue 850 m. Turn left towards St-Lô
> (D191).

Little distinguishes the terrain of Hill 108 from that of Hill 122 since the latter is a continuation of a ridge toward St-Lô. L'Émélie stands at the intersection of highways D191 and D88. Though a collection of only a few houses, it was well defended, and its capture proved costly to the 134th Regiment.

> Continue down the hill toward St-Lô (D191) into St-Georges-Montcocq. After 2.3 km,
> stop at the church on the right. (49.124486, -1.092088)

Because of its vantage point over St-Lô, the 14th-century **Église St-Georges** was heavily defended by German troops and attracted its share of American artillery fire. After the battle, the church had lost its tower, nave roof, and much of the interior. The damage was so extensive that it was not rebuilt until 1961. The church wall near the entrance stairway retains a plaque dedicated to the **134th Infantry Regiment**. The views of St-Lô from the churchyard justify the German intention to defend Hill 122 and the American need to capture it. Nothing could move in the city at the bottom of the hill without being observed from this height.

Col Thomsen sent a patrol down highway D974 into the devastated city. The route, now also part of the Voie de la Liberté, enters St-Lô near its citadel's stone wall where a commemorative plaque recognizes the 134th Regiment and 35th Infantry Division's sacrifices in liberating the city. (49.116441, -1.094194)

---

6   For actions against Hill 122, the 1st Battalion, 134th Infantry Regiment, was awarded the Distinguished Unit Citation, and the 134th Infantry Regiment was awarded the Croix de Guerre with Palm.

7   Lieutenant Colonel Alfred Thomsen was a blacksmith for the Union Pacific railroad before his National Guard unit was called up. A ferocious fighter, he led the 3rd Battalion in its attack upon Hill 122 and into St-Lô. Thomsen was wounded in Conde-s/Vire by artillery shell fragments on 30 July. He died sixteen days later in an English hospital.

> From St-Georges-Montcocq, reverse direction toward Villiers-Fossard (D191). After 2.3 km in l'Émélie, turn right away from le Mesnil-Rouxelin (D88). After1.4 km, turn left away from St-Lô (D6). After 1.4 km, turn right toward la Luzerne (D95). (49.142064, -1.054441)

Battle of Martinville Ridge
11 to 13 July 1944

Battle

On 11 July, the assault on St-Lô resumed with the 115th and 116th Regiments' attack upon Martinville Ridge east of the city. However, in the 1st Battalion, 115th Regiment's sector, the offensive was preempted by a nighttime German counterattack by an estimated 200-400 men of I Battalion, *Fallschirmjäger* Regiment 9. After they overran one company command post and threatened another, Colonel Godwin Ordway organized retreating men and rear-area personnel into infantry. The overrun companies fought on as small independent groups, and by 0730 the enemy retired.

Besides inflicting numerous casualties, the raid delayed the kickoff of the 115th Regiment's attack by five hours. When the attack did start from the fields north of la Luzerne, the German paratroopers were ready. The enemy easily gave way until the lead platoon entered the sunken road (D95). Then the mortars opened a deadly fire. The regiment's advanced stopped and its progress was minimal for the loss of almost 200 men.

The 2nd Battalion, 116th Regiment, fell against positions east of St-André from the north astride the Couvains-le Calvaire road (D59). The D95 was a natural trench and well defended. However, with the seizure of the dominant German observation summit at Hill 192 by the 2nd Infantry Division (see the end of this tour), German forces withdrew, knowing that any resistance brought down intolerable American artillery fire directed from that hilltop. The 2nd Battalion moved swiftly forward onto Martinville Ridge.

After the rapid advance of 11 July, a new German defense line slowed the American attack. Progress against the skilled and determined German paratroopers was slow and costly. Enemy guns inflicted heavy losses, especially against American tank units. General Gerhardt added the 175th Regiment, now commanded by Colonel Ollie Reed, whose grave was noted in Normandy American Cemetery, to the assault.[8] Gerhardt felt that one more push and the city would be won. However, the ridge was under observation from a ridgeline on the opposite side of the Semilly Valley to the south. Any troop movement brought instant German artillery or mortar fire.

On 13 July, the attack resumed with the 175th Regiment along the Bayeux highway. The enemy was as proficient as ever in detecting movement and in firing upon it. The regiment gained a few hedgerows and 152 more casualties. The division halted operations the next day to reconsider.

Battlefield Tour

The German front line at the opening of the final offensive ran along the sunken road from la Luzerne to west of St-Georges-d'Elle (D95). The modest country lane marked the jumping-off point for the 29th Division's attack upon Martinville Ridge and the 2nd Division's line of departure for its attack upon Hill 192. Moving east from la Luzerne

---

8   Colonel Ollie Reed was a career army officer who saw combat as a lieutenant in the First World War. He was killed on 30 July 1944 near Villebaudon at age 46. First Lieutenant Ollie Reed Jr was killed on 6 June 1944 fighting in Italy with the US 91st Infantry Division at age 25.

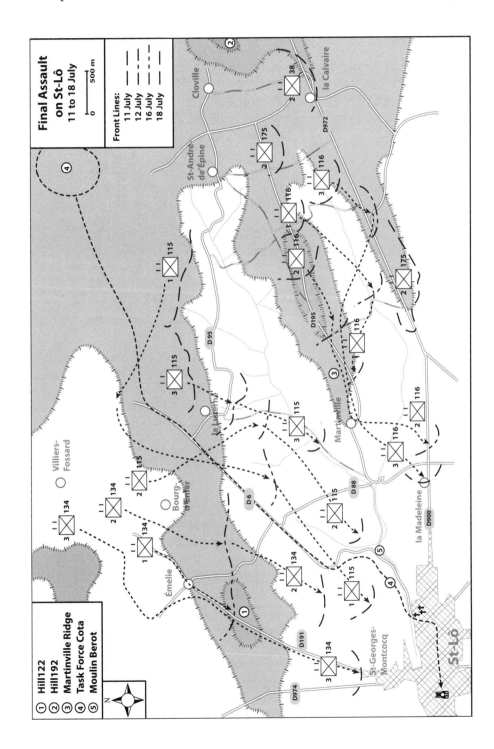

Final Assault on St-Lô
11 to 18 July

0   500 m

Front Lines:
11 July
12 July
16 July
18 July

① Hill 122
② Hill 192
③ Martinville Ridge
④ Task Force Cota
⑤ Moulin Berot

248 Fields of War: Battle of Normandy

toward St-André, the initial positions of the 3rd and 1st Battalions, 115th Regiment, stood to the north. The view to the south looks over the valley of rau de la Dollée to Martinville Ridge, the objective of both regiments. The two battalions experienced considerable difficulty overcoming German opposition between the highway and the Dollée and were effectively excluded from the next phase of the battle.

> Continue through St-André to the junction with highway D59. (49.139867, -1.005276)

The difficult advance of Major Sidney V Bingham's 2nd Battalion on 11 July centered upon highway D59 coming from the north. Despite a one-hour artillery barrage, German *Fallschirmjäger* tenaciously held its front line. Although using 'Rhino' tanks and tactics developed by General Cota, after five hours of intense fighting the equivalent of an entire rifle company was lost after a gain of only 600 meters.

The decisive assaults on Hill 192 and Purple Heart Draw by units of the 2nd Infantry Division started 200 m to the east. The end of this chapter includes a review of these engagements. If desired, they can be toured now followed by a return to this intersection to continue the tour of the attack upon St-Lô.

> Turn south in the direction of 'vers D972' (D59).

The road follows the 2nd Battalion's move against Martinville Ridge. The battalion's Company E was on the right and Company F on the left. Although generally not visible over the roadside verge and fields of crops, Hill 192 is 900 meters to the east. The height provided perfect observation of Germans positions along both sides of this roadway and, therefore, made them untenable for the enemy. When the German line broke, the pace of the advance quickened.

> After 650 m, turn west toward St-Lô (D195). (49.134932, -1.003854)

Passing through fields littered with German dead from intense artillery bombardment, Major Bingham's 2nd Battalion achieved the Martinville Ridge road at this intersection and turned west despite the presence of German troops on his left flank. The narrow country road, dirt in 1944 and not much better now, tracks the crest of the Martinville Ridge 50 meters to the south. To exploit the advance, the 3rd Battalion was committed to the attack at 1300 as it swung south to the Bayeux highway running atop the second of the three parallel ridges. Bingham advanced cautiously but against weak resistance to a line 2.2 kilometers west. He was still 1.5 kilometers short of Martinville.

> Continue 2.7 km to Point 147, where the chateau d'eau appears on the left. (49.127287, -1.03839)

By the morning of 12 July, the enemy had established a new resistance line running across the ridge. Its observation points directed accurate and deadly mortar and indirect artillery fire from German guns on the opposite side of the ridge across the Semilly Valley to the south. By the end of 12 July, Bingham's force had advanced only 500 meters to this intersection, but the rest of the regiment ground to a halt. Views of the parallel ridges north and south are possible from the cross roads.

Final Assault on St-Lô
15 to 18 July 1944

The assault by the 29th Infantry Division renewed on 15 July with the main effort along the Martinville ridge. The result was no better. General Gerhardt ordered the division to dig in for the night. Then, suddenly, the German line broke northeast of Martinville. Companies E and F, 116th Regiment, led by Major Bingham, advanced to the Bayeux road near la Madeleine, 800 meters ahead of the rest of the regiment. The Germans closed the gap, and Major Bingham and his small force became surrounded. Apparently, the Germans were unaware or unconcerned about the troops at la Madeleine while they focused their actions against the main force on Martinville Ridge.

On 17 July, despite every battalion being seriously under strength, Gerhardt ordered an all-out effort against St-Lô. Major Thomas Howie, who had recently assumed command of the 3rd Battalion, 116th Regiment, drew the assignment to push along the ridge, join Bingham's 2nd Battalion at la Madeleine, and continue into the city.

Using only bayonets and hand grenades and aided by an early morning ground fog, Howie's unit made headway and by 0730 hours it linked with Bingham's men. Howie had just completed a planning meeting with his unit commanders for a further attack upon St-Lô when he was hit by mortar shell fragments and almost instantly bled to death. He had commanded the battalion for four days.[9] A German counterattack launched that evening was crushed by timely intervention by American fighter-bombers.

Finally, at 1500 on 18 July, with the German defenses crumbling, General Cota led Task Force C, composed of 29th Division Reconnaissance troops, Shermans, and M10 tank destroyers down the Isigny highway (D6). At the large curve where the road dropped down to the plain, the 1st Battalion, 115th Regiment, which had spent the last several days in slow advance to this vicinity, joined the task force. Harassing artillery fire attempted to block their crossing of the bridge at Moulin Berot, but the advance continued until the combined forces entered the town at 1800.

The German Seventh Army commander, SS-Oberstgruppenführer and Generaloberst der Waffen-SS Paul Hausser, had decided the previous evening that available units were too weak to defend the city. His men were withdrawing southward on 18 July when Task Force C roared into the opposite end of the city. That night and the next day American troops mopped up small pockets of resistance while German artillery and mortar fire continued to fall among the ruins. By the end of 19 July, 50 percent of the 600 men in the task force had become casualties, including General Cota. The 29th Infantry Division was sent to bivouac near St-Clair-s/l'Elle on 20 July after forty-four days of almost continuous combat.

Aftermath

The battle for St-Lô had cost the 29th Infantry Division 3,000 casualties – more casualties that it had suffered on Omaha Beach. Only rarely had an enlisted man fought in both battles and survived unwounded. St-Lô was destroyed in the process of its liberation. Bulldozers plowed aside the rubble that filled the city's streets while citizens gradually reappeared from wherever they had sheltered. The German II *Fallschirmjäger* Corps formed a new defensive line to the south. For a few days, German artillery fired the

---

9   Major Thomas Howie, who had promised his men that he would be the first to enter St-Lô, posthumously received the Silver Star and *Légion d'honneur*. He is buried in Normandy American Cemetery.

occasional shell to encourage caution.

Battlefield Tour

From Point 147, continue 1.2 km to Martinville. (49.125044, -1.052413)

Martinville is merely a collection of Norman farmhouses along a sharp curve in the road. It was by-passed to the south by Bingham's force using a draw known as rau de la Pièrie. Views of St-Lô from the roadway are blocked by the ridge crest since the road does not run along its top. However, on occasion the slopes to the left and right are visible at breaks in the verge. What was initially a gradual slope suddenly accelerates down to la Planche du Bois 300 meters west of Martinville.

Continue west 750 m; turn south in the direction of 'vers D972' (D88). After 800 m, stop in the parking area on the right. (49.117169, -1.058882) Walk across the park of relatively young trees planted in a perfect grid array to the chapel. (49.117552, -1.060513)

In 1944, la Madeleine was a small crossroads village outside the limits of St-Lô. Today, it is surrounded by an Agricultural College and new housing tracts, but the tiny chapel is accessible on the opposite side of the park.

Chapelle de la Madeleine
Square des Victimes du 11 Septembre 2001
50000 St-Lô   Tel: +33 (0)2 33 77 60 35
Email: tourisme@saint-lo-agglo.fr

The small chapel is the only surviving building of a large complex constructed in the 12th century for the care of lepers. The complex fell into disuse during the French Religious Wars and, by the French Revolution, stored animal feed. The remaining chapel was acquired by the city of St-Lô in 1988. The chapel, sited near to the site of Major Thomas Howie's death, has been converted to a **Memorial to the 29th and 35th Infantry Divisions**. Displays present photographs and objects once belonging to the soldiers who liberated the city.

Open every Saturday and Sunday from 1 July through 15 September from 14:30 to 18:30.

Behind the chapel is a sculpture mounted on a plinth exacted by Robert Harding, Jr in memory of his father, 1st Lieutenant Robert J Harding, which bears the inscription: 'Who landed at D-day, fought for the liberation of St-Lô as executive officer and machine gun platoon leader of Company D, 1st Battalion, 115th Infantry, 29th Division, was wounded in action at St-Martin-de-Tallevende on August 5th, died August 6th.'

France also recognizes the modern pain of its wartime allies. The square in front of the chapel is dedicated to the **victims of 11 September 2001**. The square also holds an **NTL Totem**.

Return to the intersection of highways D195 and D88. Turn left toward le Mesnil-Rouxelin. After 100 m, turn left toward St-Lô (rue de la Planche du Bois, becomes rue

> de la Petite Suisse) and follow for 1.3 km to the junction with highway D6.
> (49.119515, -1.07784)

St-Lô

A village has occupied the cliff above a sweeping curve in the Vire River since Gallo-Roman times. The name St-Lô was adopted in the 6th century after a local saint. The town suffered greatly during the Religious Wars of the 16th century. In 1944 its population was 12,000, but few residents remained in the city after the battle because it had been 95% destroyed. After the war, Americans established the Hôpital-Mémorial France-États-Unis, at the time the largest hospital in Europe, as reparations for the city's destruction. St-Lô is the administrative capital of the Département of Manche and is now a busy city of 20,000 residents.

Office de Tourisme de la Communauté de Communes de l'agglomération Saint-Loise (49.115381, -1.098268)

Plage Verte	60 Rue de la Poterne
50000 St-Lo	Tel: +33 (0)2 14 29 00 17

The 1st Battalion, 115th Regiment, joined Task Force Cota at the top of the hill to the north. Upon hearing of the collapse of German resistance, it charged down the Isigny-St-Lô highway (D6) and across the minor bridge at the bottom of the hill toward the center of the city. A large communal cemetery is visible up the hill on the left.

> Follow highway D6 toward St-Lô-centreville as it turns left onto rue du Général Gerhardt. Stop at the entrance to the cemetery. (49.117184, -1.083033)

The plaque near the cemetery entrance simply records, in gold lettering, the fact that 'It was by this street that elements of the American 29th Infantry Division commanded by General Charles Gerhardt entered into the city.' The large stone **Blanchet Family mausoleum** stands inside the cemetery gates on the right. It was used as 115th Regimental headquarters after German gunners found the range of the previous headquarters in place du Major Howie (see below).

> Continue south and enter the roundabout; park on one of the minor streets.
> (49.115145, -1.082703)

Known in 1944 as le Carrefour de la Bascule, this intersection is now place du Major Howie. The roundabout is beautifully flowered and landscaped, making it an attractive entry into the city on the roads from Bayeux and Isigny-s/Mer. The curved stone presenting the American Stars and Stripes on the southern edge is a **Memorial to Major Howie**. A bronze bust of the major, backed by five flagpoles flying American and French flags, is prominent in the center of the stele. The inscription below the stone flag records Major Howie's last words: 'to St-Lô.' A stone walkway behind the stele is beautifully landscaped and passes among rhododendron, holly, and palms among other deciduous shrubs.

The Café – now la Cave des Amis – on the northwest corner became the **first**

American headquarters in St-Lô. The division staff attached the unit's flag to the side wall of the café proclaiming possession of the city in full view of the German observers to the southwest. All that accomplished, however, was to draw German artillery fire.

> Leave the roundabout to the west (rue de Neufbourg). After 200, turn north to enter place Ste-Croix. Proceed to the church. (49.116214, -1.085297)

Church tradition claims that the **Église Ste-Croix** descends from earlier 4th-century structures; the current Romanesque church was consecrated in 1202 as an Augustinian Abbey, although its appearance has been modified many times over the centuries. The pale yellow sandstone building stands across an open plaza north of the rue de Neufbourg, the major thoroughfare into the upper city.

As a symbol of the sacrifice entailed in capturing the city, General Gerhardt ordered that Major Howie be 'waked' where troops passing through the city could see him. The body was placed atop the stones of the destroyed belfry draped with an American flag. The body became covered with flowers placed by the city's few surviving civilians. The story caught the eye of wire-service reporters and was broadcast across the United States. Thus, Major Howie became the symbol that General Gerhardt[10] desired and became known as 'The Major of St-Lô.' A small plaque on the south side of the church commemorates the event. Fresh flowers normally adorn the plaque.

> Return to rue de Neufbourg and continue west into place général de Gaulle. (49.115544, -1.09108)

The only remnants of the ancient section of the city are the front entrance arch and doorway of the former prison, which have been transformed into a **memorial to orphans and victims of the war**. Plaques listing the names of victims of Nazi oppression are extensive and include those who were either executed or disappeared after deportation, members of the Free French, victims of crimes against humanity, and others.

> Proceed west 250 m to place Notre-Dame. It may be easier to walk, although parking in front of the church is available. (49.115403, -1.094647)

The two towers of the Flamboyant Gothic **Église Notre-Dame** made excellent observation posts and were undoubtedly used as such by the Germans. After the Americans occupied the city, artillery observers intended to occupy the church towers. While they approached, one tower, which had been weakened by American bombing and artillery, collapsed before their eyes. Shortly thereafter, German artillery brought down the second tower. The western façade of the church presents a most unusual appearance as vestiges of the ruined towers and other elements of the original facade have been preserved. The side of the church still displays an imbedded American artillery shell from the battle. Original statues and sculptures from the destroyed façade decorate the interior of the church along its north aisle.

---

10   Major General Charles Gerhardt had a reputation of being driven to success regardless of the cost. The high casualty rate suffered by the 29th Infantry Division and the numerous field officers that he relieved for not fulfilling his objectives speak testimony to the claim. After the war, Gerhardt was demoted to the rank of colonel based upon his wartime actions, although he had re-achieved his major general rank before retirement.

Walk west 230 m to Promenade des Moulleries. (49.115115, -1.097882)

The **Tour des Beaux Regards** at the tip of the medieval battlements provides a view over the Vire Valley and the fields south and west of the city. This sector was to become the next American battlefield.

Return to place général de Gaulle and proceed south to the next east-west street, rue Havin. Proceed west to the large roundabout and exit to the north. Enter the public parking area to the west. Walk back to the roundabout. (49.114863, -1.098086)

A very large memorial stone placed into the stone wall of the citadel commemorates the 450 civilian casualties of the bombardment and the destruction of St-Lô by American forces. One of the largest air attacks in the war on a French target struck St-Lô on the night of 6 June. The date is known locally as the *Nuit de Feu*, or Night of Fire. At the end of the war, the city was titled 'Capital of the Ruins' because of the extensive damage it suffered. The citizens were awarded the *Légion d'honneur* for their sacrifices. Reconstruction was not completed until 1962.

A German military hospital constructed under the citadel in 1943 was not at first open to civilians, but the Germans relented and admitted hundreds of local residents while the bombing on the night of 6/7 June became more and more intense. The steel entrance door is below ground level along the rue de la Poterne (D999), a mere 30 meters north of the citadel corner and directly below the Tour des Beaux Regards. Entering this area is possible, but it is now utilized as a sports center. (49.115175, -1.098021)

An elegant three-arch highway bridge crossing the Vire River stands below the citadel 100 meters to the west. It carries the important St-Lô-Périers highway (D900), a major east-west traffic artery and the road that marked the start line of Operation COBRA (see Chapter Twelve). (49.11514, -1.099668)

Battle of Hill 192
11 July 1944

The 29th Infantry Division's left flank was also the eastern limit of US XIX Corps. Hill 192 was the highest point on one of a series of east-west running ridges that paralleled the Bayeux highway (D972). Capture of the dominating height was assigned to the 2nd Infantry Division, V Corps. The division had been fighting against the German 3rd *Fallschirmjäger* Division for possession of the hill since mid-June at the cost of 1,253 casualties.

Like the 29th Division, the 2nd Division established teams of infantry, tanks, and engineers trained to attack the hedgerows with 'Rhino' tanks. Their objective was to use the newly developed tactics to capture the hill and sweep down its south slope to occupy the Bayeux highway. The task of capturing the hill fell to the 38th Infantry Regiment. To the east, the division's 23rd Infantry Regiment was to attack through St-Georges-d'Elle toward a road junction known as la Croix Rouge.

The Germans had not been inactive. They had established small-arms fire positions in foxholes dug into the sides of the hedgerows. All important tactical locations were registered for mortar or antitank fire. Heavier artillery was stationed south of the Bayeux highway. Hill 192 was defended by troops of the III Battalion, *Fallschirmjäger* Regiment 9. To their east was I Battalion, *Fallschirmjäger* Regiment 5. Both were experienced and well armed.

Battle

The 38th Regiment launched its attack at 0630 behind a rolling barrage supplied by division artillery and attached artillery battalions from 1st Infantry Division and V Corps. The 2nd Battalion advanced along the west slope of Hill 192. The 1st Battalion had a tougher time, but by the end of the day, it was digging in on slopes above the Bayeux highway.

To the east, 1st Battalion, 23rd Infantry Regiment, started its attack from the St-André-St-Georges road (D95), just west of St-Georges. An east-west draw holding a minor tributary of the Elle River ran 300 meters to their front and was defended by elements of the III Battalion, *Fallschirmjäger* Regiment 5. Its sides were steep enough to preclude tanks from crossing, but four tanks lined up on the hillside to support an assault by Company A. The enemy held fire until the 1st Platoon reached the bottom of the draw and then opened up. While the 1st Platoon was slowly destroyed by the withering German fire, help arrived on both flanks. 2nd and 3rd Platoons successfully swung around the draw to the west against the German western flank while two tanks moved down the highway to eliminate positions to the east. The 1st Platoon suffered 70 percent casualties. The creek valley became known as 'Purple Heart Draw.'

Although American positions experienced German artillery fire during the night, by morning the enemy had withdrawn to south of the Bayeux highway. The engagement cost the 2nd Division 69 killed, 328 wounded, and 8 missing. *Fallschirmjäger* Regiments 5 and 9 were mauled with 147 men taken prisoner.

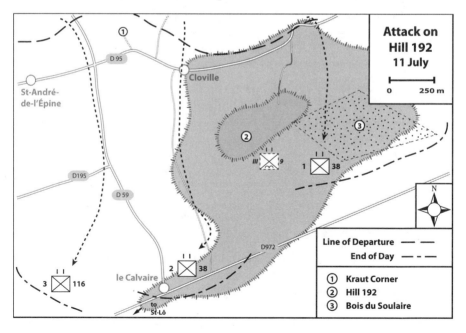

Battlefield Tour

This short tour begins on highway D95, 230 m east of highway intersection D95 and D59. (49.14066, -1.002309)

The 38th Regiment's western-most Company E had the farthest to go and almost immediately ran into German strongpoint known as **Kraut Corner**. The low ridge commanded a draw into Cloville, its eastern shoulder defended by one half of a company of German paratroopers. Direct assaults ended in failure.

The **Cloville draw** to the north of the highway, cut by a farm track, is identified by the tall, lone tree visible on the horizon. The slope to the right continues to rise in a northeast direction where the German strongpoint was located. 1st Platoon worked around the east side of the position supported by Shermans from Company B, 741st Tank Battalion. Under cover of BARs, machine guns, and light mortars, ten riflemen made the final charge. Fifteen survivors surrendered.

Continue east 150 m to the junction with highway D390 on the left (unsigned). (49.140218, -1.000443)

The minor road (D390) formed the axis of the 2nd Battalion, 38th Regiment's advance. Company E came toward the viewer on the west, Company F on the east of the road. Cloville was heavily shelled in the initial American bombardment. However, upon approaching the cluster of farm buildings, Company E faced infantry, a German 88-mm SP gun, and a PzKpfw IV hidden in the ruins about the road junction. American armor attacking down the road was silhouetted against the skyline. Nonetheless, an American tank provided the necessary support, knocking out both vehicles while the infantry cleared the ruins. After Cloville, Company E advanced quickly and reached the Bayeux highway (D972) at le Calvaire by 1700.

Continue east 800 m to a muddy track that lies on the right. (49.141243, -0.989859)

Walk up the sunken service track going to a communications tower to access **Hill 192**. The track approaches the summit in the direction of the attack of Company F, 38th Infantry Regiment. The first 100 meters of the track border a typical Norman orchard and, if one climbs the 2-meter-high hedgerow, one sees what American soldiers faced for every small square of ground gained. From the summit, views to the northwest toward the Vire River valley demonstrate the value of the position. In 1944, the vegetation had been destroyed permitting views into St-Lô that are not available today. The Bois du Soulaire, cleared later in the day by the adjacent 1st Battalion, stands to the left front on the reverse slope of the hill. In 1944, few of the trees survived American artillery in a grove the Germans used as a shelter.

A table of orientation stands beside the roadway 160 m east. (49.141939, -0.988576)

The brick and concrete **Hill 192 Table of Orientation** stands with little notice or fanfare along the side of the road slightly east of the boundary between the 29th and 2nd Divisions. The table of orientation bears a large ceramic with two views. The first provides a panoramic view from Omaha Beach to Utah Beach; the second image shows the local terrain indicating the attack of the US 2nd and 29th Divisions. The terrain to the north slopes gently downward where the attack of 1st Battalion, 38th Regiment, started. Enemy troops had crept closer to the line of departure during the American artillery preparation and laid mortar and artillery fire on American positions. In rapid succession, six tanks were disabled, and the battalion lost its support for the attack. A methodical hedgerow-by-hedgerow assault was successful until a strongpoint manned by two paratroop platoons was encountered. However, Company B, the battalion reserve, forced the enemy to withdraw. By 1330, Company B was across the crest and had entered the diamond shaped Bois du Soulaire on the southern slope. The expected enemy resistance in the wood did not materialize, due probably to the effective artillery preparation and the frequent use of dreaded white phosphorus shells.

> Continue east 1.6 km into St-Georges-d'Elle. In the center of the village, proceed to the right of the church on rue de la 2ème d'l US. The *mairie* is 110 m ahead on the right. (49.14865, -0.968972)

The 2nd Infantry Division first attacked St-Georges-d'Elle on 16 June and, in the bitter fighting that followed, the village changed hands several times. By 11 July, most of the ruined village was in American hands, but the toll of killed and wounded was high.

A polished, black-granite stele stands across the road from the school and in front of the *mairie* to honor those members of the **2nd Infantry Division** who died for freedom. The landscaped court is flanked by American and French flags.

> Return to the center of the village and proceed south in the direction of 'vers D972' (D195).

The roadway enters a deep sunken curve after exiting St-Georges. The small level area on the right, now enclosed by barbed wire strung along old concrete posts, was the site of a German stronghold that resisted American efforts to advance through the valley. (49.146408, -0.969581) Two tanks from 741st Tank Battalion moved down the road from St-Georges to bring direct fire upon German positions. As tank fire collapsed the structures' foundations, German survivors surrendered.

The sunken road widens as it approaches the bottom of **Purple Heart Draw**. Although views of the battlefield to the west are not good due to vegetation and rising terrain, the slopes and orientation of

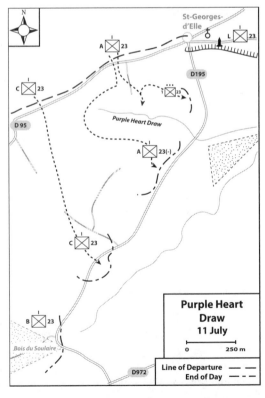

the hillsides demonstrate the danger of crossing the draw in the open. Certainly, artillery fire and German efforts to create fields of machine-gun fire had drastically removed the undergrowth in 1944. Although the battle was most intense in the field to the west, private property limits the opportunity to visit the battlefield. However, the roadway assists in understanding the topography.

The house on the left at the bottom was used by German troops to shelter machine guns providing enfilade fire into the advancing American line. (49.145578, -0.969889) By the end of the day, 1st Battalion had established a strong defensive line along the roadway, which was later renamed rue du 11 Juillet 44.

A short distance ahead is the junction with the Bayeux highway (D972) to return to St-Lô.

Chapter Twelve

Breakout and Exploitation
25 July – 19 August 1944

After the capture of St-Lô, the front lines stabilized roughly along the St-Lô-Périers road to the west and the St-Lô-Bayeux road to the northeast. Immediately west of St-Lô, the US VII Corps faced German armor of the 2nd SS Panzer, 17th SS Panzergrenadier, and Panzer Lehr Divisions and paratroops of the 5th *Fallschirmjäger* Division. Farther west, the US VIII Corps faced remnants of the 77th, 243rd, and 353rd Infantry Divisions and the 91st Airlanding Division. To the south and east of the city, the US XIX Corps faced the II *Fallschirmjäger* Corps comprised of remnants of 275th, 343rd, 352nd, and 353rd Infantry Divisions. German frontline troops were well-positioned, having turned every farm and crossroads into a strongpoint manned by tanks, antitank guns, and infantry. The troops were experienced, but weeks of almost constant combat had reduced units to a fraction of their authorized complement. Replacements were few, and their front was thinly manned and lacked the defense in depth that characterized German Army practice.

General Bradley realized that American troops had not been properly trained for hedgerow fighting. A pause after the capture of St-Lô permitted retraining to improve infantry–tank and tank–fighter-bomber communications. The result was a level of direct coordination between ground forces and aircraft that had not been achieved earlier in Normandy.

The stone walls separating the small fields were still an obstacle to rapid advance. Tank battalions, which had suffered over 50 percent losses in bocage fighting, also used the pause to add steel bars that converted their armored vehicles into 'Rhino' tanks capable of crashing through the hedgerows. This adaptation restored maneuverability to American armor and allowed it to command the battlefield. Rhino tanks could now move through fields to outflank German tanks which remained confined to roadways.

Operation COBRA
25 to 27 July 1944

COBRA's operational plan called for heavy bombers of US Eighth Air Force to destroy German positions along a 7-kilometer-wide strip south of the St-Lô-Périers road. The US 4th, 9th, and 30th Infantry Divisions were to make an initial breach between Marigny and St-Gilles; the US 2nd and 3rd Armored Divisions[1] were to pass through the leading infantry with the recently motorized US 1st Infantry Division, also available to exploit any opportunity.

Objective	To create a breech in German front line defenses
Forces	
American	Six divisions of VII Corps (Major General J Lawton Collins)
German	30,000 troops of Seventh Army (SS-Oberstgruppenführer Paul Hausser)

---

1   American armored divisions were divided into Combat Commands labeled CCA, CCB, and CCR (Reserve). Each unit was composed of an armored regiment of approximately 100 medium tanks, an armored infantry regiment, and self-propelled howitzers as an artillery element. Combat commands were further divided into task forces of varying size. Armored infantry advanced utilizing half-track carriers; by contrast, mechanized or motorized infantry advanced utilizing trucks.

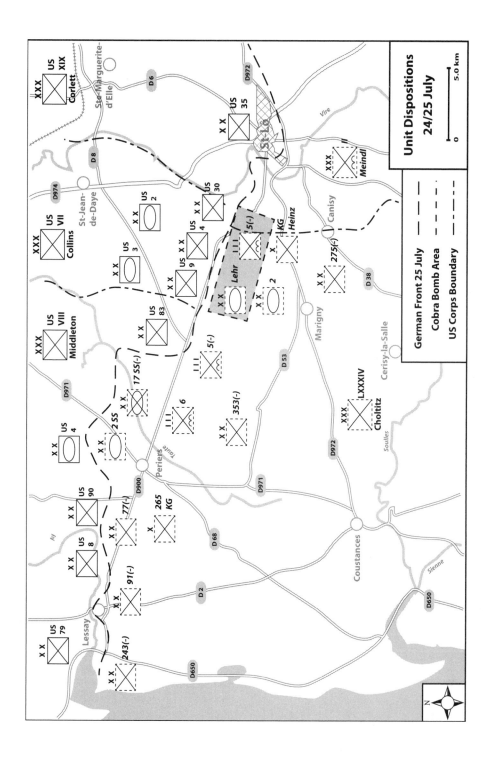

Result	A breakthrough resulted in a rapid advance
Casualties	
American	1,800 killed or wounded
German	Unknown
Location	St-Lô is 60 km west of Caen; la Chapelle-en-Juger is 10 km west of St-Lô

Battle

The massive bombing was scheduled to begin on 24 July; however, bad weather forced a recall of the aircraft targeting the German front lines. Nevertheless, three hundred planes failed to receive the recall notification and dropped their payloads onto advanced positions of the US 30th Infantry Division, resulting in 25 dead and 111 wounded.

At 0700 on 25 July, frontline American troops withdrew to positions farther back from the bombing targets. Two-and-one-half hours later, 1,978 B-17 medium and B-24 heavy bombers and 596 Thunderbolt (P-47) and Mustang (P-51) fighter-bombers dropped 3,400 tons of explosives in a concentrated 15-square kilometer area extending 8 kilometers from the bend in the Vire River and along the southern side of the Périers Road (D900). However, rather than approach the target along the front line as originally stipulated in Bradley's instructions, the bombers – crossing over American lines – came at the enemy perpendicularly. Again, bombs fell short, killing 111 American troops[2] and wounding 490 others including the entire command group of the 3rd Battalion, 47th Infantry Regiment. While dazed men stumbled about looking for the rear, some frustrated antiaircraft units fired at their own planes.

The results of the bombing on German troops were devastating. Over one thousand had been killed and a regiment of the 5th *Fallschirmjäger* Division was annihilated. In addition, Panzer Lehr Division reported that 70 percent of its 3,200 troops had been killed or incapacitated and that all of its forty-five tanks knocked out.

Although the short bombing disorganized and delayed the start of the offensive, at 1100 three American infantry divisions crossed the road to attack the crater-scared terrain that had once held Panzer Lehr Division.[3] The Germans were not all dead, however, and the Americans were subjected to artillery fire from pockets of German resistance. Cratering of roadways and congestion impeded rapid forward movement, and by day's end the leading units had advanced only 2-to-3 kilometers from their start lines.

By Normandy standards, the first day's advance was good, but not spectacular. The thin German front, however, had been penetrated, requiring General der Infanterie Dietrich von Choltitz, commander of LXXXIV Corps, and General Hausser to order infantry reserves forward to seal off the American penetrations. Hausser later ordered a counterattack by elements of 2nd Panzer Division in the direction of Marigny.

The next day, General Collins, true to his nickname of 'Lightning Joe,' sent in his armor units and the pace of the advance accelerated. German strongpoints were

---

2   One of the killed was Lieutenant General Lesley J McNair, the commanding general responsible for all organization and training of the US Army. McNair became the highest-ranking American officer killed in the war. He was 61 years of age and is buried in Normandy American Cemetery.

3   An often repeated story relates that a German General Staff officer arrived at Panzer Lehr's headquarters with orders from Generalfeldmarschall von Kluge that not a single man was to leave his post along the St-Lô-Périers road. Generalleutnant Fritz Bayerlein, the division's commander, is said to have replied, 'They are all holding their ground. They are dead! Do you understand? Dead!'

overrun, and Allied air power broke up any weak counterattack. The Americans advanced 16 kilometers south of their start point.

The American plan called for Major General Troy H Middleton's VIII Corps to maintain pressure on German LXXXIV Corps units south of Périers–Lessay road while Collins's VII Corps troops completed an envelopment of those German infantry units by passing through Marigny and taking Coutances from the east. Although the timely insertion of 2nd SS Panzer and 17th SS Panzergrenadier Divisions stopped the leading 1st Infantry Division before Coutances, VIII Corps' 4th and 6th Armored Divisions drove south from Lessay to belatedly take the city.

The US 2nd (Hell on Wheels) Armored Division, led by Brigadier General

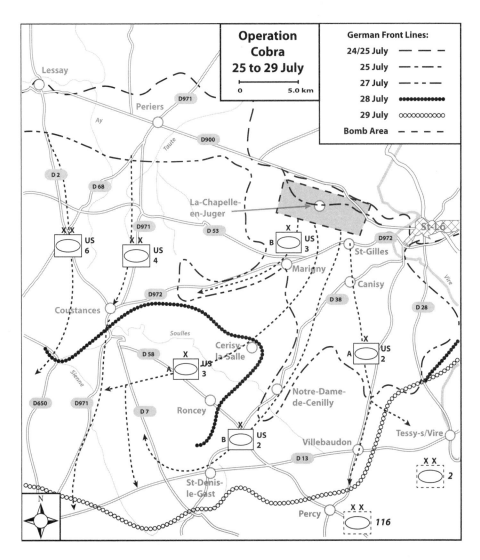

Maurice Rose's[4] CCA, broke through the German front at Canisy with the objective of protecting the left flank of the advance upon Coutances from German attack from the south and southeast. At Canisy, attack columns of CCA fanned out with one column continuing southeast toward Tessy-s/Vire and two others south toward le Mesnil-Herman and Hill 183. The following CCB, commanded by Brigadier General Isaac White, turned southwest toward St-Denis-le-Gast to set up blocking forces between Notre-Dame-de-Cenilly and Lengronne to trap the German units that had escaped from failed envelopment at Coutances. Thereafter, armored spearheads bypassed isolated German strongpoints which were dealt with by the following infantry.

Battlefield Tour

The COBRA battlefield does not present the fine tourist sites of other regions of Normandy. The area contains few notable memorials and even fewer museums since the military action for much of this region was fast and furious. The described tour proceeds generally south from the St-Lô-Périers road with east and west deviations to visit areas of selected engagements.

Leave St-Lô from the large roundabout below the citadel toward A84/Toutes Directions (D999). Follow (generally southbound) for 1.7 km to a roundabout and take the 1st exit toward Agneaux (D972). Do not enter the limited access highway N174. Enter a roundabout after 1.2 km and take the first exit toward Agneaux (rue de la Vallée Cagnon). After 230 m, turn right (unsigned, but D900e3). After 140 m, enter a roundabout and take 2nd exit toward Hébécrevon/Périers (D900). You are now on the St-Lô-Périers road. Proceed for 5.2 km to the large roundabout immediately after passing under highway N174 and stop at a convenient and safe spot. (49.136491, -1.177576

The US 30th Infantry Division's start line lay 500 meters to the north with the village of St-Gilles, 3.5 kilometers to the south, as a primary objective. Although the road network has been modified by construction of an interchange with the limited access highway, this area was the location of a German roadblock of three Panther (PzKpfw V) tanks supported by infantry along the St-Lô-Périers road. An American frontal assault by three infantry companies of the 119th Regiment supported by Sherman tanks was unsuccessful. An attempted envelopment encountered additional German strongpoints hidden in the hedgerows. Clearly not all German forces in the bombing zone had been destroyed. Eventually, infiltration and excellent tank–infantry communication destroyed a dozen enemy vehicles and eliminated the resistance. From here the 119th Infantry Regiment moved south toward St-Gilles (D77) and east to occupy Hébécrevon (D900).

Continue toward Périers (D900) for 2.2 km. Because highway D900 is too well-traveled to stop, turn left toward la Chapelle-Enjuger (D89) to a small parking space on the left just past the monument. (49.143661, -1.198958)

The **VII Corps Monument**, erected in memory of those soldiers who fought in Operation COBRA, stands along the St-Lô-Périers highway at the junction with the rural

---

4   Major General Maurice Rose was killed in action near Paderborn, Germany, on 30 March 1945 while commanding the 3rd Armored Division. He was 45 years old. General Rose is buried in Netherlands American Cemetery, Margraten, Netherlands.

road to la Chapelle and marks the approximate center of the destructive Allied bombing. An adjacent signboard displays a dramatic map of the bomb zone. A pasture directly behind bushes bordering the monument presents the remnants of bomb craters. The site is higher than surrounding ground in all directions, its elevation identifying a classic German strongpoint.

Proceed toward la Chapelle-Enjuger (D89) for 2.4 km and stop at church on the right. (49.128112, -1.215035)

The road to la Chapelle-en-Juger (alternatively spelled Chapelle-Enjuger) cuts through the bomb zone. The rural farming landscape retains scars of the bombs and rockets that fell on German positions. La Chapelle-en-Unger, a quiet little village just inside the carpet bombing zone, was severely damaged on 25 July. Most of the town's buildings became roofless walls in a sea of broken masonry. The village was liberated the next day by 8th Infantry Regiment, 4th Infantry Division, with the help of eighteen tanks to overcome stiff resistance at the entrance to the village.

The church is not the traditional Norman design because only the church's porch and bell tower survived the bombing; the remainder was rebuilt in a more modern style. The south wall of the reconstructed **Église St-Pierre** bears four stone plaques. Two plaques commemorate villagers killed in the First and Second World Wars listing them by name. Fortunately, they include only five civilian names because the town was evacuated prior to the bombing. Another plaque commemorates the American breakthrough. The largest stone is a war memorial and replaces a statue destroyed in the bombing.

Leave la Chapelle-Enjuger toward Marigny (D89). After 1.9 km turn right toward Deutsche Soldatenfriedhof 1939-1945 Marigny (unsigned, but D341, rue du Cimetière Allemand) and continue 1.0 km to the cemetery on the right. (49.11296, -1.235672)

Marigny German Military Cemetery holds 11,169 burials of German soldiers, many of whom hailed from Panzer Lehr. Additional German dead were accumulated from graveyards and field burials across the region after the war. The entry gatehouse is constructed in the form of a typical Norman church and includes a tall square tower. The verdant grave plots hold scattered groupings of German gray stone crosses that frequently ornament German military cemeteries. Graves are marked by inscribed stones that list name, rank, and dates of birth and death or 'Unbekannt' for an unidentified German soldier.

Originally the ground across the road held a separate American cemetery with 3,070 dead from Operation COBRA. Those bodies were relocated to Normandy American Cemetery in 1948. A commemorative stone recognizes the fact.

Continue 700 m; turn left toward Marigny (D29). Continue 1.6 km into Marigny. Turn left on rue des Alleux and park. (49.100315, -1.243982)

Marigny

German survivors of the bombing withdrew to establish a defensive line around Marigny. Their fierce resistance stopped the US 9th Infantry Division before the town on 25 July. On 26 July, CCB, US 3rd Armored Division, advanced on the west side of highway D29 while the 18th Infantry Regiment, 1st Infantry Division, moved along the east side.

Progress was slowed by road blocks and small pockets of resistance by the German 353rd Infantry Division. When the American troops approached Marigny, they were stopped by several PzKpfw IV and 75-mm antitank guns of the 2nd SS Panzer Division. The next day CCB circled Marigny to the west while the 18th Infantry Regiment battered directly into the town against *Fallschirmjäger* Regiment 13.[5] As the American infantry cleared Marigny, the 3rd Armored Divisions' CCA sped down the road toward Coutances.

Mémorial Cobra

2 rue des Alleux   50570 Marigny
Tel: +33 (0)2 33 56 88 67   Email: gilb.richard@wanadoo.fr
Web: http://www.si-marigny.fr/musee.php

The museum is dedicated to the people of Normandy and Operation COBRA. In three rooms, the museum presents the stories of the war years and the massive bombing and advance of 25 July 1944. The exhibits contain hundreds of documents and photographs accented by some artifacts. A video pays tribute to the event.

Open weekends June through August from 14:30 to 18:00; open Sundays in April, May, and September from 14:30 to 18:00. Free.

Return to the highway (D29, rue du Huit Mai 1945) and continue south. After 150 m in place Westport, continue straight onto highway D53 and follow that highway through a large curve to the left toward the church on the left. Continue on D53 for a total of 1.5 km to a roundabout. Take the 3rd exit toward Canisy (D972). Follow for 4.2 km to the roundabout in the center of St-Gilles and stop near the church. (49.104651, -1.175821)

Battle of the Roncey Pocket
26 to 30 July 1944

By the end of July, formerly powerful combat organizations, such as Panzer Lehr and the 2nd SS and 12th SS Panzer Divisions had been reduced to *kampfgruppe*, and the infantry divisions of LXXXIV Corps had started to disintegrate. With Allied air support severely hampering daylight road movement, the German Army in Normandy lacked the power to launch counterattacks or the mobility to seal Allied breakthroughs. German units that consisted of foreign fighters, young or old conscripts, or those with medical conditions, frequently gave ground easily or surrendered *en masse*.

For the Americans, it now became a commander's battle. The open terrain, unblocked roadways, and escape from the bocage allowed maneuverability that was the domain of the colonels and generals. Four armored divisions backed by four of America's best infantry divisions crashed south.

---

5   The regiment had been commanded by Wolf Werner Graf von der Schulenburg, who had been killed during the St-Lô fighting on 14 July. Fritz Dietlof Graf von der Schulenburg, one of the main conspirators in the 20 July Plot on Hitler's life, was hanged in Berlin's Plötzensee Prison on 10 August 1944. Friedrich Werner Graf von der Schulenburg, the ambassador to the Soviet Union when that country was attacked by Germany, was also involved in the plot. He was similarly executed on 10 November 1944.

Objective	To exploit the breakthrough in German defenses
Forces	
American	VII Corps (Major General J Lawton Collins) and VIII Corps (Major General Troy H Middleton)
German	Seventh Army (SS-Oberstgruppenführer Paul Hausser)
Result	Rapid American advancement
Casualties	
American	600 killed or wounded
German	1,500 killed and 5,200 taken prisoner
Location	St-Lô is 60 km west of Caen; St-Gilles is 7 km west of St-Lô

Battle

With the thin crust of German defenses broken, American armored columns rushed forward, ignoring weak German units on their flanks. General Collins sent his 3rd Armored Division to the southwest toward Coutances to cut behind German infantry units facing VIII Corps along the Atlantic Coast. On 28 July, Coutances was captured, but much of what was left of LXXXIV Corps had escaped to the south.

As the disorganized German Seventh Army moved southeast from Coutances, Major General Edward Brooks' 2nd Armored Division, reinforced by a battalion from 4th Infantry Division, embarked on a mission to bar enemy units retreating from the north. Speed was the primary consideration. Initially led by CCA, the division moved south encountering small, but determined, pockets of enemy resistance. The main route of advance was highway D77, which roughly parallels the Vire River valley 3 to 5 kilometers to itseast. After passing through Canisy, the division's CCB became the VII Corps' spearhead as it drove down highway D38, ignoring enemy artillery and small-arms fire. Detachments were stationed at critical road junctions forming a string of outposts supported by field artillery batteries forming an 11-kilometer-long line from Pont Brocard to St-Denis-le-Gast. Meanwhile, the division's CCA continued southeast to intercept reinforcing panzer units.

Battlefield Tour

The tour will follow the division until Canisy and then continue along the route of CCB. It will return to the actions of CCA to complete the tour of the Tessy battlefield.

The St-Gilles roundabout was a small intersection in 1944. American tanks were coming from the north when they entered the town. Combat Command A, 2nd Armored Division, composed of the 66th Armored Regiment[6] and supported by the 22nd Infantry Regiment, entered St-Gilles on 26 July. The thirty houses that comprised the village lined each side of the narrow roadway. The leading Sherman tank was met by a German PzKpfw IV, which suddenly turned a corner onto the road and into this intersection. The two tanks hurriedly exchanged fire at almost point-blank range, the American tank moving backwards seeking cover from the German panzer's more powerful gun. Finally, after several shots, a shell penetrated the PzKpfw IV, and it exploded into flames. Its crew was shot attempting to flee the burning wreckage.

---

6   The 66th Armored Regiment, 2nd Armored Division, is the oldest armor unit in the United States Army dating to the beginning of the tank service in February 1918.

The village's modern appearance and its widely-spaced buildings are the result of the utter destruction of the bombing and subsequent combat. The church porch bears a plaque to the memory of General Collins.

> Leave St-Gilles south toward Canisy (D77). Upon approaching Canisy, take notice of two minor sites.

The **railway overpass** 600 meters north of the town had been bombed and destroyed. German troops attempted to utilize the collapsed rubble and the adjacent embankments as a roadblock. The 66th Regiment's tanks bypassed the position to the west and continued their advance. Following infantry overwhelmed the German troops. (49.081519, -1.17691)

The stone gateposts and iron gate 350 meters ahead on the left mark the entrance to the **Château de Canisy**. The chateau, visible at the end of its long entrance drive, served as headquarters for Generalleutnant Fritz Bayerlein, commander of Panzer Lehr. His division had responsibility for securing the road, but the bombing left the shocked troops incapable of defending it. Although outside the carpet bombing zone, Bayerlein and his staff were forced to evacuate to the nearby woods to escape Allied fighters, which bombed and strafed the town. (49.078413, -1.17602)

> From the center of Canisy, proceed southwest toward Cerisy-la-Salle (D38), noting the described battle sites along the route.

After passing through Canisy, CCA immediately proceeded southeast. CCB turned southwest starting at 1000 on 27 July. First enemy contact was 2 kilometers southwest of Canisy at Quibou, where four Panther tanks, antitank guns, artillery, and infantry knocked out the leading American SP gun. While P-47s flew cover, the spearhead outflanked the enemy positions and regained the highway to continue toward Dangy. (49.068911, -1.193959)

The American column moved so quickly and with such determination that it never realized that in Dangy it had passed within 250 meters of Bayerlein's field headquarters where he was conducting a staff meeting. Bayerlein escaped capture for the second time by running into a nearby forest.

German armored cars at Pont Brocard were quickly overcome; however, the next morning, the 183rd Artillery Battalion found the crossroad blocked by German infantry. Artillerymen converted to infantrymen and engaged the enemy. At 1500, the arrival of Sherman tanks settled the issue and claimed 175 prisoners. Groups of German troops continued to assault American positions around the bridge through the night and into the morning of 29 July. (49.015187, -1.243773)

After the advance guard passed through Notre-Dame-de-Cenilly, 1st Battalion, 67th Armored Regiment, rounded a corner to find a formidable group of German soldiers exiting the church. Rapid machine-gun fire killed forty while the remainder scattered. German attacks on the next day were beaten off by headquarters's staff. (48.995481, -1.257935)

> Proceed 13.1 km from Canisy to la Pinetiére crossroads (highways D38 and D27). (48.987209, -1.269833)

At 0900 on 29 July, fifteen German tanks with several hundred panzergrenadiers drove into a company of 4th Division infantry holding la Pinetiére crossroads in what was the second serious attack of that day. The American infantrymen fell back to positions held by the 78th Armored Field Artillery Battalion whose 105-mm howitzers held off the enemy with direct fire until another company of infantry arrived. Again, the Germans withdrew, leaving 126 dead and seven destroyed PzKpfw IVs.

> Continue 2.9 km to les Hogues crossroads (highways D38 and D58).
> (48.96872, -1.295866)

On 29 July, Company I, 41st Armored Infantry Regiment,[7] supported by a tank company, occupied this crossroad when it heard the rumble of approaching armor. *Fallschirmjäger* Regiment 6, commanded by Oberstleutnant Friedrich August Freiherr von der Heydte, and panzers from the *Das Reich* Regiment of the 2nd SS Panzer Division, formed a column of twenty-nine tanks led by an 88-mm self-propelled gun. The pre-dawn darkness was broken by the sudden flash from an exploding Sherman, then illuminated by machine-gun tracer bullets arcing left and right. German infantry crawled along the ditches on both sides of the road while six German tanks assaulted frontally. Two more Shermans burst into flames before Sergeant Robert Lotz[8] shot the self-propelled gun's driver and gunner, thereby leaving the vehicle blocking the roadway. The fighting continued for two hours as panzergrenadier and infantryman fought with guns and knives in the dark until the enemy withdrew south toward St-Denis-le-Gast, leaving 17 dead and 151 wounded. The Americans suffered 52 casualties.

The engagements at la Pinetiére and les Hogues held up German troop movements to the southeast and created a monstrous traffic jam along the area's roadways and farm tracks while armor, trucks, and even staff cars became enmeshed in a bumper-to-bumper backup that ran for 5 kilometers in and about the small village of Roncey. When the eastern sky lightened, the Thunderbolts and Mustangs of Brigadier General Elwood 'Pete' Quesada's[9] IX Tactical Air Command roared over the stopped German columns strafing and bombing what became known as the Roncey Pocket.

> Continue 4.5 km into St-Denis-le-Gast and pause at the junction with highway D13.
> (48.940127, -1.329582)

In the darkness of the evening of 29 July, ninety armored vehicles and 1,200 men of 2nd SS Panzer and 17th SS Panzergrenadier Divisions escaping south from the Roncey pocket hit against Lieutenant Colonel Wilson D Coleman's 2nd Battalion, 41st Armored Infantry Regiment, at St-Denis-le-Gast. Panther tanks and German infantry overran

---

7   The 41st Infantry Regiment ended the war with four Presidential Unit Citations (originally named Distinguished Unit Citation). Two were awarded for actions in Normandy, the third and fourth for attacks against enemy positions at the Roer dams and during the Battle of the Bulge.

8   Sergeant Robert H Lotz received a commission to 2nd lieutenant. Killed on 13 April 1945, he is buried in Lorraine American Cemetery.

9   Brigadier General (later Lieutenant General) Elwood Richard Quesada was an early military aviation pioneer. Instrumental in developing close air support of ground forces, he received numerous medals and honors. After the war, he resigned in protest when the Air Force dismantled its Tactical Air Command. Quesada died in 1993 at age 88. He is buried in Arlington National Cemetery.

battalion headquarters. During the close contact fighting, Col Coleman fired four bazooka rockets that destroyed three enemy tanks before he was shot in the head.[10]

A confusing two-hour battle became hand-to-hand and raged through the night as isolated groups fought a determined enemy in darkness. With German troops pressuring the 41st Regimental headquarters, S/Sgt William B Kolosky, who had never before fired his weapon in combat, organized and led a mixture of clerks, radio operators, messengers, and orderlies in repelling an attack by setting up machine-gun positions and stationing men with bazookas at critical points.[11] Panther tanks forged their way through the town, but by morning American troops had regained control. Dawn of 30 July revealed 130 enemy dead, 124 wounded, and over 500 prisoners. The 41st Regiment suffered nearly 100 casualties.

Leave St-Denis-le-Gast west toward Lengronne (D13). After 2.3 km, achieve the crossroads at la Chapelle du Pont Flamba (highways D13 and D102). (48.936413, -1.36036)

A German column that had escaped the fight at St-Denis-le-Gast inexplicably turned west rather than continuing south and advanced along the road between Lengronne and St-Denis-le-Gast. At 0300, Captain Naubert Simard, a German-speaking battalion intelligence officer, was questioning prisoners when he heard approaching vehicles. Simard challenged the leading driver in German. Upon receiving the reply 'Was ist?' the Americans opened fire. The German column crashed through a roadblock into the bivouac of the 78th Armored Field Artillery Battalion at la Chapelle du Pont Flamba. Another nighttime firefight erupted. Simard rushed to a machine-gun position to rake enemy vehicles with bullets. American howitzers depressed their barrels and fired point blank at the stalled German column. Dawn brought the sight of ninety German corpses along with 200 prisoners. All German vehicles were destroyed. American casualties were eleven, including Captain Simard, who was found dead with his finger still on the trigger of his machine gun.[12]

Continue west toward Lengronne (D13). In the center of Lengronne, turn right toward Saussey / Coutances (D7). After 3.1 km, turn right toward 'vers D49' (D438). After 700 m, turn right and after 100 m stop at the memorial on the left. (48.959518, -1.38918)

As brutal as these encounters were, none matched the ferocity of the confrontation that occurred along a country lane near Grimesnil. During the night of 29/30 July, the 41st Armored Infantry manned a roadblock near le Chapitre on a rural road that paralleled the Coutances-Gavray highway (D7). Light and medium tanks of 2nd Battalion, 67th Armored Regiment, and bazooka armed engineers from the Company C, 238th Engineer Combat Battalion, were concealed behind hedgerows lining the east side of the roadway. A German

---

10   Lieutenant Colonel William Dudley Coleman was a graduate of West Point. For his leadership and courageous actions at St-Denis, he was awarded the Distinguished Service Cross. Coleman, who died at 33, is buried in Arlington National Cemetery.

11   Staff Sergeant William Kolosky, of Chicago, Illinois, was awarded a Distinguished Service Cross and later earned a Silver Star.

12   Captain Naubert Oliver Simard, a graduate of the University of Florida, was awarded the Distinguished Service Cross posthumously for his personal bravery and extraordinary heroism. He is buried in Normandy American Cemetery.

2,500-man column with tanks came from the north, attempting to escape the 2nd Armored Division trap. The American outpost line was rapidly overrun and Sergeant Hulon B Whittington assumed command. He moved between gun positions to encourage his men while ignoring German bullets whistling past. Whittington climbed atop a Sherman tank hidden in a stone barn near la Coucourie and began shouting directions to the crew inside. The Sherman's first 75-mm shell hit the leading '*Hummel*'[13] self-propelled gun at almost point blank rage causing it to spin around and block the roadway. Engineers knocked out the last vehicle, trapping the entire German convoy along the road.

Despite facing a much larger enemy force, American troops along the roadway blasted the enemy vehicles. The US 78th and 62nd Artillery Battalions fired their 27 guns for three hours onto the trapped enemy troops. When German ground troops attempted to flank American positions by moving through the fields, they were killed or captured by 41st Regiment infantry. Whittington then led his men in a spirited bayonet charge along the road to finish the resistance.[14] The carnage was horrifying. By dawn, 450 German troops were dead and 1,000 captured. Almost 100 vehicles of all types were destroyed. American losses were 51 killed and 63 wounded.

La Lande des Morts Memorial stele marks the northern extreme of the American positions. The first round from the German Hummel blew up an American half track from Company E, 67th Armored Regiment, stationed at this intersection. The German column continued along this road until trapped and destroyed between les Saulx and la Coucourie. The name 'La Lande des Morts' – The Land of the Dead – does not originate with the heavy German losses incurred during this engagement. Military actions have long been a part of the history of this productive region of France. The name refers to the death of French locals during a *chevauchée* – a raid to pillage enemy territory – launched by English troops during the Hundred Years War. The German column was along highway D49 to the south and although the roadway is visitable, it offers little of interest.

The shortest route to the next site in Roncey requires driving on difficult narrow country lanes; an easier, but longer route, is possible. Both routes appear below.

The short route: reverse direction and proceed north (D49) for 180 m. Turn right onto highway D458; after 1.5 km, proceed straight on highway D349; after 2.5 km, turn right still on highway D349; after 1.2 km, continue straight onto highway D102 and continue 800 m into Roncey. (48.989553, -1.333455) Total distance: 6.4 km.

The long route: reverse direction and proceed north (D49) for 1.2 km. Turn right toward Saussey/Coutances (D7). Proceed 4.6 km to a roundabout and take the 1st exit toward Montpinchon (D73). Proceed 3.6 km and turn right toward Roncey. Continue 4.1 km into the center of Roncey. (48.989553, -1.333455) Total distance: 13.5 km.

---

13   The *Hummel* held a powerful 150-mm howitzer mounted upon a chassis that combined elements of PzKpfw III and PzKpfw IV model tanks.

14   Sergeant Hulon B Whittington was awarded the Medal of Honor for his leadership in successfully defending the road that night. Born in Bogalusa, Louisiana, he had fought in North Africa and Sicily before fighting in France. He survived the war also earning a Silver Star, Bronze Star, French Croix de Guerre, and Belgian Fouraguerre. Whittington became a commissioned officer, rose to the rank of major, and served in Vietnam. Whittington died in 1969 at age 47, leaving two daughters and one son. He is buried in Arlington National Cemetery.

Roncey

The rapid advance of CCB, 2nd Armored Division, and the strong pressure of the 4th and 6th Armored Divisions moving from the north trapped elements of the German 243rd and 353rd Infantry Divisions, the 91st Airlanding Division, and the 2nd SS Panzer Division in and around Roncey. The concentrated men and equipment provided ideal targets for Allied fighter-bomber aircraft. Over one hundred tanks were destroyed or abandoned for lack of fuel. The village was leveled during the combat as its modern appearance attests.

A small rock along the main road bears a plaque that commemorates the **US 2nd Armored Division** and civilian victims of the fighting. The **NTL Totem** standing in front of the church describes the destruction of the town:

> The bombing and shelling of Roncey began in the afternoon of 28 July and continued without respite until the beginning of the evening of the 29th. German losses were heavy; as well as the many dead and wounded, over 250 vehicles were destroyed. Nothing much was left of the little village of Roncey: the church and 46 houses were utterly destroyed; 43 other houses were damaged and the remainder pillaged and then torched with petrol and grenades by the SS. The finishing touches to this scene of destruction were made when the Americans had to bulldoze their way through the rubble. Six civilians were killed.

Battle of Tessy-s/Vire
28 July to 2 August

General Bradley gave XIX Corps the objective of eliminating the German bridgehead across the Vire River at Tessy-s/Vire. The village sat on the west bank of the river, overlooked by high ground to the east and west, and it controlled roads that the Germans needed as supply or evacuation routes. The 1st Battalion, 66th Armored Regiment, originally moved toward Tessy-s/Vire from the northwest, but it could not penetrate the 2nd Panzer Division holding a short defensive line from Moyon to Troisgots along le Marqueran River.

Objective	To defend the breakout from counterattack from the southeast
Forces	
American	XIX Corps (General Charles H 'Cowboy Pete' Corlett)
German	2nd Panzer Division (Generalleutnant Heinrich Freiherr von Lüttwitz) and 116th Panzer Division (General der Panzertruppe Gerhard Helmuth Graf von Schwerin)
Result	The major Vire River crossing at Tessy-s/Vire was captured
Casualties	
American	Undetermined
German	Undetermined
Location	St-Lô is 60 km west of Caen; Tessy-s/Vire is 18 km south of St-Lô

Battle

General Rose split his CCA, now temporarily attached to XIX Corps, into three regiment-strength columns and fanned out to protect the eastern flank of the breakthrough from possible German counterattack. Their objective was Tessy-s/Vire.

Meanwhile, Major General Leland Hobbs's 30th Infantry Division advanced south from St-Lô toward Tessy with the 743rd Tank Battalion supporting. Generalfeldmarschall von Kluge sent the 2nd Panzer Division to shore up the depleted 353nd Infantry Division.

By 1 August, Tessy-s/Vire was under attack from the northwest by one armored battalion; from the west by two armored battalions; and from the north by Hobbs's 117th and 120th Infantry Regiments, which captured the town. German artillery on the hills to the east kept the town under fire until the 35th Infantry Division, moving south along the east side of the Vire, took the hills on 2 August.

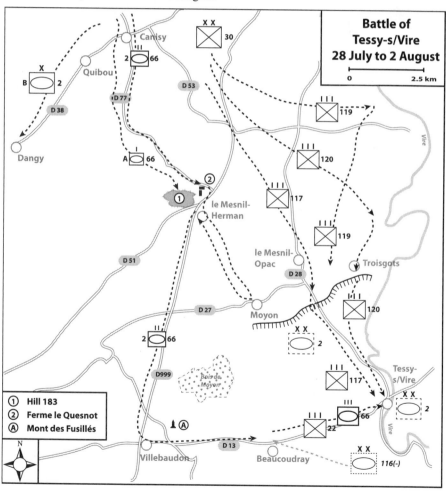

Battlefield Tour

The tour route returns toward Canisy to resume with the actions of CCA, 2nd Armored Division.

Leave Roncey toward St-Martin-de-Cenilly (D58). Follow for 3.8 km; turn sharply left toward St-Martin-de-Cenilly (D38). Continue for 11.1 km; on the opposite side of Dangy, turn right toward Soulles (D89); after 400 m, continue straight toward St-Martin-de-Bonfosse (D193) and follow for 3.5 km. Turn right (unsigned, D77). After 3.3 km, approach Ferme le Quesnot on the right. (49.033001, -1.139381)

The 2nd Armored Division's CCA, spearheaded by its 2nd Battalion, 66th Armored Regiment, advanced toward le Mesnil-Herman crossroads northeast of the village at 0200 on 26 July. Second Lieutenant George Wilson led a 24-man platoon of 4th Division infantry riding on tanks as they approached Ferme le Quesnot. They were greeted by *Panzerfaust*-armed German troops well sheltered above the deeply sunken lane. The fourth tank in the column was set aflame illuminating the three tanks ahead, which were now cut off by exploding wreckage blocking the road. Wilson's men dismounted from the tanks and eliminated one team of German tank hunters. After a brief discussion, the tanks and dismounted infantry made a scramble through German positions back up the road while the infantry randomly threw hand grenades and fired rifles over the verges and hedgerows as they ran.[15]

The crossroad was taken the next morning, but the hills surrounding le Mesnil-Herman were defended by *Fallschirmjäger* Reconnaissance Battalion 12, commanded by Hauptmann Bodo Göttsche. Göttsche's men had just arrived when the American armored column came down the highway aiming for the German 352nd Infantry Division's headquarters. Göttsche established a 'hedgehog,' or all-around defense, and held for 24 hours against all attacks. By the time he left, six Sherman tanks lay smouldering in front of his unit's guns.[16]

Continue to the junction of highways D77 and D999. Turn right at Mesnil Herman (D999) and follow for 8.4 km into Villebaudon. (48.960373, -1.166294)

The 2nd Battalion, 66th Armored Regiment, reached the crossroads at Villebaudon at approximately noon on 30 July. Its continued advance was disrupted by heavy artillery fire followed by enemy counterattacks employing numerous tanks. The German artillery pinpointed the 29th Division's 175th Regimental CP tents and effectively eliminated the command. When German infantry approached the command post, Sergeant Abe Sherman provided the necessary leadership and motivation to the non-combatant troops now forced to defend the regimental positions by shouting 'C'mon, you (expletive deleted), let's go!' With the enemy only one hedgerow away, Sherman recklessly exposed himself to enemy

---

15   Second Lieutenant George Wilson was awarded a Silver Star for his leadership. Wilson fought across France to participate in the Hürtgen Forest fighting and the Battle of the Bulge. He was the only member of Company F, 22nd Infantry Regiment, to end the war with that unit. Wilson wrote about his experiences in *If You Survive: From Normandy to the Battle of the Bulge to the End of World War II.*

16   Hauptmann Bodo Göttsche died of wounds on 11 August 1944. Göttsche is buried in Champigny-St-Andre German War Cemetery. He was 25 years old.

fire while organizing a last-stand defense of the command post.[17] The action continued for nearly thirteen hours before the last counterattack was beaten off and the crossroads secured. The enemy suffered 180 killed and 120 captured.[18]

> In Villebaudon, turn left toward Tessy-s/Vire (D13) and follow for 1.5 km to the rural road on the left. (48.959975, -1.145475) Follow the signs to the Monument des Fusillés, if desired.

On 15 June 1944, eleven members of the St-Lô postal service were executed for their systematic sabotage of German telephone lines in support of the invasion. The eleven young men had sheltered in a nearby barn awaiting rescue when they were surrounded and captured by German SS troops. The large stone Cross of Lorraine stands as a **Monument des Fusillés** to the eleven. The image on the cross represents France braving the storm from the west that will liberate the country from the invader. The bodies of the resistants were buried in two mass graves at the foot of the monument. A memorial service held every year on the first Sunday after 15 June celebrates their resistance.

> Regain highway D13 and continue 250 m to the next intersection. (48.960187, -1.142128)

On 31 July, General Rose's CCA moved east from Villebaudon, intending to capture Tessy-s/Vire. Led by the 2nd Battalion, 66th Armored Regiment, and an infantry company, it ran into serious opposition near Beaucoudray because the 116th Panzer Division was moving west along the same route. The panzers were attempting to break the American line blocking the escape of LXXXIV Corps forces trapped near Roncey. The Germans had taken strong positions in woods on the opposite side of a deep ravine. The fighting continued for 12 hours until the German troops withdrew.

> Continue east on highway D13 into Tessy-s/Vire. Turn left onto place du Marché (D177), then quickly another left onto place de l'Église to the rear of the church. (48.97264, -1.060524)

Tessy-s/Vire

Early on 1 August, the 3nd Battalion, 66th Armored Regiment, succeeded in entering the outskirts of Tessy-s/Vire. Unable to hold, it was forced back and isolated by enemy counterattacks. Later that afternoon, the 1st and 2nd Battalions, 66th Armored Regiment, with infantry from the 22nd Infantry Regiment, attacked Tessy from the west. Effective tank destroyer support eliminated seven PzKpfw IVs and PzKpfw Vs and achieved positions within 2 kilometers of the town.

Meanwhile, at 0600 on 1 August, 1st Battalion, 120th Infantry Regiment, launched its assault by fighting toward Tessy along a rural road (D177) from the northwest. The battalion's Company B encountered a German machine gun nest supported by thirty

---

17   Regimental commander Colonel Ollie Reed was killed in this action. (See Chapter Eleven)

18   Sergeant Abe Sherman was awarded a Silver Star for his leadership. He had left school at an early age to work selling newspapers on the streets of Baltimore. A veteran of the First World War, he returned to Baltimore to open a newsstand near its City Hall. Initially rejected because of his age, Sherman used political influence to rejoin the army shortly after Pearl Harbor. After the war, Sherman returned to his newsstand which he operated until his death in 1987 at age 89. He was survived by two sons, each of whom became army officers. One retired as a colonel and the other as a brigadier general.

riflemen at a bend in the road approximately 1.5 kilometers outside the town. The position was eliminated by Private Carlos Ruiz, who worked forward along the hedgerows until within range. He methodically shot the machine-gun crew while the remaining enemy troops fell back into town. When Company B entered Tessy, it came under the fire of an 88-mm antitank gun. Private Francis L Kimmel ran down the town street with his BAR until he brought the German gun under fire. With a single burst, he eliminated the gun crew.[19] With the capture of Tessy, German troops west of the Vire had lost a major escape route.

Drive around to the rear of the church to access the small park that contains a memorial stele to the **29th and 30th Infantry Divisions**.

A side tour of the British breakout effort during Operation BLUECOAT is included at the end of this chapter. To visit this battlefield, do so from Tessy-s/Vire and then rejoin the main tour at Vire. The additional round-trip distance is 75 kilometers.

To continue with the American battlefields' tour, proceed south from the center of Tessy-s/Vire toward A84/Pont Farcy/Vire (D374, becomes D21, then D52 in Pont Farcy) and follow for 22.4 km into Vire. Turn right onto Av du Général de Gaulle (D577); after 850 m, turn left onto rue d'Aignaux. A large parking area is on the left near the tourist office. (48.839614, -0.888498)

Battle of Vire
2 August to 7 August 1944

On 1 August, Bradley assumed command of the new US 12th Army Group and activated the US Third Army under Lieutenant General George S Patton Jr. General Courtney Hodges took command of US First Army, which now concentrated upon taking critical road centers at Vire and Mortain to prohibit von Kluge from shifting units to the west.

Battle

With Tessy-s/Vire captured, General Corlett's XIX Corps began its drive toward Vire with the 28th and 29th Infantry Divisions, each strengthened by an attached combat command from 2nd Armored Division. German forces slowly withdrew behind strong rear-guard actions while inflicting a serious level of casualties upon American infantry. The task of taking the city fell to the 29th Division against the 3rd *Fallschirmjäger* Division and elements of the German 353rd and 363rd Infantry Divisions.

On 5 August, an attempt to capture the town by CCA, 2nd Armored Division, ended in suburban Martilly where German artillery fire knocked out fourteen of nineteen tanks preparing to enter the city. The 116th Infantry Regiment captured lightly-defended Hill 219 west of the city. The next day, the regiment's 2nd Battalion continued the attack just before dark. In a move unexpected by the enemy, it descended the eastern side of Hill 219, forded the river, and started up the eastern side of the ravine. Although faced with steady mortar and small-arms fire from the suddenly alerted German troops, the 2nd Battalion

---

19   Private Francis Leroy Kimmel of Wolf Lake, Illinois, was killed on 8 October 1944 during fighting against the Siegfried Line in Germany. Kimmel had worked at the Ford Bomber Plant in Ypsilanti, Michigan, before enlisting in January 1943. He was one of four brothers who served in various services during the war. Kimmel is buried in Union County, Illinois.

entered the city shortly before 2200. Isolated German pockets and artillery fire from the nearby hills contested the American occupation in intense street fighting illuminated by burning buildings while bullets ricocheted off the rubble. By dawn on 7 August, the enemy had been beaten and the town liberated.[20]

Battlefield Tour

Vire

Vire is an ancient community located upon hills that overlooked the bocage. It saw the construction of a Norman keep in the 12th century by the son of William the Conqueror. The town walls were removed in 1630, but the 13th-century Porte de l'Horloge remains.

The Vire River meanders around the western and southern edges of the city. Six roadways radiated from the town center, including the best east-west route behind the German front. Repeated Allied bombings, German artillery, and house-to-house fighting destroyed 95 percent of the city's buildings.

Les Offices de Tourisme du Bocage

Square de la Résistance   14 500 Vire
Tel: +33 (0)2 31 66 28 50   Email: contact@bocage-normand.com
Web: http://www.bocage-normand.com/fr/index.htm

A tall stone, dedicated to resistance fighters of the region, stands adjacent to the tourist office. To view the Porte de l'Horloge and the Église Notre-Dame de Vire, walk south from the tourist office on rue André Halbout. After 120 m, walk around the roundabout to the right, exiting into place du 6 Juin 1944. The Porte is a short distance into the pedestrian zone. (48.838354, -0.890102)

The 13th-century **Porte de l'Horloge** was the main entrance to medieval Vire. The gateway was flanked by two dominating towers joined with a roof. The gate was protected by a wide ditch crossed by a drawbridge. A bell tower added in 1480 also served as a watchtower. The south tower now houses a memorial to the victims of the bombing. In modern times, the gate has become the symbol of the city. From behind the gateway, continue southwest on rue Saulnerie approximately 200 m to the front of the church. (48.837432, -0.891904)

Constructed upon the foundations of an earlier Romanesque chapel, the Gothic style **Église Notre-Dame** was dedicated on this site in 1272. Various enlargements and additions continued into the 16th century, but the Gothic style was retained. The church was 80 percent destroyed in the combat and bombings of 1944, postwar restoration completed in 1957.

From the tourist office, proceed south on rue André Halbout (D577a) for 120 m to the roundabout in front of the Porte de l'Horloge. Take the 3rd exit onto rue Deslongrais (D577) and follow for 1.3 km. The road changes name several times. Turn right onto Rue Charles Lemaître (the turn is signed as 'Mémorial 116ᵉ RI USA'). After 160 m, turn right onto rue de la Delotière and carefully follow for 580 m to the memorial on the right. (48.833407, -0.891529)

---

20   The 29th Infantry Division, under the command of Major General Charles H. Gerhardt, scored three major victories in a four-week period clearing the cities of St-Lô, Tessy-s/Vire, and Vire. In September, it captured its fourth urban battlefield at Brest.

German artillery continued to bombard the city from hilltop positions after the city's capture. **Hill 203**, the high point that overlooks and dominates the city center from the south, had been a German strongpoint that held excellent views of any route of approach to the German artillery positions. Before dawn on 8 August, the 116th Infantry Regiment's Company A began a mighty fire exercise to draw German attention while Companies B and C moved around the flanks. Before the sun fully illuminated the hilltop, German infantry was fleeing down the opposite side of the hill.[21] Meanwhile, the regiment's 2nd Battalion had a much easier time taking Hill 251, 1.6 kilometers to the southeast. With the capture of the two heights, the escaping enemy was caught in the middle, and few evaded death or capture.

A memorial to the soldiers of the 116th Infantry Regiment, 29th Infantry Division, occupies the high point. A large granite stele bears a plaque to the **29th Infantry Division** that bears its 'ying-yang' insignia. Two steles that flank the central monument bear plaques listing the rank and name of each of the 108 killed and 4 missing during the capture of the hill. The view down into the city presents the incredible slope that was climbed to achieve the height.

> The Avranches battlefield offers two memorials of interest, both detailing General Patton's rapid advance through the region, and two military cemeteries. They require a 90-kilometer return to the west. If desired, visitors can proceed directly to the Operation LÜTTICH battlefield 20 km to the south.

Battle of Avranches
30 to 31 July 1944

Generalfeldmarschall von Kluge, now commanding OB West, informed the German High Command that 'the left flank had collapsed.' In return, he received more orders to hold fast. Avranches was the gateway to Brittany and southern Normandy. A fact not lost to the German High Command which put every effort into holding the city.

Battle

On 28 July General Troy Middleton, under the watchful eye of General Patton serving as Bradley's deputy, ordered his VIII Corps led by his 4th and 6th Armored Divisions to drive south toward Avranches. Waves of tanks fought through German infantry in hedgerow country, and by noon the 4th Armored Division was in Coutances. The unit continued south the next day in two columns.

The western column, led by tank battalions of 6th Armored Division's Combat Command B, advanced 40 kilometers in 36 hours, achieving Avranches near dusk on 30 July. While CCB commanded the flanks, the division's CCA added its tanks to the effort and pushed into the town, but the narrow, twisting streets held enemy guns or riflemen at every turn.

During the urban fighting, Sergeant Joe Shedevy Jr, commanding an M-18 'Hellcat' of the 704th Tank Destroyer (TD) Battalion, spotted a camouflaged panzer waiting for a target. Shedevy's gunner, with the Hellcat's crosshairs on the center of the swastika, fired, and his armor-piercing shell destroyed the enemy. A second German tank, hiding behind a hedgerow, fired at Shedevy's tank but missed high. The Hellcat fired a

---

21   The 1st Battalion, 116th Infantry Regiment, was award a Presidential Unit Citation for the action. The French government awarded the battalion the Croix de Guerre with Silver Star.

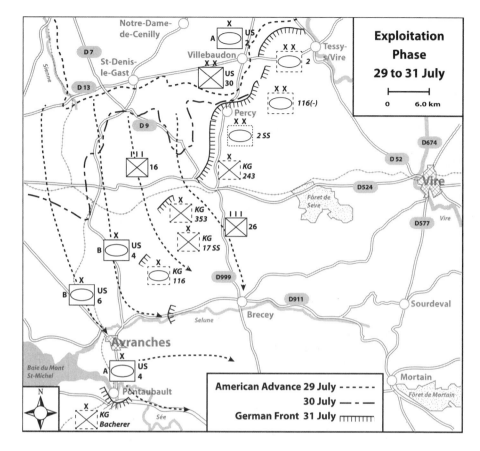

second round from its 76-mm gun and set the second panzer ablaze.[22] Two other enemy tanks quickly started to withdraw but were spotted by other tank destroyers. Both were summarily destroyed.

Captain Murray W Farmer, in command of Company F, 25th Cavalry Reconnaissance Squadron, turned his Sherman tank around a corner to find himself facing a Panther tank just 30 meters ahead. Farmer ordered his driver to ram the larger enemy, thereby blocking its gun traverse. Before the Panther could back off to fire, Farmer's men put four rounds from its short-barreled 75-mm gun into the Panther. The escaping German crew was killed by Farmer's machine gunner.[23]

The battle for the town continued through 30 July and into the 31st. A German column moved through the southern limits of the town before it came into contact with Private William Whitson of the 53rd Armored Infantry Battalion. Despite overwhelming odds, Private Whitson refused to abandon his .30-caliber machine gun, with which he raked the column, killing 50 enemy troops and destroying 25 trucks. Whitson was killed

---

22   Sergeant Joseph Shedevy died in 2007 at age 88. He is buried in George Washington Memorial Park, Paramus, NJ.

23   Captain Murray William Farmer was awarded a Silver Star. Farmer died in 2009 at age 91. He is buried in Arlington National Cemetery.

in the action.[24]

On 31 July, the commander of the German 77th Infantry Division, Oberst Rudolf Bacherer, gathered together a *kampfgruppe* and attacked Pontaubault from the east. His unit, led by 14 assault guns, turned north and fought into Avranches under a gloomy sky and a slow drizzle that kept Allied aircraft grounded. The sky cleared at noon, permitting the fighter-bombers to arrive, and the advance was over. Within minutes, all of the self-propelled guns were out of action. American tanks then attacked and drove back the German force and captured the critical Pontaubault Bridge.

Battlefield Tour

Return to the center of Vire. From the large roundabout in front of the Porte de l'Horloge, take the 4th exit onto Av du Général Leclerc (D577). After 150 m, turn left onto rue d'Aignaux (D524) and follow for 25.1 km. Turn left toward Avranches (D975) and follow for 17.7 km to a roundabout; take the 2nd exit toward Rennes/Avranches (A84/E3/E401). After 3.5, km exit toward Avranches-centre (D973). At the roundabout, take the 5th exit toward Caen/Avranches (D973). Cross back over the autoroute and, at the next roundabout, take the 1st exit toward Centreville (D7). Follow through Avranches for 1.7 km to place Patton. (48.68188, -1.355449)

Avranches

Avranches, an ancient coastal town that sits upon a 70-meter bluff at the base of the Cotentin Peninsula, controls bridges over two rivers: the Sée to the north and the Sélune to the south. As such, Avranches has seen its share of invaders through the centuries. Norsemen occupied the small fishing village in 889. The English camped nearby during one of their conquests of Normandy in 1141. It was the site of English occupation again during the Hundred Years War. Six centuries later, the Germans occupied the town in 1940.

Office Municipal de Tourisme (48.686505, -1.362637)

2 rue Général De Gaulle   50300 Avranches
Tel: +33 (0)2 33 58 00 22   Email: tourisme@avranches.fr
Web: http://www.ville-avranches.fr/
Tourisme/Decouvrir-Avranches

The Second World War museum in le-Val-St-Père is permanently closed.

The **General Patton and Liberation Memorial**, in what is now known as place Patton, commemorates the passage of the US Third Army through the city. Patton briefly established his headquarters at this road junction. The roundabout encircles an obelisk commemorating the events of the city's liberation with a large dedication to General Patton. The obelisk sits upon a large stone platform in the shape of a six-pointed star. Each of the star's points identifies a major unit of Third Army and lists the locations of the unit's major engagements. The obelisk is flanked by a bust of Patton wearing the tanker's leather helmet and the well-restored Sherman tank 'Thunderbolt,' the name of the 37th Tank Battalion's

---

24   Private William H Whitson received the Distinguished Service Cross.

command vehicle.[25] A stainless steel battle map presents Third Army's movements after the capture of Avranches. A bronze plaque also commemorates the **406th Fighter Group**, which flew 13,612 combat sorties during the Northern European Campaign and was particularly active in support of Operation COBRA.

> Leave place Patton on rue du général Patton (D7) and follow for 3.8 km. In a large roundabout, carefully take the 2nd exit toward Pontaubault (and many other towns) (D43e2). After 220 m, take the 3rd exit toward Pontaubault (D43e2) and follow for 2.0 km to the bridge. (48.631739, -1.350621)

After the savage fight for Avranches, the 37th Tank Battalion was dispatched to secure the one road bridge and two railway bridges over the River Sélune at Pontaubault. Patton drove seven divisions, over 100,000 men and 15,000 vehicles, down this one road and across this one bridge in 72 hours! Oberst Rudolph Bacherer[26] and the remaining 1,000 troops of the German 77th Infantry Division were assigned to destroy the Pontaubault bridges. Their attack was repelled amid house-to-house fighting in Pontaubault, a defeat which opened the door to Brittany and its seaports at St-Malo and Brest. Patton's forces spread out toward Brittany ports and the region's capital at Rennes. The damn had truly burst.

The original **Pontaubault Bridge** across the Sélune River was constructed in the 15th century along the path of an ancient Roman road. The current ten-arch bridge dates from 1793. A plaque on the north side of the bridge notes the German attempts to destroy the bridge and commemorates the passage of General Patton. A plaque on the south end of the bridge presents a brief history of the bridge and notes the passage of seven divisions of General Patton's Third Army. The bridge is flanked by railway bridges that were also targets of, at first American then German, bombings.

> Continue 200 m to the cemetery on the left. (48.630221, -1.350557)

On 16 July, Pontaubault was the target of Allied bombing attempting to block the movements of German reinforcements from Brittany to the Normandy battlefields. Through bombings and ground fighting, 70 percent of the village was destroyed, including most of the church. A stone block arch that once served as the entrance to the church stands in the middle of the cemetery. This single surviving part of the church presents a stark reminder of the destruction wrought upon French communities during the liberation.

A simple sign on the adjacent wall describes the courageous actions of a German soldier on 3 February 1944. Earlier that morning, three troop and munitions trains had been derailed crossing the Sélune bridge. The Germans brought the entire town's

---

25   The 37th Tank Battalion was commanded by Lieutenant Colonel Creighton Abrams. Frequently at the 4th Armored Division's spearhead, he led the division's CCA engaged in the Arracourt Tank Battle in September 1944, and the breakthrough of German defenses encircling Bastogne in December 1944. Each action earned him a Distinguished Service Cross. Abrams rose to command military forces in Vietnam for four years and later all US Army forces as Chief of Staff of the United States Army. The US Army's main battle tank, the M1 Abrams, is named after him. Abrams died in 1974 at age 59. He is buried in Arlington National Cemetery.

26   Oberst Rudolph Bacherer was captured on 15 August following the fall of St-Malo. He was a recipient of the Knight's Cross of the Iron Cross with Oak Leaves for his leadership in extracting the 77th Infantry Division from the Cotentin Peninsula. He died in 1964 at age 69.

population to the church, figuring that those not present were the saboteurs. A German soldier was selected as translator and, through subterfuge, convinced his officers that all of the townspeople were present when in fact thirteen were indeed missing. Everyone was released. After the war, the courageous soldier wrote to the townspeople to explain that he was Alsatian and, although he wore the German green uniform, he was French blue, white, and red underneath.

Continue south on rue Patton (D43e2) for 860 m to a roundabout. Take the 1st exit toward le Mont-St-Michel/Juilley (D976). After 1.3 km, enter a roundabout and take the 1st exit toward Mont-St-Michel/Courtils (D43). Follow for 5.9 km, then turn left toward Mont-St-Michel/Deutscher Soldatenfriedhof (D75). Follow for 2.3 km to the entrance drive to the cemetery. (48.61586, -1.453242)

Ossuaire Allemand Mont d'Huisnes

The Mont d'Huisnes German Military Cemetery was constructed upon a hill, the center of which holds a circular necropolis, entered via a wide staircase that leads to a passage through the mausoleum to a central, grass-covered courtyard. The 47-meter circular structure contains two stories of sixty-eight crypts containing a total of 11,956 German soldiers. The bodies were accumulated in 1961 from eleven burial sites spread across western France and the Channel Islands. A plaque on each crypt identifies the remains by name, rank, and dates of birth and death. The youngest died at age 16. Stairs in the courtyard mount an observation platform from which the ancient pilgrimage site of Mont-St-Michel, only 5 kilometers distant, is visible.

Open daily from 0830 to 1700. No admission fee.

Reverse direction (D75) and follow for 2.3 km. Turn right toward Ducey (D43) and follow for 5.9 km to a roundabout. Take the 3rd exit toward A84/Rennes (D976) and proceed 2.4 km to enter the Autoroute toward Rennes. After 10.1 km, take exit #32 toward St-James; in the first roundabout take 4th exit toward St-James (D30). Follow for 2.0 km into St-James. Turn right onto rue de la Libration (D998), then a quick left onto rue Division Leclerc (D12). After 290m, continue straight toward Hamelin (again D30). Follow for 1.0 km, noting the hairpin right turn. Turn right toward St-George-de-Reintembalt (also signed to American Cemetery, D230) and proceed 1.0 km to the cemetery entrance on the left. (48.51993, -1.301451)

Brittany American Cemetery

http://www.abmc.gov/cemeteries/cemeteries/br.php#

The cemetery was the site of a temporary American burial ground established on 4 August 1944, which, at the time, rested a short distance behind American lines. Despite the name, the cemetery is located in Normandy and holds the remains of 4,410 war dead, many of whom were killed in the Normandy fighting. The retaining wall of the memorial terrace records the names of 498 dead whose bodies were never recovered. The gray, granite Romanesque memorial chapel overlooks the burial plots and provides a stairway to a viewing platform on the tower. Significantly, the rolling, open countryside marks the end of Normandy hedgerow country and the beginning of rolling terrain of Brittany to the west and Loire Valley to the southeast.

Open daily 0900 to 1700. No admission fee.

Operation Lüttich
7 to 12 August 1944

General Bradley realized that Brittany could be captured with a minimum of forces. Accordingly, on 3 August, he ordered General Patton to change direction and clear territory south and east toward the Loire Valley.

Avranches was geographically so important that it became the objective of one of Hitler's great blunders. On 4 August, Hitler responded to von Kluge's request for a withdrawal to the Seine River with orders to launch a counteroffensive through the American front between Vire and Mortain. The objective was to recapture Avranches and to cut the Third Army's fuel supply line. Six armored spearheads from 116th Panzer, 2nd Panzer, and 2nd SS Panzer Divisions were to push west with the 1st SS Panzer Division available for exploitation. German forces could only manage to field 145 tanks – roughly an equal mix of PzKpfw IVs and Panthers – plus 32 self-propelled guns.

At Mortain, the 30th (Old Hickory) Infantry Division, relieving the 1st Infantry Division, had entered unfamiliar positions on unfamiliar terrain only four hours before the German assault. Operation Lüttich became a small unit battle with fierce close-range fighting, infiltration and counterinfiltration, punctuated by ambush and surprise. Disorganization, isolation, and lack of communications took control of the battle out of the hands of the generals.

Objective	To divide the American advance and sever Third Army's supply line.
Forces	
American	30th Infantry Division (Major General Leland S Hobbs)
German	Four weakened panzer divisions grouped into XLVII Panzer Corps (General der Panzertruppe Hans Emil Richard Freiherr von Funck)
Result	Despite an initial advance, the offensive failed.
Casualties	
American	1,800 killed or wounded
German	Uncertain; 100 tanks destroyed or abandoned
Location	St-Lô is 60 km east of Caen; Mortain is 62 km south of St-Lô

Battle

Maintaining the element of surprise, the German counterattack started without preliminary bombardment shortly after midnight on 7 August. Taking advantage of total darkness, the northern column of 2nd Panzer Division broke the American line and overran two companies of the US 117th Infantry Regiment at St-Barthélémy and made good nighttime progress along a minor road (D79) along the south bank of the River Sée, achieving le Mesnil-Adelée by 0800. It was only 24 kilometers from the coast and its objective of cutting the fuel supply to twelve US divisions. The advance was eventually contained by Combat Command B, 3rd Armored Division, which intercepted the German column with its Task Force 1 west of le Mesnil-Adelée. When the morning mist lifted, Allied air attacks hammered German columns with rocket-carrying USAAF Thunderbolts and RAF Typhoons being especially effective.

Task Force 2 from CCB, 3rd Armored Division, augmented by 3rd Battalion, 119th

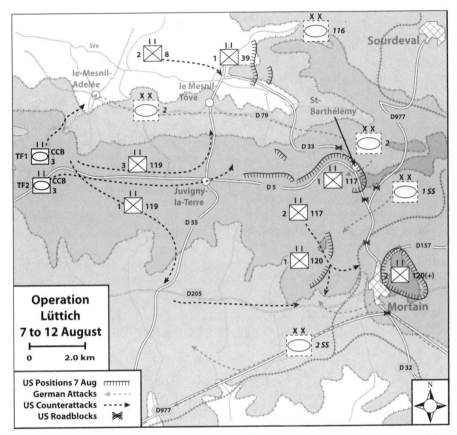

Regiment, attempted to retake le Mesnil-Tove, a village behind the German spearhead, by moving north from Juvigny, but it ran into the 1st SS Division's reconnaissance battalion and was abruptly halted. During the fighting, the CCB commander called his subordinates into a farm building for a quick orientation conference. German observers in the church tower spotted the gathering and called down artillery. A direct hit on the small wooden hut killed almost everyone in it, eliminating the unit's command structure with one blow.

The southern column of 2nd Panzer Division started late and encountered considerable resistance from the 117th Regiment in St-Barthélémy before advancing to east of Juvigny-le-Tertre.

Mortain was easily overrun by the 2nd SS Panzer Division whose two columns attacked on either side of the town. By noon, 2nd SS had advanced 7 kilometers along highway D977.

German dominance of the battlefield was frustrated by possession of strategic Hill 314 (referred to by some as Hill 317) by 2nd Battalion, 120th Infantry Regiment, strengthened by Company K of the regiment's 3rd Battalion. West of Mortain, the regiment's 1st Battalion also occupied Hill 285. The two heights afforded the Americans ideal positions from which to direct artillery and air attacks upon German troop concentrations.

During the afternoon of 7 August, General von Funck committed 1st SS Panzer Division but, after little additional progress, Funck halted the attack and his troops dug in. They were now in a defensive posture except at Hill 314. In the north, the 116th Panzer

Division's commander refused to attack because of the vulnerability of its flank and the weakness of its replacement infantry division.[27]

The fighting continued the next day and, while particularly bloody, positions changed but little. Additional units including the 629th Tank Destroyer Battalion were attached to 30th Division, and the US 35th Infantry Division was redirected toward Mortain from the southwest.

Bradley recognized the opportunity to destroy an entire enemy army. He sent the 4th Infantry Division and the remainder of the 3rd Armored Division to seal the attack front and the 9th Infantry Division to drive in the German right flank. By the next morning, they were threatening the German rear. On 9 August, Hitler replaced General von Funck with General der Panzertruppe Heinrich Karl Alfons Willy Eberbach and ordered the operation to restart on 11 August. The static warfare continued until Hitler acknowledged defeat and allowed his troops to withdraw from the salient that he had created. Mortain was recaptured on 12 August by the 320th Infantry Regiment, riding upon tanks of the 737th Tank Battalion.

Aftermath

Rather than threaten the American supply line, Hitler had driven his armies in Normandy to their destruction. The 2nd Panzer Division was annihilated, and the 1st and 2nd SS Panzer Divisions suffered serious losses of men and matériel. By 8 August, US Third Army was engaged in a deep flanking movement towards Angers and le Mans. Little remained between Patton and the Seine: no organized German units of any size, no natural obstacles, and no intercepting German air craft.

Battlefield Tour

The tour route to Mortain from Avranches travels in the opposite direction of the German 2nd Panzer Division's advance along the well-marked highway D5 through le Mesnil-Adelée and le Mesnil-Tove to St-Barthélemy. The highway follows the crest of a ridgeline that separates the Sée and Sélune Rivers, which provided natural flank protection for attacking units driving west.

From Brittany American Cemetery: reverse direction toward St-James (D230). After 1.0 km, turn right toward Hamelin (D30) and follow for 18.2 km to a roundabout on the southern outskirts of St-Hilaire-du-Harcouët. Take the 4th exit toward Mont-St-Michel (D977) and follow through the town for 5.2 km. Turn left toward Chevreville (D55) and follow for 9.8 km. Turn right toward Barthélemy/Mortain (D5) and stop after 5.6 km at the road intersection in Barthélemy. (48.680874, -0.952399)

---

27   General der Panzertruppe Gerhard Helmuth Graf von Schwerin, commander of 116th Panzer Division and a career military officer, was implicated in the 20 July assassination plot and was disheartened by German losses in Normandy. At 1600 on 7 August, he was relieved by Hausser and replaced by Oberst Walter Reinhard, Schwerin's Chief of Staff. Reinhard dutifully ordered the attack to proceed but made no progress. Later, Schwerin returned to his command to defend the city of Aachen in September 1944. When his plan to surrender that city became known to the Nazis, he was again relieved and sent to the Italian Front. Schwerin survived the war to become a military advisor to the postwar German government. He died in 1980 at age 89.

From Vire: leave Vire south toward Sourdeval/Mortain (D577). After approximately 17 km, turn right toward Brouains (D179). After 900 m, turn left toward St-Barthélémy; after 1.5 km, turn left toward St-Barthélémy (D33) and continue for 1.0 km into the village. Pass through Barthélémy to the intersection of D5 and D33, stopping near the ancient stone cross east of the highway. (48.680874, -0.952399)

The first German Panther tank rumbled up the road from Mortain toward St-Barthélémy – spelled Barthélmy in 1944 – shortly after dawn on 7 August. The south side of the town was defended by four 3-in (75-mm) antitank guns of Lieutenant George Greene's 3rd Platoon, Company B, 823rd TD Battalion. Early morning fog hid attacker and defender alike while platoon Sergeant Robert Martin aimed his antitank gun at the muzzle flashes of an approaching tank's machine gun. At a range of less than 50 meters, he fired, and the 1st SS Panzer Division tank exploded into flames. German troops spent an hour clearing the wreckage blocking the highway before sending a second Panther against Sgt Martin. In turn, he took aim and repeated his earlier performance.

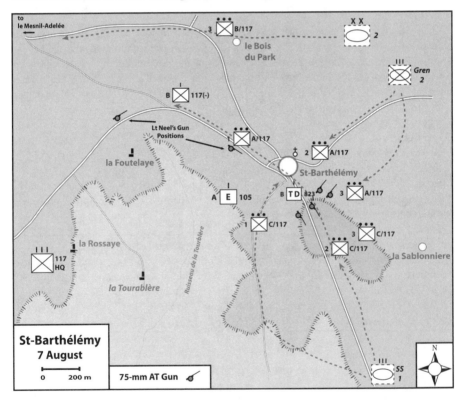

The German attack from Mortain had already stalled, but attacks from other directions continued and increased in intensity. The 2nd Panzer Division's Panzergrenadier Regiment 2 approached from the northeast using the highway and fields. Two more German tanks were knocked out, but the lifting fog exposed American guns and two of the four were destroyed in rapid succession. A third gun position was overrun and the fourth put out of action. Lt Greene and most of his men were eventually killed or captured fighting as infantry. [28]

Also defending around Barthélémy was the 117th Regiment. Companies A and C, defending positions they had occupied only the previous night, now faced a strong panzer attack by 1st SS Panzer coming from east and southeast and 2nd Panzer coming from north and northeast. By 0810, the Panthers were entering Company C's positions. By 1035, 1st Battalion's command post and the two companies had been overrun. Reserve Company B and all support personnel were committed to the defense. Survivors regrouped about a small hill to the west near Ferme la Rossaye and continued fighting despite being heavily outnumbered. The engagement continued through the next several days while small isolated units continued to resist. The regiment's 1st Battalion lost 334 men and the tank destroyer Battalion had lost 43, but elements of two panzer divisions had been delayed for six hours.

Lieutenant Lawson Neel commanded two towed 75-mm antitank guns of 1st Platoon, Company B, 823rd TD Battalion. With German troops now pouring through St-Barthélémy, Neel intended to block the roadway leaving the town to the west. He had no sooner positioned one gun at the western outskirts of the town when a Panther tank approached. Neel yelled to his men to fire immediately and the shot knocked out the tank. Accompanying German infantry fired a fusillade at the gun prompting Neel and his men to run for cover. Returning to the battalion command post, Neel took a second gun and positioned it along the highway approximately 1 kilometer west of town. From his new position, Neel and his men destroyed two more enemy tanks, whose wreckage blocked the roadway. Allied planes strafed the stalled German column stopping its progress. The 1st SS Panzer Division never proceeded farther.

Leave St-Barthélémy south toward Mortain (D5); after 1.2 km, enter a roundabout and take the 2nd exit toward Mortain (D977). The large roundabout at the junction of highways D5 and D977 was the objective of the German columns coming from the south. Proceed 1.4 km and stop near the small park on the left containing a **NTL Totem**. (48.658722, -0.947238)

An intersection of five roadways near the Cistercian l'Abbaye Blanche was held by 150 men from 117th Regiment's Company F armed with mines, bazookas, and machine guns and supported by four antitank guns of Company A, 823rd TD Battalion, all under the command of Lieutenant Tom Springfield. The entire *Der Fuhrer* Regiment of 2nd SS Panzer Division was heading their way. Fighting started at 0500 when a German reconnaissance column approached along the river track. The entire column was destroyed by 57-mm AT guns positioned near the abbey. Similarly, separate columns proceeding north across the river toward St-Barthélémy and approaching from St-Barthélémy were destroyed by 75-mm guns that covered both roadways. By 1400, the German command, now sheltering in a dairy plant near the Pont de la Vacherie, requested and received a truce to collect its dead and wounded. So far, not one American had been killed.

The attacks continued the next day, especially from the north along highway D977 where German flamethrowers made an appearance. Later, an attempt to force the position across the Cance bridge was stopped by strong small-arms fire. Sporadic attempts to force

---

28   Lieutenant George Greene received no award for his stout defense of Barthélémy. He spent eight months as a POW and nearly died during a mid-winter march through Germany. Sergeant Robert Martin was also captured and held in a German POW camp.

the roadblock occurred on 9 and 10 August to no avail. For the entire battle, the American forces, so ably led by Lt Springfield, suffered only three killed and twenty wounded. Total German losses were estimated at 220 killed or captured and eleven tanks, nine half-tracks, and dozens of other vehicles destroyed.[29]

The tree-shaded side road (D46) stretches toward the train station and was the graveyard of the German reconnaissance column on the first day of the battle. The wreckage was so dense that the route was blocked for the remainder of the battle.

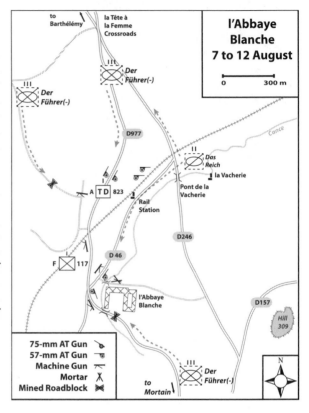

Proceed (D977) for approximately 150 meters to the bridge over the Cance River. (48.657583, -0.946321)

Private First Class Robert P Vollmer and five riflemen were covering the bridge over the Cance when he used his bazooka to destroy two approaching armored cars and a fuel truck. The group found itself outflanked, but each further enemy attempt to capture the road junction was met by tank destroyers or antitank gun fire.[30]

Continue 80 meters to the gateway on the left. Do not enter the abbey grounds. (48.657329, -0.945428)

The **Cistercian l'Abbaye Blanche,** founded in the early 12th century by a half-brother of William the Conqueror, exhibits the beginnings of the Gothic style. The wooden tower is distinctive but lacks a bell. The Romanesque cloister displays rows of arches and columns. The structure was used by religious organizations as late as 2011 when it was sold. The abbey is not generally open to visitors, but it can be partially viewed from the roadway.

29   Lieutenant Tom Springfield, from Wichita, Kansas, also participated in stopping *Kampfgruppe Peiper* near Stoumont Station during the Battle of the Bulge. He survived the war earning a Silver Star and Croix de Guerre.

30   Private Robert Vollmer was awarded the Distinguished Service Cross. He was later killed in action.

Mortain

Mortain was the starting point for the German counterattack toward Avranches. The small town, located on the southwestern fringe of hedgerow country, owes its military importance to the seven roadways the emanating therein and the rocky bluff to the east which dominated the town. From the height, observers could see 25 kilometers to the east and 32 kilometers to the west – all the way to Avranches.

Mortain was liberated by the US 1st Infantry Division on 3 August. The 30th Infantry Division had arrived only hours before the German assault and occupied their foxholes and slit trenches during the darkness of 6 August.

Office de Tourisme du Canton de Mortain (48.648915, -0.94215)

Rue du Bourg Lopin   50140 Mortain
Tel/fax: +33 (0)2 33 59 19 74   Email: mortain.tourisme@wanadoo.fr
Web: http://www.mortain-tourisme.fr/

Continue into Mortain passing the tourism office on the left; the Hotel de la Poste on the right held the 120th Regiment CP on the morning of the battle. (48.648845, -0.942464)

Isolated during the initial German assault, the regimental command attempted to join the force on Hill 314, but Lieutenant Colonel Hardaway, 2nd Battalion commander, and his staff were captured shortly after daybreak.

Proceed 600 m past the tourist office and make a sharp left turn onto rue de la 30eme Division (D157). Proceed up the hill. After 300 m, turn right onto rue de Versailles (D487e1). After and additional 350 m, turn left onto rue de la Petite Chapelle (still D487e1) and continue up the hill to the parking area on the right. (48.647134, -0.932835)

Battle

Three rifle companies from the 2nd Battalion, along with Company K, 3rd Battalion, totaling seven hundred men, became surrounded on Hill 314. Captain Reynold C Erichson assumed command despite most of his Company F's being trapped in Mortain.[31] Communications between separated groups was difficult, and the craggy, rocky mount did not permit deep foxholes. For five days the men on Hill 314 resisted every attempt to overrun their positions.

Starting at 1000 on 7 August and after the morning fog had lifted, a regimental size *kampfgruppe* from 17th SS Panzergrenadier Division launched an attack to overcome the defenders, a movement stopped by Company E supported by American artillery when forward observer 2nd Lieutenant Robert L Weiss from 230th Field Artillery Battalion radioed target coordinates to artillery units. At 1400, a second assault from the west (from Mortain) was repulsed by Company G.

On the night of 8 August, the battalion aid station was captured. A relief attempt by 2nd Battalion, 117th Regiment, entered the town to resupply the l'Abbaye Blanche roadblock but was repulsed in its efforts to reach the men on Hill 314. At 1830 on 9 August, an SS officer sent a surrender demand to Company E's commander, Lieutenant Ralph Kerley. The offer was emphatically refused despite the dwindling American ammunition

---

31   By the end of the battle, Company F had suffered almost 100 percent casualties. Only eight men survived unscathed.

supply. The subsequently SS attack overran Kerley's foxholes whereby the lieutenant called American artillery fire down onto his own positions to repulse the attack.

Just before noon on 12 August, Lieutenant Homer Kurtz, Company G, 320th Infantry, 35th Infantry Division, broke through the encircling German troops and found Lieutenant Ronal Woody to say, 'We're relieving you, sir.' Only 376 men walked off the hill. The regiment had suffered 277 killed, captured, or missing. The defense of Hill 314 has been described by historians as one of the outstanding small-unit actions of the war. [32]

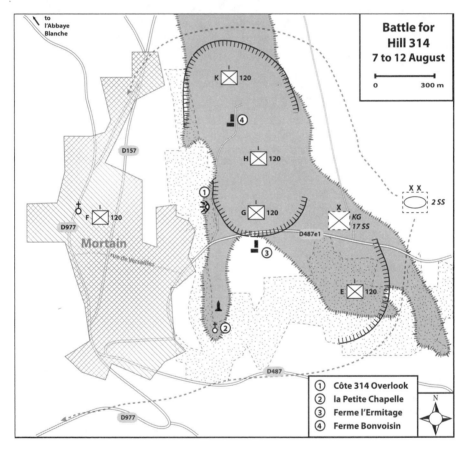

Battle for Hill 314
7 to 12 August

① Côte 314 Overlook
② la Petite Chapelle
③ Ferme l'Ermitage
④ Ferme Bonvoisin

Battlefields Tour

An **NTL Totem** stands at the beginning of the path near the roadway. A broad gravel pathway slopes gently uphill passing through a young pine forest. The new plantings are the result of the Great Storm of 1999, which struck Europe in December of that year and inflicted significant damage to forested areas. After passing into a section of mature pines that survived the storm, the path achieves a glen on the left. On the open ground, a polished

32   The 120th Infantry Regiment was awarded a Presidential Unit Citation, and the overall commander and the four company commanders received Distinguished Services Crosses. They were Captain Reynold C Erichson, overall command; Captain Delmont K Byrn, Company H; 1st Lieutenant Ralph A Kerley, Company E; 1st Lieutenant Joseph C Reaser, Company K; and 1st Lieutenant Ronal E Woody Jr, Company G.

black granite stele stands as a memorial to the soldiers of the **30th Infantry Division** and commemorates their valor, courage, and sacrifice in holding the key battleground. The inscription ends with 'They gave their lives for freedom.' The stone stands in a pattern of blocks set in the grass surface; the rectangular pattern, however, is missing blocks, perhaps representing the soldiers who could no longer answer roll call.

La Petite Chapelle (La Chapelle St-Michel) (48.643479, -0.93313)
The current chapel was constructed in 1852 to replace a hermitage founded in 1333 and restored numerous times over the centuries. The wall of the Petit Chapelle bears a plaque paying homage to the heroes of the **2nd Battalion, 120th Infantry Regiment**, who died on this hill. The stained-glass window over the doorway bears the emblem of the Supreme Headquarters of the Army Expeditionary Force.
Open daily except Tuesday in July and August from 14:00 to 18:30.

Continue to the rear of the chapel where the rocky outcropping provides the look of a natural fortress and offers the views that made this terrain so valuable. Frequently, clouds prohibit observing the valley, but on clear days locals claim that Mont-St-Michel is visible across the Baie du Mont St-Michel. The rocky surface prohibited the digging of protective foxholes. Veterans of the battle relate how an 88-mm gun fired its shells into the rocky crags, shattering the rock and shell into thousands of ricocheting shards.

> Return to the parking area and walk along the dead-end road toward la Montjoie/Cote 314M. In approximately 200 m, an additional sign indicates the route to the panorama. (Approximately 48.648449, -0.932701)

The panorama was occupied by German observers for two years before being driven off by the US 18th Infantry Regiment on 4 August 1944. Unofficial, crude signs indicate the location of the long-gone German positions. One sign identifies an American forward artillery observer's location. The depression behind the sign was the foxhole of Lieutenant CA Bartz, Battery C, 230th Field Artillery Battalion, who was stationed with Company G and reported German movements and targets until his radio batteries died midmorning on 8 August. [33]

Side Trip: British 11th Armoured Division Memorial
To achieve the final two sites on the southern shoulder of the Falaise Gap, continue east. Most highways circumvent Flers, an objective of the British Second Army and the site of a major British memorial.

> From Hill 314: reverse direction to proceed back down the hill; turn right onto rue de Versailles, then right onto rue de la 30eme Division (D157, become D25 after 17 km). Follow for a total of 33.4 km into Flers, being vigilant as the road passes through numerous villages and intersections. In the center of Flers, turn right onto rue du Docteur (unfortunately, not well signed, but situated immediately before the church on the left). In the roundabout, take the 4th exit onto rue du 6 Juin (D462). Follow through Flers for 3.2 km to a roundabout; take the 3rd exit and continue 1.2 km to the large memorial on the left. (48.787386, -0.565968)

---

33   First Lieutenant Charles A Bartz was killed later in the war.

While the Americans were swinging around to the south of the German Seventh Army and the Canadians were pushing through Falaise to the north, the British pushed in the nose of the German salient from the west and northwest. In particular, British 11th Armoured Division, now part of General Horrocks XXX Corps, led the advance against German troops retreating after the failure of Operation LÜTTICH. On 16 August, the 159th Infantry Brigade was ambushed by German artillery and three companies of panzergrenadiers defending the Pont de Vère. The Shropshire Light Infantry, supported by Cromwell tanks from the 3rd Royal Tank Regiment, forced a crossing and drove the enemy to withdraw. Flers was liberated the next day without a shot being fired.

The site now holds the **British 11th Armoured Division Memorial** – a red stone wall with bronze plaques on either end, both of which prominently display the division's 'Black Bull' insignia and commemorate those who died. The roadway immediately in front of the memorial continues north on the original highway and crosses the Pont de Vère 150 meters to the north.

Establishing the Falaise Pocket
13 to 19 August 1944

After Allied forces entered le Mans on the evening of 8 August, Allied command sent XV Corps with 2nd French and US 5th Armored Divisions and the US 80th and US 90th Infantry Divisions north toward Alençon in hopes of enveloping the German Seventh Army's rear.

Objective	To move north from le Mans and trap German forces
Forces	
American	XV Corps (Major General Wade Haislip)
German	LXXXI Corps (General der Infanterie Adolf Kuntzen) and XLVII Corps (General der Panzertruppe Baron Hans von Funck)
Result	The southern shoulder of the Falaise gap was formed
Casualties	
American	600 killed or wounded
French	Undetermined
German	Undetermined
Location	Falaise is 35 km south of Caen; le Bourg-St-Leonard is 32 km southeast of Falaise

Battle

On 11 August, 2nd French Armored Division pushed through Alençon to face the reconstituted 9th Panzer Division in the Forêt d'Écouves. Fighting continued into the forest with the slow destruction of the already weakened German unit. By the night of 11 August, the 116th Panzer Division arrived in Argentan and held the town against strong American attacks.

By 14 August, although elements of 1st SS Panzer and 2nd Panzer Divisions arrived in the Argentan sector, the entire Panzer Group Eberbach could muster only seventy tanks. Even for that reduced number, fuel and ammunition was scarce. The rapid American advance forced German commanders to commit their units in a piecemeal fashion to simply

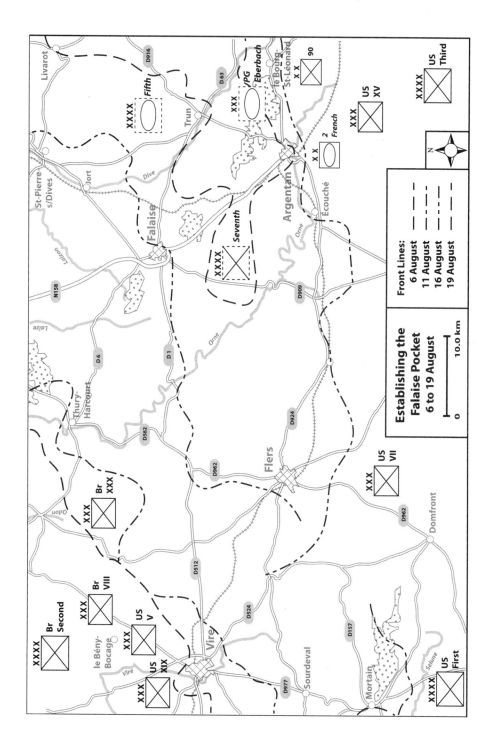

Establishing the
Falaise Pocket
6 to 19 August

Front Lines:
6 August
11 August
16 August
19 August

attempt to hold a defensive line.

With Allied forces north of Argentan, Bradley issued his controversial order to stop the advance. He reasoned that a headlong assault could result in British and American forces engaging each other. Bradley redirected two divisions eastward, leaving 2nd French Armored and US 90th Infantry Divisions holding the southern shoulder of the Argentan-Falaise gap, although Argentan remained in German hands. By 16 August, the US 90th Infantry Division moved through Forêt de Gouffern and into le Bourg-St-Leonard. The town had changed hands numerous times in a pitched battle for the ridge that overlooked the Dive River Valley. Despite the weakening of American forces resulting from their shift toward the Seine River, Montgomery altered the Canadian and American junction from between Falaise and Argentan to between Trun and Chambois. Elements of the 90th Infantry Division moved north to close the gap.

Aftermath

The conclusion of the Battle of Falaise emerges in Chapter Fifteen when Canadian, Polish, and American forces meet in and around Chambois.

Battlefield Tour

From the British 11th Armoured Division Memorial: reverse direction and proceed south toward Flers (D962). Follow for 5.3 km (take the 3rd exit in the roundabout where highways D962 and D462 divide) to a ramp toward Dreux/Flers. At the intersection, turn left toward Dreux (D924). Continue for 32.8 km into Écouché. Turn left onto Av Léon Labbé and proceed 240 m to the tank on the left. (48.715877, -0.116858)

After liberating Alençon on the morning of 12 August, General Leclerc launched two armored columns northwards. His 2nd French Armored Division reached Écouché on the evening of 12 August. At dawn the following morning, the French launched a surprise attack upon elements of the 116th Panzer Division to liberate the town and cross the Orne River.

The **M4 Sherman tank 'Massaouah'** stands at the entrance to the town as a memorial to French armored units which liberated the region. The tank belonged to 1st Company, 501st Tank Regiment, knocked out at this site during the fighting on 13 August. Three penetrations of the left-side armor owed to a German PzKpfw IV. Signboards behind the tank provide a detailed description of local fighting.

Reverse direction and regain highway D924 toward Argentan. After 6.4 km, enter a roundabout and take the 3rd exit toward Dreux (D958). After 2.4 km, enter another roundabout and take 3rd exit toward Dreux (D924). Follow for 10.3 km into le Bourg-St-Léonard. Stop at a convenient location near the roundabout in the center of the village. (48.760935, 0.106044)

Le Bourg-St-Léonard lay at the edge of the Forêt de Gouffern, which offered the Germans good concealment and a staging area for their breakout attempt. The village rests upon a ridge that forms the watershed between the Orne and Dive Rivers and provided excellent observation of the open land of the Dive River valley to the northeast, through which escaping German troops would have to pass.

On 16 August, SS Panzergrenadier Regiment 3, 2nd SS Panzer Division, supported by tanks and artillery from 116th Panzer Division, launched attacks upon US 90th Division roadblocks around le Bourg-St-Leonard. A German force of 1,100 men initially drove Company A, 1st Battalion, 359th Infantry Regiment, off the ridge, but the company regained it after dark with the help of the 712th Tank Battalion. The unit's commander, Lieutenant Colonel George Randolph, moved from tank to tank directing their fire to support the infantry.[34] The German panzers attacked again on 17 August, recapturing the village only to be driven out once again at midnight on the night of 17/18 August.[35]

The German defense was weakened by transfer of 2nd SS Panzer units to a reserve force near Vimoutiers. The 116th Panzer Division threw its last remaining force, an 80-man reconnaissance battalion, into the battle the next morning, but it was not enough to regain the village.

Little remains to commemorate the vicious fighting that occurred in the small village. A rough stone on the side of the roundabout bears a weather-worn plaque that commemorates the battle of 16-18 August. Nonetheless, the views down the ridge to the north explain the military importance of this seemingly non-descript road junction.

This chapter concludes the battlefield tours of American forces during the Normandy Campaign.

Side Trip: Operation BLUECOAT

Operation BLUECOAT
30 July to 6 August 1944

Fifth Panzer Army was holding the line from Bourguébus Ridge (see Chapter Fourteen) across the Orne River to Mont Pinçon and on to Vire. Key to Mont Pinçon was the steep western slope, which held commanding views and a Luftwaffe radar station. On 28 July, Montgomery ordered two corps to attack south from Caumont-l'Éventé with the objective of pressuring German units west of the Orne River. Success required the capture of German strongpoints at Hill 309 and Mont Picton. British forces were to continue exploitation toward Vire, if possible. The terrain was the most rugged in the Normandy bocage, and its ground rife with minefields.

---

34   Lieutenant Colonel George B Randolph was awarded the Distinguished Service Cross. A high school science teacher from Birmingham, Alabama, he enlisted in February 1941, and rose to command the 712th Tank Battalion. Randolph was later killed during a Nebelwerfer attack at Café Schumann in Luxembourg. He is buried in Luxembourg American Cemetery. Randolph was 41 years old.

35   Brigadier General William G Weaver led the defense from the front lines and at one point manned his jeep's machine gun in fire against the enemy. He was awarded the Oak Leaf Cluster to his Distinguished Service Cross. General Weaver was awarded his first Distinguished Service Cross for heroic actions during the First World War. During his career, he twice received each of the following commendations: Silver Star, Bronze Star, Legion d'honneur, and Purple Heart. Weaver retired from the army as a major general. He died in 1970 at age 82.

Lieutenant Colonel Leroy R 'Fireball' Pond was awarded the Distinguished Service Cross for taking command of his surrounded battalion during the Battle of Mont Castre in July and an Oak Leaf Cluster for personal bravery at le Bourg-St-Léonard. He later died of wounds received in December fighting in Germany. Pond also received the Silver Star, two Bronze Stars, two Purple Hearts, and the French Croix de Guerre. He was 27 years old.

Objective	To prevent German armored units from attacking the eastern flank of the American breakout
Forces	
British	VIII (Lieutenant-General Sir Richard O'Connor) and XXX Corps (Lieutenant-General Gerard Bucknall)
German	326th Infantry Division (Generalleutnant Victor von Drabich-Waechter) and 276th Infantry Division (Generalleutnant Kurt Badinski)
Result	A significant advance created a dangerous salient.
Casualties	
British	Undetermined
German	Undetermined
Location	St-Lô is 60 km west of Caen; St-Martin-des-Besaces is 25 km southeast of St-Lô

Battle

As in Operations GOODWOOD and COBRA, the battle began with an aerial bombardment of more than one-thousand bombers. The British flanking divisions made little progress due to terrain and extensive minefields. In the center, the 15th (Scottish) Division, supported by 6th Guards Tank Brigade, was initially delayed but pushed through a thin enemy front to encounter only disorganized resistance.

During the night of 30/31 July, an infantry battalion from British 11th Armored Division moved along an unguarded woodland trail to St-Martin-des-Besaces. The British path to Vire was open and sparsely defended. Although a British reconnaissance unit advanced to within 2 kilometers of the city, it abandoned that effort since the city sat in the American zone of operations – too bad.

Kampfgruppe von Oppeln, 21st Panzer Division, with Tiger tanks of Heavy Panzer Battalion 503, contained the 11th Armoured Division's advance. British attention turned east to face German units being transferred from Caen to meet the American breakout. Two companies of Tiger tanks ventured north from Vire and hit the flank of the Guards Armored Division southeast of Bény-Bocage on 2 August. The Guards lost twenty-eight Sherman and Cromwell tanks before the Tigers withdrew back to Vire. In addition, the British eastern flank was exposed by the failure of XXX Corps to advance. [36]

Thrusts by German and British armored units continued for several days while each attempted to encircle the other. By 6 August, the British breakout had been halted and contained.

Aftermath

While often overshadowed by events in the American sector, Operation BLUECOAT restricted German panzer divisions from joining the fighting farther west and occupied

---

36   Lieutenant-General Bucknall, XXX Corps commander, was dismissed on 2 August, and General Erskine and several subordinates from British 7th Armored Division were removed the next day. Bucknall was sent to command British forces in Northern Ireland, a position he held until retirement. He died in 1980 and age 86.
General Sir George Watkin Eben James Erskine commanded the 43rd (Wessex) Division in 1945. He held numerous high military positions after the war. Erskine died in 1965 at age 66.

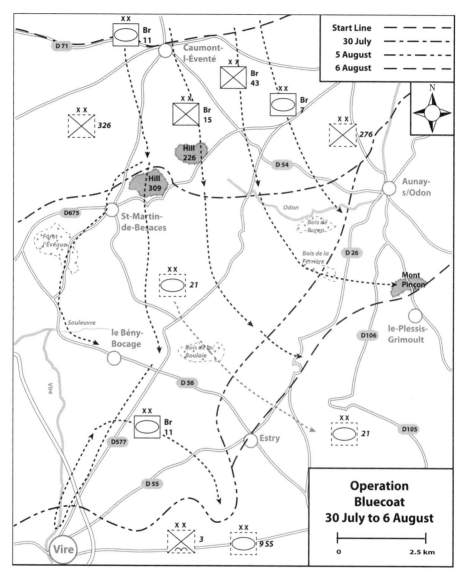

reserves that could have been added to Operation LÜTTICH. Preoccupation with the exposed 11th Armoured Division salient led British senior commanders to halt its efforts to encircle German forces and to adopt a defensive role.

Battlefield Tour

    The battle started from the British front at Caumont-l'Éventé with VIII Corps driving south. The tour does not return to that point since little remains to be seen but picks up the action 11 kilometers farther south.

From the center of Tessy-s/Vire, proceed south toward A84/Pont-Farcy (D374, becomes D21). Follow for 4.8 km, and enter Autoroute A84 toward Caen. After 17.2 km, leave the Autoroute at exit 41 toward St-Martin-des-Besaces. At the first roundabout, take the 1st exit toward St-Martin-des-Besaces (D53) and continue 1.7 km into St-Martin. Turn right onto Route de Villedieu (D675) and proceed 400 m to the museum on the left. (49.011232, -0.850089)

St-Martin-des-Besaces

St-Martin-des-Besaces was an initial objective of Operation BLUECOAT. The town was entered by British 11th Armored Division on 31 July after the capture of Hill 309 the previous day. The battle for the town was not over, however, since counterattacks by Tiger tanks and panzergrenadiers of *Kampfgruppe Rauch* from 21st Panzer Division followed. Platoon Sergeant Dennis Brookes, 5th Coldstream Guards, led his platoon in hand-to-hand fighting and later sprayed a German squad with his Bren gun inflicting numerous casualties and forcing its withdrawal. During the long battle for the town, Brookes also eliminated a German tank with a PIAT.[37] Heavy losses were incurred by both sides before the German troops withdrew at 1600.

Musée la Percee du Bocage
5 rue du 19 Mars 1962   14350 St-Martin-des-Besaces
Tel/Fax: +33 (0)2 31 67 52 78   Email: bluecoat@wanadoo.fr
Web: www.laperceedubocage.com

The museum tour starts with the impact of the German Occupation upon local civilians. It continues by relating the story of the British breakout from the dread bocage during Operation BLUECOAT from Caumont south through St-Martin-des-Besaces and on to Bény-Bocage ending on 2 August. One particularly large diorama presents the battle for this town.

Open daily except Tuesday from 3 April through September from 10:00 to 18:00. Admission fee; Normandie Pass accepted.

Reverse direction and leave St-Martin east toward Villers-Bocage (D675). After 3.2 km (from the museum), stop at the stele on the left. (49.015032, -0.809716)

On 30 July, tanks raced forward to the slopes of Hill 309, which was captured by 4th Coldstream Guards, 6th Guards Brigade, by 1900 and reinforced by 15th Scottish Division infantry. As in St-Martin, German forces launched strong counterattacks against the hill, starting with an artillery barrage at 0530 on 1 August. Thirty minutes later, *Kampfgruppe Rauch* started its move through Bois du Homme but suffered high casualties from defensive fire from Hill 309. Seven squadrons of Typhoon aircraft added their rocket fire against German armor whose assault fell apart. The 3rd Scots Guards, who had taken Hill 226 the same day, suffered a counterattack by *Panzerjäger* Battalion 654, which knocked out ten Churchill tanks but proved unable to push the British troops from the hill. The next day, the German 326th Infantry Division attacked but was bloodily repulsed when British artillery and aircraft hit the German infantry while it was assembling for the attack

---

37   Sergeant Dennis Brookes was awarded a Military Medal for personal courage.

in the Bois d'Homme.[38] A stronger attack on 1 August by 21st Panzer Division struck from the northeast, east, and south, but once again the defenders held the hill.

The memorial stele identifies Hill 309 as **Coldstream Hill** and remembers Brigadier Sir W Barttelot, commander of the 4th Coldstream Guards, which had captured the hill. Major Barttelot was promoted and put in command of the entire brigade but was killed in action on 16 August 1944.[39]

Reverse direction and proceed west toward St-Martin-des-Besaces (D675). In St-Martin, turn left onto rue de l'Église (D53), then quickly right onto a narrow lanes toward la Ferrière-Harang (D185). After 2.5 km, turn left to continue on highway D185, the approximate point where the 2nd Household Cavalry joined behind the German armored car as described below. Stay on highway D185 for an additional 3.4 km passing through the Forêt l'Évêque. Turn left toward Bény-Bocage (D56) and continue for 2.8 km to the small highway bridge. (48.947202, -0.888487)

On 31 July, the British 11th Armoured Division's reconnaissance unit, the 2nd Household Cavalry Regiment, received orders to seek out gaps in the German defensive line. The regiment's five squadrons separated and began searching the rural roads for an opening. Lieutenant DB Powle commanded the armored cars of 1st Troop, Squadron C, when, southwest of St-Martin-des-Besaces, he saw a German armored car moving rapidly south on highway D185. In a bold move, Powle trailed behind the German vehicle and followed it through German-held Forêt l'Évêque. The German vehicle turned west shortly before the bridge over le Souleuvre River. Powle continued straight to the bridge guarded by a lone German soldier. In a stroke of luck, the bridge formed the boundary between Panzer Group West and the Seventh Army; as such, neither group assumed responsibility for its protection. British armored units reinforced the small force during the day to provide the 11th Armoured Division a secure passage over the river.

The bridge bears a small plaque that identifies it as **Bull Bridge** after the insignia of the 11th Armoured Division.[40]

Continue east for 6.9 km (D56), passing through Bény-Bocage and continuing toward St-Charles-de-Percy. Turn right toward Presles (D290a) and, after 140 m, stop at the cemetery on the left. (48.927645, -0.802217)

At dawn on 2 August, the 2nd Battalion, Welsh Guards Reconnaissance unit, started the division attack towards St-Charles-de-Percy. Regrettably, it was ambushed near Catheolles. The Guard Division fought a series of intense and confused engagements south of St-Charles against *Kampfgruppe Meyer*, 9th SS Panzer Division, which included a battalion of Panther tanks and a company of SP guns. Advances were matched by retreats; at one point, three Guards battalions were surrounded at la Marvindière. After three days, the German troops withdrew from the sector to the village of Estry.

---

38   Generalleutnant Victor Paul Konrad Gustav Ludwig von Drabich-Waechter was killed in action during the attack. He was 54 years old and is buried in la Cambe German Cemetery.

39   Brigadier Sir Walter de Stopham Barttelot, 4th Baronet, is buried in St-Charles-de-Percy War Cemetery. He was 39 years old.

40   Lieutenant Powle ended the war as a lieutenant but later rose to the rank of lieutenant colonel.

St-Charles-de-Percy War Cemetery, located on the outskirts of the town, holds the graves of 809 dead from the July and August battles during Operation BLUECOAT. Many of those interred are from the Guards Regiments and fell in local battles. The cemetery is entered through a small gateway, flanked by stone shelters. The youngest burial is that of Private Edward Slater, who died on 7 August 1944 at age 17.

Reverse direction and turn right toward St-Charles-de-Percy (D56). Continue for 1.0 km into St-Charles-de-Percy. In the village, turn right to pass behind the church and continue for 240 m to the monument on the right. (48.923194, -0.789701)

The **Guards Division** memorial stele commemorates the British soldiers of the Guards Armoured Division, commanded by Major-General AHS Adair, who liberated the town during fighting from 2 to 5 August.

Reverse direction and, after 240 m, turn right toward Montchamp (D56). Continue for 1.8 km into Montchamp; turn left onto highway D290 and, after 100 m, stop at the monument on the left before the church. (48.921255, -0.766452)

A high relief engraved stone with images of four allegorical figures stands as a **Memorial to the Victims of Nazism**. The memorial, designed by world renowned artist Alfred Augustus Jannoit,[41] was erected by the twenty-seven communes of the arrondissement of Vire to commemorate local resistance fighters. The figures represent France overlooking a woman who is supporting the emaciated body of a deportee. A mourner stands on the left. The decorations around the figures all carry allegorical symbolism. A field-stone wall bears plaques of remembrance to sixty individuals who died from the occupier's tyranny. A memorial service is held each year on the last Sunday in April, near the date of the liberation of Dachau Concentration Camp.

Leave Montchamp to the north (D290). After 3.5 km, turn right toward Danvou (D298). After 3.0 km, turn left toward Danvou (D26). Follow for 3.7 km and then turn right toward le Plessis-Grimoult (D165). Follow into the center of le Plessis-Grimoult and turn sharply left toward Roucamps (D54). A white-and-green sign indicating Royal Hussars Monument-Mont Pinçon lies 100 m after this turn. After 1.3 km and opposite the communications tower on the right, turn left onto the forest road. Another white-and-green CWGC sign indicates a choppy, gravel track. Follow the track for 1.3 km, then turn left and continue an additional 350 m to the memorial below road level on the right. The route is not that followed by the Hussars tanks as described below, but it is a safer route for visitors accessing the wind-swept, flat-topped summit. Be advised that the final 2 kilometers to the Hussar memorial is a rough gravel road. (48.97133, -0.63092)

At 1340 on August 6, the British 129th Brigade, 43rd Division, supported by 13/18 Hussar tanks, assaulted Mont Pinçon. Under a cover of smoke, an artillery barrage started to creep up the slope with the 5th Wiltshire Regiment following behind. While the leading companies were crossing the Druance River, German mortar and machine-gun fire fell down onto the regiment. In minutes, their commander, Lieutenant-Colonel

---

41   Augustus Janniot was also responsible for the sixteen reliefs at the Mont Valerien Memorial outside of Paris (see Chapter Sixteen).

John Pearson, was killed and the unit became disorganized. Farther north, high casualties similarly befell the 4th Somerset Regiment.

However, two troops of Squadron A tanks found the highway D165 bridge unguarded. Shortly after 1600, they drove for the summit along a narrow, steep forest track. Despite sporadic German fire, the tanks raced to the summit to the surprise of the defenders. Witnessing their daring success, the reserve 4th Wiltshire Regiment started to climb the steep incline in a single file. A brief but bitter fight against defenders on the hillside was settled with bayonets. The Wilts achieved the hilltop and dug in.

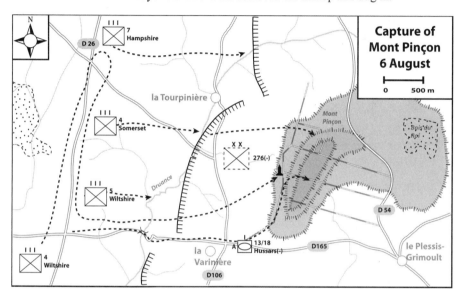

The **13/18 Hussars Monument** is slightly off the road and provides dramatic views over the surrounding countryside to the west. The top of the rose granite stone bears a bronze table of orientation, bearing the emblem of the Royal Hussars and commemorates all who served in the unit between 1922 and 1992. Battle maps beside the roadway depict the movements of infantry and armored units. An infosign provides descriptions of the local fighting.

To return to the tour at Vire, reverse direction and return to le Plessis Grimoult. Turn sharply right toward le Mesnil-Auzouf (D165). After 4.4 km, turn left toward Vire (26). Follow for 24.1 km (becomes D55) into Vire. Turn left onto Av de la Gare (D577a, becomes Av André Halbout). A large parking area sits on the right near the tourist office. (48.839614, -0.888498)

Chapter Thirteen
Battle of Caen
10 June to 20 July 1944

Late on D-Day, German reserve armor units started to receive movement orders. The gap between the 12th SS Panzer Division still arriving southwest of Caen and the German 352nd Infantry Division facing the Americans was to be filled by Panzer Lehr, commanded by Generalleutnant Fritz Bayerlein. This crack German unit, formed in 1943 from various units of elite training and demonstration troops, was probably the best equipped German Army unit with the latest armored vehicles. Panzer Lehr's difficult journey from its base near Chartres brought its leading units to the 12th SS Panzer Division's left flank at Tilly-s/Seulles on 8 June. Bayerlein's troops were being dispatched piecemeal to counter British offensive operations. It was no way to launch a concentrated armor assault to the channel as envisioned by Rommel, but both commanders realized that they had no alternative.

German commanders were severely limited in redeployment of their troops by Hitler's dictate of 'no withdrawal,' a policy which he reiterated during a 17 June meeting with von Rundstedt and Rommel. Indirectly, this mandate forced German commanders to commit their panzer forces to a purely defensive role. It also kept German forces too near the coast where they came under Allied fire from large caliber naval guns. Regardless, German defensive talents were considerable but, like a tiring boxer, they were always on their back foot responding to Montgomery's punches and jabs toward Caen.

With his first direct assaults upon Caen blocked by the timely arrival of German 21st Panzer Division and his flanking maneuver defeated at Villers-Bocage (see below), General Montgomery felt that British Second Army's revised objective was to attract German reserves to the Caen battlefield where it faced four Panzer divisions in Panzer Lehr, 12th SS, 2nd, and 21st Panzer. The action would free the US First Army to capture Cherbourg and then break out of the entrapping bocage terrain on the Allied west flank toward the Brittany ports and the open terrain in the Loire Valley.

The Battle of Caen tour begins on the western flank of British positions near Bayeux. The series of British attacks and large-scale operations aimed at capturing Caen are presented in geographic rather than chronological order to minimize traveling times. Therefore, referencing past engagements before the corresponding battlefield has been reviewed is sometimes necessary.

Operation PERCH
10 to 14 June 1944

Since the capture of Caen directly from the landing beaches proved too difficult a task, Montgomery formulated a series of set-piece attacks to capture the major Norman city. The first such operation, whose objective was to encircle Caen with a two-pincer movement utilizing British XXX Corps approaching from the west in an operation code-named PERCH and British 6th Airborne Division approaching along the east side of the Orne River in a subsidiary effort code-named TONGA. Chapter One reviewed the airborne battleground as the Battle of Bréville. British XXX Corps, led by the 50th Infantry Division, targeted occupation of the high ground east of Villers-Bocage.

The British 50th Infantry Division left Bayeux heading south toward Tilly-s/Seulles on 7 June; however, troops were fatigued from the drama of the beach assault and subsequent fighting. Their advance slowed with the increased need for rest and

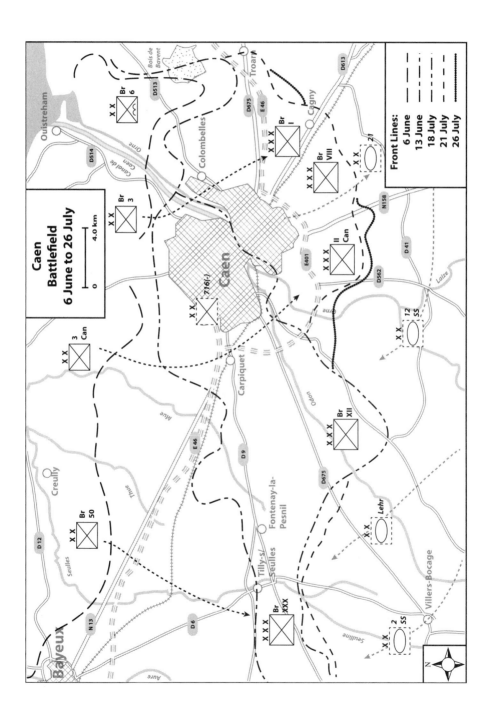

Caen
Battlefield
6 June to 26 July

Front Lines:
6 June
13 June
18 July
21 July
26 July

reinforcements. The division resumed its advance at 0830 on 10 June with their start line at the railway crossing southeast of Bayeux. The objective was to move southeast through Tilly-s/Seulles to Juvigny-s/Seulles with highway D6 as their axis of advance.

In the first days after D-Day, roving British patrols searched out enemy strengths and weaknesses while German reconnaissance units tried to fill gaps between arriving armored divisions. German resistance was spotty and easily overcome until the Germans moved stronger units into the battle zone. The terrain consisted of undulating hills sliced into innumerable parcels by streams and hedgerows of the Norman bocage. Its narrow lanes, stone walls, and tree-shaded orchards provided a multitude of positions wherein small infantry groups waged a stubborn defense based around a dug-in and camouflaged tank used as artillery or antitank gun. The tactic was to delay the British advance until a Panzer counterattack force could be assembled. Tilly-s/Seulles and nearby communities became a most telling battleground.

Battle of Lingèvres
11 to 14 June 1944

Objective	To capture the German stronghold at Lingèvres
Forces	
British	2nd Battalion, The Essex Regiment (Lieutenant-Colonel JF Higson) and 9th Battalion, The Durham Light Infantry (Lieutenant-Colonel HR Woods)
German	Elements of Panzer Lehr (Generalleutnant Fritz Bayerlein)
Result	Slow progress against an increasingly determined defense
Casualties	
British	48 killed, 201 wounded or missing
German	uncertain
Location	Lingèvres is 25 km west of Caen

Battle

A battalion of The Essex Regiment, attempting to capture Lingèvres on 11 June by moving south from Bernières, was beaten back with heavy causalities north of the village of Lingèvres. A stronger force would be necessary to dislodge the German armored infantry positioned about the minor road junction.

On 14 June, the British 50th Infantry Division's 151st Infantry Brigade attacked along a 4-kilometer front centered upon Lingèvres. It drew support from a massive bombardment by a squadron of Typhoon fighters, division and corps artillery units, Royal Naval gunfire, and even US V Corps guns firing from the west. Four companies of the 9th Battalion, Durham Light Infantry, moved along the road against Lingèvres supported by tanks of A Squadron, 4th/7th Royal Dragoon Guards, on either flank. They were met by a hail of small-arms fire from panzergrenadiers hidden in the woods north of Lingèvres. Companies A and B on the left (east) absorbed heavy casualties, especially among their officers who were targeted by German snipers. Battalion Commander Lieutenant-Colonel HR Woods[1] was killed by a mortar round. Nonetheless, Companies C and D pushed back

---

1   Lieutenant-Colonel Humphrey Reginald Woods was awarded two Military Crosses during the desert fighting in North Africa and a Distinguished Service Cross for his actions at El Alamein. Woods is buried in Bayeux War Cemetery. He died at age 28.

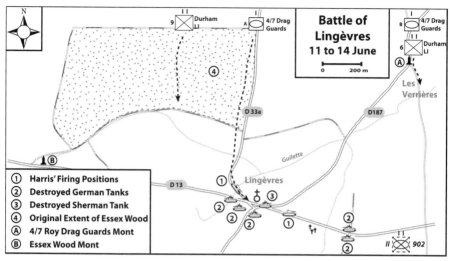

the defenders and entered the village.

The 4th Troop, A Squadron tanks, led by Lieutenant A Morrison,[2] advanced to the war memorial near the village church to control the multiple roads radiating from the town square. The troop, consisting of three 75-mm Shermans and one Sherman Firefly, held off and destroyed nine better armed and more powerful Panther tanks. That success was greeted by additional German tanks and artillery, and by 1630 the counterattack was strong enough to warrant additional air and artillery support. The village was held by the battered battalion until relieved by the 2nd Battalion, Gloucestershire Regiment, that night, but further progress was impossible. Operation PERCH was already over.

Battlefield Tour

The tour starts from Bayeux. From the ring road, proceed southeast on the Bayeux-Tilly road toward Tilly-s/Seulles (D6). Continue for 7.6 km to the small cemetery entrance on the left. Parking is possible on the wide driveway north of the cemetery. (49.209923, -0.652136)

Jérusalem War Cemetery is the smallest British Cemetery in France. It holds forty-six British soldiers, one Czech, and one unidentified body. Twenty-three of the graves belong to members of the Durham Light Infantry. They were all victims of the fighting near Tilly-s/Seulles, some having died at an Advanced Dressing Station that had been established in the nearby farm buildings. Two army chaplains are buried side-by-side, one having been killed by rifle fire while he conducted a burial service for the other. Graves appear in three curved rows to one side of the Cross of Sacrifice. The lushly landscaped perimeter reduces noise from the busy highway and brings a modicum of peace to the cemetery.

---

2   Lieutenant Alastair McLeod Morrison was awarded a Military Cross later in the war for halting a German counterattack near Arnhem, Holland. Morrison rose to the rank of major before retiring after the war. He was a noted battlefield speaker and instrumental in creating the regimental memorial near Creully. He died in 2007 at age 83.

Continue toward Tilly-s/Seulles (D6). After 900 m, turn right toward Lingèvres (D187). Follow for 2.5 km to a road junction with a monument on the right. (49.183443, -0.661315)

The **4th/7th Royal Dragoon Guards** monument marks the road junction where three Sherman tanks from B Squadron were knocked out supporting the 14 June attack by 6th Battalion, Durham Light Infantry, upon the farm hamlet of les Verrières 125 meters south. A ditch at the road junction held twelve enemy machine guns that inflicted over one hundred casualties on the men advancing through the cornfield before they were overrun. The 6th Durhams occupied les Verrières later in the day.[3]

Continue toward Lingèvres (D187) and, after 1.3 km, enter the village. Turn right toward le Haye (D13) and park near the church 100 m ahead. (49.175279, -0.672913)

Sergeant W Harris commanded a Sherman Firefly tank that took up an initial position 250 meters east. His position gave him visibility down the long slope to a depression 500 meters farther to the east toward Tilly. Harris let a captured Sherman pass to the north and focused upon two Panthers that had turned onto the highway from a side road. At a range of 400 meters, his gunner destroyed the first Panther. A second shot immobilized the second Panther. Shortly thereafter, Major J Mogg,[4] now commanding the battalion, personally destroyed the second Panther with a PIAT round.

Harris pulled back to the opposite side of the village behind a small farm north of highway D13. Later in the afternoon, He took advantage of his ambush position to destroy a third and damage a fourth Panther when they passed before him on the highway from Belle Épine (D13). He eliminated a fifth Panther trying to pass the third one blocking the highway.[5] A sixth and hidden Panther tank moved from the town center toward Longraye (D187) when it fired upon and destroyed Lt Morrison's command Sherman stationed near the memorial. Three additional Panthers likewise were knocked out to put an end to the German armor attack.

Lingèvres was destroyed during the tank battle, but it has been rebuilt in its original style. Beside the Église St-Martin, a granite stele bears a plaque in memory of the men of the **50th Northumbrian Division** who died in the battle for the village. The church holds a Roll of Honor of the servicemen killed in the action.

Continue toward le Haye for 1.3 km; turn sharp right on rural road and proceed 80 m to park entrance on the right. (49.177189, -0.689009)

The earlier attack by 2nd Battalion, The Essex Regiment, moved through one kilometer of open fields with waist-high corn. The assault went well, at first. Then German

---

3   In a locally told story, the site of the memorial was chosen because it was the temporary grave of a British soldier, believed to be Lt-Col Woods. After the fighting had moved on, a British officer arrived in a jeep and asked a local family to tend the grave of his 'cherished friend.' The family later identified the officer as General Montgomery.

4   Major John Mogg received a Distinguished Service Order for his leadership and personal actions during the battle. He survived the war, rose to the rank of general, and was knighted. He died in 2001.

5   Sergeant Wilf Harris received a Distinguished Conduct Medal, and his gunner, Trooper McKillop, was mentioned in dispatches.

Spandau machine guns, artillery, and mortars hit the leading companies from the wooded field. A frantic run put the survivors in a shallow ditch at the forest edge. Two Panther tanks appeared while German troops counterattacked. The battalion commander, Lieutenant-Colonel JF Higson,[6] called artillery down on his own positions to fight off the German assault. Despite having penetrated the bulk of the wood, the survivors withdrew the next morning under cover of smoke. The unit suffered 150 casualties of the 500 men in the attack. Days later the Durham Light Infantry suffered to retake these same stubbornly-defended orchards.

Only small sections remain of the large orchard attacked by The Essex Regiment. Originally, it ran north of the farm lane used to access the memorial park and east as far as highway D33a. Nonetheless, a small roadside park holds a memorial stele to the sacrifices of the regiment. The polished black stone is inscribed to identify this as **Essex Wood**. The rear of the stele presents a stainless steel battlefield map indicating the direction of the attack and the extent of the original orchard.

> Reverse direction and return to the church square in Lingèvres. From there, proceed east toward Tilly-s/Seulles (D13) for 2.6 km to the cemetery on the right. (49.173848, -0.638065)

Battle of Tilly-s/Seulles
8 to 19 June

Objective	To capture the town of Tilly-s/Seulles.
Forces	
British	56th Infantry Brigade (Brigadier EC Pepper)
German	Elements of Panzer Lehr (Generalleutnant Fritz Bayerlein)
Result	Successful after a long bloody battle
Casualties	
British	414 killed, wounded, or missing (including 203 men of 2nd Essex, mostly at Essex Wood)
German	uncertain
Location	Tilly-s/Seulles is 21 km west of Caen

Battle

On 11 June, the 2nd Battalion, The Gloucestershire Regiment, and 2nd South Wales Borderers moved past Bucéels toward Tilly. Shortly after passing through le Pont de la Guillette between the two towns, German tanks were spotted on the hills to the east. Despite machine-gun and mortar fire, the infantry moved into Tilly, but their supporting tanks dared not follow. Without tanks, the infantry had no answer to German armor, and although they fought to the town centre in vicious hand-to-hand combat, they could go no farther. Both battalions withdrew to high ground north of town. A repeating pattern followed as opposing forces entered into and were forced to withdraw from the town as it changed hands twenty-three times over the next five days. Amidst savage fighting and crashing salvos of naval gunfire, Tilly-s/Seulles was gradually reduced to rubble.

---

6   Lieutenant-Colonel Higson was relieved of his command that morning for not providing antitank-gun cover.

During the evening of 15/16 June, Panzer Lehr and 12th SS Panzer Divisions withdrew from forward positions along the front from Lingèvres to St-Manvieu in order to shorten their main line of defense and create divisional reserves. Although the German troops had withdrawn, shelling and booby-traps kept taking their toll. Tilly-s/Seulles remained a front-line village until mid-July. It had taken 50th Infantry Division eleven days to move the 12 kilometers from Bayeux, but it had cost Panzer Lehr dearly with over 100 tanks destroyed.

Battlefield Tour

The **Tilly-s/Seulles War Cemetery** exhibits a ceremonial stone gateway to a central aisle flanked with grave plots. The cemetery holds 990 Commonwealth and 232 German graves. The cemetery was a battlefield during the post-Tilly fighting; however, most of the burials occurred after the August breakout battles. As such, most of the dead come from British regiments and a mix of units is represented in addition to those from the local fighting.

> Continue east to the next intersection and turn right on the unnamed rural road (not the best of highways but used for only a short distance.). After 500 m, turn left (rue du 18 Juin 1944) and continue 180 m to the ruins on the left. (49.170639, -0.634407)

Tilly-s/Seulles

The destroyed house on the rue de 18 Juin 1944 on the edge of the village created a remembrance of the destruction resulting from the battle and as a memorial to those who died in the fighting. Tilly was completed destroyed and rebuilt after the war, which accounts for its uncommonly modern appearance and wide streets.

> Continue along rue du 18 Juin 1994 for 600 m; turn right to continue on the same street. Park near the chapel on the left 100 m ahead. (49.174735, -0.62672)

Musée de la Bataille de Tilly

Chapelle Notre-Dame-du-Val   14250 Tilly-s/Seulles
Tel: +33 (0)6 07 59 46 02   Fax: +33 (0)2 31 80 72 89
Email: tilly1944@neuf.fr   Web: http://www.tilly1944.com

The museum is housed in the small 12th-century Romanesque Chapel Notre-Dame du Val located in what has been renamed place de Essex Regiment. Through simple displays of artifacts, maps, photographs, and a few weapons, the museum presents the fierce battle which swirled around Tilly, Lingèvres, St-Pierre, Hottot-les-Bagues, and Villers-Bocage for three weeks in June 1944.

Open Saturdays, Sundays, and holidays from May through September from 10:00 to 12:00 and from 14:00 to 18:00. Admission fee; Normandy Pass accepted; handicap accessible.

The grounds of the museum hold several memorials to the fighting. The most dominant is the swirling polished pink granite monument dedicated to the seventy-six civilian deaths which occurred during the battle. The barrel and recoil mechanism of a **British 6-pounder antitank gun** is mounted upon stone supports garnered from the town's wreckage. Also, in front of the chapel, a stele remembers the British and Canadian soldiers who died during the June and July fighting around Tilly. A stone displaying the emblem of the **24th Lancers** lies to the left of the museum entrance. To the far left along the roadside, an iron statue of **Jeanne d'Arc** stands with its heart torn away by an errant artillery shell. A **NTL Totem** is nearby.

> Continue past the chapel to place général de Gaulle and turn left (this requires a tricky little maneuver to turn left onto a frontage road, proceed 50 m, and make a quick right to access the main street). Continue a short distance before bearing right onto rue du Stade (D13). Follow the highway for 600 m (becomes rue de la Varende); bear left to the church in St-Pierre. (49.178204, -0.618609)

The 8th Battalion, Durham Light Infantry, moved southwest from Creully on 9 June. Pushing against light reconnaissance resistance, it passed through Audrieu to Point 103, a narrow 2-kilometer-long, east-west ridgeline southeast of the village. Ahead, the company saw St-Pierre and Tilly-s/Seulles in the Seulles River Valley. German troops were waiting in St-Pierre and, when the lead company came into view, they opened fire with machine gun and mortars. A short engagement in the gardens and houses drove the German defenders from the village and established a strong position about the church, but the German infantry held onto the Seulles bridge. St-Pierre, however, was still under fire from German artillery on the hills of Fontenay-le-Pesnel to the east. The next day a German counterattack drove the British troops back through the village despite support from 24th Lancers tanks. The Sherwood Rangers replaced the depleted 24th Lancers only to fall victim to German heavy tanks that evening. British positions were being slowly surrounded and strangled, thereby forcing a withdrawal. The 10th Battalion, Durham Light Infantry, finally occupied the village several days later.

The rue de la Varende crosses the bridge held by German troops during the first day of the engagement. The church was the farthest advance of the Durham Light Infantry on 9 June.

> Proceed past the church on rue d'Audrieu (D82) for 850 m to the monument on the left. (49.182254, -0.610034)

A stone block stele carries a black stone plaque dedicated to the regimental officers of the **Sherwood Rangers** (Nottingham Yeomanry) killed by a German 105-mm shell during an officers meeting at this location.[7]

> Walk along the rue de Cristot (southeast) for 40 m to the structure on the right. (49.181833, -0.609669)

The exterior wall of this small house has been decorated with slate tiles inscribed with the insignia of British and American regiments and divisions that fought in the area during June 1944. In a place of honor near the gateway, a larger slate tile carries the insignia of the **Durham Light Infantry**.

---

7   Major MH Laycock MC, Captain GA Jones, and Lieutenant AL Head are buried in the Tilly-s/ Seulles British War Cemetery.

> Return to Tilly and continue 1.6 km south toward Juvigny-s/Seulles (D6). Turn right toward Caumont (D9) and continue 650 m to the cemetery on the right. (49.160323, -0.626339)

Hottot-les-Bagues War Cemetery lies less than 1 kilometer west of Juvigny-s/Seulles. On 11 July, the British 50th (Northumbrian) Infantry Division and British 49th Infantry Division launched Operation Maori to break the German lines. The assault failed, but weakened German units withdrew during the night of 17/18 July. The British then encircled Hottot and finally liberated the town on the evening of 19 July during fierce fighting that wrought heavy casualties. A new front stabilized south of the town, and sporadic fighting continued.

The cemetery stands upon the crest of a hill and presents a stone block entrance gate. It contains 1,006 Commonwealth and 132 German burials – including over 100 unidentified – most collected from battlefield burials in the vicinity. The German nationals lie in plot XI in the left rear of the cemetery. Plot I contains the grave of Brigadier J Hargest,[8] the liaison in the 50th Infantry Division when he was killed by mortar fire.

The liberation of Hottot on 19 July was the British 50th (Northumbrian) Infantry Division's last major action as the front stabilized. The division was sorely depleted and its men exhausted by the end of the battle. After forty-four days of fighting, it had suffered 673 killed, 3,072 wounded, and 1,236 missing, though it captured 3,000 enemy soldiers. It did not return to the Normandy fighting.

Battle of Villers-Bocage
13 June

On the morning of 12 June, Dempsey ordered Major-General GW Erskine's 7th Armoured Division to break from his attack against Tilly-s/Seulles and attempt a broad enveloping maneuver around the west flank of Panzer Lehr by moving east through Villers-Bocage, where a high ridge dominates the area and its slopes run steeply down to the Odon River to the south. Montgomery then planned to drop the British 1st Airborne Division south of Caen to establish a link between British 7th Armoured Division and British 51st Infantry Division, which was to sweep around Caen from the east.

The British 7th Armoured Division gained fame during the Second World War in North Africa, where it became known as 'The Desert Rats' for its rapid mobility. Later, while in Italy and although not part of the initial assault force, the division led the drive to Naples. Withdrawn from Italy to become part of the invasion, it landed on Gold Beach on 7 June. British 7th Armoured Division was often teamed with 50th Infantry Division to form XXX Corps. Its armored units supported 50th Division's infantry advance south from Bayeux.

---

8   Brigadier James Hargest, a New Zealand national, fought at Gallipoli in the First World War, earning a Distinguished Service Cross, Military Cross, and French *Legion d'honour*. After the war, he became a member of the New Zealand Parliament. During the Second World War, Hargest commanded a brigade in Crete, was taken prisoner in North Africa, and escaped from a POW camp in Italy. He died at age 52.

Objective	To sweep around Panzer Lehr Division to force its withdrawal
Forces	
British	7th Armoured Division (Major-General GW Erskine)
German	Elements of Panzer Lehr (Generalleutnant Fritz Bayerlein)
Result	Disastrous defeat for the British
Casualties	
British	378 killed, wounded, or missing; 27 tanks and 28 other vehicles destroyed
German	Uncertain, but 8 to 15 tanks lost
Location	Villers-Bocage is 26 km southwest of Caen

Battle

At approximately 0800, the leading element of 22nd Armoured Brigade, A Squadron, 4th County of London Yeomanry, commanded by Lieutenant-Colonel Lord Cranley, advanced up the road to stop on the high ground at Point 213 northeast of Villers-Bocage. Nine Cromwell and three Sherman Firefly tanks deployed on the soft shoulders of the road and their crews brewed tea during an officers' meeting. Unbelievably, the British tanks passed within 200 meters of the overnight laager of five Tiger I (PzKpfw VI) tanks of SS Heavy Panzer Battalion 101, led by SS-Obersturmführer Michael Wittmann. In a stunningly daring maneuver, Wittmann's tank charged out from the rural road and into the British column. After eliminating a Cromwell and a Sherman tank at the rear of A Squadron's column to his right, he turned left onto the highway toward Villers-Bocage. Driving toward the village, he fired shell after shell at point blank range, destroying three more Cromwells, three Stuarts, two command tanks, and thirteen soft-sided half-tracks and personnel carriers. Wittmann then exchanged fire with a Sherman Firefly, from which his vehicle received some damage, before withdrawing back toward the hill. The action has been cited as the most brilliant feat of tankmanship in the war.[9] Meanwhile, two other Tigers from Wittmann's company moved along a mud rut road south of the laager, engaged and eliminated the spearhead of the British force at Point 213, and eventually captured Lord Cranley.[10]

The battle for unfortunate Villers-Bocage was not yet over. B and C Squadrons, 4th County of London Yeomanry established defensive positions in Villers-Bocage centered about a Sherman Firefly in the place du général Leclerc and supported by infantry from the 131st Infantry Brigade. The expected German attack came from the north along the Tilly-s/Seulles road (D6) headed by fifteen PzKpfw IVs and Tigers from SS Panzer

---

9   SS-Obersturmführer Michael Wittmann was Germany's tank ace, having destroyed 138 tanks and 132 antitank guns mostly during fighting on the Eastern Front. For his actions at Villers-Bocage, Wittmann received the Swords addition to his Knight's Cross of the Iron Cross with Oak Leaves, one of Germany's highest military awards. Wittmann was killed on 8 August 1944 during a German counterattack near St-Aignan-de-Cramesnil. Controversy surrounds who killed Wittmann, but it has long been held that a Sherman Firefly from 1st Northamptonshire Yeomanry fired the killing shot that penetrated the Tiger tank's hull and ignited its ammunition. The entire crew died. Wittmann's temporary grave was not located until 1983, at which time he and his men were reburied in la Cambe German Cemetery. Wittmann died at age 30.

10   Lieutenant-Colonel Lord Arthur Cranley, later William Arthur Onslow, 6th Earl of Onslow, was held as a prisoner of war until the end of the war. He died in 1971 at age 57.

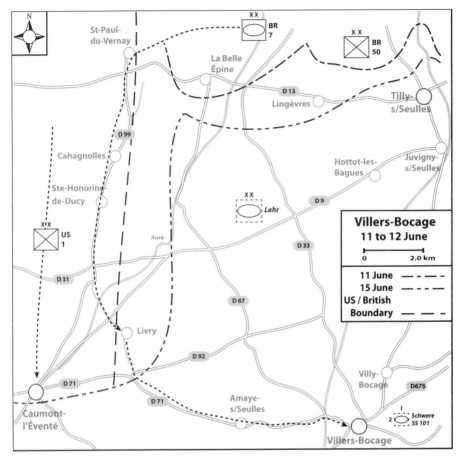

Villers-Bocage
11 to 12 June

0   2.0 km

11 June — - — -
15 June — - - —
US / British
Boundary — — —

Battalion 101. The tanks roamed the town center looking for targets. At the town's eastern end, after Wittmann's withdrawal from the village, Lieutenant W Cotton[11] established an ambush. With his four tanks and a nearby 6-pounder antitank gun, 7th Armoured exacted some measure of revenge by knocking out two PzKpfw IVs and five Tiger tanks before infiltration by German infantry forced their withdrawal.

Aftermath

As German infantry pressure increased on the men in Villers-Bocage, units withdrew under an artillery barrage and smokescreen. They formed an all-around defense on what they called the 'Island Position.' On 14 June, German troops pressured the British perimeter, almost encircling the entire position, but British and American heavy artillery kept the enemy at bay by pounding the town. After repelling a stronger attack the next day, the British started a withdrawal during the night. The British lost the chance to outflank Caen due to the daring of one experienced tanker and his comrades. The village's punishment was not complete; in the evening of 30 June, during Operation Epsom, 250 heavy bombers completed the destruction of the village by dropping 1,100 tons of bombs to interfere with assembling German armor. The ruins were finally liberated on 4 August.

---

11   Lieutenant William Cotton was awarded a Military Cross for his defense of the town.

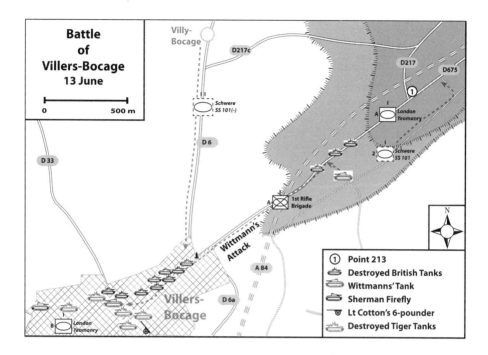

Battlefield Tour

From Juvigny-s/Seulles, proceed south toward Villers-Bocage (D6). In the eastern fringe of the town, turn left toward Caen (N175, renumbered as D675). Pass under Autoroute A84 and continue to the summit of the hill. A small sign on the right indicates Point 213 (Point 217 on modern maps). Stop along the roadway. (49.092768, -0.625733)

Point 213 shows no remains from the famous battle staged here. The road crests and flows on a long gradual slope to north and south. The position's importance for observation is obvious. The spear head of the column was trapped less than 50 meters to the northeast by two Tigers ahead and the three tanks destroyed by Wittmann to the rear. With no escape, the firefight was brief.

The rural road used by Michael Wittmann to attack the British column is 600 meters to the southwest, identified by the *Poste electrique* that still stands beside the rural road. His company's overnight laager was on the left, 170 meters along that unnamed rural road.

Reverse direction and return to the junction with the highway coming from Tilly-s/ Seulles (D6). (49.082961, -0.646021)

The approach into Villers-Bocage descends a hill typical of this region of Normandy. The **7th Armoured Division Memorial** in the intersection consists of a roughly cut, gray granite block with a bronze plaque recalling, 'with pride in gratitude those of the Seventh Armoured Division, who fought and died here for freedom on 13 June 1944.' In this intersection Wittmann and his crew abandoned his vehicle due to a damaged drive sprocket and make their escape on foot.

Continue into Villers-Bocage, following rue Clemenceau (becomes rue Pasteur) into place du maréchal Leclerc. (49.080616, -0.655414)

Villers-Bocage
The town has been rebuilt and bears little resemblance to its 1944 appearance. In the place du général Leclerc, a new Hôtel de ville and a reconstructed church face each other across an open square where British tanks and antitank guns dueled German tanks during the afternoon of 13 June 1944.

Les Offices de Tourisme du Bocage Normand
Place Charles de Gaulle   14310 Villers-Bocage
Tel: +33 (0)2 31 77 16 14
Web: http://www.bocage-normand.com/fr/index.htm

From place Jeanne d'Arc farther ahead, a Sherman Firefly tank engaged Wittmann's Tiger from the opposite end of the commercial district. Fighting brewed through the streets of Villers-Bocage for most of the day before the tanks and panzergrenadiers of Panzer Lehr and 2nd Panzer Division forced British troops to extract themselves and establish a laager north of Tracy-Bocage, 3 kilometers to the west.

Reverse direction toward Caen (D675). In the small roundabout (where the 7th Armoured Division memorial is located), take the 2nd exit and immediately in the large roundabout, again take the 2nd exit toward Villy-Bocage/Tilly-s/Seulles (D6). After 9.3 km, turn toward Fontenay-le-Pesnel (D9). After 2.2 km, enter Fontenay and turn left onto rue St-Aubin (D217). In 600 m, turn right onto rue Segrais (D217b). Follow for 260 m to the junction with Chemin de Tilly (D13), stopping at the large crucifix. (49.173217, -0.582479)

Operation MARTLET (Battle of Rauray)
(also known as Operation DAUNTLESS)
25 to 30 June 1944
A ridge south of Fontenay-le-Pesnel overlooked the line of advance to be taken during Operation EPSOM. To be successful, EPSOM required the capture this high ground to protect its western flank. The objective was assigned to the British 49th Infantry Division, in what would be its first action of the war.

Objective	To capture high ground around Rauray
Forces	
British	49th (West Riding) Infantry Division (Major-General Evelyn Barker)
German	III Battalion, SS Panzergrenadier Regiment 26 (SS-Sturmbannführer Erich Olboeter)
Result	The ridge was captured and held against repeated counterattacks

Casualties		
British	Over 390 killed or wounded	
German	45 killed, 120 wounded, and 23 missing	
Location	Fontenay-le-Pesnel is 17 km west of Caen	

Battle

At 0415 on 25 June, two infantry brigades, each supported by an attached tank unit, moved across the cornfields northwest of Fontenay-le-Pesnel and entered a heavy morning mist when they descended from Hill 102 south of Cristot. The attack stalled along the Fontenay-Juvigny-s/Seulles road (D9) when the lead units encountered enemy tank and artillery fire, especially from the bridge over the Bordel Creek. Farther west, the attack hit the boundary between Panzer Lehr and 12th SS Panzer Division and advanced over 2.5 kilometers, capturing Tessel Woods and forming a front along the Bordel Creek. *Kampfgruppe Wünsche*, formed around I Panzer Battalion of SS-Obersturmbannführer Max Wünsche's SS Panzer Regiment 12, rushed during the night to strengthen the 12th SS Division's left flank.

On 26 June, while Operation EPSOM began farther east, the fresh 1st Battalion, Tyneside Scottish, supported by 4th/7th Royal Dragoon tanks, attacked from Fontenay toward Rauray while Wünsche moved from Rauray to recover Fontenay. The two forces met head-on at dawn in an extended tank battle. Firing at close range, the Royal Dragoon Sherman Fireflys took a toll of fifteen German tanks, including, reportedly, one PzKpfw VI (Tiger) from SS Heavy Panzer Battalion 101. News of the start of EPSOM brought the German commander an order to withdraw to north of Rauray although strongpoints in Fontenay and Ferme St-Nicolas still held out.

At 0800 on 27 June, Company A, 11th Battalion, Durham Light Infantry, attacked Rauray with the objective of continuing on to Noyers-Bocage. Although much of *Kampfgruppe Wünsche* was redirected in response to Operation EPSOM, some of its positions remained manned by III Battalion, SS Panzergrenadier Regiment 26. Only six of the seventy men in the leading Durham platoons survived the next 20 minutes after they advanced into Panzergrenadier crossfire. A short, local ceasefire allowed for the recovery of the wounded. A continued attack gained Rauray that afternoon while German defenders withdrew to Bretteville. An attack on Bretteville the next day was unsuccessful, but the important ridge was held against several German counterattacks over the next two days.

Battlefield Tour

The tall Crucifix at the road junction marks the limit of the initial advance of the **11th Battalion, Royal Scots Fusiliers**, who achieved this point at 0500 on 25 June from their starting point at Boislonde 750 meters to the north. Forty men were pinned by intense machine-gun and mortar fire from fields to the north and east. A day-long battle ensued, frequently at close quarters until the arrival of Sherwood Yeomanry tanks. Fighting in the nearby buildings continued into the night while AVREs and flame-throwing Crocodiles evicted the grenadiers from their strongpoints. The Royal Scots battalion commander[12] was killed later in the fighting and was buried temporarily near the base of the crucifix. The cross remains and carries the reminders of the battle in the numerous bullets marks that still scar its surface.

---

12   Lieutenant-Colonel Alexander William Henry Montgomery-Cuninghame was killed on 3 July at age 35. He is buried in St-Manvieu War Cemetery.

Reverse direction to go southeast on highway D13. After 400 m, turn right on rue Massieu (becomes Route de Grainville, D139), passing Ferme St-Nicolas after 1.0 km. Stop at the memorial ahead on the right. (49.160758, -0.564702)

The **49th (West Riding) Division Memorial** and the cemetery to the east mark the location of intense fighting on 26 June. The memorial displays a Scottish cross covered by a stone arch. The face of an altar before the cross is engraved with the unit's 'Polar Bear' insignia, which it adopted during an earlier posting in Iceland. The back wall holds inserts with plaques presenting the various units which made up the division during their continuous and bitter fighting during the Battle of Normandy from June until August 1944.

The sometimes muddy track opposite the memorial leads directly to the cemetery. (49.160993, -0.560855)

Fontenay-le-Pesnel War Cemetery is a true battlefield cemetery holding 461 Commonwealth graves, many of them 49th Division dead from the July and August fighting, and 59 German graves of 12th SS Panzer Division (*Hitlerjugend*), largely from fighting south and west of Caen in June and July. A large number of graves at the front of the cemetery belong to the men of the Royal Tank Regiment, Royal Armoured Corps, which resulted from local armored battles. The cemetery is framed in trees, rather unusual for Commonwealth cemeteries in Europe. The Cross of Sacrifice is located on a small patio shaded by additional trees.

Return to Fontenay-le-Pesnel and turn right toward St-Manvieu-Norrey (D9). Continue for 4.4 km to the parking area on the left. A narrow path accesses the cemetery. (49.177404, -0.513922)

Operation Epsom OR The First Battle of the Odon
26 to 30 June

The Great Storm of 19 June put a temporary halt to British Second Army offensive operations until 26 June. Epsom was a combined infantry/armor assault to seize the Odon and Orne River bridges to give British armor access to the Caen-Falaise plain. With British armor south of the city, who possessed Caen would become irrelevant.

The Odon River valley, immediately to the south of the Caen-Villers-Bocage road (D675), is populated with small wooded areas, thick bushes, and some wetlands. East of the Odon, Hill 112 provides excellent observation over approaches to the Caen-Falaise plain and was the key to fighting south of Caen.

Objective	To cross the Odon River and access the Falaise Plain
Forces	
Canadian	VIII Corps (Lieutenant-General Sir Richard O'Connor)
German	Panzer Group West (General der Panzertruppen Leo Geyr von Schweppenburg)
Result	The Odon was crossed but Hill 112 could not be held

Casualties		
	British	470 killed, 2,187 wounded, and 706 missing
	German	2960 killed, wounded, or missing
Location		St-Manvieu-Norrey is 12 km west of Caen

Battle

The next attempt to outflank Caen fell to the entire British VIII Corps commanded by Lieutenant-General Sir Richard O'Connor.[13] In the rain and gloom of early morning on 26 June, sixty-thousand men and six hundred tanks passed through Canadian lines between Putot and Norrey-en-Bessin and fell upon elements of three panzer divisions – 12th SS Panzer, 2nd SS, and 21st Panzer – along a narrow front from le Mesnil-Patry to west of Carpiquet. An initial, intense bombardment by seven hundred guns, 2nd Tactical Airforce fighter airplanes, and RAF heavy bombers left the defenders only momentarily stunned. In the worst tradition of the battles at Ypres and Somme a generation earlier, three famed British divisions – the 15th (Scottish), 43rd (Wessex), and 11th Armoured – advanced across open cornfields against undamaged German positions.

After three days, the VIII Corps developed a 5-kilometer-deep salient within the enemy line. The 23rd Hussars, 11th Armoured Division, crossed the Odon to take partial possession of Hill 112 in the early morning of 28 June. It was relieved later in the day by 3rd Battalion, Royal Tank Regiment. The first German counterattack hit about 1000 from the south led by II Battalion, SS Panzer Regiment 12. Four attacks during the course of the day failed to push the British Shermans and Churchills off the hill.

On 29 June, 9th SS Panzer (*Hohenstaufen*) and 10th SS Panzer (*Frundsberg*) Divisions launched a major counterattack against the salient's western flank. The disappearance of the past two days' stormy weather allowed Allied airpower to fall against the assembled German forces. British naval units also took their toll and the German panzer advance ended with heavy losses of men and materiel. Generalmajor Hans Speidel,[14] Rommel's Chief of Staff, personally called off the attack. Moreover, the threat of pinching off the forward troops convinced General Dempsey to shut down EPSOM. The armored units were withdrawn leaving only infantry defenders. On 30 June, German troops, under a particularly effective *Nebelwerfer* barrage, reclaimed Hill 112 and its northern approaches.

Aftermath

The battle ended in a stalemate. Allied forces gained territory and attracted additional German armor to its front but still lacked the ability to conquer or encircle Caen. Panzer Group West no longer had the forces necessary to launch its planned attack to divide the British and American bridgeheads. During the battle, German Seventh Army

---

13 Lieutenant-General Richard O'Connor led British armored forces in Africa and almost destroyed a much larger Italian force in the opening days of the Western Desert Campaign. He was captured by a German reconnaissance patrol and spent two years in a POW camp before escaping in December 1943. O'Connor received a chestful of military awards during his long career. He died in 1981 at age 91.

14 Generalmajor Hans Speidel was involved in the July assassination plot on Hitler's life and was arrested by the Gestapo. He avoided trial and eventually escaped before surrendering to advancing French troops. Speidel became a historian after the war, then helped to create the postwar German Bundeswehr. In 1957 he was appointed Commander-in-Chief of NATO ground forces in Central Europe. He died in 1984 at age 87.

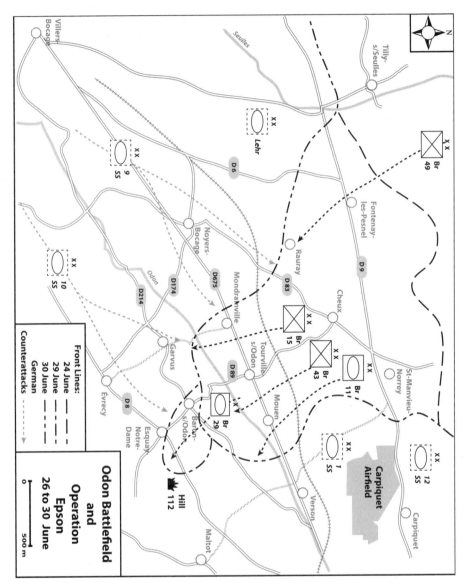

commander Generaloberst Friedrich Dollmann died of a heart attack;[15] he was replaced by
SS-Obergruppenführer Paul Hausser.

Battlefield Tour

The **St-Manvieu War Cemetery** is accessed along a narrow turfed alley and
through a gateway flanked by stone columns. An aisle runs along the right (east) side of
the grave plots. At the halfway point, a center aisle divides the cemetery and holds the
Stone of Remembrance and Cross of Sacrifice. The cemetery holds 1,627 Commonwealth

---

15   The controversy regarding Dollmann's death suggests that he committed suicide after hearing
that he was to be court-martialed because of the fall of Cherbourg.

burials, mostly from the area's battles during June and July 1944. Four grave plots in the rear corners hold 555 German burials.

> Continue 140 m and turn left toward Bretteville-l'Orgueilleuse (D83) and enter St-Manvieu. After 700 m, turn right onto rue de l'Église. After 600 m, turn left onto rue du Perron (D170) and continue for 75 m to the gated driveway on the right (private property). (49.181409, -0.501533)

On 26 June, the 15th (Scottish) Division's 44th (Lowland) Infantry Brigade led by 6th Battalion, Royal Scots Fusiliers, entered St-Manvieu at 0730. Vicious hand-to-hand fighting occurred among the village's narrow lanes and stone walls. On the eastern edge of the village, I Battalion, SS Panzergrenadier Regiment 26, headquarters had been under attack for three hours when a flame throwing Churchill Crocodile set up at the long drive to the chateau. SS-Unterscharführer E Dürr volunteered to eliminate the threat. Twice he hit the tank with *Panzerfaust* rockets without damaging it. Although wounded in the chest by machine-gun fire, he advanced a third time with a magnetic mine. Staggering from his wounds, Dürr affixed the mine to the tank but was unable to retreat before it exploded. The tank was destroyed, and Dürr was severely wounded in the legs. Bleeding profusely, he was rescued by comrades and brought to a sheltered position behind the headquarters. He died four hours later.[16] The headquarters held until dark when the men slipped through the fields to their own lines. Panzers and panzergrenadiers attacked twice to recapture the town but were repulsed both times.

> Reverse direction and continue toward Cheux (D170) for 2.5 km to the *mairie* in the center of the town. (49.165536, -0.525166)

On 26 June, 2nd Battalion, The Glasgow Highlanders, left St-Manvieu. The Highlanders reached the northern edge of Cheux at 1100 after sustaining nearly 200 casualties – 25 percent of their complement; but with tank support, the line of villages along the Route de Caen (D170) was taken from St-Manvieu through to Cheux.

The 11th Armoured Division passed through the Scottish lines, but the narrow lanes, framed by 2-meter-high verges, slowed tank movement while heavy rains turned the byways to churned mud. The crush of armored vehicles pushing their way through the narrow, rubble-filled streets of Cheux severely constrained the armor available to push onto and past Hill 112.

Cheux lacks its 1944 appearance because it has been rebuilt with a modern, less-congested road network. A special **Memorial to Operation Epsom** has been erected in front of the *mairie*. Three plaques list British Army units that participated in the battle, especially noting the first action of the 43rd (Wessex) Division. A **NTL Totem** is adjacent.

> Continue for 80 m and then turn left toward Tourville-s/Odon (D89). Follow for 2.7 km crossing over the A84/E401 and around a wide curve to the left. Soon after the curve, turn left onto Hameau de Colleville and follow the road for 2.5 km (changes name several times, finally becoming rue du major Legrand). Stop at the memorial on the left. (49.149538, -0.475845)

---

16   SS-Unterscharführer Emil Dürr was awarded the Knight's Cross of the Iron Cross posthumously. He died at age 24.

A large trio of plaques commemorates Major L Legrand,[17] a Belgian officer attached to the 23rd Hussars of the 11th Armoured Division's 29th Armoured Brigade, and the four troopers[18] of Sherman tank #149901. They all died nearby on 27 June when Major Legrand led four Sherman tanks along rue du Major Legrand, where they were hit with fire from German 88-mm guns. Three of the tanks burst into flames, including that of Major Legrand.

> Continue on rue du major Legrand until the highway junction. Turn right toward Mouen (D675). After 2.1 km, turn left onto rue de l'Église and proceed to the church. (49.149538, -0.475845)

Tourville-s/Odon and, more importantly, its bridge across the Odon was a primary objective of Operation EPSOM. The 227th Brigade, 15th (Scottish) Infantry Division, supported by tanks of the 23rd Hussars, pushed German infantry from Colleville 1.0 kilometer to the north, but was temporarily stopped by the tanks of the 12th SS Panzer Division. On the second day of the offensive, massive British firepower overcame the panzers, and 227th Brigade infantry subsequently moved onto the bridge south of the town.

The graves of six British soldiers killed in the battle stand in the church graveyard behind the west entrance of the church. The commune constructed a stone block wall behind the graves known as the **Battle of the Odon Memorial** in memory of the soldiers of the 15th Scottish, 43rd Wessex, and 53rd Welsh Divisions killed during the battle.

> Continue passing the south side of the church. After 270 m, merge left onto rue du Château; after an additional 200 m, turn left onto D89 (unsigned, but the road forward has no outlet). Proceed 270 m to the memorial on the right. (49.135638, -0.501482)

The **Monument de la 15th Division Écossais** commemorates the units and actions of the 15th (Scottish) Division, which engaged the troops and tanks of the 2nd SS Panzer Division over control of the bridges over the Odon River during Operation EPSOM. On the afternoon of 27 June, the stone bridge a short distance ahead was captured, allowing 11th Armoured Division's tanks to cross the river.

The monument, a gray granite obelisk topped by a crying lion, carries plaques on all sides from divisional units familiar from First World War engagements, including the Gordon, Seaforth, and Argyll and Sutherland Highlanders, Royal Scots, King's Own Scottish Borderers, and many more. The plaques are surmounted by the simple words 'Scotland, the Brave.'

> Continue toward Esquay-Notre-Dame (D89) and, after 800 m, cross the stone bridge over the Odon and park on the right. (49.130359, -0.499143)

The 2nd Argyll and Sutherland Highlanders supported by tanks of the 23rd

---

17   Captain Louis Henri Legrand, a Belgian officer in the 22nd Regiment d'Artillerie à Cheval, fought at the Albert Canal and was taken prisoner on 29 May 1940. He escaped (twice) before making his way to England through Spain and Portugal. He fought at El Alamein, where he received the Distinguished Service Order for his actions. His body was never recovered.

18   Trooper Walter Apps, age 30, and Trooper Arthur Salt, age 21, are buried in Bayeux War Cemetery; Trooper Alfred Howarth, age 28, is buried in St-Manvieu War Cemetery; Trooper William Blackett, age 35, is remembered on the Bayeux Memorial to the Missing.

Hussars fought house-to-house through Colleville against elements of the 12th SS Division's Reconnaissance Battalion. They seized the unblown, single-arch stone bridge at 2000 on 27 June and continued forward leaving six antitank guns to protect it.

The Odon River hardly seems worthy of the effort, being barely 3-meters wide. However, its steep and marshy banks barred a safe tank passage without a bridge. Note the narrow, winding approaches to the bridge, which limited the flow of armored vehicles. A **NTL Totem** is on the east side of the bridge.

Continue 1.1 km, then turn right toward Gavrus (D214). Follow for 1.7 km, then turn right at the 'T' junction (rue Royal Scots) and proceed 450 m and then turn right onto rue de l'Église (still D214). A stone stele under a tree on the corner commemorates the **15th (Scottish) Division**. (49.117584, -0.512677)
Follow rue de l'Église for 400 m as it passes through the village. Turn right onto rue du Moulin (D139) and continue 550 m to the Gavrus bridge. (49.122162, -0.518847)

The morning after the capture of the Tourville bridge, the 2nd Argyll and Sutherland Highlanders progressed 2.5 kilometers along the marshy banks of the Odon to capture the Pont de Mehaye at Gavrus. They held the bridge for three days under mortar and artillery bombardment until the 30 June German counterattack. It remained in German hands until 16 July. A memorial stele describes the events with an inscribed plastic infosign (French only).

Although not in chronological sequence, a review of further struggles for the Odon River and Hill 112 is convenient from this location.

Operations GREENLINE and POMEGRANATE
or The Second Battle of the Odon
15/16 to 19 July 1944

Operations GREENLINE and POMEGRANATE were subsidiary operations designed to engage the II SS Panzer Corps in a war of attrition on the west side of the Orne River while preparations for the breakthrough Operation GOODWOOD east of the Orne were completed. GREENLINE's objective was to capture Hill 112 from the village of Gavrus through Évrecy and on to the Orne River. POMEGRANATE's objective was the high ground at Point 213 east of Villers-Bocage.

Objective	To maintain pressure on German forces along the Odon front.
Forces	
British	XII Corps (Lieutenant-General Neil Ritchie) and XXX Corps (Lieutenant-General Gerard Bucknall)
German	II SS Panzer Corps (SS-Obergruppenführer Wilhelm Bittrich)
Result	No significant gains, but the operations were felt to be strategically successful.
Casualties	
British	3,500 killed, wounded, or missing
German	2,000 killed, wounded, or missing

Location	Évrecy is 16 km southwest of Caen

Battle

The assault by British XII Corps'[19] 15th (Scottish) Division, with 34th Tank Brigade and a brigade of 53rd (Welsh) Division attached, fell upon the German 277th Infantry Division holding the front line as part of II SS Panzer Corps. The nighttime attack started at 2330 on 15 July under artificial moonlight created by reflecting searchlight beams onto low-lying clouds. The 8th Battalion, Royal Scots, moved along the south bank of the Odon to capture Gavrus by 0800 and Bougy a few hours later, taking 170 prisoners. The Welsh 158th Brigade, led by the Royal Welsh Fusiliers, was to capture Évrecy but was repulsed by a strong counterattack by German 276th Infantry Division. The commitment of the 9th SS Panzer Division on 17 July wrested any gains and re-established the front line. After two days of intense fighting, the operation ended although smaller scale attacks and counterattacks of little strategic importance continued for days.

POMEGRANATE began on 16 July with the XXX Corps' 59th (Staffordshire) Division attacking on GREENLINE's right flank from Rauray against the German 276th and 277th Infantry Divisions and 2nd Panzer Division. Vendes and Hottot-les-Bagues were captured, but the assault stalled in front of Noyers-Bocage. The operation ended on 19 July.

Reverse direction and follow D139 for 2.8 km into Évrecy to the junction with highway (D8). A small park approximately 50 m to the right holds a **Memorial to the Civilian Victims** of the 15 June Allied bombing of the town and to those killed after the war by landmines. (49.100503, -0.50138)
Turn left toward Esquay-N-Dame/Caen (D8). A **NTL Totem** stands near the church cemetery ahead. Continue for 1.0 km to the memorial on the left. (49.107032, -0.491837)

During Operation GREENLINE, the 158th (Royal Welch) Brigade twice attacked Évrecy from the north (4th and 6th Battalions) and northwest (7th Battalion) on the night of 16/17 July 1944 against prepared positions of the 10th SS Panzer Division. Despite losses of one-third to one-half of 4th Battalion's forces, Évrecy was not taken until a German withdrawal on 4 August.

On the outskirts of Évrecy, the **Royal Welch Fusiliers Monument** commemorates 235 men of the regiment's 4th, 6th, and 7th Battalions who died in the June-through-August fighting and the memory of the French civilians killed in combat. The black stone plaque displays the unit's red dragon insignia. The dedication is repeated in Welsh as well as French. Beside the memorial are two beautiful white ceramic plaques mounted on gray granite pedestals which present in French and English the role of the 158th Royal Welsh Infantry Brigade in the battle for the liberation of Évrecy. The 7th Battalion's attack passed directly over the monument grounds. Grain fields behind the memorial to the west present the battlefield. Across the road, the terrain descends into the Odon Valley.

Continue for 3.0 km and stop at the memorial near the top of the hill. (49.123012, -0.461018)

---

19   Lieutenant-General Neil Ritchie had been relieved for the British Eight Army's poor performance against Rommel's Afrikakorps at Tobruk in June 1942. Redeemed by General Alanbrooke, he commanded the 52nd Division and XII Corps in northwest European fighting. After the war he held numerous high military and corporate positions. He died in 1983 at age 86.

Battle of Caen   321

Operation Jupiter or Battle of Hill 112
10 to 11 July

Caen had fallen to the Allies during Operation Charnwood (see below), but German resistance remained strong between the Odon and Orne Rivers. General Dempsey ordered Operation Jupiter, a renewed attack upon Hill 112, the boomerang-shaped, broad, flat highland that commanded observation over the wheat and rapeseed fields between the Odon and Orne Rivers. The Germans were equally keen to retain the hill which Rommel called the key to the whole of Normandy.

Objective		To expand the Odon River bridgehead with the capture of Hill 112 and nearby villages.
Forces		
	British	43rd (Wessex) Division (Major-General GI Thomas)
	German	9th SS Panzer Division (SS-Brigadeführer Sylvester Stadler) and 10th SS Panzer Division (SS-Oberführer Heinz Harmel)
Result		The hill remained in German hands.
Casualties		
	British	Over 2000 killed, wounded, or missing
	German	4,180 killed, wounded, or missing
Location		Hill 112 is 12 km southwest of Caen

Battle

The relatively fresh 43rd (Wessex) Division assumed the bridgehead between Verson and Baron-s/Odon from the 15th Division. Operation Jupiter started at 0500 on 10 July, with an impressive air and artillery barrage. The 43rd Division's 129th Infantry Brigade broke through between Verson and Baron-s/Odon to move toward the hill, held at that time by I and III Battalions, SS Panzergrenadier Regiment 22. Meanwhile, the division's 130th Infantry Brigade drove east toward Éterville and Maltot. The initial attack on Hill 112 by 5th Battalion, The Wiltshire Regiment, advanced across the open, lower slopes but could not secure the crest against machine guns and hidden riflemen. By 0800, 4th Battalion, Somerset Light Infantry, took the lead. Panzergrenadiers' slit trenches were overcome but only after suffering a crippling level of casualties to the Somerset's command structure; for example, its Company A was now commanded by a sergeant. Nevertheless, they crested the hill and entered a walled pasture, but further progress was impossible against concentrated German fire brought by the addition of two companies of PzKpfw IVs and a battalion of Panzergrenadier Regiment 29 infantry. The pasture changed hands twice before noon.

At 2230, the 5th Battalion, Duke of Cornwall Light Infantry, supported by a squadron of tanks and four 17-pounder antitank guns, launched a night attack and took the northern half of the cattle pasture against the 10th SS Panzer *Frundsberg* Division. It fought off counterattacks led by Tiger tanks of the SS Heavy Panzer Battalion 102 before finally being pushed off the top, having suffered 240 casualties – or 40 per cent of their men and most of their officers. As both sides were exhausted, neither could make any further progress. When the intense fighting eased, each side held half of a hill. As a measure of the intensity of the fighting, over fifty destroyed Churchill tanks lay scattered across the

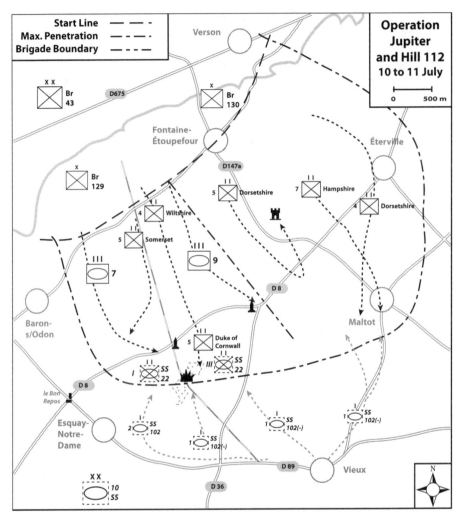

battlefield.

Aftermath

The battle for Hill 112 was one of the most horrific in Normandy. The land was pockmarked from artillery shells and bombs. Bodies lay everywhere, and the smoldering carcasses of burnt-out tanks littered the hillsides. British and German casualties were so high that replacements became difficult to obtain. The fighting power of the 9th and 10th SS Panzer Divisions was shattered. [20] Troop levels had been reduced to a small fraction of their pre-battle levels, sometimes as low as five or six men to a company.

Hill 112 remained in German hands until the American breakout in August. At that time, the Germans withdrew and the 53rd (Welsh) Division occupied the hill without a fight.

---

20   These two divisions were unexpectedly discovered to be refitting near Arnhem during Operation MARKET GARDEN in September 1944.

Battlefield Tour

The granite block stele topped with a dragon plaque commemorates the memory of all ranks of the **43rd (Wessex) Division** and marks the center of Hill 112. The site is completely surrounded by plowed fields, the devastated landscape of 1944 having returned to peaceful uses. A nearby **NTL Totem** likens the fighting on Hill 112 to that around Verdun during the First World War. The 19th-century stone cross, erected by a wealthy merchant in thanksgiving for recovery from an illness, is known as **Croix des Filandriers**; to German soldiers the site became known as the 'Hill of Calvary' for its enormous suffering.

Across chemin Haussé, an ancient Roman road also known as chemin du Duc Guillaume because it supposedly was once used by William the Conqueror, a memorial park marked with flagpoles along the highway holds a gray granite **table of orientation** indicating the positions of Allied and German units during their struggle for the hill. The location demonstrates the advantage of Hill 112 to view the Caen battlefield. Taller structures in Caen are clearly visible to the northeast, bocage to north and east, and the Caen-Falaise plain to the south. A beautifully refurbished **Churchill tank** commemorates the tank crews and support services who took part in the battle for Hill 112 from June to August 1944. (49.123229, -0.460246)

Walk south along the chemin Haussé. The wooded area behind the memorial is known as **Cornwall Wood (Bois Calloué)**, in memory of the 5th Duke of Cornwall Light Infantry, which fought so desperately to gain it. The battalion attacked from the crossroads along the line of the chemin with two companies on each side. Company B first approached the hedgerow encircling the pasture and met scything machine-gun fire that almost wiped out the company. Company A came forward supported by tanks of the Royal Scots Greys Regiment and eliminated the enemy positions. As resistance on the right was less severe, that wooded area was readily captured. A hastily organized counterattack by 9th SS Panzer Division troops failed to dislodge the Cornwall troops. By first light, the following morning, Tiger tanks moved from Esquay-Notre-Dame against the southern slopes. Their massive firepower systematically destroyed Shermans and antitank guns, halftracks, and Bren carriers of the Cornwalls. The infantry executed a disorganized withdrawal under cover of smoke. (49.119957, -0.458808)

A memorial stele has been erected along the fence line encouraging visitors to 'Respect this place, these trees – here men have suffered, many have died – honour life!' Although some of the wooded area has been altered since 1944, strands of barbed wire and pits used as shelter from artillery or aerial bombardment still remain.

Continue 1.2 km toward Caen (D8) to the next intersection. (49.127259, -0.445397)

The second part of Operation Jupiter consisted of an attack by 130th Infantry Brigade from the Odon toward the Orne River north and east of Hill 112. Each of the brigade's battalions was assigned an objective. The 5th Battalion, Dorset Regiment's target was Château de Fontaine; the 4th Battalion, Dorset Regiment, to Éterville; and 7th Battalion, Hampshire Regiment, to Maltot. They were supported by Churchill and Sherman tanks of the 44th Royal Tank Regiment. In opposition was the III Battalion, SS Panzergrenadier Regiment 1, supported by thirty tanks, including one company of Tiger tanks and forty-one *Sturmgeschütz* self-propelled assault guns.

The Château de Fontaine was taken at 0615 on 10 July, and Éterville less than two hours later. By 0955, Maltot was reported as taken, but a German counterattack led by Tiger tanks knocked out twelve Churchill tanks and drove the infantry from the town. British attacks by 5th Dorsets from Château de Fontaine and again later in the day by 4th Dorsets proved inadequate. The second attack suffered bombing by Allied Typhoons in the confused engagement. On 11 July, Panzergrenadiers fought their way into Éterville but were unable to hold the town.

A stele commemorates the **5th Battalion Dorsetshire Regiment**, which, in its first engagement, captured the Château de Fontaine, visible behind the cluster of trees 1.1 km to the north. Despite a success signal sent early in the day, Panzergrenadier holdouts continued fighting with snipers camouflaged in the farm's outbuildings, ponds, and woods until they were rooted out.

Continue toward Caen (D8) for 1.0 km. At the roundabout, take the third exit toward Fontaine-Étoupefour (D147a). Follow the road for 5.3 km, passing Château de Fontaine and crossing over the A84/E401. The road changes names several times. Stop at a convenient location on the west side of the airport. (49.167647, -0.477777)

Operation Windsor
4 to 5 July

As the battle along the Odon River died down and American forces completed the capture of Cherbourg, a short pause in Normandy offensive operations occurred. German losses incurred during the Battle of Hill 112 precluded their launching an offensive. Allied forces needed to be repositioned.

On 2 July, Hitler's displeasure with his senior commanders' repeated requests to withdraw out of range of the Allied naval guns led him to replace OB West commander Generalfeldmarschall Gerd von Rundstedt with Generalfeldmarschall Günther von Kluge. The next day, Panzer Group West commander General von Schweppenburg[21] was replaced by General der Panzertruppen Heinrich Eberbach. The 12th SS Panzer Division was now commanded by SS-Brigadeführer Kurt Meyer, succeeding SS-Brigadeführer Fritz Witt,who was killed by Allied naval fire on 14 June.[22] Of the top German commanders, only Rommel kept his position.[23]

Operation Windsor was a frontal assault upon the airport conducted by the 3rd Canadian Infantry Division. The expanse of level ground that was Carpiquet airfield had been converted into a virtual killing field by SS Panzergrenadier Regiment 26. The approaches were mined and wired. The area was dotted with pillboxes and covered by

---

21   General der Panzertruppe Leo Dietrich Franz Freiherr Geyr von Schweppenburg was a First World War cavalry officer who studied armor warfare between the wars while also serving in diplomatic roles. Schweppenburg commanded a panzer division in the Polish Invasion and a panzer corps in the Invasion of France in 1940. His panzer corps played a leading role in the drive upon Moscow during the Invasion of Russia. He was captured by American troops late in the war and held as a POW until 1947. Schweppenburg participated in the structuring of the postwar German Bundeswehr. He died in 1974 at age 87.

22   SS-Brigadeführer Fritz Witt was 36 years old when he died. He is buried in Champigny-St-André German Cemetery near Chartres.

23   On 17 July, Rommel's staff car was strafed by an Allied warplane. His wounds were serious and required hospitalization. Three days later, anti-Nazi members of the German military attempted to assassinate Hitler. Rommel's prior knowledge of the plot became known but, because of his hero reputation, he was offered the option of suicide rather than a trial that would also threaten his entire family. Rommel swallowed poison on 14 October. He was 52 years old.

crossing fire from machine guns and antitank guns. Mortars and artillery had pre-targeted every significant site.

The Canadian attack was led by four battalions of the 7th and 8th Canadian Infantry Brigades supported by tank units, five hundred artillery pieces, Typhoon fighter-bombers, and the specialized tanks of the 79th Armoured Division.

Objective	To capture the town of Carpiquet and its airfield
Forces	
Canadian	3rd Infantry Division (Major-General Rod Keller)
German	200 men from SS Panzergrenadier Regiment 25 and 150 men from I Battalion, SS Panzergrenadier Regiment 26
Result	The attack was partially successful, but it established a dangerous stalemate.
Casualties	
Canadian	123 killed, 254 wounded or missing
German	32 killed, 48 wounded, and 75 missing
Location	Carpiquet is 6 km west of Caen

Battle

At 0515 on 4 July, after a bombardment by field artillery and the nine 16-inch guns of the battleship HMS *Rodney*, three battalions of 8th Canadian Infantry Brigade attacked Carpiquet village from the west, north of the current highway D9, supported by M10 Tank Destroyers and 'Crocodile' flame-throwing tanks.

German commanders, warned of the attack by monitoring tank radio traffic, laid down a counterbarrage on advancing Canadian troops and caused substantial casualties. The special tanks, flame throwers, and AVREs, handled German strong points until the congestion of the destroyed village requiring infantry in house-to-house fighting to clear the village.

Although the village was taken, bunkers around the airport control tower and southern hanger area, stubbornly held by SS Panzergrenadier Regiment 26, presented a more difficult objective. In what amounted to a separate battle, the Royal Winnipeg Rifles crossed the fields from Marcelet. The advance created a narrow salient such that German guns from east and south could concentrate their firepower upon the Winnipegs. The hangers were taken but could not be held, and the Canadians withdrew. The repulse of the Royal Winnipeg Rifles' assault on the southern hangers led to the cancellation of the planned attack on the control buildings.[24]

The III Battalion, SS Panzergrenadier Regiment 1, supported by tanks from the 12th SS Panzer Division, counterattacked the exposed Carpiquet village salient from Franqueville at 0230 on 5 July. The panzergrenadiers stormed across the railway line but were stopped by Canadian machine-gun fire at the edge of the village. The fighting ended with the Canadians in control of the village and the northern part of the airfield and the

---

24   The handling of forces during the attack upon Carpiquet airfield, especially the lack of armored support for the Royal Winnipeg Rifles, severely damaged the reputation of Major-General Rodney Keller. His voluntary resignation was refused, but he operated under a cloud until wounded by American bombers during Operation TOTALIZE. He never again held command. Keller died in 1954 at age 53.

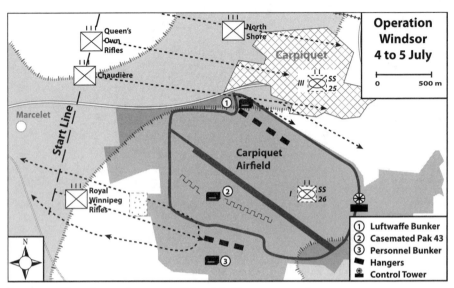

Germans still on the southern part of the airfield.

Battlefield Tour

The Royal Winnipeg Rifles attacked across this open plain from the west. Its objectives were the hangers and headquarter bunkers 1.5 kilometers to the east. The headquarters, defended by three reduced companies totaling approximately one hundred men, received support from five PzKpfw IVs sited near what is now the eastern end of the modern runway. Canadian armor support was hesitant and at first only supported the infantry movement by firing from the rear. The Winnipeg commander, Lt-Col JM Meldram, demanded closer support. One platoon of tanks advanced, but the 'Crocodiles' were easy victims for the PzKpfw IVs of SS Panzer Regiment 12.[25] The lead infantry units reached and entered the nearest airport hanger, but after hours of close quarters fighting, Lt-Col Meldram ordered a retreat of 800 meters to a small wooded area. The action was repeated in the afternoon with the Winnipegs again reaching the hangers but, against the concentrated fire, they again retreated, this time back to Marcelet. The unit suffered 132 casualties.

The hangers were visible during the approach through the open, exposed field but are now long gone. Although defensive structures remain, airport security prohibits access. The two wooded areas in the distance mark the crest of the shallow slope and provided an inadequate shelter to the withdrawing Winnipegs.

Continue (D147a) to the large traffic circle and take the second exit toward Carpiquet (D9). After 2.5 km, turn into the Aéroport de Caen-Carpiquet. Park and walk to the northwest end of the airport terminal. (49.183646, -0.459741)

The 8th Canadian Infantry Brigade began its attack on Carpiquet, moving east through the fields to the north. The Régiment de la Chaudière attacked along the line

---

25   SS-Oberscharführer Richard Rudolf was awarded a Knight's Cross of the Iron Cross for destroying six tanks in the engagement. He died in 2004 at age 81.

of the highway; the North Shore Regiment along the south side of the railway line; and the Queen's Own Rifles, the reserve battalion, in between. The village was held by one company of III Battalion, SS Panzergrenadier Regiment 25.

The battalions entered the village in line about 90 minutes after the start of the bombardment, despite heavy losses from German counterbattery fire. The Chaudière took the south part of the village and the northern airport hangers. The 'Crocodile' flame throwers cleared the concrete pillboxes on the airport.

The dark, brooding concrete of an intact **Luftwaffe personnel bunker** remains adjacent to the regional airport's terminal. The bunker was constructed substantially below ground level; the entrance trench that led to the bunker entrance has been buried. The roof held a machine-gun tobruk on one corner and an armored periscope that now is only identifiable by its damaged iron remains.

Walk to the far end of the terminal buildings. (49.182825, -0.458497)

The current terminal and control tower rest on the site of the northern hangers taken by the Regiment de la Chaudière. The 1944 control buildings were to the southeast in what is now an abandoned military complex. Between the terminal and control tower, a white-stone memorial stele to the **8th Canadian Infantry Brigade** and attached units, topped with a Canadian Maple Leaf, pays homage to 'our Canadian brothers' who fought for control of the airfield.

Exit the airport and turn right toward Caen (D9). After 800 m, stop at the stone ruin on the left. (49.184193, -0.447551)

Carpiquet

The village of Carpiquet suffered a five-hour bombardment by mortars and rockets which churned the already damaged buildings into rubble. Therefore, Carpiquet was rebuilt after the war in a more modern design. Gone are many of the stone buildings and narrow byways. However, a remnant of the village church has been preserved and now stands before a modest Norman cottage. Its plaque states: 'In remembrance of 4 July 1944, homage to the commune of Carpiquet and its Canadian liberators.' A newer plaque of black polished granite commemorates the **Fort Garry Horse**, which provided tank support during the assault on the village.

A granite block monument dedicated to the officers and men of the **North Shore (New Brunswick) Regiment** and those civilians killed in the fighting stands at the front of a small park 75 meters to the east. Nearby is the **NTL Totem**. (49.184083, -0.446499)

Continue toward Caen for 500 m, then turn left toward Authie / autoroute (D14). (49.183744, -0.440462)

This was the farthest penetration by Canadian troops on 4 July. Continued infantry advance was impossible against the artillery and mortar fire encountered in the open area ahead, and armored advance was unwise because a Flak battery with 88-mm guns was stationed 2 kilometers ahead near St-Germain-la-Blanche-Herbe. A stone memorial depicting the Maple Leaf and the flat helmet of Commonwealth troops honors the men of the **8th Canadian Infantry Brigade**, which liberated the town. Again, Major Gauvin of the Régiment de la Chaudière is given special recognition.

Continue for 2.7 km into the center of Authie (D14, then D220). (49.206574, -0.431307)

Operation CHARNWOOD
7 to 9 July 1944

German defenses now consisted of a series of strongpoints at Château de St-Louet, Gruchy, St-Contest, Galmanche, and la Bijude across an arc from Franqueville to Cambes-en-Plaine. Approaches to Buron from the north were protected by a 4.5-meter-deep antitank ditch that roughly ran along current high tension pylons.

The attack was conducted by the British I Corps, consisting of the 3rd Canadian Infantry Division, and British 3rd Infantry Division, and British 59th (Staffordshire) Division in its first action. Armor support was provided by the 27th and 2nd Canadian Armoured Brigades supplemented by specialty tanks of the 79th Armoured Division. A preliminary bombardment came from 656 divisional and army-group artillery guns. The battleship HMS *Rodney*, two cruisers, and one monitor also fired salvos.

Objective	To enter Caen and secure bridges over the Orne River
Forces	
British/	
Canadian	I Corps (Lieutenant-General John Crocker)
German	481 men of SS Panzergrenadier Regiment 25 (SS-Obersturmbannführer Karl-Heinz Milius) and 16th Luftwaffe Field Division (Generalmajor Karl Sievers)
Result	The city north of the Orne River was taken, but the enemy retained the southern sectors.
Casualties	
Canadian	330 killed, 864 wounded or missing
British	2,623 killed, wounded or missing
German	estimated at 1,400 killed or wounded; 600 taken prisoner
Location	Caen

Battle

On the night of 7/8 July, four hundred fifty Lancaster and Halifax heavy bombers dropped their loads 6 kilometers in front of Allied lines to avoid hitting their own troops. The bombs fell between the German front line and reserve troops, causing only minor military losses but killing one thousand French civilians and filling the cratered streets of Caen with impassible rubble.

On the Canadian front, fighting returned to villages that they had seen briefly on 7 June. The Stormont, Dundas, and Glengarry Highlanders now led the fight into Gruchy, and Highland Light Infantry of Canada now led against Buron and Authie. Although sometimes intense enemy resistance in the form of machine-gun fire and artillery was encountered, by day's end all objectives were occupied including the Abbaye d'Ardenne. Carpiquet airfield was captured early the next day.

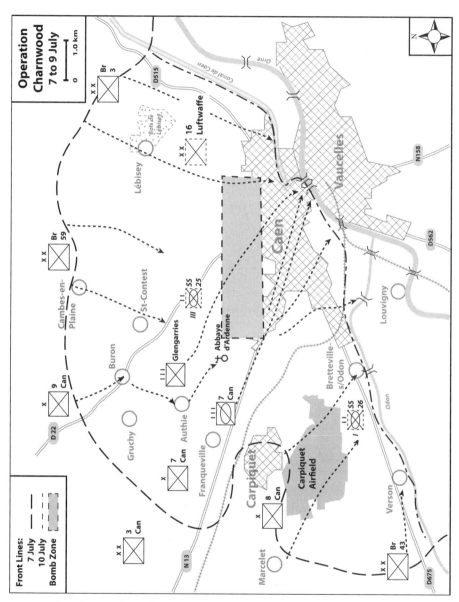

Northwest of the city, the 59th Division struck from near Hell's Corner toward St-Contest and other German strongpoints along an arc to the Caen-Luc-s/Mer railway (now highway D7). The unit entered St-Contest at 0800 but, hindered by five PzKpfw IVs coming from Buron that fell upon the Shermans of the East Riding Yeomanry, could not clear it of enemy until nightfall.

North of the city, the British 3rd Infantry Division fell against the relatively weak and inexperienced 16th Luftwaffe Field Division and took the previously difficult objective of Bois de Lébisey.

At dawn on 9 July, British and Canadian 3rd Infantry Divisions pinched out the 59th Division and entered the city center. They began the street-by-street clearing of arearguard from III Battalion, SS Panzergrenadier Regiment 25, while survivors withdrew across the Orne River. The 7th Canadian Reconnaissance Regiment reached the Orne River's north bank by 1700, but the rubble-filled street precluded passage by armored vehicles. CHARNWOOD was terminated.

Aftermath

The Germans destroyed or blocked the three Orne bridges. They established new defensive positions on Verrières and Bourguébus ridges south of the city and still blocked Allied movements toward Falaise and Paris. They also still held Hill 112's commanding position west of the city (see above). However, the five-week battle for Caen had reduced many of Germany's finest armored units to a small fraction of their former fighting capability. For example, the 12th SS Panzer Division (*Hitlerjugend*) was now the size of a battalion.

Battlefield Tour

The villages liberated at the beginning of the battle have considerably expanded with new housing developments and provide little to see except the memorials described in Chapter Three. The tour enters Caen to view memorials established to commemorate the city's liberation and to visit several of Caen's major historical sites.

The North Nova Scotia Highlanders, after suffering continuous shelling in the start line south of Buron, returned to Authie following a creeping barrage along the Buron-Authie road. They engaged a trench system north of Authie filled with enemy where Sherman tanks of the Sherbrooke Fusiliers strafed the trench lines with machine-gun fire until the infantry arrived and jumped into the trenches themselves. A bayonet and grenade fight developed with little quarter asked or given as the trenches slowly cleared. Fighting in the town continued for over an hour.

Turn right (unsigned) onto rue de l'Abbaye (D220c) and continue. The road passes the Abbaye d'Ardenne on the right. See Chapter Three for a description of the abbey.

The **Abbaye d'Ardenne**, still the headquarters of SS Panzergrenadier Regiment 25, was well-defended by machine-gun and mortar positions. Its antitank guns proved a strong threat to advancing Sherman tanks. The Regina Rifles advanced across the open fields to the south behind a moving artillery barrage; however, they fell behind the barrage due to a delay in clearing the 88-mm guns of 1st Battery, Flak Battalion 12, located in a defensive block south of Cussy, where the two leading companies suffered heavy casualties. Company D circled to the left and broke into the abbey grounds while the panzergrenadiers received permission to withdraw. The Reginas lost 200 men killed or wounded in the action.

The road becomes rue d'Authie and enters Caen. Cross the *Périphérique* and 700 m farther, stop at the monument on the left at the intersection with Av Président Cody/rue d'Isigny, difficult to see from the north. (49.19123, -0.397509)

Caen

An ancient city of major proportions, Caen sits upon the transportation and communications nexus for much of Normandy and other routes toward Falaise, Avranches, Rouen, and, eventually, Paris. The site may have been occupied as early as the 1st century. As the home of William the Conqueror, Caen is known as one of the most historic cities in France. On 26 July 1346, at the beginning of the Hundred Years War, English forces under Edward III entered Caen after a brief battle. The city remained under English occupation off and on for thirty years. After that war, Caen became a regional center of education and learning.

Allied aircraft first struck German installations in the city of 60,000 inhabitants on the morning of 6 June, bombing barracks and river bridges. The resulting fires burned for eleven days destroying whole districts of the city. Confusion and paranoia led to eighty French civilians being executed by the German garrison as saboteurs. Caen's real martyrdom, however, was to come days later, when the July bombing destroyed much of Caen's northern section. Despite liberation by Allied forces on 9 July, Caen was not fully liberated until 20 July when Operation GOODWOOD secured the southern districts, pushing German artillery beyond range one month later.

Office de Tourisme (49.183835, -0.361347)

Place St-Pierre   14000 Caen
Tel: +33 (0)2 31 27 14 14   Email: tourisminfo@caen-tourisme.fr
Web: http://www.tourisme.caen.fr

After five weeks of almost constant fighting, Allied troops had finally entered Caen. Overcoming minefields, isolated rearguards, and 88-mm gun positions, the **Stormont, Dundas and Glengarry Highlanders (Glengarries)**, accompanied by Sherbrooke Fusilier tanks, were the first Canadian battalion to enter the city. The battalion moved along the rue d'Authie to the heart of the city. A pink granite stone marks its entry point into Caen and commemorates the event.

Turn left onto Av Président Cody. After 350 m, turn right onto rue du Chemin Vert, then a quick left onto Av Robert Schuman. Follow for 650 m until a sharp left onto Av de l'Amiral Mountbatten. After 750 m, turn right onto Av du général Dempsey and in the next roundabout take the first exit onto Av du maréchal Montgomery and continue to the Mémorial de Caen parking on the right. (49.197908, -0.38376)

To approach the Mémorial de Caen from a different starting point, note the signs '*Le Mémorial*'; take exit #6 or #7 from the ring road (*Périphérique*, N814/E46) and follow the signs.

Le Mémorial de Caen

Esplanade Général Eisenhower   BP 55026, 14050 Caen Cedex 4
Tel: +33 (0)2 31 06 06 45   Email: resa@memorial-caen.fr
Web: http://www.memorial-caen.fr/

The Mémorial de Caen was constructed as an act of reconciliation for the horrific events of the 20th century. As such, it is not a war museum as much as a peace memorial. Displays present events from the start of the First World War to the fall of the Berlin Wall in a variety of displays, posters, artifacts, and films. A spiral walkway provides a timeline of events leading up to the rise of Hitler and the Second World War. A brilliant 35-minute film utilizes an effective split screen to contraposition German and Allied preparations for the D-Day invasion.

The outdoor gardens behind the building occupy the stone quarry that once housed the headquarters of Generalleutnant Wilhelm Richter, commander of the German 716th Infantry Division. Separate spaces, devoted to American, British, and Canadian designers, commemorate the French Resistance and Allied soldiers who died in Normandy and present opportunities for reflection. Mémorial Caen is a brilliantly executed and thought-provoking experience.

Open daily except Mondays 11 February through 7 November from 09:00 to 19:00; 8 November through 23 December from 09:30 to 18:00; 24 December through 5 January from 09:30 to 18:00. Closed Christmas and New Years Day. Admission fee; Normandie Pass accepted; handicap accessible.

Continue into the city by proceeding northwest on Av du maréchal Montgomery to the roundabout. Take the third exit onto Av du général Dempsey. After 350 m, turn left onto Av de l'Amiral Mountbatten. Carefully continue straight for 2 km as the name changes to rue de Rosel, then to rue St-Gabriel. Turn left onto rue Barbey d'Aurevilly, proceed 200 m and turn right onto Av du Canada. Again 200 m and turn right onto place St-Manvieu, then shortly left onto rue Bertauld and into the large place Fontette. Exit onto place Louis Guillouard and enter the large roundabout. Use the underground parking garage accessible from the large roundabout in front of the *Abbaye-aux-Hommes* and the Hôtel de ville.

Abbaye-aux-Hommes (49.181191, -0.372634)
Esplanade Jean-Marie-Louvel   14000 Caen
Tel: +33 (0)2 31 30 42 81
Web: http://www.caen.fr/abbayeauxhommes/

The large roundabout in place Louis Guillouard circulates traffic in front of the **Hôtel de ville**. The city offices, housed in the abbey buildings of the *Abbaye-aux-Hommes*, are fronted by a magnificent planned garden.

Tours of the *Abbaye-aux-Hommes* monastery buildings are available by entering the Hôtel de ville where tickets are obtained inside the main entrance. The tour includes the warming room, chapter house, and sacristy; the cloisters and the view of the church from them are spectacular. Views of the exterior rear of the church are best from the east side of the place Louis-Guillouard, where the ruins of the old St-Étienne are also located.

Open daily from 09:30 to 11:00 and from 14:30 to 16:00. Admission fee. Guided tours are available in French at 09:30, 11:00, 14:30, and 16:00.

A white stone plaque on the side of the *Center de Finances Publique* at the southwest corner of the square remembers **120 citizens of Caen and Calvados** captured from 1 to 7 May 1942 and later sent to Auschwitz-Birkenau Concentration Camp in a reprisal for actions of the French Resistance. (49.18062, -0.371143)

Walk north into place Fontette. Turn left onto rue Guillaume le Conquérant and proceed 200 m to the place Monseigneur des Hameaux on the left. (49.181828, -0.37353) The **Église St-Étienne** is the church of the former *Abbaye-aux-Hommes* Benedictine abbey. Founded in 1077, it remains one of Normandy's most remarkable Romanesque religious edifices. The abbey church was constructed by William the Conqueror as penance for his marriage against the Pope's wishes to his cousin, Matilda of Flanders. Since it was not completed until the 13th century, the architecture is a mixture of Romanesque and Gothic styles. The façade is topped by two Romanesque towers with Gothic spires. The interior stonework reflects the 12th-century Norman style, supplemented by Gothic elements especially in the ambulatory and radiating chapels. The early Gothic choir replaced the original Romanesque sanctuary. The choir once housed William the Conqueror's grave; however, it was destroyed by Huguenots during the 16th-century Wars of Religion. It was replaced in 1802 by the current inscribed marble tombstone, but William's actual remains have been lost. The abbey buildings to the south were built in the 18th century, but after the French Revolution they housed a prestigious school and now the Hôtel de ville.

In 1944, Église St-Etienne and the Hôpital du Bon Sauveur (now the *Centre hospitallier spécialisé* on rue St-Ouen) were declared non-targets to British bombers after the French Resistance had identified them as gathering points for thousands of refugees. The entreaties successfully spared those landmarks from the destruction seen by the rest of the city center.

The French flag was raised in Caen for the first time since the occupation in 1940 in this small square in front of the entrance to the Église St-Etienne. The stone **Liberation Memorial** commemorates the sacrifices of all British, Canadian, and French Resistance (FFI) forces during the liberation of the city. (49.181998, -0.373699)

Return to rue Guillaume le Conquérant and turn left. Proceed 90 m into place de l'Ancienne Boucherie to the memorial under the trees on the right. The **Canadian Battle of Normandy Monument** is on the north side of the Place de l'Ancienne Boucherie. The stele bears a metal plaque describing the liberation of the city and the celebrations that followed. It also recalls the 3,000 civilians and 3,500 Allied soldiers who died during the battle. It ends with a spirited 'Viva le Canada!' (49.182482, -0.374689)

Return to place Louis Guillouard. The ruins of the **Église St-Étienne-le-Vieux** stand on the opposite side of the roundabout from the abbey. The 10th-century church, described in its name as 'old' since it predates the abbey church of St-Étienne, stood along the walls of the ancient city and was badly damaged during the English siege of 1417. Rebuilt, it later fell into disrepair during the French Revolution and was finally closed in 1844. The nave was destroyed by German shelling in 1944. It remains partially restored, partially ruined, and inaccessible. (49.181093, -0.369445)

Leave place Louis Guillouard into place Fontette. Turn right onto place St-Sauveur then, after 200 m, left onto rue Pemagnie. Turn right onto Fos St-Julien. After 350 m, turn right onto rue de Geôle, which borders the chateau enclosure. Signs in the city center lead to the 'Château Garage' underground parking, which is conveniently located at the Porte St-Pierre entrance to the Château de Caen. Walk to the entrance to the chateau. (49.185373, -0.360787)

A circular garden along the rue de la Liberation and prominently placed near the entrance to the chateau holds a red triangle within a black triangle commemorating the **British 3rd Infantry Division**. A stone stele at the base reminds visitors that the division landed on D-Day on Sword Beach and fought its way south until the liberation of Caen on 9 July after thirty-three days of continuous combat. Other steles, identified by brigade, carry the engraved names and attached stone insignia of the various regiments that comprised the division.

Château de Caen (49.185147, -0.361739)
Le Château   14000 Caen, France
Web: http://www.chateau.caen.fr/index.htm

The chateau grounds enclose several historic structures. William the Conqueror constructed a citadel in the center of the city, repeatedly enlarged over the centuries. The château was massively damaged during the 1944 bombings and now presents only ramparts, the Porte des Champs, a dry moat, and the outlines of the foundations of the donjon. An elevator provides access to a raised terrace for views over the chateau ruins and sections of the city. Major archeological work is proceeding beside the ducal treasury (Salle de l'Échiquier).

The **Église St-Georges** was built about 1100. Modified in 1450 after the Hundred Years War and destroyed in 1944 but not rebuilt, only its nave walls remain. A plaque on a side wall honors, in French and English, the men and women of the Province of Ontario who served in the **Royal Canadian Navy**, **Canadian Army**, and the **Royal Canadian Air Force** in the Battle of Normandy in 1944.

Separate structures in the enclosure house the **Musée de Normandie** and the **Musée des Beaux-Arts de Caen**.

The chateau is generally open; the main entrance is at the Porte de St-Pierre across from the Église St-Pierre. No admission fee.

Walk from the Porte St-Pierre directly across the rue Montoir Poissonniere. (49.184251, -0.361192)

The 13th-century **Église St-Pierre** is a parish church in name only. Its enormous size and rich ornamentation give the appearance of a major cathedral. As with many urban churches, it has been enlarged and redesigned through the centuries. The impressive 78-meter-tall tower has been rebuilt since its destruction during the 1944 battle when it fell into the nave. The west façade holds a rose window and faces the entrance to the citadel. The east end presents a dramatic Renaissance appearance with ornate pinnacles and pilasters. The exterior has recently undergone a cleaning to return to its original splendor.

Operation Goodwood or Battle of Bourguébus Ridge
18 to 20 July

Operation Goodwood developed as an opportunity to use the numerical superiority of British armor in a massed attack east of the Orne River. The intermediate objective was the dominating Bourguébus ridge, 11 kilometers south of the front line, with intentions to gain the Caen-Falaise road. The terrain was not the bocage country of narrow lanes and high-walled orchards and pastures. Rather, it was shallow, sloping ground cut by a few fences. The open fields approaching the ridge were perfect tank country, and similar terrain past the ridge promised rapid movement toward Falaise, 30 kilometers to the south. However, terrain on the eastern and western flanks was much different. They were infantry country with wooded hills to the east and the extensive manufacturing suburbs of Caen on the west.

German intelligence had uncovered the plan, and Panzer Group West responded by establishing a Main Line of Resistance along the Bourguébus ridge and numerous strongpoints in the small villages and farms well supplied with assault guns, 88-mm guns, and heavy tanks. The forward positions running from Colombelles through Cuverville to Touffréville were manned by the 16th Luftwaffe Field Division, still badly depleted by losses incurred during the CHARNWOOD attack upon Caen. Behind the main line of resistance, General der Panzertruppen Heinrich Eberbach established three additional lines of defense of increasing strength, including two antitank battalions of 88-mm guns and elements of 1st SS, 12th SS, and 21st Panzer Divisions. The eastern flank of the Orne Bridgehead was defended by the German 346th Infantry Division.

The main effort passed to British VIII Corps' three armored divisions fielding approximately 1,300 tanks. The British 3rd and 51st Infantry Divisions of British I Corps provided infantry support.

Objective	To eliminate German positions south and east of Caen
Forces	
British	VIII Corps including 11th Armoured Division (Major-General GPB Roberts), Guards Armoured Division (Major-General AHS Adair) and 7th Armoured Division (Major-General GWEJ Erskine)
German	LXXXVI Corps including 16th Luftwaffe Field Division (Generalmajor Karl Sievers) and 346th Infantry Division (General der Infanterie Hans von Obstfelder)
Result	Positions on the ridge were taken, but further progress stalled.
Casualties	
British	3,474 killed, wounded, or missing; 253 tanks destroyed
German	Unknown number of killed or wounded; 75 tanks or assault guns destroyed
Location	Escoville is 12 km northeast of Caen

Battle

For three hours in the morning of 18 July, nineteen hundred medium and heavy bombers and eight hundred fighter-bombers delivered concentrated explosives on predetermined kill zones, shattering German tank battalions and panzergrenadier regiments. Three armored divisions then attacked in succession. At 0745, 11th Armoured Division led the way following a tightly-scripted rolling barrage. Initial progress against the dazed survivors of the bombing was swift; however, a traffic jam created by narrow passages through the British-laid minefield slowed the following units.

Major Hans von Luck commanded a *kampfgruppe* comprised of his Panzergrenadier Regiment 125; I Battalion, Panzer Regiment 25; five batteries of assault guns; and, most importantly, SS Heavy Panzer Battalion 503 with thirty-nine Tiger and Tiger II (King Tiger)[26] tanks. The group was responsible for holding the eastern sector of the GOODWOOD attack zone with headquarters in Frénouville. Their presence on the eastern flank of the advance further squeezed British units into a narrow front west of Cagny. By early afternoon, General Eberbach strengthened the defenses by ordering 1st SS Panzer

---

26   Tiger II was officially the PzKpfw Tiger Ausf B or Tiger B or Königstiger to German soldiers, also variously called the King Tiger or Royal Tiger by Allied soldiers. The variety of terms has led to some confusion, but they all refer to the same model.

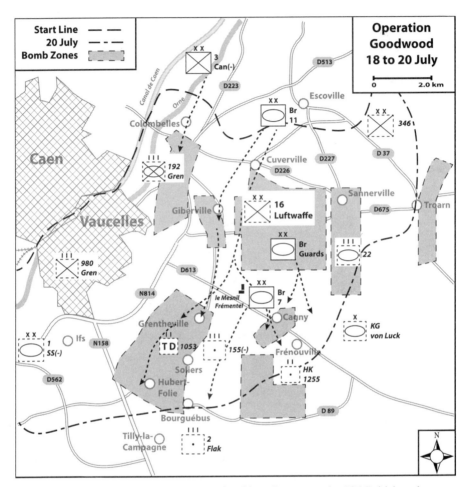

Division *Leibstandarte* from reserve onto the ridge. Consequently, 186 British tanks were destroyed that day by German artillery and antitank guns.

The next day, the battle continued with the heaviest action in the highly exposed ground north of Bras, Hubert-Folie, and Bourguébus while 11th and 7th Armoured Divisions, now fully supported by their respective infantry brigades, faced off against arriving German panzergrenadier units east and west of the Minier railway. By early evening, east of the Minier railway, Bras and Hubert-Folie were cleared with German troops withdrawing to the Verrières Ridge. The 7th Armoured Division struggled to clear Soliers and Four, but farther advance was impossible. On the eastern flanks, Guards infantry took Cagny but found Frénouville strongly defended.

On 20 July, Frénouville, after being subjected to early morning bombing, was empty of enemy troops. The 7th Armoured Division captured Bourguébus against limited opposition. By midafternoon, a torrential thunderstorm turned the battlefield into muck. GOODWOOD and the battle for Caen were essentially over but at a very questionable cost.

Aftermath

Whereas Caen was cleared of Germans, Montgomery's descriptions of his intentions during the battle for Caen remain controversial. He insisted that every attempt to take the city and the expenditure of men's lives were all part of the plan to engage Germany's best armored divisions while the Americans achieved a breakout in the west. Eisenhower believed that GOODWOOD was to achieve a decisive breakout to and down the Caen-Falaise road. Members of Supreme Allied Command accused Montgomery of slowness to respond. Whether planned or not, the British actions did keep the German armored divisions on the front lines and unavailable for a massed armored counterattack.

Battlefield Tour

The Operation GOODWOOD battlefield does not hold the museums and memorials of other Normandy areas. Despite its significance as a major tank-vs-tank engagement, not one armored vehicle remains to commemorate the events. The only physical reminders of the battle are the liberation plaques to be found in most Orne bridgehead villages. However, the terrain remains, and an understanding of Operation GOODWOOD is important. The tour focuses upon the 11th Armoured and Guards Armoured divisions.

> The GOODWOOD tour starts on the east side of the Orne River. From the Caen ring road, take exit #3a – Porte d'Angleterre toward Hérouville (D515). After 2.2 km, exit toward Colombelles (D226) and follow across the Canal de Caen and Orne River. Colombelles' industrial district is on the left immediately after crossing the canal. (49.207392, -0.310578)

As part of the subsidiary Operation ATLANTIC, the 3rd Canadian Infantry Division crossed the Orne River north of Colombelles on the morning of 18 July. It attacked the village and massive steelworks of Colombelles to capture or topple the steelwork's tall chimneys being used by German artillery observers. The aerial bombardment made a wreck of the works, but German troops survived and re-occupied the debris. Tougher than expected resistance from Colombelles slowed the leading 8th Canadian Infantry Brigade's advance whereby it fell behind the creeping artillery barrage. The battle for the steelworks lasted all day with the grounds not secured until 2200.

> From the large roundabout after crossing the canal, continue for 1.1 km to the next roundabout and take the fourth exit toward Deauville (D513). After 3.7 km, take the second exit toward Hérouvillette (unfortunately unsigned, D513a) and continue 500 m into the village. Turn right toward Escoville (D37c) and, after 850 m, turn right onto rue de l'Ormelet. Continue past the church and park near the next intersection. (49.209944, -0.245562)

A British minefield, originally placed to defend the Orne bridgehead from German counterattack, extended 5 kilometers east from the Orne River approximately through this point. Gaps were cleared to allow passage of British tanks with eight of those gaps along the southern edge of Escoville. The terrain visible to the south presents the open, fairly level field of operations available to tank units once they had squeezed through the minefield gaps.

On 18 July, after four hours of the most intense combined naval and aerial bombardment of the war, British tanks from three armored divisions, flanked by two infantry divisions, swept from the north across the fields in front of this position toward the Bourguébus ridge. The 3rd Battalion, Royal Tank Regiment, 29th Armoured Brigade, led the attack with each of its three squadrons fielding nineteen Sherman tanks.

> Turn left onto rue des Fresnets and continue 550 m to the junction with highway D227. Turn right and, after 400 m, turn right again toward Cuverville. Follow D228 south through Cuverville and Démouville. (49.192306, -0.263586)

For the first few hours of the assault, the 11th Armoured Division armor moved swiftly through the fields to the east of the highway, struggling against only the shallow craters left by the bombing while Cuverville and Démouville were taken by motorized infantry of 159th Infantry Brigade moving along the highway. Démouville was strongly defended by 500 men of a panzer battalion of 21st Panzer Division. Estimates suggest that 60 percent of enemy troops were casualties from the opening bombing, with many of the survivors too dazed to offer resistance. Hundreds of prisoners were taken and a battalion of assault guns destroyed. However, enough resistance developed to delay infantry units and separate them from the armor ahead. The lack of armor-infantry coordination produced dramatic consequences for the tank units, especially when they advanced outside the range of supporting artillery units.

> In the roundabout south of Démouville, turn left toward Sannerville (D675) and proceed 2.7 km to the parking area on the right before entering Sannerville. (49.176352, -0.22979)

Highway D675 paralleled (and was adjacent to) a no-longer existent single-track railway line from Caen to Troan. Thought to be a minor obstacle, it was anything but since the embankment rose 2 meters above the surrounding fields. Tracked vehicles struggled over the embankment while wheeled vehicles clustered around the few level crossings. The difficulty in crossing this minor elevation caused the advance to fall behind the creeping artillery barrage.

The stone arch near the cemetery entrance is a remnant of a gateway to a chateau. Although in no way connected to the cemetery, it makes a fitting identifier of the cemetery entrance. The entrance path to **Banneville-la-Campagne War Cemetery** winds for 100 meters among thickly landscaped flowering shrubs. The entrance leads directly to the war stone and a small stone shelter with a bench. The cemetery contains 2,170 Commonwealth burials, many from the GOODWOOD operation, in plots centered upon a vine-covered pergola. The two touching stones in front on the right mark the graves of four members of an RAF flight crew[27] who died together when their B-25 Mitchell bomber crashed on 23 July 1944. A counterattack in the afternoon of 18 July by six King Tiger tanks from the fields south of the cemetery was repulsed by accurate antitank gun fire from the cemetery.

> Continue 600 m to the next roundabout and take the second exit toward Cuverville (D226) entering Sannerville. After 400 m, turn right onto rue de la Renaissance and proceed 300 m to the church. (49.183162, -0.220821)

---

27   Pilot Flight Sergeant Fred Worrall, age 23; Navigator / Bomber Flight Sergeant Stanley Nunwick, age 23; Wireless Operator / Gunner Sergeant Robert Elliman; and Gunner Sergeant Cecil Smith.

The British I Corps led by British 3rd Infantry Division planned to expand the eastern flank of the Orne bridgehead toward Troan. However, the massive air assault had so demolished the villages of Touffréville and Sannerville that movement was significantly impaired. Some troops penetrated Bois de Bavent and a few troops reached Troan, but a breakout was not possible through the bridgeless, flooded valley of the Dives River.

An extensive stone memorial to the **British 3rd Division** stands at the rear of a small square adjacent to the church. Brass plaques commend the units of 'Monty's Ironsides' division, Operation GOODWOOD, and Group Captain Charles Appleton,[28] a squadron commander and Typhoon pilot shot down nearby on 12 August.

> Reverse direction and return to the junction with highway D226. Turn left back to the roundabout and take the second exit toward Troan (D675). After only 130 m, turn right toward Banneville-la-Campagne (D227) and follow for 1.9 km. At the 'T' junction, turn right toward Émieville (D225). Proceed for 1.1 km to the memorial on the right. (49.150654, -0.239103)

Villages from Sannerville to Émieville received the brunt of the heavy bombers and were reduced to dusty rubble. Émieville was laager for SS Panzer Regiment 22, and the bombing obliterated men and vehicles alike. Afterward, barely six of the regiment's PzKpfw IVs were serviceable, and the troops were so shocked that two committed suicide.

Twelve Tiger tanks of 3rd Company, SS Heavy Panzer Battalion 503, were positioned on the grounds of Manneville Haras (stud farm) when the pre-dawn aerial bombing started. The terrain east of the farm was Target zone 'H' and received a dense bombing pattern. Depending upon the season and view point, these fields still display the vestiges of craters created by the one-thousand pound bombs. However, the farm was only lightly hit, and only four Tiger tanks were destroyed.

By afternoon the Germans had established a strong blocking force running from Cagny to the northeast along highway (D255) centered approximately on this location. The firepower of the twenty-seven 88-mm PaK 43s from Antitank Battalion 1039 forced approaching Guards Armoured units to shy away to the west.

Late in the day, 2nd Squadron, Irish Guards, flanked Cagny to the east by advancing from le Prieuré Farm. When they approached highway D225, a troop of 75-mm Sherman tanks led by Lieutenant J Gorman emerged from behind a hedgerow to find three German tanks. His first shot bounced off the heavily-armored enemy and his gun jammed on the second shot. While the German tank rotated its turret toward him, Lt Gorman rammed it, his crew bailing out of the escape hatches. Gorman returned to an orchard where he took over a Sherman Firefly and re-engaged the remaining two enemy tanks with its 17-pounder gun. In a confused contest, the other two tanks were also destroyed. Lt Gorman had just beaten the first King Tiger tank to appear on a French battlefield and either two Tiger Is or two PzKpfw IVs.[29] The solitary engagement was the high point for the Guards Armoured Division that day. Delayed by vehicle traffic squeezing through the minefield gaps, slow to

---

28   Group Captain Charles Henry Appleton flew despite having only one leg. Appleton was awarded the Distinguished Service Order, Distinguished Flying Cross, and Czechoslovak Military Cross. He is buried in Banneville-la-Campagne War Cemetery. He was 38 years old.

29   Lieutenant (later Sir) John Reginald Gorman, a former member of the Royal Ulster Constabulary, received the Military Cross for his exploits just as his father had for his actions in the First World War. After the war, Gorman served in the North Ireland Assembly. His tank driver, Lance-Corporal James Baron, received the Military Medal. Baron died in 2002 at age 87.

engage the enemy, and consistently drifting away from Cagny, the division did produce an expected impact upon the battle's outcome.

The gray granite stele, inscribed with the image of Gorman's Sherman, is dedicated to those **Guards Division** members killed during GOODWOOD and adds:

'In this region one of the largest tank battles of Normandy took place. At this spot (actually, in the field directly across the road from the memorial), the destruction of the first [King] Tiger tank in Europe was executed by Lieutenant John Gorman of No. 2 Squadron, Irish Guards.'

Interestingly, there were several such claims of defeating 'the first Tiger,' but such was the huge tank's reputation among Allied tankers that British tankers assumed any dot on the horizon was a Tiger. The area is under construction for a new motorway bypass and may be substantially altered in the future.

> Continue into Cagny (D225). Turn right toward Caen (originally N13, now D613) and merge right almost immediately onto a frontage road. Continue to the church. (49.147412, -0.256199)

The 2nd Fife and Forfar Yeomanry followed behind the Royal Tank Regiment with the objective of capturing Cagny. The exposed nature of the terrain and the well-camouflaged German guns explain much of the difficulty the tankers faced in maintaining momentum.

Major Hans von Luck[30] arrived at his headquarters in Frénouville to find that no countermeasures had been taken. He jumped into his command car and sped the short distance to Cagny, where he found a Luftwaffe antiaircraft battery near the church. He ordered the battery to use its four 88-mm guns against the approaching Fife and Forfar tanks. When the airmen refused the orders of an army officer, Luck drew his pistol and famously offered the Luftwaffe officer a choice of either attacking and probably earning a medal or summary execution. The gunners acquiesced, and after being personally directed to an apple orchard behind the church (no longer existent), the four guns applied devastating fire into the flanks of the Fife and Forfar Yeomanry, setting aflame twelve tanks whose burning hulks were scattered across the fields to the west.[31] By late afternoon, pressured by approaching British infantry, the Luftwaffe guns were destroyed, and the village was abandoned.

Half new, half old, the Église St-Germain bell tower holds a plaque commemorating the units of the **Guards Division** which fought to liberate Cagny. A second plaque remembers Flying Officer John Kalen,[32] a Typhoon pilot who died when his aircraft exploded while bombing le Mesnil Frémentel on 18 July 1944.

---

30   Major (later Oberst) Hans-Ulrich von Luck und Witten was born into an old Prussian military family. He was an early proponent of armor, studying under Erwin Rommel. He fought in Poland, France (1940), Eastern Front, North Africa, Normandy (escaping the Falaise Pocket), and Siegfried Line. He was captured by Russian troops while defending Berlin during the Battle of the Halbe. After seven years in a Soviet Gulag, he returned to Germany to write his memoirs. He died in 1997 at age 86.

31   Whether the Luftwaffe officer ever received his medal is unknown.

32   Flying Officer John Kalen was a member of the Royal Canadian Air Force. He is buried in Bretteville-s/Laize Canadian War Cemetery.

Regain the Av de Paris toward Caen (D613) and immediately turn right toward Démouville (D228). Continue for 1.2 km, then turn left on a farm road. Le Prieuré Farm is visible down the farm track in the opposite direction. After 400 m, turn right and pass through Mesnil Frémentel. (49.156236, -0.269385)

The British advance crossed a hedgerow which is now the location of Autoroute de Normandie (E46/A13) and continued south achieving le Mesnil Frémentel, a former priory and walled farm complex 1.2 kilometers south of the autoroute. The farm was the headquarters of the I Battalion, Panzergrenadier Regiment 125, supported by a battery of 75-mm self-propelled antitank guns that inflicted losses upon the 3rd Battalion, Royal Tank Regiment, moving past the farm to the west with its exposed flank open to fire from behind the stone walled orchard.

At 1000, a battle group based upon the infantry of the 8th Battalion, The Rifle Regiment, supported by eleven Sherman flail tanks, attacked the western walls of the farm complex. Infantry cleared the way until a Sherman crashed the wall and entered the courtyard while firing into the buildings. It came to rest atop the German battalion command bunker. Over 130 prisoners were captured in the engagement.

After Mesnil Frémentel, turn right to regain the Route de Paris toward Caen (D613). After 800 m, take third exit toward Grentheville (D230) and continue 900 m into the village. (49.149563, -0.287222)

British tanks of the Royal Tank Regiment continued their advance southwest after running the gauntlet around le Mesnil Frémentel. The next obstacle to achieving the ridge now visible in the distance was a crossing of the dual-track Caen to Paris railway line. The first tanks approached the rail line at 0930, less than two hours since their start. West of Grentheville, a north-south Minier railway fed the steelworks at Colombelles. Positioned within the nearby chateau's grounds, *Nebelwerfer* rocket launchers exploded their flaming projectiles while a battery of self-propelled 75-mm antitank guns took on the advancing Shermans. Ten tanks quickly succumbed to the antitank gun fire while Squadron Commander Major W Close led his tanks in a mad dash through a passage under the Minier railway to the western side of the protective embankment. A polish granite stele in front of the *mairie* honors the **British 11th Armoured Division**.

Continue 1.9 km into Soliers; at the second roundabout, take the first exit onto rue de le Résistance (D89b) and continue to the railway bridge. (49.131605, -0.302736)

The leading British 3rd Royal Tank Regiment, which had advanced 10 kilometers in four hours, stopped at this point to reconnoiter Hubert-Folie just before noon. Two Bren carriers raced up the shallow slope into Hubert-Folie, around the corner of the church, and out the west side without encountering any enemy fire.

Believing Hubert-Folie was undefended, regimental commander Colonel D Silvertop ordered the ridge to be stormed along a front from Hubert-Folie to east of neighboring Bras. Hubert-Folie church's distinctive square tower provided a highly visible landmark to the British tankers. The three squadrons fell under heavy fire from antitank guns positioned on the ridge south of the village and from guns on its flanks. Eleven tanks were immediately lost and more fell in an afternoon-long engagement against German assault guns. German counterattacks down the slope from Hubert-Folie were intercepted by Typhoon fighter-bombers, and a stalemate developed. By evening the advance stopped. The regiment had lost forty-one of its sixty tanks.

Enter Hubert-Folie and continue past the church to the 'T' junction. Turn left toward Bourguébus (D120). After 170 m, turn left toward Bourguébus (D89); a **Liberation Monument** stands at the intersection. (49.131605, -0.302736)

Follow for 1.3 km into Bourguébus to the *mairie* to view the **Stèle de la Liberation** and **NTL Totem**. (49.121632, -0.298621)

Continue to the east toward Bellengreville (rue Vallée Ès Dunes, D89). Stop at a convenient high point and observe terrain to the north (left). (49.119725, -0.287533)

The 2nd Fife and Forfar Yeomanry advanced on the eastern flank of 3rd Royal Tank Regiment. Hidden among trees and shrubs and occupying the high ground, the Germans were unseen by the exposed British tankers in the fields. After crossing the Caen-Troan rail line and advancing as far as the Soliers-Four road, the tankers were caught in a cross fire from guns to their west in Soliers and to their east in the hamlet of Four. Continuing to advance toward Bourguébus, they fell victim to frontal fire of batteries of 122-mm cannon.

About midday, the reinforcing Panther tanks of SS Panzer Regiment 1 reached the Bourguébus-La Hogue road and proceeded down the hill to engage the Fife and Forfar Yeomanry. A wild melee ensued with the advantage definitely in favor of the better armed and armored Panthers. The Yeomanry were forced to withdraw.

On 19 July, the 7th Armoured Division attacked Soliers, the large community identified by the large white (school) building to the left front, and Four, the small hamlet holding several white storage tanks. Soliers was taken, and on the morning of 20 July the attack focused upon Bourguébus, which was also liberated, but attempts to move upon Verrières were firmly rebuffed by strong German forces, which included Michael Wittmann's Tiger tank unit. Rain ended the battle.

Chapter Fourteen

Battle of Verrières Ridge
18 July to 11 August 1944

The Caen-Falaise road was a first class highway that rose and fell through the gently sloping contours of fields of tall corn and wheat. The highway passed through small villages while gradually rising to a crest near St-Aignan-de-Cramesnil. The terrain was what military men called 'tank country' – open fields not cut into small plots by the dreaded hedgerows. They provided room for tanks to maneuver *en masse*, unconfined to narrow sunken lanes. Operation GOODWOOD had obtained a toe hold on the Bourguébus-Verrières Ridge, but German armor retained the higher ground and could bring tank and artillery fire down upon anything that moved on the rolling plains below. The original target of Falaise now became secondary to control of the highway subsequent to control of the ridge.

Canadian forces were facing a German Army that possessed superiority in long-range artillery weapons. Well-camouflaged German tanks, antitank guns, *Nebelwerfers*,

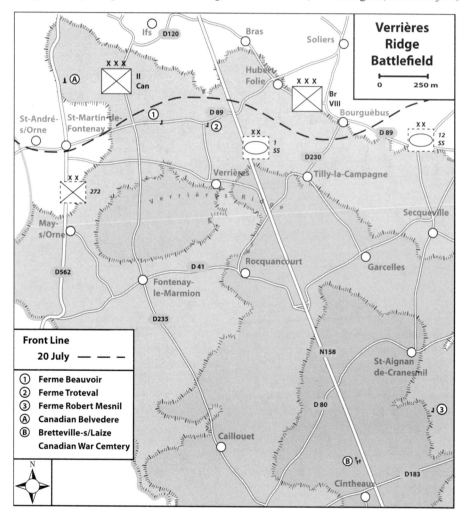

and heavy mortars provided defensive advantages in the, so called, open tank country. In addition and unknown to Allied planners, the slopes down to the Orne River were a warren of quarries, mine shafts, tunnels, and underground galleries, all of which German troops used to advantage. Panzer Group West disposed its I SS Panzer Corps and LXXXVI Corps in four defensive lines spreading 16 kilometers back from the front. To the rear was a mobile reserve of up to eighty tanks.

Allied forces were not without their advantages. Foremost was almost total air supremacy. German vehicular movement during daylight and good flying weather was nearly impossible. Canadian infantry backed by light 105-mm and heavy 150-mm artillery regiments seemed, to German troops, to possess unlimited ammunition stores. Allied manpower reserves seemed endless to German front line troops who rarely saw their casualties replaced.

Operation ATLANTIC
18 to 22 July

Separate from Operation GOODWOOD, Operation ATLANTIC utilized the infantry divisions of the newly created II Canadian Corps to clear Caen east and south of the Orne River and to establish positions on the Bourguébus-Verrières Ridge.

Objective	To liberate Caen south of the Orne River
Forces	
Canadian	II Canadian Corps (Lieutenant-General Guy Simonds), including 2nd Canadian (Major-Gen Charles Foulkes) and 3rd Canadian (Major-Gen Rod Keller) Infantry Divisions
German	272nd Infantry Division (Generalleutnant Friedrich August Schack)
Result	Leading units ascended Verrières ridge but were pushed back.
Casualties	
Canadian	1,535 killed, wounded, or missing
German	uncertain
Location	Louvigny is 6 km southwest of Caen.

Battle

While British armored divisions were attacking the Bourguébus-Verrières Ridge from the north, 3rd Canadian Infantry Division's 7th Infantry Brigade cleared the southern suburbs of Caen. Despite German small-arms fire, the Regina Rifles crossed damaged rail bridges over the Orne River and entered the Caen main railway station. A brief firefight resulted in taking sixty-nine prisoners. Canadian engineers assembled a fragile bridge and the 2nd Division's Royal Highland Regiment of Canada – also known as The Black Watch – crossed the river and advanced into Vaucelles. On the right flank, in its first action in Normandy, the Royal Regiment of Canada fought from southern Caen against German SS troops in Louvigny.

By the afternoon of 19 July, Canadian troops had advanced along a 9-kilometer front. Cormelles, the site of a massive Renault truck factory, was taken during the day by the Highland Light Infantry. The 5th Canadian Brigade had established positions as far south as Fleury-s/Orne.

The next day, during the dying throes of GOODWOOD, 6th Infantry Brigade began its attack against the German 272nd Infantry Division on Verrières Ridge. The Queen's Own Cameron Highlanders charged down a slope known as la Poudrière and into a fierce fight for St-André-s/Orne. On the opposite flank, the Fusiliers Mont-Royal captured and lost Ferme Troteval. The South Saskatchewan Regiment moved forward between the two and ran into the arriving 2nd SS Panzer Division, which hid machine guns in the tall wheat and tanks in the haystacks. Fatigue, roaming panzers on their left flank, and an afternoon thunderstorm beat the South Saks into withdrawing. Heavy German pressure and the confusion of battle forced two companies of the Essex Scottish into a disorganized withdrawal. The line eventually stabilized along highway D89 from St-André-s/Orne to Hubert-Folie.

Aftermath

The 2nd Canadian Infantry Division was bloodied in its first encounter with German armor. German soldiers, experienced in fighting on the Eastern Front, insisted that no fighting against Russian troops was as vicious and furious as that on Verrières Ridge. Recriminations roiled the senior Canadian leadership. Generals Montgomery and Simonds came under harsh criticism for their overly optimistic objectives and the severe level of casualties.

Battlefield Tour

The Verrières battlefield is difficult to tour because so many Canadian and German units engaged in large and small battles – sometimes for physically small but often tactically important pieces of terrain. This tour views selected sites that provide an understanding of the fighting.

Leave the Caen ring road (N814, *Périphérique*) at exit #9 – Porte de Bretagne toward Verson / Bretteville-s/Odon. Merge onto A84 / E401 and quickly enter a roundabout. Take 2nd exit onto Route Bretagne toward Bretteville-s/Odon (also back toward Caen-centre). After 1.5 km, turn right onto Av des Canadiens (D212). Continue for 400 m to the parking area on the right. Walk to the foot bridge at the south edge of the parking area. (49.164673, -0.406623)

The **'Bomb Alley' plaque** is mounted upon a remnant on stone wall to the left of the bridge. The plaque commemorates the Royal Regiment of Canada and the 8th Reconnaissance Regiment, which fought in the area from 16 to 20 July. The units' close contact with German 272nd Infantry Division troops less than 2 kilometers distant led to their frequent shelling by the attached SS Artillery Regiments. Thus, the location became known to them as 'Bomb Alley.'

Continue on Av des Canadiens (D212) for 100 m. Turn left onto Route du Mesnil (D212) and follow for 1 km passing straight through the next roundabout (becomes D212c). Observe the field and high stone wall on the left. Turn left (ignore the 'no entry' sign since proceeding as far as the church is permitted) to enter a tree-shaded lane framed by stone walls. Continue to the church. Do not drive past the church, as the road becomes private. (49.160232, -0.386823)

Battle of Louvigny
18 to 19 July 1944

On the night of 18/19 July, The Royal Regiment of Canada moved through the wheat fields east of les Mesnil toward Louvigny against an SS artillery regiment's headquarters centered upon a chateau and church north of the village. The walled orchard west of the church was protected by a 2-meter-high stone wall. Fort Garry Horse tanks blasted holes in the wall, and the leading Company D charged into the enclosed orchard where German troops were well sited in slit trenches and bomb craters. Two company officers were killed, where upon Sergeant OC Tryon[1] reorganized the company and led it on a flanking attack into the chateau while Company C cleared the remainder of the orchard. Brigadier S Lett,[2] the 4th Canadian Infantry Brigade commander, was badly wounded attempting to make contact with the leading units. By dawn the village was cleared with fifty-five prisoners taken, but at a cost of 111 Canadian casualties. The villagers celebrated their liberation by killing a cow, digging potatoes, and providing a noontime steak dinner for 100 welcome Canadian soldiers.

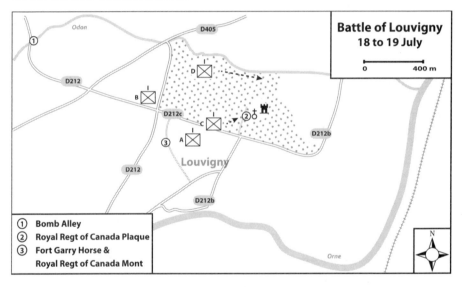

Most of the orchard's fruit trees are long gone, but the walled field across from the church identifies the location. A plaque of the south side of the church is dedicated to the 41 members of the **Royal Regiment of Canada** who died in the assault. Their names are listed, starting with the company commander Major JD Fairhead.[3]

1   Sergeant Oliver Clifford Tryon was awarded the Military Medal. Tryon died in 2005 at age 85.

2   Brigadier Sherwood Lett was awarded the Military Cross while serving in the Canadian Expeditionary Force during the First World War. Between the wars, he was a Rhodes Scholar and practiced law. He commanded the ill-fated 4th Canadian Infantry Brigade during the Battle of Dieppe in 1942, where he was wounded and for which he was awarded the Distinguished Service Order. Brigadier Lett survived his wounds and the war to oversee the agreements that ended the Indochina War in 1954. He ended his career as Chief Justice of the British Columbia Supreme Court. He died in 1964 at age 68.

3   Major James Douglas Fairhead; Captain Robert Lowe Rankin, aged 34; and Lieutenant Eric James Chellew, age 30, are buried in Bény-s/Mer Canadian War Cemetery.

> Reverse direction and return to Route du Mesnil (D212c). Turn right and follow for 500 m. Turn left onto Av des Canadiens and proceed for 180 m and park on the side road to the right. (49.158601, -0.394161)

In the small triangle park at the road junction, a rough hewn stone memorial commemorates the units that cleared the village of enemy troops. The small plaque on top remembers two members[4] of the **Fort Garry Horse** killed in the battle. The central plaque recognizes the **Royal Regiment of Canada**, support units, and the 111 casualties. The third stone plaque is a duplicate of the plaque on the church which lists all of the names of those killed in the action.

> Reverse direction and return to Route du Mesnil (D212c). Turn left and pass straight through the first roundabout. At the next roundabout (500 m), take 4th exit toward Toutes Directions/Éterville (D405). Follow for 1.9 km and enter a roundabout. Take 3rd exit onto *Périphérique Est* toward Paris/Flers/Alençon (N814). Unfortunately, this route is necessary to cross the Orne River. Good highway crossings are as scarce now as in 1944. After 3.2 km, enter exit #11 toward Flers/Fleury-s/Orne. In the roundabout, take 1st exit toward Flers/Laval (D562A). Pass straight through the next roundabout and, after 1 km, turn left onto le Grand Bargerie to access the high point. Although the gate to the parking area may be locked, the pedestrian entrance is usually open. (49.127547, -0.37493)

On 18 July, the Calgary Highlanders moved through Fleury-s/Orne and continued along the straight highway to a high point then known as la Poudrière – also known as Point 67, the north spur of the Verrières ridge. They dug in under the fire of German 272nd Infantry Division mortars and machine guns. By 1830 a panzer counterattack was approaching from the south. The tanks first hit an advanced patrol led by Lieutenant V Kilpatrick.[5] Using a single PIAT, Kilpatrick's patrol knocked out three tanks and the enemy withdrew. The Highlanders suffered 128 casualties in taking and holding the hill.

Established by the Canadian Battlefield Foundation, **Point 67** is now the location for a belvedere, or overlook, on the Canadian Verrières Ridge battlefield. The main plaque is centered upon white tiles formed into the shape of a Maple Leaf and commemorates Operation ATLANTIC, ending with the words 'Carry On.' Memorials to the Toronto Scottish Regiment,[6] Black Watch of Canada, and le Régiment de Maisonneuve[7] present their engagements in French and English with attached battle maps. A separate tableaux shows the advance of the Canadians in Operations ATLANTIC, SPRING, TOTALIZE, and TRACTABLE.

4　Captain William Edward McAleese died of his wounds in attacking Louvigny. His body was never recovered, and he is remembered on the Bayeux Memorial to the Missing. Trooper Percy Unger is buried in Bény-s/Mer Canadian War Cemetery. Unger was 23 years old.

5　Lieutenant Vernon Francis Kilpatrick was killed in that day's fighting. Kilpatrick is buried in Bretteville-s/Laize Canadian War Cemetery. He was 22 years old.

6　The Toronto Scottish Regiment was a heavy weapons unit whose machine guns and mortars were attached to other infantry units as required.

7　Le Régiment de Maisonneuve attacked the hamlet of Etavaux on 22 July during which Sergeant Benoit Lacourse led four men in a charge to destroy three machine-gun nests. Company Commander Major Jacques Ostiguy used grenades to destroy four enemy positions and rifle fire on a fifth. The Maisonneuves captured over one hundred enemy troops. Sergeant Lacourse was awarded the Distinguish Conduct Medal, and Major Ostiguy was awarded the Distinguished Service Order.

This stunning memorial was commemorated in 2000. Though much of the landscaping is immature, the quality of the memorials and its dominant position over the terrain to the north, west, and especially the view to the south up the long slope to Verrières Ridge make it the premier location to view this battlefield.

> Reverse direction to descend the hill. Turn left toward St-André-s/Orne (unsigned, D562a). After 1.2 km, turn right onto rue des Canadiens (D89) and continue 600 m into the parking area on the left. (49.116537, -0.382773)

St-André-s/Orne was first entered by the Queen's Own Cameron Highlanders of Canada during Operation ATLANTIC. At the western end of the Canadian front line, the village was under observation and bombardment from higher ground across the Orne River. It was also stubbornly defended by numerous machine-gun positions. Thus, four days later the Camerons were still fighting for control of the village which did not clear until one week later during Operation SPRING.

A large natural stone holds two plaques dedicated to officers, non-commissioned officers, and soldiers of the 4th Brigade of the 2nd Canadian Infantry Division, especially **le Régiment de Maisonneuve** and **The Black Watch of Canada**, who fought and died along the highway from St-André to May-s/Orne. The road ahead (rue des Canadiens) drops considerably while it enters the valley of the Orne.

> Reverse direction and follow highway D89 east for 3.7 km. Park near the memorial on the right. (49.120793, -0.333109)

Battle of Ferme Troteval
20 to 24 July 1944

Company B, le Fusiliers Mont-Royal, supported by five Sherwood Fusilier tanks, took Ferme Beauvoir located 550 meters to the west (and in 1944 on the north side of the highway), on the afternoon of 20 July. Accompanied by Company D, its troops dashed down a slight slope to the south toward Verrières. German infantry, hiding in the farm's cellars, re-emerged to take the Canadians from the rear. Meanwhile, Company C captured Ferme Troteval. Two Panther tanks appeared and disabled three of the Shermans before they, too, became casualties. A confused battle took place in the fields between the two farms until rain and darkness brought the fighting to a halt. On 21 July, a counterattack by two companies of 2nd Panzer Division tanks and panzergrenadiers killed or captured most of the men in the forward companies, Company B being all but eliminated. The Fusiliers were pushed out of the Troteval buildings and across the road. Ferme Beauvoir had been held.

In order to secure the start line for Operation SPRING, The Fusiliers Mont-Royal was ordered to retake Ferme Troteval. Still without replacements for casualties suffered in earlier fighting, a combined force of seventy-five men under Major J Dextraze[8] was selected for the assault. On the night of 24 July, their start was 1 kilometer to the northwest. Their advance carried them through fields of full-grown wheat. The three-pronged assault closely followed an artillery barrage. Dextraze then launched a frenzied pincer attack

---

8   Major Jacques Dextraze survived the war, during which he received a Distinguished Service Order and bar. Dextraze rose to the rank of general and became Canadian Forces chief of the defense staff.

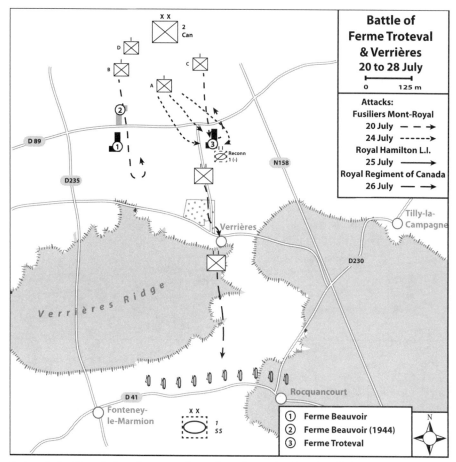

Battle of Ferme Troteval & Verrières

20 to 28 July

0   125 m

Attacks:
Fusiliers Mont-Royal
20 July   — — →
24 July   - - - - - →
Royal Hamilton L.I.
25 July   ⟶
Royal Regiment of Canada
26 July   — →

① Ferme Beauvoir
② Ferme Beauvoir (1944)
③ Ferme Troteval

N

that ended with a furious bayonet charge into the orchard and walled garden of the farm against two platoons of the 1st SS Panzer Division's Reconnaissance Battalion 1. German reinforcements from Verrières and Tilly-la-Campagne were interdicted by artillery and heavy mortar fire. German tanks appeared over the slight crest to the south but were effectively driven off with PIATs and #36 grenades.

A polished granite stele with a gilt inscription in French memorializing the sacrifice of the regiment stands outside the ancient stone walls of the farm grounds. Nearby an infosign describes the **Fusilier Mont-Royal** actions at Ferme Beauvoir and Ferme Troteval.

Operation Spring
25 July 1944

As Operation Atlantic was coming to a halt, plans were already in the making for Operation Spring, an assault whose objective was the critical high ground around Point 122 north of Cintheaux. Much of the four-phase plan, based upon nighttime attacks to avoid the German long-range antitank gun advantages, was to include the 2nd and 3rd Canadian Infantry Divisions along the west and east sides of the Caen-Falaise highway, respectively, to be followed by 7th and Guards Armoured Divisions with Tilly-la-Campagne as the initial objective.

The 1st SS Panzer Division held the front east of Verrières, and the 272nd Infantry Division, reinforced by tank and panzergrenadier battalions from 2nd and 9th SS Panzer divisions, held the front from Verrières to the Orne River. What was just another village to senior Canadian commanders was a major objective to the German High Command. To lose Tilly-la-Campagne meant to lose the ridge; to lose the ridge meant to lose Normandy – and the war.

Objective	To capture Tilly-la-Campaign, Fontenay-le-Marmion, and the crest of Verrières Ridge at Point 122
Forces	
Canadian	II Canadian Corps (Lieutenant-General Guy Simonds)
German	1st SS Panzer Division (SS-Brigadeführer Theodor Wisch) and 272nd Infantry Division (Generalleutnant Friedrich Schack)
Result	Canadian defeat
Casualties	
Canadian	450 killed and 1,100 wounded
German	uncertain
Location	Tilly-la-Campagne is 12 km southeast of Caen.

Battle

The 3rd Canadian Infantry Division attack started under artificial moonlight with an assault upon Tilly-la-Campagne by The North Nova Scotia Highlanders. Despite support from a squadron of Sherman tanks, they were forced to withdraw.

In 2nd Canadian Infantry Division's sector, the Royal Hamilton Light Infantry's assault upon Verrières was delayed, costing it the benefit of the timed artillery barrage. Nonetheless, it fought from Ferme Troteval into Verrières and repelled a German counterattack that morning and another during the late afternoon. A subsequent move by the Royal Regiment against Rocquancourt was ravaged by the combined arms of a panzer division.

The Calgary Highlanders moved on May-s/Orne, bypassing enemy positions to retain their pace behind the leading artillery barrage. Although St-Martin-de-Fontenay was declared cleared, it was not. The Black Watch advanced against Fontenay-le-Marmion despite enemy fire coming into its right flank from St-Martin and into its left flank from the ridge. They met with a ferocious German crossfire that destroyed the entire battalion. Fighting in May-s/Orne continued into the afternoon when the brigade commander ordered the Calgaries to withdraw to St-André-s/Orne. The armor advance was cancelled; SPRING was over.

Aftermath

German panzer troops launched a series of sharp armored counterattacks over subsequent days. While the Royal Hamilton Light Infantry repulsed dozens of assaults against Verrières village, the Calgary Highlanders lost May-s/Orne and St-Martin-de-Fontenay. On 27 July, the 3rd Canadian Infantry Division, which had been on the front lines since D-Day, was placed in reserve for reorganization, refitting, and replacement training.

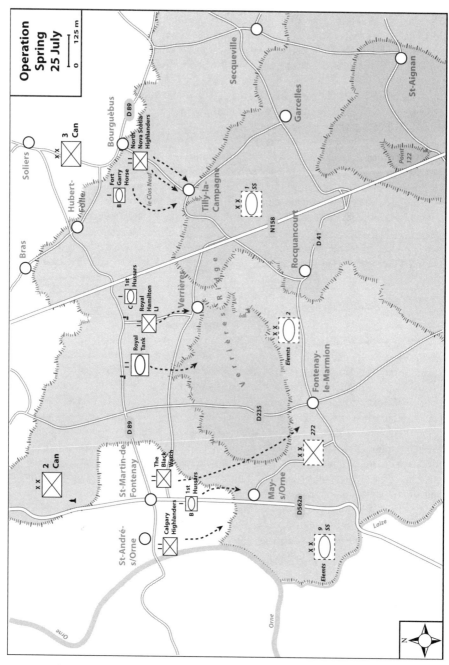

The Canadians' bloodiest day of the Battle of Normandy was a costly diversion for Operation COBRA and one that did not fool Panzer Group West. The losses resulted in more in-fighting between senior Canadian commanders. Although the more severe disaster occurred in 2nd Division, a board of inquiry was called to review 3rd Division's failure to take Tilly-la-Campagne. Brigadier DG Cunningham[9] of 9th Infantry Brigade and Lieutenant-Colonel C Petch[10] of The North Nova Scotia Highlanders were relieved of their commands. After questioning the division commander's judgment, Lieutenant-Colonel GH Christiansen, the Stormont, Dundas, and Glengarry Highlanders commander, was reassigned.

General Montgomery felt that large scale operations would fail against the concentrated German armor and instead ordered Operation BLUECOAT to the west, thereby postponing any further thrust east of the Orne River.

Battlefield Tour

The high speed and limited access Caen-Falaise highway (N158) splits the ridge and causes some inconvenience in touring the battlefield. The tour moves to the east side of the highway to review the intense fighting for Tilly-la-Campagne before returning to the west side of the highway to continue the actions of the 2nd Canadian Division.

> Leave Ferme Troteval by continuing east on highway D89. Follow the highway for 4.0 km into Bourguébus. Turn right toward Tilly-la-Campagne (D230). After 700 m, stop at the crossing farm tracks. (49.115604, -0.299914)

Battle of Tilly-la-Campagne
25 July to 8 August 1944

Tilly-la-Campagne is a modest farm community of less than 100 people. It is distinguished by its geographical position, one which allows observation of the southern districts of Caen, Bras, and Bourguébus to the northeast and Verrières to the west. Historically, its location was not lost on other commanders; in the 11th century, Duke William of Normandy fought against the English on these slopes as had Caesar's legions against Celtic tribes before him.

At 0300, the 3rd Canadian Infantry Division's North Nova Scotia Highlanders moved from the village of Bourguébus against Tilly-la-Campagne. Unknown to them, the village was defended by troops of the German 272nd Infantry Division strengthened by a platoon of four PzKpfw IVs from 7th Panzer Company, SS Panzer Regiment 1,[11] and a company of combat engineers from SS Pioneer Battalion 1.

Led by Companies C and D, the North Novas advanced across the wheat and corn fields to the west of highway D230 in an area known locally as le Clos Neuf. The troops were silhouetted by the artificial moonlight and made excellent targets for German gunners. Despite heavy casualties, they fought into the orchard north of the village to the

---

9   Brigadier Douglas Gordon Cunningham was a prewar lawyer and politician. After his removal from 9th Brigade, Brigadier Cunningham became commandant of the Royal Military College of Canada. He died in 1992 at age 84.

10   Lieutenant-Colonel Charles Petch returned to the fighting as commander of the 4th Princess Louise Dragoons in December 1944.

11   SS Panzer Regiment 1 was commanded by SS-Obersturmbannführer Joachim Peiper, who became notorious for commanding the troops that committed the Malmédy Massacre during the Battle of the Bulge in December 1944. After the war, Peiper was tried for ordering the murder of POWs and found guilty. He was sentenced to death, but the sentence was later commuted to life imprisonment. Continued controversy over the conduct of interrogations and the trial led to Peiper's release in 1956. In 1976, Peiper, then living quietly in France, was killed by what were believed to be former members of the French Resistance. He was 61 years old.

west of the buildings of Ferme Marie. While Company C was caught by German machine guns, Company D moved along the roadside and managed to lodge a few men into the first German trenches along Ferme Marie, but they, too, became casualties of the battle.

Company B circled around to the east and destroyed one of the four enemy tanks with a PIAT before its company commander was killed. Company A took the path made by Company C and reached the village outskirts before encountering an impenetrable wall of fire.

By dawn, Squadron B, Fort Garry Horse, attempted to drive Company A into the village from le Clos Neuf. German tanks buried hull-down in the rubble of the bombed village had other ideas, and they quickly destroyed eleven of the fifteen Canadian Sherman tanks. The burning tanks set the surrounding wheat on fire, killing previously wounded Canadian troops who could not escape. The North Novas held their positions all day but withdrew after dark. Casualties were high, with 61 killed, 46 wounded, and 32 taken prisoner.

Continue toward Tilly-la-Campagne passing Ferme Marie which was on the east side of the road in 1944. In the village center, turn right toward Caen (D230). Proceed 210 m past the hay barn on the right to the to the abandoned railway embankment at west edge of village. (49.111453, -0.308948)

In 1944, the straight gravel pathway on the left held a minor railway line used to ship iron ore from the mines around St-Martin-de-Fontenay to the works at Colombelles. The embankment provided some of the only shelter for attacking troops and was hotly contested during the several attacks upon Tilly. A short distance ahead, the road curves left to its junction with the Caen-Falaise highway. Straight ahead, a farm track leads to Ferme Noyer. Do not attempt to drive to the farm.

On 29 July, the Essex Scottish Regiment supported by artillery, antitank guns, and a tank troop attacked le Ferme Noyer. While the troops approached, the hedgerows around the farm grounds erupted in machine-gun fire. Officers and NCOs,[12] in a display of personal bravery, led their men in a wild charge against the farm, dropping grenades into slit trenches and shooting individual snipers. After its capture, the farm became a base for further Canadian attacks.

On 1 August, an attack by the Calgary Highlanders from Ferme Noyer reached the railway line. Three Sherman tanks from the Royal Scots Greys moved forward while the infantry entered the village. Untersturmführer Gerhardt Stiller held his fire from his well-hidden PzKpfw IV near the hay barn while the Shermans approached the road junction in front of the church. He destroyed two Shermans in quick succession, and a German mortar attack was supplemented by *Nebelwerfer* rockets. The Calgaries were pushed back to the rail embankment. A repeat attack later in the day also failed. Both sides were so battered that a brief cease-fire allowed the recovery dead and wounded.

That night the newly arrived Lincoln and Welland Regiment switched the attack line back to the Bourguébus road, but it too was beaten back. Meanwhile, the inexperienced German Infantry Regiment 1055, 89th Infantry Division, replaced the SS troops who were shifting west to face the American breakout at St-Lô. An attempt to take Tilly from le Clos Neuf on 5 August by the Argyll and Sutherland Highlanders also failed. On 8 August, after

---

12   Company Sergeant Major Les Dixon was awarded a bar to the Military Medal that he earned at Dieppe. Sergeant Charles Wold earned the Croix de Guerre, and Captain Telford Steele a Military Cross.

being isolated by advancing tank columns of Operation TOTALIZE, the fifty-one remaining German troops surrendered to the 2nd and 5th Battalions Seaforth Highlanders, British 51st (Highland) Division.

Continue following the highway (D230). After 900 m, turn right toward Soliers/St-Martin-de-Fontenay (N158, otherwise known as the Caen-Falaise Road). After 2.1 km, take the next exit toward Soliers/Bourguébus (D89). Carefully, because the exit ramp has two-direction traffic, continue to the stop. Turn right toward St-Martin-de-Fontenay (D89). After 950 m and after passing Ferme Troteval, turn left toward Hameau Verrières. Continue 850 m to the line of hedges on the right. (49.11349, -0.333281)

Battle of Verrières
25 to 28 July 1944

At 0410 on 25 July, the Royal Hamilton Light Infantry moved up the slope toward Verrières under heavy enemy machine-gun and tank fire. When Company C's commander was hit, leadership of the leading troops fell to Corporal H Sawyer, who spotted four machine guns operating in support of the German tanks along a line of hedges north of Verrières. He led a four-man section behind the enemy positions, alternately crawling and – at times – sprinting between Tiger tanks. Although wounded, Sawyer and his men eliminated all four machine-gun nests. [13] Several 17-pounder antitank guns came forward and eliminated the four enemy tanks. With the intensity of enemy fire lessened, the infantry fought into the village from opposite flanks. A quick armored counterattack was driven off by use of PIATs.

The next stage of the operation sent the Royal Regiment of Canada, supported by tanks from the 7th Armoured Division, against Rocquancourt. It gained 350 meters south of Verrières before fierce fire brought a halt to the advance. Its Company C attempted to push through but was almost annihilated in the effort. Reports indicated that the 1st SS Panzer Division had thirty tanks in hull-down positions between Fontenay and Rocquancourt.

The Royal Hamiltons, the only unit to achieve the day's objective, now came under a German armor counterattack. Eight tanks penetrated its line, a total disaster avoided by the timely intervention of a squadron of 1st Hussar tanks and rocket-firing RAF Typhoon fighter aircraft. Lesser assaults continued for three days.

Continue 300 m into Verrières; turn left, then right to access the chapel. (49.110154, -0.332401)

Canadian and French flags frame the entry to the hamlet's small stone chapel. A black stone plaque near the chapel doorway remembers the 2nd Canadian Infantry Division efforts during Operation TOTALIZE.

A brass infosign in front of the chapel commemorates the memory of the 'gallant men of the **Royal Hamilton Light Infantry**, 2nd Canadian Division.' As the infosign states, 'The RHLI was the only Canadian Regiment to gain its objective and hold on for seven days in the face of intensive fighting and relentless counterattacks by the elite German 1st SS Panzer Division. The price was high: 200 casualties, 53 of them fatal.' As the German counterattacks came through the fields to the south and southeast, the village

---

13   Corporal Harold Victor Sawyer was awarded the Distinguished Conduct Medal. He survived the war and died in 1969 at age 69.

was shelled almost into oblivion by German artillery. Walk south on the slightly uphill farm road that passes in front of the chapel to the crest of the ridge south of the village to view the terrain where the Royal Regiment's attack upon Rocquancourt was repulsed.

> Return to toward Ferme Troteval. Turn west onto D89 (unsigned) and follow for 3.0 km into St-Martin-de-Fontenay. Turn left toward May-s/Orne. After approximately 650 m, pass 'the factory' on the left. (49.110709, -0.374436)

The Calgary Highlanders moved east of highway D562 (now D562a) in their assault upon May-s/Orne. La Cité de la Mine, a complex of buildings mistakenly thought of as 'the factory' to Canadian planners, is 275 meters south of the St-Martin-de-Fontenay church. Most of the site has been redeveloped and the prominent tower, which was once used to house mine shaft machinery, no longer remains. The old water tower is still visible to the east of the highway. The Calgary Highlanders swung around the east side of the Cite de la Mine, leaving the site well defended by the German Grenadier Regiment 981 in concealed positions.

> Continue into May-s/Orne. In the town, turn left toward Fontenay-le-Marmion (D41b). After 260 m, bear left onto rue des Verrières and proceed to the end of the pavement. (49.100833, -0.367463)

The Calgary Highlanders entered May-s/Orne to find enemy troops to their rear and tank-supported enemy forces to their front. They came under fire from their own artillery and withdrew to east of St-Martin. The movement was fatal to the Black Watch, but the Calgaries were not unscathed, either. They suffered 177 casualties, including all of the company commanders.

The Black Watch left its area north of Ferme Beauvoir at 0330 and moved through St-André-s/Orne. It had to fight against German infiltrators just to achieve its start line near the St-Martin church. During the preliminary advance, Lieutenant-Colonel Stuart Cantlie,[14] battalion commander, was killed, and Major E Modzfeldt, senior company commander, was wounded. A reconnaissance patrol sent into May-s/Orne reported only light resistance – it was wrong.

At 0910, The Black Watch moved up an open slope against Fontenay-le-Marmion. Now led by a junior company commander, Major FP Griffin,[15] the battalion of 322 men fought across the open fields east of St-Martin directly against Fontenay-le-Marmion. The German main line of resistance occupied the ridge to the south and east. A support squadron of 1st Hussars lost six tanks while infantry casualties also rapidly mounted. Reportedly, 60 men may have achieved the ridge crest where they met more entrenched defenders. Unable to advance or withdraw, individuals sought their own escape. Only fifteen men safely returned; 123 were killed, 101 were wounded, and 83 were taken prisoner. It was the second worst loss by any Canadian regiment in the war, surpassed only by the Dieppe landings in 1942.

The farm track to the east is the rue de Verrières and was the Black Watch start

---

14   Lieutenant-Colonel Stuart Stephen Cantlie is buried in Bretteville-s/Laize Canadian War Cemetery. He was 36 years old.

15   Major Fredrick Philip Griffin died in the assault and is buried in Bretteville-s/Laize Canadian War Cemetery. He was 26 years old.

line. Fontenay-le-Marmion is over the slight crest to the right front (southeast). The unit crested that height to enter what is sometimes referred to as the Valley of Death, where the Black Watch troops were fully exposed to German guns to the right, left, and ahead.

> Reverse direction and turn left onto rue Fleur Terre. After 350 m, turn left onto rue de la Testé (D41b) and continue to the town exit sign. (49.096534, -0.365714)

The attack upon Fontenay-le-Marmion took place the open fields on the left where the water tower marks the northern limit of modern Fontenay. In 1944 the town was much smaller and sheltered in a depression behind the crest of Verrières Ridge.

> Continue for 750 m. Turn left toward Fontenay-le-Marmion (D41) and continue into the town. (49.093362, -0.353)

Operation TOTALIZE
8 to 11 August 1944

On 1 August 1944, the First Canadian Army became operational under the command of Lieutenant-General HDG Crerar. The army was structured around II Canadian Corps but included Allied elements such as British 15th, 49th, and 51st Infantry Divisions, temporarily the 6th Airborne Division, and the 1st Polish Armoured Division.

The enormous losses of the previous battle motivated Canadian command to seek alternative tactics for its attacks. The shrapnel and bullets of German mortars and machine guns had been the greatest source of Canadian casualties thus far in the war. Lt-Gen Guy Simonds, II Canadian Corps commander, developed the idea of stripping his 102 M7 'Priest' self-propelled guns of their main weaponry such that each vehicle accommodated ten fighting men; thus, the armored personnel carrier (APC) was born.[16] In addition, in order to blindfold the long-range German antitank gun advantage, large clouds of artificial smoke blanketed the site. To deter German armor, Allied air forces provided saturation bombing of suspected enemy armor concentrations as in operations GOODWOOD and COBRA. Finally, integrated, all-arms assault units managed a varied degree of success.

The German high command had ordered the westward movement of its panzer divisions in response to the American advance during Operation COBRA. The front line on both sides of the Caen-Falaise highway was taken over by one German infantry division strengthened during the battle by insertion of three *kampfgruppe* from SS-Brigadeführer Kurt Meyer's 12th SS Panzer Division.

Objective	To capture high ground north of Falaise
Forces	
Canadian	II Canadian Corps (Lt-Gen Guy Simonds)
German	89th Infantry Division (Generalleutnant Conrad-Oskar Heinrichs)
Result	Partial Allied victory
Casualties	
Canadian	1,256 killed or wounded; 146 tanks lost

---

16   The vehicles were officially called 'Kangaroos' after the code name of the workshop where they were modified or 'unfrocked Priests' by the troops that used them.

German	Unknown killed or wounded; 1,270 taken prisoner; 45 tanks lost
Location	Rocquancourt is 11 km south of Caen.

Battle

At 2300 on 7 August, 1,020 Lancaster and Halifax bombers dropped their bomb loads on enemy concentrations identified by red or green smoke shells fired by Canadian ground artillery. Thirty minutes later, ground troops led by a creeping artillery barrage advanced along attack lines delineated by Bofors guns firing tracers over their heads. Although some units still lost their way in the darkness, smoke, and dust, by 0900 the first objectives at St-Aignan-de-Cramesnil and Rocquancourt were occupied. The troublesome villages of May-s/Orne and Fontenay-le-Marmion, now defended by the German 89th Infantry Division, were targets of saturation bombing and captured by non-motorized infantry units.

Although several strongpoints held out, the 89th Infantry Division had been broken across a 6-kilometer front. Kurt 'Panzer' Meyer was quick to respond by sending a panzergrenadier battalion, a unit of PzKpfw IVs, a company of *Panzerjäger* IVs, Flak and *Nebelwerfer* units, and ten Tiger tanks toward Bretteville-s/Laize.

A second phase of daylight bombing by US Eighth Airforce was less stellar. Several planes dropped their loads on friendly forces, killing 65 and wounding 250, including the 3rd Canadian Infantry Division commander, Major-Gen Rod Keller. The 1st Polish Armoured Division entered the battle front at St-Aignan-de-Cramesnil and ran into a concealed *kampfgruppe*'s guns, suffering the loss of numerous tanks.

Early on 9 August, two armored forces set out in darkness toward new objectives. Halpenny Force assaulted Bretteville-le-Rabet and cleared the town by 1400. Worthington Force was assigned to capture Point 195 near Fontaine-le-Pin, the highest ground north of Falaise. Worthington became bewilderingly lost and, in the ensuing battle, was completely annihilated. TOTALIZE was over as was the battle for Verrières Ridge. The battle for Falaise was about to begin.

Aftermath

TOTALIZE gained the crest of the Verrières Ridge by advancing an impressive 16 kilometers to Point 195, but the objective of Falaise remained in German hands. Considering the massive superiority of fire-power in air and armored units and the greatly depleted enemy defensive force, more was expected. Historians have argued over reasons for the failure to achieve greater success. Criticism focuses upon high level commanders' failure to plan flexibility into the aerial bombardments, lack of reconnaissance of enemy positions, and inadequate communication between infantry and armor units.

Battlefield Tour

Leave Fontenay-le-Marmion to the east (D41); cross the new D562 and continue into Rocquancourt (becomes rue de la République). Pass the church ahead on the left and stop at the park immediately on the right. (49.094142, -0.323185)

The **Canadian Memorial Park** in Rocquancourt is beautifully landscaped with benches, mature maple trees, and a profusion of seasonal flowers and shrubs. The ground holds a stele from the town's citizens to their 'Canadian liberators and friends.'

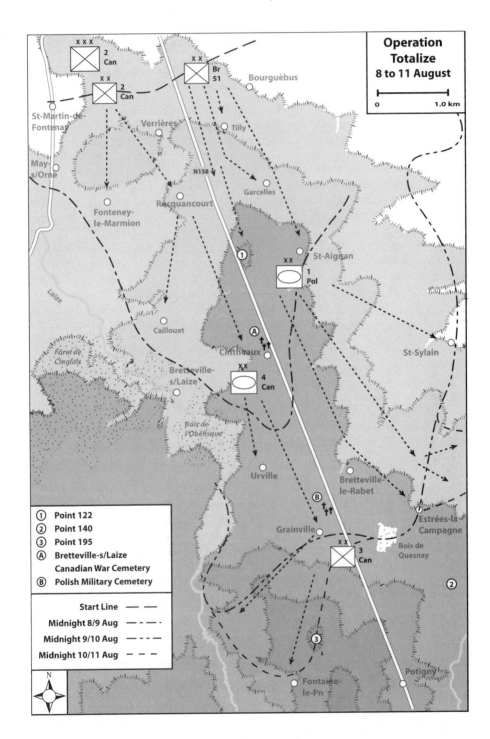

Operation Totalize
8 to 11 August

0   1.0 km

① Point 122
② Point 140
③ Point 195
Ⓐ Bretteville-s/Laize
   Canadian War Cemetery
Ⓑ Polish Military Cemetery

Start Line — —
Midnight 8/9 Aug — — ·
Midnight 9/10 Aug — — —
Midnight 10/11 Aug — — —

St-Martin-de-Fontenay
May-s/Orne
Verrières
Bourguébus
Tilly
Garcelles
N158
Fonteney-le-Marmion
Rocquancourt
St-Aignan
Laize
Caillouet
St-Sylain
Forêt de Cinglais
Cintheaux
Bretteville-s/Laize
Urville
Bretteville-le-Rabet
Bois de l'Obélisque
Grainville
Estrées-la-Campagne
Bois de Quesnay
Fontaine-le-Pn
Potigny

2 Can (XXX)
2 Can (XX)
Br 51 (XX)
1 Pol (XX)
4 Can (XX)
3 Can (XX)

N

A short stele carries an embossed plaque describing the **South Saskatchewan Regiment** and the unit's involvement in the Dieppe raid. It continues with a description of the liberation of the much contested Verrières Ridge:

> On the night of 7/8 August … attacking south from Verrières village, the South Sasks cleared Rocquancourt with mopping up completed by noon on 8 August. That afternoon two companies of the battalion with two troops of tanks from the 1st Hussars carried out a flanking attack from Rocquancourt to assist the Queen's Own Cameron Highlanders of Canada in securing Fontenay-le-Marmion. By the night of 8/9 August, Verrières Ridge was firmly in Canadian hands.

The village war memorial bears a separate plaque honoring local citizen Georges Poulard. Arrested in the night of 1/2 May 1942, he was accused of being a member of the Communist resistance that derailed a German troop train on the night of 16/17 April killing twenty-eight German soldiers and wounding nineteen in the action. [17]

Continue on rue de la République (D41). After 1.4 km, take the 2nd exit onto the ramp toward Falaise (N158), whose high speed highway can be dangerous. After 650 m past the roundabout, the highway passes Point 122, an objective of Operation TOTALIZE and the highest point on Verrières Ridge. (49.080247, -0.301394)

Take exit la Jalousie from the highway toward St-Aignan-de-Cramesnil. At the next junction, turn left toward Caen/St-Aignan-de-Cramesnil (D23). Follow for 600 m to cross over the highway and then turn right onto rue du Sept Août 1944 toward St-Aignan (D80). Almost immediately, turn right onto D183a (not signed). The road becomes a frontage road to the highway. After 1.1 km, view an insignificant field to the east of the highway. (49.066472, -0.293074)

Hauptsturmführer Michael Wittmann led four Tiger tanks toward St-Aignan-de-Cramesnil from Cintheaux. A force of over thirty Sherman Fireflys hid behind hedges and woods when Wittmann's small troop entered this field. Within minutes, the four Tigers were in flames, and Wittmann was dead. [18]

Continue 1.3 km and turn right toward Cintheaux (D183). After 350 m, turn right onto rue du Prieuré and continue 650 m to the cemetery. (49.060563, -0.291867)

The **Bretteville-s/Laize Canadian War Cemetery** in Cintheaux stands isolated amid a sugar-beet field north of the village. To enter the cemetery, pass through a double colonnade framed by two small square shelters. A center path leads directly to the Stone of Remembrance located in the center of the grave plots. Of the 2,958 soldiers buried in this cemetery 2,792 are Canadian and each of their gravestones bears the Maple Leaf emblem. Most of the burials stem from the fighting from Caen to Falaise. From the rear of the cemetery, the ground rolls down into the Laize River valley.

Near the entrance to the cemetery, but outside its boundary, a stone stele in the shape of a Maple Leaf names the place in front of the cemetery after Private Gérard Doré of

---

17   Georges Poulard was sent to the Wehrmacht prison at Royallieu near Compiègne. Poulard died in Auschwitz-Birkenau Concentration Camp on 17 August 1942. He was 41 years old.

18   Wittmann's exploits at Villers-Bocage are described in Chapter Thirteen.

the Fusiliers Mont-Royal, killed on 23 July 1944 in the attack upon Verrières. The 16-year-old soldier is considered to be the youngest Allied soldier killed in Europe during the Second World War. He is buried in Plot XVI, Row G, Grave 11.

Reverse direction and in Cintheaux turn left toward Caen (D183). On the opposite side of the highway, turn right toward Cauvicourt/Falaise (D183a). After 1.8 km, turn right toward Falaise (D132a). Enter the highway toward Potigny/Falaise (N158). Take the next exit after 2.2 km toward Grainville (D131). At the first roundabout, take the first exit and proceed to the cemetery on the left. (49.023291, -0.270034)

The **Cimetière Militaire Polonais de Lagannerie-Urville** is the only Polish Cemetery in France and holds the graves of 696 soldiers from the 1st Polish Armoured Division. The metal entrance gateway holds emblems of the various units that comprised the division. A white concrete memorial topped with a stylized Polish Eagle stands at the end of the shrub-lined center aisle. A black stone altar is part of the memorial. The graves are bedecked with French military crosses, except Jewish dead who have tombstones. Each bears an identifying plaque with the French honorific 'Mort Pour la Patrie.'

Reverse direction, and in the roundabout take the 2nd exit toward Grainville (D658). After 850 m, take the 2nd exit toward Estrées-la-Campagne. Follow this highway to and through the town for 4.7 km. When the road begins to ascend the ridge, stop at the farm track on the right. (49.017298, -0.203687)

Destruction of Worthington Force
9 August 1944

Lieutenant-Colonel DG Worthington commanded 28th Canadian Armoured Regiment – also known as The British Columbia Regiment – with the Algonquin Regiment of infantry under command. Squadron A pushed off from north of Cintheaux at 0300 on 9 August. The column was to follow a similar armor/infantry force commanded by Lieutenant-Colonel WW Halpenny, comprised of Canadian Grenadier Guards and the Lake Superior Regiment, into Bretteville-le-Rabet. While it waited for Halpenny to take Bretteville, Worthington came under fire from enemy concealed in nearby woods. Rather than sit idle while under attack, Worthington ordered the column, now led by Squadron C and his command tank, to follow the straight road it believed to be the Caen-Falaise Road. It was not. Burning wheat and haystacks gave the force meager illumination while armor and motorized infantry units became separated. Lost units wandered about looking for identifiable landmarks. One troop of Squadron B turned toward Hill 195, found itself alone among overpowering enemy, and turned back. The Algonquin's Company D veered even more left and started heading north before realizing its mistake. Most units just followed the tank tracks of the command unit through the fields of grain.

By 0700, Worthington Force, now reduced to two squadrons of the British Columbia Regiment and two companies of Algonquin infantry, reported that it had achieved its objective. However, by moving southeast instead of southwest, it was not on Hill 195 but on Hill 140 – 6 kilometers from its objective and 3 kilometers behind German lines. Unaware of the error, the Canadians consolidated and formed an all-around defense in a rectangular field surrounded by a high hedge. They were slowly being surrounded by *Kampfgruppe Waldmüller*, in turn strengthened by Tiger and Panther tanks from

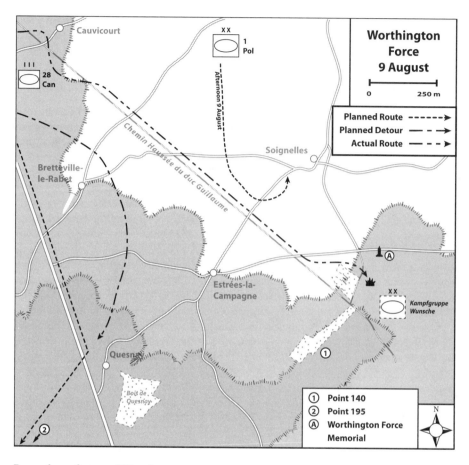

Worthington Force 9 August

0   250 m

Planned Route - - - - - ➤
Planned Detour — - - ➤
Actual Route — - - ➤

① Point 140
② Point 195
Ⓐ Worthington Force Memorial

Panzerkampfgruppe Wünsche.

Worthington placed his tanks and armored vehicles around the four sides of the field while the infantry dug trenches and established mortar positions. A day-long battle ensued with German 88-mm guns setting the perimeter vehicles ablaze and Tiger tanks firing from a small copse to the west. Requested artillery support was delivered, but to the real Hill 195. Further radio contact was then lost. An armor relief column advanced, but it turned back after being hit by massed antitank guns and losing twenty-six tanks. By noon, only seven tanks were serviceable and by 1400 only one. A Typhoon fighter attack drove off a German infantry assault.

At this time, a tank force from 1st Polish Division approached from the north. Thinking that they were German troops, the Poles opened fire upon the Canadians. The German attackers turned their 88-mm guns on the Polish and drove them off with heavy losses. The situation for the infantry was dire while they beat off repeated German infantry assaults. During a late afternoon mortar attack, Lt-Col Worthington was killed. [19] Darkness saved the few survivors who abandoned the wounded and made their way north as best they could. Forty-seven of the unit's tanks were destroyed.

19   Lieutenant-Colonel Donald Grant Worthington's body was recovered. He is buried in Bretteville-s/Laize Canadian War Cemetery.

The farm track opposite leads to the wood behind which Worthington had established his strongpoint – that is, adjacent and to the left of the smaller wood in distance. It is a long and muddy trek which retains little evidence of the momentous battle.

Continue 300 m to the memorial on the right. (49.017425, -0.199224)

The original cross was erected by order of Major-General George Kitching, 4th Canadian Armoured Division commander, a few days after Canadian troops occupied the area. The memorial commemorates **Worthington Force** and its 95 killed, 76 wounded, and 79 taken prisoner. The two polished granite steles describe the events.

Reverse direction and proceed into Estrées-la-Campagne. Turn left toward Quesnay (D260). Follow for 2.8 km passing over the Caen-Falaise highway, then turn left toward Potigny (D658). When the highway passes over the Caen-Falaise road, the large expanse of Quesnay Wood is visible on the left. (48.996325, -0.252514)

On 10 August, a final effort to reach the Laison River at Potigny fell to two battalions of 3rd Canadian Infantry Division supported by seven artillery regiments. The first objective was Quesnay Wood. However, unknown to Canadian commanders, the wood held *Panzerkampfgruppe Wünsche* and *Kampfgruppe Krause*. Entering the forest, the Queen's Own Cameron Highlanders met small-arms fire backed by tanks. The North Shore Regiment moved around the northern edge of the forest but fell victim to friendly fire. The Canadians suffered 44 killed and 121 wounded before withdrawing.

After a short distance, turn right toward Ussy (D43). Follow for 2.0 km, then turn right onto rue de Paris (unsigned rural road). After approximately 500 m, stop at the low memorial on the right. (48.978562, -0.270689)

Point 195 was finally taken without a casualty before dawn on 10 August by the Argyll and Sutherland Highlanders of Canada, led by Lieutenant-Colonel JD Stewart,[20] in one of the most brilliantly executed night advances of the war. The men crept single-file through German lines in darkness to the height where they captured the 50-man German garrison without a shot fired. By dawn they were well entrenched when a counterattack by Oberst Erich Olboeters' SS Panzergrenadier Regiment 3 was repelled. By noon, tanks from 21st Canadian Armoured Regiment arrived to provide armored support but became subjected to antitank fire from Quesnay Woods. The fighting continued throughout the day, but heavy artillery and air support defeated each German attempt to retake the hill. The Argylls were relieved that evening.

Beside the road, a stone block monument commemorates the Argylls' capture of the broad high spot of **Hill 195** immediately behind the memorial. The stone also notes the Argylls' participation in the capture of St-Lambert-s/Dives during the final closure of the Falaise Gap.

The rue de Paris continues into Fontaine-le-Pin.

---

20   Lieutenant-Colonel John David Stewart survived the was earning a Distinguished Service Cross. He became a successful businessman and politician in Prince Edward Island, Canada. Steart died in 1988 at age 78.

Chapter Fifteen

Battle of Falaise Pocket
11 to 25 August 1944

The German counterattack in Operation LÜTTICH exposed its forces to the possibility of a junction of Canadian forces moving from the north and American forces advancing from the south to form a pocket around the German Fifth Panzer and Seventh Armies. First, however, the long sought objective of Falaise had to be secured. The Canadian effort to finally capture Falaise assumed the code name TRACTABLE.

Battle of Clair Tizon
11 to 14 August 1944

In preparation for Operation TRACTABLE, General Simonds ordered General Foulkes to threaten German positions astride the Caen-Falaise road by moving south from Bretteville-s/Laize around their western flank. The route passed through Clair Tizon, a small village of a few houses on either side of a narrow, paved roadway. The village sat in the Laize River valley with higher ground to the east and west. A narrow bridge crossed the river.

Objective	To flank German forces along the Caen-Falaise road
Forces	
Canadian	2nd Canadian Infantry Division (Major-General Charles Foulkes)
German	85th Infantry Division (Generalleutnant Kurt Chill) and III Battalion, SS Panzergrenadier Regiment 26 (SS-Sturmbannführer Erich Olboeter)
Result	Clair Tizon and the bridge over the Laize were captured, but further progress was not possible.
Casualties	
Canadian	Over 79 killed, at least 260 wounded, and 3 missing
German	Uncertain; 378 taken prisoner
Location	Clair Tizon is 30 km south of Caen

Battle

A reconnaissance in force led by the 4th Canadian Infantry Brigade with the 27th Armoured Regiment under command left Bretteville-s/Laize during the night of 11/12 August. Progress was rapid as the men waded through the unharvested wheat along each side of the highway. Despite pockets of determined resistance, they advanced 7 kilometers during the first 24 hours. The reconnaissance became the main effort of II Canadian Corps because command felt that the German Army was collapsing. By 13 August, the 5th Canadian Infantry Brigade's Calgary Highlanders had advanced an additional 5 kilometers to establish a small bridgehead across the Laize River at Clair Tizon.

The force was now a major threat to German units to the north and east, which reacted accordingly, bringing artillery fire down upon the Calgaries that set two Sherman tanks ablaze. An attempt on the evening of 13 August by le Régiment de Maisonneuve to expand the bridgehead faltered among numerous casualties. On 14 August, the Canadians beat off three counterattacks by the III Battalion, SS Panzergrenadier Regiment 26, 12th

SS Panzer Division. The German troops later withdrew under threat of encirclement by Operation TRACTABLE.

Battlefield Tour

This short one-stop tour views the bridge and memorial plaques in Clair Tizon, which is a short distance from the final site of the previous chapter at Fontaine-le-Pin.

> From the place des Alliés in Fontaine-le-Pin, proceed southwest leaving the village on rue Varin. After 700 m, bear right toward highway D167 (unsigned). At the junction with highway D167, turn left and continue 1 km into Clair Tizon. At the junction with highway D6, turn right. The bridge is immediately on the right. (48.960173, -0.30663)

The 1944 bridge over the Laize River at Clair Tizon and a short section of 1944 roadway remain beside the new highway. Three flagpoles identify the location of a pink granite stele that commemorates forty-two Canadian soldiers killed during fighting at Tournebu and lists them by name and age. The village of Clair Tizon is in the commune of Tournebu, whose namesake village sits astride the main line of advance for Canadian troops before they achieved the bridge. Two memorial plaques are attached to the bridge abutments. One commemorates the advance of le **Régiment de Maisonneuve** toward Falaise and the unit's liberation of the village despite heavy German shell fire. A second plaque, unveiled only recently in 2010, commemorates the 13 August capture of the river crossing by the **Calgary Highlanders** and celebrates the leadership of its commander, Lieutenant-Colonel D MacLauchlan.[1] The plaque also notes that the engagement marked the end of one month of continuous fighting by the unit.

Operation TRACTABLE
14 to 16 August 1944

Operation TRACTABLE employed the same tactics as Operation TOTALIZE, utilizing heavy bombings, armored personnel carriers, and massed armored columns. In this instance, troops advanced in daylight rather than darkness with artillery providing smokescreens to blind German gunners. Two armored columns each supported by infantry struck east of the Caen-Falaise road against German troops holding the high ground north and west of the Laizon River valley.

Objective	To capture Falaise
Forces	
Canadian	II Canadian Corps comprised of 3rd Canadian Infantry Division and 4th Canadian and 1st Polish Armoured Divisions (Lt-Gen Guy Simonds)
German	85th Infantry Division (Generalleutnant Kurt Chill)

---

1   Despite being awarded the Distinguished Service Cross for his handling of the Clair Tizon battle, the unpopular Lieutenant-Colonel David MacLauchlan was criticized as a commander who led from the rear. In October 1944, after commanding his unit for two years and after four months in combat, MacLauchlan was relieved.

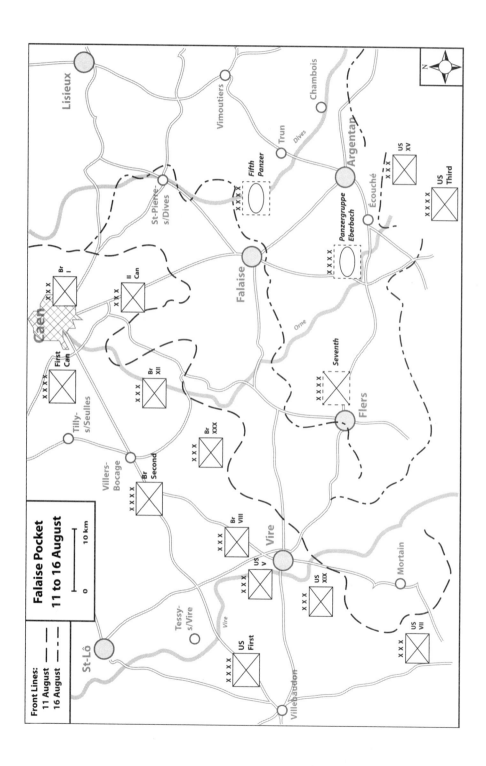

Result	Falaise was liberated and bridgeheads established across the Dives River.
Casualties	
Canadian	Uncertain
Polish	263 killed or wounded
German	Uncertain; 1,299 taken prisoner
Location	Falaise is 35 km south of Caen

Battle

Fifty-three medium bombers struck areas of suspected German concentration at 1140 on 14 August, and armoured columns started forward two minutes later. German infantry positions north of the Laizon River presented little difficulty and were quickly overcome. Although the Laizon is narrow and the water is not deep, the valley formed more of an antitank obstacle than Canadian planners had anticipated. When armored units pushed forward, they scattered looking for crossing points over the steep river banks. At 1400, 811 RAF heavy bombers struck villages on both sides of the Caen-Falaise road, including the troublesome Quesnay Wood. However, as was becoming all too common, short bombing caused three hundred Canadian and Polish casualties. Unfortunately for the attacking columns, the Canadian plan had fallen into German hands the previous day. German antitank batteries of the 12th SS Panzer Division, on the reverse slope of the ridgeline south of the Laizon, poured murderous fire upon Canadian armored vehicles. One of the early victims of German antitank fire was Brigadier EL Booth, 4th Armoured Brigade commander, killed when his tank was hit.[2] Soon the ridge was littered with burning Sherman and Churchill tanks. Nevertheless, by midnight the Canadians were within 5 kilometers of Falaise.

On the second day of the offensive, 4th Canadian Infantry Brigade was released by the enemy's withdrawal from Clair Tizon and advanced 9.5 kilometers to within 2 kilometers of western Falaise. On 16 August, Canadian infantry engaged in a two-day battle to liberate Falaise while their armor pushed southwest toward Trun.

Farther the east, the 1st Polish Armoured Division crossed the Dives River at Jort and proceeded southeast in two battle groups with Chambois becoming the divisional objective. By the night of 18 August, the two groups had crossed the Trun-Vimoutiers road, thereby blocking German escape routes toward Liverot and Vimoutiers.

Meanwhile, a crisis continued in the German High Command. On 15 August Hitler ordered General von Kluge to launch an immediate, but impossible, counterattack. Late on 16 August, while the Fifth Panzer Army, redesignated from Panzer Group West, and the Seventh Army deteriorated, Hitler relented and authorized a withdrawal behind the Dives River. The next day, Generalfeldmarschall Walter Model arrived at Army Group B headquarters and relieved von Kluge. On 17 August, von Kluge committed suicide on his way to Berlin.[3]

---

2   Brigadier Eric Leslie Booth is buried in Bretteville-s/Laize Canadian War Cemetery; he was 38 years old.

3   Generalfeldmarschall Günther von Kluge had conversations with Rommel and others regarding the planned 20 July assassination attempt on Hitler's life. He had every reason to believe that his name had come before the Führer in that context.

Battlefield Tour

From Clair Tizon, proceed toward Falaise (D6) for 10 km to a large roundabout. Take the first exit into Falaise and follow the tourist signs to Château Guillaume-le-Conquérant (D658, Route de Caen, becomes Av d'Hastings, then rue Georges Clemenceau. Turn right on D511, Bd de la Libération). (48.893206, -0.202292)

Falaise

Falaise has been occupied since pre-historic times because of its position on a high cliff – a *falaise* – above the Ante River. The rock outcropping saw its first fortifications in the 8th century during the reign of Charlemagne. In the 10th century, weakened Frankish kings gave the land to Viking invaders who created the dukedom of Normandy. Falaise became a Norman stronghold with fortifications constructed upon the cliff.

During the afternoon of 16 August, the 6th Infantry Brigade, 2nd Canadian Infantry Division, supported by twenty-four tanks of the 27th Armoured Regiment entered Falaise. The 625-man South Saskatchewan Regiment proceeded along the Caen road (originally highway D158, renamed D658), while the 667-man Queen's Own Cameron Highlanders of Canada moved in from the northwest through Porte Philippe Jean. The city had been heavily bombed three nights earlier, and armor movement was severely restricted by large bomb craters and debris-filled streets. Urban fighting at its worst ensued when the two Canadian battalions worked house-by-house to dislodge 150 SS Panzergrenadiers of the 12th SS Panzer Division supported by two Tiger tanks. By the morning of 17 August, the South Saskatchewan Regiment had reached the railway station which held the defenders' command post. At 0200 the next day, the final assault fell to les Fusilier Mont-Royal against sixty grenadiers who had dug into the *Ecole Supérieure de Jeunes Filles* along the main highway on the southern edge of the city. The fighting continued until the last resistance was overcome.[4]

Office de tourisme du Pays de Falaise (48.893587, -0.201638)
Boulevard de la Libération　　　　　　　14700 Falaise
Tel: +33 (0)2 31 90 17 26　　　　　　　Email: info@falaise-tourisme.com
　Web: http://www.falaise-tourisme.com/page_accueil.php

Note: the **Musée Août 1944** in Falaise has been permanently closed.

Château Guillaume-le-Conquérant
Place Guillaume le Conquérant　　　　　14700 Falaise
Tel: +33 (0)2 31 41 61 44　　　　　　　Email: chateauaccueil@falaise.fr
Web: chateau-guillaume-leconquerant.fr

The chateau was the birthplace of William the Bastard, later known as the Conqueror, in 1027. However, little of the original fortifications remain. The oldest sections date from William's fourth son, Henry I of England, who modeled Falaise after the stone keeps of English castles. Construction of additional fortifications continued through the Hundred Years War. The development of modern artillery meant the end of the chateau's dominance and parts of the enclosure deteriorated from neglect. It was totally abandoned

---

4　Many reports state that none of the defenders surrendered; however, in 1983 statements came to light that seventeen grenadiers in a separate building were captured the following morning (see Michael Reynolds' *Steel Inferno: I SS Panzer Corps in Normandy*).

368 Fields of War: Battle of Normandy

in the 17th century. Modern preservation efforts have saved the remaining structures. Although the city was nearly obliterated during the August 1944 bombings and assault, the chateau escaped with relatively little damage.

The enclosure tour begins through the **Porte St-Nicolas** followed by the **Main Keep**, **Small Keep**, and **Tour Talbot**. The impressive round tower is 35 meters high with walls 4 meters thick. Its top offers fine views of the city and surrounding countryside. The small chapel projects a Norman Romanesque style. An audio guide describes the various exhibition areas with much of the emphasis on William and the Normans.

Open daily February through December from 10:00 to 18:00 (19:00 in July and August). Admission fee.

Reverse direction and proceed northeast on Bd de la Libération (D511). After 600 m, turn left onto rue Georges Clemenceau (D658) and follow for 1.4 km to the large roundabout. Take the first exit toward Vendeuvre (D511). Follow the very straight road for 11.9 km.

The route to Jort follows along the high ground occupied by German units south of the Laizon River. Wind turbines visible on the left 1.2 kilometers after the large roundabout mark the location of **Hill 159**. (48.91418, -0.195951) The flat hilltop overlooked Falaise and was defended by grenadiers of the German 85th Infantry Division supported by PzKpfw IVs, Panthers, and *Jägdpanthers*[5] of *Panzerkampfgruppe Wünsche*. When Canadian Grenadier Guards and British Columbia Regiment tanks tried to capture the hill, they were bloodily repulsed. Events elsewhere made retaining the height impossible, however, and the German troops retreated into Falaise for their last stand.

Highway D511 enters a sweeping curve to the right before crossing two bridges over branches of the Dives River before entering Jort. Immediately after the second bridge, turn right onto rue Lt Paul Duhomme (D148a). After 600 m, turn right onto narrow lane (rue l'Abreuvoir) and continue to the end. The narrow lane is difficult to find because the high stone wall on the corner hides the intersection. (48.971055, -0.082768)

The 1st Polish Armoured Division, commanded by Major-General S Maczek,[6] advanced in two battle groups along the left flank of the II Canadian Corps. He targeted river crossings at Vendeuvre and Jort. The 10th Mounted Rifle Regiment, a reconnaissance unit, arrived in Jort during the night of 15/16 August to find the western of the two bridges over the river blown up and the town defended by the German 85th Infantry Division's Combat Engineer Company with three antitank guns. The Poles managed to ford two tanks 600 meters south of the bridges despite the marshy river banks. Then, using steel cables,

---

5 *Jägdpanther*: a tank destroyer built upon a PzKpfw chassis and carrying the devastating 88-mm PaK 43 cannon. Although relatively few were produced, it was a most formidable weapon.

6 Major-General Stanislaw Maczek was a career military man who fought in the First World War, the Polish-Soviet War of 1919 – 1921, in Poland in 1939, and in France in 1940. Later in the war, Maczek's forces liberated numerous towns and cities during its rush toward Germany. They captured Wilhelmshaven, Germany, and two hundred vessels of the German *Kriegsmarine* stationed in its harbor. Demobilized in the United Kingdom, his return to Poland was refused by the Polish Communist government whereby Maczek was forced into menial labor. Not until 1994 was he recognized by the new Polish government with his country's highest award, the Order of the White Eagle. Maczek died that same year at age 102. He is buried among his men in the Polish Military Cemetery, Breda, Netherlands.

the initial two tanks pulled six more Cromwell tanks across the river. Polish armor was now behind the small detachment guarding the remaining bridge. The 9th Polish Infantry Battalion waded the river to surprise the headquarters' detachment of the German infantry.

The rue de l'Abreuvoir is a short, narrow street that ends at the Dives River, where a memorial stele commemorates the crossing by the **1st Polish Armoured Division**. A simple stone bears a granite plaque simply stating that 'Here on 15 August 1944 the 1st Polish Armoured Division crossed la Dives.' It stands under the embracing branches of a huge willow tree that obviously enjoys the wet, mucky ground that was such a barrier to Polish tanks. The location is remarkable for its absolute peace and tranquility. A short distance to the north, a farm bridge crosses the river from which one can see the main highway.

Reverse direction and continue on rue l'Abreuvoir for 280 m, passing the church where the cemetery wall bears a commemorative plaque to the **1st Polish Armoured Division**. Turn right (D148). Follow the highway (D148) for 10.8 km, then turn left toward Crocy/ Trun (D63). Follow for 9.5 km (becomes D13, and rue de la République in Trun) into place du Canada in Trun. Stop near the war memorial. (48.843812, 0.032133)

Closing the Falaise Pocket
17 to 21 August 1944

The denouement of the battle for Normandy took place on the gently undulating fields of the Dive River valley. A pronounced ridge line north of Chambois dominates the terrain and overlooks the plain between Trun and Chambois. Only two improved roadways adequate for armored vehicles remained for German evacuation to the east: the Trun-Vimoutiers road (D916) and Chambois-Vimoutiers road (D16). The second of these was dominated by two hilltops both labeled Hill 262 and which became known as Hill 262 north and Hill 262 south.

The Allied noose was tightening around the German Fifth Panzer and Seventh Armies west of the Orne River when Hitler agreed to a withdrawal. The II SS Panzer Corps (2nd SS, 9th SS, and 12th SS) and 21st Panzer Division were to hold the northern flank against the II Canadian Corps. The XLVII Panzer Corps (2nd and 116th Panzer Divisions) were to hold the southern flank against the US First Army. The German Seventh Army and Panzer Group Eberbach were to conduct a fighting retreat.

On 17 August, Montgomery issued orders to II Canadian Corps to use its two armored divisions to close, at all cost, the remaining gap between Canadian and American forces. The objective was Chambois.

Objective	To link with American forces to trap the German forces west of the Dive River line.
Forces	
Canadian	4th Canadian Armoured Division (Major-General David Kitching) and 1st Polish Armoured Division (Major-General S Maczek)
German	Remnants of fifteen divisions of Fifth Panzer Army, Seventh Army, and Panzer Group Eberbach
Result	The pocket was closed after some of the fiercest fighting in Normandy.

Casualties	
Canadian	From 7 to 22 August, Canadian casualties from all units totaled 1,470 killed and 4,030 wounded or missing
Polish	325 killed, 1,002 wounded, and 114 missing (including 263 Operation TRACTABLE casualties)
German	Estimates vary, but probably 10,000 killed and 50,000 taken prisoner; approximately 50,000 escaped; thousands of vehicles were destroyed
Location	Falaise is 35 km south of Caen; Trun is 19 km southeast of Falaise

Battle

On 18 August, the advance of the 4th Canadian Armoured Division into Trun faced only slight resistance since the enemy had vacated the city. A Canadian battle group dispatched from Trun toward Chambois to close the German escape routes was stopped at St-Lambert-s/Dive, 3 kilometers short of its objective. A Polish battle group was then ordered to parallel the Canadians to the north. The Poles, traveling cross country at night, ended up in les Champeaux, 6 kilometers north of Chambois.

During 19 August, Battlegroup Stefanowicz, comprised of 1st Polish Armoured Regiment with 9th Polish Infantry Battalion attached, established positions along a steep ridgeline that dominated the terrain to the west. The Poles named their stronghold 'Maczuga' (The Mace) after the contours of the hilltop. The Chambois-Vimoutiers escape road had been effectively cut, but the Poles were similarly cut off from their supplies and communications. During the late afternoon, the 10th Polish Dragoons' reconnaissance unit moved cross country parallel to the Trun-Chambois road to enter the town. Meanwhile, Americans fought northward from le Bourg St-Léonard. That evening the Poles and Americans met at Chambois.

The small Canadian force fought into St-Lambert and held four critical river crossings under its guns for three days. The Canadians withstood repeated penetrations and attacks by considerably larger forces. The Allied tactical air forces exacted a terrific punishment upon German forces attempting to escape through the ever-narrowing gap between Canadian and Polish forces. The pressure upon German units was so intense because their daylight movement created a target-rich environment for the fighter-bombers and Allied artillery.

The 20th of August saw the fiercest combat of the battle when German Seventh Army fought east to break the encirclement while II SS Panzer Corps fought west to break the stranglehold on their comrades. Much of the German rescue effort fell against the Poles at The Mace.

The Falaise gap was finally closed on the afternoon of 21 August when 1st Hussar Regiment tanks smashed their way down the highway into Chambois and the Grenadier Guards brought relief to the Poles. In three days, Allied air forces flew 7,621 sorties and reported 5,493 destroyed or damaged vehicles, including 389 tanks. The destruction was the largest air and artillery massacre in history. Surviving soldiers fled, most of them on foot.

Aftermath

Of the 100,000 German soldiers originally in the pocket, fewer than one-half escaped, and many of those were rear-area troops, not combat soldiers. The German wounded included Seventh Army commander SS-Oberstgruppenführer Paul Hausser and

1st SS Panzer Division commander Theodor Wisch, the latter so seriously that he never returned to combat. The commanders of LXXXIV Corps and the 84th and 708th Infantry Divisions, among numerous other senior officers, were captured.

Controversy has remained, however, that Canadian or American troops did not act swiftly enough to close the pocket permitting tens of thousands of German troops to escape and fight again later in the war. That the ground campaign against the weakened but still deadly German Army in Normandy was delegated to a weak Canadian battle group, a strong but isolated Polish Division, and two companies of American infantry seems incredible. Much of such criticism must fall to senior commanders who, almost to a man, changed plans or lacked understanding of the battlefield situation. They delayed troop movements or ordered inadequate forces to perform impossible tasks. As a result, Major-General George Kitching[7] was relieved of his command of 4th Canadian Armoured Division, although some historians claim he was made a scapegoat by General Simonds.

Battlefield Tour

The tour of the Battle of the Falaise Pocket starts in Trun and includes two separate battlefields. The northern shoulder action centered upon the Canadians in St-Lambert-s/Dive, and the southern shoulder combat centered upon the Polish in Chambois and on Hill 262.

Trun

Trun Syndicat d'Initiative
Place Charles de Gaulle   61160 Trun
Tel: +33 (0)2 33 36 93 55
Web: http://www.demarchesadministratives.fr/villes/trun,61160/office-de-tourisme-trun

The crossroads town of Trun was inevitably in the German troops' path because of its control over the road to Vimoutiers. It became an RAF target during the afternoon of 18 August. Immediately after the bombing, the 4th Canadian Armoured Division, led by motorized infantry of the Lincoln and Welland Regiment, entered the town while dazed civilians and German soldiers alike emerged from the smoke and dust. Six hundred prisoners were taken that day alone. A small force left Trun that night heading for St-Lambert. The gap between the converging Allied forces was less than 8 kilometers.

The place du Canada in the center of Trun holds a particularly informative **NTL Totem** that describes the Falaise Pocket and actions surrounding Trun. The totem is near the town's war memorial, which holds a plaque commemorating the **4th Canadian Armoured Division** and its participation in the liberation of Normandy.

> Proceed through the town and continue southeast toward St-Lambert-s/Dive (D13), following the route of the squadron from the South Alberta Regiment.

---

7   Major-General George Kitching was demoted to brigadier. Later, he was assigned as staff officer for I Canadian Corps redeeming his reputation. Kitching held several high military positions after the war. He died in 1999 at age 89.

Battle of St-Lambert-s/Dive
18 to 21 August 1944

Over 100,000 German soldiers of the Fifth Panzer and Seventh Armies were ordered back from the Orne River to the Dive River with four Allied Armies and the US and RAF tactical air forces in pursuit. The meandering Dive River averages only 3 meters wide, but its steep, 2-meter-high banks made it an effective tank ditch. In order for German soldiers to escape from the closing ring, they had to cross one of the four river crossings that remained open in the St-Lambert area – bridges near the village church (Pont de l'Église) and at the Château de Quantité, a footbridge at Moulin Quantité, and a ford known as the Gué de Moissy.

Battle

At 1830 on 18 August, 15 Sherman tanks of C Squadron, South Alberta Regiment, commanded by Major DV Currie[8] with the under-strength Company B of the Argyll and Sutherland Highlanders under command, moved southeast from Trun toward St-Lambert-s/Dive. Upon entering St-Lambert-s/Dive at 2000, the two leading tanks were almost immediately destroyed by enemy antitank fire. The Canadian battle group withdrew and sheltered for the night on Hill 117, north of the village.

At 0630 on 19 August, Currie's force, slightly strengthened by the arrival of four 17-pounder antitank guns, moved on the village. Facing vastly superior numbers of enemy troops and after six hours of fierce combat, Currie's force fought to the center of the village where a German tank guarded the intersection to hold open the Pont de l'Église escape route. The tank was eventually knocked out when platoon leader Lieutenant G Armour dropped a #36 grenade into its open turret. Currie's men dug in against repeated enemy attacks. During the afternoon they were reinforced by Company C, Argyll and Sutherland and Company C, Lincoln and Welland Regiment, both also under-strength units, and eight more antitank guns. Currie's force now totaled 175 men.

On the morning of 20 August, the German 353rd Infantry Division, 2nd Panzer Division, and elements of 1st, 10th, and 12th SS Panzer Divisions, now mostly devoid of artillery support and with only a few armored vehicles, mounted a series of breakout attempts in the St-Lambert sector. During the fighting, Major IH Martin,[9] commander of Company B, Argyll and Sutherland Highlanders, twice advanced alone to call down artillery fire on German self-propelled guns. He was killed the next day while discussing the removal of wounded with a German medical officer when an artillery shell struck the group. Lieutenant Dalphé, who was acting as interpreter, was also killed in that incident.

On 21 August, much of the heavy fighting had ceased when Private EH McAllister[10]

---

8   Major David Vivian Currie, schooled as an automobile mechanic and welder, joined his local militia in 1939. Major Currie was awarded the Victoria Cross for his leadership in the battle for control of St-Lambert-s/Dive. His was the only Victoria Cross awarded to a Canadian soldier during the Normandy campaign. Major Currie survived the war, achieving the rank of lieutenant-colonel. He died in 1986 at age 73 and is buried in Owen Sound, Ontario.

9   Major Ivan Harold Martin was awarded an American Distinguished Service Cross for his inspiration and leadership under intense enemy fire. Martin is buried in Bretteville-s/Laize Canadian War Cemetery. He was 32 years old. His American DSC was one of at least twelve awarded to Canadian servicemen during the Second World War.

10   Later promoted to Lance-Sergeant, Earl Henry McAllister was killed on 20 October 1944. McAllister is buried in Bergen-Op-Zoom Canadian War Cemetery near that town in the Netherlands. He was 21 years old.

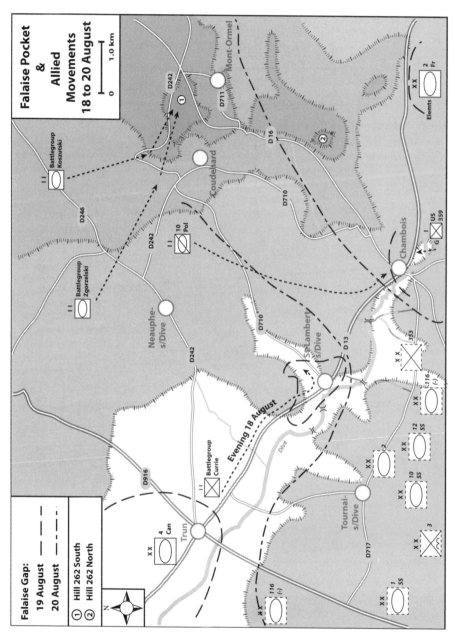

Falaise Pocket & Allied Movements 18 to 20 August

of Hamilton, Ontario, single-handedly captured 150 German prisoners. By noon, the town was completely in Canadian hands, and by 1700 the Canadians had connected with Polish forces in Chambois. Over 1,300 prisoners were taken by Currie's small force.

Battlefield Tour

     The river that flows through Normandy to empty into the English Channel is known as the Dives River in the Département Calvados and as the Dive River in Département Orne. It is the same river. France has a second river named Dive farther south in the Département Vienne.

> Before entering St-Lambert, stop at the parking area on the right, identifiable by the flags flying on the hillside beside the roadway. (48.824384, 0.069695)

The **Canadian Belvedere** is one of two established by the Canadian Battlefield Foundation. (The other overlook is at Point 67 south of Caen.) A switchback path leads from the roadside parking area uphill to the point of the overlook where visitors can view St-Lambert-s/Dive and the road to Chambois. Infosigns present the story of the battle for the village.

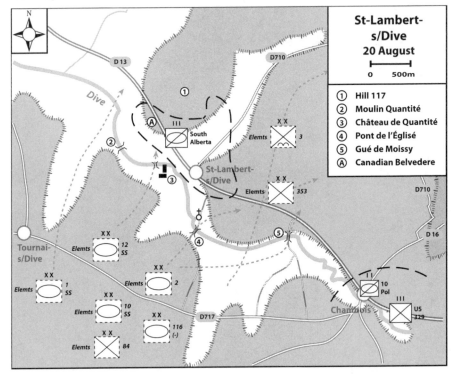

Major Currie's stronghold during the three-day battle was on Hill 117, 700 meters to the northeast. Upon that barren highpoint, he established an aid station, artillery observation post, and prisoner compound. Although the site is accessible, the belvedere location provides similar views from a more easily accessed location.

The low ridge visible to the east marks the opposite side of the Falaise Pocket occupied by Polish armored troops. The next tour site can be seen a short distance ahead near the first dwellings on the right (west) side of the highway.

> From the Belvedere parking area, continue approximate 230 m to the next intersection. (48.822548, 0.071948)

Despite fierce resistance by some German troops, others, dispirited and without resources, easily surrendered. The **Major David Vivian Currie VC Monument** marks the road junction where Currie accepted the surrender of Hauptmann Siegfried Rauch, 2nd Panzer Division, on 19 August. The dramatic encounter of Rauch advancing in a motorcycle sidecar and being waved down by Major Currie in his jeep was caught on film by a photojournalist.

The gravel road to the west leads 300 meters to Château de Quantité and a farther 350 meters to Moulin Quantité. On private property, both should be respected. The chateau possessed a farm bridge capable of supporting lighter vehicles and farm buildings used as an aid station under the protection of large Red Cross banners. The footbridge at the mill is noted for its use by the wounded commander of Seventh Army, SS-Oberstgruppenführer Paul Hausser,[11] to effect his escape from the pocket.

> Continue 450 m to the *mairie* parking on the left. (48.819355, 0.07596)

The **NTL Totem** near the *mairie* parking area describes Major Currie's efforts to capture St-Lambert-s/Dive. The intersection was kept open by a German tank – variously reported as being a Tiger, Panther, or PzKpfw IV – until eliminated by Lt Armour on 19 August. The German assault of 20 August by grenadiers of the 2nd Panzer Division temporarily regained the *mairie* and church locations, holding the escape route open for an additional six hours. Troops and vehicles using the Pont de l'Église crossed here to access the last remaining road (D710) to Vimoutiers.

> Proceed on the side road opposite the *mairie* (signed toward Aubry) for 380 m to the old church. (48.816416, 0.075724)

The 11th-century **Église de St-Lambert-s/Dive** has been closed since incurring damage during the Great Storm of 1999. The church's bell tower was used by German artillery observers during the battle. **Le Pont de l'Église** is a short distance past the church; it is one of two small bridges that cross tributaries of the Dive River that were vital for the escaping German troops. It was the only bridge crossing between Trun and Chambois capable of supporting the weight of armored vehicles.

Shortly after dawn on 20 August, the last remaining fifteen tanks of the 2nd Panzer Division overran the crossroads near the *mairie* and recaptured the bridge. The bridge over the ravine became another death trap for German troops. Under tank fire from St-Lambert, men, horses, equipment, and vehicles crashed from the bridge and lay in the river in gruesome heaps. The 2nd Panzer troops were followed by half of the 116th Panzer Division while the other half tried to escape through Trun. Those at St-Lambert found safety; those at Trun did not. Once across the bridge, the troops and few remaining vehicles turned northeast and made for Vimoutiers.

> Reverse direction and return to the highway. Turn right toward Chambois (unsigned, D13). After 1.4 km, turn right (unsigned) and continue as far as possible before stopping and walking to the ford. (48.811767, 0.090766)

---

11   SS-Oberstgruppenführer Paul Hausser was one of the founders of the Waffen-SS and served in Poland, Russia, Italy, and France. Hausser was wounded first at Stalingrad and again escaping from the Falaise Pocket. He ended the war commanding troops defending Berlin. He died in 1972 and age 92.

Although no bridge existed at this point, the gradual slope to the shallow waters of the river permitted vehicles to use **Gué de Moissy** to cross the Dive River. The Moissy ford was the last of the Dive River crossings to be captured. The ford was under the guns of British and Canadian artillery whose high explosive shells sent shards of metal into crowds of men and vehicles. Exploding fuel tanks and stored ammunition added to the destruction. Wounded horses stampeded, sometimes running in circles until they dropped. The lane was the site of death and mayhem unseen since the worst days of the Great War, earning this rural lane the German title 'Corridor of Death.'

On 20 August, German paratroopers from 3rd *Fallschirmjäger* Division led the final breakout followed by four PzKpfw IVs and three *Jägdpanzer* IVs of the II SS Panzer Battalion, 12th SS Panzer Division. Two of the tanks were hit, but the other two made their escape along with two-to-three thousand troops while under Polish and Canadian fire. The survivors met the relieving 2nd SS Panzer Division early the next morning.

A pedestrian bridge allows crossing the river to view the ford from both sides. A short walk along the farm track on the opposite side of the ford brings visitors to the open and exposed fields that German troops and vehicles had to use to approach the ford. Hundreds of men died here.

Reverse direction and return to the highway. Turn right toward Chambois (D13) and proceed 1.3 km to the center of the town. (48.805281, 0.106103)

Battle of Chambois and Hill 262
19 to 21 August 1944

By 19 August, the tattered remnants of two German Armies were being compressed by the advance of two British infantry divisions on the west, British 11th Armoured Division on the southwest, US 90th Infantry Division from the south, and 2nd French Armored Division from the southeast. The last remaining escape route was along the minor roads and farm tracks northeast of Chambois, but they were under the Polish guns on Hill 262.

Battle

A 1st Polish Armoured Division battle group comprised of 24th Lancers and the motorized 10th Dragoons, commanded by Major W Zgorzelski, secured Point 137 directly west of Hill 262 south by midday on 19 August. The unit then encountered and destroyed a German escape column on the Chambois-Vimoutiers road before continuing to the broad, forested Hill 262 north. The Polish Armoured Division's battle group Koszutski, named after its commander, Lieutenant-Colonel S Koszutski and comprised of 2nd Armoured Regiment and 8th Infantry Battalion, had become lost during its nighttime advance and was 5 kilometers north at les Champeaux. Koszutski's force, refueled and resupplied, joined Zgorzelski late that afternoon to increase the Polish force on Hill 262 to fifteen hundred men, eighty-seven tanks, and twenty antitank guns.

German infantry and paratroopers, personally led by General der Fallschirmtruppe Eugen Meindl, commander of II Parachute Corps, sheltered through the daylight hours of 19 August before beginning their breakout attempt that night. As the overnight rain ended at dawn, two single-file columns of soldiers approached Hill 262. Forward artillery observers attached to the Polish command called down the fire of two hundred guns upon the German troops.

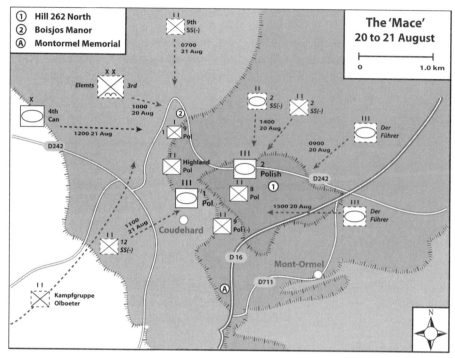

German counterattacks from outside the pocket against the Polish positions started later in the day with the 9th SS Panzer Division approaching from the north and the 2nd SS Panzer Division's *Der Führer* Regiment from the northeast. The German 3rd *Fallschirmjäger* Division attacked from the south and west to temporarily open escape corridors to the northwest of Montormel and east of Chambois. The Polish units were cut off from their supply lines and were rapidly depleting the last of their ammunition. Additional German assaults continued into the afternoon with the greatest effort being made at 1700 between highways D16 and D242.

The final German attack came on 21 August from the west and was defeated. At 1330, the sound of approaching tanks brought anxiety to the exhausted Polish infantrymen and tankmen. However, the tanks were from the Canadian Grenadier Guards. The Falaise Pocket was finally closed.

Battlefield Tour

The **Chambois Donjon** was constructed during the second half of the 12th century by Sire de Mandeville during the reign of King Louis VII. The simple 21.4-meter-high square tower was a defensive residence for Norman lords. The castle was subjected to several sieges during the Hundred Years War and was damaged during the Religious Wars and the French Revolution. It remains private property but stands as a landmark in the center of the village, visible from surrounding hillsides.

As a result of fighter-bombers attacking German vehicles passing through the town, the center of Chambois was destroyed and its streets blocked with debris. On 19

August Major W Zgorzelski's[12] 10th Polish Dragoons moved to capture Chambois. Preceded by its reconnaissance regiment, the 10th Mounted Rifles, his sixteen tanks engaged a larger German force in a thirty-minute firefight before occupying the village.

A large rough stone memorial stands next to the donjon to commemorate the **meeting of American, British, Canadian, French, and Polish forces** which secured the surrender of German troops. The **NTL Totem** is adjacent

---

Continue on the highway (D13) for 600 m to the memorial square on the right. (48.803083, 0.112846)

At 1920, Lieutenant Jan Karcz,[13] a platoon leader in the 10th Polish Dragoons Regiment, was surveying a group of troops approaching from the south when he determined that they were not German. Waving his British helmet, Karcz signaled Company G, 359th Infantry Regiment, US 90th Infantry Division, to advance. At this location, Captain Laughlin Waters[14] of Company G met Lt Karcz to accomplish the junction of US First Army from the south and First Canadian Army from the north. The union marked the first time that American and Polish troops had ever met on a battlefield. Waters and Zgorzelski then shared a bottle of liberated vodka.

The fighting was not over, however. German attacks on 20 August hit the American troops east of Chambois shortly after daybreak. Infantry, supported by a few remaining tanks and self-propelled guns, assaulted Company G's lines. The inclement weather grounded Allied fighter-bombers, but observation planes brought down Allied artillery in response.

All day long the fighting and killing continued while German soldiers pressed ahead to the east. Company E's Sergeant J Hawk directed tank destroyer fire upon German armor by repeatedly exposing himself to the enemy while attempting, in Hawk's words, to look like a fence post in the middle of the field. When finally spotted by the enemy, Hawk sought shelter behind a fruit tree in a nearby orchard, but the tank put a shell through the tree, severely wounding Hawk. He returned to combat despite shrapnel wounds in his leg. As a result of his actions, two enemy tanks were in flames and 500 German soldiers surrendered.[15] By day's end, the only Germans soldiers in Chambois were dead or in

---

12   Major Wladyslaw Zgorzelski was awarded a British Distinguished Service Order for his actions at Chambois. He was severely wounded in Holland.

13   Lieutenant Jan Karcz came from a Polish military family. Too young to fight in 1939, Karcz escaped Poland to France and later to Gibraltar. Once in England, he joined the 1st Polish Armoured Division. Later in the war, Karcz was awarded the French Croix de Guerre for liberating hostages in St-Omer; the Belgian Croix de Guerre for leading troops in liberating Ypres; and the Bronze Lion for liberating Breda, Holland. After the war, Karcz earned a degree from Oxford, England, and a PhD in Economics in the United States. He served on the US Federal Reserve Board. He died in 2009 at age 86.

14   Captain Laughlin E Waters survived the war and earned a law degree from USC. Waters became a California Assemblyman, US Attorney for Southern District of California, and later a member of the US District Court. He died in 2002 at age 87.

15   Sergeant John Druse Hawk received the Medal of Honor for his courage in exposing himself to enemy fire. Sgt Hawk recovered from his wounds to return to combat and was wounded three more times. Hawk survived the war earning four Purple Hearts, a Bronze Star, and Britain's Distinguished Conduct Medal. He exercised his GI Bill to earn a degree from the University of Washington. Hawk worked as a teacher and school principal for thirty years and, at age 88, still lives in the state of Washington.

prisoner enclosures.

Several monuments occupy the site, including a stone stele depicting two arms in a handshake with steel plaques bearing the insignia of the **1st Polish Armoured Regiment** and the **US 90th 'Tough 'Ombres' Infantry Division.** A large sign board depicts a map of Normandy and the army movements that led to the Falaise Pocket.

> Reverse direction and return to the center of Chambois. Turn right toward Coudehard-Montormel (D16, the Chambois-Vimoutiers road). Proceed for 5.0 km and then turn left into the memorial's parking area. (48.837167, 0.142736)

At midday on 19 August, the leading column of Sherman tanks of the 1st Polish Armoured Regiment met a German column of mixed armor and other vehicles along highway D16 at approximately this location. The Shermans poured fire into the disorganized enemy column trapped on the narrow road. In 30 minutes, the German units became a mess of tangled metal and dead or wounded soldiers. The burning vehicles and exploding ammunition barred the Polish from advancing toward their objective at Hill 262 south.

Two days later, while General Meindl's *Fallschirmjäger* fought up the road to join the counterattacking 2nd SS Panzer Division approaching from the opposite direction, General Meindl stopped all movement for thirty minutes. He placed his wounded soldiers on trucks and carts decked with Red Cross banners and sent them forward. In a remarkable act of humanity, the Poles understood the unspoken message and permitted the column to pass without firing. After the column passed, the war restarted.

Mémorial de Montormel

Les hayettes   61160 Montormel
Tel: +33 (0)2 33 67 38 61   Email: memorial.montormel@orange.fr
Web: http://www.memorial-montormel.org/

The Montormel Memorial overlooks the Falaise Pocket battlefield. Below the overlook, an underground visitor's center provides an explanation of the battle, using an animated map to present the movement of the opposing troops. A multi-lingual guide brings visitors to a glass-faced veranda and offers an explanation of the battle and its after-effects upon the local population. The devastation was so extensive that twenty years were required to clear the battlefield debris. A short film speaks to the 6-kilometer 'Corridor of Death' that extended from Gué de Moissy to Hill 262. Displays include rare photographs and eyewitness accounts. Walking tours of the battlefield are available.

Open daily in April from 10:00 to 17:00; open daily May through September from 09:30 to 18:00; open Wednesdays, Saturdays, and Sundays October through March from 10:00 to 17:00. Admission fee; Normandie Pass accepted.

Even if the museum is closed, its grounds make an informative visit. The Polish Memorial stands directly along the ridgeline above the underground center. A large **granite stele** identifies the historic site as the location of the final blow which destroyed German armies in Normandy. A stone **battle map** depicts the location of the armies during the critical fighting of 20 August. A **Polish M8 Light Armored Car** stands near the entryway to the terrace overlooking the battlefield. Most impressive are the views in the direction of Trun which illustrate the funnel through which German troops had to pass to escape complete annihilation. On the terrace, a **Sherman M4A1 tank** named 'Maczuga' aims its gun in the direction of the long-dead enemy soldiers who fearfully crossed the valley below. A twisted steel monument hangs on the wall of the memorial, emblematic of the destruction wrought upon German forces in the Falaise Pocket.

Follow the gravel footpath that starts behind the overlook and proceeds north for 350 meters to the 12th-century **Église de Coudehard**. An alternate view of the battlefield develops from this vantage point. The final German attack against Polish positions took place here during the late morning of 21 August. Troops from the 12th SS Panzer Division charged up the steep slope into the fire of the 9th Polish Rifle Battalion. For most of the attacking troops, the effort was suicide. (48.841178, 0.138638)

> Continue north on the highway (D16) for 1.6 km. Turn left (not well-signed, but highway D242) and continue 1.4 km to the memorial stone on the left. (48.848564, 0.140569)

The attack of 20 August by the 2nd SS Panzer Division struck against 1st Polish Armoured Regiment in this field. A Panther tank positioned atop neighboring Hill 239 destroyed five Sherman tanks in rapid succession. The German assault penetrated the Polish defensive line such that, at one point, Polish tanks were firing their coaxial machine guns at the enemy to their front while firing the turret antiaircraft machine gun at panzergrenadiers to their rear.

After the battle, the Polish strongpoint around **Hill 262 north** was the site of utter devastation. Several hundred wounded – Polish and German – overflowed the Boisjos farm buildings. In a small valley to the north, over seven hundred prisoners were kept under light guard. Roadways were blocked with burned out vehicles, unburied dead, and bloated horse carcasses. Under attack for three days without resupply, Polish troops suffered immeasurably from lack of food, water, and medical supplies. The gray granite stele marks the location of the end of the battle of the Falaise Pocket and commemorates the efforts of the Polish and Canadian armored divisions.

> Continue 400 to the building on the left. As this is private property, do not block the entrance. (48.851261, 0.137544)

The 10th-century **Boisjos manor house** towered above the valley floor offering a view of the German evacuation below. The arriving Poles found it defended by a company of entrenched German infantry. After a quick engagement, the German troops were eliminated without surrender. The house became the central bastion and command post for the Polish defense at the northwest corner of The Mace. From the tower, forward artillery observers directed fire onto enemy groups in the valley below.[16]

> Continue 230 m to the road junction. (48.853361, 0.137072)

Polish forces in The Mace came under intense pressure on 20 August. *Kampfgruppe Olboeter*, supported by a collection of four tanks and five Flak guns, moved through Gué

---

16   One such observer was Canadian Colonel Pierre Sévigny, awarded Poland's Virtuti Militari medal for his involvement in the Battle of Hill 262. Sévigny later lost a leg in the Battle of the Rhineland. After the war, he wrote an award winning book about his wartime experiences and served in the Canadian House of Commons. He ended his career as a university professor. Sévigny died in 2004 at age 86.

de Moissy during the morning of 20 August and continued battling Canadian and Polish tanks while they proceeded north on highway D710 – the presumed route. Approximately 1500 men of *Kampfgruppe Olboeter* met 120 men and six tanks of the SS Panzergrenadier Regiment *Der Führer* approaching from Champosoult at this intersection. Using their few remaining Panther tanks, they systematically destroyed several Polish Shermans and broke into The Mace's perimeter. The Poles were driven back into the woods, and the escape route to the north was temporarily reopened permitting thousands of German soldiers to escape. On 21 August, the last covering infantry of LXXIV Corps made a chaotic escape in small groups. During the afternoon the last of 2nd SS Division withdrew. The battle was over.

Additional Site: German PzKpfw VI Ausf. E (Tiger) tank

For all that is written about the dreaded German Tiger tanks, surprisingly few remain. One such example, however, is displayed near the objective of the German escape attempts at Vimoutiers – only 16 kilometers away.

> Reverse direction and return 2.0 km to the Chambois-Vimoutiers Road (D16). Follow for 9.7 km (becomes D916) into Vimoutiers. Shortly after entering the town, bear right onto rue Paul Creton. After 200 m, turn sharply right onto rue du Pont Vautier (D12). After 600 m, turn right toward Alençon (D979) and continue for 550 m to the access road on the left and stop. (48.923655, 0.214909)

Vimoutiers

On 14 June, Allied bombers dropped incendiary devices into Vimoutiers. The resulting firestorm destroyed 75 percent of the buildings and killed 170 civilians. The town remained unoccupied until German forces racing toward the Seine River passed through at the end of the Battle of the Falaise Pocket. Vimoutiers was liberated on 22 August.

Vimoutiers is a small market town with a charming place Hôtel de Ville on rue du 11 Novembre. The River Vie runs through the town center. Dairies in the region produce the famous French Camembert cheese.

Office du Tourisme

21 place de Mackau   61120 Vimoutiers
Tel: +33 (0)2 33 67 49 42
Email: ot.paysducamembert@wanadoo.fr
Web: http://www.vimoutiers.fr/Tourisme,5,0,0.html

A **Tiger I type E tank** stands upon an elevated platform beside the highway D979 east of the town. This battlefield relic represents one of the few surviving examples of this fearsome armored vehicle and one of only two in France. Symbolically, its 88-mm gun remains permanently pointed towards Vimoutiers. The ruptured top surface below the turret provides proof that German troops disabled the tank with explosive charges after it broke down attempting to climb the steep hillside. The tank remains where it has sat since 1944.

Chapter Sixteen

Liberation of Paris
19 to 25 August

The citizens of Paris had seen their share of rebellions and revolutions. Parisians were known for their forceful reaction to unwanted governments, whether those of occupiers or their own. Even after the cataclysm of Revolutionary fervor during the late 18th-century antigovernment barricades arose in the streets of Paris in 1832, 1848, and 1871.

German survivors of the Falaise Pocket failed to establish a defensive position west of the Seine River but attempted to hold the river line, especially surrounding Paris. Eisenhower was reluctant to engage in a street battle for Paris that would cause serious casualties and perhaps destroy the city. As early as 18 August, resistance posters appeared on walls throughout the city calling for a general strike and insurrection against German occupation troops. On the next day, the Free French force (*Forces Françaises de l'Intérieur*, or FFI) occupied the police station and the Hôtel de ville.

The German military governing headquarters, known as the *Kommandantur*, prepared to reap complete destruction upon Pairs. They planned to dynamite the Chamber of Deputies, the Ministry of Foreign Affairs, also known as Quai d'Orsay, the place de la Concorde, the Siemens-Westinghouse Electronics complex at Fontainebleau, all telephone centers including the underground telecommunications complex under Napoleon's Tomb in les Invalides, and all railroad stations, bridges, and power stations.

Objective	To liberate Paris without engaging in destructive urban warfare
Forces	
Allied	2nd French Armored Division (général de brigade Jacques Philippe Leclerc) and US 12th Infantry Regiment (Colonel James Luckett)
German	Twenty-thousand-man *Kommandantur Gross Paris* (General der Infanterie Dietrich von Choltitz)
Result	The German garrison surrendered after a brief battle.
Casualties	
French Army	71 killed and 225 wounded
Resistance	500 killed and 2,000 wounded
Civilians	600 killed; unknown wounded
German	3,200 killed or wounded; approximately 15,000 taken prisoner

Battle

At 0700 on 19 August, hundreds of men led by Yves Bayet, the head of a Gaullist group that had infiltrated the municipal administration, gathered in the square before the Hôtel Dieu, unfurled the French Tricolor flag, and marched into the Préfecture of Police. The building was mostly empty because the entire police force of Paris had been on strike for the past four days. Bayet's men entered the Préfecture via a door left ajar by a guard and they quickly occupied the building. By 0900, isolated pockets of fighting against German occupation troops had broken out across the city. The FFI began to occupy the *mairies* and police stations of Paris's twenty *arrondissements*. At 1530, three German tanks fired upon the Préfecture buildings. The resistors responded with Molotov cocktails – the only

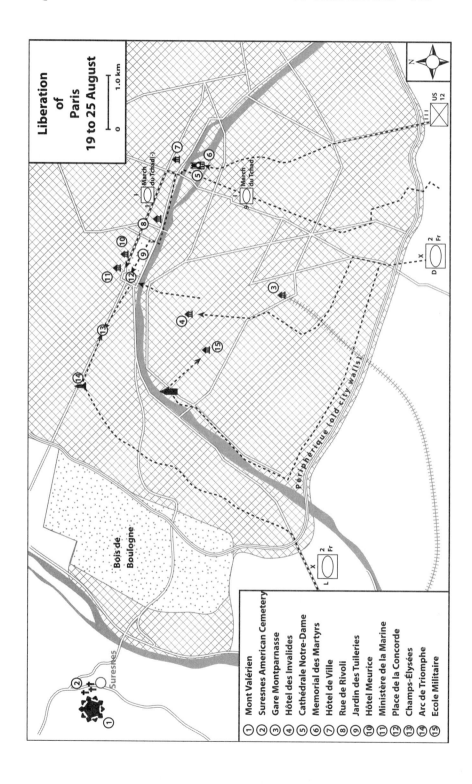

Liberation
of
Paris
19 to 25 August

0   1.0 km

N

Bois de
Boulogne

Suresnes

Marché
du Tchad(-)

Marché
du Tchad

Périphérique (old city walls)

① Mont Valérien
② Suresnes American Cemetery
③ Gare Montparnasse
④ Hôtel des Invalides
⑤ Cathédrale Notre-Dame
⑥ Memorial des Martyrs
⑦ Hôtel de Ville
⑧ Rue de Rivoli
⑨ Jardin des Tuileries
⑩ Hôtel Meurice
⑪ Ministère de la Marine
⑫ Place de la Concorde
⑬ Champs-Élysées
⑭ Arc de Triomphe
⑮ Ecole Militaire

weapon that they had against tanks. In the place du Parvis Notre-Dame, a tank burst into flames when a refilled champagne bottle burst in the open turret hatch.

The Paris *Kommandantur* received Hitler's express orders to destroy the city whereby German forces gathered the weapons capable of implementing the order. The Third Reich's largest artillery piece, a 600-mm mortar nicknamed 'Karl,' arrived from the east on its purpose-built railway platform to throw its two-and-one half ton shells into the city. The Luftwaffe command at le Bourget airfield offered to bomb districts with incendiaries. Submarine torpedoes were removed from their factory near St-Cloud and transported across the city to destroy the Palais de Luxembourg, Opera Garnier, and other civic buildings. Hitler planned to deluge the city with V-1 flying bombs. Paris was to become another Warsaw – a blackened, smoking ruin.

Desperately wishing to avoid a bloodbath and destruction of the city, the Swedish counsel general, Raoul Nordling, acted as negotiator between the FFI and the newly appointed commander of *Gross Paris*, General Dietrich von Choltitz.[1] The German commander responded favorably to the appeals of French officers and resistance emissaries and, perhaps more so, to the call of history to save the City of Light. He agreed to a cease-fire.

The next day, the Communist faction of the resistance, more organized and with more men and weapons that the Gaullist faction, instigated attacks on German soldiers throughout Pairs in an attempt to break the cease-fire. After several days of skirmishes and while the Gaullist troops of General Leclerc drew nearer to Paris, the FFI issued the call *'Aux Barricades,'* reminiscent of the 1871 Red Commune of Paris. Across the city, ripped-up paving stones and burned-out German trucks blocked major thoroughfares and small byways to important government buildings.

While preparing to plead with Eisenhower to liberate Paris, Nordling suffered a heart attack. The man who had fought for the release of French political prisoners and the salvation of Paris was out of the picture.[2] Eisenhower, faced with open insubordination by General Leclerc who had accepted conflicting orders from General Charles de Gaulle, reluctantly agreed to permit Leclerc's 2nd French Armored Division to lead Allied troops into the city. General Bradley ordered American support for Leclerc, but the only troops available and near enough to the city were a single infantry regiment from the US 4th Infantry Division.

Général Leclerc divided his division into three forces to attack Paris and his fast moving mechanized units fought through a thin defensive ring. Meanwhile, the German garrison established thirty strongpoints at key government buildings, airports, and train stations.

Tankman Capitaine R Dronne, commander of the 9th Company, Régiment de Marche du Tchad, was the first French officer to enter Paris on 24 August. At 2122, Dronne

---

1   Von Choltitz had only recently replaced General der Infanterie Karl-Heinrich Stülpnagel, a conspirator in the 20 July assassination plot against Hitler.
General der Infanterie Dietrich von Choltitz served on the Western Front during the First World War and in the *Reichswehr* during the Weimar Republic. Choltitz was awarded a Knight's Cross of the Iron Cross for capturing the Rotterdam Airport in a *coup de main* air assault in 1940. He later fought in Russia and Italy. He was considered by Hitler to be one of his most politically dependable generals. He was released by the Allies in 1947 and died in 1966 at age 71.

2   Although of Swedish nationality, Raoul Nordling was born and raised in Paris. Nordling was awarded the Croix de Guerre for his efforts to save political prisoners and the city from destruction. He died in 1962 at age 80.

and his detachment of mostly Spanish Republican soldiers entered the place de l'Hôtel de Ville with three tanks and six armored cars.[3] The signal to commence the populace uprising rang out and for the first time in four years, all of the church bells in the city rang in celebration. Paris was officially, but not militarily, liberated.

The next day, with stronger forces now available, five French Sherman tanks moved from the Hôtel de ville down the rue de Rivoli to attack German strongpoints. French infantry supported by FFI accompanied the Shermans past the arcaded shops toward the Hôtel Meurice. In a brief but sharp engagement against German garrison troops in the Tuileries Gardens and place de la Concorde, French forces led by Capitaine Jacques Branet attacked the German headquarters from three directions.[4] Accepting the inevitable, von Choltitz ordered his staff to meekly surrender. He was brought to Leclerc and signed the official capitulation document. Orders were transmitted by courier to each German strongpoint to cease resistance.[5] Paris was now truly liberated.

Aftermath

On 26 August, général Charles de Gaulle put in his claim as the government of France by laying a wreath of red gladioli at the Tomb of the Unknown, relighting the eternal flame, and then marching the length of the Champs-Élysées. The street was lined with the troops of Leclerc's division, even though some fighting still continued in northern districts of the city. When the parade of Gaullist leaders entered the place de la Concorde, shots were fired into the crowd. Whereas civilians ducked and scurried for shelter, de Gaulle did not. Without hesitation, he continued to look and walk straight ahead to the car that took him to Cathédrale Notre-Dame for the celebration of a special Mass. The shooters were never identified, but at least six people were killed. Later, shots fired from the towers of Notre-Dame peppered the place below. Random shots continued inside the great cathedral; the identity of the shooters has never been determined. After a short prayer, de Gaulle, having proven his leadership of a revitalized France, left the building. Through his actions, he had single-headedly saved the country from a vicious civil war between nationalist and communist.

On 29 August, in a show of Allied solidarity and in support for de Gaulle's government, the US 28th Infantry Division marched through Paris to cheering crowds. It passed the Arc de Triomphe, down the Champs-Élysées, and returned immediately back to the front lines.

With all of the Paris bridges across the Seine River intact and in Allied hands, the rapid pursuit across eastern France continued. Logistical issues rather than German

---

3   Capitaine Raymond Dronne was a well educated lawyer and journalist who had attended the Universities of Leipzig and Berlin. Dronne entered the French Colonial Army in 1934 and joined the Free French Forces in Africa in 1940. After the war, he was a senator and deputy in the French government. Dronne was highly decorated, including the *Légion d'honneur*, Companion of the Liberation, and Croix de Guerre with seven citations. He died in Paris in 1991 at age 83.

4   Capitaine Jacques Banet was a lieutenant of dragoons when captured in May 1940. After a year in a German POW camp, he escaped and fled to England via the USSR. Banet fought in North Africa and, after landing with Leclerc in Normandy, captured 300 German prisoners during Écouves Forest fighting. He later took part in the liberation of Strasbourg. In 1958, he fought again in North Africa, this time in Algeria. Banet was highly decorated, including the *Légion d'honneur*, Companion of the Liberation, and Croix de Guerre with six citations. Banet died in 1969 at age 55.

5   Not all German soldiers gave up so meekly, especially SS troops. The FFI frequently lynched or shot surrendering Germans and those French who had collaborated with them during the occupation. Trials of Vichy politicians continued well into 1946.

resistance halted the Allied armies when they approached the German border. Most of France was finally liberated after four years of occupation.

Conclusion

The Battle of Normandy was an enormous logistical feat for the Allied powers landing over two-million men against an entrenched defender. The troops fought through terrain almost designed to support defense against an enemy highly skilled in defensive warfare.

Despite competition for resources and incompatible personalities, the objective of defeating the enemy had remained the uppermost objective due in large part to the Supreme Allied Commander, General Dwight Eisenhower. The defeat of German forces was the result of the field leadership of General Bernard L Montgomery and the courage, tenacity, sacrifice, and ingenuity of the individual fighting men faced with the task. By the end of August, Allied forces had suffered 206,703 casualties: 124,394 American, 80,935 British Commonwealth, and 1,374 Poles.

From 6 June to 25 August, the German Army had suffered approximately 200,000 killed or wounded and an equal number taken prisoner with over one-half taken in the final month of the fighting. It had also lost 1,300 tanks, 500 assault guns, 1,500 field guns, and 20,000 other vehicles. The Battle of Normandy annihilated several of Germany's finest formations and destroyed equipment that could not be adequately replaced. Panzer Lehr, five SS panzer divisions, and three Army panzer divisions were reduced to fragments of their pre-invasion strength. Although these units were later rebuilt, they were vastly inferior to their Normandy quality.

Battlefield Tour

Paris

As a world class city, Paris has much to offer in architecture, art, music, history, shopping, and fine dining. These subjects are better covered by other tourism guides. Instead, this battlefield tour focuses upon sites important to the city's liberation in August 1944. Although tour directions are suggested, individualized routes incorporating Paris' cultural sites is recommended. The tour starts with two sites in the Paris suburbs. It then concentrates upon major sites in central Paris, accessible by foot or by Metro, the efficient Paris underground transport system. The resistance movement in Paris is commemorated by numerous white stone plaques on the walls of Parisian buildings. They identify actual locations of events during the occupation and during the Liberation of Paris. This tour describes a few examples along the tour route.

Office du Tourisme et des Congrès de Paris (48.866112, 2.333651)
25 rue des Pyramides   75001 Paris
Web: http://en.parisinfo.com/   Metro: Tuileries

The Paris Museum Pass permits an unlimited number of visits to sixty museums and monuments in Paris without waiting in the queues. Passes are available for two, four, or six-day intervals and are available in advance by internet or mail or in person at the Paris Tourist Office. See: http://www.parismuseumpass.com for more details.

Take the SNCF train from Gare St-Lazare-Versailles and exit at Suresnes station. Exit the station north to Av Franklin Roosevelt and turn right. After 60 m, turn right onto rue Worth and follow onto rue du Calvaire. Cross Bd Washington (D6) onto Promenade Jacques Baumel. Follow for 300 m into the memorial square. The total distance is 750 meters; some uphill walking is required. (48.871575, 2.213868)

Mémorial du Mont Valérien
Av du Professor Léon Bernard   92150 Suresnes
Tel: +33 (0)1 47 28 46 35   Email: info@mont-valerien.fr
Web: http://www.mont-valerien.fr/

Fort Mont-Valérien, constructed in 1841 as part of a ring of defenses surrounding Paris, withstood heavy bombardments during the Franco-Prussian War. From 1940 to 1944, Valérien was a German prison and the site of almost daily executions of its prisoners. The fort, currently home to the French 8th Signals Regiment, is open to the public on only one day per year.

A clearing outside the fort holds a memorial to French Resistance known as the **Mémorial de la France Combattante**. The memorial presents sixteen allegorical bronze reliefs representing the heroic acts of the resistance. They frame the 12-meter-high Cross of Lorraine which stands behind an eternal flame. One of the bronze doors under the cross leads to a burial crypt holding the coffins of fifteen resistance fighters. A sixteenth vault awaits the last surviving Companion of the Liberation. Little publicized, but dramatic, ceremonies take place there each 18 June, usually attended by the President of the Republic and surviving members of the Companions of the Liberation.[6]

To the left, the Mont Valérien visitor center provides information through multimedia to databases, letters, and photographs of those executed in the Île-de-France Region. Short films present images of the memorial and postwar Paris.

A path originating at the memorial leads up the hillside and passes monoliths which describe the fifteen victims entombed in the crypt. The path moves along the exterior fortification walls, eventually achieving the **Chapelle des Fusillés**, used to temporarily confine the prisoners before their execution. The chapel now houses graffiti carved by those awaiting death and the five wooded execution posts. Outside the chapel, a bronze bell inscribed with the names of the executed sits as a **Monument aux Fusillés**. A permanent exhibition '**Resistance and Repression, 1940 – 1944**' has been installed in the stables adjacent to the chapel. The path then follows the walk of the condemned to the **Clairière des Fusillés**, where the executions actually took place. The open ground bears a bronze plaque claiming 4,500 executions at Mont Valérien, but the official French archives list 1,014 men who died there.[7]

Ninety-minute guided tours are available March through June and September

---

6   The Order of Liberation is France's second highest honor granted to those individuals and organizations for outstanding service in procuring the liberation of France. Of the original 1,038 Companions, only 23 remain alive.

7   Capitaine de corvette Henri Honoré d'Estienne d'Orves is remembered as the first martyr of Free France. A naval officer, d'Orves made his way from North Africa to join Free French groups in London. He secretly returned to France to establish espionage rings in Paris. He was betrayed to German authorities by his radio operator. After a trial and legal appeals, he was executed in Valérien on 29 August 1941. A memorial stele with an emblem bearing his profile stands in place d'Estienne d'Orves in northern Paris.

through October at 09:30, 11:00, 14:30, and 16:00; July through August and December through February at 10:00 and 15:00. No admission fee, but reservations are recommended to assure access. Book reservations by telephone or internet.

Reverse direction and walk east on Promenade Jacques Baumel. After 300 m, turn left onto Bd Washington (D5). Follow for 200 m to the entrance to the cemetery. The total distance is 500 meters. (48.87198, 2.218831)

Suresnes American Cemetery
Bd Washington   92150 Suresnes
Web: http://www.abmc.gov/cemeteries/cemeteries/su.php

The cemetery is sited on the wooded eastern slope of Mont Valérien 6.5 kilometers west of Paris. Marble stairs lead to a central mall which divides the grave plots *en route* to the Memorial Chapel. Columned loggias extend on both sides of the chapel and offer views of the graves and nearby Paris.

Predominantly a First World War Cemetery, Suresnes holds 1,565 graves, and the bronze plaques in the chapel commemorate 974 servicemen missing in action. The vast majority of the burials resulted from wounds or illness in the hospitals in and around Paris. Many of the dead, including seven nurses, were victims of the influenza epidemic. Thus, only six lay in graves marked 'unknown.' A separate plot holds twenty-four unidentified burials from the Second World War, making Suresnes the only American military cemetery to honor American dead from both wars.

Open daily from 09:00 to 17:00. Closed on Christmas and New Years Day. No admission fee.

Proceed north on Bd Washington (D5) for 390 m. Turn right onto rue Fécheray and follow for 450 m to the entrance to the train station. Connect to the Paris Metro at Gare St-Lazare and take line #14 to Gare Montparnasse. (48.841404, 2.320089)

Gare Montparnasse
17, Boulevard Vaugirard
Paris

Gare Montparnasse, originally Gare de l'Ouest, is one of the six main train stations in Paris. The station became général Leclerc's headquarters on 25 August. Inside, on the main floor, stone plaques commemorate the **surrender of German troops** and the **train crew members** of the French Resistance killed during the occupation. A museum complex above the train station presents two of the most important stories of occupied France.

The museum is difficult to access; take the outdoor elevator on Bd de Vaugirand up to the Jardin Atlantique. (48.840606, 2.319574)

Musée du général Leclerc de Hauteclocque et de la Libération de Paris and Musée Jean Moulin
23, Allée de la 2e DB
Jardin Atlantique, above the Gare Montparnasse
75015 Paris   Tel: +33 (0)1 40 64 39 44
Web: www.ml-leclerc-moulin.paris.fr

The complex holds two extremely informative museums. The one on the left is dedicated to général Leclerc and the Liberation of Paris. The general's life, the Fall of France, the occupation, and the liberation of Paris are recalled in a series of modern glass-framed displays that utilize newspapers, rare photographs, and a few artifacts. On the upper floor is a not-to-be-missed 120-degree film that dramatically and artistically presents the rebellion against occupation troops and de Gaulle's defiant walk down the Champs-Élysées. The film includes English subtitles.

By descending a second stairway, visitors enter the museum dedicated to Jean Moulin. Structured similarly to the Leclerc Museum, this room presents the life of France's most famous and revered member of the French Resistance. Moulin had been a First World War veteran, lawyer, cartoonist, prefect of Chartres, and deputy. He was removed from office by the Vichy government for refusing to dismiss town mayors in his Préfecture. Moulin joined the Resistance and organized several underground groups. In June 1943, he was betrayed and arrested in Lyon where he was interrogated by the infamous 'Butcher of Lyon,' Gestapo chief Klaus Barbie. He is believed to have died in the Metz train station during his transfer to a concentration camp.[8] Others believe that he died at the hands of Barbie.[9]

Open daily except Mondays and holidays from 10:00 to 18:00. No Admission fee.

From Gare Montparnasse, take Metro line #13 to Varenne. Proceed north on Bd des Invalides; turn left on rue de Grenelle to place des Invalides. (48.857183, 2.312751)

Hôtel des Invalides
Hôtel National des Invalides   Tel: +33 (0)8 10 11 33 99
Web: http://www.musee-armee.fr/accueil.html

Hôtel des Invalides was built in 1676 as a hospital and disabled soldiers' home. The esplanade leading to the building from the place des Invalides holds rows of cannon captured by Napoleon Bonaparte at Vienna in 1805. The **Église du Dome** at the opposite end of the large complex was built shortly later and became a military necropolis during Napoleon's rule. The **Tomb of Napoleon** is directly under the dome whose side vaults hold the bodies or memorials to Vauban, Maréchal de Turenne, and Maréchal Foch.

The **Musée de l'Armée** was once a dusty old collection of manikins bearing military uniforms dating as far back as the late Middle Ages. Recent renovations have transformed the collections into interesting displays of artifacts from the two world wars

---

8   Jean Moulin's remains were relocated with great honor to the Pantheon in Paris in 1964. He was 44 years old.

9   Klaus Barbie was an SS-Hauptsturmführer and Gestapo chief in Lyon. He became notorious for personally torturing prisoners. After the war, Barbie worked for British, American, Bolivian, and German intelligence agencies. In 1983 he was extradited to France and tried for crimes against humanity. He died of natural causes while in prison in 1987. He was 77 years old.

concentrating upon the French participation. The First World War section holds such famous artifacts as a French 75-mm gun and a Renault FT17 tank among thousands of smaller pieces. The Second World War exhibit occupies three floors and starts with the Nazi invasion. The emphasis centers upon Charles de Gaulle's contribution to the liberation. Audiovisual presentations explain events, but almost all are in French only; the displays, however, are labeled in three languages.

Open daily April through October from 10:00 to 18:00; November through March from 10:00 to 17:00. Admission fee; Metro: Invalides

Unfortunately, the next site is difficult to achieve via public transportation, take a taxi to Pont des Arts on Quai de Conti. (48.857812, 2.337137)

The southern end of the pedestrian **Pont des Arts** holds two plaques attached to the wall facing Quai de Conti commemorating the actions of the Parisian underground. The first commemorates Jean Bruller, codenamed 'Vercors,' a noted author and pacifist who nonetheless joined the Resistance. Bruller founded the underground publishing concern *les Éditions de Minuit* (Midnight Press). He wrote and clandestinely distributed books prohibited by strict Nazi censorship while risking capture and deportation. [10] The Pont des Arts was used by conspirators as a meeting place to receive the works published by *les Éditions de Minuit*.

On the opposite column a plaque commemorates Jacques Lecompte-Boinet, who joined the Resistance in 1941. He became the leader of the apolitical *Ceux de la Résistance* (Those Resistors) movement in 1943 which participated in gathering intelligence and sabotage. Lecompte-Boinet led a force of several thousand men during the Liberation of Paris. [11]

Continue east along the banks of the Seine for 250 m to the intersection with rue Guénégaud. (48.856393, 2.339873)

On 17 August, Colonel J Teissier, nicknamed Colonel de Marguerittes de Lizé, established the headquarters of the FFI in this building. From it, he directed Gaullist forces during the Liberation of Paris from 19 to 28 August. De Lizé, although a non-communist and a supporter of de Gaulle, issued the order to man the barricades on 21 August. [12]

---

10   Bruller wrote humanist criticism, historical novels, and essays after the war, particularly arguing against the 1956 Soviet invasion of Hungary and the Algerian war. The *Édition des Minuit* fought French censorship in publishing a book questioning the French Army's use of torture during the Algerian War in 1958. Bruller died in 1991 at age 89.

11   Jacques Lecompte-Boinet was the grandson of First World War's général Charles 'the Butcher' Mangin, known for the disastrous Second Battle of the Aisne in 1917. After the war, Jacques Lecompte-Boinet joined the Ministry of Foreign Affairs and served numerous postings, including ambassador to Norway. He died in 1974 at age 69.

12   Colonel Jean Antoine Teissier de Marguerittes commanded the 74th Artillery Regiment in 1940 and participated in fighting in Belgium. After the surrender, he joined the *Armée Secrète* (Secret Army) and commanded the Département Seine sector of the FFI. After the war, he entered a religious order. Marguerittes died in 1958 at age 76.
Henri Rol-Tanguy was the leader of the FFI in Paris. Tanguy was a militant communist who called the general strike and led the armed uprising. He accepted the German surrender along with Leclerc. He received the *Légion d'honneur* and was a Companion of the Liberation. He died in 2002 at age 94.

> The famous Pont Neuf is 50 m to the east. (48.856379, 2.340539)

The left support on the **Pont Neuf** bears a plaque to René Revel, a Parisian police officer who participated in the capture of the Préfecture of Police on 19 August. He and a fellow resistant attacked a German car and captured the occupant's automatic weapons. Later that evening, they were guarding the Pont Neuf to block German movements across the bridge when a fellow policeman identified him to German soldiers. Revel was shot twice in the throat and died later in the Hôtel Dieu.[13]

> Cross the Pont Neuf and turn right along Quai des Orfèvres (becomes quai du Marché Neuf). Continue along the river for 580 m to enter Parvis Notre-Dame (also named place Jean Paul II). The total distance is 750 meters. (48.853576, 2.348145)

The square documents the history of Paris and, therefore, the history of France. Embedded in the square is a bronze disc marking *kilomèter zero,* the point from which all distances in France are measured. The south side of the square holds a vivid depiction of **Charlemagne**. The 1886 statue by noted designer Louis Rochet presents not only the equestrian Frankish king but also two fearsome outriders attending to their king.

The most famous Gothic edifice in the world – **Cathédrale Notre-Dame de Paris** – stands on the east side of the square. Its construction was started by Louis VII in 1182 and finished during the reign of St Louis in 1245. This building, with its magnificent galleries, flying buttresses, and grotesque gargoyles has been the symbolic church of France ever since. Views from the cathedral's tower over the rooftops of Paris and the Seine River are magnificent.

The **Préfecture of Police** lies to the west. It was the first building seized by resistants on 19 August. The huge complex was ill-defended because the police were on strike at the time. The right side of the main arch retains bullet marks from the tanks' machine guns. General von Choltitz signed a formal act of capitulation at 1515 on 25 August in the building.

The massive **Hôtel Dieu de Paris** is the oldest hospital in Paris dating to 651. Much of the current structure was rebuilt by Napoleon after a disastrous fire destroyed the previous buildings. It now occupies several city blocks and fronts the north side of the square. The Hôtel Dieu continues to provide specialized and emergency medical services to central Paris.

Two plaques that commemorate victims of the liberation are affixed to the wall of the Hôtel Dieu facing the square. One remembers police officer André Perrin, killed by the SS on 19 August.[14] A few meters to the left is a *'A Tous les Français'* plaque repeating Charles de Gaulle's stirring June 1940, radio message from London to the people of France declaring that a battle has been lost but the war goes on. Copies of this plaque populate cities all over France as a reminder of that country's darkest hour. The second plaque, 90 meters to the right, recalls Police commander Marcel Rey, who was found seriously wounded in the Metro on 19 August and later died.[15]

---

13   René Revel was awarded the *Légion d'honneur*; he was 39 years old.

14   André Perrin was 29 years old. Killed with him was police officer Abel Paillot, age 23.

15   Marcel Rey was 52 years old.

> Proceed along the south side of the Cathédrale Notre-Dame. Cross the quai de l'Archevêché and enter a small park. Continue straight to the gated entrance to the memorial. The total distance is 240 meters. (48.851741, 2.352276)

Mémorial des Martyrs de la Deportation

Ile de la Cité   75004 Paris
Square de l'Île-de-France
Email: diacparishautslieuxvisites@sga.defense.gouv.fr
Web: http://www.defense.gouv.fr/site-memoire-et-patrimoine/memoire/hauts-lieux-de-memoire/le-memorial-des-martyrs-de-la-deportation

The extensive memorial sited on the eastern tip on the Île de la Cité commemorates the 200,000 people deported from France to Nazi concentration camps during the war. Its crypt-like construction induces the claustrophobia experienced by the deportees when they were packed into train freight cars. The narrow corridor is lined with one light for each of the 200,000 deportees. An additional single light positioned at the far end of the corridor symbolizes hope.

Open daily April through September from 10:00 to 12:00 and from 14:00 to 19:00; October through March from 10:00 to 12:00 and from 14:00 to 17:00. No admission fee; Metro: Cité.

> Proceed north (right) on Quai de l'Archevêché (becomes Quai aux Fleurs) and follow the street as it curves to Pont d'Arcole. Cross the bridge and enter the place de l'Hôtel de Ville. Total distance is 650 meters. (48.856449, 2.351857)

Hôtel de ville

1, place de l'Hôtel de Ville   75004 Paris
Tel: +33 (0) 1 42 76 40 40   Web: http://www.paris.fr/english

The city government of Paris has operated from a building on this site since 1357. It has frequently seen the start of rebellions such the Commune during the French Revolution, the rebel government of 1848, and the proclamation of the Third Republic in 1870. The Red Commune burned down the building in 1871.

The current structure was rebuilt from 1874 to 1892. In a spectacular display of French art, the façade of the building displays 338 figures of famous Parisians produced by 232 sculptors, including one by Auguste Rodin. The interior holds murals by leading French painters. A day and nighttime view of the building provides a doubly rewarding experience.

After the Gaullist resistance started the Paris rebellion by occupying the Préfecture of Police, the Communist resistance responded by occupying the Hôtel de ville on 20 August. Late in the day on 25 August, de Gaulle addressed a cheering throng from a balcony of the building. His words are inscribed in a stone plaque on the low wall fronting the structure. He said, in part:

> Paris! Paris outraged! Paris shattered! Paris martyred! But
> Paris liberated. Liberated by herself, liberated by her people,
> in concurrence with the armies of France, with the support and
> concurrence of the whole of France, of fighting France, the
> only France, the true France, eternal France.

Open daily except Sunday from 10:00 to 18:00 for guided tours. Free. Metro: Châtelet les Halles

> Leave the opposite (north) end of the place onto rue de Rivoli. Although the next several sites are along the street, the Tuileries gardens lie 1.6 km ahead. Take Metro line #1 from Hôtel de Ville station at rue de Rivoli and place de l'Hôtel de Ville and exit at Tuileries station. Walk 150 m east to place des Pyramides to view the **statue of Jeanne d'Arc**. (48.863882, 2.332181)

The rue de Rivoli is named after Napoleon's 1797 victory over the Austria Army. The fashionably-arcaded shopping street borders the Louvre Palace, Tuileries Gardens, and terminates in the place de la Concorde, the largest square in Paris. The street passes through place des Pyramides, where a gilded statue of **Jeanne d'Arc** stands near the spot where she was wounded in 1429 during her unsuccessful attack upon Paris.

On 25 August 1944, French infantry with tank support received orders to move from the Hôtel de ville against German strongpoints about the Hôtel Meurice. At first, they did so to the cheering of crowds of French citizens deliriously happy at the sight of their country's soldiers returning to the city. However, when they neared the German-held Tuileries Gardens, the atmosphere changed. Along the arcades, a German tank started to position its gun to fire down the street. Sergeant M Bizier's French Sherman tank, appropriately named 'Douaumont' after the First World War Verdun fortification, fired first and the German tank exploded. The shot triggered a second explosion of rifle and machine-gun fire.

A pillbox in the corner of the gardens fired toward the advancing French infantry while a sandbagged machine gun in the place des Pyramides did the same, thereby trapping French infantry in a crossfire. Sergeant Bizier's tanks continued up the rue de Rivoli and blasted the Pyramides' position. A French tank named 'Mort-Homme' was set aflame by a hand grenade dropped into its open turret. The remaining four tanks continued to move forward toward the place de la Concorde.

> Reverse direction and walk 350 m west to le Hôtel Meurice, passing the Tuileries Gardens on the left. This section of rue de Rivoli was a major battleground on 25 August to secure German defenses in the gardens. (48.865131, 2.327996)

The Hôtel Meurice doubled as the main German headquarters. The 3rd Platoon, 1st Company, 1st Régiment of March of Tchad, led by Lieutenant Henri Karcher, moved along the arcades of rue de Rivoli and entered the hotel. With the toss of a single hand grenade, Karcher and three men captured the German headquarters staff, who meekly gave up their weapons. [16] General von Choltitz was escorted back along the rue de Rivoli through a jeering crowd to the place des Pyramids where increasingly threatening crowds demanded his immediate execution. To protect their prisoner, he was placed into a half-track and driven to the Préfecture of Police.

---

16   Lieutenant Henri Karcher was the son of a military officer killed during the first month of the Great War. Karcher became a surgeon and professor of medicine but volunteered for the infantry in January 1940. He joined the Free French Forces and fought in North Africa before landing in Normandy. After the war, he returned to medicine, then politics, becoming the Vice-President of the National Assembly. He was awarded the *Légion d'honour* and Companion of the Liberation among other medals. He died in 1983 at age 74.

Continue 350 m to the entrance to place de la Concorde. The Ministère de la Marine is the large building on the right at the north end of the place. (48.866557, 2.323523)

Ministère de la Marine, or also **Hôtel de la Marine**, was occupied by the German *Kriegsmarine* during the occupation. During the fighting in the place de la Concorde, the building's façade was riddled with bullet and shell holes. Some of the scars of the battle remain visible on the east side of the building along the rue St-Florentin. The building continues to house French Naval headquarters. The twin structure to the west is the famous Hôtel de Crillon.

Locate the memorial on the south side of the rue de Rivoli immediately before entering the place de la Concorde. (48.866275, 2.323812)

The **Mémorial des Combattants Mort de 25 August 1944** holds ten plaques positioned above niches in the wall of the Tuileries Gardens. Each plaque commemorates a soldier or civilian who died in the fighting to control the place de la Concorde. Included are Sergeant Marcel Bizien, commanding the tank 'Douaumont'; Sergeant Pierre Laigle, commanding the tank 'Montfaucon,'; Fireman Michel Mouchet; Paramedic Jean-Clause Touche; Corporal George Fontaine; pharmacist student Georges Bailley; Guy Lecomte, who died in fighting in the Tuileries Garden; Madeleine Brinet, a medical assistant; Sergeant Raymond Maestracci and soldier Antonio Lopez-Ros, who both died on the rue de Rivoli.

Continue into place de la Concorde.

The **place de la Concorde**, created during the reign of Louis XV, originally held a giant stone statue of the king and was named after him. During the French Revolution, it was renamed place de la Révolution. In January 1793, it became the site of the French Reign of Terror's guillotine and saw the execution of Louis XVI, Marie Antoinette, Madame du Barry, and revolutionary notables such as Danton, Corday, and Robespierre, among others. The square obtained its current name to represent reconciliation after the Revolution. The 3,300-year-old, hieroglyphic-inscribed **Obélisque de Louxor** from the Temple of Luxor, Egypt, stands in the center of the square. Near its base, a brass plaque marks the location of the revolutionary guillotine and the death of Louis XVI. Two beautiful fountains that represent the rivers of France and the Atlantic and Mediterranean seas of France frame the obelisk.

At 1315 on 25 August, after breaking through a barricade on the rue de Rivoli, Sgt Bizier's tank entered the place de la Concorde. A Panther tank near the entrance to the Jardin des Tuileries, disabled by a destroyed track, was engaging other Shermans approaching along the Champs-Élysées. The French tank's high explosive shells could not penetrate the Panther's armor at even such short range. While the powerful German tank slowly turned its attention to Bizien's Sherman, the French sergeant aimed his tank and deliberately rammed the Panther disabling its turret mechanism. The German crew made a hasty escape.[17]

Within 90 minutes, all five tanks moving along the rue de Rivoli were disabled,

---

17   Sergeant Marcel Bizien was killed minutes later by bullet through his neck from a sniper positioned on the roof of the Ministère de la Marine. He was 23 years old.

their crew dead or injured. However, a tank company of the 501st Régiment de Chars de Combat commanded by Capitaine G Buis moved across the place de la Concorde from the direction of the Seine River. [18] The famous square was once again French.

Proceed west along the north side of the Champs-Élysées.

The world renowned **Avenue des Champs-Élysées** starts from the Luxor Obelisk in the center of the place de la Concorde and proceeds 1.9 kilometers northwest to place Charles de Gaulle, formerly the place de l'Étoile. The street was first developed in 1616, but became central to France's military history with the construction of the Arc de Triomphe. It was the site of military parades by German forces after the Franco-Prussian War in 1871 and again on 14 June 1940, followed by the liberation parades by French and American forces on 26 and 29 August 1944. The tradition continues with a large military parade every Bastille Day on 14 July.

After 550 m, and immediately before Av de Marigny, enter the park on the right. (48.868166, 2.314591)

The **Jean Moulin Mémorial** is well hidden among trees at the intersection of the Champs-Élysées and Av de Marigny. In a grassy opening, a short metal stele dedicated to 'Jean Moulin 1899 – 1943' houses flood lamps which illuminate five metal sculptures set upon metal plinths. The sculptures are expressionistic and present a mysterious memorial to a mysterious man. Each plinth bears the emblematic image of Moulin wearing his trademark fedora and a scarf around his neck.

Cross Av de Marigny and then the Champs-Élysées. The large glass building directly ahead is the Grand Palais. (48.867517, 2.313604)

Near the corner, a **statue of général Charles de Gaulle**, depicting him striding up the famous street, stands upon a plinth inscribed with words from his famous speech declaring the liberation of Paris. The famous **Grand Palais** stands behind de Gaulle's statue. It was the largest exhibition space in Paris in 1944. On 23 August, a German Army car was ambushed from the Grand Palais while traveling along the Champs-Élysées. Shortly later, German tanks arrived and blasted the building in retaliation, setting the entire structure aflame. The curling black smoke rose above the city of two days.

A statue of France's First World War leader, **Prime Minister Georges Clemenceau**, stands among the trees across the Av Winston Churchill in the place Clemenceau.

Continue west on the north side of Champs-Élysées for 1.5 km to the stairway leading to the tunnel to the Arc de Triomphe. Alternatively, enter the Metro station near the de Gaulle statue and take Metro line #1 exiting at Charles-de-Gaulle-Étoile station. Take the tunnel to the Arc de Triomphe; the arch must be accessed via tunnels beneath the large roundabout that surrounds it. (48.87379, 2.294946)

---

18   General Georges Buis was born in Saigon, Vietnam. Buis entered tank services in 1936 and was in North Africa in 1940. After the war, he held various military and diplomatic posts in Indochina, Morocco, Iran, and Algeria. He was also a noted author. He died in 1998 at age 86.

Arc de Triomphe de l'Étoile
Place Charles de Gaulle   75017 Paris
Web: http://www.arcdetriompheparis.com/

The greatest triumphal arch in the world was designed in 1806 to celebrate the victories of Napoleon Bonaparte's Grand Armée. However, it was not actually completed until 1836, twenty-one years after Napoleon's resignation. Following the First World War, a **Tomb of the Unknown** was created under its 50-meter-high arch. The eternal flame was kindled for the first time three years later. The arch's façade bears four masterful friezes, including Francois Rude's *Departure of the Volunteers of 1792* that led to *la Marseillaise*. The inside walls bear the names of French generals and the locations of Napoleon's victories.

In sum total, the arch, its friezes, Tomb of the Unknown, and the panoramic view from the rooftop observation platform create one of the premier military attractions in Paris. A solemn ceremony commemorating the end of the First World War occurs every 11 November.

Open daily April through September from 10:00 to 23:00, October through March from 10:00 to 22:30. Admission fee for the rooftop elevator only. Metro: Charles-de-Gaulle-Etoile.

Acknowledgments

The author wishes to thank the people who assisted in researching or writing this guide. In the first rank of any author's gratitude stands his family. They alone must suffer the repeated discussions of content, presentation style, and time pressure. Research institutions provide guidance often provide new directions of investigation. The professionals and volunteers at the United States Army Heritage and Education Center, Pritzker Military Library, and the United States National Archives stand among those who added to the richness of the work. Mr James O'Loughlin did heroic work in converting the author's draft to readable and coherent text.

The superintendents of the American military cemeteries in Europe and the employees of the American Battle Monuments Commission have been singularly helpful in relating local history or suggesting important sights to be reviewed. Finally and of course, I thank the people of France who, 70 years after the events, continue to honor the American, British, and Canadian soldiers who fought for their liberation by maintaining memorials, flying flags, and organizing commemorations. In particular, I offer recognition to the members of the Adopt a Grave program for the 104,863 American soldiers buried in military cemeteries in Europe. These local citizens have taken responsibly for remembering an American soldier's sacrifice by learning, if possible, about his life and death and by adorning his grave with flowers on the soldier's birthday.

Appendices

Appendix A: Comparison of Ranks

American	British	French	German (Army)	German (SS)
			Soldat	SS-Mann
Private	Private	Soldat de deuxième classe	Obersoldat	Sturmmann
Private First Class	Lance Corporal	Soldat 1e classe	Gefreiter Stabsgefreiter or Obergefreiter	Rottenführer
Corporal	Corporal	Caporal	Unterofficier	Unterscharführer
		Caporal-chef		
		Caporal-chef (1e classe)		
		Élève sous-officier		
Specialist				
Sergeant	Sergeant	Sergent	Unterfeldwebel	Scharführer
Staff Sergeant	Staff Sergeant or Color Sergeant	Sergent-chef	Feldwebel	Oberscharführer
Technical Sergeant			Oberfeldwebel	Hauptscharführer
Master Sergeant		Adjudant	Stabsfeldwebel	Sturmscharführer
First Sergeant				
Sergeant Major		Adjudant-chef		
Command Sergeant Major				
Sergeant Major of the Army				
Second Lieutenant	Second Lieutenant	Sous- lieutenant	Leutnant	Untersturmführer
First Lieutenant	Lieutenant	Lieutenant	Oberleutnant	Obersturmführer
Captain	Captain	Capitaine	Hauptmann / Rittmeister	Hauptsturmführer
Major	Major	Commandant	Major	Sturmbannführer
Lieutenant Colonel	Lieutenant-Colonel	Lieutenant-colonel	Oberstleutnant	Obersturmbannführer
Colonel	Colonel	Colonel	Oberst	Standartenführer
Brigadier General	Brigadier	Général de brigade	Generalmajor	Brigadeführer
Major General	Major-General	Général de division	Generalleutnant	Gruppenführer
Lieutenant General	Lieutenant-General	Général de corps d'armée	General der... (Infanterie, Artillerie, Panzertruppen, etc)	Obergruppenführer
General	General	Général d'Armée	Generaloberst	Oberstgruppenführer
General of the Army	Field Marshal	Maréchal de France	Generalfeldmarschall	Reichsführer-SS

Appendix B: Unit compositions

Divisional Composition (typical and at full deployment)[1,2,3]

	Personnel	Description
American		
Infantry Division	14,253	(3) infantry regiments, artillery regiment, and cavalry reconnaissance troop
Airborne Division	12,900	(3) parachute regiments and (1) glider regiment, (2) parachute artillery battalions, (2) glider artillery battalions, and antitank, engineer and AA battalions, and a reconnaissance platoon
Light Armored Division	10,734	(3) combat commands lettered A,B, and R each with a tank battalion and armored infantry battalion, (3) artillery battalions, also cavalry reconnaissance squadron and an engineer battalion
Heavy Armored Division	14,664	(2) armored regiments, (1) armored infantry regiment, (3) armored artillery battalions, also engineer and armored reconnaissance battalion
British		
Infantry Division	18,347	(3) brigades each with (3) infantry battalions and (3) field artillery regiments, antitank, reconnaissance, and AA regiments, and machine gun and engineer battalions,
Armoured Division (before Operation GOODWOOD)	14,964	(1) armoured brigade with (3) armored regiments and (1) motorized infantry battalion; (1) infantry brigade with (3) motorized infantry battalions, also (2) artillery regiments,and antitank, AA, and armoured reconnaissance regiments, and a machine gun company
Armoured Division (after Operation GOODWOOD)		(2) brigade groups each containing (2) armored regiments and (2) infantry battalions, supported by (2) artillery regiments, and antitank, AA regiments
Airborne Division	approx. 8,000	(2) parachute brigades each with (3) parachute battalions, an antitank battery, engineer squadron and pathfinder company, also (1) airlanding brigade with (3) infantry battalions, artillery regiment and engineer company
German		(German divisions included specialized artillery regiment, and specialized reconnaissance, antitank, engineer, and signals battalions, plus division service units)
Infanterie (old)	17,000	(3) infantry regiments with (3) battalions per regiment
Infanterie (1944)	12,500	(3) infantry regiments with (2) battalions per regiment
Infanterie (2 Regiment type)	10,000	(2) infantry regiments with (3) battalions per regiment
Volksgrenadier	10,000	(3) infantry regiments with (3) battalions per regiment
Jäger	13,000	(2) infantry regiments with (3) battalions per regiment
Panzergrenadier	14,000	(2) infantry regiments and tank and AA battalions
SS-Panzergrenadier	15,000	(2) infantry regiments and a tank or assault gun battalion and AA battalion,
Panzer	14,000	(2) infantry regiments and a tank regiment and AA battalion,
SS-Panzer	17,000	(2) infantry regiments and SS tank regiment, SS rocket and SS AA battalions, less the artillery regiment
Fallschirmjäger	16,000	(3) parachute regiments and a parachute AA battalion and parachute heavy mortar battalion,
Luftwaffenfeld	12,500	absorbed into army as 1944 type infantry division

Regimental Composition (typical and at full deployment)

American	
Infantry	(3) infantry battalions each with (4) companies (lettered A-M skipping J), a cannon company with (2) SP 105-mm howitzers and (6) SP 75-mm howitzers, and a HQ company with an Intelligence & Reconnaissance Platoon,
Armored	(1) light tank battalion, (2) heavy tank battalions, and a reconnaissance company

1   Over the course of the war, changes to unit organizations were common, during an engagement support units were frequently attached or detached as the situation warranted.

2   The fighting strength of a division was considerably lower, for example an American armored Division had 5,000 combat soldiers, British armoured division approximately 7,000, but a German Waffen SS division could be as high as 12,000.

3   A division also included medical, signal, service, ordinance and military police units.

Armored Infantry	(3) armored infantry battalions with HQ, assault gun, and reconnaissance companies
Airborne (parachute and glider)	(3) parachute battalions each with (3) companies (lettered A-I)
Artillery	(3) artillery battalions each with (12) 105-mm guns (1) artillery battalion with (12) 155-mm guns,
British	
Artillery, Field	(3) batteries each with (2) troops of (4) 25-pdr guns
Artillery, Medium	(2) batteries each with (2) troops of (4) 140-mm guns
Artillery, Heavy	(2) batteries of (4) 185-mm howitzers and (2) batteries of (4) US 155-mm guns
Anti-Aircraft	(3) batteries each with (3) troops of (6) guns totalling (54) towed 40-mm light AA guns
Antitank	(4) batteries each with (8) towed 17-pdr guns and (2) towed 6-pdr guns
Tank	(3) squadrons each with (12) medium, (4) Sherman Firefly and (3) support tanks; HQ manned and additional (4) medium, (8) AA, and 11 light (Stuart) tanks
German	
Infanterie (old type)	(3) infantry battalions of (4) companies
Infanterie 1944	(2) infantry battalions of (4) companies
Volksgrenadier	(2) infantry battalions each of (3) grenadier companies and a heavy weapons company
SS-Infanterie	(2) infantry battalions of (4) companies with howitzer and antitank companies
Grenadier (mot)	(3) motorized infantry battalions with SP heavy infantry howitzer and antitank companies
Panzergrenadier	(2) motorized infantry battalions with SP heavy infantry howitzer and engineer companies
SS-Panzergrenadier	(1) armored battalion and (2) motorized infantry battalions with SP heavy infantry howitzer, half-track engineer, and AA companies
Fallschirmjäger	(3) parachute battalions and 120-mm gun and antitank companies
Artillerie in 1944 Infantry Div	(3) battalions with 105-mm howitzers and (1) battalion of 150-mm howitzers
Artillery Regiment in Volksgrenadier Divisions	(1) battalion with 75-mm antitank guns, (2) battalions with 105-mm howitzers, and (1) battalion with 150-mm howitzers
Artillery Regiment in Panzer & Panzergrenadier Divisions	(1) battalion of SP 105-mm and 150-mm howitzers, (1) battalion with 105-mm howitzers, and (1) battalion of 150-mm howitzers
Heeresküsten-artillerie	Army Coast Artillery with (2) or (3) coast artillery battalions and any number of independent batteries

Battalion Composition (typical and at full deployment)

American	
Infantry	(4) companies lettered A-M, fourth company in each battalion was heavy weapons company with machine guns and mortars; HQ Company with antitank platoon initially with (4) 37-mm and later with (3) 57-mm antitank guns, 871 men total
Armored Infantry	(3) rifle companies each with antitank platoon and a HQ company with mortar, reconnaissance, assault gun, and machine gun platoons, 1001 men total
Armored Infantry (Heavy Division)	(3) rifle companies and a HQ company with mortar, reconnaissance, assault gun, and machine gun platoons, 700 men total
Armored (Light Division)	(1) light tank company, (3) medium tank companies with a HQ company with a HQ, mortar, reconnaissance, and assault gun platoons
Armored, (Heavy Division)	(3) light tank companies with a HQ company with a HQ, mortar, reconnaissance, and assault gun platoons or (2) medium tank companies and armored reconnaissance platoon
Parachute / Glider	(3) rifle companies each with mortar squad and a HQ company with mortar and light machine gun platoons, 706 men total / 658 men total
Tank Destroyer	(3) companies each with (12) guns and a mechanized cavalry troop
Artillery	(3) batteries each with (4) 105-mm SP howitzers
Armored Artillery	(3) batteries each with (6) 105-mm SP howitzers

Armored Reconnaissance	(4) cavalry troops, lettered A to D, each equipped with (13) M8 armored cars and jeeps and a assault gun troop; E company with (8) M8 SP howitzers and light tank company with (17) M5 Stuart, or later M24, tanks
Cavalry Reconnaissance Squadron, Mechanized	(3) cavalry troops, lettered A to C, each equipped with (13) M8 armored cars and jeeps and an assault gun troop
Ranger	(6) rifle companies and a HQ company, 504 men total

British

Infantry	(4) rifle companies each with (3) platoons of (3) sections, also support company of antitank, mortar, carrier, and pioneer platoons; 821 men total
Tank	(3) squadrons each with (3) troops of (4) cruiser tanks and (1) troop of (4) Sherman Firefly, also HQ with (4) cruiser tanks, HQ squadron with (4) support troop tanks (AA, reconnaissance, etc)
Machine Gun	(12) Vickers MG and (8) 105-mm mortars
Parachute	(3) rifle companies and a HQ company with antitank platoon and (2) mortar platoons, 613 men total

Canadian

Infantry	(4) rifle companies each with (3) platoons of (3) sections, also support company of antitank, mortar, carrier, and pioneer platoons, 848 men total
Motorized	(3) motor companies each with (3) platoons of (3) sections using US half-tracks as transport, and a support company of (3) antitank and (2) machine gun platoons, 857 men total

German

Infantry	(4) infantry companies
Maschinegewehr	(machine gun battalion): (3) companies of heavy machine guns and panzerfausts plus a heavy weapons company
Scheres Granatenwerfer	(heavy mortar battalion): (3) companies each with (12) 120-mm mortars
Panzerjäger	(antitank battalion): (1) company of (12) towed 75-mm AT guns, (1) company of (14) SP 75-mm AT guns, and (1) company of (12) 20-mm AT guns
Panzer	(tank battalion): (3) companies each of (3) platoons each with (4) tanks, (2) tanks in company HQ, (6) tanks in battalion HQ, frequently also a fourth assault gun company
SS-Panzer	(SS-tank battalion): similar to tank battalion with (1) additional tank per platoon and (2) additional tanks in battalion HQ
HQ PzKpfw VI (Tiger)	(tank battalion assigned to corps): (14) Tiger tanks per company and (3) in battalion reserve
HQ PzKpfw V (Panther)	(tank battalion assigned to corps): with (17) Panther tanks per company and (3) in Bn reserve

Appendix C: German Military Units

	Commander	Allied army equivalent	Composition
Trupp			a small group dedicated to a specific task
Gruppe	Obergefreiter or Unteroffizier	British section or US squad	the smallest permanent unit in an infantry formation, usually 8-12 men
Zug	Unteroffizier, Haupt Feldwebel or Leutnant	infantry platoon	(3) gruppen and a HQ trupp
Zug, artillerie	same		a trupp with two guns
Zug, panzer	same	armored platoon	(5) tanks
Kompanie (numbered sequentially in a regiment with Arabic numerals, 1st, 2nd, 3rd, 4th company in I Batallion, etc,	Oberleutnant or Hauptmann	infantry company	(3) platoons and a kompanietrupp HQ;
Kompanie, panzer	Oberleutnant or Hauptmann	armored company	(4) panzer Zug plus a HQ
Batterie, artillery	Oberleutnant or Hauptmann	artillery battery	two zug with four guns
Schwadron, cavalry	Rittmeister	squadron	
Batallion (numbered consecutively in a regiment with Roman numerals)	Major or Oberstleutnant	infantry battalion	(3) infantry companies and a support company
Abteilung, artillery	Major	artillery battalion	three batteries totaling 12 guns
Abteilung, panzer	Major or Oberstleutnant	armored battalion	(3) light kompanie (PzKpfw III) and one heavy kompanie (PzKpfw IV)
Regiment infantry panzer,	Oberstleutnant or Oberst	infantry regiment	(3) battalions, mortar kompanie, anti-tank kompanie, support and HQ kompanie; a regiment frequently had a 13th kompanie (mortar and light artillery), a 14th kompanie (antitank) and sometimes even a 15th kompanie (engineers)
Regiment, artillery	same	artillery regiment	(4) artillery abteilungen (3 light and 1 heavy)
Regiment, panzer	same	armored regiment	(2) panzer abteilungen and a support services company
Brigade (not frequently used)	Oberst or Generalmajor		(2) motorized infantry regiments in a panzer division
Division	Generalmajor or Generalleutnant	infantry division	(3) infantry regiments, (1) artillery regiment and anti-tank, reconnaissance, and engineer battalions with support troops
Panzer Division	Generalmajor or Generalleutnant	armored division	varied but generally (2) motorized infantry regiments with (2) battalions each; (1) panzer regiment with (1) battalion PzKpfw IV and (1) battalion with PzKpfw V; (1) artillery abteilung with mix light and heavy SP guns; (1) antitank battalion
Korps	Generalleutnant	corps	2 to 4 divisions
Panzergruppe	varied		armored corps command reporting to army group
Artillerie-kommandeur or Arko	varied	corps artillery	command with large assets to support korps or armee
Armee	General der … Infanterie or Generaloberst	Army	2 or more korps
Panzerarmee	General der … Panzertruppen or Generaloberst		armored force with weak or strong armored elements
Heerestruppen			independent battalions for specialized support functions
Kampfgruppe	assumed the name of its commander	battlegroup	ad-hoc combat formation usually for identified purpose

Appendix D: Glossary of German Military Terms

	Abbreviation, acronym, nickname or literal translation	Description
Abteilung	Abt	Detachment or section, or battalion-sized unit of armor, artillery of cavalry
Abwehr		Counter-espionage service of the German High Command
Allgemeine SS	General SS	Full-time administrative, security, intelligence and police branches of the Schutzstaffel
Armeekorps		Infantry corps
Armeeoberkommando		Field Army Command
Aufklärungs Abteilung		Reconnaissance unit or battalion
Drang nach Osten	Drive to the east	Historic German desire to expand eastward
Einsatzkommando		Company-sized subunits which killed Jews, Communists and others in the Soviet Union
Eisernes Kreuz	Iron Cross	Medal awarded for valorous service
Fall Gelb	Case Yellow	Plan for invasion of the Netherlands, Belgium and France
Fall Grün	Case Green	Plan for intended invasion of Czechoslovakia
Fall Rot	Case Red	Plan for counterstrike against France in the event of an attack from the West
Fall Weiß	Case White	Plan for invasion of Poland
Fallschirmjäger		Parachute trooper
Festung		Fortress
Flakpanzer		Armored self-propelled antiaircraft gun
Flugabwehrkanone	FlaK	Anti-aircraft artillery gun
Freya radar		First operational radar in the Kriegsmarine
Führerhauptquartiere	FHQ	Official headquarters especially constructed for use by the führer
Füsilier		Light infantry, given to reconnaissance formations when the Germans reduced the number of standard infantry battalions in their divisions from 9 to 6
Gebirgsjäger		Mountain troops
Gefallen	Fallen	Killed in action
Geheime Staatspolizei	Gestapo	Secret State Police
Generalkommando		Headquarters of an army corps
Generalstab des Heeres	Gen. St.d. H.	German Army General Staff
Geschwader		Luftwaffe squadron
Granatwerfer		Mortar
Hakenkreuz	hooked cross	Swastika used by the Nazi Party
Haubitze		Howitzer
Heeresgruppen-kommando	HGr.Kdo	Army Group Command
Höckerhindernisse		Antitank defenses, Dragon's Teeth
Jagdbomber	Jabo	Fighter-bomber
Jagdgeschwader	JG	Single-engine fighter wing/group, literally: hunting squadron
Kampfgeschwader	KG	Bomber wing/group
Kampfgruppe		Army battle group usually an ad hoc task force
Kampfwagenkanone	KwK	Turret-mounted main cannon of a battle tank
Kanone		Gun as opposed to a howitzer
Kaserne		Barracks
Kübelwagen	Kübel	Open-topped military utility cars
Landsturm		Infantry of non-professional soldiers or militia
Landwehr		Territorial Army: a type of militia
Maultier	SdKfz 4	Half-track truck
Nachtjagdgeschwader	NJG	Night-fighter wing/group
Nationalsozialistische Deutsche Arbeiterpartei	NSDAP	National Socialist German Worker's Party or Nazi Party

Nebelwerfer	Nb. W, fog thrower	Multi-barrel rocket launchers used for smoke or high-explosive projectiles
Oberbefehlshaber des Heeres	Ob.d.H.	Commander-in-Chief of the Army
Oberfehlshaber West	OB West	Commander-in-Chief West
Oberkommando der Luftwaffe	OKL	High Command of the Air Force
Oberkommando der Marine	OKM	High Command of the Navy
Oberkommando der Wehrmacht	OKW	High Command of the Armed Forces
Oberkommando des Heeres	OKH	High Command of the Army and Army General Staff
Organisation Todt		Civil and military engineering group named after its founder, Fritz Todt, which built the Autobahns, Westwall (Siegfried Line), Wolfsschanze, and Atlantic Wall, notorious for its use of conscript and slave labor
Panzer-abwehrkanone	PaK	Antitank gun
Panzerfaust	tank fist	Disposable portable antitank weapon
Panzergrenadier		Mechanized infantry or a soldier belonging to a mechanized infantry unit
Panzerjäger		Tank destroyer or antitank unit fielding a variety of antitank weapons
Panzerkampfwagen	PzKpfw Armored fighting vehicle	tank
Panzerschreck	tank terror	Reloadable portable antitank weapon
Pionier (pl. Pioniere)		Combat engineer
Reichskanzlei	Reich Chancellery	Office of the German Chancellor (Reichskanzler).
Reichs-sicherheitshaupt-amt	RSHA	Reich Main Security Office or Reich Security Head Office created by Himmler to combine all German security and police departments, including the Gestapo, Kripo and SD
Ritterkreuz des Eisernen Kreuzes	Knight's Cross of the Iron Cross	Highest award for bravery
Sanität		Medical unit or medical personnel
Schützen-panzerwagen	SPW	Armored half-track or self propelled weapon
Schutzstaffel	SS	Nazi organization that grew from Hitler's personal body guard into a fourth branch of the Wehrmacht
Seelöwe, Operation		Sea Lion, plan for amphibious assault on Great Britain in 1940/41
Sicherheitsdienst der SS	SD	Security service of the SS and Nazi Party, main intelligence and counter-espionage section of the RSHA
SS-Totenkopf verbände	SS-TV	SS responsible for the concentration camps, Death's Head units
Stammlager	Stalag	German prisoner-of-war camp
Sturmabteilung	SA	Storm troopers, originally Hitler's praetorian guard (bodyguard) of Brown Shirts, disbanded
Sturmgeschütz	StuG	Self-propelled assault gun
Sturz-kampfflugzeug	Stuka	Any dive-bombing aircraft but generally associated with the Ju-87 dive bomber
Tommy		German slang for a British soldier
Unterseeboot	U-boot	Submarine
Vergeltungs-waffen-1	V1	First German vengeance weapon, pilotless, cruise missile powered by a pulse-jet engine
Vergeltungs-waffen-2	V2 or A4	Supersonic long-range rocket
Vergeltungs-waffen-3	V3	Long-range, smooth-bore gun
Volksgrenadier		Honorary title given to mostly low-grade infantry divisions formed late in the war
Volkssturm		People's defense force, mostly of boys and older men
Wacht am Rhein	Guard on the Rhine	December 1944 Ardennes Offensive, known by Americans as the Battle of the Bulge
Waffen-SS		Armed SS, military combat branch of the SS

Walküre	Valkyrie	(1) officially a Reserve Army contingency plan in the event of a breakdown in law and order, (2) failed 20 July 1944 Plot to arrest SS and Nazi officials and seize control of the German government
Wannsee Conference		Meeting held on January 20, 1942 near Lake Wannsee in Berlin in which it was made official Nazi policy to totally annihilate European Jews and other ethnic groups
Wehrmacht		Combined three branches of German armed forces
Wolfsschanze	Wolf's Lair	Hitler's Eastern Front military headquarters
Würzburg radar		German air defense radar
Zyklon-B		Commercial name for the prussic acid (hydrocyanic acid) gas used in German extermination camps

Appendix E: Armor Comparison

Tanks

	Model	Crew	Front Armor (mm)	Vehicle weight (tons)	Road Speed (kph)	Main Gun	Description, auxiliary guns
American	M26 Pershing	5	102	41.2	48	90-mm	Heavy tank, (1) 12.7-mm and (2) 7.62-mm MG
American	M3A1 Stuart III	4	38	12.7	57	37-mm	Light tank, (3) 7.62-mm MG
American	M4A4 Sherman	5	81	33	36.8	75-mm	Medium tank, (1) 7.62-mm MG
British	A22 Mark IV Churchill	5	102	38.5	27	76-mm & 40-mm	(1) 7.92-mm Besa MG, up-gunned in succeeding marks
British	A27L Cruiser Mark VIII Centaur	5	76	28.4	43	6-pounder	(2) 7.92-mm Besa MG,
British	A27M Cruiser Mark VIII Cromwell	5	76	27.5	51	6-pounder	(2) 7.92-mm Besa MG, upgunned with 75-mm
British	A30 Cruiser Challenger	5	101	32	51	76.2-mm	(1) 7.62-mm MG
British	A34 Cruiser Comet	5	101	35	46	77-mm	(2) 7.92-mm Besa MG
British	Crusader I	5	40	18.5	43	40-mm	(2) MG
British	Firefly	4	81	33	40	17-pounder	up-gunned American Sherman
French	Char B-bis	4	60	32	28	75-mm & 47-mm	(2) 7.5-mm MG
French	Hotchkiss H-35	2	40	10.43	27	37-mm	(1) 7.5-mm MG
French	Hotchkiss H-39	2	40	11.9	36	37-mm	(1) 7.5-mm MG
French	Renault R-35	3	45	14.3	41	37-mm	(1) 7.5-mm MG
French	Souma (S-35)	3	40	19.2	40	47-mm	(1) 7.5-mm MG
German	PzKpfw 38(t)	4	25	9.25	42	37-mm KwK L/40	Czech Skoda LT-38, (2) 7.92-mm MG
German	PzKpfw III J	5	77	22	40	50-mm Kwk	Medium Tank, up-gunned, (2) MG 34
German	PzKpfw IV Model H	5	60	22	32	75-mm KwK 40 (L/43)	Medium Tank, (2) 7.92-mm MG 34
German	PzKpfw V (Panther) G	5	100	45.5	48	75-mm KwK 42 (L/40)	Heavy Tank, (2) 7.92-mm MG 34
German	PzKpfw VI (Tiger I)	5	100	56	36	88-mm KwK 36 L/56	Heavy Tank, (2) 7.92-mm MG 34
German	PzKpfw VI (Tiger II or Königstiger)	5	150	68	39	88-mm KwK 43 (L/71)	Heavy Tank (2) 7.92-mm MG 34

Hobart's Funnies[4]

Model	Chassis	Function
AVRE Bobbin	Churchill	Place canvas carpet over sand to provide tanks with traction
AVRE Fascine	Churchill	Carried bundle of branches to be dumped in antitank ditches
AVRE Petard	Churchill	Fired 18 kgm mortar shell against blockhouses
AVRE Small Box Girder	Churchill	Carried extendable bridge to cross ditches
Crab	Sherman	Mine clearance with rotating drum of chains in front
Crocodile	Mark VII	Flame thrower with fuel in towed trailer
Duplex Drive DD	Sherman	Swimming tank with collapsible canvas screen to land ashore on D-Day

---

4   Specially modified tanks for the D-Day invasion (and afterward) developed for British 79th Armoured Division by armor expert General Sir Percy Hobart.

Tank Destroyers

	Model	Gun	Max Armor (mm)	Description / armament
American	M-10 Wolverine	76-mm	37	(1) 12.7-mm MG, later up-gunned with 90-mm gun
American	M-18 Hellcat	76-mm	12	(1) 12.7-mm MG
American	M-36	90-mm	50	(1) 12.7-mm MG
British	A30 Avenger	17-pounder	101	(1) 7.7-mm Bren MG on AA mount
British	M10 Achilles	17-pounder	37	Upgunned American M10
German	Elephant	88-mm Stu K 43 (L/71) or 88-mm Pak 43/2	185	Formerly known as Ferdinand, mounted on Pz Jäger Tiger P chassis
German	Jagdpanther	88-mm Pak 43/3 or 43/4	100	Mounted on Pz Jäger Panther chassis, (2) 7.92-mm MG
German	Jagdpanzer IV	75-mm Pak39 L/48	100	Mounted on Pz Kpfw IV chassis
German	Jagdtiger	128-mm Pak 44 (L/55)	150	Mounted on Pz Jäger Tiger B chassis, (2) 7.92-mm MG
German	Nashorn (Rhinoceros)	88-mm Pak 43	30	On hybrid Pz Kpfw III and IV chassis

Index